Beverly C. White, R.N., m.a.
New Mexico SIDS Project
Office of the Medical Investigator
UNM School of Medicine
Albuquerque, NM 87131

505-277-3053

SUICIDE
IN THE
YOUNG

Edited by

Howard S. Sudak
Amasa B. Ford
Norman B. Rushforth

John Wright • PSG Inc
Boston   Bristol   London
1984

Library of Congress Cataloging in Publication Data
Main entry under title:

Suicide in the young.

   Includes bibliographical references and index.
   1. Suicide.   2. Youth — Suicidal behavior.   I. Sudak,
Howard S.   II. Ford, Amasa B.   III. Rushforth,
Norman B.   [DNLM: 1. Suicide — In adolescence.   2. Suicide
— In infancy and childhood.   HV 6546 S9485]
RJ506.S9S87   1984   616.85'8445'0088055   83-23782
ISBN 0-07236-7059-5

Published simultaneously by:
John Wright • PSG Inc, 545 Great Road, Littleton,
Massachusetts 01460, USA
John Wright & Sons Ltd, 823–825 Bath Road,
Bristol BS4 5NU, England

International Standard Book Number: 0-07236-7059-5

Library of Congress Catalog Card Number: 83-23782

CONTRIBUTORS

PAUL J. AMBROSINI, MD
Research Fellow in Child
  Psychiatry
Instructor of Clinical Psychiatry
Columbia University College of
  Physicians and Surgeons
New York State Psychiatric
  Institute
New York, New York

MICHAEL S. ARONOFF, MD
Clinical Assistant Professor of
  Psychiatry
Cornell University Medical College
White Plains, New York

RICHARD C. BEDROSIAN, PhD
Director, Massachusetts Center
  for Cognitive Therapy
Westborough, Massachusetts

SHAHIM CARRIGAN, PhD
Child Psychiatric Services
Department of Psychiatry and
  Behavioral Sciences
University of Louisville School
  of Medicine
Louisville, Kentucky

JOHN CLARKIN, PhD
Associate Professor of Clinical
  Psychology in Psychiatry
Cornell University Medical College
Director of Psychology
  Department
New York Hospital–Cornell
  Medical Center–Westchester
  Division
White Plains, New York

RUTH CORN, MSW
Lecturer in Social Work in
  Psychiatry
Cornell University Medical College
Assistant Director of Social Work
  Services for Staff Development
New York Hospital–Cornell
  Medical Center–Westchester
  Division
White Plains, New York

ANN DERRICK, RN
Child Psychiatric Services
Department of Psychiatry and
  Behavioral Sciences
University of Louisville School
  of Medicine
Louisville, Kentucky

DAVID C. DOLEN, MD
Child Psychiatric Services
Department of Psychiatry and
  Behavioral Sciences
University of Louisville School
  of Medicine
Louisville, Kentucky

NORMAN EPSTEIN, PhD
Assistant Professor
Department of Family and
  Community Development
University of Maryland
College Park, Maryland

PAMELA R. FAIN, PhD
Assistant Professor of Preventive
  Medicine
Creighton University School of
  Medicine
Omaha, Nebraska

PAUL FINE, MD
Associate Professor of Psychiatry
  and Pediatrics
Creighton University School of
  Medicine
Omaha, Nebraska

PRUDENCE FISHER, MS
Research Social Worker
New York State Psychiatric
  Institute
New York, New York

AMASA B. FORD, MD
Professor of Epidemiology and
  Community Health
Professor of Family Medicine
Associate Professor of Medicine
Associate Dean for Geriatric
  Medicine
Case Western Reserve University
  School of Medicine
Cleveland, Ohio

CALVIN J. FREDERICK, PhD
Professor, Department of
  Psychiatry and Behavioral
  Sciences
University of California at
  Los Angeles
Chief, Psychology Service
Veteran's Administration Medical
  Center
West Los Angeles-Brentwood
  Division
Los Angeles, California

RICHARD C. FRIEDMAN, MD
Clinical Associate Professor of
  Psychiatry
Cornell University Medical College
Associate Attending Psychiatrist
New York Hospital-Cornell
  Medical Center-Westchester
  Division
White Plains, New York

ERNA FURMAN
Assistant Clinical Professor of
  Child Therapy
Case Western Reserve University
  School of Medicine
Cleveland Center for Research in
  Child Development
Hanna Perkins School
Cleveland, Ohio

G. DAVIS GAMMON, MD
Clinical Instructor of Psychiatry
Department of Psychiatry
Yale University School of
  Medicine
New Haven, Connecticut

WILLIAM H. HILL, ACSW
Department of Social Work
University Hospitals of Cleveland
Cleveland, Ohio

PAUL C. HOLINGER, MD, MPH
Associate Attending Physician
Psychomatic and Psychiatric
  Institute PPI
Michael Reese Hospital and
  Medical Center
Rush-Presbyterian-St Luke's
  Hospital
Chicago, Illinois

STEPHEN W. HURT, PhD
Assistant Professor of Psychology
  in Psychiatry
Cornell University Medical College
Staff Psychologist
New York Hospital–Cornell
  Medical Center–Westchester
  Division
White Plains, New York

KAREN JOHN, BA
Associate in Research
Department of Psychiatry
Yale University School of
  Medicine
New Haven, Connecticut

KEVIN W. LUKE, BS
Research Fellow
Senior Medical Student
Rush Medical College
Chicago, Illinois

MATILDA S. McINTIRE, MD
Professor of Pediatrics
Director of Ambulatory
  Pediatrics
Creighton University School of
  Medicine
Omaha, Nebraska

JEROME A. MOTTO, MD
Professor of Psychiatry
University of California Medical
  School, San Francisco
Associate Director of Psychiatric
  Consultation–Liaison Service
University of California, San
  Francisco Medical Center
San Francisco, California

GEORGE E. MURPHY, MD
Director, Psychiatry Clinic
Department of Psychiatry
Washington University School of
  Medicine
St. Louis, Missouri

JACK NOVICK, PhD
Adjunct Associate Professor
Wayne State Medical School
Supervising Analyst
Michigan Psychoanalytic Institute
Senior Staff and Co-Director of
  Psychology Unit
Arbor Clinic, Inc.
Ann Arbor, Michigan

DANIEL OFFER, MD
Professor of Psychiatry
Pritzker School of Medicine
University of Chicago
Chairman, Department of
  Psychiatry
Michael Reese Hospital and
  Medical Center
Chicago, Illinois

VERNON D. PEARSON, Jr, BA
Child Psychiatric Services
Department of Psychiatry and
  Behavioral Sciences
University of Louisville
  School of Medicine
Louisville, Kentucky

vi

CYNTHIA R. PFEFFER, MD
Assistant Professor of Psychiatry
Cornell University Medical College
Chief, Child Psychiatry Inpatient
  Unit
The New York Hospital–
  Westchester Division
White Plains, New York

DAVID P. PHILLIPS, PhD
Professor
Department of Sociology
University of California,
  San Diego
San Diego, California

JOAQUIM PUIG-ANTICH, MD
Associate Professor of Clinical
  Psychiatry
Columbia University College of
  Physicians and Surgeons
New York State Psychiatric
  Institute
New York, New York

HARRIS RABINOVICH, MD
Research Fellow in Child
  Psychiatry
Instructor of Clinical Psychiatry
Columbia University College of
  Physicians and Surgeons
New York State Psychiatric
  Institute
New York, New York

JOSEPH RICHMAN, PhD
Associate Professor
Department of Psychiatry
Albert Einstein College of
  Medicine
New York, New York

CHARLOTTE P. ROSS
Executive Director
Suicide Prevention and Crisis
  Center of San Mateo County
San Mateo, California

NANCY M. RUSHFORTH, BA
Research Assistant
Department of Biology
Case Western Reserve University
  School of Medicine
Cleveland, Ohio

NORMAN B. RUSHFORTH, PhD
Professor and Chairman
Department of Biology
Associate Professor of Biometry
Case Western Reserve University
  School of Medicine
Cleveland, Ohio

DAVID SHAFFER, MD, BS,
  MRCP, FRC Psych
Chief, Division of Child
  Psychiatry
New York State Psychiatric
  Institute
Professor of Clinical Psychiatry
  and Pediatrics
Columbia University College of
  Physicians and Surgeons
New York, New York

MOHAMMAD SHAFII, MD
Professor of Psychiatry
Director of Child Psychiatric
  Services
Director of Child Psychiatry
  Training Program
University of Louisville School
  of Medicine
Louisville, Kentucky

MARK I. SOLOMON, PhD
President, Bereavement Services
  of Alberta
Alberta, Canada

HOWARD S. SUDAK, MD
Professor of Psychiatry
Case Western Reserve University
  School of Medicine
Chief, Psychiatry Service
Veteran's Administration Medical
  Center
Cleveland, Ohio

JAMES M. TOOLAN, MD
Old Bennington, Vermont

PAUL D. TRAUTMAN, MD
Deputy Director of Training
Division of Child Psychiatry
Columbia University College of
  Physicians and Surgeons
New York, New York

MYRNA M. WEISSMAN, PhD
Professor of Psychiatry and
  Epidemiology
Yale University School of
  Medicine
New Haven, Connecticut

J. RUSSELL WHITTINGHILL,
  ACSW
Child Psychiatric Services
Department of Psychiatry and
  Behavioral Sciences
University of Louisville
  School of Medicine
Louisville, Kentucky

CONTENTS

ACKNOWLEDGMENT

The editors wish to acknowledge the tireless and skillful typing, organizing and coordinating of Mrs Myrna Andell which greatly facilitated the preparation of this book.

FOREWORD

Society has a special stake in the suicide rate of the young that transcends even the personal tragedy of suicide in young people. Long before social and behavioral scientists made us aware that suicide like crime, drug and alcohol abuse were barometers of social stress, almost all cultures intuitively recognized youthful suicide as a threat to social cohesiveness which should concern everyone.

The feelings individuals have about life, what they live for and the circumstances under which they would prefer not to live involve a delicate balance of the personal and the social. The recent rise in suicide among the young in Western cultures seems to reflect psychosocial changes — sexual, familial and demographic — that have appeared to make it harder for families to raise children and for children to grow up.

Until recently, what little psychosocial understanding there was in studies of suicide was reflected in the presentation of suicide statistics which showed differences in rates among different age groups, between blacks and whites, and between the sexes. That those differences might reflect differences in motivation as well was little understood. By focusing on the suicide of the young, the editors of this volume have helped to define them as a special group.

The recognition by the editors and contributors of the specific psychological as well as demographic features of suicide among the young enables them to make observations and conclusions that are more valuable than those generalizations applicable to suicide at all ages and in all cultures. One result is finely detailed case histories which have the unique stamp of Western suicidal adolescents. The psychodynamics of suicide are set in a context of the characteristic adolescent concerns with identity, sexuality, and the meaning of life. The ultimate adolescent task is to shape a life separate and independent from their families. The reader will become aware of the irony that those youngsters whose relationships with their families are most disturbed often have the most difficulty in separating from them.

Despite the wealth of epidemiological information it contains, this book is primarily clinical in nature. The individual contributors and the editors are aware of the methodological problems implicit in the various ways of studying suicide and, in particular, of the difficulty of integrating data from such different disciplines as demography and psychology. In such problems also lie possibilities and the present volume takes a step in a direction that is likely to be increasingly productive.

HERBERT HENDIN, MD, Director
Center for Psychosocial Studies
New York Medical College and
VA Medical Center
Montrose, New York

INTRODUCTION

Deaths are always painful for families and friends, but some are more tragic than others. Suicide, with its inevitable legacies of self-recriminations, hurt, bewilderment, guilty relief and inexpressible rage, plays particular havoc with survivors. Cruelest of all suicides are those of children and adolescents. There are at least three major reasons why this should be so. First is its prematurity—why kill one's self when so much of life is yet to come? How can we account for giving up hope when, at least to the observer, so much potential for change exists? We cannot understand closing out options in the face of a capricious fate which we, whom are not depressed, know can profoundly change our perspectives from one moment to the next.

The second reason concerns our singular emotional investments in our children. That we see ourselves in our children; express ourselves through them, take pride, even vicarious pleasure, in them and their achievements does not make us poor parents. It would be surprising if this were not the case. These are some of the major psychological and existential reasons we procreate: to afford ourselves some approximation of immortality; to provide continuity; and, perhaps, to add meaning to our own brief lives. Biologically, of course, it appears that we reproduce because such activity affords us instinctual pleasure, but we may also agree with the assertion that, from an evolutionary or teleological point of view, we can all be viewed as rather elaborate support systems for our reproductive organs—existing primarily to allow our gonads to reach maturity, fertilize, and propagate the species. Dawkins puts this in more modern terminology in terms of support systems for gene replication.[1] Thus, the death of a child robs us not only of the child but also of a large part of ourselves. No wonder we cannot cope readily with such a massive loss.

The third reason such deaths are particularly devastating to parents has to do with our sense of responsibility for our children. Even if a child develops a purely physical problem (eg, a severe cold, a bad case of measles, a broken arm) we tend to reproach ourselves. We should not have let him or her play with another whom we suspected might be infectious or we should not have let him or her swing so high. Imagine what room we leave ourselves to feel guilty when the issue appears psychological rather than physical. Perhaps we cannot control the neighbor's germs or a faulty link in a swing-set, but surely we are responsible for how our children *feel* from moment to moment. "If my child is unhappy, it must be my fault. If my child is so apparently unhappy that he or she attempts to kill him or herself, then, surely, where else is the blame to go? What monstrous parenting I must have provided to make life appear so awful to my child." There is no one left to blame, except one's spouse, and such a displacement is yet another bitter sequel frequently left to the survivors. Even if the act is viewed as an angry rejection of the parents by the child, the pain is not significantly lessened. Whether we have made our children mad or sad, their reaction still leaves us with the same terrible sense of responsibility.

For these and, undoubtedly, countless other reasons, suicidal deaths of children and adolescents exact an awesome toll on parents, siblings and friends. Small wonder that, in the Cleveland Survivors Group, consisting of parents, children, siblings, or spouses of people who have suicided, it always appeared that it was the parents who had the most difficult time reconciling themselves to their overwhelming pain!

It is as an attempt to investigate these issues that this book is addressed, to seek answers to the questions: why do children and adolescents kill themselves or make suicide attempts and what can be done to prevent them? There is, of course, no one answer. The simplest, and perhaps, most comforting, would be a biological explanation: a number of children, adolescents, and adults suffer from depressions that are, in part, biologically or genetically predetermined and the suicidal act is merely the expression of such a biochemically induced, underlying, affective state. This view could decrease some of our guilt (except that those parents bearing such "bad" genes could still feel guilty for having transmitted them). It might, however, enable us to focus less on what we did wrong as parents and allow more hope regarding promising organic treatment strategies for others so afflicted. Such an explanation is too simple since, even if it is correct, it ignores the issue of why some depressed children attempt suicide while others, with presumably similar genetic predispositions, do not. Similar genotypes do not necessarily insure similar outcomes.

Suicide is an "act," a complex behavior and, as such, cannot be fully understood from a single point of view. First of all, we have to decide what level of understanding we are seeking. From which vantage point do we want to approach the problem? The categories are as diverse as one's imagination allows, and many have obvious relevance: political, economic? Certainly, we can try to understand suicide rates transnationally according to political systems, unemployment rates, distribution of wealth, etc. Spiritual factors? Numerous studies of effects of formal religion and informal and personal religious beliefs and suicide rates have been carried out. Sociological and social-psychological approaches to suicide are in abundance, ranging from Durkheim's classical work on *Suicide*[2] to more recent work such as Gibbs' on *Status Integration*.[3] The focus may shift from larger (nations, races, religions) to smaller groups (ethnic groups, occupational groupings) and, ultimately to the family. Much of the work in this present volume will focus on discrete epidemiological issues (age, race, population and cohort studies, role of the family, temporal effects, etc), which at present appear to be the most promising avenues of inquiry regarding suicide, but we will also focus at the level of the suicidal individual and his or her intrapsychic processes.

Even a perspective at the individual level does not greatly simplify the task of understanding, however. This is particularly so, intrapsychically, because complex behavioral acts, as Robert Waelder[4] indicated, are "multiply-determined," ie, they do not occur unless many disparate needs are met. Instinctive needs (often libidinal as well as aggressive); existential issues; ego and superego needs; past, present, and future (or no future) agendas; unconscious as well as conscious motives; all play their parts. It is not enough to proceed only a step beyond the most superficial questions. For instance, lay persons often ask "Why would Marilyn Monroe, or Hemingway (or some other notable) commit suicide? . . . He or she had everything to live for." Superficial explanations are to be found in near-to-the-surface motives such as "perhaps she felt she was running out of beauty or youth" or "perhaps he was afraid he was getting too old and 'running out of macho'." Possibly, so, but such explanations account for only a fraction of the total motivational complex strong enough to drive someone to suicide.

Some readers may wonder how contradictory wishes are believed to exist side by side without canceling one another out and with both sides remaining active. For example, how can infantile wishes still be active in adolescence and adulthood — often wishes which, if fulfilled in reality, would appear to cause us more pain than pleasure? Such paradoxes, however, follow the normal operating principles of our unconscious mental life. For instance, how can we consider libidinal contributions to behavior which is as apparently unloving and nonerotic as suicide? Again, multiple psychic layers and diverse motivations may all play roles. At the conscious level, of course, we are familiar with lovers' suicides, such as those of Romeo and Juliet. Unconsciously, the suicidal behavior may be partly motivated by a wish to rejoin a departed, loved parent or other love object, or represent an identification (out of love) with someone who has suicided, or it may relate to primitive erotic pleasures emanating from early childhood development. An enormous number of possibilities exist and, for any given individual, a "thorough understanding" of the underlying motives for his or her suicidal behavior would entail attempts to gain such multilayered, multifaceted data.

Rarely are we in the position of understanding human behavior to these depths — particularly so for completed suicides, since the decedents cannot provide direct answers to our queries. We have to infer some motives, extrapolate from other cases, and piece together clues as best we can from families and friends.

Another issue more complex than it appears at first pertains to the basic question of what is meant by suicidal behavior. Are we referring to any self-destructive behavior? If so, we would then have to so classify the deaths of delirious or demented patients who jump out of their 10th floor hospital windows because they were confused and thought the building was on fire. Since there was not conscious intent to die but rather a misguided attempt to escape and live, most authorities would classify these as accidental, not suicidal. What of a delusional schizophrenic patient whose voices tell him or her to shoot him or herself and then he or she will be reincarnated, immortal, and free of torment? Again, since a conscious attempt to die was not the primary motive, some people would question labeling this as suicide.

What of behavior which appears either to be less lethal or in which the intent to die seems less marked such as suicide attempts rather than completed suicides (note that the term, "successful suicide," ought to be eschewed lest it add credence to the view that a person who has not died has "failed" and to the irony that a completed suicide would be viewed as a "success")? There are scales of lethality and intent, and these may be helpful in appraising suicide attempts. The term "suicide gesture" has become pejorative and connotes behavior even less indicative of a wish to die than "suicide attempt." Implicit in the term "gesture" is the (dangerous) suspicion that the individual is merely trying to manipulate his or her environment. Such a view is potentially dangerous because it simplistically allows one not to feel concerned enough; ignores the complexity of human behavior; and overlooks the role of other unconscious factors (besides any possible manipulativeness) as discussed earlier. Some British suicidologists[5] prefer the more neutral term "parasuicide" to cover all kinds of attempts.

What of other human behavior, clearly self-destructive, without a conscious wish to die? Obviously, a continuum could be conceived with "normal" risk-taking at one end and profound risks at the other, eg, the diabetic patient who refuses insulin; the patient with severe coronary artery disease who continues to smoke heavily; the alcoholic patient with known hepatic disease or esophageal varices who continues to drink. Some risk-taking is inevitable in everyday behavior, though few of us might agree as to where ordinary risk-taking leaves off and foolhardiness begins. Shneidman[6] refers to such behavior as "subintentional," thereby stressing the lack of conscious desire for self-harm.

The relationship between depression and suicidal behavior is not an invariable one. If one studies retrospectively a sample of completed adult suicides, one finds that most of the decedents were suffering either from a major affective disorder or at least had a significant amount of depressed feelings. Demographically they are more likely to be males, older, white, and widowed, divorced or single. Conversely, studying a sample of adult suicide attempters reveals a much lower incidence of major affective disorders and a higher incidence of personality disorders. They are more apt to be female, and young (15 to 40 years old). Obviously, these do not represent two entirely distinct populations, since there is some overlapping (eg, a profoundly depressed individual may be fortuitously saved from an otherwise lethal suicide attempt; a transiently and minimally depressed psychopath may die when his or her "expected" rescuer fails to appear or the combination of pills ingested was more potent than anticipated).

When we consider children and adolescents and the relation of their suicidal behavior to depressions, we find the relationship more obscure than with adults. Psychoanalytically oriented theorists in the past traditionally held that a true, adult-model depression was not possible until adolescence (ie, not until a relatively mature superego was present). This view has been increasingly challenged by others who maintain that not just psychologically, but also biologically, childrens' depressions may be no different from adults (cf, Ambrosini's study in Chapter 6). Although the contributors to this book generally subscribe to the concept of bona fide depressive disorders in children, it is well to keep in mind that, just as with adults, not all suicidal children and adolescents are depressed. We should also note that there are important statistical differences between child/adolescent suicides and those of adults. Most notably, boys *attempt* (as well as complete) suicide more frequently than do girls,[7] whereas women much more frequently attempt suicide than do men.[8] Perhaps males are more "truly" suicidal than females across all ages, but male children and adolescents have less access to effective means to implement their desires. It is only in the youthful group that the number of male attempts exceeds the female rate. The theory usually held to account for the greater female rate of attempts (and the greater male rate of completions) in adults is that women are allowed more impulsivity and latitude of emotional expression so that, when upset, they utilize anything available, and this is likely to be an agent of a relatively low order of lethality. In addition, females typically seek means which are viewed as neither painful nor disfiguring and these factors militate against more quickly lethal means such as guns, knives, hanging, jumping in favor of slower agents such as pills (which have a greater margin of safety due to the time available for rescue between the act and death). Men, in contrast, are allowed less open emotional expression but, when depressed, are apt to brood for longer periods of time, affording them the opportunity to select methods of greater lethality. Do male adolescents, like male adults, utilize firearms more frequently than do females or are there other significant differences in the modes of the methods employed by the two sexes?

Another area of difference between youthful and adult suicide relates to the frequent tendency of childhood suicidologists to group together as "suicidal," suicide attempters as well as those children who have only threatened suicide or talked about it. Since suicidal ideation is so common in adults, people who have merely "thought about it" are not generally grouped with attempters. Also, marked racial differences exist for adults (with the white rate two to three times the non-white for both attempts and completions), but there is some evidence that these differences are less marked in children and adolescents. The racial disparity in adults is usually explained by the "vicissitudes of aggression" hypothesis — namely, that groups who externalize their aggressive feelings will have high homicide and low suicide rates, while groups who internalize their aggression will have low homicide and high suicide rates. In youth, the relationship between suicide and homicide may be more direct than inverse; ie, violence, both internal and external, is more characteristic of youth.

This book is divided into three major sections: Epidemiology and Etiology; Diagnosis; and Prevention, Intervention, and Postvention. Under Epidemiology and Etiology, we will consider both cohort and population studies; the interrelatedness of suicide and other acts of violence, temporal or suggestion effects; biological factors; general epidemiological data plus some more specific studies. We have attempted to adhere to a somewhat more rigorous standard of epidemiological quality and quantity than is usually found in the psychiatric literature. The section on Diagnosis includes material on how suicidal children present themselves to pediatricians as well as to mental health workers; devotes a number of chapters to the diagnosis and appraisal of suicidal risk; and considers diagnostic subgroups at particular risk for suicidal behavior. Under Prevention, Intervention, and Postvention we will present longitudinal studies of treatment; consider individual, group, cognitive, and family approaches to inpatient and outpatient children and adolescents; and look at programs in schools to help prevent suicidal behavior as well as deal with its after-effects. There are obvious overlaps among the sections since our contributors were given considerable latitude regarding boundaries between major sections. There are also some inevitable redundancies as authors frequently refer to common principles, theories, or background data. At the end of each section, the editors have reviewed the chapters in that section and added material as appropriate.

We have attempted to select from the available approaches those which currently appear to hold the most promise for increased understanding in this field and for treatment implications. We hope our contributions represent a broad enough spectrum of opinions, are comprehensive enough to acquaint the reader with what is most relevant in the field, and are lucid enough to provide the reader some clarity and better focus regarding this distressing subject.

HOWARD S. SUDAK, MD
AMASA B. FORD, MD
NORMAN B. RUSHFORTH, PhD

REFERENCES

1. Dawkins R: *The Selfish Gene*. New York, Oxford University Press, 1976.
2. Durkheim E: *Suicide*. Spalding VA, Simpson G (trans). New York, The Free Press, 1951.
3. Gibbs JP, Martin WT: *Status Integration and Suicide*. Eugene, Oregon, University of Oregon Books, 1964.
4. Waelder R: The principle of multiple function. *Psychoanalytic Q* 1936;5: 45–62.
5. Kreitman N, Schreiber M: Parasuicide in young Edinburgh women, 1968–75. *Psychol Med* 1979;9:469–479.
6. Shneidman ES, Farberow NL (eds): *Clues to Suicide*. New York, McGraw-Hill, 1957.
7. Mattsson A, Seese LR, Hawkins JW: Suicidal behavior as a child psychiatric emergency: Clinical characteristics and follow-up results. *Arch Gen Psychiatry* 1969;20:100–109.
8. Sudak HS, Sterin G, Hauser H: Suicide rate of callers to a poison information service. *Am J Psychiatry* 1975;132:1212–1214.

Section I. EPIDEMIOLOGY/ETIOLOGY

CHAPTER 1

COHORT STUDIES
OF SUICIDE

MARK I. SOLOMON
GEORGE E. MURPHY

The relationship between suicide and age has, for more than a century, been studied by profile analysis. Using this method, researchers have compared the suicide rates of various age groups, usually in five- or 10-year aggregates, at a particular point in time, over a series of time periods. They have consistently noted that suicide is rare in children, tends to increase steadily with age, and declines somewhat among older people, particularly among women. Also, using this method, recent research has indicated an increase in the suicide rates of adolescents and young adults over the past generation.

In this chapter the cohort analysis method of studying the relationship between suicide and age will be discussed. First, the difference between profile analysis and cohort analysis will be explained. Second, we will briefly examine the results of two cohort analyses of suicide rates, the Alberta study by Solomon and Hellon and the United States study by Murphy and Wetzel. Finally, various implications of the cohort analysis method for the epidemiology of suicide will be suggested.

From the 19th century onward, researchers have employed profile analysis to study the relationship between suicide and age. By selecting a particular year or series of years, these researchers have compared the suicide rates of various age groups, typically grouping data in five- or 10-year aggregates. Using such data from 1848–1857 in Europe, Durkheim[1] showed that suicide was rare in children and that the rate increased steadily with age while varying substantially in magnitude from one country to another.

Since Durkheim's time until recently, researchers had consistently noted a similar trend both regarding the rarity of completed suicide in young persons[2-6] and in the direct positive relationship between suicide and age, particularly in white males.[7-17] Suicide rates among older women were lower than in some younger age groups.[8,13] Until the 1950s, the suicide–age profile had remained remarkably stable. Recently, however, the profile has changed. In this chapter we will first examine what profile analysis shows us about these changes. Then we will examine a newer method, cohort analysis, for what it can tell us additionally. Specifically, we will examine the results of two cohort analyses of suicide rates, the Alberta study by Solomon and Hellon[18] and the United States study by Murphy and Wetzel.[19]

PROFILE ANALYSIS

Profile analysis is the traditional method of studying the relationship between suicide and age. Using this method, researchers have selected a year for analysis and have then calculated age-specific suicide rates. These rates usually are expressed as numbers of suicides per 100,000 population within each age group. Rates are most commonly reported in five-year and 10-year age groups; for some purposes, 20-year aggregates may be used. Once the rates have been calculated, a profile is constructed so that the rates of the various age groups can be compared at a given time (age-specific rates). Because of pronounced sex differences in suicide, rates are most commonly reported separately for each sex (sex–age-specific rates). Further breakdown by race, region, etc permit more specific comparisons.

Another use for profile analysis is in tracing changes in suicide–age profiles over time within a particular jurisdiction. Profiles are drawn at successive points in time and changes in the profiles can be noted. It is by this method that several recent studies have identified an increasing rate of suicide among adolescents and young adults.[20-29] Frederick[20] called attention to the fact that in the United States between 1955 and 1975 the greatest increases in suicide rates were in the 20- to 24-year age group. Rates for this age group had, by 1975, equaled or exceeded the rates for all other age groups under 40 years of age. Peck and Litman[23] showed that by 1973 a bimodal distribution in suicide rates had occurred in Los Angeles County, with peaks at ages 20 to 29 and 50 and older. Stack,[29] analyzing 1975 data, noted that in Detroit younger persons had the highest rates of suicide. The conclusion reached on the basis of profile analyses has been that while suicide rates once increased directly with age, there has been a shift in the profile, with rates among adolescents and young adults approaching those of the traditionally higher risk, older age groups.

This trend is clearly visible in Tables 1-1 through 1-3, where data from Canada are presented. (Data for persons aged 60 and over are aggregated because they are uninformative for present purposes.) Between 1951 and 1977, there were 4315 suicides registered in Alberta Vital

Table 1-1
Age-Specific Combined Suicide Rates per 100,000 Population Averaged for Five Years Surrounding Census Years, 1951–1976, Alberta*

Age Group	Census Year					
	1951	1956	1961	1966	1971	1976
15–19	1.61	3.0	3.8	6.0	15.2	20.0
20–24	7.9	4.8	7.9	13.7	18.9	29.5
25–29	4.2	8.2	10.4	11.1	14.6	19.9
30–34	10.2	9.8	12.6	15.1	18.0	17.6
35–39	11.9	10.9	12.0	17.1	15.9	20.0
40–44	12.9	18.3	13.8	19.3	22.9	22.1
45–49	21.3	15.3	18.0	18.2	22.7	23.5
50–54	27.0	26.8	18.3	17.9	23.2	35.3
55–59	19.8	27.3	18.4	29.1	20.9	18.8
60+	19.3	24.3	21.4	18.3	15.1	19.0

*Sources: 1) for suicides: Alberta Vital Statistics, 2) for population:
a) *Population by Five-Year Age Groups and Sex for Canada and Provinces, 1921–1971.*
Catalogue No. 92-715, Table 7, Statistics Canada, 1973, and b) *Census Data for Base Year 1976.* Research and Planning Division, Dept. of Social Services and Community Health, Government of Alberta, 1977.

Table 1-2
Age-Specific Male Suicide Rates per 100,000 Population Averaged for Five Years Surrounding Census Years, 1951–1976, Alberta*

Age Group	Census Year					
	1951	1956	1961	1966	1971	1976
15–19	3.2	4.4	6.8	11.1	24.0	31.4
20–24	10.5	7.6	13.6	24.0	29.6	46.0
25–29	7.9	12.6	16.4	14.9	23.7	30.1
30–34	13.9	14.4	22.4	24.1	24.7	24.2
35–39	17.6	13.5	20.9	23.7	22.7	27.8
40–44	14.4	30.0	22.4	26.2	30.0	31.6
45–49	31.0	23.1	28.9	27.2	33.6	33.3
50–54	38.9	37.9	30.3	28.2	36.2	50.0
55–59	31.7	34.8	29.6	45.5	32.7	28.8
60+	30.5	36.9	33.6	28.7	24.7	29.5

*See footnote to Table 1-1.

Statistics, 3386 suicides by men and 929 suicides by women. All but 48 were 15 years old or older. Age-specific suicide rates were calculated for men and women combined (Table 1-1) and for men (Table 1-2) and women (Table 1-3) separately by averaging the numbers of suicides for the five years surrounding each census year, except that for 1951 and 1976 shorter periods were used for averaging since the full five-year data spread was not available. During this period in Alberta, the overall suicide rate doubled from 8.9/100,000 to 18.0/100,000.

Table 1-3
Age-Specific Female Suicide Rates per 100,000 Population Averaged for Five Years Surrounding Census Years, 1951–1976, Alberta*

Age Group	Census Year					
	1951	*1956*	*1961*	*1966*	*1971*	*1976*
15–19	0.0	1.5	0.8	0.9	5.8	7.9
20–24	5.4	2.0	2.2	3.8	8.1	12.4
25–29	0.8	3.3	3.9	7.4	5.8	9.5
30–34	6.5	5.1	1.7	5.2	11.0	10.9
35–39	6.3	8.2	3.0	10.0	8.5	12.0
40–44	11.1	5.5	5.0	12.3	15.0	11.7
45–49	9.1	5.7	6.5	9.5	11.4	12.2
50–54	10.5	12.7	4.4	7.3	10.8	20.9
55–59	4.2	17.8	4.5	10.4	8.5	17.1
60+	3.9	8.0	6.7	7.0	4.5	9.0

*See footnote to Table 1-1.

Reading Table 1-1 vertically, it can be seen that beginning in the 1956 period suicide rates increased steadily from 25 to 55 years of age. By 1966 the suicide rate for the 20- to 24-year age group had become double digit, and by the 1971 period the same had become true for the adolescent population in Alberta. The leveling off of the distribution was progressive. By 1976, the distribution had become nearly bimodal, with rates among the younger age groups approximating those of the traditionally higher risk, older ages.

Reading Table 1-1 horizontally, one can observe that increases in age-specific rates in Alberta have been greater among the younger than among the older age group. The suicide rate for those 15 to 19 years old increased 1250% from 1.6/100,000 to 20.0/100,000 between the 1951 period and the 1976 period. Changes in rates among successively older age groups were significantly smaller over the same time period (Spearman's r_s = .952, P < .01).

Tables 1-2 and 1-3 show that the changes in suicide-rate profiles were not specific to one gender: nor were age-specific changes in rates. Increases in rates were significantly smaller among both older males (r_s = −.940, P < .01) and older females (r_s = −.891, P < .01) than among the younger age groups.

The question of the accuracy of official suicide rates must be raised when viewing changes in rates over time within a jurisdiction. It is possible that changes in attitudes, changes in coroners or medical examiners, or changes in methods of death certification over time could contribute to the observed changes in the suicide–age profiles. But one would have to show that those who are involved in the death certification process had, over the period observed, become more likely to certify an equivocal death as suicide and that this tendency had become more pronounced when the deceased was young. Where this question has been examined it has not been found to be the case.

Brugha and Walsh[30] compared coroners' records in Dublin from 1900 to 1904 with a similar series for 1964 to 1968 and found that there was no tendency for suicides in the latter period to be classified more freely than in the former period. Sainsbury and Barraclough[31] showed that differences between coroners' districts in England and Wales are independent of the coroner who determines the verdict. Reporting errors affected demographic groups equally. In Alberta between 1951 and 1977 there was a consistent system for determining manner of death. There is no reason to assume that as time went on coroners became more likely to certify a death as suicide when the person was young and less likely to certify a death as suicide when the person was older than 55 years of age.

If the vagaries of suicide ascertainment are an unlikely source of the observed statistical trends, are we simply observing a byproduct of rapid social change? During the years under consideration, the Province of Alberta underwent a very large socioeconomic transformation. The predominantly agrarian economy had one of the lowest per capita incomes in the provinces. With the discovery of oil-bearing sands in the north, the development of petroleum, petrochemical and related industries balooned per capita income to among the highest, while the influx of workers actually doubled the population.[32] These changes might well be thought to account for the changing pattern of suicide rates. To evaluate this possibility, we make a third use of profile analysis by comparing age- and sex-specific suicide profiles across jurisdictions. Data from the United States over the same time period offer a much larger population base; one that did not experience such sweeping changes.

Figure 1-1 illustrates the traditional age-specific profiles for white and nonwhite males and females in the United States for the year 1950. The sharply rising suicide rate with age for white males overshadows the others, where age-rate trends are less striking. This pattern held true for several decades, until the mid-1950s. Figure 1-2 shows for the United States in 1975 what has just been described for Alberta — a steep rise in the suicide rate for the young as well as a decline in rates at later ages. The rate for nonwhite males even exceeds that of white males in the 25- to 29-year age group! Meanwhile, suicide rates for women show an earlier upward trend to a higher level and a more pronounced peak, followed by a decline. For white women, the peak is in the 40- to 50-year age range, while for nonwhite women it occurs as early as ages 25 to 29. Little should be made of the fluctuation in rates for nonwhites after the age of 44, as those for nonwhite males are based on fewer than 100 suicides per year nationwide in each five-year interval and fewer than 50 for nonwhite females.

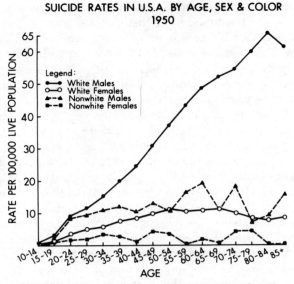

SUICIDE RATES IN U.S.A. BY AGE, SEX & COLOR
1950

Calculated from Vital Statistics of the United States for 1950.

Figure 1-1

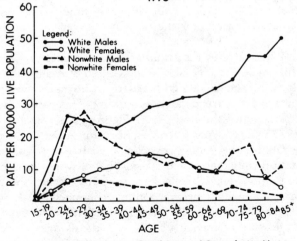

SUICIDE RATES IN U.S.A. BY AGE, SEX & COLOR
1975

Source: Mortality Statistics Branch, National Center for Health
Statistics, Vital Statistics of the United States, (published
& unpublished data).

Figure 1-2

Tables 1-4 and 1-5 display the data numerically for white males and females, to show the similarity in trend to that observed in Alberta. (The dates chosen for presentation, 1950, 1960, 1970, correspond to the decennial census years in the United States. Rates given for the halfway points between them are based on official population estimates.) For white males, the suicide rate in the 15- to 19-year age group has more than tripled in the 25-year span. For white females it has nearly doubled. Thus, although the changes are somewhat smaller in magnitude and proportion for the United States white population, they are most pronounced in the young and decrease with age, as in Alberta over the same period of time.

The nonwhite population of Alberta is too small to generate stable serial rates. In the United States that population represents 10% to 14% of the total and is predominantly black. Progressive urbanization of blacks over the past half century has been associated with gradually rising suicide rates among black males (Table 1-6). The change has been most striking in the younger age groups in the last 20 years. The rate between ages 15 and 29 has more than doubled. Indeed, as previously seen in Figure 1-2, the rate for nonwhite males even exceeds that for white males in the 25 to 29 age group. The rate change for nonwhite females is

Table 1-4
Age-Specific United States White Male Suicide Rates per 100,000 Population by Year in Five-Year Intervals

Attained Age	Year					
	1950*	1955†	1960‡	1965§	1970‖	1975¶
15–19	3.7	3.9	5.9	6.3	9.4	13.0
20–24	9.4	8.6	11.9	13.9	19.3	26.8
25–29	11.9	12.6	13.8	16.5	19.8	25.1
30–34	15.8	12.8	15.9	18.9	20.0	23.5
35–39	20.1	16.4	19.6	21.8	21.9	22.8
40–44	24.9	23.2	24.3	25.0	24.6	26.1
45–49	31.2	28.3	30.2	26.7	28.2	29.1
50–54	37.4	35.7	37.6	35.2	30.9	30.2
55–59	43.5	41.5	39.9	40.3	34.9	32.0
60+	53.4	48.2	44.7	41.9	39.2	37.1
Annual Rate	19.0	17.2	17.6	17.4	18.0	20.1

*Rates calculated from deaths from each cause (p 118) and from enumerated population residing in the continental United States by age, race and sex (1945) listed in Table 2.21 p 56, Vital Statistics of the United States (VSUS), 1950.
†Rates calculated from deaths for each cause (pp 98–99) VSUS 1955 and from Table 5-3, pp 5-12, 13, VSUS 1960.
‡From Table 5-12, pp 5-202, 203, VSUS Vol II, Part A, Mortality, 1960.
§From Table 1-9, pp 1-20, 21, VSUS Vol II, Part A, Mortality, 1965.
‖From Table 1-8, pp 1-24, 25, VSUS, Vol II, Part A, Mortality, 1970.
¶Op cit, 1975.

Table 1-5
Age-Specific United States White Female Suicide Rates per 100,000
Population by Year in Five-Year Intervals

	Year					
Attained Age	1950*	1955†	1960‡	1965§	1970‖	1975¶
15–19	1.9	1.4	1.6	1.8	2.9	3.1
20–24	3.5	2.6	3.1	4.3	5.7	6.9
25–29	5.1	3.9	4.8	6.6	8.6	8.0
30–34	5.4	5.7	6.7	8.7	5.5	10.0
35–39	7.5	5.8	8.2	11.7	12.2	11.4
40–44	8.9	7.4	8.1	12.3	13.8	13.9
45–49	9.9	9.6	10.8	13.2	13.5	14.0
50–54	11.1	10.9	11.1	14.0	13.5	13.6
55–59	10.4	10.7	10.8	13.4	13.1	12.7
60+	10.2	9.5	9.4	9.6	9.3	11.0
Annual Rate	5.5	4.9	5.3	6.6	7.1	7.4

*–¶ See footnotes to Table 1-4.

Table 1-6
Age-Specific United States Nonwhite Male Suicide Rates per 100,000
Population by Year in Five-Year Intervals

	Year					
Attained Age	1950*	1955†	1960‡	1965§	1970‖	1975¶
15–19	2.2	3.7	3.4	5.2	5.4	7.0
20–24	8.4	8.6	7.8	13.1	19.4	23.6
25–29	9.4	8.4	12.6	14.9	20.1	27.6
30–34	10.8	10.6	13.2	13.5	19.4	20.9
35–39	12.3	9.4	14.7	15.3	13.9	17.2
40–44#	10.5	10.9	12.2	14.8	11.4	14.8
45–49	13.2	9.3	13.2	14.2	16.5	14.1
50–54	10.2	11.7	12.3	12.8	11.3	11.5
55–59	16.8	12.7	16.8	12.9	12.3	13.0
60+	14.6	12.7	13.9	15.2	10.0	11.2
Annual Rate	7.0	6.1	7.2	7.7	8.5	10.6

*–¶ See footnotes to Table 1-4.
#Rates at this and older ages are based on fewer than 100 suicides per year nationwide.

neither very striking nor very stable (Table 1-7), because of the relatively small number of suicides. (It is not known why nonwhite females have such distinctly lower suicide rates. "Cultural factors" are implicated, but that is not really an explanation.) Not only for nonwhite males who may have undergone substantial social changes but also for whites of both sexes, who in general have not, *there has been a striking and steady rise in suicide rates, selectively affecting the young.* This allows us to conclude that over the past generation or so the changes in the age distribution of suicide rates are not particular to Alberta, but are general throughout North America.

Research indicates that these cross-jurisdictional comparisons are valid. Sainsbury and Barraclough[31] found that suicide rates of immigrants into the United States were highly correlated with the suicide rates of their countries of origin even though the certification systems differed considerably among countries. Ross and Kreitman[33] found no age-related tendency to misclassify cases in an exchange of sudden-death case files between English coroners and Scottish Crown Counsel. The methods of certification in England and Scotland are quite different. Sainsbury and Jenkins[34] recently reviewed several studies designed to measure the accuracy of official suicide statistics. Though they acknowledged that suicide is underreported, these authors concluded that the underreporting is random, at least to the extent that temporal and cross-jurisdictional comparisons are valid.

We would not contend that deaths are always correctly certified. We would, however, maintain that the trend toward increasing suicide rates among young persons in North America and the changes in the suicide-age profiles over time are real and not an artifact of the certification processes employed by various jurisdictions or within jurisdictions over time.

The general conclusions that are reached using profile analysis are that: 1) traditionally, suicide rates increased directly with age, continuously for white males and only up to the middle years for white

Table 1-7
Age-Specific United States Nonwhite Female Suicide Rates per 100,000 Population by Year in Five-Year Intervals

Attained Age#	Year					
	1950*	1955†	1960‡	1965§	1970‖	1975¶
15–19	1.5	1.3	1.5	2.4	2.9	2.1
20–24	1.8	2.8	1.6	4.0	5.5	6.0
25–29	2.0	2.9	3.1	5.6	6.0	6.8
30–34	3.7	2.6	3.8	6.4	5.6	6.0
35–39	2.7	2.0	3.4	4.4	4.5	5.4
40–44	1.6	1.5	4.0	4.0	4.1	4.5
45–49	4.2	2.9	2.7	3.7	4.0	4.0
50–54	3.8	2.6	3.9	4.6	5.1	5.1
55–59	0.7	1.5	3.7	2.3	1.8	3.9
60+	2.1	2.8	3.6	2.9	3.1	3.4
Annual Rate	1.7	1.5	2.0	2.5	2.9	3.3

*–¶See footnotes to Table 1-4.
#Rates at each age based on fewer than 100 suicides per year nationwide.

females, 2) over the past 20 years, suicide rates among adolescents and young adults of both sexes have increased progressively so that suicide rates no longer increase directly with age, and 3) this trend is general across North America. To say that suicide rates increase with age is ambiguous, and it is this ambiguity that gives rise to the need for cohort analysis.

COHORT ANALYSIS

If, by saying that suicide rates increase with age, one means that during a particular time period suicide rates among older people are higher than among younger people, then profile analysis is a sufficient method for studying the suicide–age relationship. Comparisons can be made among age groups during a specified year or time period or within a particular age group over several time periods. If, however, one means that as people get older their suicide risk increases, then profile analysis is not sufficient. One must follow the same age cohorts over time as they age. Those who were 15 to 19 years of age in 1976 do not belong to the same cohort as those who were in the same age range in 1951. Nor were those who were aged 50 to 54 in 1956 in the same cohort as those who were 30 to 34 years old that year.

In cohort analysis one takes into account the fact that those people who were between the ages of 15 and 19 in 1951 are the same cohort of people who were 20 to 24 in 1956, 25 to 29 in 1961, and so forth. To find out if suicide risk increases with age, the changing rates must be observed within this and subsequent cohorts as they age. If suicide rates do not increase with age, one would expect an irregular pattern of rates. If, however, suicide rates do increase directly with age, one would expect that for each cohort, rates at each successive age would be higher than those at younger ages.

In profile analysis, tables are read vertically and horizontally, as previously discussed. In cohort analysis, the same data can be used, and the pertinent rates for a given birth cohort can be followed by reading diagonally downward to the right. For greater clarity, the most interesting data have been realigned in Tables 1-8 though 1-12. Tables 1-8 and 1-9 display birth cohort data for Alberta males and females, while Tables 1-10 and 1-11 contain the comparable data for United States white and nonwhite males, and Table 1-12 for white females. Taking Table 1-8 for example, the first column on the left presents the oldest birth cohort, Alberta males born between 1932 and 1936. Reading vertically, it can be seen that for this cohort suicide rates increased directly with age. For each successive five-year period, their rate was higher than when they were younger. Reading horizontally, it is clear that males born in each succeeding quinquennium had a higher suicide rate at ages 15 through 19

Table 1-8
Cohort-Specific Male Suicide Rates per 100,000 Population of Alberta

Attained Age	Period of Birth of Cohort					
	1932–36	1937–41	1942–46	1947–51	1952–56	1957–61
15–19	3.2	4.4	6.8	11.1	24.0	31.4
20–24	7.6	13.6	24.0	29.6	46.0	
25–29	16.4	14.9	23.7	30.1		
30–34	24.1	24.7	24.2			
35–39	22.7	27.8				
40–44	31.6					

Last figure in each column is for 1976.

Table 1-9
Cohort-Specific Female Suicide Rates per 100,000 Population of Alberta

Attained Age	Period of Birth of Cohort					
	1932–36	1937–41	1942–46	1947–51	1952–56	1957–61
15–19	0.0	1.5	0.8	0.9	5.8	7.9
20–24	2.0	2.2	3.8	8.1	12.4	
25–29	3.9	7.4	5.8	9.5		
30–34	5.2	11.0	10.9			
35–39	8.5	12.0				
40–44	11.7					

Last figure in each column is for 1976.

Table 1-10
Cohort-Specific White Male Suicide Rates per 100,000 Population
of the United States

Attained Age	Period of Birth of Cohort					
	1931–35	1936–40	1941–45	1946–50	1951–55	1956–60
15–19	3.7	3.9	5.9	6.3	9.4	13.0
20–24	8.6	11.9	13.9	19.3	26.8	
25–29	13.8	16.5	19.8	25.1		
30–34	18.9	20.0	23.5			
35–39	21.9	22.8				
40–44	26.1					

Last figure in each column is for 1975.

than did those born at any earlier time since 1932. Moreover, as each birth cohort aged (columns), it continued to show a higher suicide rate than its predecessors. The same is true for Alberta females, as seen in Table 1-9. The trends are clear and consistent. Within each cohort, suicide rates increased directly with age. Columns are progressively

Table 1-11
Cohort-Specific Nonwhite Male Suicide Rates per 100,000 Population of the United States

Attained Age	Period of Birth of Cohort					
	1931–35	*1936–40*	*1941–45*	*1946–50*	*1951–55*	*1956–60*
15–19	2.2	3.8	3.4	5.2	5.4	7.0
20–24	9.2	15.8	13.1	19.4	23.6	
25–29	12.6	14.9	20.1	27.6		
30–34	13.5	19.4	20.9			
35–39	13.9	17.2				
40–44	14.8					

Last figure in each column is for 1975.

Table 1-12
Cohort-Specific White Female Suicide Rates per 100,000 Population of the United States

Attained Age	Period of Birth of Cohort					
	1931–35	*1936–40*	*1941–45*	*1946–50*	*1951–55*	*1956–60*
15–19	1.9	1.4	1.6	1.8	2.9	3.1
20–24	2.6	3.1	4.3	5.7	6.9	
25–29	4.8	6.6	8.6	8.0		
30–34	8.7	5.5	10.0			
35–39	12.2	11.4				
40–44	13.9					

Last figure in each column is for 1975.

shorter because successive birth cohorts have not yet reached the later ages. Late data are lacking because of a nearly four-year lag in the publication of vital statistics. The missing data points make clear the uncertainty as to whether this trend will continue, despite the consistency of the existing data.

Turning to data for the United States we can observe a similar trend, although the actual rates are lower. Precisely the same relationships hold true for white and nonwhite males and nearly so for white females in the United States during the same period (Tables 1-10 through 1-12). It is again clear that each five-year birth cohort since 1950 has not only attained the age of 15 to 19 with a higher suicide rate than that of the preceding five-year cohort but it continues to exhibit a higher rate than its predecessor in each subsequent quinquennium.

COMMENT

What we learned from profile analysis is that younger people are exhibiting a growing risk for suicide. Cohort analysis warns us that if past trends continue these younger people will carry this elevated risk as they age. When recent cohorts enter the traditionally high-risk ages of 50 and older, we might predict that suicide rates could be extremely high compared to rates for the older age groups in the past.

But this prediction must be made cautiously. We have been able to observe cohorts over only a limited number of years. For the younger cohorts we could trace their rates for only one or two five-year periods. Profile analysis indicated a leveling off or even a decline in suicide rates among older age groups in the past generation. It is possible that as younger cohorts age their rates will level off or decline as well. But even if this occurs, the leveling off can be expected to occur at a higher rate than previously, since rate increases have been higher among younger than among older persons both in Alberta and in the United States. This could result in an increasingly higher lifetime risk for suicide.

While we have shown that in recent years suicide risk is cohort-specific once a cohort enters the 15- to 19-year age group and that this risk increases as cohorts age, we have not addressed the question of why suicide rates have been steadily increasing among adolescents and young adults over the past generation in North America. In the next chapter Holinger and Offer discuss a population model for predicting adolescent suicide rates.

REFERENCES

1. Durkheim E: *Suicide*. Glencoe, IL, Free Press, 1951. Originally published in 1897.
2. Dizmang L: Self-destructive behavior in children: A suicidal equivalent, in Farberow NL (ed): *Proceedings: Fourth International Conference for Suicide Prevention*. Los Angeles, Delmar Publishing Co, 1968, pp 316–320.
3. Faigel HC: Suicide among young persons: A review of its incidence and causes and methods for its prevention. *Clin Pediatr* 1966;5:187–190.
4. French AP: Family dynamics, childhood depression and attempted suicide in a 7-year-old boy. *Suicide* 1975;5:29–37.
5. Shaffer D: Suicide in childhood and early adolescence. *J Child Psychol Psychiatry* 1974;15:275–291.
6. Stearns AW: Cases of probable suicide in young persons without obvious motivation. *J Maine Med Assoc* 1953;44:16–23.
7. Bakwin H: Suicide in children and adolescents. *J Pediatr* 1957;50:749–769.
8. Dublin LE: *Suicide: A Sociological and Statistical Study*. New York, Ronald Press, 1963.
9. Gardner EA, Bahn AK, Mack M: Suicide and psychiatric care in the aging. *Arch Gen Psychiatry* 1964;10:547–553.
10. Jacobziner H: Attempted suicides in children. *J Pediatr* 1960;56:519–525.
11. Peck ML: Suicidal motivations in adolescents. *Adolescence* 1968;3:109–118.
12. Perlstein AP: Suicide in adolescence. *NY State J Med* 1966;66:3017–3020.
13. Sainsbury P: Suicide in old age. *Proc R Soc Med* 1961;54:266–268.
14. Sainsbury P: Suicide in later life. *Gerontol Clinic* 1962;4:161–170.

14

15. Sims M: Sex and age patterns in suicide rates in a Canadian province: With particular reference to suicides by means of poison. *Life Threat Behavior* 1974;4:139–159.
16. Yacoubian JH, Lourie RS: Suicide and attempted suicide in children and adolescents. *Clin Proc Children's Hosp* 1969;25:325–343.
17. Zilboorg G: Considerations on suicide, with particular reference to that of the young. *Am J Orthopsychiatry* 1937;7:15–31.
18. Solomon MI, Hellon CP: Suicide and age in Alberta, Canada 1951–1977: A cohort analysis. *Arch Gen Psychiatry* 1980;37:511–513.
19. Murphy GE, Wetzel RD: Suicide risk by birth cohort in the United States, 1949–1974. *Arch Gen Psychiatry* 1980;37:519–523.
20. Frederick CJ: Current trends in suicidal behavior in the United States. *Am J Psychother* 1978;32:172–200.
21. Jacobziner H: Attempted suicides in adolescence. *JAMA* 1965;191:101–105.
22. Klagsbrun F: *Too Young to Die*. Boston, Houghton Mifflin, 1976.
23. Peck M, Litman R: Current trends in youthful suicide, in Bush JA (ed): *Suicide in Blacks*. Los Angeles, Fanon Research and Development Center, 1975.
24. Ramsay RF: Is it just attention getting?: A study of teenage suicide. *Alberta Counsellor* 1976;6:24–31.
25. Brooke EM: *Suicide and Attempted Suicide*. Public Health Papers No. 58. Geneva, Switzerland, World Health Organization, 1974.
26. Ross M: College student suicide. *Sci Psychoanal* 1970;17:94–102.
27. Toolan JM: Suicide in children and adolescents. *Am J Psychother* 1975;29: 339–344.
28. *Prevention of Suicide*. World Health Organization Public Health Papers No. 35. Geneva, WHO, 1968.
29. Stack S: Suicide in Detroit 1975: Changes and continuities. *Suicide Life Threat Behav* 1982;12:67–83.
30. Brugha T, Walsh D: Suicide past and present: The temporal constancy of under-reporting. *Br J Psychiatry* 1978;132:177–179.
31. Sainsbury P, Barraclough B: Differences between suicide rates. *Nature* 1968; 220:1252.
32. Hellon CP, Solomon MI: Suicide and age in Alberta, Canada, 1951 to 1977. The changing profile. *Arch Gen Psychiatry* 1980;37:505–510.
33. Ross O, Kreitman N: A further evaluation of differences in the suicide rates of England and Wales and of Scotland. *Br J Psychiatry* 1975;127:575–582.
34. Sainsbury P, Jenkins JS: The accuracy of officially reported suicide statistics for purposes of epidemiological research. *J Epidemiol Community Health* 1982;36:43–48.

CHAPTER 2

TOWARD THE PREDICTION OF VIOLENT DEATHS AMONG THE YOUNG

PAUL C. HOLINGER
DANIEL OFFER

The authors examine the relationship between suicide, homicide, motor vehicle accident, and nonmotor vehicle accident mortality rates, and population changes among adolescents and young adults (15 to 24 year olds). Significant positive correlations are found between adolescent and young adult suicide, homicide, and nonmotor vehicle accident mortality rates, and the changes in the proportion of 15 to 24 year olds in the population of the United States between 1933 and 1976; significant negative correlations are found between motor vehicle accident mortality rates and the changes in the proportion of adolescents and young adults in the United States population. These results expand the authors' previous study by examining other forms of self-destructive behavior (homicide and accidents) in addition to suicide, and by enlarging the age range. These results suggest that the violent death rates for the adolescent and young adult age group can be predicted, a finding which may have important public health consequences.

Suicide is the third leading cause of death among adolescents (following accidents and homicides, respectively[1]), and adolescent suicide rates have doubled over the period 1961 to 1975 and tripled between 1956 and 1975.[2-4] In an attempt to better understand time trends in suicide rates, we recently examined the relationship between suicide rates and population changes among adolescents.[5] Significant positive correlations were found between adolescent suicide rates (15 to 19 year olds), changes in the adolescent population, and changes in the proportion of adolescents in the population of the United States in 1933–1975. In contrast, the suicide rate of an older age group (65 to 69 year olds) was inversely, but not significantly, related to shifts in that population. The results suggested that the suicide rates for the adolescent age group could be predicted, a finding which would have important public health consequences.

However, attempting to understand man's self-destructive tendencies by studying only suicide may be a limited approach. Clinical and epidemiologic data suggest that homicides and accidents, in addition to suicides, may reflect self-destructive tendencies.[6] The purpose of this chapter is to relate adolescent and young adult homicide and accident rates, as well as suicide rates, to changes in the adolescent and young adult population and changes in the proportion of adolescents and young adults in the total population in the United States during the 20th century. Implied is the following question: Is it possible to predict the time trends in suicide, homicide, and accident rates among adolescents and young adults, and can such a predictive model logically imply effective intervention?

LITERATURE

An extensive literature review of suicide, homicide, and accidents among adolescents and young adults is beyond the scope of this chapter and has been presented elsewhere.[2,6] The general idea that changes in the population may be related to suicide, homicide, and accident rates has some support in the literature in addition to the correlations described above.[5] Wechsler[7] found that rapidly growing communities tended to produce significantly higher rates of suicide, and Gordon and Gordon's[8] results supported Wechsler's data. Klebba,[9] discussing the increase in homicide among the young, suggested an etiologic connection between the rising rates of homicide and the increases in the adolescent population over the past two decades. On the other hand, Levy and associates[10-12] found negative or insignificant correlations between both population density and crowding and suicide rates.

Two investigators have made important contributions to the potential prediction of violent death rates by studying separate aspects of the problem. Easterlin[13] has examined in some detail the relationship between population changes and a variety of variables, although with little mention of violent deaths. Brenner,[14,15] for example, has demonstrated the negative correlations between economic changes and various causes of mortality, including suicide and homicide (ie, utilizing unemployment rates, he found that the worse the economy, the higher the mortality rates). Others have more directly begun to relate population changes, economic changes, and violent death rates and suggest the potential for prediction.[16,17] However, there is a lack of systematic research focusing on the potential for a population model to predict the patterns of violent deaths and the relationship of this predictive model to economic changes.

METHODOLOGY

Two major types of methodological problems occur when using national mortality to study violent death patterns: 1) under- and overreporting, and 2) data classification. Underreporting may cause reported suicide data to be at least two or three times less than the actual figures.[18-21] The underreporting may be intentional or unintentional. In intentional underreporting, the physician, family, friends, etc, may contribute to covering up a suicide for various reasons: guilt, social stigma, insurance or pension benefits, malpractice, and so on. Unintentional underreporting refers to deaths labeled "accidents" (eg, single car crashes and some poisonings), which were actually suicides but were unverifiable as such due to the absence of a note or other evidence. In the case of homicide, the rates measure those killed; homicide rates in the younger age groups say nothing about the age of the killers. Therefore, the homicide rate among young people may reflect suicidal tendencies through the eliciting of homicide rather than indicating externally directed aggression. In the case of accident rates, overreporting may occur and may be intentional (covered-up suicides classified as accidents) or unintentional (deaths of "accident-prone" individuals that represent suicide).

Two types of data classification problems exist. One involves classification at the national level and the changes in this classification over time. The changes in federal classification over time have been outlined in government reports.[22-28] There has been little change over the century in federal classification for suicide, homicide, and motor vehicle accidents; accidents excluding motor vehicle accidents have shown a slight tendency toward a decrease in the number of deaths listed as non-motor vehicle accidents over the sixth (1949–1957), seventh (1958–1967) and eighth (1968–1977) Revisions of the International Classification of Diseases.* The second type of data classification problem concerns classification at the local level; eg, the legal issue in which some localities may require a suicide note as evidence of suicide, thereby both decreasing numbers and biasing results so that only the literate could be listed as having committed suicide.

Studies of violent deaths in the young involve additional methodological problems. There may be greater social stigma and guilt

---

*Comparability ratios for the sixth, seventh and eighth Revisions were, respectively, for suicide 1.00, 1.03 and 0.9472; for homicide 1.00, 1.00 and 0.9969; for motor vehicle accidents 1.00, 1.00 and 0.9921; for accidents excluding motor vehicle accidents 0.93, 0.95 and 0.9250; and for accidents (total) 0.95, 0.97 and 0.9570. Comparability ratios were not calculated by the government prior to the sixth Revision because of the nature of the available data and the difficulty quantifying the classification changes. The comparability ratios and discussions of these changes can be found in the references listed above in the Methodology section. Comparability ratios are calculations of the extent to which mortality rates for a cause of death may differ from one Revision to the next solely on the basis of reclassification of deaths. A comparability ratio of 1.00 indicates, usually, that the number of deaths attributed to a cause of mortality in the later Revision is essentially the same as for the earlier Revision; a ratio of less than 1.00 indicates that fewer deaths were attributed to the later Revision, while a ratio of greater than 1.00 indicates that more deaths were attributed to the later Revision due to classification changes.

surrounding suicide in childhood and adolescence because of the intense involvement of the parents at that age and the issue of parents failing and being "bad parents." In addition, it may be much easier to cover up suicide in the younger age groups. Poisonings and other methods of suicide are more easily conceived of as accidents in those age groups than in older age groups.

The data used are for the complete population, not samples: they include all suicides, homicides, and accidental deaths among 15 to 24 year olds that occurred in the United States between 1933 and 1976 (1933–1976 for correlations; 1933–1978 for graphs).* Sources of population, suicide, homicide, and accident data are the same as the sources for population and suicide data in our earlier report.[5]

Data for the years prior to 1933 are not included because it was not until 1933 that data from all states of the United States were included in the mortality statistics (Alaska was added in 1959 and Hawaii in 1960). It also should be noted that the data used in this chapter are age-specific mortality rates (deaths/100,000 population) of persons 15 to 24 years old, not simply number of deaths. Although it might be assumed that the number of deaths from a particular cause will increase with increases in the population, the mortality *rates* do not necessarily increase with an increase in population because the denominator is constant (ie, deaths/100,000 population).

RESULTS

Figure 2-1 shows the changes over time in mortality rates for suicide, homicide, motor vehicle accidents, and nonmotor vehicle accidents, for 15 to 24 year olds, and the population and the proportion of 15 to 24 year olds from 1933–1978 in the United States. The mortality rates, populations changes, and proportion of this age group in the population can be seen to be rather parallel, except for the opposing trends seen for motor vehicle accident rates. The changes in the mortality rates might be real, they might be artifact (ie, resulting from changes in reporting and classification over time), or they might be both. However, the changes in the suicide, homicide, and motor vehicle accident rates do not appear to be due to changes in federal classification; the nonmotor vehicle accident rates are slightly lower due to an artifact in federal classification, and the recent leveling-off of rates is in actuality a slight increase. (For a more

---

*Figures 2-1 through 2-5 use national mortality data from 1933–1978, while the correlations utilize data from 1933–1976; this discrepancy is due to the fact that the data for 1977 and 1978 were not available when the correlations were calculated, but were available to be included in the graphs.

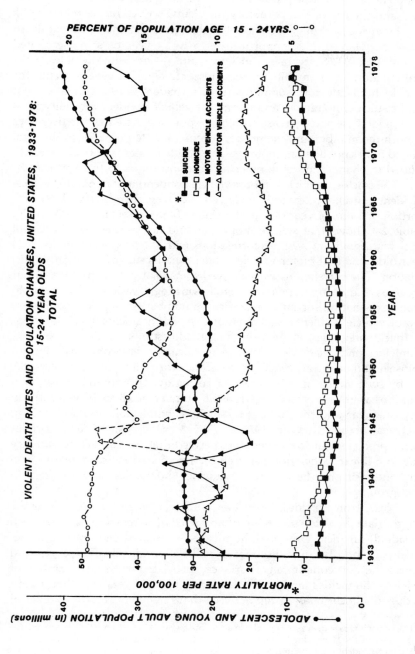

Figure 2-1

complete discussion of problems in classification of data on the federal level and the use of comparability problems, see references 6 and 28.*)

Figures 2-2 through 2-5 show the changes over time in violent death rates, population and proportion of 15 to 24 year olds in the United States, 1933–1978, by race and sex: white males, white females, nonwhite males, and nonwhite females, respectively. The general trends for suicide, homicide, and nonmotor vehicle accident rates are parallel: that is, the suicide, homicide, and nonmotor vehicle accident mortality rates tend to increase and decrease with corresponding increases and decreases in both the number and the proportion of 15 to 24 year olds in the total United States population; motor vehicle accident rates tend to be inversely related to changes in the number and proportion of 15 to 24 year olds.

The suicide, homicide, motor vehicle accident, and nonmotor vehicle accident mortality rates for 15 to 24 year olds were correlated with the proportion of 15 to 24 year olds in the United States population, 1933–1976. Table 2-1 shows that suicide, homicide, and nonmotor vehicle accident rates had significant positive correlations with the proportion of 15 to 24 year olds, and that motor vehicle accidents had a significant negative correlation. The correlations were derived somewhat differently than in our previous study.[5] In this review, the following logic was used. The most obvious explanation for an increase in the number of suicides, homicides, motor vehicle accidents, and nonmotor vehicle accidents in any one year is that there might have been more adolescents to die by suicide, homicide, and accidents in that year. Clearly, these obvious relationships should be linear, assuming constant proportions of the adolescents die by such violent means of death. To remove this obvious effect, correlations were performed between the number of 15 to 24 year olds in any one year and the number of suicides, homicides, and accidents in that year across the years 1933 to 1976. On the basis of these correlations, predicted suicide scores were derived that contain all the variance due to a linear association between the number of 15 to 24 year olds in any one year and the number of suicides, homicides, and accidents in that group.

Next, from suicides, homicides, and accidents in any one year the appropriate predicted scores were subtracted. The remainders were called "residual suicides," "residual homicides," "residual motor vehicle accidents," and "residual nonmotor vehicle accidents." These residual scores cannot contain any variance associated with the number of suicides, homicides, and accidents among 15 to 24 year olds that in turn is due to a linear relationship between those numbers and the number of

---

*The sharp increase in nonmotor vehicle accidents among 15 to 24 year olds occurring during the early 1940s was due to an increase in air transport deaths within the United States borders (Accident fatalities in the United States, 1943. *Vital Statistics–Special Reports*, vol 21, no 7. Washington, DC, Dept. of Commerce [Bureau of the Census], 1946).

21

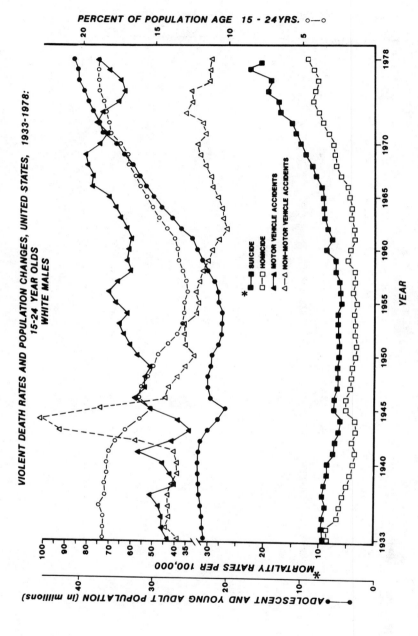

Figure 2-2

22

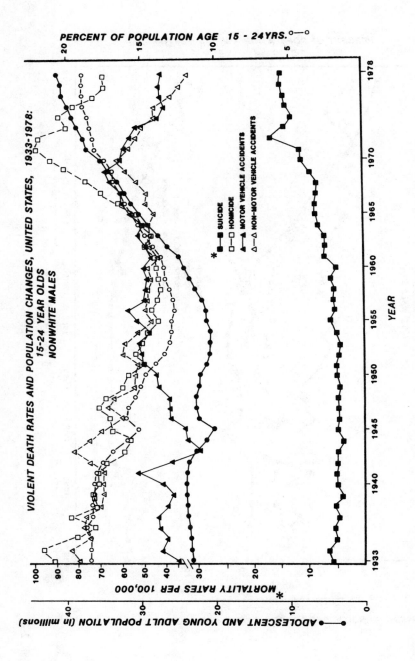

Figure 2-3

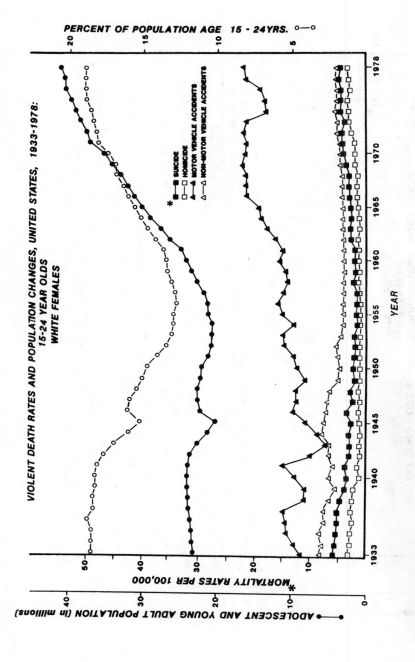

VIOLENT DEATH RATES AND POPULATION CHANGES, UNITED STATES, 1933-1978:
15-24 YEAR OLDS
WHITE FEMALES

PERCENT OF POPULATION AGE 15 - 24YRS. ○—○

* ■ SUICIDE
□—□ HOMICIDE
▲—▲ MOTOR VEHICLE ACCIDENTS
△—△ NON-MOTOR VEHICLE ACCIDENTS

YEAR

*MORTALITY RATES PER 100,000

●ADOLESCENT AND YOUNG ADULT POPULATION (in millions)

Figure 2-4

24

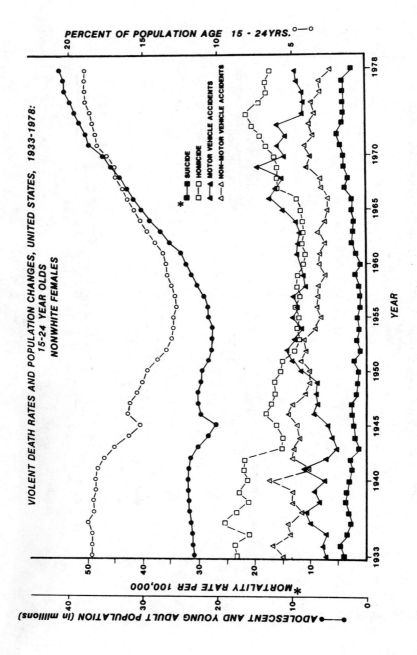

Figure 2-5

15 to 24 year olds in the general population. These residual scores expressed as a mortality rate by division by the corresponding population of 15 to 24 year olds were then correlated with the proportion of 15 to 24 year olds in the general population across the years 1933 to 1976. The resulting correlations are presented in Table 2-1. There is a notable reduction in the variance in suicide, homicide, and accident rates that can be explained on the basis of the methodology presented above. It should be mentioned, however, that at issue is the potential prediction of groups, not individuals (ie, the purpose is not to establish a 1:1 correlation with individuals).

DISCUSSION

The data suggest that significant positive correlations exist between adolescent and young adult rates of suicide, homicide, and nonmotor vehicle accidents, and changes in the proportion of adolescents and young adults in the United States. A significant negative correlation exists between motor vehicle accident rates and changes in the proportion of 15 to 24 year olds. That is, increases and decreases in the proportion of 15 to 24 year olds in the population are temporally related to corresponding increases and decreases in suicide, homicide, and nonmotor vehicle accident mortality rates for those ages, with motor vehicle accident rates being inversely related to the proportion of 15 to 24 year olds. These findings enlarge our previous study[5] in two important ways. First, homicide, motor vehicle accidents, and nonmotor vehicle accidents, in addition to suicide rates, are shown to be significantly correlated with the population changes in the younger ages. Second, there is evidence that these relationships exist in most race and sex breakdowns and in the 15- to 24-year-old age group rather than the 15 to 19 year olds.

One must always keep in mind the multidetermined nature of the various forms of violent death and question whether or not such single-variable relationships are spurious. The importance of the above findings

Table 2-1
Correlation Coefficients for Proportion of 15–24 Year Olds
in the Population and Violent Death Rates for 15–24 Year Olds,
United States, 1933–1976.

	Suicide	Homicide	Motor Vehicle Accidents	Nonmotor Vehicle Accidents
Proportion of 15–24 year olds in US population	.46*	.49*	−.60*	.52*

*Correlation significant at $P < .001$.

lies in the potential for prediction of suicide, homicide, and accident rates among specific age groups. Inasmuch as the population of children and preadolescents decreased throughout the late 1960s and 1970s,[29,30] we would expect the population trends for 15 to 24 year olds to shift and begin decreasing in the late 1970s and 1980s. We would also predict that suicide, homicide, and nonmotor vehicle accident death rates among 15 to 24 year olds would decrease simultaneously with the population decrease in that age group, and that the motor vehicle accident death rates would increase. These data should be related to Brenner's[14,15] and Easterlin's[13] work. Brenner demonstrated that indicators of economic instability and insecurity, such as unemployment, were associated over time with higher mortality rates, including suicide and homicide. His explanation for this association was that the lack of economic security is stressful: social and family structures break down and habits that are harmful to health are adopted. Some data show that suicide, homicide, and accident rates are parallel over time and may all reflect self-destructive tendencies to some extent,[6] and Brenner's model suggests a reason for the parallel rates: economic cycles. Easterlin[13] has related population increases in specific age groups with worsening economic conditions in those age groups. Turner et al[31] have reported increases and decreases in economic conditions among adolescents and young adults which correspond clearly to the decreases and increases, respectively, in the youthful population data presented in this chapter.

With respect to these relationships between violent deaths, the economy, and population changes, one must be curious about the significant negative correlation between motor vehicle accidents and the population changes among 15 to 24 year olds, particularly inasmuch as this finding is in opposition to the trends found in this chapter between youthful population changes and suicide, homicide, and nonmotor vehicle accident death rates. While further research is necessary to enhance the understanding of this phenomenon, the finding regarding motor vehicle accidents may relate to the economy and the youthful age group involved: during times of economic prosperity, there may be more opportunity for youngsters to own or use (and die in) motor vehicles, while in an economic depression such opportunity for motor vehicle use may be less for youngsters but remain high enough for older age groups to account for their increased motor vehicle accident death rates.

These data appear to suggest that while the behavior of a single individual may be unpredictable, the violent death rates for populations over time are predictable. Gedo and Goldberg[32] have discussed the conceptual problems involved in trying to understand the data and findings of one scientific discipline by using models derived from data of a very different scientific discipline. Specifically, they described the potential for error in applying metapsychological propositions about intrapsychic phenomena to social psychology and vice versa. The data presented here lend themselves to potential intervention on a public health level. However, the specifics of the intervention on a social level seem discernible only when one attempts to bridge the epidemiology–intrapsychic gap and hypothesize about what, on an intrapsychic level, could account for the epidemiologic data presented.

Therefore, in a previous paper,[5] we made some preliminary remarks to explain these epidemiologic relationships on a clinical basis and justify our suggestion for interventions. Two psychodynamic explanations, not necessarily mutually exclusive, were advanced: one involved a competition, self-esteem, and failure cycle, and the other a process of progressive isolation. The intervention and prevention of increased rates of suicide, homicide, and accidents seem implied by the intrapsychic models and involve addressing the need for more services (psychiatric) and positions (job, high schools, college enrollments, etc) sooner and cutting the time lag between the adolescent and young adult population changes and society's response. Such intervention is possible with this population model because the changes in the population of 15 to 24 year olds can be predicted years ahead of time by the population figures for children and preadolescents.

It also should be noted that these epidemiologic data appear to be consistent with data from questionnaires and interviews with samples of normal adolescents. In studying thousands of adolescents, Offer et al[33] noted that the self-image of adolescents was better in the early 1960s than in the late 1970s for every category tested except the sexual sphere. These differences correspond closely to the smaller numbers of adolescents in the late 1950s and early 1960s, and the larger numbers of adolescents in the mid-to-late 1970s.

In summary, although the relationship between the economy and mortality rates is well documented (bad economic conditions are related to higher mortality rates),[14,15] one cannot predict future mortality rates from this relationship because, without considering population variables, one does not know what economic conditions will be like in the future. On the other hand, the population model suggested in this chapter may allow future predictions, not only of violent death rates,[5] but also of economic conditions[13] for certain age groups, because the population shifts for certain age groups are known years ahead. Finally, this predictive cycle perhaps becomes even more complete when one considers that the birth rate in the United States (which is responsible for most of the relevant population changes) tends to be inversely related to economic changes in the United States (ie, high and low birth rates correspond to good and bad economic conditions, respectively).[31]

Thus, the interrelationship of these variables becomes clearer: from the birth rate comes relevant population changes; these population changes appear to influence economic conditions (ie, unemployment); economic conditions (and the population changes) tend to influence not only changes in violent death rates, but also changes in the birth rates, thus completing the cycle. The potential for prediction of violent death rates seems to occur by breaking into the cycle and extracting the data on population changes.

ACKNOWLEDGMENTS

This study was supported in part by the Harold W. Schloss Memorial Fund. The authors gratefully acknowledge the assistance of Eric Ostrov, PhD, JD and Kenneth Howard, PhD in the statistical analysis.

REFERENCES

1. Holinger PC: Violent deaths among the young: Recent trends in homicide, and accidents. *Am J Psychiatry* 1979;136:1144–1147.
2. Holinger PC, Offer D: Perspectives on suicide in adolescence, in Simmons R (ed): *Social and Community Mental Health*. Greenwich, CT, Jai Press, 1981, vol 2, pp 139–157.
3. Holinger PC: Adolescent suicide: An epidemiological study of recent trends. *Am J Psychiatry* 1978;135:754–756.
4. Holinger PC: Self-destructiveness among the young: An epidemiological study of violent deaths. *Int J Soc Psychiatry* 1981;17:277–282.
5. Holinger PC, Offer D: Prediction of adolescent suicide: A population model. *Am J Psychiatry* 1982;139:302–307.
6. Holinger PC, Klemen EH: Violent deaths in the United States, 1900–1975. *Soc Sci Med* 1982;16:1929–1938.
7. Wechsler H: Community growth, depressive disorders, and suicide. *Am J Sociology* 1961;67:9–16.
8. Gordon RE, Gordon KK: Social psychiatry of a mobile suburb. *Int J Soc Psychiatry* 1960;6:89–106.
9. Klebba AJ: Homicide trends in the United States, 1900–1974. *Public Health Rep* 1975;90:195–204.
10. Levy L, Herzog AN: Effects of crowding on health and social adaptation in the city of Chicago. *Urban Ecology* 1978;3:327–354.
11. Levy L, Herzog AN: Effects of population density and crowding on health and social adaptation in the Netherlands. *J Health Soc Behav* 1974;15:228–240.
12. Herzog AN, Levy L, Verdonk A: Some ecological factors associated with health and social adaptation in the city of Rotterdam. *Urban Ecology* 1977;2:205–234.
13. Easterlin RA: *Birth and Fortune*. New York, Basic Books, 1980.
14. Brenner MH: Mortality and the national economy: A review, and the experience of England and Wales, 1936–76. *Lancet* 1979;2:568–573.
15. Brenner MH: *Time Series Analysis of Relationships Between Selected Economic and Social Indicators*. Springfield, VA, National Technical Information Service, 1971.

16. Seiden RH, Freitas RP: Shifting patterns of deadly violence. *Suicide Life Threat Behav* 1980;10:195–209.
17. Peck M, Litman RE: Current trends in youthful suicide. *Tribune Media* 1973; 14:13–17.
18. Seiden RH: Suicide among youth: A review of the literature, 1900–1967. *Bull Suicidology* 1969 (suppl).
19. Kramer M, Pollack ES, Redick RW, et al: *Mental Disorders/Suicide*. Cambridge, Harvard University Press, 1972.
20. Toolan JM: Suicide and suicidal attempts in children and adolescents. *Am J Psychiatry* 1962;118:719–724.
21. Toolan JM: Suicide in children and adolescents. *Am J Psychother* 1975; 29:339–344.
22. Dunn HL, Shackley W: Comparison of cause-of-death assignments by the 1929 and 1938 revisions of the International List; Deaths in the United States, 1940. *Vital Statistics–Special Reports* vol 12, no 14, 1944.
23. Faust MM, Dolman AB: Comparability of mortality statistics for the fifth and sixth revisions: United States, 1950. *Vital Statistics–Special Reports* vol 51, no 3, 1963a.
24. Faust MM, Dolman AB: Comparability ratios based on mortality statistics for the fifth and sixth revisions: United States, 1950. *Vital Statistics–Special Reports* vol 51, no 3, 1963b.
25. Faust MM, Dolman AB: Comparability of mortality statistics for the sixth and seventh revisions: United States, 1958. *Vital Statistics–Special Reports* vol 51, no 4, 1965.
26. Classification of terms and comparability of titles through five revisions of the International List of Causes of Death. *Vital Statistics — Special Reports* vol 19, no 13, 1944.
27. Death rate by age, race, and sex: United States, 1900–1953. *Vital Statistics–Special Reports*, vol 43. Washington, DC, US Government Printing Office, 1956.
28. Klebba AJ, Dolman AB: Comparability of mortality statistics for the seventh and eighth revisions of the International Classification of Diseases, United States. *Vital and Health Statistics*, series 2, no 66. Washington, DC, US Government Printing Office, 1975.
29. Grove RD, Hetzel AM: *Vital Statistics Rates in the United States: 1940–1960*. Washington, DC, US Government Printing Office, 1968.
30. *Vital Statistics of the United States, 1961–1978: Mortality*. United States Department of Health, Education and Welfare, Public Health Service, National Center for Health Statistics, Washington, DC, US Government Printing Office.
31. Turner CW, Fenn MR, Cole AM: A social psychological analysis of violent behavior, in Stuart RB (ed): *Violent Behavior: Social Learning Approaches to Prediction, Management and Treatment*. New York, Brunner/Mazel, 1981.
32. Gedo J, Goldberg A: *Models of the Mind*. Chicago, University of Chicago Press, 1973.
33. Offer D, Ostrov E, Howard KI: *The Adolescent: A Psychological Self-Portrait*. New York, Basic Books, 1981.

CHAPTER 3

SUICIDE IN YOUNG
MINORITY GROUP PERSONS

CALVIN J. FREDERICK

Racial minority groups have been undervalued and underserved for years with respect to the recognition of self-destructive behavior and the special need to provide mental health services for addressing this problem in these populations. The percentage increase in suicidal deaths among young nonwhite males, specifically black males, has exceeded that of young white males for over a decade (through the 1970s). Moreover, the percentage of all suicidal deaths that occur below age 25 is greater for both sexes for nonwhites in general and for blacks in particular than it is among whites.

Analysis of the methods of suicide reveals major similarities in those used by white and black adolescents and young adults. Both groups utilize firearms as the predominant mode regardless of sex. Suicide and deaths from alcoholism are prevalent in young Native American Indians. (Self-destruction involving drinking and driving is an acute problem in this and other minority groups. Many alcohol-related traffic accidents may be direct or indirect suicides.) A study in the District of Columbia showed that blacks have high drug addiction rates, excessive suicide attempt rates, and greater rates of violent death, including suicides. These findings highlight the need for concentrating more research, innovative training and treatment efforts in relation to these increasingly vulnerable populations.

The increasing suicide rate in young persons of all races and both sexes has been particularly acute over the past two and one-half decades in the United States as noted by the author,[1-3] and others.[4,5] In the last few years additional attention has been focused upon suicide in young blacks and other racial minorities,[6-8] due in part, perhaps, to the expressive voices of such groups along with a continuing emphasis upon issues of discrimination. Several decades ago, the recorded suicide rates among blacks, in particular, were low in comparison with rates among whites.[9] In 1959, the United States suicide rate for white persons of all ages was 11.2 per 100,000 compared with 4.5 for nonwhites of all ages and 3.4 for blacks. The lower black suicide rate was postulated to be due to a number of factors,[5,10] such as the presence of tightly knit and supportive family groupings, a philosophical acceptance of lower socio-economic status, and inaccurate counting procedures of the incidence of deaths among blacks since local governments often did not want to spend funds for autopsies on poor, minority groups. However, Peck and Litman[5] suggest a relationship between higher rates of suicide in black youth in the late 60s and early 70s and the increase in adolescent suicide in general. More recent data show greater relative increases in the suicide rates of young black males, aged 15 to 19 and 20 to 24 years than for their white counterparts.

SOME CONCEPTS OF SUICIDE
CONCERNING RACIAL MINORITIES

Most attempts to account for the lower incidence of suicide among blacks have been conjectural. Because of the low suicide rate reported among black populations a few decades ago, it was sometimes assumed that one important set of factors was the built-in restraining influence of the "solid black family unit" along with an "acceptance" of the stresses of a lower socioeconomic status. Henry and Short,[11] Breed,[12] and Maris[13] all have alluded to this in some manner. Davis[10] held that these ties have been weakened, especially among younger blacks, to the point where increased suicidal behavior can be explained by it. Hendin[4] suggested that blacks have been so beaten emotionally that they may have less fear of dying than whites and, consequently, may engage in greater risk-taking behavior, including violence. Numerous periods in jail (resulting in haunting penal records) could have caused many blacks to give up and forsake striving for a better life. Putative, harsh child-rearing practices in single family homes may have made many black children suffer at the hands of their frustrated and unwed mothers as another possible contributing factor. While the phenomenon of upward mobility and equal rights in the marketplace has helped economically, black sole-support mothers continue to operate under emotional and psychological stress.

It is not unlikely, in some instances, that the stresses of racism and discrimination against blacks and other minorities have produced a closeness and cohesive spirit in these groups which has helped to mitigate self-destructive behavior. On the other hand, the opportunity for greater acceptance in the marketplace, more opportunities for education and greater expectations for upward mobility may have resulted in heightened frustrations in many blacks who have not developed the coping skills to adjust to such changing circumstances. Increased status and higher standards of living have, by no means, been rapid or automatic. Long hours of work and impatience with bureaucratic business protocol have been realistic obstacles in pathways to success. Many blacks have not learned how to maneuver through such troublesome facets of business life. Feelings of despair and depression can follow quickly in the wake of such events, with suicide as a possible consequence, particularly if there is a history of, and an acceptance of, violence (sanctioned by example) in the early lives of minority group persons. Depending upon past learned associations and personality type, such group-sanctioned violence can be turned outward, against others, or inward, against the self. Homicide among blacks has continued to increase even more rapidly than suicide rates.[14]

Bohannan,[15] an anthropologist, and Durkheim,[16] a French sociologist, emphasized the value of social ties. Bohannan commented that suicide among African tribes is generally low due to the presence of strong familial and cultural ties. For persons in their 20s and 30s, the presence of disease is the leading cause of suicide among Africans, whereas quarrels with a spouse or lover is the second most prominent cause. However, for those under 20 years of age, quarreling with spouse or lover was found to be the most frequent cause. Durkheim spoke of several types of suicide, but the one which is applicable for our purposes he called "anomic." This emphasized that a normlessness existed, which caused suicide to vary inversely with the degree of integration of the individual into his or her subgroup. He felt that moving abruptly from one social status or life-style to another created severe stressors which could lead to suicide since the person felt like an outcast. When Malinowski[17] described his studies of primitive societies, he emphasized the importance of "institutions." An institution, for him, was a group of people united by the process of seeking common purposes and goals. Its presence or absence could be vital in suicidal acts.

In Durkheim's terms anomic suicide is a societal indicator of inadequate regulations and laws in the social institutions of the locale involved. In Malinowski's thinking, suicide is found in societies, subcultures or familial situations where the institution, as he defined it, is not adequate to hold people to united goals and purposes. In the author's view these concepts overlap, and are, at least, in part both applicable as reasons which contribute to the increase in suicide among young persons of all races in the United States today.

There is no simple answer to the question of why there has been such a marked increase in suicidal behavior among young persons in western society. Suicide is a function of a number of factors; it varies with socioeconomic conditions, social forces and structures, intrapersonal and interpersonal stress, cultural mores, physical and mental health. The influence of any given factor will vary with time and situation. Suicide rates have not been stable, but have varied with national conditions. Traditionally, they have increased prior to war and decreased during and after a war. They appear to have increased during economic depressions and decreased with a more favorable economy.[11]

In 1975, Davis[10] reported on a national study of black suicide completed for a doctoral dissertation. In suggesting an explanation for the increasing incidence of suicide reported among young blacks, he looked at the role of weakened communal ties in the family and focused on the "isolating effects" of emigration and living alone. He viewed such effects as limiting access to the alleged cohesive, positive relationships within black communities, which appeared to have functioned as a protection or buffer against suicidal acts. Davis also sought to determine what relationship might exist between black suicide and educational level (which he equated with social class status). While it was found that emigration and educational level showed a strong positive correlation with black suicide rates, no relationship was noted between these rates and living alone. Davis' principal finding indicated a statistically significant association between weakened social relationships (alienation from established communal and family ties) and the incidence of suicide among blacks.

SUICIDE RATES BY COLOR AND SEX: RECENT NATIONAL DATA

There is currently a heightened focus on the increase of suicide among younger age blacks. Black male suicide occurs most frequently among persons below the age of 35; following that, it tends to decrease. This is not the case with white males, who show a fairly direct increase with age. While elderly white males still have the highest suicide rates, the recent relative rate increase has been greatest among the younger age groups.[1,6] In general, for the three racial categories, suicide rates have increased over the past 12 years in nearly every age grouping and sex category among younger individuals. Only those 10 to 14 years old in the nonwhite female category and black males have shown decreases. While the greatest increases in rates have also occurred in the 10–14 age ranges, especially among various female categories and nonwhite males, the numbers of deaths are relatively small. For example, an increase in rate of 100% for black females in the 10–14 age range represented only three suicides in 1979 with an increase in rate from 0.1 in 1968 to 0.2 in 1979. Although a consistent upturn in death rates from any cause must be reason for some concern, it is prudent to assess the influence of small numbers upon the statistical outcome.

Table 3-1 shows numbers and rates for the year 1979 as well as the percent change in suicide rates by color and sex for persons between the ages of 10 and 24 years from 1968 through 1979. Rates of suicide for non-

Table 3-1

Numbers, Rates and Percent Change in Suicides for Younger Age Groups by Race, Age and Sex, United States, 1979

	10–14 Years			15–19 Years			20–24 Years		
	N	Rate	%Δ	N	Rate	%Δ	N	Rate	%Δ
Total, Both Sexes	151	0.8	33	1788	8.4	68	3458	16.4	71
Total Male	103	1.1	22	1452	13.4	72	2793	26.5	78
Total Female	48	0.5	150	336	3.2	45	665	6.3	34
White, Both Sexes	139	0.9	50	1602	8.9	68	3000	16.7	72
White Male	94	1.2	20	1305	14.3	72	2422	26.8	77
White Female	45	0.6	200	297	3.4	55	578	6.5	38
Nonwhite, Both Sexes	12	0.4	33	186	5.4	59	458	14.6	70
Nonwhite Male	9	0.6	100	147	8.5	81	371	24.6	81
Nonwhite Female	3	0.2	−33	39	2.3	4	87	5.3	23
Black, Both Sexes	7	0.3	0	132	4.4	57	354	13.1	66
Black Male	4	0.3	−25	100	6.7	76	289	22.5	83
Black Female	3	0.2	100	32	2.1	17	65	4.6	9

Calculations by the author based upon data supplied by the National Center for Health Statistics.

%Δ = Percent change over the 12-year period from 1968–1979 in annual rates.

whites and specifically blacks are lower than those of whites for these younger age groups.

Of greater concern are the steadily increasing suicidal deaths occurring in young persons aged 15 to 19 and 20 to 24 years, particularly the latter. The numbers of suicides as well as the rates and percentages of increase are of interest. The increase in rates over the past decade or so for adolescent and young adult males has exceeded 70%. The rate for nonwhites, including blacks, has shown a remarkable rise of more than 75% among those 15 to 19 and 20 to 24 years of age over the past 12 years. These relative increases during this period of time are greater for nonwhite males, and specifically blacks, the largest component of this population, than those found in the white population. Although this fact is worthy of note, the reader should again be mindful of the smaller numbers upon which the minority group data are based. While the percentage of increased change is greater for minority group males, the reverse was obtained for females, with the white females showing a greater relative increase. The trends in increasing rates for all groups of adolescents and young adults should alert health policy planners to address themselves to this issue in these populations.

The relative importance of suicidal deaths among the young as a cause for national concern is shown in Table 3-2, which reveals that one fifth of all suicides in the United States are found in persons under 24 years of age, with 22% of all male self-destructive deaths occurring below this age. Whites comprise the bulk of the suicides in all categories by numbers and percentages of total deaths. However, it is another matter when we consider the percentage of deaths occurring within each racial category. The relative frequency of suicide in the young of minority races is apparent from the figures shown in Table 3-2. This is particularly evident for suicides in the 20–24 year age range, where the percentage of all suicides among blacks and nonwhites of both sexes exceeds the comparable percentages for whites.

For nonwhite males, 21% of all suicides occur in that age group (20% in the case of black males) compared with 14% for white males. For females aged 20 to 24 years, comparable figures are 17% for nonwhite, 17% for blacks and 9% for whites. The lower percentages for young whites reflect, to a large extent, the higher rates of suicide in white adults, peaking in the middle years in females, and increasing steadily with age in males (see Chapter 1). Suicide rates for nonwhites, and specifically blacks, are almost as high as those of whites for the age range 20–24 years, but are substantially smaller in the older age groups. These figures result in a higher proportion of nonwhite and black suicides in the younger age range, emphasizing the greater relative importance of young suicides in minority populations.

Table 3-2
Numbers of Deaths from Suicide and Percentage of All Individual Deaths by Race and Sex for Persons 15–19 and 20–24 Years, United States, 1979*

	Total Suicides	15–19 Years Of Age			20–24 Years of Age		
		No. of Suicides in Each Subgroup	% Total of Subgroup	% Total	No. of Suicides in Each Subgroup	% Total of Subgroup	% Total
Total							
Both Sexes	27,206	1939	—	7	3458	—	13
Male	20,256	1555	—	8	2793	—	14
Female	6950	384	—	6	655	—	10
White							
Both Sexes	24,945	1741	7	6	3000	12	11
Male	18,504	1399	8	7	2422	14	12
Female	6441	342	5	5	578	9	8
All Nonwhite							
Both Sexes	2261	198	9	.7	458	20	1.6
Male	1752	156	9	.7	371	21	1.8
Female	509	42	8	.6	87	17	1.2
Black							
Both Sexes	1812	139	8	.51	354	20	1.3
Male	1428	104	7	.51	289	20	1.4
Female	384	35	9	.50	65	17	0.9

*Computations derived by the author from data provided by the National Center for Health Statistics.

METHODS USED IN SUICIDE: COMPARISONS OF BLACK AND WHITE YOUTH

An analysis of the various methods used in suicide indicates that, in general, few major differences exist between whites and blacks among adolescents and young adults. Among United States white youngsters of both sexes aged 10 to 14 years in 1979, firearms and explosives constitute the most prominent mode of suicide, followed by hanging and strangulation, and ingestion of solid and liquid substances. All three of these methods are equally prevalent in blacks for this age group, but these figures are based on very few cases.

Table 3-3 gives the percentages of suicide by various methods for adolescents aged 15 to 19 years and young adults aged 20 to 24 by sex for United States whites and blacks in 1979. For both age groups and both races, taken individually and when combining both sexes, firearms and explosives are the predominant mode, a result due almost exclusively to firearm use. The second most frequently used method of suicide is by hanging, strangulation, or suffocation, followed in third place by ingestion of solid and liquid substances, primarily barbiturates and tranquilizers. Proportionately more black males than white males hang themselves or die by jumping from high places or drowning, whereas relatively more white males use firearms or die utilizing carbon monoxide. A higher proportion of females poison themselves, employing barbiturates and tranquilizers, irrespective of race. Firearms, however, are utilized in a majority of female suicides both for white and black adolescents as well as young adults. Although more black adolescent males (29.0%) employ hanging than whites of the same sex (16.2%), the opposite obtains for females in that age group since a higher proportion of white females (12.1%) use that method to take their lives than black females (6.2%). Inasmuch as guns are used in the largest percentage by far of suicidal deaths for adolescents and young persons, it is clear that access to such lethal means is readily available for those in the younger age groups as well as in the more adult age ranges.

DEATHS FROM SUICIDE AND ALCOHOLISM: NATIONAL DATA ON NATIVE AMERICAN INDIANS

It is well known that young male American Indians and Eskimos have strikingly high death rates from both alcohol and suicide. The author has personally witnessed an appalling incidence of alcohol abuse among Eskimo males 13 to 15 years of age in Alaska and among black youth of comparable ages in metropolitan areas in the inland 48 states.

Table 3-3
Percentage of Suicides by Method in the United States for 1979 for Adolescents (Aged 15–19 Years) and Young Adults (Aged 20–24 Years) by Race and Sex

	Code*	White			Black		
		Total	Male	Female	Total	Male	Female
Solid and liquid substances	950	7.3 (9.5)	3.8 (6.3)	22.6 (23.0)	9.1 (7.3)	3.0 (4.8)	28.1 (18.5)
Domestic gas	951	0.1 (0.2)	0.2 (0.3)	0.0 (0.0)	0.0 (0.0)	0.0 (0.0)	0.0 (0.0)
Other gases and vapors (CO)	952	6.4 (7.3)	6.6 (7.2)	5.4 (7.8)	1.5 (1.1)	2.0 (1.4)	0.0 (0.0)
Hanging/strangulation/ suffocation	953	15.5 (14.1)	16.2 (15.6)	12.1 (8.0)	23.5 (19.2)	29.0 (21.8)	6.2 (7.7)
Drowning	954	0.9 (1.6)	0.6 (1.5)	2.4 (2.1)	4.5 (4.2)	5.0 (4.2)	3.1 (4.6)
Firearms and explosives	955	64.6 (60.9)	67.7 (63.1)	50.8 (51.6)	53.0 (56.2)	54.0 (55.7)	50.0 (58.6)
Cutting and piercing	956	0.6 (1.0)	0.6 (1.1)	0.3 (0.7)	0.8 (0.6)	0.0 (0.7)	3.1 (0.0)
Jumping	957	2.6 (3.3)	2.2 (2.8)	4.0 (5.0)	3.8 (6.8)	5.5 (6.9)	6.2 (6.2)
All other		2.1 (2.1)	2.0 (2.1)	2.3 (1.9)	3.8 (4.5)	4.0 (4.5)	3.1 (4.6)

*9th Revision ICD Code; data supplied by the National Center for Health Statistics. Percentage data in parenthesis refer to persons 20–24 years of age. International Classification of Diseases (ICD).

The likelihood of such very young persons living past their 20s has diminished markedly with the increases in substance abuse from drugs and alcohol.[6,17]

The problems of suicide and alcohol-related deaths begin at very young ages among Native American Indians, as seen in Table 3-4. Both suicides, per se, and deaths from alcohol begin to appear before the age of 15 and are prevalent in the age groups 15–24. Suicide rates for this population are highest in this age group, whereas deaths from alcohol continue to climb up to ages 45 to 54 years. Native American Indian suicide rates show a ratio greater than the one based both on United States nonwhites and all races combined for the younger age groups. This holds up through age 44 compared with all races, and up through age 64 compared to nonwhite. In the case of deaths from alcoholism, such ratios are larger than the ones for all ages, dramatizing the alarmingly high death rates for this racial group. Native American Indian death rates from alcoholism show a shockingly large ratio compared with all males in the United States and with nonwhite persons; those ratios being 19.8 and 8.8 to 1, respectively. Thus, for this minority group deaths from alcohol are an acute problem in the young.

Self-destruction involving drinking and driving is an important problem not only for Native American Indians but for young persons in all racial groups. Vehicular accidents are a leading cause of death for teenage males. Many of these adolescents lose their lives in alcohol-related traffic accidents. Drug abuse also accounts for a significant number of vehicular deaths because concentration becomes impaired.

Alcohol consumption also pays a significant role in suicidal deaths. James[18] indicated that between 25% and 37% of all persons committing suicide had some level of alcohol in their blood at the time of the act. While it is difficult to ascertain a precise figure for overt suicidal traffic fatalities, it is known that between 30% and 50% of these fatalities show alcohol involvement. Because deaths from alcohol, per se, are not listed among the causes of death, no exact numbers of teenage deaths from this cause, either accidental or overtly suicidal, are available. It is probable, however, that persons in these younger age ranges lose their lives in significant numbers due to alcohol and traffic accidents which may be direct or indirect suicides. Although controversial, the reduction, in some states, of the legal age from 21 to 18 years for the purchase of hard liquor and of the driving age to 16 years probably contribute to this problem. Death rates due to accidents in the 16- to 24-year age range have increased following such changes in the law.

DRUG ABUSE AND SUICIDE:
A STUDY OF YOUNG BLACKS

A study of drug addicts instituted by the author[19] in cooperation with the District of Columbia Narcotics Treatment Administration

Table 3-4

Age-Specific Death Rates from Suicide and from Alcoholism for Native American Indian and all Races in the United States, 1977-1979*

Age	Suicide Rates					Death Rates from Alcoholism				
	Native American Indian	Nonwhite	All Races, U.S.	Ratio: Indian to Nonwhite	Ratio: Indian to All Races, U.S.	Native American Indian	Nonwhite	All Races, U.S.	Ratio: Indian to Nonwhite	Ratio: Indian to All Races, U.S.
5-14	1.0	0.3	0.4	3.3	2.5	0.1	0.0	0.0	–	–
15-24	44.7	8.9	12.4	5.0	3.6	7.9	0.9	0.4	8.8	19.8
25-34	41.8	13.9	16.7	3.0	2.5	71.2	10.7	2.9	6.7	24.6
35-44	28.9	10.3	15.8	2.8	1.8	129.9	35.7	11.6	3.6	11.2
45-54	14.5	8.6	17.1	1.7	0.8	158.7	47.5	22.8	3.3	7.0
55-64	11.6	6.9	18.1	1.7	0.6	137.3	47.9	26.8	2.9	5.1
65-74	5.1	6.7	18.8	0.8	0.3	56.2	26.2	20.1	2.1	2.8
75-84	7.5	8.0	22.6	0.9	0.3	29.9	14.1	8.8	2.1	3.4
85+	7.6	6.3	18.6	1.2	0.4	7.6	4.9	3.2	1.6	2.4

*Rates per 100,000 population annually taken from 1977-1979 interpolating 1978 midpoint figures.

Native Americans (Indian population) includes Alaskan natives.

Deaths from alcoholism based upon *International Classification of Diseases*, 8th ed.

Alcoholism includes deaths from alcohol, alcoholic psychosis, and cirrhosis with mention of alcohol.

In 1979 this classification included alcohol dependent syndrome and chronic liver disease.

Data provided by Vital Events Branch, Office of Program Statistics, DRC/IHS.

revealed significant differences when comparing black and white groups on a number of indices including depression, attitudes toward death and suicide attempts. Ninety-five percent of a sample of some 100 hard-core addicts, 15 through 26 years of age, were black. These subjects were comparable in socioeconomic status, age, social history and length of addiction to white addicts. Although the population in the geographical area was predominantly black, the sample still exceeded the expected figure by 25%. Black controls were the only subjects among four other control groups who showed no differences from an experimental group of addicts on two scales measuring depression and attitudes toward expected forms of violent death, including suicide. Thirty-nine percent of those on methadone and 65% of the addicts in an abstinence group were clinically depressed as measured by the Zung Depression Scale. The suicide completion rate for persons 25 years of age and younger is 8.5 per 100,000 population annually. A generally accepted procedure for calculating suicide attempts in the population is to multiply the number of completions by a factor of 10. Thus, when the expected suicide attempt rate of 85 per 100,000 was assessed for persons under 25 years of age, black controls alone were comparable to drug addicts, with figures 16 times greater than the national rate for age-adjusted averages in one year. Over a 12-year span, black controls and addicts alike were 200 times in excess of the national rate for all persons of similar ages.

The study suggests that being black adds to both the risk of addiction and the probability of self-destructive behavior. This position is supported by higher addiction rates, excessive suicide attempt rates, and greater rates of violent death, including suicide, for young blacks in this community. In the minds of many blacks such a death was foreordained, as measured by a morbidity attitude scale developed by the author. Blacks often seek conformity and accepted status via addiction, but instead find a lack of satisfaction and heightened feelings of loneliness. Although tension was reduced early on, the addiction liabilities soon exceeded any gains since any initial peer group acceptance was outweighed by loneliness and depression. Addiction does not provide a suitable exit from frustrating life situations. Although avenues of upward mobility have offered some opportunities for personal development, negative attitudes and decreased self-image often prevail, leading to still greater despair. An earlier notion, that poor and disadvantaged persons accepted their lot so completely that few mental health problems existed, is clearly not tenable, particularly for young blacks.

DIAGNOSTIC AND TREATMENT CONSIDERATIONS

Discernible diagnostic clues present themselves in different ways among specific minority group populations. Classical signs of depression may not become manifest in teenagers and young children. The younger the child the more likely behavioral disturbances are to appear and to mask any clues to depression. Differences in cultures and color can also complicate the picture. Preliminary data, yet unpublished by the author and colleagues in studying Vietnam veterans, suggests that blacks and Hispanic young people often act on their distress by alternating between withdrawal, irritability and rebellion, while Native American Indian youth are often more consistently repressed, presenting a picture of veiled hostility and resentment which can be missed by the naive therapist. Although a crisis intervention worker or psychotherapist need not be of the same cultural group as the person under stress to be helpful, some knowledge of the mores or cultural attitudes of another culture can be crucial to effective services.

Innovative therapeutic procedures based upon available knowledge are often in order when dealing with persons in extreme crisis. Various adaptations of behavior therapy principles, the learning of new responses to old stimuli and incorporating the assistance of appropriate, significant-other persons, are procedures which can be more effective than traditional forms of psychotherapy in mental health emergencies.[20,21]

While general knowledge of crisis intervention procedures may be useful in working with suicidal persons, a special sensitivity to, and information about, racial and cultural beliefs and attitudes can be of paramount importance in effective intervention and treatment.

REFERENCES

1. Frederick CJ: Current trends in suicidal behavior in the United States. *Am J Psychother* 1978;32:172–200.
2. Frederick CJ: Self-destructive behavior among younger age groups. DHEW Pub. No. (ADM)78-365, 1978.
3. Frederick CJ: Drug abuse: A self-destructive engima. *Md State Med J* 1973; 22:19–21.
4. Hendin H: *Black Suicide*. New York, Basic Books, 1969.
5. Peck ML, Litman RE: Current trends in youthful suicide. *Med Trib* 1973; 14:11.
6. Frederick CJ: *Suicide, Homicide, and Alcoholism Among American Indians*. Rockville, MD, National Institute of Mental Health, 1973.
7. Breed W: The negro and fatalistic suicide. *Pacific Soc Rev* 1970;13:156–162.
8. Seiden RH: We're driving young blacks to suicide. *Psychol Today* 1970;4:3–8.
9. Prudhomme C: The problem of suicide in the American Negro. *Psychoanal Rev* 1938;25:187–204, 372–391.
10. Davis R: A statistical analysis of the current reported increase in the black suicide rate. Unpublished dissertation, Washington State University, Pullman, Washington, 1975.
11. Henry AF, Short JF: *Suicide and Homicide*. Glencoe, IL, Free Press, 1954.
12. Breed W: Suicide, migration and race: A study of cases in New Orleans. *J Soc Issues* 1966;22:30–43.
13. Maris R: *Social Forces in Urban Suicide*. Homewood, IL, Dorsey Press, 1969.

14. Weiss NS: Recent trends in violent deaths among young adults in the United States. *Am J Epidemiol* 1976;103:416–422.
15. Bohannan P: *African Homicide and Suicide*. Princeton, NJ, Princeton University Press, 1960.
16. Durkheim E: *Suicide*. Glencoe, IL, Free Press, 1951.
17. Malinowski B: *Crime and Custom in Savage Society*. London, Kegan Paul, 1926.
18. James I: Blood alcohol levels following successful suicides. *Q J Stud Alcohol* 1966;27:23–29.
19. Frederick CJ, Resnik HLP, Wittlin BJ: Self-destructive aspects of hard core addiction. *Arch Gen Psychiatry* 1973;28:579–585.
20. Frederick CJ: Suicide prevention and crisis intervention in mental health emergencies, in Walker CE (ed): *Clinical Practice of Psychology*. New York, Pergammon Press, 1981, pp 198–213.
21. Shneidman ES, Farberow NL, Litman RE: *The Psychology of Suicide*. New York, Science House, 1970.

CHAPTER 4

INCREASING SUICIDE RATES IN ADOLESCENTS AND YOUNG ADULTS IN AN URBAN COMMUNITY (1958–1982): Tests of Hypotheses from National Data

NORMAN B. RUSHFORTH
AMASA B. FORD
HOWARD S. SUDAK
NANCY M. RUSHFORTH

Suicide rates have risen in Cuyahoga County, Ohio over the period 1958–1982, due to substantial increases of suicide in persons under age 40 years. These increases were large in adolescents (15 to 19 years) and young adults (20 to 24 years), particularly white males in the city of Cleveland, although increases were also observed for whites and nonwhites of both sexes in this city and its suburbs.

A cohort analysis showed that suicide rates tended to increase with age, and successive cohorts had higher suicide rates at each age. This latter effect holds for white males over the past two decades, but there appears to be a lower suicide rate for the most recent cohort (those born in 1962–1965 attaining age 15–19) for the other race — sex subgroups.

For white males, suicide rates have increased in a somewhat parallel manner for firearm and nonfirearm deaths for both adolescents and young adults. Rates for city white males have increased much more than those in the suburbs for both age groups, irrespective of the mode of death. In the case of city nonwhite males, however, firearm rates were much greater than the death rates for all other modes of suicide combined.

The observed increases in rates of suicide have accompanied major population shifts in Cuyahoga County over the past two decades. While there was an increase in the county population from the 1960 to 1970 census, it dropped in 1980 to 91% of the initial level. The city of Cleveland lost both whites and nonwhites, while the nonwhite population in the suburbs rose dramatically, and the white suburban population increased in the 1960s and then decreased in the 1970s. Similar shifts occurred in

adolescents and young adults, but the net effects resulted in increasing pro-
portions of these segments of the population in 1970 and 1980, compared
with baseline levels in 1960. Increasing suicide rates among young persons
over the two decades were associated with such proportionate increases in
their population. These patterns were quite clear for the first decade but
less so in the subsequent 10-year period. These data provide partial support
for a hypothesis by Holinger and Offer suggested in Chapter 2 of this book,
based on national United States data, that increased suicide rates in
adolescents and young adults are significantly and positively correlated
with increased proportions of individuals in these age groups in the total
population.

Recent studies have shown that the rate of suicide among young persons in several countries has risen over the past 25 years.[1-5] Parasuicide
(attempted suicide) also has increased in frequency in the young during
this period.[6,7] In the United States, increasing suicide rates among
adolescents and young adults are just one example of a recent dramatic
rise in the rates of violent death of the young. Since 1960, death rates
among young adults from motor vehicle accidents, homicide and suicide
have risen.[8-10] All three types of violent death may represent to varying
degrees lethal outcomes of suicidal tendencies.[9]

Cohort analyses of national rates of suicide for the United States and
Australia were undertaken recently.[4,11] For the United States data over
the past 25 years, each successive birth cohort starts with a higher suicide
rate and, at each successive five-year interval of age, has a higher rate
than the preceding cohort had at that age.[11] The Australian data showed
similar trends, together with some transient decreases in suicide rates.
These short-term declines have been explained as effects resulting from
legislation introduced in 1967 restricting the prescription of sedatives.[4]
Similar results to those found in the United States were noted by
Solomon and Hellon in earlier cohort studies of suicide for the Canadian
Province of Alberta, covering the period 1951 to 1977.[3]

Two hypotheses have been offered recently to explain the increasing
suicide rates of young persons, using macroanalyses of United States national suicide data. Boyd[2] examined the various modes of suicide and
showed that the age-adjusted rate of suicide by means of firearms had
risen continuously over the period 1953 to 1978. The corresponding rate
of suicide by all other means had remained the same over this time span.
This result corresponded with earlier findings that the rise in suicide rate
among the relatively young was primarily a result of firearm deaths.[12]
Boyd[2] suggests that increases in the frequency of suicide might in the
future be controlled by restricting the sale of handguns, since they account for the vast majority of suicides by firearms.

A second postulate to explain the observed increases in young
suicides stems from the studies of Holinger and Offer.[12] They found

significant positive correlations between adolescent suicide rates, changes in the adolescent population size, and changes in the proportion of adolescents in the population of the United States over the period 1933–1976.[13] The studies were extended to include young adults, and similar relationships were noted for homicide and nonmotor vehicle accident mortality rates in Chapter 2 of this book. Holinger and Offer suggest economic and psychodynamic factors related to such correlations and propose that the relationship may be useful for predicting violent death rates in the young over time, alerting us to the need for increased intervention on a public health level.

A primary purpose of the present analysis was to apply a cohort analysis, similar to those previously undertaken for United States and Australian national data, and the provincial data for Alberta in Canada, to suicide rates by race and sex, for persons below the age of 40, for Cuyahoga County, Ohio. We wished to determine if the results observed for the larger geographic regions held also for the young of this northcentral United States urban community. The subdivision of the county into the city of Cleveland and its suburbs, together with the relatively large nonwhite component of the population, made possible cohort analyses for several subgroups of this population.

A second goal of our study was to evaluate the hypotheses suggested: 1) by the work of Boyd,[2] implicating firearms as the predominant mode resulting in the recent increased suicide rates of young persons in the United States; and 2) from studies by Holinger and Offer,[13] proposing that increases in the proportions of adolescents and young adults resulted in the elevated suicide rates of these groups.

METHODS

Cuyahoga County, Ohio ("county") consists of the city of Cleveland ("city") and an adjacent collection of 38 cities, 18 villages, and four townships ("suburbs"). All known or suspected violent deaths (accidents, homicides and suicides) in the county must be investigated by the Cuyahoga County Coroner's Office. Since 1936, Samuel R. Gerber, MD, JD has been County Coroner. Under his direction, the professional staff has provided a set of unusually complete and uniform records, based on consistent criteria for verdicts.

Annual suicide rates were calculated using data from coroner's records for the number of deaths and from United States Census Bureau publications for population figures. The latter included a special census for the city of Cleveland carried out in 1965. Average annual suicide rates were calculated for five-year periods centered around the decennial census years, ie, 1958–1962 (1960), 1968–1972 (1970) and 1978–1982 (1980), using actual census figures as denominators. For the five-year periods 1963–1967 (1965) and 1973–1977 (1975), the city, suburban and county populations were estimated by linear interpolation of the decennial census figures, except for the period 1963–1967 (1965) for the city of Cleveland, where population data from the special census were utilized. Fatalities are tabulated according to the location of the suicide incident (city vs. suburbs) rather than the residence of the victim or the place of birth. Race is designated as white or nonwhite; the nonwhite county population was 98.7%, 97.3% and 92.6% black in 1960, 1970 and 1980, respectively.

RESULTS

Sex, Race and Location of Suicide Victims: All Ages

Before inspecting changes in the suicide rates of young adults over the 25-year time span of the study, it is useful first to consider the changes in 1) population sizes and 2) overall rates of mortality from suicide during this period. The number of suicide victims and age-adjusted suicide rates for the total county population, as well as those based on race and sex for the county, city and its suburbs are given in Table 4-1. Age-adjusted rates based on the total United States population in 1970 as the standard population, tended to be somewhat lower than the crude rates for the later periods of the study, indicating an increasing proportion of the county population in the older age groups.

Changes in population size The population figures given at the foot of Table 4-1 depict not only changes in the county population, but also rather dramatic relative changes in the racial composition of the county, the city and its suburbs during the period of the study. While the total county population rose from 1,647,895 in 1960 to 1,721,300 in 1970, during the next decade it decreased to 1,498,400 in 1980. Thus, by 1980 the population in the county had dropped to 91% of the 1960 baseline level. Large changes in the racial composition of the county occurred over this period. The white population decreased so that in 1980 it was 81% of the size in 1960, whereas the nonwhite county population increased, achieving a level of 142% of the respective baseline value.

The relative changes in the racial composition of the city of Cleveland and its suburbs were more pronounced and were characterized by a major movement of both white and nonwhite residents from the city to the suburbs. In the city the white populations decreased to 74% and to 49% of baseline levels by 1970 and 1980. In contrast, the nonwhite city populations increased to 116% of 1960 values by 1970. During the next decade, however, the nonwhite city populations began to decline, so that by 1980 they were 105% of the baseline sizes. Dramatic shifts in the nonwhite population in the suburbs occurred over the 20-year period: the nonwhite population jumped markedly in the 1960s so that by the end of

Table 4-1
Annual Suicide Rates† in Cuyahoga County (Ohio) by Race and Sex (1958–1982): Number and Age-Adjusted Annual Rate*

Group and Location of Suicide	1958–1962		1963–1967		1968–1972		1973–1977		1978–1982	
	No.	Age-Adjusted Rate	No.	Age-Adjusted Rate	No.	Age-Adjusted Rate	No.	Age-Adjusted Rate	No.	Age-Adjusted Rate
City of Cleveland										
White Males	350	21.4	310	22.7	272	23.6	282	29.0	289	35.8
Nonwhite Males	36	6.0	52	9.7	73	11.4	109	17.3	117	18.8
White Females	95	5.2	116	7.6	111	8.7	112	10.5	99	11.3
Nonwhite Females	18	2.7	15	2.0	36	4.6	38	5.0	40	5.2
Suburbs of Cleveland within Cuyahoga County										
White Males	220	13.0	266	13.4	313	14.0	370	16.9	386	17.8
Nonwhite Males	1	5.2	5	6.8	11	9.8	28	14.1	28	10.1
White Females	109	5.1	171	7.1	200	7.6	226	8.8	195	7.5
Nonwhite Females	1	7.4	0	0.0	6	6.8	11	5.2	12	4.5
Cuyahoga County										
White Males	570	17.0	576	17.1	585	17.3	652	20.6	675	22.6
Nonwhite Males	37	5.9	57	9.5	84	11.3	137	16.7	145	16.1
White Females	204	5.2	287	7.3	311	7.9	338	9.3	294	8.5
Nonwhite Females	19	2.9	15	1.8	42	4.7	49	5.0	52	4.8
Total	230	10.0	935	10.9	1022	11.5	1176	13.7	1166	14.0

*Age adjusted with United States population in 1970 as standard population.
†Victims/100,000 population. Census figures for county population: 1960 = 1,647,895; 1970 = 1,721,300; 1980 = 1,498,400:

	City				Suburbs			
	WM	NWM	WF	NWF	WM	NWM	WF	NWF
1960	304,679	122,115	318,263	130,993	370,412	2,683	395,944	2,806
1970	219,088	137,088	238,996	155,731	444,001	21,399	481,664	23,333
1980	146,460	122,801	160,804	143,757	391,177	48,229	431,525	53,647

the decade the level reached 815% of initial level, and continued to rise in the 1970s so that by 1980 the population had reached a value of 1856%. On the other hand, white suburban population increased during the 1960s but fell during the 1970s. In 1970 and 1980 the respective population sizes for white were 121% and 107% of those in 1980.

Changes in suicide rates   Suicide rates within this urban community also changed during this period of shifts in subgroup populations. Using successive five-year intervals, and midcensus estimates of population size, average annual age-adjusted suicide rates were found to increase steadily for the total population of Cuyahoga County, from an initial rate of 10.0 victims per 100,000 for 1958–1962 to a value of 14.0 in 1978–1982 (a relative increase to 140% of the baseline rate). The largest increases in the total county suicide rates occurred between 1968–1972 and 1973–1977, when the rates jumped from a level of 11.5 to 13.7. This pattern was observed for white males, the subgroup with highest rates of suicide throughout the entire study period. However, for the other three subgroups, rates peaked by 1973–1977 and decreased somewhat for the last five-year interval of the study (1978–1982).

Increasing suicide rates for all four race-sex subgroups are observed for the city of Cleveland (Table 4-1). White males have the highest rates, increasing from a value of 21.4 in the baseline period (1958–1962) and attaining a rate of 35.8 in 1978–1982, 167% of the baseline rate. However, the greatest relative increase in suicide rates in the city occurred for non-white males. In 1978–1982 the rate of 18.8 was 313% of the initial level of 6.0 for 1958–1962.

For the suburbs, white male rates were highest throughout the study period, increasing from a level of 13.0 to 17.8, a relative increase of 137% of the baseline values. These rates were considerably lower than those of white male rates for the city of Cleveland, ranging from 50% to 61% of the respective city rates. For the other three suburban race–sex subgroups, rates were lower in 1978–1982 than in the previous five-year period, 1973–1977. Rates for the two nonwhite suburban groups, however, are based on small numbers of suicides, particularly in the first three periods of the study.

Suicide Rates for Persons under Age 40 Years

The major emphasis in the present chapter is on the changing patterns of suicide mortality by race and sex in adolescents and young adults in a large metropolitan county. As a next step, after examining suicide rates at all ages, it is instructive to focus on rates under the age of 40 years. In Table 4-2, the county age-specific suicide rates by five-year intervals of age are given by race and sex for the five time periods under investigation. The table depicts increasing suicide rates for all groups in

Table 4-2

Age-Specific Annual Suicide Rates for Persons under Age 40 per 100,000 Population by Race and Sex for Cuyahoga County

Attained Age	1958–1962 (1960)	1963–1967 (1965)	1968–1972 (1970)	1973–1977 (1975)	1978–1982 (1980)
White Males					
15–19	4.7	4.9	5.7	15.7	21.6
20–24	14.7	15.5	18.9	34.2	41.5
25–29	16.1	11.0	21.4	30.8	36.6
30–34	12.7	13.7	19.9	20.9	33.6
35–39	15.1	20.9	26.4	30.0	28.2
Nonwhite Males					
15–19	0.0*	1.7*	4.9*	17.5	9.0
20–24	2.9*	13.7	37.4	40.7	37.8
25–29	13.7	4.8*	17.0	37.1	36.4
30–34	17.6	24.1	24.4	36.3	40.3
35–39	11.6	14.2	19.4	23.9	28.4
White Females					
15–19	0.4*	1.8	2.0	8.7	4.4
20–24	1.5*	4.9	5.3	10.9	4.0
25–29	5.0	6.8	9.7	9.6	14.8
30–34	3.0	8.6	9.3	10.4	12.0
35–39	5.9	9.2	16.8	17.0	13.6
Nonwhite Females					
15–19	2.4*	1.6*	6.8	11.0	4.2*
20–24	6.6*	0.0*	2.7*	8.2	9.2
25–29	1.8*	7.3*	16.2	8.0	11.2
30–34	6.8*	3.5*	8.8	6.0*	6.6
35–39	1.8*	5.0*	6.8	3.4*	15.4

*Number of victims < 5.

1978–1982 compared with those in 1958–1962, except for nonwhite females aged 30 to 34. It should be noted, however, that rates for groups of nonwhite females are based on fewer than five victims for most periods, resulting in widely fluctuating values. The data from Table 4-2 are plotted in Figure 4-1 both as: a) cross-sectional curves (left) displaying the age profiles of suicide rates for the five periods surveyed, and b) cohort curves (right) showing the relationships of suicide rate and age for successive cohorts. The dramatic increases in suicide rates for both white males and nonwhite males in Cuyahoga County in recent cohorts are evident. Such trends give rise to the observed changes in the age profiles. Increases for females are considerably smaller and patterns less systematic.

Since it was observed that suicide rates in white males were considerably higher in the city of Cleveland than in the adjacent suburbs within the county, age-specific rates were investigated both in the city

52

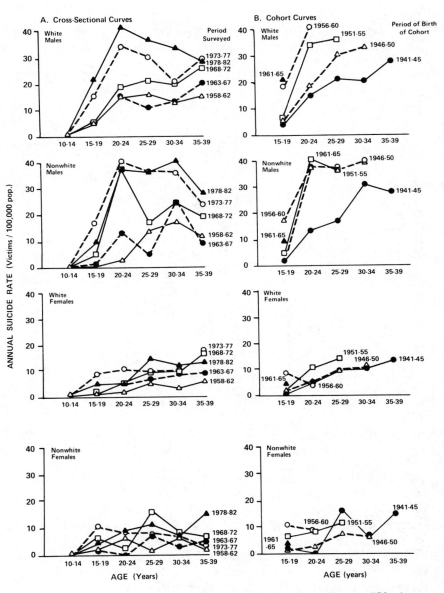

Figure 4-1 Age-specific annual suicide rates for Cuyahoga County (Ohio).

and in the suburbs. Table 4-3 gives the cohort-specific suicide rates in the city and suburbs for both white males and females, and in the city for nonwhite males and females. These age-specific rates for five-year age groups are presented for successive cohorts as a function of period of

Table 4-3
Cohort-Specific Rates† for the City of Cleveland and Its Suburbs within Cuyahoga County, Ohio

	Period of Birth of Cohort									
	1941–1945		1946–1950		1951–1955		1956–1960		1961–1965	
Attained Age	C	(S)	C	(S)	C	(S)	C	(S)	C	(S)
White Males										
15–19	2.2*	(6.6)	4.0*	(5.5)	5.6	(5.8)	21.5	(13.5)	30.6	(18.6)
20–24	17.4	(13.8)	26.0	(14.5)	28.1	(26.6)	60.3	(32.9)		
25–29	25.6	(19.1)	41.1	(25.7)	60.4	(26.0)				
30–34	39.4	(13.0)	52.2	(26.9)						
35–39	52.4	(20.9)								
Nonwhite Males										
15–19	0.0*		1.9*		4.1*		18.9		9.2	
20–24	15.5		30.7		41.9		43.8			
25–29	15.7		41.4		45.0					
30–34	35.2		37.3							
35–39	43.3									
White Females										
15–19	0.0*	(0.8*)	1.0*	(2.4*)	4.4*	(1.0*)	12.1	(7.4)	5.2*	(4.1)
20–24	4.5	(5.3)	7.4	(4.0)	14.9	(8.7)	7.5	(2.4*)		
25–29	6.5	(11.4)	12.6	(8.3)	18.0	(13.4)				
30–34	5.7*	(12.2)	24.7	(7.9)						
35–39	19.5	(11.9)								
Nonwhite Females										
15–19	2.5*		1.7*		6.5		10.8		4.2*	
20–24	0.0*		3.2*		5.9*		9.7			
25–29	17.8		8.9		13.0					
30–34	6.3*		6.3*							
35–39	18.8									

*Number of suicide victims < 5. †Victims/100,000 population: City (Suburbs).

53

birth for the cohorts in the same manner as Tables 1-8 through 1-12 in Chapter 1 by Solomon and Murphy. Reading down successive columns indicates that, in general, suicide rates increase with age for each cohort. Reading across the columns for white males and nonwhite males at each attained age, successive cohorts have higher suicide rates at a given age. Note, however, the drop in suicide rate for nonwhite males aged 15 to 19 for the most recent cohort (ie, nonwhite males born in 1961–1965). In the case of white females and nonwhite females aged 15 to 19, suicide rates have decreased for the most recent cohorts and for ages 20 to 24 rates have decreased for the white female cohort born in 1956–1960. The table clearly shows the higher suicide rates for males for each cohort when compared with corresponding rates for females, and the consistently, often strikingly higher rates in the city as compared to the suburbs, where the data permit comparisons.

Suicide Rates for Adolescents and Young Adults

The suicide rates for adolescents attaining the age of 15 to 19 years and young adults attaining the age of 20 to 24 years are presented in Figure 4-2 as a function of the period of birth. These data, obtained form Table 4-3, depict the changing mortality rates of the five successive cohorts. For both adolescent and young white males, suicide rates increase in successive cohorts, attaining a much higher level in the city than in the suburbs. The rates for city nonwhite males increase in a similar manner, but decrease in the cohorts most recently attaining the age of 15 to 19 years. For white females in the city and suburbs, and city nonwhite females, with successive cohorts, rates increase to a lesser degree than they do in males and then decrease. These graphs clearly depict the increasing vulnerability of young males to suicide over the time period under investigation. In contrast, female rates have increased to a much lesser extent before returning to lower levels. Their rates have remained considerably lower than those of adolescent and young adult males.

Firearm Suicide Rates for Adolescent and Young
Adult Males

To investigate further the dramatic increase in mortality rates for adolescent and young adult males, an assessment was made of the use of firearms as a mode of suicide. This was suggested not only by the results of our own studies of violent death in Cuyahoga County showing an increasing use of firearms in homicides,[14] accidental firearm fatalities[15] and suicides,[16] but also by recent articles by Boyd[2] reporting that the increasing rate of suicide among persons in the United States under the age of 40 years from 1953 to 1978 was related to increases in the proportion of suicides by means of firearms.

55

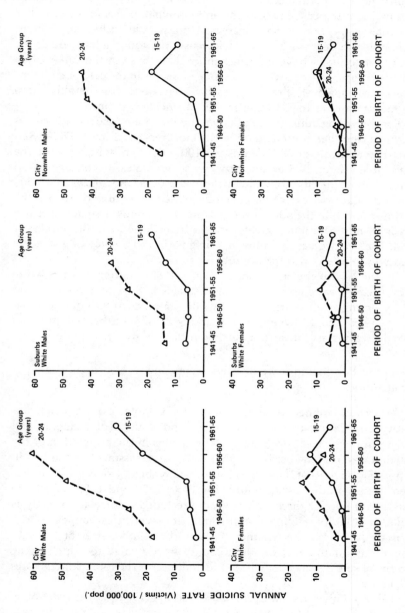

Figure 4-2 Suicide rates for adolescents (15–19 years) and young adults (20–24 years) by race and sex for the city of Cleveland and suburbs in Cuyahoga County (Ohio).

Figure 4-3 depicts the changes in annual suicide rates by firearms and all other modes for adolescents (15–19 years) and young adults (20–24) for white males in the city and suburbs and nonwhite males in the city. For white males, suicide rates have increased in a parallel fashion for firearm and nonfirearm deaths for both adolescents and young adults. Rates for the city white males have increased more than those in the suburbs for both age groups, irrespective of the mode of death. In the case of city non-white males, however, firearm rates have increased considerably more than the death rates for all other modes of suicide combined.

For the young adult group of city nonwhite males, a dramatic rise in firearm suicides has continued up to the most recent period (1978–1982), giving rise to a rate of 33.7 deaths per 100,000, slightly higher than the comparable rate of 29.5 attained by city white males. In this age group mortality rates for city nonwhite males using other modalities of suicide increased to a lesser extent and even decreased to a value of 10.1 in the last time period. In the adolescent group of city nonwhite males, firearm rates increased to a much greater extent than those for other modes of suicide, before decreasing in the last time period to a value of 7.6, compared with a rate of 1.6 for nonfirearm suicides.

By the end of the study period (1978–1982), among city nonwhite males, firearms were used as a mode of suicide in 83% of adolescent and 77% of young adult deaths. In city white males, corresponding percentages were 50 and 49, whereas 42% and 50% of suburban white males utilized firearms as a means of suicide in the last five-year period.

Changes in Population Sizes of Adolescents and Young Adults

In view of Holinger and Offer's report in Chapter 2 of the significant positive correlation between adolescent and young adult suicide and changes in the proportion of 15 to 24 year olds in the population of the United States over the period of 1933–1976, an assessment of changes in the population sizes of these age groups in Cuyahoga County was undertaken, based on the census figures for 1960, 1970 and 1980. While the limited data base of three census years precluded a correlation analysis similar to that of Holinger and Offer, it nevertheless appeared appropriate to investigate whether shifts in the relative sizes of the subpopulations for this metropolitan county were related to the changing patterns of suicide rates, in light of the findings for the total United States population.

Table 4-4 gives the numbers of adolescents (15–19 years) and young adults (20–24 years) and their percent of the total populations by race and sex for the city of Cleveland and its suburbs. Comparisons may be made of the changes in population size for these two age groups with

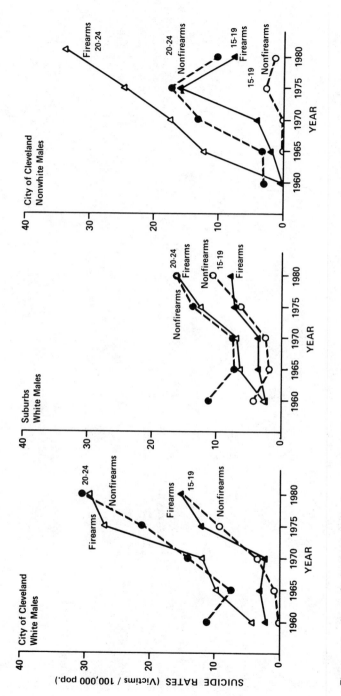

Figure 4-3 Annual suicide rates by firearms and other modes for adolescents (15–19 years) and young adults (20–24 years).

Table 4-4
Number of Persons by Race and Sex in Age Groups 15–19 Years and 20–24 Years and All Ages in the City of Cleveland, Its Suburbs in Cuyahoga County, Ohio for the Census Years 1960, 1970, 1980

| Age/Sex/Race Group | Number (Percent of Total of All Ages) | | | | | |
| | City of Cleveland | | | Suburbs | | |
	1960	1970	1980	1960	1970	1980
White Males						
15–19	18,635 (6.1)	18,021 (8.2)	11,748 (8.0)	24,210 (6.5)	41,627 (9.4)	35,516 (9.1)
20–24	19,524 (6.4)	18,486 (8.4)	15,595 (10.6)	14,407 (3.9)	29,023 (6.5)	34,024 (8.7)
All ages	304,679	219,088	146,460	370,412	444,001	391,177
Nonwhite Males						
15–19	6955 (5.7)	14,482 (10.6)	13,085 (10.7)	147 (5.5)	1917 (8.6)	4753 (9.9)
20–24	6637 (5.4)	9129 (6.7)	11,863 (9.7)	156 (5.8)	1557 (7.3)	4006 (8.3)
All ages	122,115	137,088	122,801	2683	21,399	48,229
White Females						
15–19	20,958 (6.6)	18,296 (7.7)	11,557 (7.2)	24,829 (6.3)	41,445 (8.6)	34,173 (7.9)
20–24	22,717 (7.1)	21,638 (9.1)	15,964 (9.9)	18,025 (4.6)	35,145 (7.3)	33,626 (7.8)
All ages	318,263	238,996	160,804	395,944	481,644	431,525
Nonwhite Females						
15–19	8063 (6.2)	15,417 (9.9)	14,190 (9.9)	184 (6.6)	2094 (9.0)	4844 (9.0)
20–24	8926 (6.8)	12,621 (8.1)	14,487 (10.1)	170 (6.1)	2123 (9.1)	4982 (9.3)
All ages	130,993	155,731	143,757	2806	23,333	53,647

those for the total population given at the bottom of Table 4-1. For city white male and female adolescents and young adults, shifts in the population size mirrored those of the total populations: population sizes decreased between 1960 and 1970 and still further in the next decade. By 1980, the numbers of city white adolescents and young adults ranged from 55% to 80% of those in 1960. In the case of city nonwhite males and females aged 15 to 19, the population shifts in size were similar to those of the total population; increasing between 1960 and 1970 but falling somewhat in the following decade. By 1980, city nonwhite male and female adolescents numbered 188% and 176% of baseline population sizes. It should be noted, however, that for the two nonwhite adolescent groups the population size roughly doubled between 1960 and 1970 — a far greater relative increase than for young adult or total populations of nonwhite males or females. For city nonwhite males and females aged 20 to 24, the population size increased in the 1960s and then further in the 1970s, so that in 1980 these population sizes were 179% and 162% of baseline values.

In the city of Cleveland, for each of the three census years, there were more females than males among adolescents, young adults, and persons of all ages, except for white adolescents in 1980. There were more females than males in the suburbs at each point in time, except for white adolescents and young adults in 1980 and white adolescents in 1970. It must be pointed out, however, that census figures underreport blacks living in urban communities and such underreporting is probably considerably greater in the case of males.[17]

Shifts in the suburban population sizes for nonwhite adolescents and young adults were similar to those described previously for total populations of all ages for both sexes; between 1960 and 1970 populations increased tenfold and then more than doubled again in the next decade. Undoubtedly much of the increase reflected the migration of inner city blacks to the suburbs, characteristic of many large United States urban communities. In the case of whites, the patterns were less clear-cut. For both suburban white males and females in the age group 15–19, trends in population size paralleled those of the total populations; an increase in the 1960s followed by a decline in the following decade. For suburban white females in the age group 20–24, similar population shifts occurred, whereas the numbers of white young males continued to increase in the 1970s following a twofold increase in the previous decade.

The net effects of shifts in population sizes, expressed as Δ_p, are shown in Table 4-5. There were increases in the proportions of adolescents and young adults in all populations, irrespective of race, sex or location (city vs. suburbs) between 1960 and 1970. Similar increases for the young adults aged 20 to 24 years were seen in all eight subgroups between the 1970 and 1980 census years. In the case of adolescents, only

Table 4-5
Changes in Suicide Rates (Δ_s) and Changes in the Population Size
Proportions (Δ_p): 1960–1970 and 1970–1980 for Adolescents Aged
15–19 Years and Young Adults Aged 20–25 Years

	1960–1970		1970–1980	
	Δ_p	Δ_s	Δ_p	Δ_s
Adolescents Aged 15–19 Years				
City				
White Males	+2.1	+ 3.4	−0.2	+25.0
Nonwhite Males	+4.9	+ 4.1†	+0.1	+ 5.1*
White Females	+1.1	+ 4.4	−0.5	+ 0.8†
Nonwhite Females	+3.7	+ 4.0*	0.0	− 2.3*
Suburbs				
White Males	+2.9	− 0.8	−0.3	+12.8
Nonwhite Males	+3.1	+10.4†	+1.3	− 2.0†
White Females	+2.3	+ 0.2†	−0.7	+ 3.1
Nonwhite Females	+2.4	+ 9.6†	0.0	− 5.5†
Young Adults Aged 20–24 Years				
City				
White Males	+2.0	+10.6	+2.2	+34.3
Nonwhite Males	+1.3	+27.3*	+3.0	+13.1
White Females	+2.0	+ 6.5*	+0.8	+ 0.1
Nonwhite Females	+1.3	− 3.5†	+2.0	+ 6.5*
Suburbs				
White Males	+2.6	+ 0.6	+2.2	+18.4
Nonwhite Males	+1.5	+77.1*	+1.0	−57.1*
White Females	+2.7	+ 1.8*	+0.5	− 1.6*
Nonwhite Females	+3.0	0.0†	+0.2	+ 8.0†

*One of the rates used in determining Δ_s based on fewer than 5 victims.
†Both of the rates used in determining Δ_s based on fewer than 5 victims.

two of the subgroups increased, two remained unchanged and four had a decreasing proportionate population size in 1980 compared with the value 10 years earlier.

Thus, the population shifts over the two decades resulted in increasing proportions of young adults, whereas increases in the adolescent fraction of the population were restricted to the 1970s. It is against this background of relative changes in adolescent and young adult population sizes (Δ_p) that the corresponding changes in suicide rates (Δ_s) in this urban community can be assessed as a test of Holinger and Offer's hypothesis.

Inspection of Table 4-5 indicates that for the eight subgroups of young adults only city nonwhite females had a decrease in suicide rates in 1970 compared with baseline rates in 1960. For six of the seven other subgroups an increasing suicide rate accompanied an increasing proportion of young adults in the population. For the period 1970 to 1980, two groups (nonwhite suburban males and suburban white females) showed a drop in suicide rate, whereas the remaining six subgroups had simultaneous increases in suicide rate and proportionate population size. For adolescents, comparing 1970 values with 1960 shows positive values of Δ_s accompanying positive values of Δ_p, except for suburban white males who show a decrease in the suicide rate. Thus, in seven of the eight subgroups, for the first decade of the study increasing suicide rates are associated with increasing proportions of adolescents in the total population. The relationship completely breaks down for adolescents over the period 1970 to 1980, several suicide rates and population size proportions decreasing, in no apparently systematic fashion.

Caution must be used in evaluating the data of Table 4-5, since the suicide rates in many cases are based on less than five victims. However, for the period 1960 and 1970, a sign test in which $P(-\Delta_p, +\Delta_s$ or $+\Delta_p, -\Delta_s) = 1/2$ and $P(+\Delta_p, +\Delta_s$ or $-\Delta_p, -\Delta_s) = 1/2$ may be applied for 1960–1970 changes for the adolescent, young adult and both groups combined. The probability of obtaining the observed association of $+\Delta_p, +\Delta_s$ signs under a random mechanism is $8(1/2)^8 = 0.031$ for adolescents and $7(1/2)^7 = 0.055$ when the groups are young adults considered separately, and $105(1/2)^{15} = 0.003$ when the observations for the two age groups are pooled. The P value for two-tailed tests of Holinger and Offer's hypothesis is 0.007 for pooled observations. Thus, the observed association of increases in the suicide rate and proportions of adolescents and young adults between 1960 and 1970 are consistent with the hypothesis. Data for the following decade, however, fail to support it.

Since Holinger and Offer pool their data for age groups 15–19 and 20–24 to form a larger group of individuals aged 15–24 years, the data in the present study were combined in a similar fashion, giving rise to the data presented in Table 4-6. Here, as in Table 4-5, Δ_p and Δ_s are given, but for eight subgroups rather than 16. In addition, the ranks of the difference for Δ_p and Δ_s are also given for the two time intervals, 1960–1970 and 1970–1980. As expected, on the basis of the data in Table 4-5, for the period 1960 to 1970, increases in suicide rate accompany increases in the proportion of the population aged 15 to 24 years. In the period 1970 to 1980, two subgroups, suburban nonwhite males and white females, depart from the pattern of positive values for both Δ_p and Δ_s, seen in the other six subgroups. Applying a sign test to these data results in two-tailed P values of .008 for the period 1960 to 1970, again supporting the hypothesis of a positive association between an increasing proportion of 15–24 year olds in the population and an increasing rate of suicide in this age group. Application of the test to changes in relative population size and suicide rates between 1970 and 1980 for this age group resulted in a corresponding P value of 0.289, affording no support for the hypothesis.

Table 4-6
Changes in Suicide Rates (Δ_s) and Changes in the Population Size
Proportions (Δ_p) for Adolescents and Young Adults Aged 15-24,
1960-1970 and 1970-1980

	1960-1970		1970-1980	
Group	Δ_p (Rank)	Δ_s (Rank)	Δ_p (Rank)	Δ_s (Rank)
City				
White Males	+4.2 (7)	+ 5.9 (3)	+2.0 (2.5)	+32.7 (1)
Nonwhite Males	+6.1 (1)	+13.7 (2)	+3.1 (1)	+10.4 (3)
White Females	+3.0 (8)	+ 5.5 (4)	+0.4 (6)	+ 0.5 (7)
Nonwhite Females	+5.0 (5)	+ 1.0*(6.5)	+1.9 (4.5)	+ 1.3 (5)
Suburbs				
White Males	+5.5 (2.5)	+ 0.0⁺(8)	+1.9 (4.5)	+16.3 (2)
Nonwhite Males	+4.9 (6)	+40.3*(1)	+2.0 (2.5)	−26.7 (8)
White Females	+5.1 (4)	+ 1.0*(6.5)	−0.2 (8)	+ 0.8 (6)
Nonwhite Females	+5.5 (2.5)	+ 4.7†(5)	+0.2 (7)	+ 1.4*(4)

Δ = differences (rank of difference).
*One of rates used in determining Δ_s based on less than 5 victims.
†Both of rates used in determining Δ_s based on less than 5 victims.
⁺Positive when second decimal place is considered.

A more stringent test of the hypothesis was undertaken by determining the Spearman Correlation Coefficient[18] for the two sets of data. If, as Holinger and Offer suggest, there is a positive association between suicide rates and population size proportion, other things being equal, a significant positive correlation between the algebraic values of Δ_p and Δ_s in Table 4-6 would be anticipated. The Spearman Rank Correlation Coefficient calculated for the two time periods resulted in nonsignificant values of r = −0.24 for 1960-1970 and r = +0.31, for 1970-1980. Thus, no support for the hypothesis is obtained on the basis of this analysis.

DISCUSSION

The present study portrays the large increases in rates of suicide for teenagers (15-19 years) and young adults (20-24 years) in Cuyahoga County, Ohio over the period 1958-1982. Although increasing rates have been observed in both sexes for whites and nonwhites in the city of Cleveland and its suburbs in this county, the most dramatic rise in suicide has been that of city young white males. A question requiring further research is why the rates for this group have been almost double those for suburban young white males over the 25-year period. Clearly, our data depict the increasing vulnerability of young males to suicide in this urban community, pointing to another question requiring more attention. What factors predispose young females, particularly nonwhite females, to have much lower rates than their male counterparts? The differences in rates appear to continue to diverge, since white male suicide rates and those of nonwhite males using firearms have risen further in 1978–1982, while they have fallen for female groups.

Focusing on suicide in white adolescents and young adult males, we find that the pattern of rising suicide rates seen in Cuyahoga County parallels that seen in other populations.[3,11] Table 4-7 summarizes the suicide rates for males, aged 15–19 and 20–24, in populations that are either exclusively white or predominantly so, from several studies of different geographic locations. Apart from England and Wales, where rates decreased somewhat in 1970 for both groups and in 1975 for teenagers, the data show a consistent pattern of successive increases in mortality for suicide from the mid-1950s to the present time. It should be noted that the rates for England and Wales have risen again by 1980, and their drop in the late 1960s was relatively small compared with those of older age groups.[20] Such decreases in suicide rates in the United Kingdom have been attributed to the removal of carbon monoxide (CO) from domestic gas in the 1960s. Kreitman found that the drop in CO suicide, a predominant mode in Britain, was sufficiently large to lower the total suicide rate at all ages, but in doing so it concealed an increase of suicide by other means in young males.[20]

Firearms as a Means of Suicide

The widespread phenomenon of rising suicide rates of young males, seen in Table 4-7, suggests that attributing such increases in the United States primarily to a greater propensity to use firearms as a mode of self-destruction, as suggested by Boyd,[2] may be an oversimplification. In populations outside the United States, suicide by firearms constitutes a small component of the total suicide rate, yet some of their rates have risen more than those of the United States, eg, Alberta, Canada. Our own studies of Cuyahoga County show an increasing use of firearms in homicidal[14] and accidental deaths,[15] which we have attributed to the continued availability of handguns. This factor, however, is only one of a large number of interacting variables leading to escalating rates of suicide among the youth of this urban community. The present study clearly shows that for white males, both in the city and the suburbs, teenage and young adult, increasing rates of nonfirearm suicides have closely paralleled those by firearms. In city nonwhite males of both age groups, however, the predominant mode of self-destruction is increasingly the use of a handgun. These groups also bear an increasing death rate by firearms for homicides and accidents.

For the United States, the role of the handgun in suicide is undoubtedly an important factor because of its predominant use by males,

Table 4-7
Mean Age-Specific Suicide Rates for Males Aged 15–19 and 20–24 Years Taken from Population Studies for Various Time Intervals Within the Period 1950–1980*

Population (Study)	1950	1955	1960	1965	1970	1975	1980
Australia (Goldney and Katsikitis*)		6.1 (11.5)	4.5 (15.6)	5.9 (14.9)	6.9 (19.7)	9.4 (22.5)	11.1
Canada Alberta (Solomon and Murphy, Chapter 1)	3.2 (10.5)	4.4 (7.6)	6.8 (13.6)	11.1 (24.0)	24.0 (29.6)	31.4 (46.0)	
Ontario (Sims[a])	5.1 (7.8)	3.3 (10.7)	4.4 (11.6)	6.6 (14.9)			
England and Wales (Medical Statistics Unit, UK Office of Population Census and Surveys)			3.0 (7.6)	4.0 (9.6)	3.2 (8.2)	3.0 (9.3)	4.0 (9.7)
United States White (Solomon and Murphy, Chapter 1)	3.7 (9.4)	3.9 (8.6)	5.9 (11.9)	6.3 (13.9)	9.4 (19.3)	13.0 (26.8)	
Cuyahoga County, Ohio: White			4.7 (14.7)	4.9 (15.5)	5.7 (18.9)	15.7 (34.2)	21.6 (41.5)
City of Cleveland			2.2 (15.4)	4.0 (17.4)	5.6 (26.0)	21.5 (48.1)	30.6 (60.3)
Suburbs of Cleveland (present study)			6.6 (13.9)	5.5 (13.8)	5.8 (14.5)	13.5 (26.6)	18.6 (32.9)

*Suicide victims/100,000 population: males aged 15–19 (20–24).

its increasing use by both sexes, and its high lethality. This has suggested a means of reducing the suicide rate through restricting the sale of this weapon.[2,21] While reducing the availability of handguns would result in a long-term decline in homicidal and accidental death by handgun, we conclude, along with others,[22,23] that the reduction in suicide rates would be limited. Examples may be found of only transient declines in self-inflicted deaths following the restriction of a frequently utilized means of suicide: 1) detoxification of the domestic gas in Basel, Switzerland was followed by a temporary reduction in the suicide rate, which returned to its previous level as a result of an increasing number of deaths by drowning;[24] 2) reductions in the numbers of suicides of young persons in Australia by poisoning, attributed to the restriction of sales of sedatives, appear to have decreased overall suicide rates only for a short time period, since total rates soon began to rise again;[4] 3) detoxification of gas in the United Kingdom appears to have led to only a transient decline in youthful suicides.[20] For individuals with a strong and continuing intent of self-destruction, substitution of an alternative means of suicide presumably results when another mode becomes less available. If such persons constitute a large fraction of the population of suicidal deaths, only small, long-term gains in the reduction of suicides may be expected. However, in the case of such a lethal mode as firearms, substitution of a slower method of self-destruction, such as poisoning, may lead to a reduction in mortality in cases in which intervention in the suicidal event may result in saving a life.

Factors Affecting Cohorts

Apart from the increasing availability of handguns to teenagers and young adults, several other factors appear to have influenced successive cohorts, possibly giving rise to the elevated rates of suicide we have observed in these groups. Such influences, shown from many previous studies to be related to suicide, may be grouped in the broad categories below. The categories, however, should not obscure the fact that suicide results from multiple interacting causal factors.

1. Increasing rates of suicide attempts.[6,7,25]
2. Larger cohort sizes resulting in effects due to a greater proportion of young persons in the population;[13] increased competition for jobs with a resultant increase in failure for some youth;[26] relative decline in income for young people compared to their parents.[26,27]
3. Greater alienation of the young due to social disorganization within urban communities:[28] increased migration and social mobility;[28,29] deteriorating neighborhoods and rapidly expanding suburbs;[30,31] increased criminal victimization;[8,26,28] larger rates of youth unemployment.[26,32]

4. Long-term effects of family and personal disorganization;[27,28] increased divorce rates among parents, creating large numbers of single-parent families;[26,27] decreased marriage rates among young adults and decreasing birth rates for those married;[26,29] increased illegitimate pregnancy;[27,28] breakdown of family patterns emphasizing religious beliefs and traditional moral values;[33] rising rates of child abuse;[34,35] increasing exposure to violence as a means of problem solving (eg, through the mass media);[36,37] increased alcohol consumption and attendant family problems;[27] rising rates of drug abuse.[28]

The cumulative effects of many of these factors may result in a poorer self-image in the young, and a perception of decreased ability to handle the increased stresses imposed upon them.[27,38] Increasing rates of violent death in young persons are dramatic indicators of social pathology in contemporary society.

Data exist on a national level showing increases in many of the above factors associated with the observed elevation in youthful suicide rates. Stronger evidence of relationships might be gained for Cuyahoga County in future studies relating temporal changes in these factors to those of suicide in young persons. Such investigations are planned for this urban community, first by determining a typology of local suicide (together with other forms of violent death), and then relating the emerging types to social and economic variables in temporal and spatial analyses. Data from Cuyahoga County, uniformly reported in detail over several decades, affords an opportunity to test postulates derived from many studies of larger populations. Confirmed hypotheses could elucidate further relationships and point to ways to reduce the rising tide of violent death in our young.

ACKNOWLEDGMENTS

The authors gratefully acknowledge Dr. Samuel R. Gerber and the staff of the Cuyahoga County Coroner's Office, particularly Dr. Lester Adelson, Chief Deputy Coroner, for their assistance in this study. We wish to also thank Mr. Morgenstern for his programming services and Mrs. Dixon of the Medical Statistics, United Kingdom Office of Population Censuses and Surveys for providing the data for England and Wales used in Table 4-7.

REFERENCES

1. Frederick CJ: Current trends in suicidal behavior in the United States. *Am J Psychother* 1978;32:172–200.
2. Boyd JH: The increasing rate of suicide by firearms. *N Engl J Med* 1983; 308:872–874.

3. Solomon MI, Hellon CP: Suicide in Alberta, Canada 1951–1977: A cohort analysis. *Arch Gen Psychiatry* 1980;37:511–513.

4. Goldney RD, Katsikitis M: Cohort analysis of suicide rates in Australia. *Arch Gen Psychiatry* 1983;40:71–74.

5. Sainsbury P, Jenkins J, Levey A: The social correlates of suicide in Europe, in Farmer R, Hirsch S (eds): *The Suicide Syndrome*. London, Croom Helm, 1982.

6. Aiken RCB, Buglass D, Kreitman N: The changing patterns of attempted suicide in Edinburgh 1962–67. *Br J Prev Soc Med* 1969;23:111–115.

7. Wexler L, Weissman MM, Kasl SV: Suicide attempts 1970–75: Updating a United States study and comparisons with international trends. *Br J Psychiatry* 1978;132:180–185.

8. Weiss NS: Recent trends in violent deaths among young adults in the United States. *Am J Epidemiol* 1976;103:416–422.

9. Holinger PC: Violent deaths among the young: Recent trends in suicide, homicide, and accidents. *Am J Psychiatry* 1979;136:1144–1147.

10. Ford AB, Rushforth NB: Urban violence in the United States—Implication for health and for Britian in the future: Discussion paper. *J Roy Soc Med* 1983;76:283–288.

11. Murphy GE, Wetzel RD: Suicide risk by birth cohort in the United States, 1949–1974. *Arch Gen Psychiatry* 1980;37:519–523.

12. Boor M: Methods of suicide and implications for suicide prevention. *J Clin Psychol* 1981;37:70–75.

13. Holinger PC, Offer D: Prediction of adolescent suicide: A population model. *Am J Psychiatry* 1982;139:302–307.

14. Rushforth NB, Ford AB, Hirsch CS, et al: Violent death in a metropolitan county: Changing patterns in homicide (1958–75). *N Engl J Med* 1977;297:531–538.

15. Rushforth NB, Hirsch CS, Ford AB, et al: Accidental firearm fatalities in a metropolitan county (1958–1973). *Am J Epidemiol* 1974;100:499–505.

16. Ford AB, Rushforth NB, Rushforth NM, et al: Violent death in a metropolitan county. II. Changing patterns in suicides (1959–1974). *Am J Public Health* 1979;69:459–464.

17. Bureau of the Census: Conference on Census Undercount. Washington, DC, US Government Printing Office, 1980.

18. Milton JS, Tsokos JO: *Statistical Methods in the Biological and Health Sciences*. New York, McGraw-Hill, 1983, pp 443.

19. Sims M: Sex and age differences in suicide rates in a Canadian Province: With particular reference to suicide by means of poison. *Life Threat Behav* 1974;4:139–159.

20. Kreitman N: The coal-gas story: United Kingdom rates, 1960–1971. *Br J Prev Soc Med* 1976;30:86–93.

21. Browning CH: Suicide, firearms and public health. *Am J Public Health* 1974;64:313–317.

22. Newton GD Jr, Zimring FE: Firearms and violence in American life. A staff report submitted to the National Commission on the Causes and Prevention of Violence. Washington, DC, US Government Printing Office, 1969.

23. *Prevention of Suicide*. Geneva, World Health Organization, Paper No. 35, 1968.

24. Stengel E: *Suicide and Attempted Suicide*. Baltimore, Penguin, 1964.

25. Weissman MM: The epidemiology of suicide attempts, 1960–1971. *Arch Gen Psychiatry* 1974;30:737–746.

26. Esterlin RA: *Birth and Fortune: The Impact of Numbers on Personal Welfare*. New York, Basic Books, 1981.
27. Waldron I, Eyer J: Socioeconomic causes of the recent rise in death rates for 15–24 year olds. *Soc Sci Med* 1975;9:383–396.
28. Ford AB: Casualties of our time. *Science* 1970;167:256–263.
29. Fuchs VR: *How We Live: An Economic Perspective on Americans from Birth to Death*. Cambridge, Harvard University Press, 1983.
30. Wheeler H: Community growth, depressive disorders and suicide. *Am J Social* 1961;67:9–16.
31. Gordon RE, Gordon KK: Social psychiatry of a mobile suburb. *Int J Soc Psychiatry* 1960;6:89–106.
32. Brenner H: Estimating the social costs of national economic policy: Implications for mental and physical health, and criminal aggression. Vol 1, Paper No. 5 in *Achieving the Goals of the Employment Act of 1945 – Thirtieth Anniversary Reviews*. Washington, DC, US Government Printing Office, 1976.
33. Schall M: *Limits: A Search for New Values*. New York, CN Potter, 1981.
34. Oliver JE, Cox J, Buchanan A: The extent of child abuse, in Smith SM (ed): *The Maltreatment of Children*. Baltimore, University Park Press, 1980, pp 121–153.
35. Gil DG: *Violence Against Children: Physical Child Abuse in the United States*. Cambridge, Harvard University Press, 1970.
36. Somers AR: Violence, television and the health of American youth. *N Engl J Med* 1956;294:811–817.
37. Rothenberg MB: Effect of television violence on children and youth. *JAMA* 1975;234:1043–1046.
38. Offer D, Ostrov E, Howard KI: *The Adolescent: A Psychological Self-Portrait*. New York, Basic Books, 1981.

CHAPTER 5

TEENAGE AND ADULT TEMPORAL FLUCTUATIONS IN SUICIDE AND AUTO FATALITIES

DAVID P. PHILLIPS

Using time series regression analysis, this chapter systematically examines the impact of day of the week, month of the year, and holidays on certain types of daily United States mortality: 1) teenage suicides, 2) adult suicides, 3) teenage auto accident fatalities, and 4) adult auto accident fatalities. Teenage suicides differ markedly from the remaining three groups in their response to the temporal factors examined. The last three groups are very sensitive to temporal factors, while teenage suicides are barely responsive. Some implications of this finding are discussed.

In the study of suicide, one can discern two main types of statistical analysis. In the first, "cross-sectional" approach the researcher examines relationships among many variables at *one* point in time. For example, the researcher might study a group of suicides and nonsuicides at a given time and seek to determine whether the suicides differ from the non-suicides with respect to such variables as sex, race, age, or marital status. In the second, "time-series" approach the researcher examines relationships among many variables at a series of *different* points in time. Here, the researcher typically seeks to discover whether the fluctuation in suicide over time is correlated with changes in other variables, eg, the monthly unemployment rate.

Both styles of research are evident in studies of adult suicide. In the study of teenage suicide, however, time-series analyses are very rare.

In this chapter I will try to redress the balance to some extent. In the main, I will seek to determine whether a time-series approach holds promise in this analysis of teenage suicides. Secondarily, I will try to illustrate standard time-series regression techniques, for the benefit of the reader who may be unfamiliar with the power, subtlety, and convenience of these approaches.

This chapter will examine the impact of three different types of temporal variables on teenage suicide: 1) day of the week; 2) month of the year; and 3) holidays. It will be instructive to compare the temporal fluctuation of teenage suicides with the temporal fluctuation in three other groups: a) adult suicides; b) teenage auto accident fatalities; and c) adult auto accident fatalities. These comparisons will help us to determine whether temporal factors play an unusual role in teenage suicides.

METHODS OF ANALYSIS

An excellent, elementary introduction to time-series regression analysis is provided by Ostrom.[1] Useful, advanced treatments appear in Johnston[2] and Rao and Miller.[3] For applications of time-series techniques to daily suicide and auto fatalities, see Bollen and Phillips.[4,5] These two articles employ techniques essentially identical to those used in the current paper.

Computerized information on all United States daily suicides is provided by the National Center for Health Statistics, and distributed by the Inter-University Consortium for Political Science Research. As of this writing, the latest available information from the latter source is 1977, the year examined in this chapter.

To assess the effect of each day of the week on suicide, one can proceed as follows. A 0–1 dummy variable was constructed for all days that were Mondays; another such dummy variable was constructed for Tuesdays; and in general a separate dummy variable was coded for each day of the week, with Sunday being the omitted variable. Similarly, to assess the impact of the monthly variables, a 0–1 variable was coded for each month of the year, with December being the omitted variable.

Finally, a dummy variable for holidays was constructed. As in previous research,[4,5] I have examined the effect of the six legal public holidays which are celebrated in all states on the same date: New Year's Day, Memorial Day, Independence Day, Labor Day, Thanksgiving, and Christmas. Many of these holidays actually extend over several days, typically, a "holiday weekend." For example, this is true for Labor Day and Memorial Day. Even July 4, not ordinarily associated with a holiday weekend, fell on a Monday in 1977, and thus the July 4 holiday period actually extended from Saturday, July 2 through Monday, July 4. A "holiday period" was thus defined as beginning with the first day of the holiday and ending with the last day of that holiday. Any day falling in the holiday period was coded "1"; all other days were coded "0".

This chapter uses a single dummy variable to consider the impact of holidays in general. If one wished to provide estimates of the impact of each separate holiday, one would need to construct a dummy variable for each holiday. This type of analysis has been provided by Phillips and Liu,[6] Bollen and Phillips,[5] and Bollen.[7]

Sometimes the effect of a holiday may persist for several days after the end of a holiday period and start several days before the true beginning of the holiday period. In order to discover "lagged" and "leading" effects of this sort, additional holiday variables were constructed in the following manner. The dummy variable, HOL(1), was coded "1" for all days immediately following a holiday period; for all other days it was coded "0". Thus, for example, December 26 was coded "1" for HOL(1), as was July 5. Similarly, the dummy variable, HOL(2), was coded "1" for all days that were two days after the end of the holiday period; otherwise it was coded "0". For example, December 27 and July 6 were coded "1" for this variable. Parallel procedures were used to code all the related holiday variables, HOL(−3), HOL(−2), HOL(−1), HOL(1), HOL(2), and HOL(3). HOL(−3), for example, is coded "1" for all days falling three days before the beginning of the holiday period.

The number of suicides on a given day may be correlated with the number of suicides one or two days later, *even after* other temporal factors are corrected for. This could happen, for example, if some social factor prompts many people to attempt suicide on (say) May 3. A surge of suicide attempts on this day may result in a rise in suicides on May 3 (from firearm suicides) and on May 4 and 5 (from slower-acting forms of suicide, like poisoning). The net effect of this lag in poisoning deaths would be to create a correlation between the number of suicides on May 3, 4, and 5, even after other temporal factors are corrected for. In order to discover "lagged" effects of this sort, the lagged endogenous variables, SUI(1) and SUI(2), were constructed. SUI(1) measures the effect of suicides at time t on suicides one day later. SUI(2) is defined in parallel fashion.

The techniques just described will be used in the next section to assess the impact of temporal variables on four demographic groups: 1) adult suicides; 2) teenage suicides; 3) teenage auto fatalities; and 4) adult auto fatalities. To my knowledge, no previous research using United States daily mortality data has systematically compared seasonal fluctuations in the four groups just mentioned. (However, see Phillips and Liu[6] and Bollen and Phillips[5] for an examination of United States daily fluctuations for suicides in all ages combined; see also Bollen[7] for a comparison of suicide and auto temporal fluctuations for all ages combined. These papers review earlier work, which typically do not cover the entire United States, but instead describe small, geographically limited samples.)

RESULTS

Adult Suicides

Table 5-1 shows that 34% of the variance in United States adult suicides, 1977, is "explained" by the temporal factors under study. This means that all temporal variables combined exert a substantial, though not a dominant influence on United States adult suicides.

Thus far we have been looking at the impact of all temporal variables combined; it is also valuable to look at the impact of each temporal variable, considered separately. This is easy to do because the regression analysis in Table 5-1 displays the impact of each temporal variable, correcting for the impact of all the others. (This is one of the features which makes regression analysis so useful.)

In addition, the regression analysis in Table 5-1, allows us to determine whether the impact of any given variable is statistically significant, *provided* that there is no serial correlation between the residuals in the regression equation. Conventionally, one tests for serial correlation with the Durbin-Watson statistic. This test is not appropriate, however, when lagged endogenous variables are included in the regression equation, as they are in Table 5-1.[8] Durbin[9] suggested two other tests of serial correlation for use with lagged endogenous variables. The first of these (Durbin's h-test) cannot be used here because $Tvar(b^*)$ is greater than 1. Consequently, Durbin's second test has been substituted. For the data in Table 5-1, this test reveals no evidence of first-order serial correlation among the residents. After the effect of other variables is corrected for, $e(t-1)$ is not significantly correlated with $e(t)$ ($t = -.59$). A clear, elementary discussion of this and related tests appears in Ostrom.[1] More complete discussions can be found in Durbin[9] and in Johnston[2]. Evidence of higher order serial correlation was sought by the methods described by Bollen and Phillips[5]; no such evidence was uncovered.

Turning now to Table 5-1, we notice that the number of adult suicides at any given time is not significantly correlated with the number of suicides one or two days later. Second, we can see that the day of the week is significantly associated with the fluctuation of adult suicides. On Monday, adult suicides are markedly higher than on any other day of the week. The average Monday in 1977 had 12.33 more suicides than the average Sunday (the omitted day-of-the-week variable). The next highest number of suicides occurs on Tuesday, with the average Tuesday displaying 5.56 more suicides than Sunday. In general, the number of suicides seems to decline quite smoothly from a peak on Monday to a low on Sunday.

Next, we can see that adult suicides are significantly affected by monthly variables, with suicides being unusually low in January and December (the omitted variable). In general, United States adult suicides

Table 5-1
U.S. Adult Suicides Regressed on Day-of-the-Week, Month, and Holiday Variables, 1977

Regressand

ADULT SUICIDES

Regressor	Regression Coefficient	t-Statistic
Intercept	59.59	11.73*
SUI(1)	.04	.77
SUI(2)	− .02	− .42
Monday	12.33	7.14*
Tuesday	5.56	2.94*
Wednesday	4.02	2.12*
Thursday	3.34	1.85
Friday	2.54	1.43
Saturday	1.04	.60
January	− .64	− .27
February	10.89	4.37*
March	11.77	4.80*
April	11.25	4.50*
May	10.87	4.59*
June	8.54	3.59*
July	10.78	4.47*
August	10.21	4.25*
September	9.69	4.04*
October	9.57	3.99*
November	4.00	1.76
HOL(−3)	−3.41	− .89
HOL(−2)	−3.18	− .83
HOL(−1)	−2.36	− .62
HOLIDAY	−9.53	−4.05*
HOL(1)	12.94	3.42*
HOL(2)	6.59	1.70
HOL(3)	−2.69	− .71

Standard deviation of y about regression line = 8.704, 336 d.f.
R^2 = 38.7%
R^2 = 34.0%, adjusted for d.f.

ANALYSIS OF VARIANCE

Due to	D.F.	S.S.	M.S. = S.S./D.F.
Regression	26	16076.13	618.31
Residual	336	25458.14	75.77
TOTAL	362	41534.27	F = 8.16

*Significant at 0.05 level or better, two tail test.
NOTE: In all tables and in the text, an "adult" has been defined as a person aged 20 or more; a "teenager" has been defined as a person aged 13 to 19.99.

appear to be relatively high in February through May, and relatively low in the latter part of the year (September through December).

Finally, we see that United States adult suicides drop significantly and substantially in the holiday period. During the holiday, there are 9.53 fewer suicides per day than in nonholiday periods. This finding also holds for suicides of all ages combined.[5-7] These authors (Bollen, Phillips and Liu) examined daily suicides for the entire United States. Other authors, who examined much smaller, geographically limited samples, typically have not found significant drops in suicide during the holiday period. For a current review of the literature on this topic, see reference 7.

It is also interesting to examine the behavior of suicides before and after the holiday period. Adult suicides appear to drop for several days before the holiday period and rise above normal for several days after the holiday is over. It is interesting to note that the total rise in adult suicides in the three days after the holiday period ($16.84 = 12.94 + 6.59 - 2.69$) very nearly cancels the total *drop* in suicides in the holiday period and the three days preceding it ($-18.48 = -3.41 - 3.18 - 2.36 - 9.53$). Phillips and Liu,[6] who were the first to report this phenomenon, speculate on some possible explanations for it.

Finally, it might be appropriate to mention the influence of one other set of time-series variables, though they are not explicitly examined in Table 5-1. A series of reports has shown that, correcting for the effect of other temporal variables, suicides increase briefly but markedly just after publicized suicide stories, either fictional[10] or nonfictional.[5,11,12] The more publicity given to these stories, the more suicides increase, and the increase occurs primarily in the geographic area where the suicide story is publicized. In addition, auto fatalities also rise significantly after publicized suicide stories, both fictional[10] and nonfictional.[12-14] The steepest rise occurs for single car crash fatalities. Motto has shown what might be considered the inverse of these findings: during a newspaper strike in a city, suicide rates in that city sometimes fall,[15,16] though not always.[17] Motto attributes this drop to the absence of newspaper suicide stories during the newspaper strike.

Teenage Suicides

Table 5-1 showed that adult suicides are substantially influenced by temporal variables, which explained 34% of the variance. The picture for *teenage* suicides is markedly different. Table 5-2 shows that only 4% of the variance in teenage suicides is explained by temporal factors, taken as a whole. Remarkably, these temporal variables have a trivial impact on teenage suicides.

For the most part, the individual temporal variables, considered separately, are also unrelated to teenage suicides. For example, in con-

Table 5-2
U.S. Teenage Suicides Regressed on Day-of-the-Week,
Month, and Holiday Variables, 1977

Regressand

TEENAGE SUICIDES

Regressor	Regression Coefficient	t-Statistic
Intercept	6.24	9.07*
SUI(1)	.13	−2.46*
SUI(2)	.13	−2.36*
Monday	−.42	−.86
Tuesday	.20	.40
Wednesday	.01	.02
Thursday	−.08	−.17
Friday	−.43	−.86
Saturday	−.30	−.61
January	1.56	2.34*
February	2.26	3.32*
March	1.90	2.86*
April	1.36	2.06*
May	1.04	1.62
June	−.34	−.52
July	.49	.76
August	.20	.31
September	1.22	1.90
October	1.10	1.68
November	1.02	1.59
HOL(−3)	.39	.36
HOL(−2)	.91	.84
HOL(−1)	−1.45	−1.35
HOLIDAY	.28	.42
HOL(1)	1.00	.94
HOL(2)	.24	.22
HOL(3)	1.60	1.51

Standard deviation of y about regression line = 2.477, 336 d.f.
R^2 = 10.9%
R^2 = 4.0%, adjusted for d.f.

ANALYSIS OF VARIANCE

Due to	D.F.	S.S.	M.S. = S.S./D.F.
Regression	26	253.12	9.735
Residual	336	2061.45	6.135
TOTAL	362	2314.57	F = 1.587

*Significant at 0.05 level or better, two tail test.

trast to adults, teenagers do *not* commit suicide significantly more often on one day of the week than on any other. The monthly pattern of teenage suicides is also weak and blurred. Only four months (January through April) display significantly unusual levels of suicide — suicides are significantly high for this period. Finally, teenage suicides do not fluctuate significantly around the holidays, in marked contrast to adult behavior. These strong differences between adult and teenage suicide patterns may be worth pursuing, and will be discussed further at the end of this chapter.

One other adult-teen difference might be mentioned briefly. In contrast to adult suicide, there is a significant, negative correlation between the number of teenage suicides on one day and the number one and two days later. As noted earlier, statistical significance can be calculated, provided there is no serial correlation among the residuals. The test for serial correlation, originally applied to the data in Table 5-1, was used once again for the data in Table 5-2. No evidence of serial correlation was found: e(t) was not significantly related to e(t−1) ($t = -.97$).

Teenage Auto Fatalities

In contrast to teenage suicides, teenage *auto fatalities* are markedly affected by temporal factors, which explain an extraordinarily large, 71% of the variance (Table 5-3). (Compare this with 4% for teenage suicides.)

Considered singly, nearly all the individual temporal variables have a significant impact on teenage auto deaths. Unlike suicides, auto fatalities are unusually *low* at the beginning of the week. Auto deaths increase quite smoothly to a peak at the end of the week, on Saturday and Sunday. Auto fatalities are significantly low during January and February, and significantly high May through November, reaching a peak in July and August. Not surprisingly, holiday periods have a very different effect on auto fatalities than they do on suicides. Teenage auto deaths *rise* markedly during the holiday period; before and after this period there is no significant fluctuation.

No evidence of first-order serial correlation of the residuals was found, when this was sought by the methods described earlier. For teenage auto fatalities, the regression coefficient relating e(t) with e(t −1) is not statistically significant ($t = -1.07$). For adult auto fatalities there is also no evidence of serial correlation among the residuals ($t = -.42$).

Adult Auto Fatalities

We noticed earlier that teenage and adult suicides behave very differently with respect to temporal variables. This is not so with auto fatalities, where the teenage and adult patterns are very similar. Because of this similarity, Table 5-4 can be discussed briefly.

As with teens, a large proportion of the variance in adult auto fatalities is explained by temporal factors (75.6%). Adults, like teens, suffer a relatively small number of auto fatalities at the beginning of the

Table 5-3
U.S. Teenage Auto Fatalities Regressed on Day-of-the-Week,
Month, and Holiday Variables, 1977

Regressand
TEENAGE AUTO FATALITIES

Regressor	Regression Coefficient	t-Statistic
Intercept	30.54	10.95*
AUTO(1)	.04	.81
AUTO(2)	−.01	−.25
Monday	−15.30	−9.98*
Tuesday	−16.09	−8.86*
Wednesday	−14.87	−7.95*
Thursday	·13.46	−7.37*
Friday	−7.22	−4.13*
Saturday	5.51	3.60*
January	−7.73	−4.15*
February	−5.04	−2.74*
March	−.35	−.20
April	3.12	1.75
May	6.88	3.83*
June	9.21	4.88*
July	14.18	7.01*
August	10.06	5.21*
September	7.13	3.93*
October	7.41	4.01*
November	3.49	1.99*
HOL(−3)	−2.40	−.82
HOL(−2)	−.56	−.19
HOL(−1)	3.83	1.32
HOLIDAY	4.42	2.45*
HOL(1)	1.62	.56
HOL(2)	−1.63	−.57
HOL(3)	.91	.32

Standard deviation of y about regression line = 6.671, 336 d.f.
R^2 = 73.1%
R^2 = 71.0%, adjusted for d.f.

ANALYSIS OF VARIANCE

Due to	D.F.	S.S.	M.S. = S.S./D.F.
Regression	26	40632.56	1562.79
Residual	336	14952.76	44.50
TOTAL	362	55585.33	F = 35.12

*Significant at 0.05 level or better, two tail test.

week, and many more at the end of the week. Both adult and teen auto fatalities peak in July and August, and drop in the first two months of the year. Fluctuation around holiday periods is generally similar for adults and teens, but adult auto fatalities are significantly high just before the holiday period, and this is not true for teenagers.

78

Table 5-4
U.S. Adult Auto Fatalities Regressed on Day-of-the-Week, Month, and Holiday Variables, 1977

Regressand

ADULT AUTO FATALITIES Regressor	Regression Coefficient	t-Statistic
Intercept	101.92	10.30*
AUTO(1)	.24	4.38*
AUTO(2)	−.12	−2.26*
Monday	−23.87	−6.64*
Tuesday	−22.79	−5.34*
Wednesday	−22.94	−5.13*
Thursday	−18.16	−4.13*
Friday	4.97	1.20
Saturday	26.25	7.71*
January	−27.05	−5.98*
February	−17.44	−4.12*
March	−10.49	−2.64*
April	−6.60	−1.68
May	−2.06	−.55
June	7.81	2.03*
July	10.60	2.78*
August	13.30	3.36*
September	5.49	1.45
October	10.50	2.69*
November	5.41	1.43
HOL(−3)	−4.66	−.73
HOL(−2)	−.32	−.05
HOL(−1)	20.76	3.27*
HOLIDAY	9.41	2.34*
HOL(1)	12.01	1.92
HOL(2)	−2.40	−.38
HOL(3)	3.75	.59

Standard deviation of y about regression line = 14.61, 336 d.f.
R^2 = 77.3%
R^2 = 75.6%, adjusted for d.f.

ANALYSIS OF VARIANCE

Due to	D.F.	S.S.	M.S. = S.S./D.F.
Regression	26	244749.9	9413.5
Residual	336	71756.4	213.6
TOTAL	362	316506.4	F = 44.07

*Significant at 0.05 level or better, two tail test.

In sum, teenage suicides contrast markedly with the other three demographic groups studied. These three groups are substantially or dominantly influenced by temporal variables; only teenage suicides are not.

DISCUSSION

Perhaps teenagers are not immersed in the social world of work, and perhaps it is this "work world" which lends special significance to Mondays (when adult suicides are so high), and holidays (when adult suicides are so low). If this hypothesis is correct, then other groups which are not immersed in the work world should behave like teenage suicides and display little seasonal fluctuation in mortality. Future research might profitably compare seasonal fluctuations in suicide for the following groups: 1) retired persons; 2) the unemployed (perhaps distinguishing long-term from recent unemployed); 3) housewives; 4) working and nonworking teenagers. If the "work world" argument is correct, then many of these groups should display similar "nonpatterns" of temporal suicide mortality.

However, one should bear in mind the fact that temporal factors significantly affect teenage *auto fatalities*. This casts some doubt on the "workworld" argument, or, at the very least, suggests that this argument is oversimplified.

This chapter has examined the influence of temporal factors on four groups: 1) teenage suicides, 2) adult suicides, 3) teenage auto accident fatalities, and 4) adult auto accident fatalities. The last three groups are markedly affected by temporal factors; only the first group is not. Why should teenage suicides behave so differently from the other groups examined? The answer to this provocative question may shed light on an important social problem — teenage suicide.

REFERENCES

1. Ostrom C: *Time Series Analysis: Regression Techniques.* Beverly Hills, Sage, 1978.
2. Johnston J: *Econometric Methods.* New York, McGraw-Hill, 1972.
3. Rao P, Miller R: *Applied Econometrics.* Belmont, CA, Wadsworth, 1971.
4. Bollen KA, Phillips DP: Suicidal motor vehicle fatalities in Detroit: A replication. *Am J Sociol* 1981;87:404–412.
5. Bollen KA, Phillips DP: Imitative suicides: A national study of the effects of television news stories. *Am Sociol Rev* 1982;47:802–809.
6. Phillips DP, Liu J: The frequency of suicide around major holidays: Some surprising findings. *Suicide Life Threat Behav* 1980;10:41–50.
7. Bollen KA: Temporal variations in mortality: A comparison of U.S. suicides and motor vehicle fatalities, 1972–1976. *Demography* 1983 (forthcoming).
8. Nerlove M, Wallis K: Use of the Durbin-Watson statistic in inappropriate situations. *Econometrics* 1966;34:235–238.

9. Durbin J: Testing for serial correlation in least-squares regression when some of the regressors are lagged dependent variables. *Econometrics* 1970;38: 410–421.
10. Phillips DP: The impact of fictional television stories on U.S. adult fatalities: New evidence on the effects of violence in the mass media. *Am J Sociol* 1982; 87:1340–1359.
11. Phillips DP: The influence of suggestion on suicide: Substantive and theoretical implications of the Werther effect. *Am Sociol Rev* 1974;39:340–354.
12. Ganzeboom HBG, de Haan D: Gepubliceerde zelfmoorden en verhoging van sterfte door zelfmoord en ongelukken in Nederland 1972–1980. *Mens en Maatschappij* 1982;57:55–68.
13. Phillips DP: Motor vehicle fatalities increase just after publicized suicide stories. *Science* 1977;196:1464–1465.
14. Phillips DP: Suicide, motor vehicle fatalities, and the mass media: Evidence toward a theory of suggestion. *Am J Sociol* 1979;84:1150–1174.
15. Motto JA: Newspaper influence on suicide. *Arch Gen Psychiatry* 1970;23: 143–148.
16. Blumenthal S, Bergner, L: Suicide and newspapers: A replicated study. *Am J Psychiatry* 1973;130:468–471.
17. Motto JA: Suicide and suggestibility — The role of the press. *Am J Psychiatry* 1967;124:252–256.

CHAPTER 6

BIOLOGICAL FACTORS AND PHARMACOLOGIC TREATMENT IN MAJOR DEPRESSIVE DISORDER IN CHILDREN AND ADOLESCENTS

PAUL J. AMBROSINI
HARRIS RABINOVICH
JOAQUIM PUIG-ANTICH

*Investigation of phenomenology, biological factors and phar-
macological response in major depression in children has validated the syndrome's existence in prepuberty. Although there is not a total concordance
in the neuroendocrine and polysomnographic parameters investigated, the
evidence to date suggests that prepubertal and adolescent major depression
is associated with dysfunction of several neuroregulatory systems. Completion of ongoing studies of TRH/TSH, cortisol, and growth hormone will
greatly enhance our knowledge about childhood and adolescent MDD.*

*The important variable of age may account for the differences previ-
ously described. The age factor is apparent in adult MDD, particularly in
cortisol hypersecretion and polysomnographic variables. Within the adult
sample of major depressives, there is a greater likelihood of abnormal cortisol secretion and sleep architecture abnormalities with advancing age. In
this chapter, the authors present data comparing biological indices of
depression in children and adolescents to those in adults. Recommendations are made regarding psychopharmacological treatment for those
children and adolescents for whom such therapy appears indicated.*

This chapter will report on the current state of assessment, biological
factors, and pharmacological treatment of children and adolescents with
the syndrome of Major Depressive Disorder (MDD). A discussion of
MDD in a text on suicide in children is relevant because suicidal behavior
is so often a symptom of the depressive syndrome. Thus, the data
presented here pertain to children exhibiting the syndrome of MDD and

not merely depressive or suicidal symptoms. A syndrome is a group of symptoms which occur together and constitute a recognizable condition. The criteria for the syndrome of MDD are listed in Table 6-1.

The distinction between the syndrome of MDD and mere depressive symptoms is important because only approximately one third of those children identified through a psychiatric screening as having depressive symptoms fit criteria for MDD when clinically interviewed.[1] The prevalence of MDD increases up to 80% in those children with serious suicide intent or attempts.[2] In other words, a great majority of suicidal youngsters suffer from a MDD, of which suicidal ideation and behavior are just symptoms.

Morbid preoccupations with death wishes or feelings that one would be better off dead frequently precede suicidal behavior but, in themselves, are not considered suicidal ideation unless actual thoughts of suicide also are present. As suicidal ideation worsens, the individual may mentally rehearse a death plan and then progress to suicidal gestures or attempts.

Suicidal behavior refers to actions which have the potential for serious self-injury or harm. Suicidal gestures frequently involve a secondary gain to manipulate some other person(s) or produce a dramatic effect. Assessment of suicidal ideation and behavior also must include an evaluation of the lethality (ie, method, threat to life) and the intent or seriousness of the act (ie, likelihood of rescue, purpose of the attempt). Decisions to hospitalize are made by judging the severity of intent and lethality, and intent to attempt again.

Not all self-destructive behaviors, however, are suicidal. For example, the self-mutilation seen with Lesch-Nyhan syndrome or the impulsive behavior seen in conduct-disordered children with low intellect occur without the intent to harm or kill oneself. A similar pattern also may be seen in some deluded schizophrenics, manic psychotics, or during clouded consciousness which accompanies organic psychotic states produced by drug abuse. Delusional children and adolescents with self-destructive tendencies are all at great risk and require protection from themselves. As with nondelusional children, delusional children and adolescents can only be considered suicidal if they threaten or engage in self-destructive behavior and, in clear consciousness, have a wish to die. Thus a child who, convinced he can fly, jumps off a window, even if the action is ultimately self-destructive, cannot be considered truly suicidal.

Children, adolescents, and adults who suffer from depressive disorders are the group most likely to harbor suicidal ideation or display suicidal behavior. Epidemiological studies of adult suicide victims and adult suicide attempters show a strong association between suicide and psychiatric disorder. The most common diagnosis is depressive disorder followed by chronic alcoholism, a disorder which may have familial

Table 6-1
Research Diagnostic Criteria for Major Depressive Disorder[14]*

A.	Dysphoric mood or pervasive loss of interest or pleasure
B.	At least four of the following eight items of depressive syndrome:

    1) Poor appetite, weight loss, increased appetite or weight gain
    2) Sleep difficulty or sleeping too much
    3) Loss of energy, fatigability or tiredness
    4) Psychomotor agitation or retardation
    5) Loss of interest or pleasure in usual activities
    6) Excessive or inappropriate guilt
    7) Diminished ability to think or concentrate
    8) Recurrent thoughts of death or suicide, or any suicidal behavior

C. Duration of dysphoric features at least two weeks
D. Sought or was referred for help or impairment in functioning
E. No signs suggestive of schizophrenia
F. Does not meet the criteria for schizophrenia, residual subtype

*A.–F. are all required.

links to depressive disorder. In the only psychological postmortem study with an epidemiological sample of child and adolescent suicide victims, Shaffer[3] reported only four of 31 children lacked evidence of psychiatric symptoms in their records. Thirteen of the children were noted to have "depressed mood or fearfulness." There was a high prevalence of depression and suicidal behavior among the victims' parents and siblings. The most common precipitant was a disciplinary crisis.

Carlson and Cantwell's recent work[2] in an outpatient sample of children and adolescents studied the relationship between suicidal behavior and depression. They assessed the group on the basis of the intensity of their suicidal ideation and behavior. Eighty-three percent of the most severely suicidal group met diagnostic criteria for a depressive disorder; and, the frequency of depressive disorder was significantly greater than in the mild and moderate suicidal groups. Three quarters of subjects in the severe group had families with depression, depression spectrum disorders, or alcoholism. This study found that a majority of depressed children and adolescents had suicidal ideation. Others who have studied suicidal ideation (as opposed to attempted or completed suicide) have also noted this association.[4-6]

In depressed individuals, suicidal ideation and behavior generally abate with the remission of the depressive disorder. This pattern occurs whether the remission is induced pharmacologically or happens spontaneously. Suicidal ideation and behavior act no differently than the other associated symptoms of the depressive disorder because they are an integral part of this syndrome. Nevertheless, a few patients remain prone to make suicidal statements and gestures even after recovery from the depressive syndrome, usually with at least a partial goal of manipulating the environment.

Adult depressive symptoms were described in adolescents and children during the 1950s and 1960s, but it was believed that children lacked the cognitive capacity to suffer an "adult-like depression." When considered at all, "childhood depression" was classified among the neurotic or emotional disorders. At present, the existence of major depressive illness in children and adolescents is no longer controversial. Numerous studies have repeatedly found children fitting symptomatic criteria for depression loosely derived from adult diagnostic criteria among clinic groups[7] and also in total population samples.[8] In addition, Pearce,[9] and Kovacs and Beck[10] have independently shown that the items of the depressive syndrome tend to cluster in children with the presence of depressive mood. As more rigorous assessment methods and diagnostic criteria for depressed children were established, MDD in childhood received greater acceptance as a nosological entity distinct from neurotic syndromes. This historical change is now reflected in the official American Psychiatric Association classification of Mental Disorders (DSM-III).

It has been our goal to validate further the diagnosis of MDD in prepuberty and adolescents by studying depressed children and appropriate controls along several psychobiological parameters which are characteristically altered in adult MDD. These include psychosocial relationships, sleep physiology, neuroendocrine rhythms, hormone responses, family prevalence of affective disorders, natural history, and response to antidepressant medication. In adults, this strategy has particularly supported the existence of a genetic and hormonal component in affective disorders.

Genetic transmission of affective illness is compatible with data from families of adult probands which show familial aggregation of the illness. It has received further support from a higher concordance rate in monozygotic than in dizygotic twins regardless of home environment.[11] Recent analyses of family histories in our sample of prepubertal major depressives strengthens the evidence for this genetic link. We found a significantly higher prevalence of depression spectrum disorders within first-degree relatives of MDD probands than within those of both normal and pathological controls. Within adult proband samples, familial aggregation is negatively correlated with age of onset. Thus, the prepubertal onset of MDD may reflect a greater genetic loading for affective disturbances. This emerging pattern in the family histories of prepubertal major depressives strengthens the validity of this syndrome in children.

Biological correlates of adult MDD have been established over the past two decades. These correlates include abnormalities in neuroendocrine systems, particularly of the hypothalamic-pituitary axis (HPA). The secretion of hormones by the HPA is influenced by several neurotransmitter systems, among them norepinephrine and serotonin. Deficiencies of these neurotransmitters are implicated in the pathogenesis of MDD. Thus, studying hormone responses of provocative tests affecting the HPA could indirectly assess the functional status of the hypothalamic catecholaminergic system.

Recent advances in child psychiatric research have identified several of the psychobiological abnormalities of adult MDD in both children and adolescents. However, one-to-one concordance with adult findings does not occur because age and sexual maturation also influence these variables. Once these are taken into account, one can see that the biological correlates of prepubertal MDD are quite consistent with the adult data.

Pharmacological treatment of adult MDD has greatly reduced the morbidity of this disorder. Antidepressant medication is an essential component in the comprehensive treatment of adult major depressive disorders. Studies supporting the efficacy of antidepressants in prepubertal MDD have only recently been reported.[12] The therapeutic response to tricyclic antidepressants (TCAs) in prepubertal MDD is pharmacologically similar to that shown in adult depressives. Children tolerate antidepressants well, exhibiting the same spectrum of clinical and cardiovascular side effects as adults. Furthermore, response of the depressive syndrome in prepuberty is highly correlated with serum tricyclic levels as is the case in adult depressives. Similar work with adolescents is proceeding.

Systematic research of genetic and biological factors, and the pharmacological response of children with MDD has led to the validation of this syndrome in youngsters. Continued research efforts are essential in order to clarify the influence of age, genetic predisposition and environmental factors in the etiopathogenesis of major depressive illness and suicidal behavior throughout the lifespan on those afflicted with MDD.

Evaluation Methods

Assessment of prepubertal MDD necessitates a valid and reliable method to identify a group of children with this syndrome. In a pilot study of a sample of children, Puig-Antich et al[13] found it possible to use unmodified research diagnostic criteria (RDC) for major depressive disorder in adults.[14] A clinical evaluation instrument, the Schedule for Affective Disorders and Schizophrenia for School-Age Children (K-SADS) was subsequently developed. The K-SADS is designed to record the chronology and symptoms of the child's present psychiatric state and systematically evaluate RDC criteria for MDD. The Kiddie-SADS-P (K-SADS-P), derived from the adult SADS,[15] is an effort to reduce information variance in both the descriptive and diagnostic evaluation process. This interview is in a semistructured format which allows the clinician flexibility to elicit information about the symptom spectrum of the child. Symptom ratings are obtained by interviewing, individually, the parent and then the child. Each symptom is rated for the most severe point in the episode and for the week preceding evaluation; this is important as a baseline from which to measure change. Finally, summary ratings which include all sources of information (parent, child, school and chart) are arrived at for each item.

A second form of this instrument is available (K-SADS-E) and is designed to evaluate the past and current episodes of psychopathology for epidemiological or retrospective clinical research in children and adolescents from age 6 through 16 years. Although the K-SADS title refers only to affective disorders and schizophrenia, symptoms related to conduct and emotional disorders are also included.

The K-SADS also provides symptomatic criteria for diagnosing major depressive subtypes. These include the endogenous subtype which depends mostly on the severity of dysphoric mood and anhedonia and on the presence of "vegetative" symptoms. Specifically, at least six of the following 10 symptoms should be present: pervasive anhedonia, lack of reactivity of the depressed mood to environmental change, worsening of mood in the morning, excessive guilt, psychomotor changes, early morning awakening, poor appetite, weight loss, loss of interest or pleasure, and distinct quality to depressed mood. The diagnosis of psychotic subtype depends on the presence of mood-congruent hallucinations or delusions experienced in clear consciousness. The atypical subtype, very rarely found before adolescence, is defined by the presence of reactivity of mood plus at least two of the following: excessive sleeping, extreme bodily inertia or feeling of leaden paralysis, increased appetite or weight, and rejection sensitivity. These adolescents are potentially most vulnerable to suicidal ideation and behavior whenever they feel rejected, as a consequence of an event which rightly or wrongly they interpret this way.

The K-SADS represents a departure from traditional child psychiatric practice because it aims for symptomatic assessment by means of a verbal interview, rather than a play interview. The majority of previous clinical research with children and adolescents relied heavily on parent and teacher reports for assessment of psychiatric disorder or behavioral deviance in the child. The play interview with the child assesses psychodynamic conflicts but generally not symptoms. Contrary to widespread opinion, symptomatic and psychodynamic assessments of the child are neither mutually exclusive, nor at odds with each other. They are simply complementary. Both parent and child reports are essential because crucial symptoms of depression are "inner" symptoms (eg, mood state, anhedonia, suicidal ideation) which can only be accurately reported by the child while the parent is more aware of "outer" symptoms (eg, weight loss, guilt, and reactivity of dysphoric mood). With this emphasis on symptoms, the reliability of childrens' reports is an increasingly important issue. Rutter and Graham[16] and Herjanic et al[17] studied this issue and found children to be reliable reporters.

BIOLOGICAL CORRELATES

Biological variables consistently reported as abnormal in adult endogenous MDD include among others: growth hormone (GH) hyporesponsiveness to insulin tolerance testing (ITT), desipramine, and clonidine; cortisol hypersecretion; cortisol nonsuppression to dexamethasone; blunted thyroid-stimulating hormone response to thyroid-releasing hormone (TRH/TSH); and polysomnographic abnormalities. These parameters are all abnormal during an active episode of MDD; yet, the cortisol variables return to baseline following full clinical recovery. Neither sleep nor GH have been systematically restudied in recovered adult depressives.

Although the work in prepubertal and adolescent MDD has closely paralleled that performed in adult depressives, the data available do not show total concordance in the neuroendocrine and polysomnographic results. The abnormalities reported in prepubertal and adolescent MDD during active illness include: GH hyporesponsiveness to insulin-induced hypoglycemia[18]; cortisol nonsuppression to dexamethasone[19]; and elevated GH during sleep.[20] The abnormalities found upon full clinical recovery include persistence of the GH abnormalities during insulin hypoglycemia and sleep, and shortened first REM period latency. The similarities and differences between adult and child depressives will be detailed below.

Growth Hormone

Growth hormone response to insulin-induced hypoglycemia is a provocative neuroendocrine test which assesses the integrity of the hypothalamic-pituitary axis. It is performed by injecting 0.10 units of regular insulin intravenously and sampling for glucose and growth hormone, every 15 minutes for two hours following infusion.

In a recently completed study of 46 prepubertal children in a drug-free state during active illness, 60% of those with endogenous depression, 35% with nonendogenous MDD and 12% of nondepressed neurotics hyposecreted GH.[18] When all children with MDD were combined, approximately 50% significantly hyposecreted GH, and this test correctly identified the endogenous subtype, with a sensitivity of 65% and specificity of 88%.

These findings are similar to results reported in adult endogenous MDD. Approximately 50% of endogenously depressed postmenopausal women hyposecrete GH in response to the ITT. Menstrual status is an important variable in assessing the GH response to insulin hypoglycemia because estrogens potentiate the GH response to a variety of stimuli.[21] It is conceivable, therefore, that the estrogen status of premenopausal women, young men and adolescents could mask what otherwise would be a blunted GH response. (In fact, the test does not appear sensitive in premenopausal adult women.) Assessment of the GH response to insulin-induced hypoglycemia must be performed in each of these distinct groups to fully understand its pattern in MDD across ages. Our group is currently investigating the GH-ITT in adolescents.

The remaining question, however, is whether a blunted GH-ITT test is a constant neuroendocrine response in depressives or exists only during active illness and normalizes upon recovery. This change differentiates a marker of illness (state dependent) from a marker of predisposition (state independent) if the finding existed before the episode. Our group subsequently investigated the GH-ITT response in 18 recovered prepubertal MDDs who were in a drug-free state for at least one month in order to clarify the dynamic status of this test upon recovery.

The results of this study[22] revealed that endogenous depressives continued to significantly hyposecrete GH to ITT when compared to the other subjects, while there were no significant differences between recovered nonendogenous depressives and nondepressed neurotic children. Approximately 57% of recovered endogenous subjects were found to continue to hyposecrete GH. The pre-post correlations were very high. The strength of these findings is that the endogenous MDDs in recovery are segregated from the nonendogenous depressives and the neurotics by the GH-ITT test. This type of study is not yet available in adults or adolescents with endogenous depressions.

A second abnormality of GH observed in prepubertal MDD is increased secretion during sleep. This aspect of GH secretion has not been adequately studied as yet in adult depressives. GH hypersecretion, found both during active illness[20] and upon full clinical recovery,[23] was not dependent on any polysomnographic differences among studied subjects. It occurred in both the endogenous and nonendogenous depressives when compared to psychiatric controls and normal children.

In summary, GH abnormalities in prepubertal MDD are: 1) GH hyporesponsiveness to insulin hypoglycemia, 2) GH hypersecretion during sleep, 3) persistence of most GH abnormalities after full clinical recovery. These data suggest that these neuroendocrine parameters are state independent and may fulfill criteria for a marker of predisposition for prepubertal MDD. The persistent neuroendocrine dysfunction in prepubertal chidren with a past history of MDD is likely to reflect specific neuroregulatory abnormalities in the limbic-hypothalamic systems which underlie the predisposition of affective episodes.

Cortisol Secretion

Cortisol hypersecretion is the most extensively investigated biological variable analyzed in adult MDD. Approximately 50% of adult endogenous depressives hypersecrete cortisol[24] when studied through a 24-hour period as compared to normals. In addition, hypersecretors have an increased number of secretory episodes, increased total cortisol secretion, and increased time each day during which cortisol secretion occurs. These parameters appear to be independent of emotional arousal and distress; they also normalize upon recovery.

The first report of cortisol hypersecretion in children fitting criteria for MDD was noted in two prepubertal endogenously depressed subjects.[25] During active illness, these children had an increased mean cortisol level, more secretory episodes, increased amount of secretory time and excess secretion during evening and early morning hours. This hypersecretory pattern disappeared with recovery.

Our group subsequently expanded this work to include 62 subjects during active illness and eight normal controls.[26] Plasma cortisol concentrations were not significantly different among the diagnostic groups. Within the depressives, about 10% did hypersecrete cortisol when compared to themselves upon recovery. Although cortisol hypersecretion occurs in some prepubertal MDD children, its rate is much lower than in adults. This pattern is consistent with the influence of age in hypersecretion of cortisol in adult endogenous MDDs. The older the endogenous depressive, the higher the chances of cortisol hypersecretion. Thus, the prepubertal data is not identical to, but consistent with data for adults with the same diagnosis, once the effects of age are taken into account.

Dexamethasone Suppression Test

The Dexamethasone Suppression Test (DST) assesses states of excessive cortisol secretion, by inhibiting cortisol secretion through negative feedback at the hypothalamic-pituitary axis. In this test, dexamethasone (1 mg) is given orally at 11 PM, followed by 4 PM and 11 PM cortisol sampling the next day. Serum cortisol levels should decrease to < 5 μg/dL. Sensitivity for lack of cortisol suppression during a DST in adult endogenous depressives is approximately 65%; specificity (true negatives) approaches 95%.[27] In the adult population, the DST is gaining wider acceptance as a diagnostic procedure to positively identify inpatient endogenous depressives because of its high specificity and normalization upon recovery. It is much less sensitive among outpatient, nonendogenous MDDs.

Poznanski et al[19] reported results of the DST in 18 prepubertal depressive and neurotic children. The dose of dexamethasone used was

0.5 mg, which yields approximately the same proportion of steroid to body weight as the 1-mg dose in adults. Fifty-six percent of the depressives escaped cortisol suppression, while 89% of the nondepressives had a normal DST. The sensitivity of the DST in prepubertal endogenous MDD was 63%, specificity was 90%. These data are also consistent with DST data in adult endogenous MDD, where no age effects have been found.

Present data on the cortisol secretion in prepubertal MDD reveal the following: 1) hypercortisol secretion occurs rarely in MDD children. Prevalence of this biological variable appears to be age dependent, ie, there is a greater likelihood of excessive cortisol secretion with increasing age; 2) the dexamethasone suppression test can reliably identify 50% to 60% of children with an endogenous depression; 3) the DST may be a useful clinical test to verify the diagnosis of prepubertal and perhaps adolescent MDD.

Polysomnography

Sleep disturbances are commonly reported in adult MDD and polysomnographic abnormalities are now well established. The most commonly reported disturbances during active illness are the following: 1) shortened REM latency,[28] 2) increased REM density,[29] 3) decreased delta sleep,[30] 4) decreased sleep efficiency,[30] and 5) abnormal temporal distribution of REM sleep during the nocturnal sleep episode.[31]

Studies assessing clinical sleep disturbances and all night polysomnographic parameter in prepubertal MDD, neurotics, and normals by our group[32] during active illness found that two thirds of the depressives report difficulty falling asleep or persistent middle night awakenings; approximately one half of the endogenous group had early morning awakening; and a minority reported an increase in total time asleep in the 24-hour day. Clinical sleep disturbances in depressives were more prevalent and more stable across time compared to the nondepressed groups.

Analysis of the overall sleep stage architecture variables and a detailed analysis of REM sleep parameters failed to show any polysomnographic abnormalities in the depressed groups which could be ascribed specifically to prepubertal major depression. The REM sleep analysis showed no abnormalities of REM latency or density in either the endogenous or nonendogenous groups which are specific for adult MDD. Young, Knowles et al[33] recently corroborated this finding in 12 children ages 7 through 13 diagnosed as depressed by Weinberg criteria.[34]

Our group restudied these same children when fully recovered from their depressive episodes for at least six weeks and drug free for at least one month.[35] Approximately one quarter of the recovered depressives continued to report some difficulty falling asleep but generally sleep continuity measurements improved in the depressives during recovery. An unexpected finding was a highly significant shortening of the first REM period latency upon recovery. The recovered depressives also had a significantly shorter mean first REM period latency than both groups of controls and a larger number of REM periods. These results suggest that shortened first REM period latency may be a marker of trait present in prepubertal MDD only during recovery. The increase in the number of REM periods is probably secondary to the shortened first REM period latency without changes in either length of REM period cycles or total sleep time.

It remains uncertain if the REM sleep results reported in prepubertal MDD are at variance with adult data because not enough information exists in adult recovered depressives. However, the first few pilot studies in which adult depressives were compared to themselves when ill showed a short first REM period latency during illness which did not normalize upon recovery. If the discrepant results from depressed adults and prepubertal patients are replicated, it would suggest that neuroregulation of affectivity and its psychobiological sleep correlates undergo a significant alteration during puberty.

The data on polysomnographic variables in prepubertal MDDs show the following: 1) during active illness there are no specific sleep abnormalities characteristic of adult MDD; 2) on recovery compared to themselves while ill, prepubertal depressives show a mild, but significant improvement in a variety of sleep continuity measures; 3) on recovery, they exhibit a shortened first REM period latency and a greater number of REM periods. It is suggested that shortened REM latency may be a trait marker for prepubertal MDD.

Thyrotropin-Releasing Hormone

Several investigators[36,37] reported that some adult euthyroid depressed patients had a deficient or blurred serum thyrotropin (TSH) response to intravenous thyrotropin-releasing hormone (TRH). The TSH response varies with both age and sex of the subject. In depressed adults, it may remain blunted upon clinical recovery.[38] The only reported data in adolescent depressives is a retrospective study by Greenberg et al.[39] They found that five of 17 adolescent depressives had a blunted response. Follow-up data after remission of the depressive syndrome was not available. Our group is actively testing prepubertal and adolescent major depressives with the TRH/TSH test. Studying this test in children may help isolate the effects of sex and age on the TRH test and clarify its usefulness in studies of depression.

PHARMACOTHERAPY

Recent evidence suggests that pharmacotherapy of prepubertal major depression is likely to be an effective treatment modality.[11,12] In fact, it may be the initial treatment of choice. The indications for drug treatment are a firm diagnosis of major depressive disorder using DSM-III criteria and no EKG, cardiovascular or other serious medical abnormalities.

Most children in our studies are treated with imipramine (IMI) because of greater experience and knowledge of its therapeutic and toxic effects in children. Initially IMI is administered in three equally divided daily dosages calculated on a milligram per kilogram of body weight per day schedule. The first dose is 1.5 mg/kg/day and this is subsequently raised every third day to 3, 4 and 5 mg/kg/day. Preceding each increase, EKG, blood pressure and clinical side effects are assessed. Because IMI induces cardiac conduction changes, the medication should not be increased if the following EKG variables are exceeded: 1) resting heart rate > 130 per minute, 2) PR interval > 0.21 msec, and 3) QRS widening > 130% baseline.

In addition, systolic blood pressure > 145 or diastolic blood pressure > 95 mmHg are also indications to lower the dose of IMI. Unacceptable clinical side effects would also preclude increasing dosage. Therefore, with any excessive EKG or clinical side effects, IMI should be decreased to the previous dose level.

Plasma tricyclic levels are important for proper pharmacological treatment, since clinical response correlates with threshold plasma levels in prepubertal children with MDD.[11,12] Blood samples are obtained when maintenance oral dose is reached. The samples should be drawn at least eight hours after the last dose, after at least three days on the same dose, and drawn through a syringe (the rubber top of the vacutainer tubes interferes with adequate quantitative analysis).

Imipramine is metabolized to desipramine (DMI) and the combined IMI and DMI levels significantly predict clinical response better than the level of either compound alone.[11] Maintaining plasma levels over 200 ng/mL maximizes effectiveness of treatment. A second factor which contributes to clinical pharmacological response is the presence of depressive hallucinations and/or delusions. Those children with psychotic depression need serum levels over 350 ng/mL for an adequate response. A phenothiazine also may be needed in these cases.

Imipramine toxicity includes cardiac conduction abnormalities and noncardiovascular symptoms (eg, dry mouth, abdominal pain, constipation, nightmares, insomnia, urinary retention, headaches, sweating, tiredness). Particularly troublesome may be orthostatic hypotension, chest pain, a rare syndrome of cognitive impairment, irritability and agitation, and anticholinergic blockade. In these situations, IMI dose should be lowered or discontinued. Changing medication to DMI may alleviate the anticholinergic symptoms and lessen the PR interval effects, but it has similar QRS effects, in our experience.

Overdose of tricyclics causes cardiac arrhythmias, seizures, coma and death. Emergency medical care is mandatory. It should include: 1) ipecac or gastric lavage up to 18 hours after ingestion, using large volumes for lavage since a significant percentage of the circulating drug is secreted in gastric juices; 2) activated charcoal 50 to 100 mg in 8 oz of water, administered every two hours by mouth or through a nasogastric tube (use lower amounts for children less than 40 kg); 3) admission to an intensive care unit for a minimum observation period of 24 hours. EKG monitoring is mandatory because the QRS complex is the best gauge of cardiotoxicity.

The following procedures are not helpful in managing acute overdose of tricyclics: 1) dialysis, since most of the drug is protein bound; 2) induced diuresis; 3) acidification of the urine because this increases the risk of cardiac arrhythmia; and finally, 4) intravenous physostigmine is not an antidote for tricyclic overdose. It may clear the sensorium if anticholinergic delirium is present, but it will have no effect on cardiotoxicity nor seizure prevention.

Acute tricyclic withdrawal may be associated with nausea, vomiting, abdominal cramps, drowsiness/fatigue, decreased appetite, tearfulness, apathy/withdrawal, headache and agitation.[40] A flu-like illness with gastrointestinal symptoms may also appear. The acute administration of 25 mg of IMI by mouth will generally alleviate most of these symptoms within one to two hours. This dose can be repeated as needed. Tapering withdrawal over two weeks will prevent most of these difficulties from occurring.

We treat prepubertal MDD children with antidepressants for a minimum of five weeks. At this time, assessment of response should focus on the signs and symptoms of the depressive syndrome, because tricyclics will not directly ameliorate the child's psychosocial functioning. Nonresponders at five weeks should be checked for medication compliance and plasma level. Those who are receiving 5 mg/kg/day and have low maintenance plasma levels can be slowly titrated to 7 mg/kg/-day if there are no clinical contraindications, with EKG and blood pressure monitoring as previously described. If there is no response within another month, reassessment of diagnosis is indicated. When the plasma level cannot be raised to an effective range, switching to DMI, nortriptyline or MAO inhibitors may be indicated.

Prepubertal responders at five weeks are maintained on tricyclics for three additional months. One month after discontinuation of medication, each child should be reevaluated for relapse of depressive symptoms. If relapse occurs, tricyclics can be reinstituted following the same titration schedule.

Studies of the effectiveness of TCAs in adolescent major depression are ongoing, but no conclusions have been reached as yet. Thus, the data described here cannot be simply transposed to adolescent depressives.

ACKNOWLEDGMENTS

Supported in part by grants MH-30838 and MH-30839 from the NIMH and from grants 5-T32-MH 16434-02 and 5-T32-MH 15144-06.

REFERENCES

1. Carlson GA, Cantwell DP: A survey of depressive symptoms, syndrome and disorder in a child psychiatric population. *J Child Psychol Psychiatry* 1980; 21:19–25.
2. Carlson GA, Cantwell DP: Suicidal behavior and depression in children and adolescents. *J Am Acad Child Psychiatry* 1982;21:361–368.
3. Shaffer D: Suicide in childhood and early adolescence. *J Child Psychol Psychiatry* 1974;15:275–291.
4. Guze S, Robins E: Suicide and primary affective disorder. *Br J Psychiatry* 1970;117:437–438.
5. Miles CP: Conditions predisposing to suicide: A review. *J Nerv Ment Dis* 1977;164:231–247.
6. Goldney RD, Pilowsky I: Depression in young women who have attempted suicide. *Aust NZ J Psychiatry* 1980;14:203–211.
7. Welner Z, Welner A, McCrary MD, et al: Psychopathology in children of inpatients with depression: A controlled study. *J Nerv Ment Dis* 1977;164: 408–413.
8. Rutter M, Tizard J, Whitmore K: *Education, Health and Behavior*. London, Longman, 1970.
9. Pearce JB: Childhood depression, in Rutter M, Hersov L (eds): *Child Psychiatry*. London, Blackwell, 1977.
10. Kovacs M, Beck AT: An empirical-clinical approach toward a definition of childhood depression, in Schulterbrandt JG, Raskin H (eds): *Depression in Childhood*. New York, Raven Press, 1977.
11. Baron M, Klotz J, Mendlewicz J, et al: Multiple-threshold transmission of affective disorders. *Arch Gen Psychiatry* 1981;38:79–84.
12. Puig-Antich J, Perel JM, Lupatkin W, et al: Plasma levels of imipramine (IMI) and desmethylimipramine (DMI) in clinical response to prepubertal major depressive disorder: A preliminary report. *J Am Acad Child Psychiatry* 1979;18:616–627.
13. Puig-Antich J, Blau S, Marx N, et al: Prepubertal major depressive disorder: A pilot study. *J Am Acad Child Psychiatry* 1978;17:695–707.
14. Spitzer RL, Endicott J, Robbins E: Research Diagnostic Criteria: Rationale and reliability. *Arch Gen Psychiatry* 1978;35:773–782.
15. Spitzer RL, Endicott J: *Schedule for Affective Disorders and Schizophrenia (SADS)*. New York State Psychiatric Institute, 1978.
16. Rutter M, Graham P: The reliability and validity of the psychiatric assess-

ment of children: The interview with the child. *Br J Psychiatry* 1968;114: 563–579.

17. Herjanic B, Herjanic M, Brown F, et al: Are children reliable reporters? *J Assoc Child Psychol Psychiatry* 1975;3:41–48.

18. Puig-Antich J, Novacenko H, Davies M, et al: Growth hormone secretion in prepubertal major depressive children: I. Response to insulin-induced hypoglycemia during a depressive episode: Final report. (Submitted for publication.)

19. Poznanski EO, Carroll BJ, Banegas MC, et al: The dexamethasone suppression test in prepubertal depressed children. *Am J Psychiatry* 1982;139:321–324.

20. Puig-Antich J, Goetz R, Davies M, et al: Growth hormone secretion in prepubertal major depressive children: II. Sleep-related plasma concentrations during a depressive episode. (Submitted for publication.)

21. Merimee TJ, Fineberg SE: Studies of the sex based variation of human growth secretion. *J Clin Endocrinol Metab* 1971;33:896–902.

22. Puig-Antich J, Novacenko H, Davies M, et al: Growth hormone secretion in major depressive children: III. Response to insulin-induced hypoglycemia after recovery from a depressive episode in a drug-free state. (Submitted for publication.)

23. Puig-Antich J, Goetz R, Davies M, et al: Growth hormone secretion in prepubertal major depressive children: IV. Sleep related plasma concentrations in a drug-free recovered clinical state. (Submitted for publication.)

24. Sachar EJ: Neuroendocrine abnormalities in depressive illness, in Sachar EJ (ed): *Topics in Psychoneuroendocrinology*. New York, Grune & Stratton, 1975.

25. Puig-Antich J, Chambers W, Halpern FS, et al: Cortisol hypersecretion in prepubertal depressive illness: A preliminary report. *Psychoneuroendocrinology* 1979;4:191–197.

26. Puig-Antich J, Novacenko H, Davies M, et al: Cortisol secretion in prepubertal major depressive children during a depressive episode. (Submitted for publication.)

27. Carroll BJ, Feinberg M, Greden JF, et al: A specific laboratory test for the diagnosis of melancholia: Standardization, validation, and clinical utility. *Arch Gen Psychiatry* 1981;38:15–22.

28. Kupfer D: REM latency: A psychobiological marker for primary depressive disease. *Biol Psychiatry* 1976;11:159–174.

29. Coble P, Kupfer DJ, Spiker DG, et al: EEG sleep and clinical characteristics in young primary depressives. *Sleep Res* 1980;9:165.

30. Kupfer DJ, Foster FG: EEG sleep and depression in Williams RL, Karacan I (eds): *Sleep Disorders: Diagnosis and Treatment*. New York, John Wiley & Sons, 1979.

31. Vogel GW, Vogel F, McAbee RS, et al: Improvement of depression by REM sleep deprivation: New findings and a theory. *Arch Gen Psychiatry* 1980; 37:247–253.

32. Puig-Antich J, Goetz R, Hanlon C, et al: Sleep architecture and REM sleep measures in prepubertal children with major depression. A controlled study. *Arch Gen Psychiatry* 1982;39:932–939.

33. Young W, Knowles JB, MacLean AW, et al: The sleep of childhood depressives: Comparison with age matched controls. *Biol Psychiatry* 1982;17: 1163–1168.

34. Weinberg WA, Rutman J, Sullivan L, et al: Depression in children referred to an educational diagnostic center. *J Pediatr* 1973;83:1065–1072.

96

35. Puig-Antich J, Goetz R, Hanlon C, et al: Sleep architecture and REM sleep measures in prepubertal major depressives during recovery from the depressive episode in a drug-free state. *Arch Gen Psychiatry* 1983;40:187–192.
36. Prange AJ, Wilcon IC, Lara PP, et al: Effects of thyrotropin-releasing hormone in depression. *Lancet* 1972;2:999–1002.
37. Kirkegaard C: The thyrotropin response to thyrotropin-releasing hormone in endogenous depression. *Psychoneuroendocrinology* 1981;6:189–212.
38. Loosen PT, Prange AJ: Serum thyrotropin response to thyrotropin-releasing hormone in psychiatric patients: A review. *Am J Psychiatry* 1982;139:405–416.
39. Greenberg R, Extein I, Rosenberg G, et al: The Thyrotropin-Releasing Hormone Test and the Dexamethasone Suppression Test in Adolescent Depression. Washington, DC, Am Acad Child Psychiatry, 1982.
40. Law W, Petti T, Kazdin AE: Withdrawal symptoms after graduated cessation of imipramine in children. *Am J Psychiatry* 1981;138:647–650.

CHAPTER 7

THE EPIDEMIOLOGIC PATTERNS OF SELF-DESTRUCTIVENESS IN CHILDHOOD, ADOLESCENCE, AND YOUNG ADULTHOOD

PAUL C. HOLINGER
KEVIN W. LUKE

This study examines both the age of onset of various self-destructive behaviors (suicides, homicide, and accidents) as well as the changes in the mortality rates throughout childhood, adolescence, and young adulthood. This investigation utilizes national mortality data and studies suicide, homicide, and accident rates by one-year age intervals for 0–30 years, by sex, and by race, from 1968–1977. The data suggest that suicide, homicide, and accident rates for all sex and race combinations have similar patterns by age and increase throughout the early, middle, and late adolescent years and into young adulthood. Furthermore, violent death rates for males, in addition to being higher than corresponding rates for females, tend to start increasing at the same or earlier ages than female rates. These data call into serious question two ideas found in the literature: first, that suicide rates increase primarily at one or two specific and/or circumscribed ages in youth (eg, at 10 to 11 years of age and/or at 15 to 16 years); and, second, that physiologic changes in puberty are primarily responsible for the increase in suicide rates (an idea implying that the increase in female suicide rates should occur one to two years earlier than in males in accordance with the earlier onset of physiologic changes in puberty in females).

Increasing evidence seems to justify the idea that suicide among youth is a serious public health problem in the United States. Suicide is the third leading cause of death among adolescents, following accidents and homicide, respectively.[1] Adolescent suicide rates have doubled over the years between 1961 and 1975, and tripled over the 1956–1975 period.[2,3]

However, studying only suicide may be a limited approach in attempting to understand self-destructive tendencies among youth.

97

Clinical[4-6] as well as epidemiologic[7] studies have suggested that a variety of behaviors in addition to suicide could be considered self-destructive. More specifically, mortality trends in homicides and accidents, as well as in suicides, may be useful in understanding self-destruction among the young: evidence exists that many homicides are victim-precipitated and represent suicides;[8] some "accidental" deaths may be due to accident-proneness and risk-taking which reflect depression and suicidal tendencies;[4,9-11] and a small percentage of motor vehicle deaths have been shown to be suicides.[12] A more detailed review of the literature dealing with the controversy regarding the extent to which homicide and accidents, in addition to suicide, represent self-destructive tendencies has been presented elsewhere.[7]

The purpose of this descriptive epidemiologic study is to examine the patterns of suicide, homicide, and accidents among the young by one-year age intervals. Three variables will be examined: age (one-year intervals, from 0 to 30 years); race (white and nonwhite); and sex (male and female). The focus will be on the nature of the changes in mortality rates from 0 to 30 years of age.

LITERATURE

The literature on this topic will be divided into two parts: epidemiologic studies dealing with the shift in suicide rates between childhood and adolescence; and four areas (puberty, cognition, socialization theory, and conceptualization of death) from which hypotheses may be derived regarding the age of onset of overt self-destructiveness and the shift in suicide rates from childhood to adolescence. The focus of this brief literature review will be on suicide, inasmuch as there is a paucity of studies dealing with these problems (ie, the shifts in rates) in terms of homicide and accidents. However, the homicide and accident data presented in this chapter will be related, together with the suicide findings to the issues raised in this examination of the literature.

Epidemiologic Studies Dealing with the Shift in Suicide Rates between Childhood and Adolescence

In the literature on suicide there exists the persistent idea that there is a sharp rise in the suicide rates between childhood and adolescence, a qualitative shift that is different from any increases before or after. Zilboorg[13] presented data which he felt suggested that "the age of puberty seems to be the crucial period as far as the development of active self-destructive drives are concerned." Zilboorg, in reviewing some of Durkheim's[14] data, felt it indicated a sharp rise in the rate of suicide somewhere around the age of 15 or 16. Similarly, Bakwin[15] suggested that suicide was rare under 10 years of age and remained infrequent until about 15 years or age, "when a sharp rise in both boys and girls takes place." However, the conclusions reached by these investigations are marked by a serious methodologic problem: namely, that the age of this "sharp rise" is just the cut-off point in the age interval for the suicide data (eg, before and after 16 years, or 10 to 14 years and 15 to 19 years).

Seiden[9] presented data for five-year age intervals (5–9, 10–14, 15–19, 20–24 years), and noted the rarity of suicide before age 15. He reported that the rate rises acutely during ages 15 to 19, when "there is an eight- to tenfold increase, and at age 20–24 the suicide rate doubles again." Holinger[3] also studied youthful suicides by five-year intervals, reporting 1975 rates of 0.5 (10–14 year olds), 7.6 (15–19) and 16.5 (20–24) per 100,000. These rates were approximately double those of 15 years previously. Thus, in 1975, suicide rates for 15 to 19 year olds were 15 times those of 10 to 14 year olds, and rates for 20 to 24 year olds were twice those of the 15–19 group.

Missing from the literature, however, are more precise epidemiologic studies which better describe the nature and magnitude of these shifts in suicide rates from childhood to young adulthood. The studies above suffer from the methodological problems involved with using five-year intervals, and the "shift" in rates noted in the literature at 15 or 16 years of age may be due to the fact that those years provide the cut-off points for most of the data using five-year intervals. There are few studies in which this shift in suicide rates are examined by one-year age intervals.

Hypotheses Regarding the Shift of Suicide Rates from Childhood to Adolescence

Four areas will be examined briefly in order to derive hypotheses regarding the shift in suicide rates from childhood to adolescence. These four areas do not exhaust the possible sources of ideas regarding this shift, nor is an exhaustive literature review of each intended. Rather, the four areas will be examined in order to add different perspectives from other scientific disciplines and hopefully aid in understanding the past epidemiologic studies and the epidemiologic data presented here.

Puberty Puberty is perhaps best conceptualized as a complex process, a combination of physical and psychological changes. Development of secondary sex characteristics, changes in levels of various hormones, physical growth, and onset of menarche and ejaculation of seminal fluid are physical aspects of this process. The biological changes occurring in puberty have recently been reviewed in detail by Petersen and Taylor.[16] Marshall and Tanner's work[17-19] is of particular importance in evaluating the various physical changes of puberty and the ages at which they occur. To briefly summarize a massive amount of data, Marshall and Tanner[18] noted that peak height velocity is reached, on the average, nearly two years later in boys than in girls, and that pubic hair appears one and one-half years later in boys than in girls; however, the boys' genitalia begin to develop only about six months later than the girls' breasts. A rough age range for this complex process of puberty, then, would appear to be about 11 to 13.5 years for girls and 13 to 15 years for boys.

The task now is to make an hypothesis about the shift in suicide rates from childhood to adolescence based on the influence of puberty. There would appear to be a genuine sex difference. One might, based on the data on puberty, hypothesize an increase in suicide among girls to occur from 11 to 13.5 years and among boys to occur from 13 to 15 years. This assumes that the increase in suicides would be related to the middle of the process of puberty, an assumption which, of course, may not be valid. The beginning or ending of puberty might be more disruptive and conducive to suicide. In addition, this type of hypothesizing takes into account only the majority of boys and girls going through puberty; one might suspect that an increase in suicide at this age is due to those who go through the process of puberty much earlier or much later than the majority of their peers. For example, an increase in suicide rates at age 12 to 13 among girls might result from the suicides of girls who have not experienced the physiologic changes their peers have. Thus, social factors as well as physiologic factors could account for an increase of suicide found in relation to the age range of physical changes in puberty.

Cognition   There has been much recent attention given to advances in the understanding of cognition, and as many of those important steps appear to coincide to some extent with the postulated shift in self-destructiveness, it seems appropriate to examine the relationship of cognition and self-destructiveness. The work of Jean Piaget is most central to the current task. The general structure of Piaget's ideas on the development of thought do not require detailed discussion here.[20-26] In particular, we are concerned with the shift from the concrete operational period (6/7 years to 11/12 years) to the level of propositional or formal operations (11/12 years to 14/15 years), when the adolescent becomes capable of abstract thought. Petersen[25,26] noted four approaches to examining cognitive functioning: intelligence, cognitive abilities, academic achievement, and cognitive development. Cognitive abilities involve mathematical skills, spatial ability, and verbal ability. She stated Piaget's contributions are primarily in the area of cognitive development as opposed to the other three areas of cognitive functioning. Of particular importance in Petersen's[16,25,26] work and the efforts of others is the recognition of potential sex differences in cognitive functioning. Of the four areas of cognitive functioning, only measures of intelligence appear not to have sex-related differences.[27] With respect to cognitive abilities, boys may be more proficient in mathematical and spatial skills and girls in verbal skills.[25-27] Complex sex differences also occur in achievement.[25,26] Finally, in cognitive development, boys may show earlier evidence of formal operations.[28]

To summarize, the weight of the evidence appears to suggest the age range of 12 to 14 years as the interval during which the most important aspects of cognition appear (in terms of our study). Sex-related differences are difficult to interpret. Although girls reach puberty sooner, socialization and cognitive studies suggest that, in general, boys may develop the capacity for more mature cognition sooner. Hence, if one assumes a relationship between the onset of such cognitive capacities and the onset of overt self-destructiveness, one might predict from these data an increase in completed suicides to occur between 12 and 14 years of age. Taking sex differences into account, one might expect the increase to occur at 12–13 years in boys and 13–14 in girls.

Socialization theory The particular focus here is on socialization theory, and the literature is specific to modern Western culture. It is necessary to see in what age range socialization theory suggests the greatest degree of disruption as one moves from "childhood" to "adolescence." While there is much literature on socialization in adolescence (although relatively less than for other age groups), none of it specifically relates the disruptive effects of adolescence to the emergence of overt suicide in that age group.[29-37] This literature does, however, go into some detail with respect to the various factors involved in the shift from childhood to adolescence. For example, such factors include: shift from family activities to peer relationships; shift to heterosexual interests; assumption of a variety of adult or adult-like roles; biological changes of puberty; shift from parental values to peer, teacher, and/or societal values; and so on. In addition to describing these various factors involved in the transition from childhood to adolescence, this literature makes a reasonable attempt at isolating an age range at which this process may be said to occur. The bulk of the evidence suggests that 12 to 14 years of age is most disruptive regarding the shift from childhood to adolescence, and that one might predict the increase of suicide at that age range. However, interesting work by Roscow[38] points to a later age range as a possibility. Regarding sex differences, inasmuch as puberty assumes such importance in the definition of the onset of adolescence, one would predict a slightly earlier age range for females (12–13 years) than for males (13–14 years), as based on socialization literature.

Conceptualization of death Another body of literature that needs to be examined in terms of its relationship to overt self-destructiveness is that dealing with the conceptualization of death. Earlier studies[39-43] suggested that children did show an interest in and fantasies about death, and Anthony's work indicated that, contrary to popular opinion, death was a common topic for young minds. In a developmental study of the child's conceptualization of death by Nagy[44] three major stages were described: the first stage (about 3 to 5 years of age) highlights the denial of death as a regular and final process (death as a departure, temporary, with living and lifeless not yet distinguished); the second stage (about 5 to 9 years) suggests death is personified (death is an eventuality, but outside us and not universal). The third stage (after 9 to 10 years) indicates death is recognized as a process which takes place in all of us, and it is seen as inevitable. Although the consensus seems to be that the bulk of the data tend to support Nagy's findings,[44,45] many critiques and modifications of her work exist.[46] In addition, increasing literature on children with terminal illnesses[47] suggests that even young children who are terminally ill have conceptualizations of death thought to occur only in older children. Haim[48] stressed the discrepancies in the studies, noted that even young children often showed a solid conceptualization of death, and suggested that adult denial plays an essential role in the apparent absence in the child of a preoccupation with death.

In generating an hypothesis about the age of increase of self-destructiveness based on the capacity of conceptualization of death, the bulk of the literature seems to suggest that the child begins to conceive of death as inevitable and nonreversible at about age 10. Therefore, one would hypothesize the increase in suicides to occur around 10 years of age. It may be that prior to 10, the child does not kill himself because death is seen as temporary and reversible (ie, suicide offers no real solution to a distressed child under 10 years of age who sees death as temporary and reversible; nor does suicide under those conceptualizations pack any real wallop for vengeance against a mother or father or other important person who has hurt and disappointed the child in some way). The literature does not seem to suggest a sex difference, so it is hypothesized that the increase in suicide after age 10 occurs the same for males and females. One must also relate this literature to work on cognition discussed earlier. Conceptualizations of death may change in subtle and unexamined ways around 13 to 15 years old, when the adolescent has been shown to be more capable of formal operations.

METHODOLOGY

The methodologic problems can be divided into two parts: general (national mortality and census data) and specific (problems with the presentation of the data in this particular chapter).

General Serious methodologic problems exist in using national mortality and census data. These include under- and overreporting, misclassification, and changes in national classification over time. More detailed discussions of these problems have been presented elsewhere.[1,2,49]

Specific The national mortality data utilized in this study are all deaths by suicide, homicide, motor vehicle, and nonmotor vehicle accidents in the United States, for the years between 1968 and 1977, by each year. The source of these mortality data is The National Mortality Data Tapes from the National Center for Health Statistics. The only exception to this is the year 1972; only 50% of the deaths for that year were

Table 7-1
Suicide Rates Per 100,000 Population

Age (Years)	White Male	White Female	Nonwhite Male	Nonwhite Female
0(0–11 Mos)	0.0	0.0	0.0	0.0
1	0.0	0.0	0.0	0.0
2	0.0	0.0	0.0	0.0
3	0.0	0.0	0.0	0.0
4	0.0	0.0	0.0	0.0
5	0.0	0.0	0.0	0.0
6	0.0	0.0	0.0	0.0
7	0.0	0.0	0.0	0.0
8	0.0	0.0	0.0	0.0
9	0.0	0.0	0.1	0.0
10	0.2	0.0	0.1	0.0
11	0.4	0.1	0.2	0.0
12	0.8	0.1	0.2	0.3
13	1.7	0.4	0.6	0.5
14	3.0	1.0	1.2	1.1
15	4.7	1.7	2.1	1.9
16	8.3	2.4	4.2	2.2
17	11.2	2.9	6.1	2.8
18	14.9	3.7	9.8	3.5
19	17.7	4.4	14.0	3.7
20	19.7	5.1	16.4	5.2
21	23.2	6.0	21.5	6.4
22	23.5	6.2	21.8	5.8
23	24.9	6.7	24.0	5.7
24	23.4	6.9	22.7	7.7
25	23.5	7.4	23.9	6.6
26	22.1	8.2	22.6	6.9
27	21.9	8.0	22.2	6.4
28	22.1	8.4	24.0	6.0
29	21.9	8.7	22.8	5.8
30	20.3	8.4	20.1	4.9

reported on the data tapes, so in compiling the results for this paper those numbers were doubled. The population data used to derive the mortality rates are the resident population of the United States, 1968–1977, which does not include armed forces overseas. The source of the population data is Current Population Reports No. 441 and 721.[50]

Mortality rates for the years 1968–1977 by one-year age intervals were calculated in two ways. First, all deaths during 1968–1977 (for a particular cause of mortality, for each age (eg, age 5, 6, 7), by race and sex, were added up; similarly the population for a particular age for each year 1968–1977 (by race and sex) was added. The number of deaths for each age (by race and sex) were then divided by the population for the appropriate age (by race and sex) and a mortality rate was derived for

Table 7-2
Homicide Rates Per 100,000 Population

Age (Years)	White Male	White Female	Nonwhite Male	Nonwhite Female
0(0–11 Mos)	2.8	2.5	9.2	8.7
1	2.2	1.9	8.4	7.7
2	1.8	1.3	7.3	6.8
3	1.4	1.2	4.1	3.9
4	1.0	0.9	3.2	2.3
5	0.7	0.7	1.7	1.8
6	0.7	0.5	2.1	1.4
7	0.5	0.5	1.3	1.2
8	0.5	0.6	1.6	1.4
9	0.5	0.5	1.7	1.3
10	0.5	0.5	1.7	1.0
11	0.6	0.4	1.9	1.1
12	0.7	0.7	3.0	1.9
13	1.0	0.8	5.5	2.7
14	1.5	1.0	11.3	3.9
15	2.6	1.5	20.9	6.2
16	4.7	2.2	36.6	8.5
17	6.6	2.6	54.6	11.7
18	9.2	3.3	67.3	15.1
19	10.8	3.7	85.7	19.5
20	11.3	3.7	96.6	21.3
21	13.0	3.8	120.1	23.1
22	13.8	4.3	130.9	26.2
23	14.2	3.9	141.3	26.9
24	14.2	3.9	144.0	26.5
25	14.5	3.7	146.9	25.7
26	14.6	3.6	146.4	27.0
27	14.2	3.9	148.4	25.7
28	14.7	3.5	151.7	27.1
29	13.9	3.7	143.4	25.9
30	13.6	3.4	130.0	23.4

each age by race, sex, and cause of death. Second, mortality rates (by age, race, sex, and cause of death) were derived for each year (eg, 1968) using the appropriate mortality and population data for that year. This gave mortality rates for each of the 10 years, and these were averaged together to give an overall mortality rate for the 10 years, 1968–1977. The rates presented here are derived using the first method (see Tables 7-1 through 7-4) because it was felt that the averaging over the 10 years might distort the data by giving equal weight to years having less population. Two findings, however, are noteworthy: 1) the results of the two methods are virtually identical; and 2) the patterns of the mortality rates are very similar from one year to the next, eg, the age, race and sex patterns of mortality of 1968 compared to 1969.

Table 7-3
Motor Vehicle Accident Rates Per 100,000 Population

Age (Years)	White Male	White Female	Nonwhite Male	Nonwhite Female
0	8.5	8.5	8.5	9.6
1	10.9	10.4	13.7	10.9
2	11.5	9.6	16.6	12.7
3	12.2	8.9	18.4	11.7
4	11.2	8.2	18.6	12.1
5	12.3	8.3	21.8	14.2
6	12.5	8.1	19.2	11.4
7	12.1	7.6	17.3	9.3
8	10.7	6.4	14.7	8.2
9	9.7	6.0	12.8	7.7
10	9.1	5.2	10.8	5.6
11	9.3	5.1	9.9	4.2
12	10.5	5.5	10.5	4.7
13	13.4	7.2	12.5	5.2
14	19.0	10.0	14.0	5.7
15	28.7	15.7	18.0	8.4
16	53.3	22.9	29.6	9.5
17	73.9	26.3	38.7	13.5
18	94.3	29.9	52.5	15.3
19	93.4	26.3	59.2	15.2
20	85.1	22.5	61.8	14.1
21	87.9	21.1	69.2	16.4
22	81.5	18.7	72.5	17.1
23	71.3	16.6	72.4	16.2
24	62.8	14.7	68.6	15.0
25	58.2	14.4	63.7	14.0
26	52.1	13.3	66.9	12.5
27	47.6	12.5	62.8	13.0
28	43.7	11.5	64.8	14.3
29	43.5	11.6	61.1	14.8
30	38.6	10.8	51.0	13.1

Table 7-4
Nonmotor Vehicle Accident Rates Per 100,000 Population

Age (Years)	White Male	White Female	Nonwhite Male	Nonwhite Female
0	38.8	28.4	86.7	73.1
1	26.5	19.0	46.1	38.9
2	23.8	14.5	34.0	28.6
3	19.8	10.3	30.4	21.0
4	15.0	8.2	23.1	16.0
5	12.5	6.6	16.4	12.9
6	11.0	5.7	16.6	9.6
7	10.4	4.9	17.9	9.0
8	10.6	4.6	18.9	8.0
9	10.7	4.0	19.2	6.6
10	10.3	3.9	20.0	6.8
11	11.2	4.2	19.5	7.9
12	12.4	4.3	21.8	7.2
13	16.3	4.5	24.7	6.7
14	20.6	4.6	30.2	6.9
15	23.9	4.8	36.0	6.7
16	27.8	5.0	39.7	7.4
17	31.0	5.7	42.1	8.1
18	35.0	6.1	47.0	9.7
19	36.6	6.2	50.9	9.7
20	35.5	5.6	49.6	10.1
21	37.3	5.8	51.7	11.0
22	35.8	5.9	56.6	12.5
23	35.1	5.4	57.1	13.3
24	33.2	5.5	61.1	12.3
25	33.5	5.3	57.0	12.1
26	31.4	5.6	60.9	11.8
27	31.3	5.4	53.4	12.0
28	30.9	5.5	60.3	12.7
29	30.3	5.8	57.2	12.7
30	28.8	5.3	54.0	11.3

RESULTS

Figure 7-1 shows the suicide rates by age, race and sex by one-year age intervals from 0–30 years old, for the United States, from 1968–1977. Several familiar patterns can be seen: male rates are higher than female, and white rates higher than nonwhite. The rates tend to increase from early adolescence until the mid-20s, when they level off. Figures 7-2, 7-3 and 7-4 present data for homicide, motor vehicle, and nonmotor vehicle accidents, respectively. In Figure 7-2, homicide, male rates are higher than female, and nonwhite rates higher than white. After high rates in infancy, there is a decrease until adolescence when the rates begin to

107

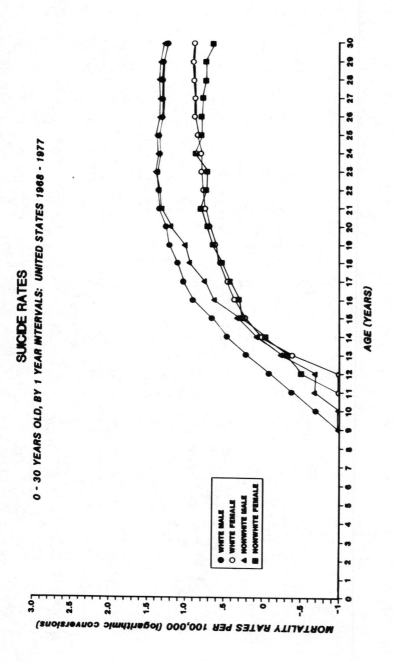

Figure 7-1

108

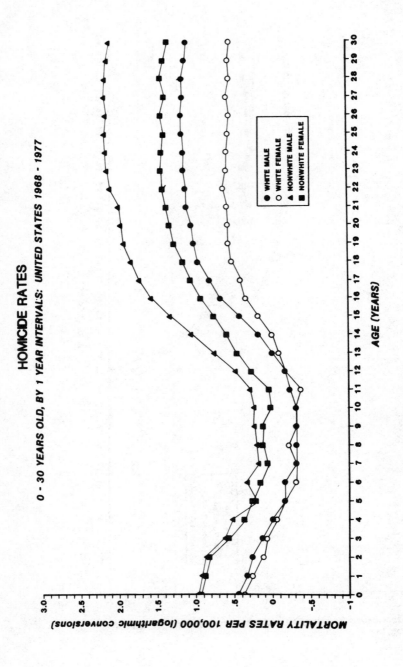

Figure 7-2

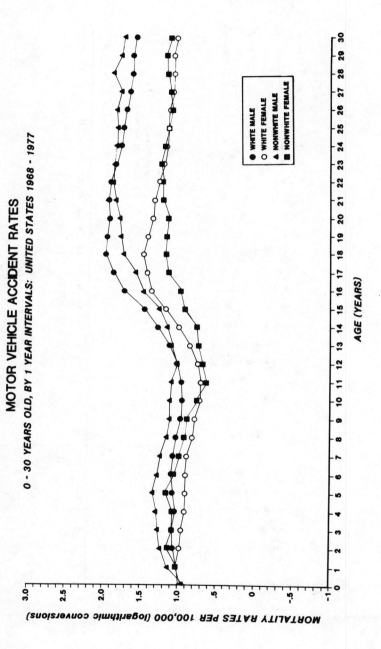

MOTOR VEHICLE ACCIDENT RATES

0 - 30 YEARS OLD, BY 1 YEAR INTERVALS: UNITED STATES 1968 - 1977

Figure 7-3

110

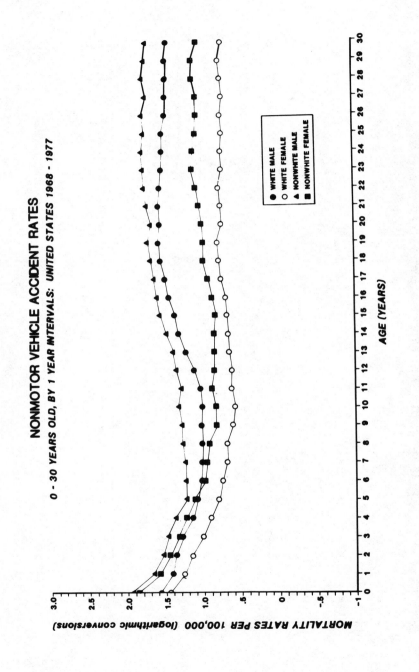

NONMOTOR VEHICLE ACCIDENT RATES

0 - 30 YEARS OLD, BY 1 YEAR INTERVALS: UNITED STATES 1968 - 1977

● WHITE MALE
○ WHITE FEMALE
▲ NONWHITE MALE
■ NONWHITE FEMALE

AGE (YEARS)

MORTALITY RATES PER 100,000 (logarithmic conversions)

Figure 7-4

increase to a peak in the late 20s. In Figure 7-3, motor vehicle accidents, male rates are higher than female, and nonwhite rates tend to be higher than white rates except from about 12 years to the early 20s, when white rates are higher than nonwhite. After about the first six years of life, the rates tend to decrease slightly throughout childhood and begin increasing again in adolescence to peak in late teenage years for whites and early 20s for nonwhites. In Figure 7-4, nonmotor vehicle accidents, male rates are higher than female, and nonwhite rates are higher than white. The rates tend to decrease throughout childhood, begin increasing in adolescence, and peak in the late teens and early 20s for whites, and early to mid-20s for nonwhites.

DISCUSSION

The data presented in this chapter describe the epidemiology of suicides, homicides, motor vehicle, and nonmotor vehicle accidents, by one-year age intervals from 0 to 30 years old, race, and sex, for the United States, from 1968 to 1977. Motor vehicle accident death rates tend to have the highest rates, followed by nonmotor vehicle accidents, suicides, and homicides, respectively, except for the nonwhite male and female homicide rates which have rates higher than the other causes from about age 17 to 30. Male rates are higher than female rates for every cause of death, and at every age, except for infant (0–1 year) deaths due to motor vehicle accidents. Nonwhite rates tend to be higher than white rates except for suicide rates at all ages and motor vehicle accident rates from about age 12 through the early 20s.

These data also elucidate the nature of the changes in suicide, homicide, and accident rates from infancy to 30 years of age. Three points are particularly noteworthy. First, the suicide rates, for example, tend to increase throughout adolescence (early, middle, and late adolescence), before a relative leveling off in the 20s. Whether one calls this phenomenon a rapid increase occurring over a relatively small number of years (eg, from ages 12–20), or characterizes it as a longer, steady increase across the span of adolescence depends on one's perspective and theoretical framework. These data do, however, call into question the idea that sharp increases in suicide rates occur at specific ages such as 10–11 years and again at 15–16 years. Second, these data seem to aid in clarifying the issue of the importance of physiologic changes in puberty and increases in suicide rates. Inasmuch as most evidence suggests that females reach physiologic puberty one to two years prior to males, one might expect the changes in suicide rates to occur earlier in females. The data presented in this chapter suggest that male and female suicide rates begin increasing at about the same time, with male rates perhaps beginning even a little earlier. Third, it should be noted that the increases in homicide and accident rates throughout adolescence seem to be more similar than dissimilar to the changes in suicide rates. Virtually all the rates, regardless of cause of death, race, or sex, start to increase around 10 years of age and level off (or begin a decrease) around the very late teenage years to mid-20s. In addition, homicide, nonmotor vehicle accidents, and, to a lesser extent, motor vehicle accident rates all show the similar trend of a decrease in rates from infancy until the rise in rates begins at about 10 years.

Finally, perhaps a conceptualization that acknowledges multiple interacting variables is most appropriate for understanding something as complex as the onset of overt self-destructiveness in human beings. Therefore, one might ask how the four theoretical categories discussed above (puberty, cognition, socialization, conceptualization of death) fit the data. In a general sense, all may be relevant in that they correspond to the data by tending to suggest an increase in self-destructiveness occurring in early or middle adolescence. More specifically, cognition and conceptualization of death seem more useful than puberty and socialization in regard to sexual differences. The data presented here suggest that the onset of overt self-destructiveness occurs at about the same ages in boys and girls, with perhaps a very slightly earlier onset in boys. These findings are more consonant with cognition and conceptualization of death than with puberty and socialization theories.

REFERENCES

1. Holinger PC: Violent deaths among the young: Recent trends in suicide, homicide, and accidents. *Am J Psychiatry* 1979;136:1144–1147.
2. Holinger PC, Offer D: Perspectives on suicide in adolescence, in Simmons R (ed): *Social and Community Mental Health*. Greenwich, CT, Jai Press Inc, 1981, vol 2, pp 139–157.
3. Holinger PC: Adolescent suicide: An epidemiological study of recent trends. *Am J Psychiatry* 1978;135:754–756.
4. Freud S: *The Psychopathology of Everyday Life*. London, The Hogarth Press, 1960 (1901).
5. Menninger KA: *Man Against Himself*. New York, Harcourt, Brace & Co, 1938.
6. Farberow N: *The Many Faces of Suicide*. New York, McGraw-Hill, 1979.
7. Holinger PC, Klemen EH: Violent deaths in the United States, 1900–1975. *Soc Sci Med* 1982;16:1929–1938.
8. Wolfgang ME: Suicide by means of victim-precipitated homicide. *J Clin Exp Psychopathol* 1959;20:335–349.
9. Seiden RH: Suicide among youth: A review of the literature, 1900–1967. *Bull Suicidology* 1969 (suppl).
10. Kaplan HB, Pokorny AD: Self-derogation and suicide—II: Suicidal responses, self-derogation and accidents. *Soc Sci Med* 1976;10:119–121.
11. Selzer ML, Payne CE: Automobile accidents, suicide, and unconscious motivation. *Am J Psychiatry* 1962;119:237–240.

12. Schmidt CW, Shaffer JW, Zlotowitz HI, et al: Suicide by vehicular crash. *Am J Psychiatry* 1977;134:175–178.
13. Zilboorg G: Considerations on suicide, with particular reference to that of the young. *Am J Orthopsychiatry* 1937;7:15–31.
14. Durkheim E: *Suicide: A Study in Sociology*, Spaulding, Simpson (trans). New York, The Free Press (MacMillan Publishing Co), 1897 (1951).
15. Bakwin H: Suicide in children and adolescents. *J Pediatr* 1957;50:749–769.
16. Petersen AC, Taylor B: Puberty: Biological change and psychological adaptation, in *Handbook of Adolescent Psychology*. New York, Wiley, 1978.
17. Marshall WA, Tanner JM: Variations in pattern of pubertal changes in girls. *Arch Dis Child* 1969;44:291–303.
18. Marshall WA, Tanner JM: Variations in the pattern of pubertal changes in boys. *Arch Dis Child* 1970;45:13–23.
19. Tanner JM: Sequence and tempo in the somatic changes in puberty, in Grumbach MM, Grave GD, Mayer FE (eds): *Control of the Onset of Puberty*. New York, Wiley, 1974.
20. Flavell JH: *The Developmental Psychology of Jean Piaget*. New York, Van Nostrand Reinhold Co, 1963.
21. Society for Research in Child Development: *Cognitive Development in Children*. Chicago, University of Chicago Press, 1970.
22. Inhelder B, Piaget J: *The Growth of Logical Thinking*. London, Routledge & Kegan Paul, 1958.
23. Basch MF: Developmental psychology and explanatory theory in psychoanalysis, in *The Annual Journal of Psychoanalysis*. New York, International Universities Press, 1977, vol 5.
24. Evans RI: *Jean Piaget: The Man and His Ideas*. New York, Dutton, 1973.
25. Petersen AC: Differential cognitive development in adolescence, in Sugar M (ed): *Female Adolescent Development*. New York, Brunner/Mazel, 1979.
26. Petersen AC: Hormones and cognitive functioning in normal development, in Wittig MA, Petersen AC (eds): *Sex-Related Differences in Cognitive Functioning: Developmental Issues*. New York, Academic Press, 1979.
27. Macoby EE, Jacklin CN: *The Psychology of Sex Differences*. Stanford, Stanford University Press, 1974.
28. Dulit E: Adolescent thinking a la Piaget: The formal stage. *J Youth Adolesc* 1972;4:281–301.
29. Clausen JA: Perspectives on childhood socialization, in Clausen JA (ed): *Socialization and Society*. Boston, Little Brown & Co, 1968.
30. Clausen JA: *Socialization and Society*. Boston, Little Brown & Co, 1968.
31. Coleman JS: *The Adolescent Society*. New York, The Free Press of Glencoe, 1961.
32. Eisenstadt SN: Archetypal patterns of youth. *Daedalus* 1962;Winter:28–46.
33. Broom L, Selznick P: *Sociology*. New York, Harper & Row, 1973.
34. Goslin DA (ed): *Handbook of Socialization: Theory and Research*. Chicago, Rand McNally, 1969.
35. Hollingshead AB: *Elmtown's Youth*. New York, Wiley & Sons, 1949.
36. Campbell EO: Adolescent socialization, in Goslin DA (ed): *Handbook of Socialization: Theory and Research*. Chicago, Rand McNally, 1969.
37. Nash SC: Sex role as a mediator of intellectual functioning, in Wittig MA, Petersen AC (eds): *Differences in Cognitive Functioning: Developmental Issues*. New York, Academic Press, 1979.
38. Roscow I: *Socialization to Old Age*. Berkeley, University of California Press, 1974.

39. Piaget J: *The Language and Thought of the Child*, Warden M (trans). New York, Harcourt Brace & Co, 1926.
40. Schilder P, Wechsler D: The attitudes of children toward death. *J Genet Psychol* 1934;45:406–451.
41. Bender LL, Schilder P: Suicidal preoccupations and attempts in children. *Am J Orthopsychiatry* 1937;7:225–243.
42. Anthony S: *The Child's Discovery of Death*. London, Routledge, 1940.
43. Anthony S: *The Discovery of Death in Childhood and After*. London, Allen Lane, The Penguin Press, 1971.
44. Nagy MH: The child's view of death, in Feifel H (ed): *The Meaning of Death*. New York, McGraw-Hill, 1959, pp 79–98.
45. Kastenbaum R: Death and development through the lifespan, in Feifel H (ed): *New Meanings of Death*. New York, McGraw-Hill, 1977, pp 17–45.
46. Feifel H (ed): *New Meanings of Death*. New York, McGraw-Hill, 1977.
47. Bluebond-Langner M: Meanings of death to children, in Feifel H (ed): *New Meanings of Death*. New York, McGraw-Hill, 1977, pp 47–66.
48. Haim A: *Adolescent Suicide*, Smith AMS (trans). New York, International Universities Press, 1974.
49. Klebba AJ, Dolman AB: Comparability of mortality statistics for the seventh and eighth revisions of the International Classification of Diseases, United States. *Vital and Health Statistics*, series 2, no 66. Washington, DC, US Government Printing Office, 1975.
50. *Vital Statistics of the United States, Mortality, 1950–1975*. US Department of Health, Education and Welfare, National Center for Health Statistics. Washington, DC, US Government Printing Office.

CHAPTER 8

ATTEMPTED SUICIDE IN ADOLESCENCE:
The Suicide Sequence

JACK NOVICK

This chapter reports psychoanalytic research on seven adolescents who had each made at least one serious suicide attempt, and presents a replication of the findings using the psychoanalytic material of another adolescent suicide case. The investigation demonstrated that attempted suicide in adolescence is not an impulsive act but the end point in a pathological regression. In each of the cases the suicide attempt appeared in the context of severe, long-standing disturbance; depression, feelings of abnormality, and suicide thoughts had been present for a long time. The regression started, in each case, with the experience of failure in the attempt to separate from mother. Age-appropriate sexual impulses were experienced by these adolescents as hostile separation and a sadistic oedipal triumph. Subsequent events led to regressive intensification of a sadomasochistic tie to mother and displacement of the experience of rejection and anger from mother to another person. Following displacement, guilt was no longer an inhibiting factor and the suicide plan was put into action. At the time of the attempt, all the adolescents denied the reality of death and thought of suicide as a positive, brave action producing multiple results. The importance of elucidating the elements of the suicide sequence in the treatment of suicidal adolescents is discussed.

Soon after her 18th birthday, Mary drove her car down a steep embankment. The car was completely destroyed, Mary suffered severe internal injuries and nearly died. After recovering from major surgery, she told her psychiatrist that she had intended to kill herself. I saw Mary and her parents soon after she left the hospital. Near the start of the interview mother said, "I refuse to feel guilty," and remained fairly silent, as did Mary, for the rest of the session. Father, a tall, tree-trunk of a man, did most of the talking and the women nodded assent when I looked at them for additional comments. The whole family referred to the suicide attempt as "the accident," and apparently viewed it as an impulsive,

115

rebellious bit of behavior to be appropriately punished and not repeated. The parents had insisted that Mary use her college savings toward paying for a new car as this would help impress her with the unacceptability of her actions.

Mary was the second of two children, with a brother three years older. The elder child had always rebelled, fought with the parents and failed at school, whereas Mary was seen as a high-achieving person who had always done well at school and was well behaved. She was said to have had many friends, to have played on the school teams and in general to have been well adjusted and happy, with a secure future in the professional career she had chosen. The parents said that they were completely surprised by the event. It was totally out of character and they could see no reason why she had done it. Even when I saw Mary alone she had little to add to our understanding of her serious suicide attempt. She claimed that she too had no idea why she had done it, and said that while driving she had suddenly felt that it would be better if she were dead. She was having difficulty with her superior at work, and felt unjustly criticized by her but, at the same time, felt that she was not doing well enough. The referring psychiatrist had ruled out psychosis or a major biological depression, a view that concurred with my assessment and that of another psychiatrist I had called in for a second opinion and a drug consultation. So why had she made a serious suicide attempt? What was the risk of a further attempt? What was the treatment of choice?

When I recommended four-times-per-week psychoanalysis, father went back to the referring psychiatrist to ask, "What kind of nut is Novick? Are they still doing psychoanalysis?" Aside from his personal issues, which were then addressed, he did well to ask about psychoanalysis. Psychoanalysis is not commonly used with adolescents and almost never with suicidal young people.

There is a vast literature on suicide and attempted suicide, for, as Baechler comments, "It is probable that suicide is the most unremittingly studied human behavior."[1] Except for the epidemiological data on suicide and attempted suicide which underscores the increasing incidence of the problem, the vast literature offers little assistance to the clinician.[2-4] Given the nature of the topic, it is understandable that there are few studies based on clinical case material, but even research into attempted suicide in adolescence has relied almost entirely on demographic data, interview data obtained immediately subsequent to the event, and sometimes on clinical material obtained from brief interventions with suicidal adolescents. Hurry[5] and Kernberg[6] provide notable exceptions to the meager clinical literature on the topic.

The value of psychoanalysis as a research technique has often been questioned by those outside the field, and of late the research value of psychoanalysis has been put under very severe test by sophisticated arguments from within. Without entering into these stimulating and controversial issues, such as natural versus humanistic science, the search for meaning (hermeneutics) versus the explication of general scientific laws, nomothetic versus idiographic science, narrative versus historical truth, etc, this writer will present a research project on attempted suicide in adolescence conducted by analysts using five-times-a-week psychoanalysis both as a method of treatment and as a method of investigation. Mary's material is used to illustrate and amplify the research findings.*

METHODS

It is now almost ten years since my colleagues and I began to summarize the results of a research project based on the psychoanalysis of adolescents who had attempted suicide. This report, completed in 1976, has not been published in toto as yet, but brief descriptions, summaries and references to this research have appeared in the literature.[5,7-10] Subsidized, five-times-a-week psychoanalysis was offered to nonpsychotic adolescents who had made medically serious suicide attempts. We were thus excluding those who made suicide threats, where the attempt did not require medical intervention to save the person's life, or where an ongoing psychotic process obscured the issue of intentionality.

The final sample consisted of seven adolescents, three females and four males ranging from 14 to 19 years of age. Analysts wrote detailed weekly reports on each case. These reports were circulated to the other members of the group, and all the analysts met weekly for two hours to discuss each patient and to evolve a conceptual and technical approach to the topic. We started with the assumption that attempted suicide in adolescence is always a sign of severe pathology. There are many who tend to romanticize suicide; to see it as an expression of free will. One of the current best sellers in France is a book on techniques of suicide. Alvarez[11] traces the differing attitudes toward suicide and the attraction suicide has for the young and the creative. However, in an earlier study on adolescents who came to a walk-in center my colleagues and I[12] found that adolescents who had made a serious suicide attempt showed more signs of current disturbance, a history of greater childhood disturbance, and a higher incidence of parental disturbance than the nonsuicidal adolescents who had come for psychological help. The psychoanalytic project on attempted suicide further confirmed this finding as each of the seven subjects proved to have been severely disturbed from childhood on.

The same was true in Mary's case. Near the end of her first year of analysis, Mary was attending college but did nothing more than study

---

*Mary is the pseudonym of a young woman seen in analysis while she was attending university in England. I would like to thank Mary for permission to use material from the first three years of our work together.

for her courses. She lived at home, totally dependent on her mother for everything from shopping to laundry. She turned down all offers of friendship and spent weekends and evenings alone in her room. When she was not studying, she stayed up late at night rearranging the furniture or spending hours trying to decide which side of the desk to put her pencils on. She sat silently at meals, hardly said anything to her father, and spoke only when asked direct questions. She was 19 years old, fully developed sexually but always dressed in bib overalls, sneakers and loose-fitting sweatshirts. She wore her hair closely cropped and looked like a young boy. Her inhibited behavior and strange appearance were the overt signs of her disturbance; I was more concerned about the continuing danger that she might either kill herself or suffer a psychotic breakdown and have to be hospitalized.

Nevertheless, at this point in her treatment her father, under pressure from mother, told Mary that he and mother were very pleased with her progress, that they felt she was now a "normal girl," that she seemed to be doing well and perhaps she should think of stopping her analysis or at least cutting down. They were intelligent, college-educated, professional people. Defenses, of course, have no respect for class or intellectual distinctions. Gross denial of pathology was the hallmark of this family, and a major focus of analytic work was Mary's view that only she knew that the story of her being a normal child from a normal family was untrue. It she were to reveal to anyone how disturbed she and her mother had been, and still were, terrible consequences would ensue. It is risky to base an assessment of parental pathology on the patient's distortions of memory and the selective acuity of projections, but Mary's description of mother as "weird" probably comes close to the mark. Mother's barely concealed hostility to her daughter and her extreme obsessionality were evident during my meetings with the parents, and over the years the family had completely acceded to her pathological concerns with cleanliness and security.

Most striking, however, was mother's inability to tolerate the slightest sign of hostility. In her constant preoccupation with defending against both her own hostility and that of others mother seemed completely out of touch with Mary's ordinary needs. This could be seen in many examples from current and past behavior and also in Mary's identification with an inattentive, unresponsive, affectless mother. Mary told me that she had always considered herself as neuter, neither male nor female. Although signs of severe problems in sexual identity had appeared at puberty, including serious menstrual dysfunction of probable psychogenic origin, Mary's identity problem was more basic. As we learned from the analytic work, her choice was not between male and female but between life and death. Neuter did not refer to gender identity but to existence. Repeatedly, in treatment, Mary's response to stress was to "tune out, go blank, become a zombie." We came to call this "a little suicide" and she said that she could remember long periods of time, going back to childhood, when she would function like a robot, with no feelings. "When I tune out," she said, "it's as if I'm not there." Mary's memories of childhood showed signs of a lifelong difficulty in experiencing and maintaining feelings of pleasure in achievement. She had what Krystal[13] has referred to as "anhedonia"—we called it the "big deal" response. She would work with enormous energy out of a near panic that she would fail. When she achieved her A or A+, she would feel a brief period of relief and then say to herself "big deal" and forget about her accomplishment. The disturbance in her ability to tolerate and experience affect and her feeling of being a "robot, a zombie" are typical signs of a post-traumatic reaction which have led me to hypothesize that infantile trauma is part of Mary's history.

THE FOCAL RESEARCH

It does not require the effort and power of psychoanalysis to demonstrate that attempted suicide represents a breakdown in normal adolescent development and appeared, both in Mary and in the other adolescents in our research, in the context of severe, long-standing disturbance. As important as this finding may be, a psychoanalytic project should be able to tell us much more about attempted suicide in adolescence. An immediate obstacle, one shared by most psychoanalytic research projects, related to the volume of material generated by psychoanalysis. We devised a method, called "focal research," in part as a response to the challenge of dealing with large amounts of data. The weekly reports on each case contained many references to suicide. Most of these suicide references related to the actual attempt, some were threats or plans for further attempts and some were intellectualized comments on the nature of death. Each suicide reference was extracted from the weekly reports and put on a separate piece of paper. It was noticed that these comments varied in frequency, and the focal research was an attempt to study both the content and the context in which these suicide thoughts appeared. Examples of such comments, taken at random from each of the seven cases, are as follows:

Female Case #1: "I had told my school friends that I wanted to kill myself but they didn't believe me."

Female Case #2: "When I took the tablets I felt nobody cared for me."

Female Case #3: "It may sound paradoxical but I think of suicide as my lifeline. Suicide is my way out. Without it I would become dependent on life."

Male Case #4: "Suicide people don't really believe they will die."

Male Case #5:   "I always feel that it is something I might try again. I'm frightened of doing it again and frightened of the pain but it's something I can't give up."

Male Case #6:   Patient reported that while at his parents' home for the weekend he had made a trial run, taking six aspirins to see if he could swallow them one after the other. The next day he tried to kill himself.

Male Case #7:   "I think I must have been in a mad, insane mood. I can't even remember what happened or how I came to turn the gas on, so I think I must have been crazy."

On the same page as the extracted comment, note was made of the immediate context, the larger context and, finally, space was allotted for speculations. The immediate context included proximal interventions by the analyst, the patient's material and affective state prior to and subsequent to the suicide thought and such events as an upcoming vacation, a weekend break, etc. The larger context referred to events which took place over a span of time, such as the developing and predominant transference relationship, emerging changes within the patient, shifts in defenses and the increasing dominance of certain phase-specific dynamics. The section on speculations allowed the analyst to associate freely to the material and to see whether certain hypotheses could be borne out by subsequent material. In doing the focal research analysts worked in pairs, each abstracting the suicide comment and content on the other analyst's case. A pilot study using pairs of analysts working independently on one case showed almost perfect agreement on the abstracted suicide items and on the immediate context for the emergence of these suicide thoughts. Surprisingly, there was also very high agreement between the analysts on the larger context for the emerging suicide thoughts.

As a further measure of the reliability of the findings, two measures of internal consistency were used. Each analyst wrote a detailed metapsychological portrait of the case in treatment. The sections and subheadings of this portrait were based on Anna Freud's metapsychological profile[14] as extended for adolescents by Laufer.[15] The analyst who was doing the focal research could then check the dynamic picture emerging from the focal research with the metapsychological profile written by the analyst of the case, and, finally, the analyst of the case would evaluate the focal research findings for consistency with his own clinical view of the case.

RESULTS

An immediate and striking finding of the focal research was the extent to which significant bits of information concerning the actual suicide attempt were not available until well into the analysis. For each case an enormous amount of additional information emerged during the course of analysis compared to what was elicited by direct questions soon after the suicide attempt. Often, the new information came in response to an interpretation, especially a transference interpretation. In an earlier publication[10] this writer referred to one of the seven cases, a 19-year-old who had claimed that his suicide attempt was precipitated by a rejection from the university of his choice. Near the end of his first year of analysis, my interpretation of his attempt to force me to reject him led to his remembering that he had applied to the university knowing that the deadline had passed. Similarly, in Mary's case the meager information available soon after the suicide attempt was considerably augmented by memories recovered following analytic intervention. For example, she recalled, in the third year of her analysis, that the car she had smashed was her mother's; mother had loved the car and Mary had hated it.

The focal research provided two sets of information: 1) suicide thoughts (which include memories of the actual attempt, attitudes and fantasies about suicide, etc) and 2) the context in which these thoughts emerged. We hypothesized that the thoughts and memories did not emerge at random but related to specific dynamic patterns discernible in the immediate and larger context of the flow of material. We found in all seven cases that suicide thoughts emerged in relation to: 1) fear of or feeling of abandonment, 2) fear of or wish for engulfment, and 3) fear of or guilt over what were felt to be omnipotent aggressive wishes toward mother. The details of this finding and many others of the suicide research such as distinctions between a suicide act and a suicide thought and the multidetermination of such thoughts and acts await the publication of the full report, but in this chapter the author wishes to present another of the major findings of the focal research, *the suicide sequence*. Material from the case of Mary, who was seen subsequent to the study, will be used in an attempt to test the reliability of the findings and exemplify the steps in the suicide sequence.

THE SUICIDE SEQUENCE

Mary and her parents viewed her suicide attempt as an impulsive act, out of character with a previous well-functioning personality and precipitated by some person or event outside the immediate family. This characterization of the suicide attempt is similar to the one presented by the adolescents in the research project and is not an unusual view. In a recent syndicated newspaper article (*Ann Arbor News*, May 7, 1981, Dallas [AP], Leigh Shirley) the reporter wrote of a 16-year-old boy who had shot himself with his father's favorite shotgun. Father described him as "popular, played football, just a normal, teenage kid." This view of adolescent suicide has attained the power of a myth, and one of the major findings of the focal research was to contradict this myth. In every case we found a consistent sequence of psychological steps leading to a suicide attempt. In a previous publication the suicide sequence was summarized as follows: "The suicide attempt in each of the cases was not a sudden act but the end point in a pathological regression."[10]

The focal research enabled us to combine the memories of the suicide attempt with the dynamic context for the recall of these events to arrive at a first approximation of the steps in the regressive sequence leading to the suicide attempt. Bearing in mind all the limitations and controversies concerning the accuracy of reconstructions the author would like to present the steps in the sequence and use the material from Mary's case to test the findings. The numbered sections in this text refer to the steps in the sequence as described in the unpublished report.[16]

1. For a considerable period prior to the suicide attempt, the adolescents had felt depressed, sexually abnormal, and had suicidal thoughts. The focal research shows that depression and feelings of sexual abnormality can coexist with suicidal thoughts without in themselves motivating the act of suicide.

When Mary reached puberty her feelings of nonexistence were expressed as feelings of sexual abnormality. She frequently constructed mental lists of "impossibles." The order of "impossibles" changed during our work together, but for years the top three remained unaltered — sex, marriage, and babies. Much later in the analysis she admitted with embarrassment that during junior and senior high school she sometimes had fantasies about boys, thought of talking to certain boys but was sure that they would find her "weird and unattractive." Mary was potentially an attractive young woman and as the analysis progressed and she gathered courage to take charge of her own body, there were times when she allowed herself to be quite feminine and pretty. It was evident, however, that from early puberty on she had felt sexually abnormal and incapable of becoming a mature, sexual woman.

Regarding feelings of depression preceding the suicide attempt, Mary reported that she had been "feeling bad" for at least four years. Her father, a professional, had accepted a position in another part of the country and Mary had to leave her friends and her school. She said that she had felt "bad" ever since and had never been able to make the kind of friends she had before the move. "Feeling bad" was Mary's term for an undifferentiated state of dysphoria; as she slowly became able to differentiate and verbalize her feelings, she could talk about her anger at her parents, especially her father, for not having considered her feelings or her needs and for never having talked to her about the move.

As to preexisting morbid fantasies and suicidal thoughts, the material revealed that for many years Mary had been preoccupied with thoughts of death and dying. Father traveled frequently and since childhood Mary had worried that he might die. She was surprised when she had reached her 18th birthday and realized that she had never thought of herself as being 18. She felt this indicated that she probably thought she would not live to be 18.

Some aspects of her memories regarding the actual attempt are still unclear, but there is evidence for a preexisting suicide plan from another source. The year after the start of treatment, just before the anniversary of her suicide attempt, Mary was in a state of visible anguish and "feeling bad." She was spending many hours in her room, not sleeping at night, and defending vigorously against conscious awareness of any angry feelings toward her parents. I mentioned the anniversary, the reemergence of suicide thoughts and, when she agreed that such thoughts were in her mind, I asked if she were making concrete plans for such an event. Following extraction of wisdom teeth her dentist had prescribed a powerful pain killer. Mary told me that she had been refilling the prescription for weeks and saving the pills for her next suicide attempt. As we found with the seven adolescents in the project, so, in Mary's case, depression, feelings of sexual abnormality and suicidal thoughts could be present for considerable time without leading to an actual attempt. This finding suggests that there is a more complicated link between depression and adolescent suicide than usually noted in the literature. As will be demonstrated, it requires more than depression and a suicide plan to lead to a suicide attempt. Erna Furman, in Chapter 15, arrived independently at a similar conclusion.

2. The sequence leading to the suicide act is precipitated in all cases by external events which impose on the adolescents the responsibility of taking a step that represents to them the breaking of the tie to the mother.

In Mary's case the suicide attempt was preceded, first, by her leaving home to go to college and then by her 18th birthday. Both these external events symbolized independence and adulthood, a phase she had never imagined entering. During the course of analysis, many external independent moves were seen to represent for Mary the complete severing of ties to mother, actions which she felt were totally unacceptable. Moving out of her house to a dorm precipitated suicidal thoughts. Going to a party or even imagining buying her own television set was felt by her to be an act of extreme defiance which was followed by suicidal thoughts. In her third year of analysis she planned to return to the city of her childhood home in order to visit her old high school friends. She first arranged a change in her analytic schedule, then went through all the other necessary steps. On her way to the travel agent she realized that this final step would mean that she had done it all without her parents. She knew that she should feel pleased; instead, she felt terrible. "It wasn't right." When I suggested that this was what she might have felt when she was away at college, she recalled a moment of panic when she had realized that her winning a scholarship meant she did not need her parents for anything.

> 3. In all cases the adolescents fail to make such a step. The external event and the experience of failure make the adolescents conscious of their dependency on their mothers.

In Mary's case the failure which occupied most of the first year of analysis was her inability to stay away at college. The college was highly competitive and she had attained a place and a full scholarship by beating out a long list of female applicants. The college not only symbolized independence from mother but would, in fact, have made her independent since she would not need them for any financial support. During the period of extreme difficulty at college, she felt very close to her mother and appreciative of mother's support. She felt that it was father who wanted her to stay. She left college after six weeks and returned to her parental home. Following the start of analysis, she attended a local college but remained at home and had her mother do everything for her from cooking to laundry. Mary felt totally dependent on mother, would panic at the thought of traveling to a different place without her, and allowed mother to select and buy all her clothes. It was only during her third year of analysis, at the age of 20, that Mary began to allow herself to shop independently. A psychology of will and action must encompass the paradox of adolescent suicide. Mary's behavior underscores the fact that these young people are often incapable of the simplest actions such as buying clothes or going to a party. On the other hand, they are capable of self-destruction, an avenue of activity not open to other young people, even those who are otherwise seriously disturbed.

> 4. The failure to make the normal adolescent move away from the parent throws the adolescent back into an intense infantile relationship with mother, which on a descriptive level could be termed a sadomasochistic relationship. . . . The female adolescent, terrified of being abandoned by mother, will submit to her and create situations in which she is repeatedly forced to do so. . . .

This summary paragraph from the adolescent attempted suicide study is condensed and requires much amplification. It was an attempt to state as concisely as possible that the preexisting relationship with the mother is very primitive and that failure to separate and become autonomous throws the adolescent back into that primitive relationship.

The analytic material, especially during the periods of repeated suicidal crisis, allowed us to reconstruct the relationship between Mary and her mother prior to the suicide attempt. It had revolved around

Mary's total inability to contain the slightest negative thought about her mother. The anger was, as she termed it, a "hot potato." She dealt with her anger mainly by turning it against herself and displacing it onto some other object. Since childhood, anger at her elder brother had been an accepted outlet and often she and mother joined together to criticize and attack him. Prior to the suicide attempt, aggression was displaced onto her father and then onto the superior at work. In the analysis I was frequently the recipient of her displaced aggression. This occurred concomitant with regression to a state of helpless submission in which Mary saw herself as totally inadequate and her mother as perfect.

The state of total submission to a powerful, idealized mother who could do no wrong was epitomized in Mary's hairstyle. Mary wore her hair in a highly unusual style. It was shorter than that of most boys, clipped behind the ears and the back of the neck, a "short back and sides," reminiscent of the style of haircut worn by men in the 1950s. Well into the analysis, in the context of talking about her inhibited exhibitionism, her wish to wear pretty clothes but her fear and inability to do so, I inquired about her hairstyle. I wondered about it and asked if she were aware that it was cut unusually short. She said that her brother and father had said that her hair was very short. Her friends had also said so, but her mother thought it was a good length. Mary then looked at me, smiled ruefully and said, "But she would, you know, since she cuts my hair."

The sadomasochistic battle centered on who owned Mary's body and it could be safely inferred that toilet training was achieved in a traumatizing, unempathic manner. Mary commented on mother's rough, "no nonsense" handling of her niece and said that mother would have been a good animal trainer but a bad child raiser. Mary's fear of making a mess was a focus of considerable work, and links could be drawn between her fear of losing bladder or bowel control and her severe constriction of affect and activity. At one point, when discussing her inability to tolerate ambivalent feelings, she said that she thought such feelings were messy. She said, "I always thought feelings should be neat and tidy."

5. In this state of heightened consciousness of their dependency all sexual and aggressive preoccupations become a source of anxiety. There is evidence in the memories of the external event that these adolescents become at least dimly aware of the incestuous nature of their fantasies.

In Mary's case one could see repeatedly how her extreme dependency and submission served to defend against her primitive rage at mother. However, the dependency intensified her anger, which in turn made dependency more necessary but more unacceptable. As she gradually learned to tolerate her feelings and began to recognize anger directed at her mother, she said often, "If I'm angry at someone else I still have mother, but if I'm angry at mother then I'm all alone." Regarding incestuous fantasies breaking through prior to the suicide attempt, it is evident that the oedipal situation is a source of enormous anxiety for Mary, especially because of the aggression involved in the rivalry. To take a minor example: Mary always performed extremely well at school, but seldom had any pleasure in the results. It was a problem we focused on, and it was linked with her inability to dress in a pretty way, to take pride in herself or to exhibit herself in an appropriate fashion. Following this work, she explained that when she brought back a good grade father was appreciative and seemed to understand the nature of the effort involved and the achievement in the grade. Mother, on the other hand, expressed her pleasure by immediately comparing Mary's high grades with her own academic difficulty when she went to college. Mary felt that there was a rivalry, that mother felt beaten, and then Mary began to wonder if this was why she could take only momentary pleasure in her academic achievements and then dismissed them as "big deal."

Clearer evidence of a link between positive oedipal fantasies and suicide thoughts emerged in what came to be seen as a repeated pattern in which good feelings about me and father emerged in the context of criticism of her mother. When she criticized her mother, she then felt good about me. During one of these periods, she dreamed that she was going on a trip with her father and that her mother had floated off alone in a balloon. There was a period of about two weeks in which she and father shared giggly jokes and teased each other. She worked hard in treatment, and brought much material related to her feeling that her mother was "weird" and unusual. The situation then became unbearable. She began to "feel bad," she refused to talk in treatment, father and I became the "bad guys" and she again became totally dependent on mother and highly suicidal. As I linked this repetitive pattern to the sequence preceding the suicide attempt, she at first denied that there had been any positive feelings for her father. But she then remembered that she had been able to make an important intervention in regard to the father's feelings about the elder brother, an intervention which father still describes as having been enormously important. Further, it seemed that Mary's intervention had altered the balance of forces within the family. It had brought father, Mary, and elder brother close together and excluded mother. Mary had completely forgotten about this event which had happened just before her actual suicide attempt.

As the work progressed, the influence of persisting sadistic sexual theories became explicit and were seen to have had an important influence on Mary's inability to retain positive oedipal fantasies. In her dreams, associations and memories, sex involved intensely sadistic attacks eventuating in death or destruction.

6. The next event in the sequence was the attempt, once again, to break away from their mothers by appealing to another person. The appeal took the form of a suicide threat. The appeal to the other person is an attempt by the adolescent to get out of a highly dangerous situation, one in which both sexual and aggressive wishes are threatening to break through to consciousness.

As yet, there is no evidence in Mary's case that she had threatened suicide and had appealed to some person outside the family for help. Mary's material both amplifies and clarifies the points in the sequence outlined from the suicide research. Her material indicates that the aborted move to someone outside the family is not simply an emergent step in the sequence but a repetitive pattern that occurs with increasing frequency in the adolescents' frenzied attempt to defend against aggressive feelings toward mother. There is an attempt to break away from the dangerous dependency, but very quickly the person toward whom they turn as an ally comes to be seen as an enemy. Disappointment, hurt and anger toward mother are quickly displaced, and the person who could help them is seen as the person who drives them into a more intense dependency on mother.

This is what I have described in another publication as a "negative therapeutic motivation;"[10] when it appears in treatment it becomes a means of displacing failure, blame and anger onto the therapist and intensifying the primitive tie to the again-idealized mother. Did this happen prior to Mary's suicide attempt? Her memory was somewhat fuzzy, but repeatedly in the course of treatment each moment of suicidal crisis — and there were many — was preceded by just such a point in the sequence. Friends who seemed eager to help would be regarded with suspicion and anger. She would be invited away for a weekend and then imagine getting sick so that she would have an excuse not to go. Most ominous, and a sign that suicidal thoughts and wishes were in the forefront, was when I became the "bad guy," when she would come to the session determined not to talk to me, when she deliberately kept things secret. During a session filled with stubborn silence she said, "I feel as if I'm a POW and you're trying to make me talk." It was at these times that my anxiety increased, and I would then tell her of my concern that she was thinking about and intending to kill herself.

The suicide research summarized this section of the sequence as a series of steps of appeal to an outside object to take them away from the intense and dangerous tie to the mother. In Mary's case it was apparent that it was a lifelong pattern of oscillation between mother and nonmother. During the analysis, one could see the oscillation occurring with increased frequency and intensity as, with each return to mother, Mary's anger at her intensified. Displacement as a defense was no longer sufficient. Mary's material revealed reasons for this. Even while locating all the negative feelings on the external object, Mary was aware that she was doing this for mother's sake. In Mary's view, and there seemed to be some justification for this perception, it was mother who could not tolerate separation, mother who could not accept or absorb any aggression or criticism. Mary had been dimly aware of this before but, during analysis, she became conscious of an intense feeling that all her sacrificing of an external life was done for mother. To return to a submissive dependency on mother and still feel unattended to, unappreciated and unloved, intensified her rage even further and led to an ever-increasing frequency of oscillation between mother and nonmother.

7. In the sequence of actual events we now have a breakthrough of aggressive feelings toward mother by both girls and boys. In the case of girls it is a breakthrough of conscious aggressive feelings toward mother accompanied by extreme guilt reactions. The guilt was intensified by an event which confirmed the girls' feelings of omnipotent aggression. The girls experience a conscious choice between killing themselves or killing their mothers. As a result of the breakthrough of aggression, both boys and girls experience a fear of loss of control over their impulses.

For much of the first year of her analysis, Mary denied that she had been angry with her mother before the suicide attempt. However, Mary's repeated pattern of dealing with her anger at her mother during analysis made her aware of how she had distorted her memory of the events prior to the attempt. During her sessions, any remark critical of mother would be followed, at times in the same session, by Mary "feeling bad," becoming highly self-critical, and "tuning out" or "becoming a zombie." She would stop feeling and thinking. A voice in her mind kept saying, "you've said enough, you've gone too far, you better stop now." The next day Mary would be agitated and very anxious about school or angry about something a friend had said. When I pointed out the displacement and the fact that only the day before she had been critical of her mother, she would react with genuine surprise, having completely forgotten that she had said those things about her mother. Eventually, my supposition that this "whitewash" might have occurred in relation to her feelings prior to the suicide attempt brought some confirming material. The most intense and sustained feeling of anger centered on her reactions to her birthdays. Her 18th birthday had occurred a week and a half prior to the suicide attempt; during analysis we saw her reactions to her 19th and 20th birthdays as repeating the reactions before the suicide attempt. Mary and her father had birthdays two days apart, and it was a family custom, initiated by mother, to hold their birthday parties on the same day. This was but one of the many features of her birthday which left

Mary feeling unattended to, uncared for and unloved. The birthday celebration and the presents seemed perfunctory, slapdash and performed out of duty rather than caring. This young woman, who had a remarkable memory for academic subjects, could not remember what she had received on her 18th or 19th birthdays. During the analysis, the breakthrough of rage at mother immediately following the birthday was evident, expressed in the analysis and immediately followed by self-criticism, "feeling bad," agitated attempts to displace the anger, and then another suicide crisis in which she was overwhelmed by suicidal wishes and close to putting suicidal plans into action.

In relation to the issue of loss of control, Mary regarded everything in extremes. In her view she had to become a zombie (ie, totally devoid of wishes), or she would be swept away by impulses and move directly into omnipotent action. In her dreams she never just felt angry but continued to hit until the person was killed. The zombie reaction was termed a "little suicide," and I suggested that she was killing a part of herself. She responded by saying that if she did not kill herself she would kill someone else. Regarding the finding that some external event confirmed the adolescent's fantasy of omnipotent aggression, there was no evidence by the third year of treatment that anything had occurred specifically in relation to mother just before the suicide attempt. What probably did occur was a breakdown in Mary's strenuous denial of mother's severe pathology, her "weirdness," her vulnerability, and the marital difficulties of the parents. When, after an extended period of work, Mary found the courage to confront mother over an incident of intrusive behavior, mother reacted by crying, running away, and not returning for hours. When Mary took charge of her own body, including doing her own hair, moving to her own apartment and in general acting more independently, mother became busy cleaning out the attic and would not come down to greet Mary when she returned for a weekend visit. Mary asked father about mother's behavior and he told her that they were involved in a mother-daughter game. It became evident that the family had for years been playing a more serious game, that of protecting mother and denying her pathology.

8. The adolescent will now feel in a state of intense panic and deadlock. Suicide thoughts which had been present for a considerable period of time will now become the solution. It is considered a positive, brave action. It is a solution to the conflict, a way out of the dilemma. Unable to make the normal adolescent moves, the wish to positive action is transferred to the suicide attempt.

In Mary's case suicide as a positive, brave action and a solution to an insoluble dilemma was addressed from the very beginning and interpreted as such. She confirmed my interpretation and when, for example,

I suggested that it would be wise if I kept the pills she had saved for her next suicide attempt, she agreed to give them to me but said that she would hate herself for doing it. It was her only way out. It was a positive action, she said, one she could not think of giving up. She described her suicide attempt as an overpowering surprise to her parents, and it became clear that the attempt represented, in part, an acting out in reverse form of the experience of having been surprised and thus unprepared and overwhelmed. Her parents had been completely taken by surprise; she had kept all thoughts and suicide plans secret from them. During the analysis, I found myself especially uneasy at moments when the suicide crisis seemed to have passed. When I first verbalized my disquiet and my concern that she was thinking of suicide she said, "I was just thinking that this would be a good time to do it—I mean, everyone thinks the worry is over." It became apparent that suicide as an overwhelming surprise was a derivative of what Laufer[17] has termed a "central masturbation fantasy" and, in turn, could be traced to repeated primal scene exposure and a persistent lack of parental protection from other overwhelming experiences. Note, in the chapter by E. Furman, the role of parental pathology in the exposure to traumatic situations and "the persistence (in the suicidants) of intense unfused early aggression in its sexualized sadomasochistic form. . .". At another point, Mary agreed that her suicide was an attempt to change her parents and went on to say that she had achieved many of her aims by attempting suicide. For the first time, her parents had paid attention to her and had expressed their love and devotion. In fact, she was in analysis only because of her suicide attempt and the analysis was being supported by her parents.

9. Totally preoccupied with suicidal impulses, the adolescent turns once more to the outside world, not for help but in order to deal with guilt in reaction to aggressive feelings about mother. Material on the suicide event indicates that unconsciously the adolescent provokes a rejection and the focal research shows that they are compelled to do so. There is an unconscious need to take the blame away from mother and put it on some person outside the home. By provoking rejection at the hands of someone else the conscious awareness that the suicide is an aggressive attack on mother is avoided. This is a decisive move because the blame is located on some external object, the guilt no longer acts as an inhibiting factor and the suicide plan is put into action.

In Mary's case we know that consciously she experienced the suicide attempt as due entirely to a difficult relationship with a superior at work. She was critical of this superior and felt criticized by her. She felt that she was not living up to the expectations of the superior, but at the same time this woman had disappointed her. All her feelings of rage, rejection and abandonment had been displaced from mother onto this female authority figure, and consciously the act was precipitated only by her feelings about this female superior. She had been preoccupied with thoughts about her superior, anxiety about work and self-hatred for having failed to remain at college. She had not thought of her parents or brothers nor felt any pangs of conscience for intending to kill herself.

10. Consciously, at the time of the actual suicide attempt, the adolescent saw the event as producing multiple results. It would reassert their control over external events, over people and over their bodies. The world would be sorry for having mistreated them and they would achieve a bodily state where there was no experience of aggressive or sexual feelings.

Mary's fantasies about the effect of her suicide on other people and on her own impulses was a central theme from the beginning of her analysis; various aspects recurred repeatedly in her words, actions, and dreams. Most prominent was the fantasy that by killing herslef she would make others "feel bad." She would force them to pay attention to her, to feel sorry for having neglected her and not having paid attention. Their reaction, she imagined, would be one of total surprise and guilt. They would say, "Oh, we never knew, we never suspected."

11. In the memories of the circumstances of the actual attempt there are many details to indicate that the adolescent had experienced an altered ego state, a psychotic state, at the time of the attempt. In all cases the adolescent did not experience any conscious concern or feelings of guilt in relation to their parents. Further, there is a total denial of death as evident in the conscious fantasies that they would not only achieve their aims through the suicide but would be around to observe and to benefit from the changes effected by their deed. This denial of death was related to the ever-increasing regression in which they had given up completely any feelings of ownership of their body; the body was something which did not belong to them. It was a source of unwanted impulses, both aggressive and sexual, something intruded upon, controlled by and belonging to mother. Finally, analysis showed that as part of the ego regression the mother they wish to destroy becomes the mother who wishes them dead, and suicide then is not an attack but a submission to the wishes of mother. Thus, we see that the adolescents not only deny the reality of death but see it as a state of peace and being at one with their mothers.

All this was very true of Mary; in her case projection of her death wishes seemed to fall on very fertile ground. Mary felt that her mother did not like her children, that she wished that she had never had any. As Mary became more observant and more capable of containing these observations and bringing them to treatment, we began to see many things which, as Mary said, "make one think." A particularly vivid example was the following: a psychiatric patient had committed suicide by jumping from a bridge. Within a day of the event, Mary's mother was driving Mary to a shopping center and took a roundabout route which passed over that bridge. Then, according to Mary, mother mentioned casually, as if commenting on the weather, that she had heard a rumor that a psychiatric patient had jumped off that bridge the other day.

12. In many cases the very choice of method will itself be of dynamic significance and not just fortuitous.

In her third year of analysis Mary mentioned that the suicide attempt was made with mother's car, a car which mother loved and Mary hated.

13. Immediately following the suicidal act the adolescent will feel a state of calm, of relief and release from all tensions.

This was true in Mary's case. She felt an enormous sense of relief and total calm while waiting for the ambulance to arrive. She knew that she would not die, she said. She felt that she had finally accomplished something. She had done a powerful, brave thing, something most people could not do. She had shocked everyone and forced them to pay attention to her and now everything would be different.

DISCUSSION

The material from Mary's case appears to confirm the results of the study of seven adolescents who had each attempted suicide. From the psychoanalytic material of Mary's case, we can replicate the finding that the suicide attempt was not a sudden act but the end point of a pathological regression. Suicide thoughts had been present for a considerable period prior to the attempt. The regression started with her experience of failure in the move toward independence from mother. Subsequent events then led to an intensification of her tie to mother and a displacement of the experience of rejection and anger from mother to an external object. Once the experience of rejection and blame was displaced, guilt was no longer an inhibiting factor, and the suicide plan was put into action. At the time of the attempt, Mary thought of suicide as a way to change the external world, mother and self. Suicide was considered a positive, brave action, producing multiple results including the restoration of positive self-regard. Reality of death was denied and the death wish was projected onto mother.

In addition to replicating the findings from the psychoanalytic study of attempted suicide in adolescents, the material from Mary's analysis amplifies some of these findings. Here are summarized some points in the sequence which can be looked at in the somewhat different light cast by the analytic material emerging in Mary's case.

Relationship with mother prior to suicide attempt: The emphasis on the adolescent's fear of abandonment and engulfment, though correct, does not sufficiently emphasize the importance of primitive aggression. In Mary's case it was not rejection or abandonment in themselves which were crucial components, but the omnipotent rage which would break through if these events were to occur. Her intense anxiety consequent upon each developmental step was not primarily a fear of abandonment, but a fear of enjoying and preferring the nonmother to her own mother. This would break down her denial of her mother's pathology and unleash Mary's primitive and omnipotent rage. For example, as a way of saving money mother provided only powdered milk at home. Mary could not remember having had whole milk until she was a school child and then she was shocked and thrown into a panic on finding out how much she loved milk.

Dependency intensifying anxiety: Although it is true in Mary's case that the experience of complete dependence on mother intensified fear of drive expression, especially hostility, her material underscored another, possibly more important reason for the association between increased dependency and heightened anxiety over hostile wishes. Mary experienced her dependency as a giving up for mother. It was "a little suicide" with the same motives of self-sacrifice in order to change mother into a caring, loving mother. Mother's failure to change intensified Mary's primitive rage. Concomitant with defenses against the rage was an ever-increasing self-sacrifice of autonomy and feelings of separate existence which made Mary even more dependent. Suicide was the ultimate sacrifice of a separate self, with the fantasy that this surrender to total dependency would create the wished for "purified pleasure dyad"[10] free of hostility from either partner.

Provoking rejection: Regarding the step in the sequence in which the adolescent provokes rejection, Mary's material emphasized that this was an old pattern of oscillation between mother and nonmother objects such as sibs, father and teachers. For her, there was a lifelong pattern of splitting the ambivalent feelings, displacing negative feelings onto some object other than mother, and thereby retaining the illusion of a purified mother-child dyad. Such a history of intermittent involvement with others might be looked for in other cases.

Projection of death wishes onto mother: Mary's material indicated that her conviction that mother wished her dead was not just a projection but had a substantial basis in reality. Mary's material should make us sensitive to the intense death wishes of mothers of suicidal adolescents. Looking back over the material of the seven suicide cases, including one of my own cases, there is abundant evidence that the intense hostility and death wishes of mothers played an important role in the suicidal behavior of the adolescents. Hurry,[5,8] in her excellent summary of suicide in adolescents and her detailed clinical presentation of one of the suicidal patients from the study, demonstrates the importance of this factor.

Turning the aggression against the self: Although this mechanism in suicide was described by Freud in *Mourning and Melancholia*[18] and noted in an earlier report on the suicide study,[7] insufficient emphasis was placed on this factor in the final summary of the research. In Mary's case the mechanism by which it was accomplished could be seen. It was via an identification with the hated part of the mother that the instinctual vicissitude of turning aggression against herself could not only defend against but also express her hostility towards mother. An important shift in the treatment was when these identifications could become a focus of the analytic work. As one of many examples: mother had put the envelope containing Mary's grade reports in Mary's desk without showing them to father. On the weekend, Mary discovered the grades in her desk and thought to herself that mother did not want father to see the grades. She said to me, "So then I did the same as mother did. I put them back into the desk." She then completely forgot about the grades and about the incident. That weekend she was "feeling bad" and felt angry and critical of herself for not doing what she imagined she should be doing for school.

Affect regression: In cross-validating the regressive sequence with Mary's material I was struck with how much of our work and material centered on the history and vicissitudes of her feelings, especially her anger, toward her mother. In my attempt to conceptualize the material I was stimulated by the highly original views of Orgel[19] and the series of critical papers on affect and trauma by Krystal.[13,20] Orgel postulates that the suicidant, in infancy (6 months to 15 months), has been deprived of a primary love object who could "absorb his waves of aggression." Krystal writes about a progressive response to trauma termed "lethal surrender." Starting with anxiety, it progresses to catatonoid states, aphanisis and potentially to psychogenic death.[13] It would be useful to look at the suicide sequence in relation to its infantile roots and to the sequence described by Krystal.

SUMMARY AND CONCLUSIONS

What answers and general conclusions can we draw from the adolescent suicide study and the cross-validation of the findings using material from Mary's analysis?

First, I believe that we have demonstrated that the "focal research" as described is a fruitful way of handling the vast amount of analytic data and provides, at least for topics such as suicide, a way of replicating and cross-validating previous studies.

The amount of significant data which emerged after the initial interviews and often not until late in the analysis casts serious doubt on those studies that rely solely on interview data subsequent to the suicide attempt. The value of psychoanalysis for obtaining a more complete picture of an event appears to be demonstrated in the study.

Finally, the study demonstrates that suicide is best viewed as the result of a complex interaction of many factors taking place over a long span of time and leading, by a sequence of steps, to this pathological solution.

The findings presented here emerged from a study using psychoanalysis as a research tool. But psychoanalysis is also a therapeutic technique and, as such, this study leads to certain technical suggestions regarding the treatment of adolescents who have made serious suicide attempts. Initially the family, the adolescent, and even the referring person may try to deny the seriousness of the attempt and may speak of it as a one-time occurrence totally out of character with the adolescent's usual good behavior. This should be addressed quickly with the adolescent and the family. The one action these adolescents are capable of is suicide. To the adolescent, suicide represents a positive, powerful solution to all their conflicts and they will be reluctant to give it up. The aggression in the attempt should be verbalized, as this may produce some guilt in regard to the suicide attempt. Without guilt, there is little to stop the adolescent from repeating the attmept. The multiple motives in the attempt and the unreality in the fantasy that the adolescent will actually be around to reap the rewards should be taken up. The lifelong pattern of displacing negative feelings from mother to others may soon become a problem in the therapy. This will be especially true around weekends and vacations. If the adolescents can construe the analyst as the bad object, the one who rejects and abandons them, then they are free once more to kill themselves without guilt.

The finding that a suicide attempt is the end point of a regressive sequence was a major result of the focal research. The author's subsequent work has been influenced by this result and he actively engages the young person in a search for the elements of the suicide sequence. In Mary's case it took almost three years to elucidate the crucial elements of the sequence. In her third year of analysis she could become conscious of the fact that the precipitating event of leaving home meant a sadistic oedipal triumph over mother and, with her integration of this last bit of knowledge concerning the first step in the sequence, the issue of suicide receded to make way for more pressing neurotic conflicts about becoming a mature, adult woman.

To undertake the treatment of an adolescent who has made a suicide attempt is a responsibility that entails a ceaseless struggle. Litman[21] notes that there are references to suicidal symptomatology in all of Freud's published case histories except that of "little Hans." Many of Freud's cases, especially his earlier ones, were adolescents, and Freud's experience with suicidal young people might be one of the factors influencing his shifting views on aggression and his final adoption of the theory of the death instinct. One cannot work with suicidal adolescents without being impressed with the power of their wish to kill themselves. The positive value they put on suicide and the power of this force is caught in a poem by Sylvia Plath, written before she killed herself.

> Dying
> Is an art, like everything else.
> I do it exceptionally well.
>
> I do it so it feels like hell.
> I do it so it feels real.
> I guess you could say I've got a call.
>
> (in Alvarez)[11]

To counter this force, we have to call on all our experience, our tolerance and the support of our colleagues. In 1926, discussing a young patient, Freud said, "What weighs on me in his case is my belief that unless the outcome is very good it will be very bad indeed: What I mean is that he would commit suicide without any hesitation. I shall therefore do all in my power to avert that eventuality."[22]

ACKNOWLEDGMENTS

The study reported in this paper was conducted at the Centre for Research into Adolescent Breakdown, London, England and supported by the Grant Foundation. The director of the Centre is Dr. Moses Laufer who was responsible for initiating the research program. The members of the research group were: Dr. M. Friedman, Dr. M. Glasser, Mrs. A. Hurry, Mrs. E. Laufer, Dr. M. Laufer, Dr. J. Novick and Dr. M. Wohl. The chairman of the group was Dr. M. Glasser. I would like to acknowledge my gratitude and debt to the members of this group and especially to Mrs. E. Laufer with whom I shared the excitement of evolving a research method. As ever, I owe an incalculable debt to Kerry Kelly Novick for her clinical acumen and editorial skill.

REFERENCES

1. Baechler J: Suicides. New York, Basic Books, 1979.
2. Haim A: Adolescent Suicide. New York, International Universities Press, 1974.
3. Otto U: Suicidal behavior in childhood and adolescence, in Anthony EJ, Chiland C (eds): The Child and His Family. New York, John Wiley & Sons, 1982, vol 7.

4. Petzel SV, Riddle M: Adolescent suicide: Psychosocial and cognitive aspects, in Feinstein S, et al (eds): *Adolescent Psychiatry*. Chicago, University of Chicago Press, 1981, vol 9, pp 343–398.
5. Hurry A: My ambition is to be dead. *J Child Psychother* 1977;4:66–83.
6. Kernberg P: The analysis of a fifteen-and-a-half-year-old girl with suicidal tendencies, in Harley M (ed): *The Analyst and the Adolescent at Work*. New York, Quadrangle, 1974.
7. Friedman M, Glasser M, Laufer E, et al: Attempted suicide and self-mutilation in adolescents: Some observations from a psychoanalytic research project. *Int J Psychoanal* 1972;53:179–183.
8. Hurry A: Part II. Past and current findings on suicide in adolescence. *J Child Psychother* 1978;4:69–82.
9. Novick J: Walk-in clinics for adolescents. *J Child Psychother* 1977;4:84–89.
10. Novick J: Negative therapeutic motivation and negative therapeutic alliance. *Psychoanal Study Child* 1980;35:299–320.
11. Alvarez A: *The Savage God*. London, Weidenfield & Nicholson, 1971, p 3.
12. Hurry A, Novick J, Laufer M: A study of 84 adolescents who have attempted suicide. Report to the Department of Health and Social Security, Center for the Study of Adolescence, London, England, 1976.
13. Krystal H: Trauma and affects. *Psychoanal Study Child* 1978;33:81–116.
14. Freud A: Assessment of childhood disturbances. *Psychoanal Study Child* 1962; 17:149–158.
15. Laufer M: Assessment of adolescent disturbances: The application of Anna Freud's diagnostic profile. *Psychoanal Study Child* 1965;20:99–123.
16. Hurry A, Laufer E, Novick J, et al: Attempted suicide in adolescents. Center for the Study of Adolescence, Report to Grant Foundation, New York.
17. Laufer M: The central masturbation fantasy, the final sexual organization, and adolescence. *Psychoanal Study Child* 1976;31:297–316.
18. Freud S: Mourning and Melancholia, in *The Complete Psychological Works of Sigmund Freud*, Strachy J (trans), standard ed. London, Hogarth Press, 1957, vol 14, pp 237–260.
19. Orgel S: Fusion with the victim and suicide. *Int J Psychoanal* 1974;55:532–538.
20. Krystal H: The activating aspects of emotions. *Psychoanal Contemp Thought* 1982;5:605–648.
21. Litman RE: Sigmund Freud on suicide, in Shneidman E (ed): *Essays in Self-Destruction*. New York, Science House, 1967.
22. Freud S: *Psychoanalysis and Faith*. New York, Basic Books, 1963, pp 101–102.

CHAPTER 9

METHODS FOR INVESTIGATING SUICIDE IN CHILDREN AND ADOLESCENTS: An Overview

PRUDENCE FISHER
DAVID SHAFFER

The authors point out that a model viewing suicide as the consequence of the distortion of perception or judgment which characterizes individuals who are psychiatrically ill is the most useful and valid framework for conceptualizing its causes. Using this model, they examine different ways of obtaining information about child and adolescent suicides. The validity and reliability of official statistics are discussed. Official statistics are shown to be useful in generating hypotheses and gaining new perspectives on suicide. The study of suicide attempters is dismissed as a method of learning about victims as the two populations differ. Likewise, the study of those in treatment at time of death is dismissed as too limited. The authors recommend the "psychological autopsy" technique, used successfully in three large adult studies, as it showed considerable psychopathology among the victims. Some similar, smaller child and adolescent studies are reviewed in detail.

Suicide, the third leading cause of death among adolescents aged 15 to 19 in the United States, poses a puzzle to clinicians. We know from summary mortality statistics that the incidence increases with age and that it is more common in boys. However, we know relatively little else about the youngsters who kill themselves. Are they psychiatrically ill or does the pressure of circumstances lead otherwise normal adolescents to suicide? Do they make their decision in clear consciousness or when intoxicated? What gives them the notion of suicide? Is this an option available to all or does firsthand experience with family or friends enhance the possibility that it will be used? How many suicides have previously threatened or attempted to kill themselves? Could the knowledgeable clinician have predicted their death and perhaps intervened to prevent it?

Clinicians and researchers seek answers to these questions in a variety of ways, and this chapter seeks to examine their usefulness and the type of information that can be obtained from them. The research methods that have been used may reflect different research opportunities or different conceptual models.

MODELS OF SUICIDE

The path to suicide has been considered in a number of broadly different ways. These include: 1) suicide as the result of an individual's internal or subconscious conflicts (the "psychological model"); 2) suicide as a logical behavior which follows from a particular individual's position in society and life situation (the "sociological model"); and 3) suicide as the consequence of an individual's psychiatric illness (the "disease model").

The *psychological model* explains suicide as the outcome of such intrapsychic dynamics as the need to identify with or join a deceased love object, the internalization of anger, or of interpersonal goals such as manipulations to either gain love or inflict punishment. Freud,[1] Abraham,[2] Zilboorg,[3] and Toolan[4] present detailed suggestions of such dynamic models. Because a psychological model is often unique to an individual, it requires a detailed knowledge about the subject's thinking before death and lends itself to a study through case reports of individuals in psychiatric treatment.

While it may be that the clinical observations which have led to the formation of many psychological theories were sound, their causal relationship to suicide is unclear. Such phenomena as self-denigratory thought and morbid preoccupations with deceased loved ones can frequently be reversed with antidepressant medication and therefore seem more likely to be a consequence, rather than a cause, of a disturbance of mood. While the act of suicide may retain some logical consistency when seen in the light of these distorted perceptions, the causal chain may originate with an alteration of affect (ie, the disease model) rather than with the disturbed perceptions as might be suggested in some of the dynamic psychological models.

A separate problem is that the case material upon which intrapsychic models are based is likely to be biased. Individuals who commit suicide during the course of intensive psychological treatment are unlikely to be representative of the total suicide population. Most suicides are not receiving treatment at time of death,[5] and we do not know the ways in which these untreated suicides differ systematically from those who are in treatment.

The *sociological model* holds suicide to be an intended or understandable behavior given an individual's life situation or position in society. It originates with Durkheim[6] and includes such concepts as a lack of social integration or anomie, group dynamics that foster or lessen identification with society and political-economic pressures such as cycles of unemployment. Translated into individual terms, suicide is the "only solution" that will logically allow escape from an intolerable situation.[3] The basic problem, the first link in the causal chain, is a social or political one, and individuals are seen to be responding to social forces beyond their control. This model does not stand alone, of course. No one has suggested that all individuals enduring an anomalous position in society or a particular stress will seek a suicidal solution. It becomes one element in an act that is determined multifactorially and therefore interacts with both the psychological and disease models. Studies carried out based on the sociological model usually relate mortality statistics to other measurable population variables (eg, total population fluctuations, unemployment rates, ethnic mixtures in geographic units, immigration patterns, migration, crime and divorce rates).[7] Such studies are potentially useful in generating hypotheses about change in suicide rates.

Sociological studies are usually correlational, however, and when one variable (eg, unemployment rate) varies, other factors may be varying with it, or the variation may occur against a backdrop of more general change so that causal inferences may not be justified.

The *psychiatric disease model* supposes that suicide occurs as a consequence of the distortions of perception and judgment that characterize a disturbance of mental state brought about by a psychiatric illness such as depression or an intoxication, eg, alcohol or drug use. Suicide is not in itself a disease but rather a symptom or sign of the underlying condition. A number of different research strategies have been used to support this model. Because suicide occurs infrequently, *prospective* studies of a general, unselected population are impracticable. Large numbers of individuals would have to be studied for many years in order to arrive at a reasonable number of deaths. However, a high-risk strategy can be more efficient; ie, a smaller group of at-risk individuals can be studied to arrive at a number of deaths sufficiently large to be suitable for study. Prospective studies have been carried out on patients with depression and schizophrenia,[8] suicide attempters,[9] and those who had contacted suicide prevention centers.[10] Each of these is able to provide reliable premorbid diagnostic information but will not provide information about the significant number of suicide victims who do not fall into the particular high-risk group being studied.[11]

An alternative way to study the disease model is to use the *"psychological autopsy"* technique, in which inquiries are made about manifest behaviors that were apparent or utterances that were made before death. This information is used to reconstruct a diagnosis or the precipitants of death. Such studies are clearly more practicable than prospective studies

142

in unselected groups and they provide diagnostic information about all conditions that might lead to suicide. Much of the information that we have on psychiatric disease in adult suicides derives from such studies, eg, that by Robins et al in 1959,[12] who investigated 134 consecutive suicides in the St. Louis area and concluded that 94% of their sample were psychiatrically ill. A study in 1960 by Dorpat and Ripley[5] of 108 suicides in the Seattle area found none to be without psychiatric illness and a British study in 1974 conducted by Barraclough et al[13] of 100 consecutive suicides found 93% to be mentally ill. Depression, followed by alcoholism, was the most common psychiatric disorder in all of these investigations.

As indicated above, none of the models is necessarily incompatible with the others. Possible examples of how the models could be integrated would be cases in which social factors (eg, unemployment or minority status) bring with them a reduction of social support which then impairs resistance to stress and increases the likelihood of depression and with it, suicide, although at each step only a minority of those at risk will be affected. Alternatively, it could be that genetically determined affective disturbance or alcoholism lead to interpersonal difficulties and social drift to an anomalous position in society, which may tie in to a vicious cycle of isolation and distortion of thoughts.

METHODS FOR LEARNING ABOUT ADOLESCENT SUICIDE

As indicated above, information about the characteristics of suicide in children and adolescents can be obtained in several ways: 1) by a study of mortality statistics (used in sociological and psychiatric models); 2) by inference from studies of children or adolescents who attempt suicide (used in sociological and psychological models); 3) by the intensive study of youths who commit suicide while under psychiatric care (used in psychological models); and 4) by psychological autopsies of consecutive suicides in a given geographical area (used in psychiatric models).

Official Statistics

Official statistics pro
suicide victims as well a:
month in which the dea
from these data.

Age   There is a dire
suicide in children, adole
States only two children

the ages of 10 and 14 died from suicide. This yields an annual mortality rate of .81 per 100,000 in 10 to 14 year olds or .55% of all suicides at all ages. In other words, the suicide rate in this group is much less than expected, for this group makes up 8.5% of the total population of the United States.[14]

In the same year, 1367 adolescent boys and 319 girls aged 15 to 19 died from suicide, an annual rate of 7.64 per 100,000. This age group accounts for just under 10% of the population but accounts for only 6.18% of all suicides. The suicide mortality rate for 15 to 19 year olds is almost 10 times higher than that of the younger group but remains smaller than would be expected if suicidal death were distributed evenly across all age groups. Childhood suicide rates in other countries expressed as a proportion of all suicides are strikingly similar.[14] These data suggest that there are age-related factors that either protect the very young from suicide, or conversely, increasingly predispose individuals to suicide as they grow older.

There are a number of possible explanations why children should be less prone to suicide than their elders. The first is that affective illness is the most common cause of suicide; although it does occur in children and adolescents, it is probably less prevalent in this group than among adults. A second is that the intense and multiple social support systems that characterize childhood and adolescence reduce isolation and extend emotional support which may prevent the occurrence of effective suicide acts. A third general possibility is that a certain degree of cognitive maturity is required before a child experiences feelings of despair and hopelessness and that this maturity develops as a part of that stage of cognitive development referred to by Piaget as "formal operations."

Sex Suicide is more common in males than in females at all ages.[15,16] A number of explanations have been offered for this finding. Gould[17] suggests that females in our society enjoy less cultural sanction to show angry or aggressive feelings which would include suicide. Other suggestions include a six-linked preference for so-called "passive" methods such as overdose ingestion. These female-type methods may in turn be less effective than the typical male methods such as hanging and shooting.

There is also a suggestion that there is an interaction between sex, psychiatric disorder and suicidal behavior. Thus, boys who attempt suicide have been found to have more severe psychiatric disorders than girl attempters.[18] If suicidal behavior is shown in the context of more serious disturbance in males than in females, then greater suicidal intent and a higher mortality rate will follow, although the reason for the initial association has still to be explained.

Ethnicity Mortality from suicide in different ethnic groups and in different countries can be obtained from official statistics. Suicide is generally more common in whites than in nonwhites in all age groups. Given that blacks tend to experience more stress than their white counterparts, it has been suggested[14] that they too (like younger children) may enjoy some "protective" factor. Two hypotheses have been proposed. The first, based on the original Freudian dynamic model, is that there is a reciprocal relationship between inwardly and outwardly directed aggression. It follows that because black adolescents have a high rate of delinquency (ie, outwardly directed aggression), they should be expected to show low rates of suicidal behavior (ie, inwardly directed aggression). Breed, however, found that 50% of the blacks who attempted suicide had recently been in trouble with the law, compared with only 10% of whites.[19] Shaffer[11] also noted that a majority of children who commit suicide manifested antisocial behavior before their deaths. Likewise, Chiles et al[20] have noted a high prevalence of depression in delinquent adolescents. Thus, suicide and depression appear to be related directly, rather than inversely, to aggression.

The second hypothesis is that even though blacks must endure more external stress than whites, cultural factors or convention make suicide a less acceptable behavior. For example, Bush[21] suggested that blacks have more effective social support systems than whites. Gibbs and Martin[22] suggested that status integration may be enhanced by racial discrimination and narrowed job opportunities and this may, in turn, reduce the likelihood of suicide among blacks.

To determine whether a measure of protection from suicide is provided by the black subculture, Shaffer and Fisher[14] compared the suicide rate of black adolescents living in what is likely to be a traditional setting (ie, the American South) with blacks residing in the industrialized Northeast and Northcentral states, where it is reasonable to assume that varying degrees of deculturation have occurred. The comparison demonstrated that while blacks living in the South had substantially lower rates than Southern whites, blacks and whites in the North had similar rates. A likely explanation is that Northern blacks either experience a loss of protection through deculturation or, and this seems less probable, that they experience some qualitatively different and more specifically suicide-promoting stress than their Southern counterparts.

Secular changes Secular changes in rates emerge from official statistics. In an examination of adolescent suicide rates from 1964 to 1977,[23] Shaffer and Fisher[14] showed that although rates in 10 to 14 year olds have remained almost stable, the rate among 15 to 19 year olds has risen dramatically (125% for males, 70% for females). Rapid increases in rate during a given time period (as is found among older adolescents and young adults) could be due to a "period effect" which usually follows from a change in some external influence or from a change in reporting procedures. Examples of external influences could be factors that increase stresses which result in initiating suicidal behavior or changes in the accessibility of the means of suicide (eg, Kreitman[24] reported a reduction in the suicide rate after the introduction of nontoxic household gas to replace coal gas in certain areas of the United Kingdom). Finally, for those cases in which a method does not result in instant death, differences in the quality or availability of a given treatment technique may lead to varying survival rates. The effects of treatment quality or availability may be inferred by comparing mortality rates for underdeveloped and developed countries. Thus, Sathyavathi[11] noted that 53% of the completed adolescent suicides in India were alive at the time of discovery as compared with only 6% in Shaffer's British series,[13] suggesting that mortality from methods that are not immediately lethal is greater in India than in the United Kingdom. Changes in treatment availability over time are likely to have reduced rather than increased the suicide rate.

A "period effect" would most likely affect all age groups. This does not appear to have been the case over the past two decades. Murphy and Solomon (see Chapter 1 of this volume), suggest that the changes are specific for certain generations born since the mid-1940s and there is an increased predisposition to suicide at all ages born since that time (ie, that the increase in rate is a cohort effect). In an earlier paper, Murphy and Wetzel[26] reviewed the official statistics for the last 30 years in this country. They found that not only does each successive generation (five-year cohort) start out with a higher suicide rate than the one preceding it, but that it maintains higher rates at every age interval. The authors conclude that the rise in suicide rate is the result of very early and lasting causes, rather than of societal changes.

These findings do not support the suggestion by Holinger and Offer[27] who examined the relationship between changes in the size of the adolescent (age 15 to 19) population and changes in the adolescent suicide rate. A significant positive correlation was noted on which the authors based a predictive "population" model. As the proportion of adolescents in the population increases (decreases), so will the adolescent suicide rate increase (decrease). Yet, the suicide rate has been rising for other age groups as well. The young adult-to-adolescent suicide ratio has shown no tendency to diminish[14] as would be expected if this population model were sufficient to explain the rise in adolescent suicide. The authors use a much older (aged 65 to 69) group for comparison purposes and explain the group differences as resulting from different pressures and supports. However, the age-incidence curve for suicide has, with the exception of the depression years, shown a decline in incidence after age 60, since records were first kept. A more appropriate comparison group would be young adults and, in these, secular increases have been even greater than among adolescents.

Season The season or month of death can be obtained from official statistics. Changes from season to season in a mortality rate can indicate acute environmental influences. Proportionately, more young adolescents have been shown to commit suicide during the school year than during their summer vacations.[11]

Method The method used by a victim to commit suicide may be extracted from official data. From 1973 to 1977 the most common method in the United States for adolescent suicide[23] was firearms and explosives, followed closely by hanging, strangulation, and suffocation. Both of these were used primarily by boys. These were also the most common causes of "undetermined" death. Poisoning was the third most common suicide method and it was also high on the list of deaths whose cause was undetermined as suicidal or accidental. There is a marked sex difference in the choice of method; females tend to use less certainly lethal methods, eg, drug overdose.

Validity of official statistics Conclusions drawn from mortality statistics will be limited by their reliability and validity. Many authors have suggested that because both social stigma and pecuniary loss (eg, the invalidation of life insurance benefits) are associated with suicide it is systematically underreported. The first factor is particularly likely to hold for child suicide in which parents or school may be held responsible for the child's death. Misreporting can take the form of underreporting, which could erroneously support the conclusion that suicide in childhood is a rare event, or it could be idiosyncratic or biased.

Underreporting has been studied in adults by Wilkins[10] who used a sample frame of 1311 persons who contacted a suicide prevention program in Chicago. Death certifications examined 19 months later revealed that 17 of them had died; four were certified as suicide. Each case was reinvestigated and Wilkins found the true suicide rate to be between two and three times the official rate.

The International Classification of Diseases incorporates a designation of cause of death, "undetermined whether death is accidental or purposefully inflicted." Shaffer[11] reviewed coroners' records for children aged 10 to 14 for whom this verdict was given in the United Kingdom. He found the number of cases designated "undetermined" was very small but he concluded that most of these deaths were probably suicides. Even so, the rate in children remained very low and was confined to children aged 12 and older.

Barraclough[28] has suggested that by combining the categories of "suicide" and "undetermined" one is most likely to arrive at the "true" suicide rate. Shaffer and Fisher[14] calculated that if this was done for the United States statistics (they examined mortality data from 1973–1977), the rate per 100,000 for 10 to 14 year olds would be increased from .81 to 1.21 and in 15 to 19 year olds from 7.64 to 9.16. In the over-20-year age group the increase would be from 16.91 to 19.48. Child suicides would still account for under 1% of all suicides (ie, they would remain a rare phenomenon) and adolescent suicide still occurs at a lower than expected rate, considering the size of the population.

It is also possible that child and adolescent suicides are more likely to be misclassified as accidental than similar deaths in adults. However, when Shaffer[11] reviewed coroners' inquest dispositions on a cohort of children who died from the same causes as suicide victims, he found that most of the accidental deaths were in the infant and toddler age groups; it seemed reasonable that these were not suicidal.

Study of Suicide by Examining Attempted Suicide

Attempted suicide is thought to be at least eight times as frequent at all ages as completed suicide and considerably more so in children and adolescents.[16] Survivors can be studied directly and may be able to explain to the investigator their reasons and feelings at the time of the attempt. It has therefore been tempting for those interested in completed suicide to study suicide attempters and to generalize from them to suicide victims, the assumption being that suicide victims and suicide attempters will exhibit similar personality traits and problems. Amir,[29] for example, in a study in Israel grouped attempted and completed suicides together for the purpose of data analysis.

However, there is convincing evidence that completed and attempted suicide victims differ significantly from each other. Studies in adults that have examined this include the study by Segal and Humphrey[15] who examined data from consecutive suicide victims (N = 90) of all ages in New Hampshire over a 13-year period (1955–1967) and compared them with suicide attempters (N = 103) hospitalized at the state's only inpatient psychiatric facility. Even though the attempted suicide sample was unlikely to be representative of all who attempted suicide during this period as it included a disproportionate number of attempters who had used more lethal methods (which might be expected to *diminish* differences between the two groups), substantial differences were noted. Attempters tended to be younger; 70% of the attempters were under age 40 as compared to only 26% of the victims. The victims were usually male (75%), and the attempters, female (54%). Victims used highly lethal methods approximately 80% of the time and only 13% of the attempters used such methods. Other studies[16,30] have yielded similar observations.

Shneidman and Farberow[16] compared suicide victims (N = 768) with attempted suicide (N = 2652) for a one-year period in Los Angeles County and found significant demographic differences. Victims were older and were predominantly male. Methods used within sexes were very different, with the most popular method among male victims being gunshot to the head (35%) a method rarely used by male attempters (2%). The reasons for their behavior were also different.

The same authors[16] separated the groups with respect to possible reasons for suicide (as provided by witnesses to the deputy coroner). Depression was common in both, but suicide completers much more often suffered from a clear physical or mental illness.

Both Shneidman and Farberow[16] and Segal and Humphrey[15] suggested that because of such differences suicide victims and persons who attempt suicide should not be grouped together. Shneidman and Farberow[16] note that the modal attempter is likely to be female, in her 20s, and uses barbiturates, whereas the modal victim is likely to be male, in his 40's or older, and uses a more violent means. They suggest that investigators looking at attempted suicide should not "match their data from committed suicides on the assumption that the two are essentially the same."

There have been no comparative studies of completed and attempted suicide in childhood or adolescence so that differences between the groups have to be deduced from separate reports on representative samples of each. Looked at in this way, it appears that the differences found in adults are also found in adolescents. Bergstrand and Otto[31] have described a total population of adolescent suicide attempters admitted to Swedish hospitals from 1955 to 1959. Of the 1727 patients, 20% were male and 87% made attempts by ingesting drugs. In Shaffer's study[11] of a consecutive British series of completed child suicides, 70% were male and 67% of boys used a highly lethal method as compared to only 13% of the girls.

Bergstrand and Otto[31] were able to obtain the reason for the suicide attempt in almost 1300 of their cases. The most important precipitating circumstance was love problems (30%), followed by family problems (25%) and mental illness (14%). School problems were considered a precipitating circumstance in only 6.2% of the sample. This was in contrast to Shaffer[11] who found "disciplinary crisis" (usually related to school) as the most frequent precipitant.

Bergstrand and Otto[31] also looked at the number of previous attempts made by their sample. Approximately 10% of their sample had made an earlier attempt and 5% had made several attempts. Previous attempts were much more common in males. In Shaffer's British series almost half were known to have made a previous suicide threat or attempt.

Because of different classification approaches, personality variables are difficult to compare. The most frequent personality types among the approximately 500 children for whom information was available in the Swedish study were termed infantile and hysteroid, either alone or in combination. The most common personality descriptions in Shaffer's sample were paranoid, impulsive, self-critical, or uncommunicative. Of these children, 75% showed antisocial and/or affective symptoms.

Bergstrand and Otto were able to obtain adequate family information on 927 cases. They found that the home environment was "entirely" normal in only 4% of their cases. Usually one or more problems were present. Fifteen percent of the sample had alcoholism in one or both parents, 28% had a mentally ill parent, and 44% came from broken homes. These findings are similar to those of Shaffer.[11]

One must conclude, therefore, that the differences between those who attempted suicide and those who ultimately become suicide victims are such that it is not reasonable to draw inferences about one from the other. A number of authors[15,16,30] have concluded that they are different events occurring in somewhat overlapping populations.

Study of Youths Who Commit Suicide While under Psychiatric Care

How are we to find out more about the clinical picture shown by children and adolescents who commit suicide? Some investigators have examined individual case reports of children or patients who committed suicide after a psychiatric evaluation or during treatment.[32-34] As we noted above, such studies will, by definition only, include patients whose deaths occurred during or after a psychiatric evaluation, and the only available data[11] suggest that a minority of successful child suicides have previously seen a psychiatrist or physician before their death. Sanborn et al[35] warned that the generalizability of studies of suicidal adolescents who have been institutionalized or hospitalized is limited. They note that studies using such populations report a disorganized home environment and an excess of parental loss for the adolescent suicide victim. However, parental loss is prevalent in psychiatric patients,[36] and a poor home environment may act to increase referral to a psychiatrist or psychiatric facility. Thus, one cannot know whether parental loss or home disorganization is characteristic of a suicidal syndrome or is simply a reflection of the locus of treatment. Furthermore, in such cases the reporter (ie, the therapist) is giving an account of a "failed" treatment case which may, in turn, increase a likelihood of reporting bias or interpretation.

Psychological Autopsies of Consecutive Suicides

Robins et al[12] have argued that a way to circumvent many of the above problems is through a comprehensive clinical study of a sizeable group of unselected consecutive suicides. In this type of study one would be able to indicate a) what proportion of suicides show clinical evidence of psychiatric disturbance before death; b) what factors are helpful in predicting suicide; and c) how often the presuicidal person has been perceived to have a clinical problem. In their study of a consecutive sample (N = 134) of people who committed suicide in the St. Louis area during a one-year period, information was collected from primary informants and employees, medical and psychiatric histories, and hospital, social service and police record searches "to reach the most accurate possible psychiatric diagnosis of the sample."[37] Five principal diagnoses were made: affective disorder (47%), alcoholism (25%), organic brain syndrome (4%), schizophrenia (2%), and drug dependence (1%). A small number were thought to be psychiatrically ill, but no diagnosis could be made; 2% of the sample were considered clinically well, and 4% were terminally medically ill.

Assigning a diagnosis allowed somewhat sharper predictive statements to be made. For example, white males over age 65 with a diagnosis of major affective disorder could be predicted to be at high risk for suicide, whereas a black female, under age 30, diagnosed as neurotic would seem to be a very low risk. Diagnosis was also related to the clinical features of the suicide. Of the 69% of subjects who had previously indicated suicidal intent, three fifths of those diagnosed alcoholic and two fifths of those diagnosed as having an affective disorder made specific suicidal threats. Fewer than one fifth of the remaining subjects did this. Of the women diagnosed as having an affective disorder, 33% had made previous attempts, compared to only 9% of depressed men. The likelihood of a suicide victim having had previous psychiatric care was also affected by diagnosis. For example, 70% of those diagnosed as having affective disorder had received psychiatric care in the year before their death; only 40% of the undiagnosed group and of those diagnosed alcoholic or having another psychiatric disorder had received care.

Affectional relationship loss as a predictor of suicide also became more important when correlated with diagnoses. Forty-eight percent of those diagnosed alcoholic had suffered divorce, separation or death of spouse, bereavement of a close friend or relative, or separation from a relative during the 12 months preceding the suicide, as compared with only 25% of the undiagnosed group, 14% of the affective disorder group, or 17% of the rest. Thirty-three percent of the alcoholics suffered such a loss within the six weeks prior to the suicide. Fifty-four percent of the whole sample had received psychiatric care within a year of the suicide, but all of the women with an affective diagnosis had been treated.

Another study of adults which showed the significance of psychiatric diagnosis in suicide was that conducted by Dorpat and Ripley[5] who investigated 114 consecutive suicides in Seattle from July 1, 1957 to July 1, 1958. None of their sample was thought to have been free of psychiatric illness. Interesting interactions were noted between age and diagnosis. Twenty-seven percent were regarded as alcoholic (most common in the 40- to 60-year age group), 18.5% psychotic depression (most common in patients over 60), 12.0% psychoneurotic depression,

12.0% schizophrenia (most common in the group under age 40), 9.5% personality and sociopathic disorders, 4.3% chronic brain syndrome, 3.5% other psychiatric disorders, and 16% an unspecified illness.

A third adult study of psychiatric diagnosis in suicide victims was carried out by Barraclough et al[13] in 100 consecutive suicides in Great Britain. Information was obtained from interviews with relatives or persons close to the victim and available supporting records. Like the other two studies, the investigators found the majority of victims to be men and older persons. Ninety-three percent of the victims were diagnosed as being mentally ill, 70% were diagnosed as suffering from depression, 15% as suffering from alcoholism, and 8% as suffering from another psychiatric disorder.

By establishing a diagnosis, Barraclough et al[13] were able to compare suicide victims to other populations with similar psychiatric conditions. Victims diagnosed as being depressed resembled other depressed patients except that they were eight times more likely to have attempted suicide. Similarly, alcoholic victims were found to be older than the non-suicidal alcoholics and a history of attempted suicide was six times as common. Other interactions with diagnosis were found with reference to suicidal threat. The authors note that threats by an alcoholic, especially if he had made a previous attempt and if his current domestic life is in disarray, warrant serious attention.

CHILD-ADOLESCENT TOTAL POPULATION STUDIES

Few diagnostic studies have been carried out on children and adolescents. The most comprehensive was that of Shaffer[11] who studied a wide range of records on a consecutive series of child suicides (N = 30) aged under 15 in England and Wales over a seven-year period. The data Shaffer examined included inquest deposition, educational and medical records, and, where available, the psychiatric and social welfare records of the dead children and the medical and psychiatric records of the deceased children's parents and siblings. His study was facilitated by the existence in Great Britain of extensive standardized medical records available through a central source.

Detailed examination of the records provided information on a number of areas; the most frequent precipitant was a "disciplinary crisis" which occurred in 11 cases (36% of the sample). In five of these cases the child had been informed by his teacher that his parent was to be told of truanting or antisocial school behavior; in the other six, the child was anticipating either court action or some sort of punishment at school. Four suicides followed a fight with another child, three followed a dispute with a parent, and two followed being dropped from a sports team. Two

152

others seemed precipitated by fantasy models. In three cases the child's interaction with a psychotic parent apparently was a causal factor. In six others there was some bereavement (not necessarily recent) that had affected the child. This included two cases of parent loss and four cases of grandparent loss. Seven of the children died within two weeks of their own birthday.

As was found in the Robins[12,37] and Barraclough[13] studies, many (46%) of Shaffer's[11] series had previously discussed, threatened or attempted suicide (the majority within 24 hours of their death). The author felt this was probably an underestimate of the true number. He noted that those children who killed themselves after a disciplinary crisis were less likely to have attempted or threatened suicide previously than those whose deaths followed other precipitants. Again, interpretation of this is difficult, as threatened or contemplated suicide may be a fairly common event in early puberty. Leese,[38] Lukianowitz,[39] and Mattsson et al[40] all report that between 6% and 10% of referrals to their child psychiatry clinics are for attempted or threatened suicide.

Shaffer[11] found that over half of his male victims (12 children) were not in school on the day before their death. Four were on holiday, but the other eight were absent even though school was in session. Three of these were chronic school refusers but the other five had been absent for less than a week. This finding verifies that of previous studies by Stanley and Barter[41] and Teicher and Jacobs[42] who noted a similar phenomenon among suicide attempters.

IQ estimates were available on 28 children. Shaffer noted that there was an excess of children with above average intelligence. Likewise, all but two of the children in his series were above the 50th percentile for height — and a disproportionate number were tall or very tall for their age. The author noted that his sample was unusual in their physical and intellectual precocity.

Shaffer[11] attempted to group behavior and emotional characteristics of the children through interviewing their classroom teachers. He was able to derive four separate categories: 1) oversensitive to criticism and irritable (N = 9); 2) impulsive, volatile, erratic (N = 6); 3) quiet, thought to be uncommunicative, difficult to get to (N = 9); 4) perfectionist, high standards, self-critical, afraid of making mistakes (N = 6); and 7) none of the above (N = 6). The first category overlaps with the others, but all the others are exclusive. Although these were described retrospectively as enduring traits of the child, it is possible that some of the descriptions related to circumscribed periods of disturbance such as a major depressive episode which stood out in the information recollection as being a permanent feature of the child's personality.

Shaffer additionally assessed the prevalence of antisocial and emotional symptoms among the children. Twenty-two of his sample were reported to have antisocial symptoms; 21 exhibited affective symptoms and 17 exhibited both. This is of particular interest since Rutter et al[43] have noted that children who have conduct disorders are often unhappy or miserable. Shaffer speculated as to whether the children's depression was being manifested in this way.

Thirty percent (nine children) of Shaffer's sample were either in treatment with a psychiatrist or on the waiting list to receive treatment from a psychiatrist. Of these, only two had been referred for attempted suicide. Six other children were recognized as having conduct or emotional problems at school. These children had been seen by either probation or welfare services.

Unlike the adult studies, Shaffer's sample did not manifest many physical illnesses. Only two (7%) of the children suffered from any sort of chronic illness.

Most of Shaffer's sample (all but two) were living at home with either one or both parents at the time of death. The exceptions were one child who was psychiatrically hospitalized and another child who was living with close relatives.

Seven (33%) of the children were living with only one parent. Of these "broken homes," six had been the result of a divorce after which two of the mothers died. The other home was broken due to the death of the mother shortly before the child's suicide. Unfortunately, these figures cannot indicate the quality of the intact marriages. The author concluded that these may be judged as not being particularly happy because at the time of his investigation (one to four years post death of child) six more sets of parents had either separated from one another or divorced. Of course, the impact of their child's suicide would place an additional burden on these couples.

Fifty-five percent of Shaffer's sample (16 families) had a family member who had either consulted a psychiatrist or received treatment for an emotional problem from a general practitioner prior to the child's suicide. In four of his cases, either the parent or the sibling of the child was reported as having exhibited suicidal behavior. Furthermore, there were three cases of attempted suicide *after* the child's death. Eight of the dead boys' fathers and one of the mothers were described as alcoholic.

Shaffer's findings differ from those found in adults. Antisocial behavior and "getting into trouble" are significant features in adolescents and children which have not been reported in adults. Their diagnostic significance, ie, whether they form part of an affective disturbance, is not certain.

In a smaller but somewhat similar study embracing an older age group Sanborn et al[35] attempted to describe and evaluate the lives of each adolescent suicide (aged 10 through 19) in New Hampshire over a two-year period (N = 10). These researchers used records of the child obtained from the police, medical examiners, and school as well as actually interviewing the victim's family, relatives, friends and other significant persons in his life.

The ratio of males to females in this study was 9:1. Method of suicide was not reported. Eight were enrolled in school at the time of their death. Of the other two, one was a housewife, and one was a marine. Five had shown some difficulty in school adjustment. Only one was a good student. Three were "average" and four were "poor." Only four of the schools reported (after the child's death) that they had noticed anything in the victim that might indicate something was wrong. Four of the victims (40%) previously had threatened suicide. All of the youngsters came from intact families. However, the authors learned through their family interviews that eight families experienced significant family/marital discord prior to the child's death. Only two families described themselves as being happy families. Family history information was incomplete, but a third of those for which there was information had a family history of suicide.

The authors did not attempt to make diagnoses on the sample. They noted that, sometimes, unhappiness or depression had been reported in the victims but not to such a degree that would differentiate them from other people. Most of the suicides appeared to be impulsive rather than planned.

A third study of consecutive adolescent suicides, which also included the 20–25 age group, was conducted during a seven-year period on an Indian reservation by Dizmang et al.[44] This study also highlighted the importance of the relationship between suicide and behavior disturbance. One-half of all suicides occurring in this population were in this adolescent-young adult age group. Comparisons were made with a control group matched for age, sex, degree of Indian blood, and a history of no personal or nuclear family suicide attempts or behavior. Although no diagnoses, sex differences or method information was provided, some interesting differences between the two groups were noted.

Seventy percent of the suicide group had more than one significant caretaker before age 15, compared with 15% of the control group. Forty percent of the caretakers of the suicide group had been arrested five or more times, compared to 7.5% of the control group caretakers. Fifty percent of the suicide group had experienced loss of a family member by desertion or divorce as compared with 10% of the control group; 80% of the suicide group had been arrested one or more times in the year prior to death, compared to 27.5% of the nonsuicidal group (most arrests being for such offenses as intoxication, glue sniffing, and rowdy or aggressive behavior). The two groups did not differ significantly on the lifetime total of arrests, but the suicidal group was likely to have been arrested at an earlier age; 70% of the suicide group had been arrested at least once by age 15 as compared with only 20% of the controls. Seventy percent of the suicide group had attended boarding school at some time compared with 30% of the controls.

Dizmang et al[44] concluded that the suicide group had had a more chaotic and unstable childhood than the nonsuicidal group. The authors explained this finding as a consequence of the white man's intrusion into Indian culture which has resulted in both cultural and family disorganization.

Jan-Tausch[45] studied all public school students in the State of New Jersey known to have comitted suicide from 1960 to 1963 (N = 41). Data were derived from school records and interviews from school personnel. The ratio of male to female was 3.6:1. Students ranged in age from 7 to 19; only one victim was 7, two were 10, and two were 11. The intelligence of the victims was found to be average to superior. Many more (15 children) were in the superior range than might have been expected, yet most (29 children) were poor achievers, with over one fourth of the sample being reading retarded.

Subjects were classified by "personality." Approximately 75% of the sample were considered aggressive or withdrawn. None was viewed as having a close friend or confidant.

SUMMARY

Three theoretical frameworks for conceptualizing the causes of suicide were discussed: a psychological, a sociological, and a disease model. In practice it is usually possible to integrate elements from all three models to fit an individual case.

Different methods of studying suicide were examined. These include:

1. The use of official mortality statistics which provide suggestive information about age, sex, method and secular trends. The reliability and validity of these were examined and underreporting was noted to be more of a problem than was idiosyncratic or biased reporting.

2. The study of suicide attempters. We have found much evidence that shows the two populations to be very dissimilar, although somewhat overlapping, and this raises doubts about the use of this method of study as a technique for learning about completed suicide. However, attempted suicide is in itself an important diagnostic entity which requires a major research endeavor.

3. Examining individual case reports of patients who committed suicide while in psychiatric treatment or after having had a psychiatric evaluation. This is applicable to the very few victims who have been in well-described treatment, and the elements of sample bias make this method of questionable value.

4. The study of a consecutive sample of victims using the "psychological autopsy" technique has proved valuable. Three postmortem studies using psychological autopsies on large adult samples are presented in detail. Each found at least 93% of their sample to have been psychiatrically ill. Similar, much smaller studies on child and adolescent samples, using far fewer victims, are also reviewed.

ACKNOWLEDGMENTS

Preparation of this material was assisted by grants from the William T. Grant Foundation, from NIMH Psychiatry Education Branch Grant #MH07715-19, and NIMH Research Training Grant #5T32MH16434-03.

REFERENCES

1. Freud S: *Mourning and Melancholia*, standard ed. London, Hogarth Press, 1957.
2. Abraham K: Notes on the psychoanalytic investigation and treatment of manic depressive insanity and allied conditions, in Jones E (ed): *Selected Papers*. London, Hogarth Press, 1927, pp 137–156.
3. Zilboorg G: Consideration on suicide with particular reference to that of the young. *Am J Orthopsychiatry* 1936;7:15–35.
4. Toolan JM: Suicide and suicide attempts in children and adolescents. *Am J Orthopsychiatry* 1962;118:719–724.
5. Dorpat TL, Ripley HS: A study of suicide in the Seattle area. *Compr Psychiatry* 1960;1:349–359.
6. Durkheim E: *Suicide*. New York, Free Press, 1951.
7. Boor M: Relationship of 1977 state suicide rates to population increases and immigration. *Psychol Rep* 1981;49:856–858.
8. Pokorny A: Suicide rates in various psychiatric disorder. *J Nerv Ment Dis* 1964;139:499–506.
9. Ettlinger RW: Suicides in a group of patients who had previously attempted suicide. *Acta Psychiatr Scand* 1964;40:363–378.
10. Wilkins JL: Predicting suicides. *Am Behav Sci* 1970;14:185–201.
11. Shaffer D: Suicide in childhood and early adolescence. *J Child Psychol Psychiatry* 1974;45:406–451.
12. Robins E, Murphy GE, Wilkinson RH Jr, et al: Some clinical considerations in the prevention of suicide based on a study of 134 successful suicides. *Am J Public Health* 1959;49:888–899.
13. Barraclough BM, Bunch J, Nelson B, et al: A hundred cases of suicide. *Br J Psychiatry* 1974;125:355–373.
14. Shaffer D, Fisher P: The epidemiology of suicide in children and young adolescents. *J Am Acad Child Psychiatry* 1981;20:545–565.
15. Segal BE, Humphrey J: A comparison of suicide victims and suicide attempters in New Hampshire. *Dis Nerv Syst* 1970;31:830–838.
16. Shneidman E, Farberow N: Statistical comparisons between attempted and committed suicides, in Farberow N, Shneidman E (eds): *The Cry for Help*. New York, McGraw-Hill, 1965.
17. Gould RE: Suicide problems in children and adolescents. *Am J Psychother* 1965;19:228–246.
18. Otto U: Suicide attempts in adolescence and childhood. States of mental ill-

ness and personality variables. *Acta Paedopsychiatr* 1964;31:397–411.

19. Breed W: The negro and fatalistic suicide. *Pacific Soc Rev* 1970;13:156–162.
20. Chiles JA, Miller ML, Cox GB: Depression in an adolescent delinquent population. *Arch Gen Psychiatry* 1980;37:1179–1186.
21. Bush JA: Suicide and blacks. *Suicide Life Threat Behav* 1976;6:216–222.
22. Gibbs JP, Martin WT: *Status Integration and Suicide*. Eugene, University of Oregon Press, 1964.
23. National Center for Health Statistics: *Vital Statistics of the United States, 1964–1978, Inclusive*, vol II, parts A and B. US Department of Health and Human Services, Mortality Statistics Branch (published and unpublished data).
24. Kreitman N: The coal gas story. *Br J Prev Soc Med* 1976;30:86–93.
25. Sathyavathi K: Suicide among children in Bangalore. *Indian J Pediatr* 1975; 42:149–157.
26. Murphy GE, Wetzel RD: Suicide risk by birth cohort in the United States, 1949 to 1974. *Arch Gen Psychiatry* 1980;37:519–523.
27. Holinger PC, Offer D: Prediction of adolescent suicide: A population model. *Am J Psychiatry* 1982;139:302–307.
28. Barraclough B: Are the Scottish and English rates really different? *Br J Psychiatry* 1972;120:267–273.
29. Amir A: Suicide among minors in Israel. *Isr Ann Psychiatr Relat Discip* 1975; 11:219–269.
30. World Health Organization: *Suicide and Attempted Suicide*. Geneva, World Health Organization, Public Health Papers, 58, 1974.
31. Bergstrand OG, Otto U: Suicidal attempts in adolescence childhood. *Acta Paedopsychiatr* 1962;31:397–411.
32. Holinger PC: Suicide in adolescence. *Am J Psychiatry* 1977;134:1433–1434.
33. Kallman FJ, DePorte E, Feingold L: Suicide in twins and only children. *Am J Hum Genet* 1949;1:113–126.
34. Rachin S, Milton J, Pam A: Countersymbiotic suicide. *Arch Gen Psychiatry* 1977;34:965–967.
35. Sanborn DE, Sanborn CJ, Cimbolic P: Two years of suicide: A study of adolescent suicide in New Hampshire. *Child Psychiatry Hum Dev* 1974;3: 234–242.
36. Gregory I: Studies of parental deprivation in psychiatric patients. *Am J Psychiatry* 1958;115:432–442.
37. Robins E: *The Final Months*. New York, Oxford University Press, 1981.
38. Leese SM: Suicidal behavior in twenty adolescents. *Br J Psychiatry* 1969; 115:479–480.
39. Lukianowicz N: Attempted suicide in children. *Acta Psychiatry Scand* 1968; 44:415–435.
40. Mattsson A, Seese LR, Hawkins JW: Suicidal behavior as a child psychiatry emergency—Clinical characteristics and follow-up results. *Arch Gen Psychiatry* 1969;20:100–109.
41. Stanley EJ, Barter JT: Adolescent suicidal behavior. *Am J Orthopsychiatry* 1970;40:87–93.
42. Teicher JD, Jacobs J: Adolescents who attempt suicide: Preliminary findings. *Am J Psychiatry* 1966;122:1248–1257.
43. Rutter M, Tizard J, Whitmore K: *Education, Health and Behavior*. London, Longmans, 1970.
44. Dizmang LH, Watson J, May PA, et al: Adolescent suicide at an Indian reservation. *Am J Orthopsychiatry* 1974;44:43–49.
45. Jan-Tausch J: *Suicide of Children 1960–1963*. Trenton, NJ, New Jersey Public Schools, Department of Education, 1964.

CHAPTER 10

THE CAUSES OF SUICIDE:
Review and Comment

AMASA B. FORD
NORMAN B. RUSHFORTH
HOWARD S. SUDAK

The stark fact of suicide compels us to search our hearts and minds, and especially our consciences, for an explanation. The need to understand is particularly exigent when the victim is young. What extraordinary stress, what perverse longing, what inexpressible, disordered mechanism of the body could possibly drive an adolescent or young adult to such an act?

The previous chapter has touched on leading theories of suicide causation, most of which have been developed to explain suicide in general, but not with specific reference to the age group that is the subject of this book.

Since the incidence of suicide has been rising recently in this particular group differently from the pattern in the rest of the population, it will be useful to review the new evidence presented in the first nine chapters, not so much to decide whether it fits previous theories, but rather to see whether it leads to any new hypotheses that will help to explain why increasing numbers of our young people are deciding to end their lives prematurely. Initially, therefore, we will briefly restate the main findings from each of the previous chapters, dividing the evidence into rough categories of external and internal causation, the latter including both biological and psychodynamic mechanisms. Then, we will examine first what we have learned about social and environmental factors in the causation of suicide from the epidemiologic perspective. Second, we will consider what light is cast on possible endogenous causes by evidence from the study of individuals. Finally, we will direct attention to the study of intermediate level phenomena — relationships with family and friends — as one promising approach to a better understanding of these distressing suicides.

In the process of assembling and interpreting contributions to this book, the editors have had a previous impression strongly reinforced, namely, that no single mechanism is adequate to explain the tragedy of a young person's suicide, but, rather, that powerful external forces, transmitted from the larger society through family and peers, impel a biologically or psychologically vulnerable individual to the final, drastic step.

EXTERNAL CAUSES

The first five chapters have presented new or reanalyzed population-based information, documenting and exploring the recent rise in suicide rates among young people. This epidemiologic approach essentially continues the long series of studies initiated in 1897 by Durkheim.[1]

In Chapter 1, Solomon and Murphy review and extend studies of suicide in Alberta and the United States for the years 1950–1975. Using cohort analysis, they show that, in both populations, since 1950 each birth cohort has exhibited a higher suicide rate than the preceding one in every five-year segment of the life span for which data are available. We seem to be experiencing not only a rise in suicide rates among young people, but also sustained elevations as successive cohorts age.

Holinger and Offer, in Chapter 2, suggest one possible use for such data. They examine suicides, homicides, and accidental death rates in the United States for 15 to 24 year olds and changes in these rates from 1933 through 1978. Positive correlations are demonstrated between these rates on the one hand and changes in the proportion of 15–24 year-olds in the population on the other, except that the correlation between motor vehicle mortality and population percentage is negative. The authors interpret these findings to show that "violent death rates for the adolescent and young adult age group can be predicted."

The reader should be aware of some of the differences between the cohort and population models cited above. To exaggerate these for illustrative purposes, the former model implies a fixed, constant rise in rates across successive cohorts; the latter implies a more plastic situation, with suicide rates varying with shifting proportions of adolescents in the general population. It is easier to fit the population model to theories that interpret suicide rates as representing a barometer of psychosocial distress. One may, of course, synthesize the two models by viewing different cohorts as being exposed to differing psychosocial stresses (perhaps quite early in their lives), with resulting different rates of suicide, which may be sustained in a given cohort as its members age.

The special case of suicides among minority young people is considered by Frederick in Chapter 3. Using mainly United States data for 1968 to 1979, ages 5 to 24, by race, he shows that suicide rates have been increasing among young blacks, although they remain lower than white rates, and that suicide rates among young American Indians are alarmingly high. He also cites evidence of high rates of substance abuse among blacks and of alcoholism among Indians, which, he suggests, may influence the suicide rates. (Alternative explanations of differences in suicide rates in different ethnic groups are presented in Chapter 9.)

Focusing on a particularly reliable set of data from a midwestern metropolitan community for 1958 through 1982, the editors, in Chapter 4, confirm the rising and sustained suicide rates for young males in successive cohorts that have been observed previously in the United States, in Alberta, and elsewhere. They also call attention to a possible decrease in suicides for the most recent cohort, divergent trends for males and females, and a striking increase in suicide rates and the use of firearms as the means of committing suicide among young nonwhite males.

In the final epidemiologic study, Chapter 5, Phillips uses 1977 United States data for teenagers (13 to 19 year olds) and adults to examine temporal patterns of suicides and auto accident fatalities. He finds that teenage suicides are not clearly related to day of the week, month of the year, or holidays, whereas much of the variance in auto accident fatalities, at all ages, and of adult suicides as well, can be explained by such temporal factors.

INTERNAL CAUSES

Although a sharp separation between external and internal factors cannot always be made, the distinction can serve an analytic purpose and can be defended on the grounds that the "epidemiologic" data are population based, whereas the next three chapters are based mainly on the study of individuals and clinical studies.

Biological Factors

Ambrosini and colleagues (Chapter 6) describe clinical studies of major depressive disorder in children and adolescents, compared to confirm the existence of major depression in children, associated with abnormalities of several hormonal systems. They also show that some of the biological variables are age-related. Although these early studies are far from providing a simple explanation of suicide, they do point toward objective biological markers that may be useful in identifying vulnerable individuals and that strengthen the possibility of a biological factor in depression and suicide.

Psychodynamic Factors

In Chapter 7, Holinger and Luke set forth four explanatory models of suicide (and other self-destructive behavior) in young people, ie, that these deaths might be related to puberty, to developing cognition, to socialization, or to the conceptualization of death. They test these models by comparing the ages at which each of the developmental changes takes place most rapidly with changes in suicide rates, by year of life from birth to age 30, using United States data for 1968 through 1977. They find steady (ie, not abrupt) increases in suicide, homicide, and accident rates for all sex and race combinations through the early adolescent and middle adolescent years. The findings appear to be "more consonant with cognition and conceptualization of death than with puberty and socialization theories." Inconclusive though this study is, it raises interesting questions about whether there may have been recent changes in specific biological, intellectual, and social developmental patterns that occur during adolescence which, in turn, can be correlated with the rise in suicide rates.

In Chapter 8, Novick presents a lucid account of psychodynamic patterns that he and his colleagues have observed in common in the psychoanalytic study of young people who have attempted suicide. An interesting point in this pattern is the importance of a precipitating interpersonal event in the life of an individual with preexisting psychopathology.

Finally, Fisher and Shaffer's review of the literature on methods of investigating childhood and adolescent suicides (Chapter 9) finds that individual cases can be shown to develop out of a mixture of psychological, sociological, and disease elements. They recommend a blend of epidemiologic and case study methods, namely the "psychological autopsy" of series of consecutive suicides, as the most promising avenue for future research.

THE EPIDEMIOLOGIC PERSPECTIVE

Durkheim used the crude epidemiologic methods and data of the 19th century to develop his theories of egoistic, altruistic, and anomic suicide. Today, with better data, computers, and more refined statistical methods, we ought to be able to test his theories or replace them with more accurate new theories. Some advances have indeed been made, as, for example, our ability to observe, much more precisely, temporal changes in suicide rates. But our understanding of the whole problem has not advanced nearly as well as Durkheim hoped when he set us on this road nearly 100 years ago. In part, the explanation lies in technical problems that set limits to the uses of epidemiologic data and, in part, in the probability that an advance in understanding will be more likely to come from detailed studies of interpersonal relationships and the individual than from further study of populations.

Are We Seeing the Whole Picture?

Population-based data have some inherent weaknesses that limit the conclusions that can be drawn from them.

Reliability of official statistics Durkheim accepted the figures published by European governments with little skepticism, although he was concerned about the definition of suicide. Subsequent investigators, however, have properly questioned the reliability of such figures. Holinger and Luke in Chapter 7, and Fisher and Shaffer in Chapter 9, for example, point out that there are serious methodologic problems in the use of mortality and census data for the United States and the United Kingdom, including under- and overreporting, misclassification and changes in official definitions. Most of these problems tend to reduce the reported numbers of suicides, and the resulting errors may be large enough to invalidate international comparisons[2,3] or comparisons between social groups in the United States.[4]

A specific problem is whether some deaths classified as accidents or homicide are really suicides. Holinger (Chapters 2 and 7; 5) adduces evidence that death from self-destructive behavior is more prevalent than is indicated by suicide rates alone. But, at least one detailed study shows that the error due to suicides being misclassified as accidents is probably very small.[6] In spite of the fact that suicide is likely to be one of the most unequivocal forms of death, official statistics must be used and interpreted with caution, as Fisher and Shaffer conclude after their review of the literature (Chapter 9). Individual reports should include an assessment of the reliability of the data reported.[7]

Scale of survey The epidemiologic approach also entails a methodological dilemma: large numbers of a relatively rare event are needed in order to attribute statistical significance to observed differences, while, at the same time, merging of data from different locations and times may obscure important demographic and temporal relationships. For example, international comparisons, such as those presented in Chapter 1, can help in recognizing general patterns and differences (the data, incidentally, show consistently higher suicide rates in male cohorts born in Alberta since 1947 than in comparable cohorts in the United States, although the authors do not comment on this point). A narrower focus, on regions of the United States,[8] metropolitan areas (Chapter 4), or racial groups (Chapter 3), for instance, allows for finer discrimination, although the problem of small numbers always sets limits to how many different categories can be examined. Thought must be given to comparisons that are lost when a narrow range of data is selected. This consideration applies to some of the chapters under review that examine suicide rates for only the younger part of the population.

Can we really understand racial differences among youths, for example, without taking into account the fact that suicide rates continue to rise with age among white males, while they decline after the age of 30 among black males?[7] This observation has led to the formulation of a "survivor" hypothesis to explain the relatively low rates of suicide among older blacks[9] and American Indians,[10] and this hypothesis, in turn, puts suicide among young minority males in perspective as one manifestation of multiple stresses associated with minority status.

Are Suicide Attempts Different from Completed Suicides?

A particularly knotty problem in the study of suicide is posed by the fact that victims of completed suicide cannot be studied, and detailed premortem psychiatric or other clinical information is rarely available in any uniform way. One may be inclined, therefore, to turn to studies of survivors of attempted suicide, as in Chapter 8 and later chapters. Before accepting information obtained from attempters as equivalent to what might have been obtained from actual suicides, however, we must ask how closely the two groups resemble each other. Fisher and Shaffer, after reviewing the literature, come to the conclusion that "they are different events occurring in somewhat overlapping populations" (Chapter 9). Studies of attempted and completed suicide in defined populations indicate that the two groups differ and should not be grouped together.[11,12] A special term for attempted suicide, "parasuicide," has been introduced in Britain in recognition of these differences, and suicide has been found to be epidemiologically associated with certain factors, such as social disorganization, that are different from others, such as poverty, that are associated with parasuicide.[13,14] A commonly observed difference is that attempters are more likely to be young and female and completed suicides male and older. Even those who attempt suicide are not a single, homogeneous group.[15-17]

Although the weight of evidence seems to be against taking suicide attempters as representative of actual suicides, the overlap is great enough that something undoubtedly can be learned about the general problem from the study of this related group. Farmer comments, "Within the broad area of self-harm there are undoubtedly many subcategories, but a primary division on the criterion of fatality may not be the most appropriate,"[18] while Shafii suggests that there is a continuum (Chapter 17).

Is Prediction Possible?

The assertion by Holinger and Offer that violent death rates among the adolescent and young adult age group can be predicted raises hopes that such studies can provide guidelines for clinical practice and suicide prevention. Unfortunately, there are two stubborn statistical problems in the way. The first is the distinction between prediction for groups and for individuals, which the authors recognize, claiming only that we can make estimates of how many such deaths will occur in this population in the immediate future, but not that we can predict who the victims will be.

The second statistical obstacle to predicting mortality rates, even for groups, is that, in dealing with events as rare as suicide (approximately 10 per year per 100,000 population in the age group under consideration), the sampling error is comparable in magnitude to the rate being predicted. For example, the highest correlation shown in Table 2-1 of Chapter 2, that between motor vehicle accidents and proportion of adolescents and young adults in the population, is .60. Such a correlation "explains" only 36% of the variance, giving a wide margin of error for predictions on which to base clinical and policy decisions. Efforts to test this hypothesis, using data from a metropolitan community (Chapter 4), provide only partial support.

Pokorny has clearly demonstrated the statistical limits to predicting suicide among individuals in a prospective study of 4800 patients for whom extensive clinical and survey data were available. He concluded that "identification of particular persons who will commit suicide is not currently feasible, because of the low sensitivity and specificity of available identification procedures and the low base rate of this behavior."[19] Murphy, in a commentary on this study, further explains the statistical constraints and gives another example of an unsuccessful effort to overcome them.[20] He also points out that, even though accurate prediction is not possible in our present state of knowledge, the description of trends and patterns does have value as a guide to the clinician's thinking about individual cases. Clinically, a more useful formulation than exact prediction is to describe individuals in terms of risk factors, a concentration of which in one case raises the probability of suicide, even though it does not predict the event.

Can More Be Learned from Future Epidemiologic Studies?

Case prediction seems out of the question, although epidemiologic studies clearly provide some guidance in the treatment of suicide attempters and the prevention of suicide in high-risk populations. Perhaps future epidemiologic studies will be more fruitful if we look to them, as Durkheim did, for a better theoretical understanding of the suicide problem rather than unrealistically expecting them to be directly applicable in practice. The cohort studies, for example (Chapters 1, 4 and 10), suggest the possibility of examining relationships between the rising and sustained suicide rates we are observing among young people and the specific historical and social events successive cohorts have experienced. Holinger and Offer have explored one such idea, namely the relationship between the sharp demographic changes of the baby boom generation and rates of violent death among the young. They also suggest in their discussion that economic changes may be a mediating factor between population changes and mortality rates. This is a possibility that could be explored, adding economic and unemployment variables to the correlation analysis. Brenner, for example, has shown that higher suicide rates are associated with declines in percapita personal income and increases in unemployment and inflation, and he calls for more economic "microscopic level" research, especially for cities.[21]

Additional social variables that can be quantitated and which might prove to be correlated with the youthful suicide rate — variables that have changed during the years of rising suicide rates — include increasing divorce rates, teenage pregnancies, single-parent families, childlessness, alcohol and drug abuse, unemployment, and military service in Vietnam. On the basis of one such study, Waldron and Eyer concluded that a major cause of the recent increase in suicides among 15 to 24 year olds was "an increase in potentially overwhelming life problems."[22] Although such analyses of multiple variables are complex, modern statistical techniques and computers make them more feasible, and the 1980 census data are finally becoming available as a basis for testing and extending our conceptual understanding of the problem addressed by this book.

The specter of a possible nuclear holocaust has loomed over the world since 1945, casting a particularly dark shadow on the young. Considering the overwhelming importance of this issue, it is striking how little research has been done on its impact on young people and their behavior.[23] Could this explain some of the recent rise in suicides among adolescents and young adults? At the very least, future studies should include this concern among other possible causes of youthful suicide.

Another avenue of epidemiologic study that has been only tentatively explored is the possibility that "epidemics" of suicide among young people can be initiated or reinforced by suggestion in news stories or events portrayed by entertainment media.[24,25] Certainly, we know that cultural factors can contribute powerfully to the suicide of young people, as in the Japanese phenomenon of "Examination Hell" (shiken jigoku).[26,27] Cross-cultural studies with the United States (American Indians, for example) and between nations, combining epidemiologic and anthropologic approaches, could increase our understanding, with due attention to the problems of comparability noted above.

Epidemiologic studies have made it abundantly clear that there are factors external to the biological and psychological processes within the individual that have measurable effects on suicide rates among young people. The most difficult research challenge in the field remains to examine both exogenous and endogenous factors in the same set of individuals.

STUDY OF THE INDIVIDUAL

The epidemiologic perspective portrays disease as the action of an *agent* on a *host* under specific conditions of the *environment*. Although suicide is certainly not directly analogous to infectious or toxic illness, it is closer to trauma, which has been profitably analyzed using the epidemiologic model. Can we identify a specific agent that is instrumental in producing suicidal behavior? And what are the characteristics of the individual that make him or her vulnerable? Chapters 6 through 8 examine these questions.

A biological basis Although a specific suicidogenic agent seems improbable, by moving a step back in the possible chain of causation, Ambrosini, Rabinovich, and Puig-Antich have been able to assemble some objective evidence for the existence of a biological disorder underlying Major Depressive Disorder in childhood and adolescence, which they show to be closely similar to adult depression. Family histories suggest that there may be a genetic component to depression in both children and adults. An abnormal growth hormone response to hypoglycemia is frequently observed in depressed children and adults, and abnormalities of cortisol secretion can be demonstrated fairly consistently in both age groups. Response to medication is also similar at all ages.

Adolescent changes The surge of hormonal changes that takes place during puberty, especially if they are unbalanced or out of normal sequence, could well set the stage for those suicides that result from depression. Holinger and Luke interpret the data in Chapter 7 as showing "steady" increases in suicide and other violent death rates through the early and middle adolescent years. Our interpretation differs. Even though there may not be a sharp change at a specific age, the figures actually show dramatic increases in rate during these years. For suicides, these increases follow upon near-zero rates in the first 10 years of life and are followed in turn by a very much reduced rate of increase, after about age 15 for females but not until about age 21 for males, at which point slight decreases in rate actually appear (Chapter 7, Figure 7-1; see also Chapter 9). The adolescent increases are very large: Holinger and Luke comment that suicide rates for white males increase 21-fold between 12 and 16 years of age.

The authors also state that they are not able to demonstrate an exact relationship between the average age at which maximum increases occur for suicides, as compared to ages of maximum change in biological puberty, cognition, socialization, or conceptualization of death. This negative finding may be explainable on technical grounds. A major difficulty is the unavoidable impreciseness of timing some of the functions, such as socialization and conceptualization. We have also noted the statistical problems associated with measuring rates of infrequent events. Holinger and Luke have merged data for the 10 years 1968–1977 in order to obtain larger numbers of suicides to analyze by individual year of life. Unfortunately, this decade, as shown in Chapters 1 and 4, has been one in which large changes in age-specific suicide rates have been taking place. Thus, in an effort to cope with the discrimination problem of low rates, the authors may have introduced a confounding temporal bias. The possibility remains to be examined, probably by other than traditional epidemiologic methods, that some disorder of the biological and psychosocial changes which are such prominent features of adolescence can cause or contribute to the increase in suicide that occurs at this stage of life.

The psychopathology of adolescent suicide   The psychoanalytic study of young people who have made medically serious suicide attempts (Chapter 8) is at a descriptive and hypothesis-generating stage of scientific investigation. The difficulty of generalizing from a very few cases seems intrinsic to the psychoanalytic method. The claim of "cross-validation" when patterns identified in seven cases are also seen in another subject analyzed by one of the same investigators is probably not justified, but the information presented can be considered as evidence of some degree of reproducibility of findings. The psychodynamic sequence described is logical, and the evidence of disordered personal relationships and psychological processes stretching back long before the suicidal attempt is convincing. Novick presents a warning, applicable to some of the other research presented in this book, that single interviews immediately after the event must be interpreted with great caution and may not reveal the "real" reasons for the step that was taken.

FAMILY RELATIONSHIPS

The study of suicide has tended to focus on a search for either large-scale, exogenous factors or small-scale, mainly endogenous ones. Evidence presented in several of the chapters reviewed here, arising from both population statistics and case studies, suggests that more knowledge about transactions on an intermediate scale, that of family relationships, may be essential to a better understanding of adolescent and young adult suicides.

Epidemiologic and social analytic studies, reported here and elsewhere,[22,28,29] suggest that the recent rise in such suicides has been temporally correlated with, and may have been contributed to by recent changes in the structure and stability of the family. Similar correlations also have been noted in other countries.[30,31] Psychological autopsies and psychoanalysis point strongly in the direction of disordered family relationships and accompanying regressive responses to the adolescent and young adult task of becoming a person independent of the family. There is evidence, some of which will be presented in later clinical chapters, that the families (and peers) of youthful suicides are also at risk and may have contributed to the event in complex and poorly understood ways. More multidisciplinary, detailed studies of family relationships appear to be promising avenues of future investigation[30] and could lead to a better knowledge base for family therapy.

In the practice of medicine, the physician is regularly required to make diagnostic and therapeutic decisions, even though information about the patient and understanding of the pathogenesis of disease is incomplete. Nearly 100 years of study of the cause of suicide still leaves us with a fragmentary set of explanations, but suicides and attempted suicides continue to occur, with distressingly greater frequency among young people. The next two sections of the book will therefore deal with the state of the art of diagnosis, treatment, and prevention of this phenomenon.

REFERENCES

1. Durkheim E: *Suicide: A Study in Sociology*. Glencoe, Illinois, The Free Press, 1951. (First published in French in 1897.)
2. Barraclough B: Differences between national suicide rates. *Br J Psychiatry* 1973;122:95–96.
3. World Health Organization: Suicide statistics: The problem of comparability. *WHO Chronicle* 1975;29:188–193.
4. Warshauer ME, Monk M: Problems in suicide statistics for whites and blacks. *Am J Pub Health* 1978;68:383–388.
5. Holinger PC, Klemen EH: Violent deaths in the United States, 1900–1975. *Soc Sci Med* 1982;16:1929–1938.
6. Jenkins J, Sainsbury P: Single-car road deaths – disguised suicides? *Br Med J* 1980;281:1041.
7. Ford AB, Rushforth NB, Rushforth N, et al: Violent death in a metropolitan county: II. Changing patterns in suicides (1958–1974). *Am J Pub Health* 1979;69:459–464.
8. Farberow NL, MacKinnon DR, Franklyn LN: Suicide: Who's counting? *Pub Health Rep* 1977;92:223–232.
9. Seiden RH: Mellowing with age: Factors influencing the nonwhite suicide rate. *Int J Aging Hum Dev* 1981;13:265–284.
10. McIntosh JL, Santos JF: Suicide among minority elderly: A preliminary investigation. *Suicide Life Threat Behav* 1981;11:151–166.
11. Shneidman E, Farberow N: Statistical comparisons between attempted and committed suicides, in Farberow N, Shneidman E (eds): *The Cry for Help*. New York, McGraw-Hill, 1965.
12. Segal BE, Humphrey J: A comparison of suicide victims and suicide attempters in New Hampshire. *Dis Nerv Syst* 1970;31:830–838.
13. Buglass D, Duffy JC: The ecological pattern of suicide and parasuicide in Edinburgh. *Soc Sci Med* 1978;12:241–253.
14. Kreitman N, Philip AE, Greer S, Bagley CR: Parasuicide. *Br J Psychiatry* 1970;116:460–461.
15. Henderson AS, Hartigan J, Davidson J, et al: A typology of parasuicide. *Br J Psychiatry* 1977;131:631–641.

170

16. Hawton K, Osborn M, O'Grady J et al: Classification of adolescents who take overdoses. *Br J Psychiatry* 1982;140:124–131.
17. Hawton K, O'Grady J, Osborn M, Cole D: Adolescents who take overdoses: Their characteristics, problems and contacts with helping agencies. *Br J Psychiatry* 1982;140:118–123.
18. Farmer RTD: The relationship between suicide and parasuicide, in Farmer R, Hirsch S (eds): *The Suicide Syndrome*. London, Croom Helm, 1980, pp 19–37.
19. Pokorny AD: Prediction of suicide in psychiatric patients. *Arch Gen Psychiatry* 1983;40:249–257.
20. Murphy GE: On suicide prediction and prevention. *Arch Gen Psychiatry* 1983;40:343–344.
21. Brenner H: Estimating the social costs of national economic policy: Implications for mental and physical health, and criminal aggression. Vol 1, Paper No. 5, in *Achieving the Goals of the Employment Act of 1946 — Thirtieth Anniversary Review*. Joint Committee Print (94:2), US Congress. Washington, DC, US Government Printing Office, 1976.
22. Waldron I, Eyer J: Socioeconomic causes of the recent rise in death rates for 15–24 year olds. *Soc Sci Med* 1975;9:383–395.
23. Beardslee W, Mack J: The impact on children and adolescents of nuclear developments, in American Psychiatric Association: *Psychosocial Aspects of Nuclear Developments*. Washington, DC, American Psychiatric Association, 1982, pp 64–93.
24. Phillips D: Motor vehicle fatalities increase just after publicized suicide stories. *Science* 1977;196:1464–1465.
25. Phillips D: Airplane accident fatalities increase just after newspaper stories about murder and suicide. *Science* 1978;201:748–750.
26. Iga M: Suicide of Japanese youth. *Suicide Life Threat Behav* 1981;11:17–30.
27. Ishii K: Adolescent self-destructive behavior and crisis intervention in Japan. *Suicide Life Threat Behav* 1981;11:51–61.
28. Tishler CL, McKenry PC, Morgan KC: Adolescent suicide attempts: Some significant factors. *Suicide Life Threat Behav* 1981;11:86–92.
29. Fuchs VR: *How We Live*. Cambridge, MA, Harvard University Press, 1983, pp 108–111.
30. Brooke EM (ed): *Suicide and Attempted Suicide* (Public Health Papers, No. 58). Geneva, World Health Organization, 1974.
31. Paerregaard G: Suicide in Denmark: A statistical review for the past 150 years. *Suicide Life Threat Behav* 1980;10:150–156.

Section II.   DIAGNOSIS

CHAPTER 11

CLINICAL ASSESSMENT OF SUICIDAL BEHAVIOR IN CHILDREN

CYNTHIA R. PFEFFER

This chapter discusses the clinical interview evaluation of suicidal potential in children. Some factors discovered to be specifically associated with childhood suicidal behavior are outlined. The clinical evaluation should focus on determining the presence and degree of depression in the child; the child's concepts, experiences, and thoughts about death; and family interactions and suicidal tendencies in important family members. In addition, the author argues that current data do not seem to support a hypothesis that suicidal behavior among children is a result of normal developmental turmoil. Instead, any signal of a child's proclivities toward suicide should be taken seriously and evaluated by trained mental health professionals. Finally, issues are pointed out that increase a clinician's personal responses and attitudes in work with suicidal youngsters. Understanding these feelings will increase the objectivity of the evaluation of suicidal potential in children.

One of the most important factors for prevention of suicidal action in children rests on the ability to recognize individuals at risk for suicidal behavior. This chapter will explore the approaches to clinical assessment of chilhood suicidal risk. It will discuss the necessary ingredients for a proper evaluation of preadolescents that include comprehensive knowledge of the phenomena and clinician's feelings, biases, and responses toward suicidal tendencies in children. Information from empirical research as well as my clinical experience working with large numbers of suicidal children will be the basis of discussion. Furthermore, I will argue against the hypothesis that suicidal tendencies of children arise from normal developmental turmoil.

LITERATURE REVIEW

Although completed suicide in prepubertal children is relatively low,[1,2] a comprehensive assessment of suicidal impulses in children is warranted. Suicidal impulses are expressed frequently by children in the forms of suicidal ideas, suicidal threats, and suicidal attempts.[3-5] Such statements as "I want to kill myself" are not uncommon among children. Actions such as a child holding a knife to his chest with the intent to kill himself are frequent frightening situations. Ingesting harmful substances is a familiar method of self-harm in youngsters. Jumping from heights, one of the most common suicidal techniques, has been reported widely.[3,4,6]

To date, most research on suicidal behavior in children has been conducted with psychiatric patient populations. These studies seem to conclude that suicidal behavior is a common symptom among psychiatric patients. For example, among psychiatric inpatients who were 6 to 12 years old, it has been documented that 72% of the children expressed suicidal ideas, threats or attempts.[3] In addition, the degree of severity of suicidal behavior seems to be less among less disturbed psychiatric outpatients. Among psychiatric outpatients, 33% of a randomly selected sample of children showed suicidal tendencies.[4]

At present, there is no empirical evidence to support the possibility that expression of suicidal impulses is a normal developmental process synonymous with episodes of transient developmental turmoil. In fact, there is some evidence against this. Shaffer,[2] in a systematic review of the coroner, school, medical, psychiatric, and social service reports of 31 children who committed suicide in England and Wales from 1962 to 1968, discovered that 46% of the children had previous suicidal thoughts, threats, or attempts. Eight of the children signaled their suicidal tendencies within 24 hours of their deaths. Shaffer believed that the number of children with previous history of suicidal tendencies was a definite underestimate.

Although it is evident that, among child victims of completed suicide, a high percentage showed earlier evidence of suicidal tendencies, it is not understood what distinguishes children who show suicidal ideas, threats, or attempts but did not commit suicide from those children who eventually commit suicide. It has been reported that there is approximately a 100:1 or 50:1 ratio between suicide attempts and completed suicide in children and adolescents.[7] However, until systematic studies provide more data about why some youngsters who attempt suicide do not go on to commit suicide, it is not wise to assume that suicidal behavior can be attributed to a phase of developmental turmoil. Rather, it is preferable to consider any suicidal communication as a signal of potential danger and of underlying psychiatric disorder.

Shaffer's study[2] showed that 30% of the children were seeing a psychiatrist or were on a waiting list for a psychiatric clinic at the time of their death. Six more children were recognized as having a conduct disorder or emotional problems at school, although they were not referred to a psychiatrist. His studies determined that a high percentage had associated psychiatric symptoms. Twenty-two children had antisocial symptoms and 21 children had emotional or affective symptoms. Seventeen of the children showed a combination of antisocial and emotional symptoms. That these children were emotionally disturbed argues against suicide being a phase of developmental turmoil.

There is very clear and convincing evidence that depression is related to childhood suicidal behavior. Studies of psychiatric inpatient and outpatient children show that acute and chronic depressions significantly correlate with the severity of suicidal preoccupations and actions.[3,4] These studies pointed out that depression is one of the most important risk factors for suicidal ideas, threats, or attempts in children.

Another study[8] validated the interactive effects of depression on suicidal tendencies in children. Carlson and Cantwell interviewed 102 children and adolescents, who were 6 to 16 years old and randomly selected from a psychiatric population. Severity of depression was assessed by clinical interview and by means of the Children's Depression Inventory, which is a self-rating scale. Severity of suicidal tendencies was evaluated by the interview and by the responses indicated on the Children's Depression Inventory Scale. For analysis of data, the children were divided into groups. Group A consisted of children who denied suicidal ideation in the interview and the self-report scale. Group B consisted of children who denied suicidal ideation on the self-report scale but admitted to thoughts in the interview. Group C children admitted to suicidal ideation on the interview and responded on the self-report scale that "I think about killing myself but would not do it." Group D children rated themselves as severely suicidal in the interview and checked off on the self-report scale that "I would like to kill myself" or "I would kill myself for sure if I had the chance."

The results of the study indicated that 45% of the total sample were in Group A. They were significantly younger than Group D children and contained more outpatients. The depression of Group A children was significantly lower than for Group C and Group D children. Forty-five children were in Group B and C combined. Their ages and depression ratings were on a continuum between children with no suicidal ideation and those with severe suicidal ideation. They were significantly more depressed than Group A children. Thirty-three percent of these children met criteria for major affective disorder. Twenty-four families of these 45 children had either depression alone, depression and alcoholism, or alcoholism alone. Group D contained 12 children who seriously felt like killing themselves. They were severely depressed. Eighty-three percent met the criteria for major affective disorder. Eight of these 12 children had families with either depression, depressive spectrum disorders or alcoholism alone. Among the 102 children and adolescents, 22 made a suicide attempt and significantly more of this group were adolescents. Only five preteens made suicide attempts. Thirty percent of these attempters were chronically depressed. Fifty percent of the families of the attempters had depression and other psychopathology.

The most important conclusion of the study was that there is a direct association between feeling depressed and feeling suicidal. It was determined that 63% of the patients who were depressed were suicidal compared to 34% who were suicidal but not depressed. However, there seemed to be a clearer relationship between suicidal ideation and depression than between suicidal attempts and depression. The reasons for this difference are yet to be more systematically studied.

Although depression is considered a major risk factor for suicidal tendencies in children, not all depressed children are suicidal. Also, little has been done to study systematically what distinguishes depressed children who will become suicidal from those who will not. The fact that depression, a defined psychiatric disorder, is so much related to suicidal behavior in children is an additional argument against the hypothesis that suicidal behavior is a normal developmental event. Instead, it can be argued that suicidal behavior is associated with the occurrence of psychiatric disorders of children.

One recent study was among the first to delineate differences between groups of suicidal depressed children, depressed children, and children with other psychiatric disorders.[5] Seventy-six child psychiatric inpatients, aged 5 to 14 years, were studied. In a review of medical records, the children were evaluated for measures of life stress and symptomatology during their total life span, during four defined developmental periods, and during the year preceding hospital admission. It was determined that the suicidal children experienced greater amounts of stress as they matured than the depressed children or children with other types of psychopathology. Specific family disruptions involving losses of important people were notable among the suicidal children. This study may lend more support to the notion that suicidal behavior is not a stage of developmental turmoil but rather a disturbance that arises because of specific environmental situations which produce pathological degrees of stress for the child.

Most studies of family contributors toward suicidal tendencies in children have not been systematic and usually lack adequate comparison groups. An exception to this was a study that investigated the psychopathology of parents of suicidal youngsters.[9] Parental psychological stress and disorders were systematically studied among 46 adolescent suicide attempters and 46 adolescent nonsuicidal individuals. The purpose of the study was to determine difference in factors relating to parental self-image. All the adolescents who were studied were seen at an emergency room of a large urban children's hospital. Parents of the adolescents were interviewed and a self-esteem questionnaire was administered.

The results indicated that the fathers of the suicidal attempters were significantly more depressed, had lower self-esteem, and consumed more alcohol than fathers of the nonsuicidal adolescents. The mothers of the adolescent suicide attempters were significantly more anxious, had more suicidal ideas, and consumed more alcohol than the mothers of the nonsuicidal youngsters. This study not only upheld the significance of depression and suicidal behavior among the parents of the suicidal youngsters, but amplified areas to be assessed in risk determination of suicidal children. It also pointed out that suicidal youngsters grow up in environments that hamper the child's healthy, adaptive functioning. Such children live with chronic turmoil and long-standing interactions with disturbed parents. These facts make it less likely that the appearance of suicidal behavior in children arises from normal developmental pressures. Instead, suicidal behavior seems to be the child's adaptive responses to disturbed environmental situations.

METHOD OF CLINICAL INTERVIEWING FOR CHILDHOOD SUICIDAL POTENTIAL

Studies are beginning to indicate that suicidal tendencies in children are not the result of normal developmental turmoil but are the outcome of a psychopathological process. Therefore, it is important that any expression of suicidal tendencies in children be taken very seriously and be considered a signal of intolerable stress.[10] Suicidal behavior in children requires, at the very least, exploratory psychiatric intervention. Given our current, newly acquired, body of knowledge about this phenomenon, it is preferable to err on the side of caution and consider any form of self-destructive expression, even if it is a child's fleeting statement, a serious concern that warrants professional assessment.

It has been clearly documented that the three factors of the child's depression, the child's preoccupations with death, and family suicidal tendencies are specific risk factors for suicidal behavior in children.[3,4] These factors must be systematically inquired about during the psychiatric assessment of suicidal potential of children. In fact, the variables and their component parts should be assessed whenever a child is evaluated psychiatrically.

The diagnosis of depression in children has been validated by many systematic studies.[8,11-15] There is consensus that analysis of the different research criteria used to study depression in children such as that developed by Cytryn and McKnew, Weinberg, Kovacs, and DSM-III show a striking overlap.[12] It has become a more accepted conclusion that childhood and adult diagnostic criteria for affective disorders are similar. Furthermore, the DSM-III manual is a valid instrument to be used for diagnosing childhood affective disorders. In addition, the concept of masked depression has been increasingly dispelled.[13] Such symptoms as hyperactivity, temper tantrums, delinquency, learning disabilities, psychophysiological disorders[16,17] previously believed to be symptoms of masked depression seem to be either only presenting symptoms or congruent additional diagnoses.

Carlson and Cantwell[13] proposed that for children with depression, behavior problems seem less severe and seem to postdate the onset of depressive symptoms. In children with both diagnoses and in children with behavior disorders alone, behavior problems were chronic and of greater magnitude. More recently, Puig-Antich[18] corroborated this impression in his findings which indicated that among children with major depressive disorder, one-third also fit the criteria for conduct disorder. In fact, successful treatment of the mood disorder with imipramine was followed by a decrease in conduct disorder in the majority of patients. It was noted that the appearance of the conduct disorder never preceded the onset of dysphoric mood. In addition, it was observed during a preliminary follow-up study of the patients that a recurrence of the depressive syndrome was always followed by a reappearance of a conduct disorder.

For clinical diagnosis of childhood depression, familiarity with DSM-III criteria is essential. According to DSM-III criteria,[19] the diagnosis of major depression in children, as in adults, includes dysphoric mood or loss of interest or pleasure in all or almost all usual activities and at least four of the following that have been present nearly every day for two weeks: poor appetite or weight loss, insomnia or hypersomnia, psychomotor agitation or retardation, loss of energy, fatigue, feelings of worthlessness, self-reproach, expressions of guilt, decreased ability to think or concentrate, recurrent thoughts of death, suicidal ideation, or suicide attempts. Chronic depression in children that is less severe than major depression is considered a dysthymic disorder. In children it includes a variety of symptoms similar to that for major depression but manifested for at least one year's duration. However, the degree of severity of symptoms is less than for major depression.

The evaluation of a child's current beliefs and concerns about death is essential in determining risk for suicidal behavior. The importance of a child's beliefs about death rests on the deterrent forces that may exist if a child believes death is final. Conversely, if death is considered temporary or pleasant, a child may be more inclined to take suicidal action. Death concepts and preoccupations in children fluctuate and are affected by the child's ego state. Therefore, if the child is under great stress, cognitive appreciation of the finality of death may change to a more regressed level in which the child believes death to be reversible. Consequently, it is not the age-expectable state of development that is important in assessing suicidal risk, but rather the actual level of ego functioning at the time of assessment for suicidal potential that must be determined.

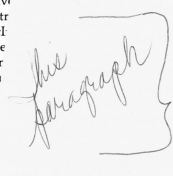

Child _____ _____ or attempts seem to be more preoccupi _____ deaths of friends or relatives and have _____ ith death than nonsuicidal psychiatr _____

McI _____ here are differences in ideas about de _____ lal children and that age is not the main _____ out death. They determined in 598 you _____ ages 13 to 16 years, 20% still conside _____ be cognizant, 60% thought of a spirit _____ ed that death was final. Among 18 you _____ had definite suicidal ideas, their concep _____ greater beliefs in temporariness of dea _____

C _____ out death and clinicians should not he _____ ersations. Dreams, fantasies, experien _____ death themes that can be readily elicite _____ ensitivity is advisable in talking with ch_____ _____ process of discussion the reward of obtaining a deeper understanding of a child's dilemma will be forthcoming. The following brief vignette will illustrate how discussion of a child's death preoccupations led to uncovering his suicidal tendencies.

Albert, an 11-year-old boy, was referred because of severe behavior problems in school that were thought to be related to his learning disabilities. His parents denied knowledge of any suicidal tendencies in their child. However, in the initial phase of the introductory meeting with Albert, he focused on his worries about an aunt who died several years before, another aunt who had a serious illness, and concern that his mother would get sick and die. His therapist was alerted by the child's intensity and repetitious remarks about death and, as a result, inquired whether "he ever thought about his own death or wished that he would die?" He then stated that often at school he thinks about "running to the classroom window and jumping out. I know that it would kill me because my classroom is six floors up."

It is essential that clinicians always ask children about their suicidal tendencies. Any child who is in psychiatric evaluation should be asked about this. Examples of the kinds of questions that can be asked are: "Did you ever feel that things were so upsetting that you wished you would die? Have you been feeling so sad, angry, or upset that you thought of killing yourself? Did you ever want to commit suicide?" The questions should be asked in a variety of ways so that the child will fully understand the issues of inquiry. In addition, they must be asked sensitively and directly. Inferences are not sufficient in this type of evaluation. In fact, children feel more comfortable when they know that suicide can be spoken about openly. Furthermore, questions should be presented simply. "Have you thought of killing yourself? Did you ever want to commit suicide?" This helps the child focus directly on the issue and not be distracted by other issues or concepts.

There is a consensus that unbearable family disruption enhances the risk in children of both psychiatric disorders and suicidal behavior. Shaffer[2] discovered that, among the 31 children who committed suicide, seven came from broken homes which were predominantly due to divorce. Six sets of parents who were living together at the time of the child's death separated or divorced between one and four years after the death of the child. Whether the break-up of these families was due to parental problems predating the child's death or subsequent to the child's death is unknown. Another form of family turmoil among the families studied by Shaffer was the degree of mental illness among the parents. Fifty-five percent of the families had one or more persons who consulted a psychiatrist or received treatment for emotional symptoms. In four cases, a parent or sibling demonstrated suicidal behavior. In three additional cases, there were suicide attempts among first-degree relatives. Unfortunately, comparison groups of families were not part of Shaffer's study so that understanding the full meaning of these facts awaits further investigation using index and comparison samples.

Among psychiatric inpatient and outpatient children, one specific family factor for childhood suicidal ideas, threats, and attempts was a history of suicidal behavior among the parents.[3,4] Gathering a history of parental suicidal behavior is often difficult. Because of family dynamics, social stigma, and lack of initial trust, parents are secretive about their own suicidal proclivities. In addition, family dynamics may be such that the child's suicidal tendencies result from an acting out of parental conscious or unconscious wishes. One form of ominous family interactions was highlighted by Sabbath.[21] He talked about the concept of the expendable child. In this concept, the child perceives the parents' conscious and unconscious wishes to be rid of the child or for the child to die. The child feels that he is to blame for family problems and acts out parental wishes by suicide.

I have observed that it is possible for some parents to acknowledge having suicidal tendencies only after the child's suicidal impulses have abated. This may be due to a shift in family dynamic equilibrium when the child is no longer acting out the parental suicidal wishes. Interviews with the parents alone and in the presence of the child should be performed during any evaluation of a potentially suicidal child. The clinician is able in such interviews to assess direct and indirect aspects of communication, preoccupations, themes, and ability of the family to gain insight into their style of relating which may be contributing factors to increased suicidal risk for a child.

DISCUSSION

The clinical assessment of suicidal risk requires that a methodical inquiry be used and that it integrate a clinician's skill in speaking with children, knowledge of suicidal phenomena, and conscious and unconscious attitudes to issues of death and suicide. Unfortunately, many clinicians have not acquired the necessary skills for such diagnostic work primarily because of lack of sufficient familiarity with suicidal phenomena in children, lack of experience working with suicidal children, and a variety of conscious and unconscious feelings and perceptions about suicide and dying. The earlier sections of this chapter discussed information that is useful for the clinician's basis of knowledge.

Very little has been written about the conscious attitudes and unconscious feelings or countertransference feelings of therapists who work with suicidal children. Yet, this issue is one of the most important factors in insuring the proper evaluation of suicidal youngsters. The most common and problematic reaction of clinicians is intense anxiety generated by being involved with a suicidal child. Anxiety arises most because of the fear of unpredictability that a suicidal child may suddenly act out his or her suicidal impulses. Another worry of clinicians stems from lack of sufficient ability to forecast definitively which child may attempt or commit suicide. A third form of anxiety arises from feelings of responsibility for the safety of a suicidal child. In addition, anxiety occurs when decisions have to be made about the immediate therapeutic course of intervention of a suicidal child.

All children who consult a psychiatrist should be evaluated for suicidal impulses. This principle is the same as that used in the format for the psychiatric mental status examination of adults. There is now firm evidence that among preadolescent psychiatric patients, suicidal threats or attempts are relatively common. Therefore, any clinical biases of the therapist about suicidal behavior in children must be suspended in order to insure that an objective account of a child's suicidal state is obtained; and any other personal reactions on the part of the therapist need to be understood and contained.

Unfortunately, far too often, clinicians do not embark upon a systematic evaluation of children's suicidal tendencies. Frequently, an unstructured interview approach is used and only clinical inferences are made about the degree of suicidal risk. Many clinicians hesitate in having an open conversation about suicide with their child patients because clinicians fear that such discussions will frighten the child or facilitate converting the child's ideas into suicidal action. Other clinicians deny suicidal tendencies in their patients because of their own conscious or unconscious reactions about death, rejection, hostility, and responses to parental figures. Finally, many clinicians worry that they may not be able to intervene appropriately.

Intense anxiety has been clearly acknowleged by one child psychoanalyst[22] who said that "A child's vehement expression 'If I die they'll start loving me' makes me shudder, and I feel safe only if this stage has subsided" (page 838). This statement depicts an almost universal concern of clinicians working with suicidal patients. The contribution of a clinician's conscious and unconscious personal experiences, wishes, and fantasies in fostering his or her levels of anxiety must be understood through processes of self-analysis, peer supervision about work with suicidal patients, and personal therapy. The hardest task for a therapist is to resolve those personal factors that increase anxiety in working with suicidal patients. Nevertheless, the more objectivity a therapist has about himself or herself and about the characteristics of suicidal behavior in children, the better equipped he or she will be in working with suicidal youngsters.

Fears that children will make use of discussion about suicide by acting out these tendencies is quite unfounded. Children who are not suicidal will respond appropriately to questions about suicidal impulses. They will respond openly and directly. In addition, most children who have suicidal proclivities will acknowledge them. In fact, such children may find it quite comforting and even surprising to know that someone is able to talk with them about such scary notions. Discussion of suicidal tendencies can help toward reaching a resolution of these feelings.

Speaking to children about death or about self-destructive wishes ought not be a therapeutic taboo. This principle was clearly demonstrated in the systematic studies of Koocher[23] when working with children dying of terminal illness. He noted that children are capable of speaking about death and that they find it helpful to know that there are no barriers to this type of discussion. In fact, the basic premise of any psychotherapy is to maximize open discussion, make use of objective self-analysis, and reach new insights through enhancing self-awareness. Direct communication is of paramount importance in work with suicidal children. Some of the dynamic aspects of suicidal behavior are based upon the child's inferences and nonverbal perceptions that he or she is disliked, bad, and blameworthy.[21] Open dialogue between child and therapist may improve the child's sense of trust, self-esteem, and working through of confusing fantasies and perceptions.

When a therapist agrees to see a suicidal child, he or she must be well prepared to intervene immediately and in a variety of ways. Several basic principles must be followed. It is wise for a therapist not to see too many suicidal individuals at any given time especially since the degree of a therapist's anxiety may reach intolerable proportions. Sufficient time is required to interview the child and parents satisfactorily; to assess the type of therapeutic alliance that can be developed between child, parent and therapist; and to plan for the next therapeutic action. Finally, the therapist must have available a variety of therapeutic modalities that can be invoked immediately. Most importantly, the therapist should have the services of a psychiatric or pediatric hospital unit available, if this should be indicated, to insure greater safety of the child.[10] Knowing that backup services exist will help allay the anxiety of clinicians who work with suicidal children.

The therapist should fully understand that total responsibility for the well being and safety of a suicidal child does not rest entirely with the therapist. The primary responsibility of self-preservation is held by the child and his family. All must openly acknowledge this responsibility in order to develop a genuine atmosphere in the work to diminish the child's self-destructive tendencies. However, if this responsibility is not accepted by the child or his parents, the safety of the child can less adequately be insured without the use of a round-the-clock therapeutic environment such as that offered in a hospital setting.

This brief discussion outlines some of the personal and strategic factors that apply in work with suicidal youngsters.

REFERENCES

1. Holinger PC: Adolescent suicide: An epidemiological study of recent trends. *Am J Psychiatry* 1978;135:754–756.
2. Shaffer D: Suicide in childhood and early adolescence. *J Child Psychol Psychiatry* 1974;15:275–291.
3. Pfeffer CR, Conte HR, Plutchik R, et al: Suicidal behavior in latency-age children: An empirical study. *J Am Acad Child Psychiatry* 1979;18:679–692.
4. Pfeffer CR, Conte HR, Plutchik R, et al: Suicidal behavior in latency-age children: An outpatient population. *J Am Acad Child Psychiatry* 1980;19:703–710.
5. Cohen-Sandler R, Berman AL, King RA: Life stress and symptomatology: Determinants of suicidal behavior in children. *J Am Acad Child Psychiatry* 1982;21:178–186.
6. Bender L, Schilder P: Suicidal preoccupations and attempts in childhood. *Am J Orthopsychiatry* 1937;7:225–234.
7. Jacobziner H: Attempted suicides in children. *J Pediatr* 1960;56:519–525.
8. Carlson GA, Cantwell DP: Suicidal behavior and depression in children and adolescents. *J Am Acad Child Psychiatry* 1982;21:361–368.

9. Tishler CL, McKenry PC: Parental negative self and adolescent suicide attempts. *J Am Acad Child Psychiatry* 1982;21:404–408.
10. Pfeffer CR: Psychiatric hospital treatment of latency age suicidal children: *Suicide Life Threat Behav* 1978;8:150–160.
11. Cantwell DP, Carlson G: Problems and prospects in the study of childhood depression. *J Nerv Ment Dis* 1979;167:522–529.
12. Cytryn L, McKnew DH, Bunney WE Jr: Diagnosis of depression in children: A reassessment. *Am J Psychiatry* 1980;137:22–25.
13. Carlson GA, Cantwell DP: Unmasking masked depression in children and adolescents. *Am J Psychiatry* 1980;137:445–449.
14. Puig-Antich J: Affective disorders in childhood. *Psychiatr Clin North Am* 1980;3:403–424.
15. Kashani JH, Hussain A, Shekim WO, et al: Current Perspectives on childhood depression: An overview. *Am J Psychiatry* 1981;138:143–153.
16. Glaser K: Masked depression in children and adolescents. *Am J Psychotherapy* 1967;21:565–574.
17. Toolan JM: Depression in children and adolescents. *Am J Orthopsychiatry* 1962;32:404–415.
18. Puig-Antich J: Major depression and conduct disorder in pre-puberty. *J Am Acad Child Psychiatry* 1982;21:118–128.
19. American Psychiatric Association Committee on Nomenclature and Statistics: *Diagnostic and Statistical Manual of Mental Disorders*, ed 3. Washington, DC, American Psychiatric Association, 1980.
20. McIntire MS, Angle CR: The taxonomy of suicide and self-poisoning — A pediatric perspective, in Wells CF, Stuart IR (eds): *Self-Destructive Behavior in Children and Adolescents*. New York, Van Nostrand Reinhold Co, 1981, pp 224–250.
21. Sabbath JC: The suicidal adolescent — The expendable child. *J Am Acad Child Psychiatry* 1969;8:272–289.
22. Lowental U: Suicide — The other side: The factor of reality among suicidal motivations. *Arch Gen Psychiatry* 1976;33:838–842.
23. Koocher GP: Talking with children about death. *Am J Orthopsychiatry* 1974;44:404–411.

CHAPTER 12

STRUCTURED ASSESSMENT OF PSYCHIATRIC DIAGNOSIS AND OF PSYCHOSOCIAL FUNCTION AND SUPPORTS IN ADOLESCENCE: A Role in the Secondary Prevention of Suicide

G. DAVIS GAMMON
KAREN JOHN
MYRNA M. WEISSMAN

In this chapter, we consider the role that the structured assessment of psychiatric diagnosis and psychosocial functioning may play in the identification of the suicidal adolescent. Structured diagnostic and psychosocial assessment, until recently considered solely the domain of clinical research, may profitably be incorporated into the battery of psychological tests routinely administered to troubled children and adolescents who present to the mental health professional for psychiatric evaluation and treatment. In support of the feasibility and clinical utility of this approach to the identification of the suicidal youth, we present data from a pilot study of a small sample of hospitalized adolescents in which we pretested a structured assessment battery. In addition to finding the assessment battery useful, we found a remarkable lack of consistency between the patients' clinical diagnoses and diagnoses arrived at by other means.

The Magnitude of the Problem: The Age Group at Risk

Because suicide in children under the age of 5 has not been reported and rates for 5 to 14 year olds are consistently low (less than 1.5/100,000 annually) and have not varied appreciably in recent years,[1-2] we will restrict our attention to adolescents between the ages of 15 and 19 years (though structured assessment techniques may be useful adjuncts to traditional evaluation methods in the younger adolescent and latency age child, as well). For the 15- to 19-year-old group, the risk of suicide has trebled in the past 20 years, and death by suicide now approaches an annual rate of eight per 100,000 among adolescents, ages 15 to 19.[2] While this rate is only about one-half that reported for the general population,[2] suicide has become the third leading cause of death of adolescents in the United States,[3] and thus a public health problem of considerable magnitude for which prevention strategies are sorely lacking.

Levels of Prevention: Where to Intervene

There are at least two levels of prevention: primary and secondary.[4] Primary prevention implies understanding and modifying the causes of a condition so that it occurs with decreased frequency or not at all. Secondary prevention implies intervention in a disease process to modify its outcome — either through its cure, amelioration, or arrest.

Attempts to understand the causes of suicide have resulted in a variety of etiologic models that might explain the occurrence of suicidal behavior. Holinger and Offer[5] have suggested that these models encompass four general categories: 1) sociocultural or socioeconomic; 2) psychodynamic or intrapsychic; 3) diagnostic or psychopathologic; and 4) biologic. That no single etiologic model is sufficient to explain the cause of suicide is exemplified by the findings from a study by Paykel and associates.[6] In their study suicidal ideation was found to be quite common in the general population, but only a small fraction of individuals with suicidal ideation had actually attempted suicide. Several variables were found to intervene between suicidal ideation and suicidal behavior in Paykel's sample, and were analogous to three of Hollinger and Offer's suggested models: 1) sociocultural factors, eg, social isolation; 2) psychological factors, eg, character structure; and 3) nosological factors, eg, affective illness. However, there were complex interactions among the three variables that proved elusive, and unifactorial models could not explain the occurrence of suicidal behavior in that general population sample — though they were useful in identifying "at risk" subgroups. The authors concluded that more complex multifactorial probabilistic models based on further research are required if we are to have a less rudimentary notion of cause.[6]

Moreover, many of the putative causes of suicide, and therefore potential targets of primary prevention, touch on the fundamental structure of modern life. For example, some years ago Durkheim[7] identified the lack of social integration, the absence of a cohesive value system, and the variety of social transitions required of an individual, as factors in society that contribute to an increase in self-destructiveness. A life-style that includes geographic mobility, separation from the extended family, and a high frequency of divorce and single parent families has evolved since

World War II in the United States and in Europe, and as a consequence has contributed to social isolation and the weakening of available social and emotional ties. The family, church, and schools, which once served to integrate young persons into a social group and provided models of behavior and values, are less available as effective resources, and no ready remedy is apparent. In this context, modern industrial society constitutes a high-risk environment quite resistant to modification. Currently, secondary level intervention thus appears to be the only practical approach to the prevention of suicide among young people.

Of the etiologic models or explanatory frames, the diagnostic or nosological is most proximal to the suicidal act. Much suicidal behavior, whether completed or not, occurs within the context of a discrete psychiatric disorder,[5,6,8-16] usually a major affective disorder or schizophrenia, often in conjunction with or complicated by alcohol/substance use/ dependency disorders or specific personality disorders. The timely identification of such disorders offers promise as a means to identify adolescents at risk for suicidal behavior, and provides an opportunity for secondary prevention through psychosocial and/or somatic therapies. Moreover, social maladjustment or an inadequate support system may increase the risk of suicide,[6,15] and preventive intervention directed toward the improvement of the adolescent's social adjustment and social supports might serve to modify the risk of suicide in the context of a major psychiatric disorder. Recently developed research instruments now permit the reliable and structured assessment of diagnostic and social variables in adolescence.

STRUCTURED ASSESSMENT IN ADOLESCENCE

Application of Formal Diagnostic Criteria to Adolescents

Although there has been a debate about the prevalence of affective disorders among adolescents, as well as about the usefulness of the formal diagnostic assessment with this age group, increasing evidence demonstrates the reliability, validity, and clinical utility of the nosological approach in this population. Because adolesence has been viewed traditionally as a period of great psychological and behavioral instability, clinicians have found it difficult to distinguish normal from psychopathological development, and symptoms and dysfunctional behaviors often have been considered to be transient and mutable.[17-19] From this perspective, descriptive, nosological diagnosis has been considered of limited validity.

On the other hand, epidemiologic studies of adolescent groups have provided little support for the concept of adolescent turmoil as a phenomenon.[20-23] Several specific findings emerged from these and other studies[24-28] that support the utility of descriptive diagnosis for clinical work and psychiatric research. First, only a small portion of adolescents have been found to manifest significantly impaired psychosocial adaptation.[20-23] Second, symptoms, behavioral disturbances, and impaired psychosocial adaptation do not appear to be benign and transitory phenomena, but rather appear predictive of the persistence of such disturbances in adulthood.[24-28] When descriptive diagnoses are assigned to such patients, these diagnoses are likely to agree with those made with similar criteria later in adulthood.[24-26, 28]

Other recent studies have demonstrated the reliability of formal descriptive diagnosis in adolescence, based on strictly specified diagnostic criteria,[29-32] as well as the validity of specific disorders, the occurrence of which in adolescence was widely doubted or regarded as extremely rare.[33-35] Strober and Carlson,[33] for example, reported their experience with the use of 13 DSM-III categories to classify the psychiatric illness of 95 adolescents consecutively admitted to UCLA. There was complete agreement for more that 75% of the cases, and levels of agreement for Schizophrenia and Major Affective Disorders were comparable to those achieved in recently reported adult samples. Other studies by the same group[34,35] have examined predictor variables such as treatment response, cross-sectional symptom patterns, and family-genetic factors. These studies support the validity of using adult diagnostic criteria for the diagnosis of unipolar depressive and bipolar syndromes in adolescence. Other recent studies have examined a variety of issues bearing on the validity and frequency of occurrence of major affective disorders in adolescence.[36,37]

Structured Interviews and
Specified Diagnostic Criteria

One of the major advances in recent years in psychiatric diagnosis has been the development of structured diagnostic interviews that have been designed for use in conjunction with highly specified sets of diagnostic criteria to generate formal descriptive diagnoses. These interviews and diagnostic systems, when employed by trained clinical interviewers, reduce the several sources of variance[38] that compromise the reliability and measurement validity of clinical diagnoses generated by more informal clinical interviews.

The success of such approaches in facilitating the acquisition of highly reliable diagnostic information was perhaps the major impetus for the development of the third edition of the *Diagnostic and Statistical Manual* of the American Psychiatric Association (DSM-III).[39] This manual, developed by a task force of experts under the leadership of Robert Spitzer, was designed to provide researchers and clinicians with well-operationalized sets of criteria that define the major psychiatric disorders of children and adults. To the extent that it was possible, the task force based the criteria on clinical, epidemiological, and genetic-biochemical data that had supported the construct validity of such disorders.

The DSM-III[39] employs a multiaxial diagnostic system. All of the mental disorders are coded on Axes I or II, while on the remaining axes, physical conditions, psychosocial stressors and psychosocial functioning within the year prior are coded. The disorders listed on Axis II are the personality disorders and the specific developmental disorders. The other mental disorders and conditions are included in Axis I. The DSM-III permits the concurrent diagnosis of multiple disorders on Axes I and II. The DSM-III, Axis I diagnostic criteria were those used in the pilot study to be described below.

Several structured diagnostic interviews have been developed recently for use in conjunction with the DSM-III to obtain diagnostic information directly from children and adolescents and/or from parents about their children. Such information is used to make a wide variety of DSM-III diagnoses. The interviews include the Schedule for Affective Disorders for School Aged Children,[40-42] available in present (Kiddie-SADS-P) and epidemiological (K-SADS-E) versions, the Diagnostic Interview for Children and Adolescents (DICA)[30-32,43] and the Child Assessment Schedule (CAS).[44-46] In addition, the center for Epidemiological Studies (CES) is currently developing an interview for use by lay interviewers, the Diagnostic Interview Schedule for Children (DIS-C).[47,48] Although the DIS-C is still being developed, it appears quite promising for use in epidemiologic studies and in clinical settings in which highly trained interviewers are not available.

For use in the pilot study, we chose the K-SADS-E for the following reasons: 1) the K-SADS-E assesses both current and lifetime diagnoses; 2) at the time of the study, the K-SADS-E was completely developed, while the DICA and the DIS-C were still under development, and psychometric data on the CAS had not yet been reported; 3) what psychometric data were available suggested the K-SADS-E was a strong instrument capable of collecting highly reliable and valid diagnostic data. Moreover, our experience with the K-SADS-E tended to confirm the promise of this interview. However, for various clinical and research applications the other interviews may be equally or more appropriate. The K-SADS-E is described in detail in the methods section below.

Social Adjustment and Its Measurement

The presence of relatively intact social adjustment (ie, adequate role functioning and social network) has appeared to "protect" individuals from depression,[49] and, in the context of a major affective disorder, to modify the risk of suicide.[6] Unfortunately, research exploring the influence of social adjustment on mental illness and suicidal behavior has been restricted to adults, probably because the development of quantitative, empirical research methods to assess social functioning in children and adolescents has lagged behind the development of methods in adult psychiatry.

Weissman and associates have identified 28 measures for the assessment of adult social adjustment in clinical and in psychiatric epidemiology studies, scales that reasonably meet criteria for reliability, validity and utility.[50,51] We have recently examined measures of social competence — the construct of social functioning usually employed in the child and adolescent psychosocial literature as the analog of social adjustment — and have found no measures of social functioning in children and adolescents that meet similar criteria.

Moreover, within the child competence literature, we found that instruments typically were designed to measure the relative competence of children with severe handicaps, or a child's school performance. An exception to this is the social competence section of Achenbach's Child Behavior Checklist.[52-58] We could find no articles in which social competence or social adjustment instruments were said to assess the influence of social competence on the risk for the acquisition of psychiatric disorders or for suicidal behavior in adolescents or children. While many anecdotal reports describe various aspects of social adjustment in the context of a psychiatric disturbance in this age group, few have considered its influence in a systematic way. To fill an apparent need for a social adjustment instrument for use with children and adolescents, we devised one that we included and tested in our pilot study of adolescent inpatients. This instrument, the Social Adjustment Inventory for Children and Adolescents (SAICA), is described in the methods section below.

Achenbach's Child Behavior Checklist[52-58] and the SAICA each provide a means to identify areas of relative social dysfunction in young people who present for evaluation or treatment, areas that might then become the target of subsequent intervention. Achenbach's Child Behavior Checklist is considerably briefer to complete than the SAICA, and is given as a self-administered questionnaire to a parent (if the child is aged 4 to 18) and/or a child (if the child is aged 11 to 18), whereas the SAICA is a semistructured interview administered by a trained clinician. The Child Behavior Checklist may therefore be preferable for use in many clinical and research settings in which a more exhaustive evaluation of social functioning is not required. The SAICA, on the other hand, may be given to a child (aged 6 to 18), his parent, or both, and provides a more detailed assessment of social functioning and of social supports. Moreover, while the Child Behavior Checklist provides an assessment of the child's social functioning only for the past year, the SAICA may be administered retrospectively to construct a chronological profile of social adjustment.

Both instruments have advantages over informal clinical evaluation of social functioning in that they permit a highly reliable and relatively complete assessment of social functioning over a broad range of areas, such as academic performance, peer relations, and leisure activities. Informal clinical evaluations may overlook important areas of social functioning or assess areas of adjustment less uniformly.

PILOT STUDY: THE ASSESSMENT OF ADOLESCENT INPATIENTS

Methods

Setting The study was conducted at a small university-affiliated psychiatric hospital that specializes in the residential care of adolescents and young adults.

Sample Twenty-one adolescents (aged 13 to 18) were inpatients on the hospital's ward at the time of study (March–June, 1981). The criteria for admission to the study were that patients be between the ages of 13 and 18 years, inclusively, that the patient and his/her mother agree conjointly to participate, and that there be no evidence of organic mental disorder. Seventeen of 21 patient-mother pairs (81%) who were eligible to participate at the time, entered the study. Three of 21 patients were judged by the staff as too disturbed to participate — though some actively psychotic patients were able to participate — and one patient refused. Therefore, 17 patients: 13 males and four females, fully participated in the study.

Assessments The battery included demographic, medical, developmental, familial, and psychosocial assessments. The K-SADS-E and SAICA were used to determine a patient's diagnoses and social adjustment, respectively, through interviews with patients and their mothers. Four highly trained raters blind to each other's findings interviewed mother, child, or reviewed the hospital chart. Patients, mothers, and selected hospital staff independently completed self-administered reports. Study design, self-administered reports, training, and evaluation procedures are described elsewhere (GD Gammon, K John: YPI Pilot Study Protocol: Pretest of Reliability and Validity of Child Assessment Batteries, 1981, unpublished).

The Schedule for Affective Disorders and Schizophrenia for School-Aged Children and Adolescents, Epidemiologic Version (the Kiddie SADS-E or K-SADS-E) is a semistructured, diagnostic interview that was developed by Puig-Antich and associates[41] for administration to 6 to 18 year olds. Structured similarly to the Schedule for Affective Disorders and Schizophrenia, Lifetime Version (SADS-L), from which it was adapted, the K-SADS-E is intended for use by highly proficient clinical raters, who have received from 10 to 15 hours of training in its administration. The interview takes about 15 minutes with subjects who have no clinical disorders, and no longer than 60 minutes with subjects who have multiple disorders.

The K-SADS-E is designed to generate RDC and DSM-III diagnoses (both current and lifetime) for the nonaffective, nonorganic psychoses, major affective disorders, panic disorder, phobic disorders, obsessive-compulsive disorder, and alcohol/substance use disorders, and DSM-III diagnoses for infantile autism, anorexia nervosa, attention deficit disorder, conduct disorder and overanxious disorder of childhood. The presence of suicidal ideation, the number and severity of suicidal attempts, and the seriousness of the subject's suicidal intention are also assessed.

Puig-Antich et al[40] performed reliability and validity work on the K-SADS-P, which assesses current psychiatric status,[41] and Orvaschel et al recently reported on the validity of the K-SADS-E in a group of prepubescent children (6 to 13 years old).[42]

The Social Adjustment Inventory for Children and Adolescents is based conceptually on a modification of the model of social role adjustment used in adult scales and, as such, can produce data on social adjustment potentially comparable to those derived from adult scales. Within such a conceptual framework, social role adjustment constitutes the transactions of the person with the social environment. These role transactions are varied and complex, but since they are performed in relatively well-specified circumstances, the assessment of social role adjustment should provide a sensitive and valid index of social adjustment in children and adolescents.

The SAICA is a 78-item, semistructured interview with well-defined anchor points, which takes from 10 to 60 minutes to administer, depending on the age of the subject (ie, the number of grade spans covered). It is suitable for school-aged subjects (6 to 18 years of age) or it may be administered to parents about their children. Social role adjustment is assessed in the four areas in which a child or adolescent typically transacts: school, spare-time activities, relations with peers (including heterosexual for subjects 12 to 18 years old), and home life. Each role area is comprised of items that assess both competent behaviors demanded of and potential problem behaviors within that role. This division of items was adopted to yield assessments of role performance from very competent to incompetent and of problem behaviors from absent to severe (each on a four-point scale). Currently, scores for each of 11 subscales can be obtained as well as an overall score. With further work, useful factors or clusters also may be identified. These subscales are as follows:

- *School Academic*: a score derived from the subject's academic performance and "track" assignment.
- *School Social*: a score based on the subject's relations with classmates and teachers.
- *School Problems*: a score based on the presence and severity of 11 problem behaviors at school.
- *Spare-time Activities*: a score based on a subject's participation in eight kinds of spare-time activities.
- *Spare-time Problems*: a score based on the presence and severity of seven spare-time problems.
- *Peer Relationships*: a score based on five normative behaviors with peers.
- *Peer Problems*: a score based on 11 peer problem behaviors.
- *Peer Heterosexual Adjustment*: a score based on four normative and four problem heterosexual behaviors.
- *Sibling Relations*: a score based on three normative and six problem peer relations items.
- *Parent Relations*: a score based on three normative behaviors with each parent (six items).
- *Home Problems*: a score based on four home adjustment problem items.
- *Total Score*: the arithmetic mean of all subscale scores.

Because the SAICA has been developed only recently, its psychometric properties have not been fully established. In the pilot study, the SAICA questions were administered iteratively to patients and their mothers for grades 1–3, 4–6, 7–9, and 10–12 to produce retrospective and current assessments of social adjustment.

Diagnostic sources   Five sets of diagnoses were used in the study:

1) *Patients by K-SADS-E interview*. A single interviewer conducted all patient interviews. Diagnostic information obtained from the patient was recorded on a precoded scoring sheet from which DSM-III and RDC diagnoses were made.

2) *Mother by K-SADS-E interview*. Two interviewers blind to chart and patient diagnosis interviewed the mothers. Diagnostic data were recorded on a second copy of the precoded scoring sheet.

3) *Chart diagnoses*. Another independent rater exhaustively reviewed all relevant clinical materials contained in the charts, and coded all symptoms and information about clinical course from which DSM-III and RDC diagnoses could be made onto a third precoded scoring sheet.

4) *Clinician diagnoses from chart review*. The chart reviewer also recorded diagnoses that hospital clinicians gave to a patient in the course of the hospitalization in a special section of the third precoded scoring sheet.

5) *Best estimate diagnoses.* After the completion of data collection and processing, three independent diagnosticians reviewed all sources of information (including family history and treatment response — variables not considered in the other diagnoses) and generated a separate set of RDC and DSM-III best estimate diagnoses.

Assessment of suicidality In the K-SADS-E, a subject is asked about the presence of, or a past history of suicidal ideation or behavior. Five levels of severity may be scored: 1) not present; 2) recurrent thoughts of death; 3) wishes to be dead; 4) specific suicidal ideation; 5) suicidal behavior. If suicidal behavior is present, the subject is asked about the number of such behaviors and age at each attempt; the severity of the act is rated from 1 to 6 (no danger to very extreme), and the subject's intent is estimated on a six-point scale (obviously no intent to every expectation of death). From these data, we constructed a six-point summary scale that was inserted on the precoded scoring sheet: 0 = suicidal ideation denied; 1 = mild suicidal ideation (life not worth living; recurrent thoughts of death); 2 = moderate ideation (wishes to be dead); 3 = serious ideation (specific thoughts of suicide, usually a plan); 4 = suicide gesture (serious but not life-threatening, definite intent but ambivalent); 5 = suicide attempt (life-threatening, serious intent). Because clinicians' descriptions of suicidal ideation or behavior were the basis for the chart review ratings, there were only four suicidality scores to be compared.

Results

Demographic variable Table 12-1 presents the basic demographic variables. All patients were between 15 and 18 years of age. The mean age of patients at the time of interview was 17.1 years. Males outnumbered females by approximately three to one, which is typical of the unit and reflects the increased risk of hospitalization in adolescent males. Social classes (Hollingshead) I and II were somewhat over represented, and the IQ (WISC-R) distribution was skewed rightward with a mean of 110. No relationship between any of the demographic variables and patients' diagnostic status was evident.

Feasibility of instrument administration All patients and their mothers were able to complete the interviews and self-administered reports. Even when multiple diagnoses were present, the K-SADS-E was completed within 90 minutes, and the SAICA took no longer than 60 minutes to administer. In several instances patients and mothers remarked on the usefulness of the interviews in helping them to review the patient's history.

Agreement between diagnostic sources for primary diagnoses Table 12-2 presents primary diagnoses from each diagnostic source. Inspection of the table suggests that concordance of primary DSM-III

Table 12-1
Patients by Sex, Age, Social Class, and IQ (N = 17)

	Percent
SEX	
Males	76
Females	24
Total	100
AGE	
15 Years	24
17 Years	30
18 Years	46
Total	100
IQ (WISC FULL SCALE)	
87–99	25
100–109	25
110–119	25
120–135	25
Total	100
SOCIOECONOMIC STATUS (Hollingshead)	
I and II	58
III	18
IV and V	24
Total	100

diagnoses derived from the structured interview of patient and mother, respectively, was high. Only in cases 1, 5 and 11 was there substantive discrepancy.

The agreement between primary DSM-III diagnoses derived from chart review and hospital clinicians' diagnoses was not as good. The principal source of discordance was found in the five cases (patients #3, 8, 15, 16 and 17) that were assigned primary DSM-III, Axis I diagnoses from the chart review and DSM-III, Axis II (personality disorder) diagnoses from clinicians. A limitation of the chart review — as well as of the K-SADS-E and other structured diagnostic instruments — is that it has not been designed to collect clinical data from which Axis II diagnoses can be made.

The agreement between primary DSM-III diagnoses derived either from patients or their mothers and chart diagnoses, whether from chart review or from clinicians, was disappointing. The major source of discordance was in the diagnosis of Bipolar (I) Disorder and Atypical Bipolar (II) Disorder. Although structured interviews yielded six cases of bipolar disorder, hospital sources failed to identify a single case. While

Table 12-2
DSM-III Diagnoses from All Sources

Patient #	Structured Interview		Hospital Chart		Summary
	Patients	Mother	Chart Review	Hospital Clinicians	Best Estimate
1	Schizoaffective Disorder	Schizophrenia	Schizophrenia	Schizophrenia	Schizoaffective Disorder
2	Major Depressive Disorder (Recurrent)	Major Depressive Disorder (Recurrent)	Major Depressive Disorder	Major Depressive Disorder	Major Depressive Disorder (Recurrent)
3	Major Depressive Disorder (Recurrent)	Major Depressive Disorder (Recurrent)	Major Depressive Disorder	Borderline Personality Disorder	Major Depressive Disorder (Recurrent)
4	Conduct Disorder	Conduct Disorder	Conduct Disorder	Conduct Disorder	Conduct Disorder
5	Atypical Bipolar (II) Disorder	Major Depressive Disorder		Atypical Depression	Atypical Bipolar (II) Disorder
6	Bipolar (I) Disorder	Bipolar (I) Disorder	Schizophrenia	Atypical Psychosis	Bipolar (I) Disorder
7	Conduct Disorder	Conduct Disorder	Conduct Disorder	Conduct Disorder	Conduct Disorder
8	Atypical Bipolar (II) Disorder	Atypical Bipolar (II) Disorder	Conduct Disorder	Borderline Personality Disorder	Atypical Bipolar (II) Disorder
9	Schizoaffective Disorder	Schizoaffective Disorder	Schizophrenia	Schizophrenia	Schizoaffective Disorder
10	Conduct Disorder	Conduct Disorder	Conduct Disorder	Conduct Disorder	Conduct Disorder
11	Major Depressive Disorder (Recurrent)	Conduct Disorder	Conduct Disorder	Conduct Disorder	Major Depressive Disorder (Recurrent)
12	Conduct Disorder	Conduct Disorder	Conduct Disorder	Conduct Disorder	Conduct Disorder
13	Atypical Bipolar (II) Disorder	Bipolar (I) Disorder	Major Depressive Disorder	Major Depressive Disorder	Atypical Bipolar (II) Disorder
14	Schizophrenia	Schizophrenia	Schizophrenia	Schizophrenia	Schizophrenia
15	Atypical Psychosis	Atypical Psychosis	Conduct Disorder	Narcissistic Personality Disorder	Atypical Psychosis
16	Bipolar (I) Disorder	Bipolar (I) Disorder	Atypical Psychosis	Narcissistic Personality Disorder	Bipolar (I) Disorder
17	Bipolar (I) Disorder	Bipolar (I) Disorder	Major Depressive Disorder	Borderline Personality Disorder	Bipolar (I) Disorder

the use of Axis II primary diagnoses also was a source of discordance between diagnoses derived from structured interviews and hospital clinicians' diagnoses, when the clinician data in the charts were reviewed, DSM-III, Axis I diagnoses were made for these cases that were generally in good agreement with those made by structured interview.

When primary DSM-III diagnoses made from structured interviews were compared with the summary or best estimate diagnoses, agreement was high. Diagnoses from patient interviews agreed completely with the best estimate diagnoses, and, consequently, sources of discordance between diagnoses from mother interviews and best estimate diagnoses were the same as those between diagnoses derived from interviews of patients and their mothers.

Discordance between diagnoses from hospital charts and best estimate diagnoses was high. The sources of discordance were the same as those that accounted for the discordance between diagnoses from structured interviews and those from hospital charts.

Multiple diagnosis Clinicians frequently assigned patients Axis II personality diagnoses, even though the chart review demonstrated that enough clinical data existed in the charts to assign Axis I diagnoses in all but one case (#5). Although the validity of personality diagnoses in adolescents is in question and is reflected by the criterion that excludes persons under 18 years of age from many DSM-III personality disorder diagnoses, it was conceivable that clinicians assigned these diagnoses because personality dysfunction represented a major focus of treatment at this residential, psychoanalytically oriented treatment facility. To examine this possibility, we assessed patients by secondary diagnoses from each diagnostic source.

For these analyses, the best estimate diagnoses were taken as a criterion against which other diagnostic sources were compared. This approach seemed reasonable, because the best estimates were constructed by independent diagnosticians using all available diagnostic information from charts and direct research interviews of patients and their mothers. Moreover, Leckman and associates[59] have demonstrated recently the validity of using best estimates—constructed similarly to those in this study—as a criterion of the validity of diagnostic sources. Their results suggest that diagnoses derived from structured interviews of subjects agree very well (Kappa = .95) with those constructed by best estimate diagnosticians.

Table 12-3 presents: 1) the number of best estimate DSM-III diagnoses patients received; 2) best estimate DSM-III primary diagnoses by rank order of frequency among patients; and 3) best estimate DSM-III secondary diagnoses by rank order of frequency among patients. Patients tended to have multiple diagnoses, many of which preceded by several years the onset of the primary disorder. The mean number of

Table 12-3
**Patients by Number of Best Estimate DSM-III Diagnoses Received
and by Best Estimate Primary and Secondary DSM-III Diagnoses**

Number Best Estimate DSM-III Diagnoses:	*N*	*Percent*
1	0	0
2	1	6
3	3	18
4 or more	13	76
Total	17	100

DSM-III Primary Disorder (Best Estimate):	*N*	*Percent*
Conduct Disorder	4	23
Major Depressive Disorder	3	18
Bipolar (I) Disorder	3	18
Atypical Bipolar (II) Disorder	3	18
Schizoaffective Disorder	2	11
Schizophrenia	1	6
Atypical Psychosis	1	6
Total	17	100

DSM-III Secondary Disorders (Best Estimate):	*Number of Patients Affected**
Conduct Disorders	12
Substance Use/Dependency Disorders	11
Anxiety Disorders	7
Cyclothymic Disorder	7
Alcohol Use/Dependency Disorders	6
Dysthymic Disorder	5
Major Depressive Disorder	2
Attention Deficit Disorders	2
Atypical Psychosis	1
Other	0

*All but one patient received two or more secondary diagnoses.

disorders diagnosed by best estimate for each patient was 4.6, with a
range of 2 to 8.

Data from structured interviews with patients agreed well with the
best estimate, yielding a mean number of 4.5 diagnoses per patient, with
a range of 3 to 8. Interviews with patients' mothers yielded a mean
number of 3.6 diagnoses, with a range of 2 to 9. The chart review yielded
a mean number of 2.0 diagnoses with a range of 1 to 3, and the mean
number of clinician diagnoses was 1.8 with a range of 1 to 3. The number
of secondary diagnoses, then, were nearly as great through patient interview as through best estimate sources, and there were slightly fewer
through mother interview, but there were many fewer assigned through
chart review.

Among primary diagnoses, affective disorders occurred with
greatest frequency (9, 54%). Bipolar (I) and Atypical Bipolar (II)

Disorders were unexpectedly frequent in this sample (6, 36%), while the frequency of the nonorganic, nonaffective psychoses was low (2, 12%) for a long-term, residential sample. Two patients (12%) had a mix of prominent affective and psychotic features that were such that a clear diagnosis of affective disorder or nonaffective psychosis could not be made, and they were assigned the DSM-III residual category of Schizoaffective Disorder.

Conduct problems were very frequent in these studies, as well. Conduct Disorder was the primary diagnosis of four (23%) patients, and a secondary diagnosis in 12 (71%) patients. Substance and Alcohol Use/Dependency Disorders were commonly encountered as secondary diagnoses (11, 65%; and 7, 41%).

The three patients with a primary diagnosis of Major Depression satisfied DSM-III criteria for Dysthymic Disorder, as had one bipolar patient in the year before the onset of bipolar illness. Five bipolar patients also met criteria for Cyclothymic Disorder; in each case the disorder preceded the onset of frank bipolar disorder by at least one year. Two of four patients with a primary diagnosis of Conduct Disorder satisfied DSM-III criteria for Major Depressive Disorder, and another satisfied those for Dysthymic Disorder.

Agreement, sensitivity and specificity: Best estimate diagnoses vs. other diagnostic sources   To assess the significance of the less frequent identification of secondary diagnoses by chart sources, we compared best estimate diagnoses with diagnoses from other diagnostic sources for the eight most frequently assigned primary or secondary diagnostic categories.

Table 12-4 presents agreement, specificity and sensitivity for the eight most common diagnostic categories and for all these categories combined, when the best estimate served as the criterion against which the four other sources were assessed. Percent agreement uncorrected for chance was calculated for each specific diagnostic category because cell sizes were often too small (< 5) to warrant use of Cohen's Kappa or intraclass correlation coefficients as measures of agreement, and Kappa[60] was calculated for the eight categories combined. Since the number of primary diagnoses was small compared to the number of secondary diagnoses, primary and secondary diagnoses were combined for purposes of calculation.

Diagnoses derived from patient interviews agreed acceptably with the best estimate diagnoses. The slightly lower level of agreement between best estimates and mothers arose in part because mothers identified milder affective disorders and anxiety disorders less frequently than their offspring. This finding is not surprising in view of the often nondramatic nature of these disturbances and the well-known reticence of adolescents to confide information about their internal lives to their

Table 12-4
Percent Agreement, Sensitivity and Specificity of Primary
and Secondary DSM-III Diagnoses for All Other
Diagnostic Sources vs. Best Estimate*

	Best Estimate vs.			
DSM-III Diagnosis	*Patient*	*Mother*	*Chart*	*Clinician*
Schizoaffective	100%	100%	94%	100%
Disorder or	SN = 1.00	SN = 1.00	SN = 1.00	SN = 1.00
Schizophrenia	SP = 1.00	SP = 1.00	SP = .93	SP = 1.00
(N = 3)†				
Bipolar Disorder	100%	94%	65%	65%
(I and II)	SN = 1.00	SN = .83	SN = .00	SN = .00
(N = 6)†	SP = 1.00	SP = 1.00	SP = 1.00	SP = 1.00
Major Depressive	94%	82%	76%	59%
Disorder	SN = 1.00	SN = .00	SN = .40	SN = .20
(N = 5)†	SP = .92	SP = .92	SP = .92	SP = .75
Dysthymic or	100%	76%	47%	35%
Cyclothymic	SN = 1.00	SN = .67	SN = .25	SN = .08
Disorder	SP = 1.00	SP = 1.00	SP = 1.00	SP = 1.00
(N = 12)†				
Conduct Disorder	94%	100%	59%	41%
(N = 16)†	SN = .94	SN = 1.00	SN = .56	SN = .38
	SP = 1.00	SP = 1.00	SP = 1.00	SP = 1.00
Anxiety Disorders	100%	59%	59%	59%
(N = 7)†	SN = 1.00	SN = .29	SN = .00	SN = .00
	SP = 1.00	SP = .90	SP = 1.00	SP = 1.00
Alcohol Use or	100%	82%	71%	71%
Dependency	SN = 1.00	SN = .50	SN = .17	SN = .17
Disorder	SP = 1.00	SP = 1.00	SP = 1.00	SP = 1.00
(N = 6)†				
Substance Use or	100%	82%	82%	71%
Dependency	SN = 1.00	SN = .73	SN = .73	SN = .45
Disorder	SP = 1.00	SP = 1.00	SP = 1.00	SP = 1.00
(N = 11)†				
Summary for all	K = .97	K = .70	K = .37	K = .22
Diagnoses‡	SN = .99	SN = .73	SN = .39	SN = .26
(N = 66)†	SP = .98	SP = .97	SP = .97	SP = .96

*Readers should be aware that, with several small sample sizes (eg, 3, 5, 6), percent agreement, sensitivity, and specificity are less meaningful than with larger groups.
†N is the number of cases or disorder (primary and secondary) identified by best estimate.
‡Kappa is reported because cell sizes are large (> 5).

parents. Mothers usually seemed apprised of alcohol and substance abuse, but they often could not estimate the severity. For this reason, they identified alcohol and substance use/dependency disorders less frequently than did their offspring.

Inspection of the sensitivity and specificity for the eight most commonly assigned diagnostic categories and for those eight categories combined revealed a marked reduction in overall concordance between best estimate and clinical source. Two related factors were found to account for these findings: 1) most patients were assigned multiple diagnoses by the best estimate diagnosticians and through the interviews with patients and mothers; however, multiple diagnoses rarely were assigned through chart review or by clinicians; and 2) several disorders were not identified by hospital clinicians, ie, bipolar (mentioned earlier), secondary affective, anxiety, and alcohol and substance use disorders; and descriptive information found in the charts was often insufficient to permit the diagnosis of these same disorders. We had hypothesized that clinicians frequently made an Axis II primary diagnosis rather than an Axis I primary diagnosis because the personality disorder was the focus of treatment, but that Axis I disorders would be identified concurrently and regarded as secondary. This was not the case. Although the charts sometimes contained information necessary for Axis I diagnosis, they were not noted by clinicians, and therefore explained much of the discordance between best estimate and clinician.

Suicidal ideation and behavior in the sample The six-point scale that we constructed to rate patients' suicidality was found to constitute a continuum. That is, whatever score a patient obtained, the preceding scale items were found to be invariably present. Therefore, each patient was given a scale score (0–5) that represented his/her highest level of suicidal ideation or behavior.

Table 12-5 compares the number of patients who were assigned each of the six suicidality scores by each information source. Best estimate and patient sources agreed that nine patients engaged in suicidal behavior and that two others had suicidal ideation. Scores derived from mother interviews also agreed reasonably with best estimate scores. However, in one case the mother was unaware of a drug overdose that her child had taken before hospitalization. Agreement was poorer between scores based on clinical source and the best estimate. The primary reason for the discrepancy seemed to be that hospital clinicians seldom noted past suicidal ideation or behavior in the charts. From our subsequent discussions with the staff, it became evident that clinicians often had not

Table 12-5
Patients' Suicidality Scores by Source of Information

Suicidality Score	Structured Interview		Clinical	Summary
	Patient Number	Mother Number	Chart Number	Best Estimate Number
0 = Suicidal Ideation Denied	6	7	8	6
1 = Mild Ideation	0	0	0	0
2 = Moderate Ideation	1	1	2	1
3 = Serious Ideation	1	1	0	1
4 = Gesture	5	4	6	5
5 = Attempt	4	4	2	4
Total	17	17	17	17

systematically inquired about such previous episodes and were unaware of them. Consequently, two moderately serious attempts that had occurred some time before hospitalization had gone unidentified by hospital staff. However, once patients were hospitalized, clinicians seemed well apprised of their suicidal activity. It was our impression then that just as hospital physicians frequently underdiagnosed affective disorders — perhaps because they did not inquire about symptoms systematically — they were unaware of suicidal ideation and past behavior unless a patient volunteered the information.

Table 12-6 presents the number of patients with and without each of six DSM-III diagnoses by suicidality score. Five of these diagnostic groups, 1) Schizophrenia or Schizoaffective Disorder; 2) Bipolar (I) and Atypical (II) Bipolar Disorders; 3) Major Depressive Disorder; 4) Alcohol Use/Dependency Disorder; and 5) Substance Use/Dependency Disorder, were selected because the adult psychiatric literature provides support for each as a risk factor for suicide,[8-16] though support from the adolescent psychiatric literature is less substantial. An association between antisocial personality disorder and suicidal behavior also has been suggested.[15] Since Conduct Disorder is the analog of Antisocial Personality Disorder for children and adolescents in the DSM-III, Conduct Disorder is also included in the table.

Because Major Depressive Disorder and Conduct Disorder were frequently secondary diagnoses in this sample, and Alcohol and Substance Use/Dependency diagnoses occurred only as secondary diagnoses, considerable diagnostic overlapping is present among these patients. Nonetheless, several trends emerge. In two of the three patients with Schizophrenia or Schizoaffective Disorder suicidal ideation was present, and one schizoaffective patient made a serious suicide attempt during a period of severe depression before his hospitalization. Suicidal ideation was present in five of the six patients with a primary diagnosis of Bipolar Disorder. One of these patients made repetitive suicidal gestures and three had made serious attempts. The two most seriously suicidal patients in this sample who had made numerous life-threatening attempts suffered Bipolar Disorder. Four of the five patients with Major Depressive Disorder had experienced suicidal ideation, and three had made gestures. Of six patients with a diagnosis of Alcohol Use/Dependency Disorder, five had made attempts or gestures. This group included four of the five bipolar patients, and one of the schizoaffective patients. Conduct Disorder is so frequent a diagnosis (16 out of 17) that it is difficult to discern a trend. The presence of any of the first five diagnostic categories in these patients, however, does appear to be associated with an increased risk of suicidal ideation and suicidal behavior. Because of the sample size, absence of a suitable control group, and the high degree of diagnostic overlapping, statistical analysis, of course, was not feasible, and so firm conclusions cannot be drawn.

Table 12-6
Patients by Best Estimate Suicidality Score and Best Estimate Diagnoses (Primary and Secondary)

Best Estimate Suicidality Score	Schizoaffective or Schizophrenia Number Patients: With	Without	Bipolar (I and II) Number Patients: With	Without	Conduct Disorder Number Patients: With	Without	Alcohol Use/ Dependency Number Patients: With	Without	Substance Use/ Dependency Number Patients: With	Without	Major Depression Number Patients: With	Without
0 No Ideation (N = 6)	1	5	1	5	6	0	1	5	3	3	1	5
1-3 Mild to Serious Ideation (N = 2)	1	1	1	1	2	0	0	2	2	0	1	1
4 Suicide Gesture (N = 5)	0	5	1	4	4	1	2	3	3	2	3	2
5 Suicide Attempt (N = 4)	1	3	3	1	4	0	3	1	3	1	0	4
Total (N = 17)	3	14	6	11	16	1	6	11	11	6	5	12

There appears to be a correlation between suicidality score and the number of diagnoses a patient received. The patients who had denied suicidal ideation had an average of 3.6 diagnoses; patients who only suffered suicidal ideation had an average of 4.5 diagnoses, and patients who had engaged in suicidal behavior had an average of 5.4 diagnoses. While, again, the sample is too small for statistical significance to emerge, a trend may be evident.

Social adjustment and the risk of suicide Levels of correlation between patients' and their mothers' reports on each of the subscales for the four time periods were generally acceptable. Total score correlations ranged from .53 to .76. Nonetheless, because of our limited experience with the SAICA and the small sample size, our results must be restricted to impression and anecdote. In the two most suicidal patients (#5 and 17) whose hospital courses were characterized by unrelenting suicidal ideation and frequent suicidal behavior, social adjustment on all subscales was very poor. The subjects did poorly in school, though both were bright, had poor relations with teachers, and hung around with an antisocial peer group. After school the subjects had few leisure-time activities except for the use of drugs, occasional antisocial peer group activities, and spent much time alone. Their relations with their families (parents and siblings) were strained and distant. These patients manifested manifold problem behaviors as well as the relative absence of competent behaviors. Neither the patients nor their families appeared to have much in the way of institutional or community ties.

While the pattern of social adjustment for these two patients was relatively extreme, even for this group of severely ill hospitalized patients, in the other suicide attempters the picture was relatively similar. The absence of stable peer ties and constructive leisure activities, and the presence of hostile or distant family relations were marked.

The patients who had experienced no suicidal ideation frequently presented a different picture of social adjustment. Patient 2, for example, suffered episodes of severe major depression with melancholia. Outside the episodes of illness, however, his social adjustment was much more intact. He had several close friends, many leisure-time activities — he was a good musician — was involved in various community activities, and had relatively few problems with his immediate family. Patient 16, though he eventually developed bipolar illness, had had good premorbid social functioning. He did well in school, was appreciated by teachers and peers and had several close friends. Although his relations with his parents were strained, several older male surrogates looked after him.

One additional impression is that after the onset of a major psychiatric disorder in adolescence, social adjustment appeared to decline. Perhaps this is because the disorder inhibits the successful completion of the developmental tasks of adolescence. The effects of this decline may conceivably increase the risk of suicide as well.

Discussion

Reliability of the K-SADS-E and validity of diagnostic sources The diagnoses derived from K-SADS-E interviews of patients and their mothers agreed well with the best estimate diagnoses and with each other; the sources of discordance were largely due to the differences in information available to patients and their mothers about the patient's psychiatric course. This source of diagnostic disagreement has been labeled information variance by Spitzer, Endicott and Robins,[38] and cannot be reduced by interviewing technique.

Although diagnoses made by clinicians from clinical interviews of subjects traditionally have been used as criterion measures of the validity of semistructured interviews, Kappa coefficients of agreement, when such a criterion measure has been used, have usually been in the range of 0.25 to 0.56.[61] As our study suggests, these disappointing results may reflect upon the inaccuracies of clinical interviews. While clinicians in this study focused on personality diagnosis, they frequently appeared to miss Axis I disorders, even though sufficient diagnostic information often was available in the charts from which Axis I diagnoses could be made. These considerations justify the use of best estimate diagnoses as a criterion measure of the measurement validity of the four other diagnostic sources considered in our study. Agreement, sensitivity and specificity, when best estimates are taken as the criterion against which patient and mother K-SADS-E interviews are compared, are acceptable despite the small size of the sample.

While diagnoses from the K-SADS-E interviews agree well with best estimates, and sensitivity and specificity are generally reasonable, similar coefficients for diagnoses from hospital sources are much lower. The sources of disagreement are due to the marked underdiagnosis of bipolar disorder and of secondary disorders by clinicians. Secondary diagnoses such as the milder affective disorders, alcohol and substance use/dependency disorders, and conduct disorders that should constitute specific treatment focuses in their own right were frequently missed.

Another important source of disagreement was the frequent diagnosis of DSM-III Axis II personality disorders. Although there is still some question about the construct validity of personality disorders in this age group, personality dysfunction may certainly constitute an important focus of treatment in a setting of this sort. Unfortunately, no diagnostic instruments for which reliability and validity have been established are currently available for making all the DSM-III Axis II personality diagnoses, though some are under development and appear promising. For this reason, we could not examine the validity of clinicians' diagnoses of DSM-III, Axis II personality disorders.

Clinical use of structured interviews Our findings suggest that structured interviews may complement the usual clinical interviewing techniques in the identification of disorders that account for significant risk of suicide in adolescence. While our sample may be peculiar for the large number of secondary disorders per patient, the results are consistent with those of other studies that suggest the frequent underdiagnosis of psychiatric disorders such as affective disorders in adolescence.[24,25]

Our findings also suggest that structured interviews are useful in the identification and quantification of suicidal ideation and behavior. Although hospital clinicians were able to accurately identify suicidal behavior that occurred while the patient was hospitalized, they were often unaware of suicidal behavior that occurred prior to hospitalization and of suicidal ideation that occurred both prior to and during hospitalization.

Patients' social adjustment and suicidality could not be statistically associated in this small sample, but examination of cases revealed that patients with the greatest degree of social isolation were most suicidal. Consistent with the adult literature that suggests that social adjustment may modify the risk of suicide in the context of the predisposing psychiatric disorders, patients with schizophrenia, schizoaffective disorders, affective disorders and alcohol and substance use/dependency disorders, who had the highest suicidality scores, also were the most impaired in their peer and family relations and in their capacities for positive spare-time activities. While a good clinical interview might identify such deficits, formal structured assessment of social adjustment permits a systematic appraisal.

CONCLUSION

From this pilot study and current epidemiologic data, a provisional portrait of the adolescent at risk for suicide emerges. He or she is between the ages of 15 and 19, often has an affective disorder, schizophrenia or schizoaffective disorder, complicated by behavioral problems — often satisfying criteria for conduct disorder — and by substance or alcohol abuse. He or she is often socially isolated, with impaired peer and family relations and a dearth of spare-time activities. He or she has often had past episodes of psychiatric disorders and a long history of psychosocial difficulties. Suicidal ideation and behavior frequently have been present in the past, usually during episodes of psychiatric disorder.

Whether such a patient has had psychiatric contact in the past, or present for evaluation for the first time, the clinician who typically performs the evaluation appears prone to focus on intrapsychic difficulties and personality dysfunction and may miss severe Axis I disorders that may be quite treatable — with concomitant risk reduction — and may miss concurrent and past suicidal behavior and current suicidal ideation.

Thus, while a good clinical interview may be sufficient to identify the suicidal adolescent, it appears that the structured assessment of psychiatric diagnosis, potential suicidality, and social adjustment and psychosocial supports may represent an invaluable adjunct to the traditional clinical evaluation.

ACKNOWLEDGMENT

This work was supported in large part by the Yale Mental Health Clinical Research Center (MHCRC), NIMH Grant MH30929. In addition, Dr. Gammon received support from the Research Training in Psychosocial Epidemiology Grant, NIMH2T32 MH14235. We would like to thank Gary L. Tischler, MD, Director, Yale Psychiatric Institute (YPI), and the YPI staff for their generous assistance in the conduct of the study described. We would also like to thank Brigitte A. Prusoff, PhD for her help with the analysis of the data reported.

REFERENCES

1. Petzel S, Cline DW: Adolescent suicide: Epidemiological and biological aspects, in Feinstein S, Giovacchini P (eds): *Adolescent Psychiatry.* Chicago, University of Chicago Press, 1978, vol 6, pp 239–266.
2. Shaffer D, Fisher P: The epidemiology of suicide in children and young adolescents: *J Am Acad Child Psychiatry* 1981;20:545–565.
3. Holinger PC: Violent deaths among the young: Recent trends in suicide, homicide, and accidents. *Am J Psychiatry* 1979;136:1144–1147.
4. Gruenberg EM: Epidemiology, in Kaplan HI, Freedman AM, Sadock BJ (eds): *Comprehensive Textbook of Psychiatry,* ed 3. Baltimore, Williams & Wilkins Co, 1980, pp 531–548.
5. Holinger PC, Offer D: Perspectives on suicide in adolescence, in Simmons RG (ed): *Research in Community and Mental Health.* Greenwich, Connecticut, JAI Press Inc, 1981, vol 2, pp 139–163.
6. Paykel ES, Myers JK, Lindenthal JJ, et al: Suicidal feeling in the general population: A prevalence study. *Br J Psychiatry* 1974;124:460–469.
7. Durkheim E: *Suicide.* Glencoe, NY, Free Press of Glencoe, 1951.
8. Baraclough BM, Bunch J, Nelson B, et al: An hundred cases of suicide: clinical aspects. *Br J Psychiatry* 1974;125:355–373.
9. Robins E, Murphy GE, Wilkinson RH, et al: Some clinical considerations in the prevention of suicide based on a study of 134 successful suicides. *Am J Public Health* 1959;49:888–899.
10. Spalt L: Suicide behavior and depression in university student psychiatric referrals. *Psychiatr Q* 1980;52:235–239.
11. Goldney RD, Plowsky I: Depression in young women who have attempted suicide. *Aus NZ J Psychiat* 1980;14:203–211.
12. Schuettler R, Huber G, Cross G: Suicid und suicidrersuch im Verlauf Schizophrener Erkronkungen. *Psychiatr Clin* 1976;9:97–112.
13. Garfinkle BD, Froese A, Hood J: Suicide attempts in children and adolescents. *Am J Psychiatry* 1982;139:1257–1261.
14. Ervin FR: Evaluation of organic factors in patients with impulse disorders and episodic violence, in Smith WC, Kling A (eds): *Issues in Brain Behavior Control.* New York, Spectrum, 1976.

206

15. Garvey MJ, Sponen F: Suicide attempts in antisocial personality disorder. *Compr Psychiatry* 1980;21:146–149.
16. Sainsbury P: *Suicide in London: An Ecological Study*. Maudsley Monograph No. 1, London, Chapman and Hall, 1955.
17. Blos P: *On Adolescence*. New York, Free Press, 1962.
18. Erikson E: The problem of ego identity. *J Am Psychoanal Assoc.* 1956; 4:56–121.
19. Freud A: Adolescence as a developmental disturbance, in Chaplon G, Lebovici S (eds): *Adolescence*. New York, Basic Books, 1969.
20. Douvan E, Adelson J: *The Adolescent Experience*. New York, Wiley, 1966.
21. Offer D: *The Psychological World of the Teenager*. New York, Basic Books, Inc, 1968.
22. Offer D, Offer JL: *From Teenager to Young Manhood*. New York, Basic Books, Inc, 1975.
23. Rutter M, Graham P, Chadwick OFD, et al: Adolescent turmoil: Fact or friction. *J Child Psychol Psychiatry* 1976;17:35–56.
24. Hudgens RW: *Psychiatric Disorders in Adolescents*. Baltimore, Williams and Wilkins, 1974.
25. King LJ, Pittman GD: A six year follow-up of sixty-five adolescent patients. *Br J Psychiatry* 1969;115:1437–1441.
26. Masterson JF: The psychiatric significance of adolescent turmoil. *Am J Psychiatry* 1968;124:1540–1544.
27. Weiner I, DelGaudio A: Psychopathology in adolescence. *Arch Gen Psychiatry* 1976;33:187–193.
28. Welner A, Welner Z, Fishman R: Psychiatric adolescent inpatients: Eight to ten year follow-up. *Arch Gen Psychiatry* 1979;36:698–700.
29. Strober M, Green J, Carlson G: Reliability of psychiatric diagnosis in hospitalized adolescents. *Arch Gen Psychiatry* 1981;38:141–144.
30. Herjanic B, Herjanic M, Brown F, et al: Are children reliable reporters? *J Abnorm Child Psychol* 1975;3:441–448.
31. Herjanik B, Reich W: Development of a structured psychiatric interview: Agreement between child and parent on individual symptoms. *J Abnorm Child Psychol* 1982;10:307–324.
32. Reich W, Herjanik B, Welner Z, et al: Development of a structured psychiatric interview: Agreement on diagnosis comparing child and parent. *J Abnorm Child Psychol* 1982;10:325–336.
33. Strober M, Carlson G: Bipolar illness in adolescents with major depression: Clinical, genetic and psychopharmacologic predictors in a three-to-four year prospective follow-up investigation. *Arch Gen Psychiatry* 1982;39:549–555.
34. Strober M, Burrouhs J, Salkin B, et al: Ancestral secondary cases of psychiatric illness in adolescents with mania, depression, schizophrenia and conduct disorder. *Biol Psychiatry*, in press.
35. Strober M, Green J, Carlson G: Phenomenology and subtypes of major depressive disorder in adolescents. *J Affect Disord* 1981;3:281–290.
36. Puig-Antich J: Affective disorders in childhood: A review and perspective. *Psychiatr Clin North Am* 1980;3:403–424.
37. Gammon GD, John K, Pothblum E, et al: Identification of bipolar disorder in adolescents with a structured diagnostic interview: The frequency and manifestations of the disorder in an inpatient sample. *Am J Psychiatry*, in press.
38. Spitzer RL, Endicott J, Robins E: Clinical criteria for psychiatric diagnosis and the DSM-III. *Am J Psychiatry* 1975;132:1187–1192.
39. American Psychiatric Association Task Force: *Diagnostic and Statistical Manual of Mental Disorders*, ed 3 (DSM-III), Washington, DC, APA, 1980.

40. Chambers W, Puig-Antich J, Tabrize MA: The ongoing development of the Kiddie-SADS. Paper presented at the 25th Annual Meeting of the American Academy of Child Psychiatry, San Diego, 1978.
41. Puig-Antich J, Orvaschel H, Tabrizi MA, et al: *The Schedule for Affective Disorders and Schizophrenia for School-Age Children — Epidemiologic Version (Kiddie-SADS-E),* ed 3. New York, New York Psychiatric Institute and Yale University School of Medicine, 1980.
42. Orvaschel H, Puig-Antich J, Chambers WT, et al: Retrospective assessment of child psychopathology with the K-SADS-E. *J Am Acad Child Psychiatry,* in press.
43. Herjanic B, Welner Z: Diagnostic interview for children and adolescents (DICA). St. Louis, Washington University School of Medicine, 1981.
44. Hodges K, Kline J, Fitch P, et al: The Child Assessment Schedule: A diagnostic interview for research and clinical use. *Catalog of Selected Documents in Psychiatry,* 1981;11:56.
45. Hodges K, Stern L, Cytryn L, et al: The development of the Child Assessment Schedule for research and clinical use. *J Abnorm Child Psychol* 1982; 10:173–189.
46. Hodges K, McKnew D, Cytryn L, et al: The Child Assessment Schedule (CAS) diagnostic interview: A report on reliability and validity. *J Am Acad Child Psychiatry* 1982;21:468–473.
47. Robins L, Helzer J, Croughan J, et al: *The NIMH Diagnostic Interview Schedule, Version 3,* ADM-42-12-79. Washington, DC, US Government Printing Office, 1980.
48. Costello AJ, Edelbrock CS, Kessler MD, et al: Structured interviewing: A progress report on the NIMH Diagnostic Interview Schedule for Children (DIS-C). Presented at the 29th Annual Meeting of the American Academy of Child Psychiatry, Washington, DC, 1982.
49. Myers JK, Lindenthal JJ, Pepper MP: Social integration and psychiatric symptomatology. *J Health Soc Behav* 1975;16:421–428.
50. Weissman MM. The assessment of social adjustment: A review of techniques. *Arch Gen Psychiatry* 1976;33:1111–1115.
51. Weissman MM, Sholomskas D, John K: The assessment of social adjustment: An update. *Arch Gen Psychiatry* 1981;38:1250–1258.
52. Achenbach TM: *The Child Behavior Checklist and Child Behavior Profile.* Burlington, VT, University of Vermont, 1980.
53. Achenbach TM: The Child Behavior Profile: I. Boys age 6–11. *J Consult Clin Psychol* 1978;46:478–488.
54. Achenbach TM, Edelbrock CS: The Child Behavior Profile: II. Boys age 12–16 and girls aged 6–11 and 12–16. *J Consult Clin Psychol* 1979;47: 223–233.
55. Achenbach TM, Edelbrock CS: An empirically based system for assessing children's behavioral problems and competences. *Int J Ment Health* 1979;7:24–42.
56. Edelbrock CS, Achenbach TM: A typology of child behavior profile patterns: Distribution and correlates for disturbed children aged 6–16. *J Abnorm Child Psychol* 1980;8:441–470.
57. Achenbach TM, Edelbrock CS: Behavioral problems and competences reported by parents of normal and disturbed children aged 4–16. *Monographs of the Society for Research in Child Development,* 46, Serial No. 118. Chicago, University of Chicago Press, 1981.
58. Achenbach TM, Edelbrock CS: *Youth Self-Report — for Ages 11–18.* Burlington, VT, University of Vermont, 1981.

59. Leckman JF, Sholomskas D, Thompson WD, et al: Best estimate of lifetime psychiatric diagnosis: A methodologic study. *Arch Gen Psychiatry* 1982; 39:879-883.
60. Fleiss JL: *Statistical Methods for Rates and Proportions*, ed 2. New York, John Wiley & Sons, 1982, pp 217-225.
61. Hedlund JL, Vieweg, BW: Structured psychiatric interviews: A comparative review. *J Oper Psychiatry* 1981;12:39-67.

CHAPTER 13

THE SERIOUSLY SUICIDAL ADOLESCENT: Affective and Character Pathology

RICHARD C. FRIEDMAN
RUTH CORN
MICHAEL S. ARONOFF
STEPHEN W. HURT
JOHN F. CLARKIN

This chapter reviews recent changes in the concept of normalcy during adolescence and then proceeds to discuss developments in the diagnosis of the affective disorders. Our research has focused on the relationship between psychiatric diagnosis and history of attempted suicide in adolescent inpatients. Such patients (obviously) represent the more severely suicidal part of a hypothetical severity spectrum and are not representative of all suicide attempters.

Almost all of these individuals meet DSM-III or RDC criteria for some type of Depressive Disorder. The diagnosis of Adjustment Disorder with Depressed Mood appears to occur infrequently among such adolescents. Although many seriously suicidal adolescents suffer from Major Depression, a goodly number appear to have Dysthymia. This fact, taken in conjunction with the observation that Dysthymia may progress to Major Depression during adolescence, strongly suggests that some dysthymic adolescents suffer from a more malignant type of Affective Disorder than is generally appreciated.

We present a brief synopsis of the literature on personality traits of individuals who engage in parasuicidal activity. It is apparent that these traits are similar to the group of behaviors that characterize the Borderline Personality Disorder (BPD) diagnosis in DSM-III. Psychiatric thinking that led to the establishment of the criteria for Borderline Personality Disorder (BPD) is presented in historical context. The diagnosis of BPD places more weight on parasuicidal behavior than on any other Axis II disorder in DSM-III. We present preliminary findings that suggest that (as may be expected) both adolescents and adults who manifest an Axis I Depressive Disorder and Axis II BPD are an especially suicidal subgroup of patients.

The difficulties inherent in applying the BPD criteria to adolescent patients are explored. We feel that, in general, it is clinically useful to do so.

The subtype(s) of Axis I Depressive Disorder(s) and Axis II Personality Disorder (or disorders) must be clearly delineated in order for accurate diagnosis and effective treatment to occur. Depressive Disorders may coexist with Personality Disorders other than BPD during adolescence. Particularly in younger patients, early forms of these Personality Disorders may be difficult to detect. The motivation for parasuicidal activity often differs between the various Axis II conditions. Clinical summaries illustrate commonly occurring Affective Disorder–Personality Disorder interactions with emphasis on the motivation for atempted suicide. These summaries also provide examples of a particularly complex diagnostic problem: coexistence of a Depressive Disorder, BPD, and an additional Personality disorder. The chapter concludes with a discussion of principles of treatment of the seriously suicidal adolescent.

The idea that adolescence is "normally" characterized by dysphoria, lability and unpredictability has had great currency among mental health professionals during the past 75 years. For instance, Anna Freud[1] wrote (1958):

Adolescence is by its nature an interruption of peaceful growth, and . . . the upholding of a steady equilibrium during the adolescent process is in itself abnormal . . . adolescence resembles in appearance a variety of other emotional upsets and structural upheavals. The adolescent manifestations come close to symptom formation of the neurotic, psychotic or dissocial order and merge almost imperceptibly into almost all the mental illnesses.

A recent report by Offer et al[2] illustrates that many mental health professionals even today share this view of "normal adolescence." A self-image questionnaire designed to assess self-concept was administered to mental health professionals who were instructed to complete the form with the same responses that would be given by a mentally healthy, well-adjusted adolescent of the same sex. The results revealed their beliefs that most normal adolescents (presumably in good mental health) actually have low self-esteem, are deeply unhappy, and have great difficulty in coping with relationships. This, however, is *not* an accurate picture of mentally healthy adolescents, and data from a variety of sources suggest that the term "normalcy" has the same meaning during teenage years as it does at any other time of life.[3] It did not seem reasonable to us, therefore, to consider certain adolescents "normal" who manifest symptom clusters that satisfy criteria for syndromes of psychopathology. Consequently, we set out to test this widely held notion that adolescents are basically psychologically different from adults in that they do not commonly suffer the affective disorder syndromes diagnosed in adults. To accomplish this, we felt that the detailed study of seriously depressed and suicidal adolescents would deepen our understanding of specific aberrant adolescent behavioral phenomenology and might contribute to the identification of an adolescent subpopulation at risk for psychiatric crisis. We were, therefore, led to the major focus of our research, the relationship between psychiatric diagnosis and attempted suicide in adolescent inpatients.

Suicide is the most serious consequence of depressive illness, affecting as many as 15% of depressives,[4] and clinical depression, itself, is common in the population at large. The adolescent suicide rate in the United States has greatly increased in recent years and is now the third leading cause of death among 15 to 24 year olds. Holinger[5] has reported that between 1961 and 1975 suicide rates increased by 124% in the United States in the 15- to 19-year-old group. Carlson and Strober,[6] among others, have observed that the diagnosis of affective disorders in adolescents is often overlooked. It is interesting to note that this occurs despite the fact that many adult depressives retrospectively report the occurrence of depressive disorders in their adolescent years that were not identified as such then. Therefore, evidence suggested that clinical entities comparable to adult depression occur during adolescent years and with a frequency greater than had previously been appreciated.

With suicide rates climbing in this population, and with the well-documented association between depression and suicide in mind, we turned to our depressed adolescent population for clues to any possible associations between affective disorder and the seriously suicidal adolescent. Although our population consisted of adolescent inpatients, who may not necessarily be representative of all adolescent suicide attempters, our studies,[7-9] have led us to conclude that important associations do exist; namely, that depressed adolescents with borderline personality disorder are at particular risk for seriously suicidal activity, and some adolescents carrying a diagnosis of dysthymic disorder are at risk for developing a more serious affective disorder subsequently. These conclusions are based on data from a review of the medical records of 76 adolescents consecutively discharged during one year from the inpatient services of the New York Hospital–Cornell Medical Center–Westchester Division (NYH-CMC-WD) and an additional series of 88 adolescent inpatients recruited from consecutive admissions to a special inpatient research and treatment unit.

With regard to identifying our patients diagnostically in the chart review study, we used the Diagnostic and Statistical Manual-III (DSM-III),[10] a system that reflects the most recent thinking and codification of psychiatric diagnosis in American psychiatry. DSM-III is based on a multiaxial evaluation in which every case is assessed on five different "axes," each of which refers to a different area of information. Axis I refers to clinical syndromes such as Affective Disorders, Schizophrenia,

212

and Organic Mental Syndromes. Axis II is concerned with personality of character disorders such as Obsessive, Histrionic or Borderline. Axis III refers to the presence of concomitant physical disorders, Axis IV to the presence of psychosocial stressors, and Axis V to the estimation of ability to adapt and cope. Each case, then, is evaluated on all axes and a multileveled diagnostic statement is formulated. For the purposes of these studies, we will look at the first two axes in an attempt to clarify the relationship between psychiatric syndromes and underlying personality structure in adolescents at risk for suicide.

Affective Disorders (Axis I) are defined, according to DSM-III, as those disorders in which there is a primary mood disturbance and associated behavioral dysfunction. There are three subgroups of Affective Disorders. In the studies reported below, we focus on two subtypes of these: Major Depressive Disorder and Dysthymia (a subtype in which the symptoms are similar to those of Major Depressive Disorder but less severe and of chronic duration). With regard to the Axis II (Personality/Character) disorders, diagnostic criteria refer to the characteristic of an individual's long-term functioning as opposed to more acute or episodic disturbances of behavior. Two Axis II diagnostic groups in particular, Borderline and Histrionic, are of interest here. Borderline Personality Disorder refers to characterological dysfunction in five of eight areas including 1) impulsivity or unpredictability in at least two areas that are potentially self-damaging, eg, drug abuse, gambling, 2) a pattern of unstable interpersonal relationships, 3) inappropriate intense anger or lack of control of anger, 4) identity disturbance, 5) affective instability, 6) intolerance of being alone, 7) physically self-damaging acts, and 8) chronic feelings of emptiness or boredom. The diagnosis of Histrionic Personality Disorder requires the presence of overly dramatic behavior and characteristic disturbances in interpersonal relationships as indicated by two of the following criteria: 1) perceived by others as shallow, 2) egocentric and inconsiderate of others, 3) vain and demanding, 4) dependent and helpless, and 5) prone to manipulative suicidal attempts, threats or gestures.

A DIAGNOSTIC PROFILE
OF ADOLESCENT INPATIENTS

In our initial study we reviewed charts of 76 adolescents, ages 13 to 19 years, who had been consecutively discharged from the inpatient services of NYH-CMC-WD in 1980. DSM-III diagnoses (Axis I and II) were made by the research team on the basis of documented symptomatology, independent of clinical diagnoses assigned by staff therapists. We applied a modification of the primary-secondary nosological format to those adolescent patients identified as having affective disorders.[11] That is, a "primary" affective disorder is defined as one not preceded by any other DSM-III disorder; a "secondary" disorder has a history of an antecedent disorder (other than an affective one). We were interested in determining the incidence of affective disorders in this population and in determining whether the onset of Axis II personality disorders was preceded by, simultaneous with, or followed by the onset of Axis I affective disorders. Additionally, we recorded the frequency and lethality of suicide attempts over each patient's lifetime using the Schedule for Affective Disorders and Schizophrenia (SADS).[12] In this system, one rates the suicide attempt on a scale of 0 (no information) to 6 (extreme) in order of increasing medical seriousness of the suicide attempt. For instance, "a scratch on the wrist" is rated 2 while "cuts throat" is rated 5, and "respiratory arrest"or "prolonged coma" is rated 6.

The distribution of the total number of adolescent inpatient diagnoses is summarized in Table 13-1. As can be seen, many patients had both personality disorders and affective disorders. Interestingly, however, in every instance but one, the type of personality disorder manifested by patients with affective disorders was Borderline Personality Disorder (BPD). The data in Table 13-1 are organized to reflect the presence of affective and nonaffective diagnoses and the concomitant presence or absence of BPD. The relationship between the presence of BPD and affective disorder diagnoses was significant ($X^2 = 7.91$, P < .005). All patients with BPD also met criteria for an Affective Disorder. It is also interesting to note that the sex distribution in the affective group without BPD was 50/50, while 83% of the affective group with BPD were females. In the nonaffective disorder group, there were 19 males and 12 females, all without BPD.

Significant relationships were also observed between lifetime occurrence of suicide attempts, medical lethality of suicide attempts and psychiatric diagnosis. These relationships are illustrated in Table 13-2. Of the total group of 45 patients with Affective Disorders, 27 patients (60%) made at least one suicide attempt. Only one patient (3%) in the nonaffective group of 31 patients made such an attempt ($X^2 = 25.43$, P < .001). It should be noted that suicide attempts were common among dysthymic patients as well as those suffering from Major Affective Disorders, and only patients with Primary Major Depression and Primary Dysthymia ever made severe or extreme attempts.

Table 13-3 further delineates the relationship between lifetime suicidal acts and BPD. All of the affective/borderline patients (N = 12) had a history of at least one suicide attempt. In contrast to this, the incidence of suicide attempts in the simple affective group was considerably lower (48%) ($X^2 = 7.58$, P < .01). With regard to severity of attempt, 50% of the affective/borderline patients had attempts rated as moderate to extremely lethal (SADS 4 or above), while only 11% of the

Table 13-1
DSM-III Diagnoses of Adolescent Inpatients: Total N = 76

	Coexisting Borderline Personality Disorder			Without Coexisting Border-line Personality Disorder		
	Male	Female	N	Male	Female	N
AFFECTIVE DISORDERS: TOTAL N = 45						
Major Depression	1	4	5	5	5	10
Primary Dysthymia	1	4	5	6	5	11
Secondary Dysthymia	0	2	2	3	3	6
Atypical Depression with Psychotic Features	0	0	0	1	1	2
Bipolar Disorder, Manic	0	0	0	0	2	2
Bipolar Disorder, Depressed	0	0	0	1	0	1
Schizoaffective Disorder	0	0	0	0	1	1
Subtotal	2	10	12	16	17	33
NONAFFECTIVE DISORDERS: TOTAL N = 31						
Schizophrenia	0	0	0	9	2	11
Anorexia Nervosa	0	0	0	0	5	5
Adjustment Disorder with disturbance of conduct	0	0	0	1	2	3
Conduct Disorder, socialized, nonaggressive	0	0	0	0	1	1
Conduct Disorder, socialized, aggressive	0	0	0	2	0	2
Oppositional Disorder	0	0	0	1	0	1
Gender Identity Disorder	0	0	0	0	1	1
Passive-Aggressive Personality Disorder	0	0	0	1	1	2
Attention Deficit with Hyperactivity	0	0	0	3	0	3
Antisocial Personality Disorder	0	0	0	2	0	2
Subtotal	0	0	0	19	12	31

simple affective group had attempts rated in this range (Fisher's exact = 2.25, P < .02). All patients diagnosed as Primary Dysthymia/BPD had histories of suicide attempts, whereas only 55% of the Primary Dysthymia/non-BPD group had such histories.

Our findings about the prevalence of Major Depressive Disorders in adolescents are in keeping with current studies.[5,13] Carlson and Cantwell[14] observed that 22.5% of children and adolescent outpatients in a different geographical setting had major depressive illness. The finding that 21% of our sample had major depressive illness is similar. Furthermore, since many of our patients met criteria for Dysthymia, it is possible that many subjects in Hudgens'[15] earlier meticulous study would (presently) meet DSM-III criteria for Dysthymia as well.

One important observation of our study was a sequential relationship between Primary Dysthymia and Major Depressive Disorder. We found that four patients with Major Depressive Disorder had Dysthymia as their initial manifestation of affective illness. One other patient with Major Depressive Disorder had Cyclothymia as her first Affective Disorder diagnosis. There were no patients, however, diagnosed with Dysthymia who had Major Depression as their first affective episode. This observation is in keeping with the report of Akiskal et al[16] that Primary Major Affective Disorder develops frequently in adults who present initially with "neurotic depression." It is clear that followup studies are needed to determine the frequency and course of Major Affective Disorders evolving in adolescents with diagnoses of Dysthymia or Cyclothymia. Considering the high incidence of suicide attempts

Table 13-2
Diagnoses: Lifetime Suicide Attempts of Adolescent Inpatients and Lethality of Most Severe Attempt

| | Patients Making Attempts | SADS Medical Lethality Rating | | | | |
		Minimal 2	Mild 3	Moderate 4	Severe 5	Extreme 6
DIAGNOSIS: AFFECTIVE DISORDERS						
Major Depression (N = 15)	10	0	5	3	1	1
Primary Dysthymia (N = 16)	11	3	5	2	0	1
Secondary Dysthymia (N = 8)	4	3	0	1	0	0
Atypical Depression with Psychotic Features (N = 2)	1	0	1	0	0	0
Bipolar Disorder Manic (N = 2)	0	0	0	0	0	0
Bipolar Disorder Depressed (N = 1)	1	0	1	0	0	0
Schizoaffective Disorder (N = 1)	0	0	0	0	0	0
Subtotal (N = 45)	27	6	12	6	1	2
DIAGNOSIS: NONAFFECTIVE DISORDERS						
Schizophrenia (N = 11)	1	0	1	0	0	0
Other (N = 20)	0	0	0	0	0	0
Subtotal (N = 31)	1	0	1	0	0	0

Table 13-3
Adolescent Inpatients: Simple Affective vs. Affective/Borderline Disorders and Lifetime Suicidal Behavior

	Major Depression (N = 10)	Major Depression + Borderline (N = 5)	Primary Dysthymia (N = 11)	Primary Dysthymia + Borderline (N = 5)	Secondary Dysthymia (N = 6)	Secondary Dysthymia + Borderline (N = 2)	Total Simple Affective (N = 27)	Total Affective/ Borderline (N = 12)
Number of patients ever making attempts	5	5	6	5	2	2	13	12
Total number of attempts	8	11	9	6	3	2	20	19
Mean attempts per patient	1.6	2.2	1.5	1.2	1.5	1.0	1.5	1.6
Number of patients with multiple attempts	2	3	2	1	1	0	5	4
Number of patients with moderate to extremely lethal attempts (SADS 4 or above)	1	4	2	1	0	1	3	6

associated with Dysthymia as well as the possible progression from Dysthymia to Major Depression, we suggest that the condition of Dysthymia, diagnosed during adolescence, should not be considered insignificant or benign. DSM-III emphasizes the mild nature of impairment in its definition of Dysthyma. We would stress that Dysthymia may be a disorder with serious consequences, especially if the onset is during childhood or adolescence.

Our data further revealed evidence of the relationship between BPD and Affective Disorders in adolescents, analogous to the data of Stone's[17,18] and Akiskal's[19] recent studies. Thus, every patient diagnosed BPD in our study (N = 12, Table 13-1) met criteria for an Affective Disorder. In patients with Dysthymia, BPD and the Affective Disorder had a simultaneous onset in five cases; Dysthymia occurred first in one case and BPD occurred first in one case. However, in every case of patients with Major Depression, the affective illness clearly occurred earlier. Akiskal et al[16] have stated that an Axis II Personality Disorder diagnosis often develops after an Axis I Affective Disorder. Our data certainly support this observation. It is intriguing to consider whether BPD would have developed had the Affective Disorder been diagnosed and treated at its onset.

The data collected in Tables 13-2 and 13-3 illustrate the importance of making both Axis I and Axis II diagnoses in order to evaluate the clinical significance of suicide attempts. For example, the affective/borderline patients, accounting for only 27% of the affective illness group, had made 48% of the attempts. Furthermore, 67% of patients who ever made a suicide attempt of moderate lethality (SADS 4 or above) were diagnosed affective/borderline. It is also interesting to note that the only Secondary Dysthymia with a SADS lethality score of 4 was a borderline patient. This association between BPD and attempted suicide requires further replication.

Space does not allow us to discuss the relationship between familial psychopathology and adolescent suicidal behavior in detailed fashion. However, as Table 13-4 illustrates, there were only nine patients who had parents who suffered from depression. All parents who had been *hospitalized* for depression had offspring in the Major Depression group. Furthermore, every patient with BPD and Major Depression had a parent with an affective disorder. All suicides of first- or second-degree relatives in the sample were reported to occur among families of patients diagnosed as either Primary Dysthymia or Major Depression.

It has been reported that successful suicide among adolescents has increased recently for unknown reasons, and published figures underestimate the actual prevalence.[20] One way of increasing the likelihood that truly suicidal adolescents will be detected is by being particularly attentive to psychiatric diagnosis. Patients who are both

Table 13-4
Adolescent Inpatients Whose Parents Have Been Treated for Depression: N = 9

Diagnoses of Adolescent Patients	Father	Mother
Major Depression		
Female*		D²
Female*		D²
Male*		D¹
Female*	D¹	
Female*		D³
Male	S	D²
Primary Dysthymia		
Female		D¹
Female		D¹
Conduct Disorder, Socialized, Aggressive		
Male		D¹

D = Depression.
¹Outpatient psychiatric treatment received for Depression.
²Psychiatric hospitalization for Depression.
³Treatment was ECT; unknown if received in hospital or outpatient.
S = Death by suicide.
*Borderline Personality Disorder.

depressed and borderline should be evaluated carefully. Often these patients make suicide attempts in a histrionic manner. In our sample, the great majority of borderline depressives were female. As clinicians, we have observed an unfortunate tendency to regard the female adolescent suicide attempter as manipulative, dramatic and not seriously ill. Our data suggest that this stereotype does not do justice to the complexities of the clinical presentation of these patients.

RELATIONSHIPS AMONG BPD DEPRESSION AND SUICIDAL BEHAVIOR

In our next set of observations, also using the DSM-III format, we looked at 53 adolescent patients recruited from consecutive admissions to a unit specializing in the treatment of depression in adolescents and young adults at the NYH-CMC-WD over a one-year period. We were interested in following up our observations about relationships between psychiatric diagnosis and suicidal behavior. It should be pointed out that the criteria for arriving at the diagnosis of BPD are weighted towards *self-destructive* behavior. Physically self-damaging acts are components of DSM-III diagnostic criterion 7 and may also be found in criterion 1.

The only other personality disorder diagnosis that takes the presence of parasuicidal behavior into account is Histrionic Personality Disorder, which has only a single criterion for such.

Despite the idea that one might expect depressed patients also suffering from BPD to be more suicidal in frequency and severity of suicide attempts than depressed patients not suffering from BPD, empirical support for this, other than that from our own medical records study, is lacking. Therefore, we studied diagnosis and suicidal behavior in the 53 patients noted above. In this investigation, 50% of the sample were adolescents (aged 14 to 18 years). The remaining 50% were young adults (aged 19 to 30 years). The two subgroups were comparable to each other with respect to diagnostic profile and history of suicide. Data on suicidal behavior and lethality were collected by independent clinicians blind to diagnostic considerations. Lifetime suicide attempts were graded according to the SADS[12] criteria for medical lethality.

Table 13-5 summarizes the distribution of Axis I affective diagnoses and Axis II diagnoses. It should be noted that no patient had an Axis II disorder without an Axis I disorder, while seven patients had depression without an Axis II disorder. Suicidal history, by diagnosis, is summarized in Table 13-6. A comparison was made of the overall prevalence of suicide attempts, the frequency of multiple suicide attempts, and the SADS medical lethality scores for the most life-threatening attempt. Thirty-three of 36 patients with depression and BPD made one or more suicide attempts. Successful suicide occurred in two of these patients. The frequency of suicide attempts in this group was significantly greater than among those patients with depression and other Axis II disorders (Fisher's exact, $P < .007$), and significantly different from the prevalence of attempts among depressives with no Axis II diagnosis (Fisher's exact, $P < .008$; all Fisher tests one-tailed). When the "depressed/other Axis II"

Table 13-5
Depressed Adolescents: Relationship of Axis I and Axis II Diagnoses

		Axis II Diagnoses		
N	Axis I Diagnoses	Borderline*	Other Axis II†	Without Axis II
42	Major Depressive Disorder	28	10	4
3	Bipolar Disorders	3	0	0
1	Schizoaffective Disorder	0	0	1
7	Dysthymic Disorders and Atypical Depressions	5	0	2

Total N = 53

*Concomitant Axis II disorder was diagnosed in four of these patients.
†Compulsive, Avoidant, Mixed, Histrionic, other (Masochistic) and Schizotypal.

220

Table 13-6
Depressed Adolescents: Diagnosis of Suicidal Behavior

	Number and Percentage of Patients Who Have Ever Attempted Suicide	Maximal SADS* Lethality Scores		
		1–2	3–4	5–6
Major Depressive Disorder and BPD (N = 28)	26 (93%)	2	14	10†
Other Depressive Disorders and BPD (N = 8)	7 (88%)	0	6	1
Major Depressive Disorders and Other Axis II Disorders (N = 10)	6 (60%)	3	0	3
Other Depressive Disorders Without Axis II Disorders (N = 7)	4 (57%)	2	1	1
Total N = 53				

*SADS Medical Lethality
0 = No information
1 = No danger, eg, no effects, held pills in hand
2 = Minimal, eg, scratch on wrist
3 = Mild, eg, took 10 aspirins, mild gastritis
4 = Moderate, eg, took 10 Seconals, had brief unconsciousness
5 = Severe, eg, cuts throat
6 = Extreme, eg, respiratory arrest or prolonged coma
†Includes two patients who suicided during treatment.

and "depressed/no Axis II" groups were combined to form a depressed/ non-BPD group and compared to the "depressed/BPD" group, the difference in the increased frequency of suicide attempts in the latter group was significant (Fisher's exact, $P < .003$). Lethality of suicide attempts was likewise significantly related to Axis II pathology. While 31 of 36 "depressed/ BPD" patients made mildly to extremely lethal attempts (SADS 3 or greater), only three of 10 patients did so in the "depressed/other Axis II" group (Fisher's exact, $P < .002$). Two of seven patients in the "depressed/no Axis II" group made attempts of similar severity in contrast to the 31 of 36 "depressed/BPD" patients (Fisher's exact, $P < .002$). Of particular note is the fact that patients in the "depressed/BPD" group made more seriously lethal attempts than all other groups of Axis II patients combined ($X^2 = 14.54$, $P < .001$). Thus, depressed patients with BPD had a higher frequency of suicide attempts as well as more lethal attempts than depressed patients with other Axis II disorders or without Axis II pathology.

If we look at the personality traits of individuals who engage in parasuicidal behavior who were studied prior to the development of DSM-III, we can hypothesize that many would be diagnosed today as having BPD. A number of investigators[21-26] have described chronic anger and hostility in suicidal patients, along with impulsivity, inability to cope with frustration, and interpersonal relationships fraught with friction and disruption. These characteristics are similar to the DSM-III criteria for BPD of impulsivity and unpredictability in self-damaging areas, unstable, intense interpersonal relationships, affective instability, and an inability to control anger. Our study suggests that a pathosynergistic effect may occur between Axis I depression and Axis II BPD with regard to suicidal behavior. The principal support for such an association, prior to our own research, had been an investigation carried out exclusively on adolescents by Crumley.[27] In addition, it would appear that the "border" delineated in the DSM-III definition of BPD is a "border" between extremely malignant and somewhat less malignant affective disorders.

SIMILARITIES OF DEPRESSIVE DISORDERS IN ADOLESCENTS AND YOUNG ADULTS

In order to further sharpen and perhaps get a more precise perspective on the relationship between diagnosis (particularly of type of depression) and suicidal behavior in adolescents and in young adults, we changed our diagnostic frame of reference from the DSM-III to another diagnostic system, the Research Diagnostic Criteria (RDC).[28] In this investigation the SADS was administered to patients during the first week of hospitalization by an investigator independent from treating clinicians. RDC diagnoses were then determined on a subset of 44 patients manifesting suicidal behavior who were selected from a consecutive series of 88 depressed patients admitted to the unit. There were 20 females and four males in the adolescent suicide attempters group and 17 females and three males in the young adult group (see Table 13-7). With

Table 13-7
RDC Study: Diagnoses for Adolescent and Adult Suicide Attempters

	Adolescent (N = 24)		Adult (N = 20)		Total (N = 44)	
	N	%	N	%	N	%
*Affective Disorders**						
Major Depression	17	71	20	100	37	84
Manic Disorder	3	13	1	5	4	9
Hypomanic Disorder	0	0	1	5	1	2
Schizoaffective, Depressed	3	13	0	0	3	7
Minor Depressive Disorder	3	13	0	0	3	7
Intermittent Depressive Disorder	1	4	0	0	1	2

*Columns do not add to Total N as patients may receive multiple diagnoses using the RDC.

regard to the various subtypes of Major Depressive Disorder, there were no important differences between adolescent and young adult patients concerning frequency of psychotic, endogenous, agitated, retarded or situational subtypes of depression. The mean lethality scores for the two groups, using the SADS criteria, were virtually identical (see Table 13-8). In the adolescent group, 67% made serious attempts (scores of 4 to 6) compared with 75% in the young adult group. Finally, there were no differences between the two groups with regard to suicidal intent scores.

Recent studies have suggested that adolescents suffer from major syndromes of depression previously thought to occur predominantly in older patients.[8,14,29,30] We found that affective disorder diagnoses in both adolescent and young adult patients hospitalized following suicide attempts associated with depressed mood were similar. This similarity is interesting since depressed mood can be found in disorders ranging from Adjustment Reaction to Major Depression, psychotic subtype. These data provide further support for the importance of the association between clinical depression and suicidal behavior in adolescents.

A principle that has emerged from our work to date is that suicide attempts represent only one of a complex set of symptomatic behaviors in adolescents suffering from severe affective disorders. It would be inaccurate to conclude, from the material we have presented above, that all adolescents who make suicide attempts are depressed.[31-33] It is apparent, however, that a subset of suicidal adolescents do suffer from serious affective illnesses, and that a majority of hospitalized depressed adolescents have been suicidal. From the clinical point of view, it is important to establish whether the adolescent who has made a suicide attempt, or

Table 13-8
RDC Study: Description of Suicidal Behavior as Related to Age Group

	Mean SADS Lethality Score of Current Suicide Attempt	Mean SADS Intent Score of Current Suicide Attempt	% of Patients With Prior Attempts	% of Patients With Attempts (Ever) With Serious* Lethality
Adolescents (N = 24)	3.8 (SD = 1.5)	3.5 (SD = 1.7)	58	67
Adults (N = 20)	4.0 (SD = 1.2)	3.7 (SD = 1.7)	75	75
Total (N = 44)	3.9 (SD = 1.3)	3.6 (SD = 1.7)	66	70

*SADS rating of 4 to 6.

threatened suicide, suffers from affective illness. Like Carlson and Cant-well,[14] we agree that depressive symptomatology can readily be elicited by a knowledgeable clinician when it is present, even in cases in which it appears to be "masked" by other behaviors.

SOME FURTHER DIAGNOSTIC AND TREATMENT CONSIDERATIONS

In keeping with the previous section of this chapter, our description of treatment will focus on the adolescent patient whose suicide attempt has occurred in the context of some type of Axis I affective disorder. We recognize that it may be difficult to determine whether hospitalization is indicated. We assume that an appropriate decision to hospitalize has been made, however, and our emphasis is on subsequent intervention.

Following admission to the hospital, immediate examination of the patient must be carried out. The therapist should contact "significant other" individuals at this time in order to obtain as complete a history of the suicidal crisis as possible. Family members, former therapists, and sometimes peers, may provide valuable information. The patient should be examined alone, and with key members of his or her interpersonal environment, if possible. Evaluation of data from all sources concerning the patient's past behavior, taken in conjunction with the examination of mental status and interaction of patient with significant others, should clarify the determinants of the suicidal crisis that led to hospitalization. These data provide the basis for determining the degree of immediate supervision required to maintain the patient's physical safety. The most suicidal adolescents require constant (ie, within arm's length) presence of staff members(s) at all times.

As we have emphasized throughout this chapter, many adolescents hospitalized following suicide attempts suffer from underlying Axis I mental disorders. Often these disorders have not been previously diagnosed. Personality disorders which may be present can impair the capacity to cope with such underlying affective disorders. Affective disorders in turn may interact with personality disorders. A central principle of our therapeutic approach is that Axis I Affective Disorders must be vigorously treated whether or not Axis II Personality Disorders are simultaneously present. A bias frequently encountered among clinicians is that Axis II conditions are of psychogenic origin and therefore require psychotherapeutic intervention only; conflicts must first be "worked through" in psychotherapy before the affective disorder can be effectively treated. The Axis I Affective Disorder is treated as being secondary in importance to the Axis II Personality Disorder. This type of therapeutic strategy assumes that the suicide attempt is totally determined by unconscious emotional forces which must be treated with confrontation, clarification, interpretation, and the positive effects of a therapeutic relationship.

We have found, however, that many suicidal patients experience such severe impairment of ego functioning due to affective symptoms that they are not immediately able to engage in productive psychotherapeutic work. We recommend that the same diagnostic guidelines used during adulthood be used for the prescription of thymoleptic and neuroleptic medication during adolescence. It has become clear that many patients require both psychotherapy and pharmacotherapy.[34] Pharmacotherapy may relieve the debilitating symptoms of the affective disorder, and thereby enable the patient to experience the motivation, concentration, and the capacity to reason and form relationships, all of which are essential components of the psychotherapeutic process. With appropriate diagnosis and subsequent use of psychotherapy or psychotherapy with pharmacotherapy, the great majority of patients can be successfully treated for the present episode of illness. Two forms of treatment of the suicidal adolescent that additionally may be useful under the proper circumstances are electroconvulsive therapy and long-term intensive psychotherapy. Each of these treatments requires outcome studies during the adolescent phase of life.

Once a suicidal crisis has been decompressed and the underlying conditions leading to persistent suicide risk following hospitalization ameliorated, a decision must be made about the duration of hospital treatment. At this point, a distinction should be made between the minimal time compatible with survival following discharge, and the optimal time required for treatment of the underlying disorder. It is important to emphasize that hospital treatment must lead to adaptational change in order to be successful. Apparent amelioration of factors predisposing to attempted suicide may result simply from temporary institutional internment of the patient. Since a patient must not be discharged into an environment where suicidal crises will rapidly occur, the clinical team must decide whether such improvement, in fact, reflects adaptational change. As a general rule, adaptational improvement results from treatment of patient and significant others, usually family members. Sometimes, however, adolescents come from environments of neglect or abuse that require change, and placement of such patients in secure posthospital living conditions is also required.

SUMMARY

In this chapter we have focused on the relationship between attempted suicide and affective psychopathology in two subgroups of suicide attempters whose adaption has been impaired to the degree that they have required hospitalization on a specialized inpatient unit in addition to one subgroup of a hospitalized adolescent population studied by chart review. We concluded that a subgroup of suicidal adolescents suffer serious affective illness. These Axis I Affective Disorders occur earlier in life than previously believed, and can be brought to the attention of caretakers and mental health professionals as a result of suicide attempt. Therefore, the importance of early diagnosis of depression seems self-evident.

We additionally concluded that an interaction effect occurs between Axis I Depression and Axis II BPD with regard to suicidal behavior, and that the "border" alluded to in BPD is between malignant and less malignant affective disease. Studies are needed from settings other than the private northeastern hospital where our work was carried out. Such research would not only allow for the replication of our general observations about relationships between affective disorders and parasuicidal behavior, but also the association with character pathology, particularly BPD, which we have stressed. Still other studies are needed to determine the frequency with which affective disorders occur in general among *all* adolescent suicide attempters. *Prospective* research on suicide attempters might also elucidate the frequency with which affective disorders *ultimately* develop in adolescents who do not meet criteria for such disorders at the time of a suicide attempt.

ACKNOWLEDGMENT

The authors would like to gratefully acknowledge the most helpful assistance of Ms. Pat Cobb in the preparation of this manuscript.

REFERENCES

1. Freud A: Adolescence. *Psychoanal Study Child* 1958;13:255–278.
2. Offer D, Ostrov E, Howard KI: The mental health professional's concept of the normal adolescent. *Arch Gen Psychiatry* 1981;38:149–152.
3. Rutter M: *Changing Youth in a Changing Society.* Cambridge, Harvard University Press, 1980.
4. Robins E, Guze SB: Classification of affective disorders: The primary-secondary, the endogenous-reactive and the neurotic-psychotic concepts, in William TA, Katz MA, Shields JA Jr (eds): *Recent Advances in the Psychobiology of the Depresive Illnesses.* Washington, DC, US Government Printing Office, 1972, pp 283–293.
5. Holinger PC: Adolescent suicide: An epidemiological study of recent trends. *Am J Psychiatry* 1978;135:754–756.
6. Carlson G, Strober M: Affective disorders in adolescence. *Psychiatr Clin North Am* 1979;2:511–526.
7. Friedman RC, Clarkin JF, Corn R, et al: DSM-III and affective pathology in hospitalized adolescents. *J Nerv Ment Dis* 1982;170:511–521.
8. Clarkin JC, Friedman RC, Hurt SW, et al: Affective and character pathology of suicidal adolescents and young adult inpatients. Paper presented to the American Association of Suicidology, Fifteenth Annual Meeting, New York, April 17, 1982.
9. Friedman RC, Aronoff MS, Clarkin JF, et al: Suicidal behavior in depressed borderline patients. *Am J Psychiatry,* in press.

226

10. American Psychiatric Association: *Diagnostic and Statistical Manual of Mental Disorders*, ed 3. Washington, DC, American Psychiatric Association, 1980.
11. Feighner J, Robins E, Guze S, et al: Diagnostic criteria for use in psychiatric research. *Arch Gen Psychiatry* 1972;26:57-63.
12. Endicott J, Spitzer RL: A diagnostic interview: The schedule for affective disorders and schizophrenia. *Arch Gen Psychiatry* 1978;35:837-844.
13. Puig-Antich J: Affective disorders in childhood: A review and perspective. *Psychiatr Clin North Am* 1980;3:403-424.
14. Carlson G, Cantwell DP: Unmasking depression in children and adolescents. *Am J Psychiatry* 1980;137:445-449.
15. Hudgens RW: *Psychiatric Disorders in Adolescence.* Baltimore, Williams & Wilkins, 1974.
16. Akiskal HS, Bitar AH, Puzantian VR, et al: The nosological status of neurotic depression. *Arch Gen Psychiatry* 1978;35:756-766.
17. Stone MH: *The Borderline Syndromes: Constitution, Personality and Adaptation.* New York, McGraw-Hill, 1980.
18. Stone MH: The borderline syndrome: Evaluation of the term, genetic aspects and prognosis. *Am J Psychother* 1977;31:345-365.
19. Akiskal HS: Subaffective disorders: Dysthymic, Cyclothymic and bipolar II disorders in the "borderline realm." *Psychiatr Clin North Am* 1981;4:25-57.
20. Bakwin RM: Suicide in children and adolescents. *J Am Med Wom Assoc* 1973;28:643-650.
21. Crook T, Raskin A, Davis D: Factors associated with attempted suicide among hospitalized depressed patients. *Psychol Med* 1975;5:381-388.
22. Lester D: Suicide as an aggressive act: A replication with a control for neuroticism. *J Gen Psychol* 1968;79:83-86.
23. Nelson VR, Nielson EC, Checketts KT: Interpersonal attitudes of suicidal individuals. *Psychol Rep* 1977;40:983-989.
24. Richman J, Charles E: Patient dissatisfaction and attempted suicide. *Community Ment Health J* 1976;12:301-305.
25. Vinoda KS: Personality characteristics of attempted suicide. *Br J Psychiatry* 1966;112:1143-1150.
26. Weissman M, Fox K, Klerman GL: Hostility and depression associated with suicide attempts. *Am J Psychiatry* 1973;130:150-154.
27. Crumley FE: Adolescent suicide attempts. *JAMA* 1979;241:2404-2407.
28. Spitzer RL, Endicott J, Robins E: Research diagnostic criteria: Rationale and reliability. *Arch Gen Psychiatry* 1978;35:773-782.
29. Puig-Antich J, Blau S, Marx N, et al: Prepubertal major depressive disorder: A pilot study. *J Am Acad Child Psychiatry* 1978;17:695-707.
30. Strober M, Green J, Carlson G: Phenomenology and subtypes of major depressive disorder in adolescence. *J Affective Disorders* 1981;3:281-290.
31. Jacobs J: *Adolescent Suicide.* New York, Wiley & Sons, 1971
32. Hawton K, O'Grady J, Osborn M, et al: Adolescents who take overdoses: Their characteristics, problems and contacts with helping agencies. *Br J Psychiatry* 1982;140:118-123.
33. Hawton K, O'Grady J, Osborn M, et al: Classification of adolescents who take overdoses. *Br J Psychiatry* 1982;140:124-131.
34. Weissman MM, Myers JK, Thompson D: Depression and its treatment in a US urban community. *Arch Gen Psychiatry* 1981;38:417-421.

CHAPTER 14

SUICIDE IN MALE ADOLESCENTS

JEROME A. MOTTO

Limited empirical data are available regarding the psychosocial characteristics of adolescents who die by suicide. This discussion presents findings from a project that attempts to overcome some of the obstacles to obtaining such data. It reports the prospective study of a sample of 335 adolescents (aged 10 to 19) known to be at high risk for suicide by virtue of their admission to a hospital due to a depressive or suicidal state. The 122 male subjects in this sample, including 11 (9%) suicides, were examined in detail. The variables most closely associated with a suicidal outcome included: clear communication of intent and actively seeking help in those who had made a suicide attempt, fears of losing mind or having a rare disease, over five hours sleep, negative or mixed attitude toward interview when first seen, financial resources over $100, moderate ability to communicate with others, feelings of hopelessness, and apathy-psychomotor retardation. Though the methodological problems inherent in this research area are not completely solved, the empirical nature of the observations provide us with a perspective that has not previously been available.

Suicide in the young has long held a special place among the concerns of society and of the behavioral science community. One of the best known psychiatric discussions of our time was the symposium on suicide in students which was presented by the Vienna Psychoanalytic Society[1] in 1910. Then, as now, a perceived increase in suicide among young people created renewed interest in self-destructive behavior and the tragedy of its appearance early in life.

In spite of this interest, little systematic research was reported during the next 50 years. Balser and Masterson[2] observed in 1959 that the only discussion they could find in the literature was a single report in 1954[3] on four cases of suicide attempt. In order to provide a background for their paper on adolescent suicide, they were obliged to use data derived from adults and children.

Recent decades have seen a sharp increase in reports on suicide in adolescents, most of which have been theoretical or clinical in nature, and focused on suicidal ideation and behavior rather than on completed suicide.[4-10] A recent review of the past 20 years (1960–1980) of research on child and adolescent suicide by Berman and Cohen-Sandler[11] found only two data-based studies on the characteristics of those who completed the act.[12-13] Both of these reports are compromised by the usual problems of retrospective design, lack of comparison groups, noncomparable subjects, and descriptive rather than statistical analysis of data. Berman and Cohen-Sandler conclude that the paucity of empirical studies may account for contradictory and confusing statements that have appeared in the literature, and that in spite of the many studies undertaken, "glaring methodological weaknesses — leave our understanding . . . only slightly advanced from twenty years ago." Special note is taken of ill-defined samples, lack of controls or comparison groups, vague outcome criteria and absence of statistical analysis. Petzel and Cline[14] also pointed out, in an extensive epidemiological review, that "research on suicide in youth is complicated by . . . a scarcity of studies using adequate sampling and control techniques and by the limitations imposed by retrospective data."

That few statistical investigations have been done may, in part, reflect an appropriate focus on the importance of individual, family and social dynamics in the persons studied. At the same time, it is clear that efforts to identify any generalizable principles by statistical means have been seriously hampered by the practical difficulties of gathering adequate samples, finding controls, obtaining a wide spectrum of data, maintaining prolonged followup, and having access to detailed outcome information. For example, Mattsson et al[5], having observed that no followup data on suicidal emergencies in child psychiatry had yet been published, followed 75 suicidal youngsters who had first been seen in a suicidal state. When only three repeated suicide attempts and no suicides had occurred after one year of followup, they acknowledged that their data could "contribute little to the scanty knowledge of the long-term personality formulation of children with a history of suicidal acts." Similarly, Cohen-Sandler et al[15] followed up 76 subjects for five months to three years (mean 18 months) and found no known suicides to examine.

Both male and female subjects participated in the present study, but the universally observed preponderance of male suicides in the adolescent age group, which was seen clearly here, suggested that statistical observations would only be meaningful in the male subgroup. In this regard it is of interest that during the two years of the Mattsson et al[5] investigation, there were seven suicides in persons under age 18 in the

Cleveland area, the locale of their study. All seven were adolescent males. Welner et al,[6] in St. Louis, found that five of the six suicides in their followup of adolescent inpatients were male, with a mean followup period of 9.4 years. Similarly, Sanborn et al[12] report that in their sample of adolescent suicides recorded in New Hampshire during the two-year period, 1968–1970, 10 of 11 suicides were males.

This report represents an effort to overcome the problems of precise sample definition, sample size, limited data base, suitable comparison group and clear outcome criterion. Though these problems are not completely solved, the empirical nature of the observations may provide us with a perspective that has not been previously available.

METHOD

Definition of the Sample

For the five-year period, 1969–1974, persons were identified who were admitted, because of a depressive or suicidal state, to any of nine psychiatric inpatient settings in San Francisco. Such persons were considered to represent a high risk for suicide on the basis of prior reports.[16,17] The facilities included five mental health center inpatient units, two psychiatric wards at the University of California, San Francisco, Medical Center, and two private hospital psychiatric services, one of which was primarily for adolescents. Of the 3005 persons who satisfied these criteria for admission to the study, 335 were aged 10 to 19, of whom 213 were female and 122 were male.

It is this sample of 122 males aged 10 to 19 that is the focus of attention in this discussion. Their ethnic background was primarily Caucasian, with blacks predominating in the nonwhite categories (Table 14-1).

Table 14-1
Ethnic Distribution of Males
Aged 10–19 in Sample

Ethnic Group	Number	Percent
Asian	2	1.6
Black	14	11.5
Hispanic	6	4.9
Native American	1	0.8
White	94	77.0
Mixed	3	2.5
Other	2	1.6
Total	122	

Seventy-six (62.3%) had made a suicide attempt, precipitating their admission. The other 46 presented with other suicidal manifestations or severe depression.

Procedure

An extensive evaluative interview was carried out with each subject, and ratings determined for 101 psychological, social and epidemiological variables (Appendix). The information gathered constituted a detailed clinical inquiry, but included no items that would not be found in any thorough psychiatric examination. This procedure generally required two to four hours, and was often carried out in more than one session. Information from the subject was supplemented by ward staff, medical records and, when available, family members. The investigators shared and discussed the data with members of the ward staff, but did not enter actively into the treatment or management of the subjects.

An annual review of the State Death Registry was subsequently carried out for the 10-year period, 1969 through 1978. This served to identify those subjects who died in California, and state residents who died elsewhere, during a 4- to 10-year followup period after discharge from the hospital. Information from death certificates, coroners' records, families, health care personnel, and health care records were reviewed to determine which deaths were due to suicide.

Eleven suicides and three nonsuicidal deaths were identified. The suicides represented 9.0% of the sample and approximately 20.0% of the suicides in this age/sex group in San Francisco during the 10-year period of the study, 1969–1978. With a mean followup time of seven years, the suicide rate was 1.3% per year. The ethnic distribution of the suicides was two black, eight white, and one Asian subject.

For the 11 suicidal deaths, the mean elapsed time from hospital discharge to suicidal death was 38 months, ranging from one and one-half to 90 months. The three nonsuicidal deaths were not included in subsequent procedures, leaving a final total of 119 subjects for further study.

Using the entire set of 119 subjects, the 101 psychosocial and epidemiological variables explored in the initial interview were examined for their individual association with the outcome variable, completed suicide. The procedures used were those outlined in detail in 1976 by Heilbron and Bostrom.[18] Interval scale variables were examined using the Mann-Whitney statistic. Categories of nominal variables were combined in a pattern previously obtained in an analysis of adult subjects, in which the categories were ordered according to the observed proportions of suicides, and those with similar proportions collapsed together. The proportions of suicides in the higher risk categories were compared to the proportion in the lower risk categories using Fisher's exact test. Because three nominal variables produced two different dichotomizations, a total of 104 analyses of association were carried out.

RESULTS

The screening process resulted in the identification of nine variables showing a significant association with suicidal outcome (P < .05), as shown in Table 14-2. Two of these variables are related to a current suicide attempt: clear communication of intent, and help having been actively sought before the attempt was made. Four variables are clinical considerations often associated with severe emotional disturbances: fear that one is losing one's mind or is the victim of a strange disease, sleep pattern, severe feelings of helplessness and hopelessness, and the presence of apathy and psychomotor retardation. Two variables reflect subjective judgments by the interviewer: the presence of a negative or ambivalent attitude toward the interviewer on the subject's part, and the subject's capacity to communicate with others. Lastly, one variable reflects the demographic question of financial resources, with any level greater than $100 indicating high risk. The resources of the parents, if available to the youngster, were included in determining the response category.

The sleep item is paradoxical in that the high-risk category is the reporting of six or more hours of sleep per night, contrary to an expected loss of sleep time. For the fear variable, the statistical program indicates both a high and an intermediate level of risk, based on the distribution

Table 14-2
Variables with Statistically Significant Association with Suicidal Outcome (P < .05)

Variable	High Risk Category	N	Suicides	P Value
1. Communication of intent, if attempt made	Clear	12	4	.014
2. Fear of losing mind or rare disease	Questionable, mild	18	2	.018
	Moderate, severe	17	4	
3. Help sought before suicide attempt	Actively sought help	20	5	.019
4. Sleep	Six or more hours	85	11	.020
5. Attitude toward interview	Negative or mixed	50	8	.033
6. Financial resources	Over $100	50	8	.033
7. Ability to communicate with others	Moderate	63	9	.042
8. Feelings of hopelessness	Severe	22	5	.045
9. Apathy — psychomotor retardation	Mild, moderate or severe	64	9	.047

shown in Table 14-3. It must be kept in mind that all subjects are considered a "high risk" from a clinical point of view, but can be further ordered as to relative risk into higher and lower categories.

The ratings of the subjects' ability to communicate with others did not suggest a continuous influence on outcome as anticipated. Those with "high" communication skills showed the lowest risk as expected, but an intermediate level of risk was found in the "low" category of communication, while those with "moderate" communication skills were in the highest risk group, as indicated in Table 14-4.

Eight additional variables were found to be associated with suicidal outcome at a level that approached the usual standard for statistical significance (P values between .05 and .10), as indicated in Table 14-5. None of these variables assumes that a suicide attempt has been made, but three reflect data elicited in assessing the present risk of suicide: the presence of moderate or severe suicidal thoughts, the presence of moderate or severe suicidal impulses, and no action having been taken to implement a contemplated suicide. Two variables require subjective judgments by the interviewer: low or moderate ability to communicate with the interviewer, and low ability to relate to others in school, social or family life. One clinical variable indicates minimal or no drug abuse, one variable specifies one prior psychiatric hospitalization, and one demographic description indicates a birth rank order of fourth or more.

Two of these high-risk indicators are contrary to expectations: the absence of any preparatory action toward a contemplated suicide attempt, and minimal or no drug abuse. The latter is consistent with the

Table 14-3
Distribution of Variable: Fears of Losing Mind, Cancer, Rare Disease

Response Category	Nonsuicide	Suicide	Total	Percent Suicide	Risk Category
None	79	5	84	6.0	Low
Questionable or mild	16	2	18	11.1	Intermediate
Moderate or severe	13	4	17	23.5	High

Table 14-4
Distribution of Variable: Ability to Communicate with Others

Response Category	Nonsuicide	Suicide	Total	Percent Suicide	Risk Category
High	20	0	20	0	Low
Moderate	54	9	63	14.3	High
Low	34	2	36	5.6	Intermediate

Table 14-5
Variables Associated with Suicidal Outcome at a Level Approaching Statistical Significance (P = +.05 < p < .10)

Variable	High Risk Category	N	Suicides	P Value
1. Presence of suicidal thoughts	Moderate or severe	55	8	.062
2. Action toward contemplated attempt	None	36	6	.071
3. Ability to communicate with interviewer	Moderate or low	95	11	.074
4. Drug addiction or abuse	None or mild	63	8	.090
5. Prior psychiatric hospitalization	One prior hospitalization	29	5	.094
6. Birth rank order	Fourth or more	20	3	.097
7. Presence of suicidal impulses	Moderate or severe	59	8	.097
8. Ability to relate to others	Low	59	8	.097

findings of Sanborn et al,[12] who found that only one of their 11 suicide subjects had a history of drug use, and Shaffer[13] makes no mention of drug abuse in his sample of 21 male suicides.

The absence of preparation for a contemplated attempt suggests that those who go on to suicide are the more impulsive and unpredictable youngsters. We could also speculate that those who are willing to trust a caring adult with information about preparatory activity are able to relate well enough to find some stabilizing support. Those who are unable to trust helping persons in this way may be considered more vulnerable, and for some subjects the rating of "none" for this variable may be more indicative of such distrust than anything else. In any case, the six suicides of 36 subjects in this category provide ample clinical evidence that we cannot find any reassurance in a negative response to this inquiry.

DISCUSSION

Methodology

The consistently negative assessment of the results of past studies of adolescent suicide has generated an understandable pessimism about the potentials of this area for systematic investigation. Rigorous reviews of the field[11,14,19] not only point out the severe methodological weaknesses that contribute to the problem, but also acknowledge the practical obstacles involved. For example, in assessing risk, how can a control sample be generated for validation purposes when every high-risk individual must, on ethical grounds, be provided all possible treatment resources?

Even investigators seem dispirited in reporting that, ". . . apart from outright threats of suicide, there was little or nothing that could be found that acted consistently as an indicator of suicide . . .. Perhaps part of the difficulty lies in the inherent nature of suicide in this age group. . . highly impulsive, spur-of-the-moment . . .".[12] Neuringer[19] states flatly that "all efforts to identify the specific behavior of suicides in adolescents are doomed to disappointment," because of the likelihood that such behavior springs from "the general emotional disequilibrium found in any disturbed adolescent." He suggests that the general level of pathology may be a better indicator of risk than specific behavior, and whether suicidal behavior will occur may depend upon "luck or happenstance."

If we nonetheless persist in efforts to clarify the problem, the first task is to define our population clearly, which can be accomplished largely by focusing on completed suicide within a specific age range. This avoids the inevitable ambiguity of "suicidal behavior," which has plagued so many studies, and which Neuringer[19] suggests we relinquish as a phenomenon to be considered for risk assessment. As data accumulate, it should be possible to refine our age categories into pre-, early, middle and late adolescence in order to reflect the progressive developmental tasks which generate the conflicts of these specific periods of life. The age range of 10 to 19, used here and by Sanborn et al,[12] provides a starting point for this process. It is also consistent with public health statistical data, which are often reported for age groups 10 to 14 and 15 to 19.

To study the antecedents of a completed suicide requires that we gather our data before the event to obtain known or hypothesized outcome-relevant data. This can only be addressed by a prospective design, and the identification of a high-risk population willing to participate in the data-gathering process. Such an approach dictates that a great many persons be included who will not go on to suicide, but who can subsequently serve as a closely parallel comparison group for those persons who do.

A prospective design also requires that sufficient time be taken to include enough persons to obtain observations regarding suicidal outcome in the quantities required for statistical treatment. The five years of data-gathering and four- to 10-year followup utilized here only partially satisfied this need. More elaborate statistical programs were not considered appropriate for the size of this sample, hence we are restricted in the procedures we can use.

As a last methodological consideration, when persons other than the investigators are responsible for the treatment and management of subjects, the influences brought to bear are those of time and the resources of the health system and of society at large. Since these cannot usually be controlled, or even monitored, it is very difficult to determine the influence of a "treatment variable" in determining outcome. This issue remains a major problem thoughout the field of studies in suicide.

Specificity of High-Risk Variables to Male Adolescents

A question of special interest here is whether the variables found in our sample would apply to females in the same clinical circumstances and 10- to 19-year age range. The four suicides found in our sample of 213 females do not permit statistical treatment, but some descriptive comparisons are possible. With an overall suicide proportion of 1.9% (0.3% per year), two (4.4%) of the 45 female adolescents with severe hopelessness and four (3.3%) of the 123 exhibiting apathy and psychomotor retardation went on to suicide. These rather tenuous associations are the only evidence that the high-risk variables derived from the sample of adolescent males are applicable to adolescent females.

Perhaps of greater usefulness is the observation that of the 27 females rated "high" in "ability to communicate with others," none suicided. Similarly, none of the 20 male adolescents in this category did so, suggesting the possibility of using communication skills as a low-risk indicator. Applying this to the item, "ability to communicate with interviewer," we find the same result, with no suicides among the 24 males or 36 females. In this regard, Sanborn et al[12] comment that eight of the 10 families of the adolescent suicides they studied were marked by severe discord, and that a major problem of these families appeared to be in communication. An intriguing aspect of this issue is that the "moderate" rating for ability to communicate was consistently associated with the highest incidence of suicide, both for males and females. One wonders if those adolescents who communicate well tend to use verbal channels to provide for their needs, those with few verbal skills find a substitute method, and those with only moderate skills just struggle on without developing other alternatives.

A comparison of our sample of adolescent males with a sample of 535 males, aged 20 to 29, using the same selection criteria, reveals overlap with two risk items from Table 14-2: "help sought actively before a current suicide attempt" and "severe feelings of hopelessness." These two items are the only ones in Table 14-2 that show a strong association with suicide in a sample of males in all age groups (N = 1329), suggesting that these are the least age-specific of the high-risk indicators. The judgment of whether feelings of hopelessness are "severe" is a subjective decision for which clear criteria are not available, but in practice this has not presented difficulties. Although hopelessness has long been recognized as an antecedent to suicide, its role as distinct from other depressive symptoms has only recently been emphasized by Beck.[20]

The roles of hopelessness and communication skills may be closely related, in that problems with communication can generate or intensify a sense of alienation that makes one especially vulnerable to feelings of hopelessness. Peck and Schrut[21] describe a sample of college student suicides as being made up of students who were more hopeless, more isolated, and less likely to communicate to others that they needed help. This "loner" category of suicidal adolescent is most troublesome because the persons involved tend to provide so few clues, and often come from intact families without evident pathology.[21] Shaffer[13] also refers to this pattern by noting two categories in his sample of suicides, aged 12 to 14, those who led a "solitary, isolated existence," and those prone to "aggressive or violent outbursts." The clinical observation of high risk in youngsters who seem alienated and alone has long been noted.[22,23]

Variables Significantly Associated With Suicide

If we were to assume no differences in any of the characteristics between the suicides and the nonsuicides, the large number of comparisons made using a P value of .05 would lead us to expect several items to be significant by chance alone. The estimated number would be $104 \times .05 = 5$ significant at the 5% level, and the same number significant at the 10% level but not at the 5% level. Nine variables were found at the $P < .05$ level (Table 14-2), and eight variables with a P value between .05 and .10 (Table 14-5). Thus, the majority of the items that have been identified as indicating "high risk" may have arisen by chance.

The two high-risk items which imply that a suicide attempt preceded our clinical interview, "clear communication of intent" and "help sought actively before attempt" (Table 14-2), give us reason for both hope and dismay. It appears that ample notice of an impending suicidal action was given in these instances, but that the needs of these youngsters were greater than the available resources could meet. We are aware of how demanding and difficult suicidal youngsters can be,[24,25] and that too often such expressions as "wanting attention," "suicidal gesture" and "manipulative" are used in evaluating them. The 36% of the suicides in our sample who had clearly indicated their intent before completing the act, compares remarkably closely with the 40% reported by Sanborn et al[12] and 46% found by Shaffer.[13]

The item "fear of losing mind or having rare disease" (Table 14-2) brings to mind the intense need of the growing youngster to be seen as the same as his/her peers, without "defect" and without question of developing into a competent adult. Difficulty understanding the effects of emotional turmoil, and the awful threat associated with the stigma of "craziness" can generate a panic state of suicidal proportions.

The item "hours of sleep per night" (Table 14-2), with high risk indicated by six or more hours of sleep, seems contrary to expectation. It is of interest that the same high-risk variable was derived for a general adult population aged 18 to 70, using elaborate statistical methods including a validation procedure.[26] It seems likely that sleep disturbance is an indicator of intensity of depression or anxiety, but that the degree of suicide risk is not directly related to the presence of these states. Whatever the explanation for this, it seems clear that empirically we cannot take reassurance from an apparently "normal" sleep pattern.

Financial resources (Table 14-2) also vary directly with suicide risk, with the lowest risk among those who have no available funds or who are in debt. This relationship was also found to be a high-risk indicator in a large adult sample, as mentioned in the preceding paragraph.[26] Most of the ratings reflect parental resources available to the adolescent if needed.

The observation by an interviewer that the adolescent takes a negative or ambivalent attitude towards the interview (Table 14-2) may indicate a communication problem or difficulty relating to other persons, both of which are high-risk items included in Table 14-5. Shortcomings in the interviewers' skills may play a role as well. The suggestion must be considered that an underlying mixture of guilt, fear, resentment and especially dependent-independent conflict interferes with the expression of a desire for help, posing an obstacle to the rapport that is so necessary to create a positive atmosphere in the interview situation.

The item "apathy-psychomotor retardation" (Table 14-2) is likely to be a reflection of the related variable, "feelings of hopelessness," discussed above. Whether a manifestation of a depressive state, a thought disorder or some other pathological process, from the point of view of suicide risk, it has the advantage of visibility with little potential for concealment. It is during recovery from such a state that suicide risk is said to be increased, but a conservative approach would accord it a great deal of respect at any stage.

Traditional High-Risk Variables

Some variables have been repeatedly identified, in clinical studies, as related to "suicidal behavior," and are conspicuous by their absence from Tables 14-2 and 14-5. The most obvious omission is the background of a "broken home." Though this characteristic is one of the most consistent findings in studies of depression and suicide attempts, both in adolescents[4,5] and adults,[27-29] Sanborn et al[12] found that in all 10 cases of adolescent suicide in their study, the youngster had been living with both natural parents at the time of death. Shaffer[13] found in his study that only four (19%) of the 21 male suicides came from a broken home. It would be necessary to know the proportion of broken homes in this age group (10–14) in the population at large to assess its role here.

Stanley and Barter[30] emphasized the specific nature of the family disruption, observing that the threats of divorce or separation were more frequent among the parents of suicidal adolescents, as compared with nonsuicidal adolescents. The likelihood of protracted tension and hostility in the home preceding such a break may suggest greater and more prolonged stress on a growing youngster, with a greater likelihood of self-destructive patterns resulting. The reasoning is clear, but the data are not insofar as completed suicide in adolescents is concerned. Except for the two studies mentioned above,[12,13] reports comparing completed and attempted suicide focus primarily on adult populations.[28] Jacobs[31] suggests that the crucial issue is not simply disruption of the family in early life, but the stability of the ensuing pattern, and especially whether disruptive events continue to occur after the onset of adolescence.

In the present study, the data suggest that in high-risk adolescent males, the history of a broken home is more closely associated with completed suicide than with no suicide, as seen in Table 14-6. The numbers are too small to examine separately for each category, but we see that 4% (2 of 50) of the subjects rated "no broken home" went on to suicide, while 13% (9 of 69) of those in the "broken home" categories did so. Another way of stating this is that of the 11 suicides, 82% (9) came from a broken home, while of the 108 nonsuicides, 56% (60) came from a broken home. The distribution of the high-risk adolescent female sample is included in Table 14-6 for comparison.

Table 14-6
Distribution of Variable, "From Broken Home," by Sex and Outcome

Response Category	Males 10–19		Females 10–19	
	N	Suicides(%)	N	Suicides(%)
1. No broken home*	50	2 (4)	74	2 (3)
2. Death of father	14	2 (14)	15	1 (7)
3. Death of mother	6	0 (0)	10	0 (0)
4. Death of both parents	1	0 (0)	2	0 (0)
5. Separation, father left	11	1 (9)	34	1 (3)
6. Separation, mother left	2	0 (0)	5	0 (0)
7. Divorce, father left	25	3 (12)	51	0 (0)
8. Divorce, mother left	2	2 (100)	3	0 (0)
9. Separation or divorce both parents left	5	1 (20)	10	0 (0)
10. Other	3	0 (0)	6	0 (0)
Totals	119	11	210	4

*This category included for comparison purposes only.

Alcohol and drug abuse are frequently mentioned in discussions of adolescents who display "suicidal behavior," but the relationship to completed suicide in our sample is not statistically significant. The use of drugs is related at a level approaching significance, however, and in a way contrary to expectations. Table 14-5, item #4, indicates that, paradoxically, mild or no drug abuse is related to a higher level of suicidal outcome than to other categories of drug use, though the actual distribution (Table 14-7) suggests that when drug use is "severe," the risk is also high. The numbers of suicides in these categories, however, are not large enough to provide more than suggested possibilities. These observations are consistent with the view that for some young people, drugs at moderate levels may provide a pain-reducing function that helps them to survive until they develop better coping skills or their life situation is changed sufficiently to permit them to manage without drugs. If their situation does not improve, drug use may increase until it creates more pain than it alleviates, and the risk of suicide rises.

A history of prior suicidal behavior is a very visible indication of potential risk, and is customarily regarded as an important consideration in all age groups. In our sample, six (8.8%) of the 68 subjects who reported no prior suicide attempts went on to eventually suicide, while five (9.8%) of the 51 with a history of one or more attempts did so. This difference is not great enough to be very helpful in either risk assessment or clarifying patterns of behavior in this population. It is of interest that Sanborn et al[12] found no evidence of a prior suicide attempt in any of the adolescent suicides they studied. Shaffer[13] stated that 14 (46%) of his 30 subjects had previously "discussed, threatened or attempted" suicide. He adds the pertinent observation that those youngsters who killed themselves following a disciplinary crisis were less likely to have attempted or threatened suicide previously than those whose deaths were not precipitated in this way.

It is quite possible that we were not always provided completely accurate information by these young people, and that a better historical

Table 14-7
Distribution of Variable: Drug Abuse

Response Category	Nonsuicide	Suicide	Total	Percent Suicides
No drug abuse	32	5	37	13.5
Mild drug abuse	22	3	25	12.0
Moderate drug abuse	26	1	27	3.7
Severe drug abuse	15	2	17	11.8
Sporadic drug abuse	12	0	12	0
Prior history only	1	0	1	0
Total	108	11	119	

marker would be prior psychiatric admissions, a variable that did approach statistical significance (Table 14-5, #5). We might assume that a number of prior admissions were due to suicidal states, and that such admissions were less likely to be concealed than suicide attempts. Subjects with no prior psychiatric hospitalization showed a 6.6% incidence of subsequent suicide (4 of 61), while those with one or more prior admissions had a 12.1% incidence (7 of 58).

The presence of emotional disorder in the family is another frequent association with suicide risk that does not rank high in this empirical approach. In other studies of completed suicides, Sanborn et al[12] report two families with identified emotional disorder of 10 subjects. Shaffer[13] found evidence of mental illness in nine families and alcoholism in eight families of the 21 male suicides in his sample.

The subjects reported here reveal 37 instances of functional emotional disorder in the family. Six of these 37 subjects (16.8%) went on suicide, as compared with four suicides (6.8%) in the 59 subjects with no disorder recognized in the family. These differences are consistent with our expectations, but the numbers are too small to make inferences with any confidence. Of 22 subjects with alcoholism in the family, one (4.4%) suicided. The distribution of emotional disorders found in the entire sample are indicated in Table 14-8.

The presence of depression has traditionally been a major concern as regards suicide. That it does not appear in an empirical study is probably accounted for by the vagaries of diagnostic criteria and the fact that young people so often present their conflicts in ways other than the usual depressive pattern. Shaffer[13] found a "depressed mood or tearfulness" the most frequent symptom in his sample, present in seven of his 21 male subjects. Sanborn[12] refers to frequent unhappiness and depression in his sample, but could not differentiate these states from "the unhappy and

Table 14-8
Distribution of Variable: Emotional Disorder in Family

Type of Disorder	Nonsuicide	Suicide	Total	Percent Suicides
No disorder	55	4	59	6.8
Alcoholism	22	1	23	4.4
Antisocial	2	1	3	33.3
Neurosis, affective	9	2	11	18.2
Neurosis, other	1	0	1	0
Neurosis, mixed	6	0	6	0
Psychosis, affective	4	0	4	0
Psychosis, other	5	2	7	28.6
Other	4	1	5	20.0
Total	108	11	119	

depressed moments of everyday living that everyone else manages to cope with." Most of the studies of the relationship of depression and suicide in adolescents have been in subjects other than completed suicides.[5-7] A recent systematic investigation of this question by Carlson and Cantwell[32] found depression in one half of the subjects who attempted suicide, emphasizing the problem of recognizing the risk of suicidal behavior in youngsters who do not manifest depressive symptoms.

CONCLUSIONS

In spite of the severe methodological obstacles to an empirical approach to studying suicide in adolescents, some progress may be possible in clarifying this difficult area. If we aim for "predicting adolescent suicidal behavior,"[19] we are almost certain to be disappointed. A more realistic goal would be to provide a clinically relevant set of data-based observations, indicating how youngsters in a suicidal state who go on to kill themselves differ from those in a suicidal state who do not have this outcome. The characteristics involved can provide only an estimate of risk, not a prediction of suicide as such, and must serve at best as a supplement to the overall evaluation of the adolescent. Intuitive judgment and respect for the uniqueness of each individual must always be the final determinants in utilizing clinical observations.

In view of Balser and Masterson's[2] lament in 1959 that they could find no studies of completed suicide in adolescents and only one report on adolescent suicide attempts in the psychiatric literature, and Berman and Cohen-Sandler's[11] finding that in the ensuing 20 years, there were only two published "data-based" reports, it would seem that this field has been much neglected. Even a hasty review assures us that this is not the case. It is true, however, that the many studies available to us tend to focus on clinical analysis of suicide attempts or on epidemiological data. Very few consider completed suicide and even fewer conform to an experimental design. The reasons for this are clear and realistic but not insurmountable. Long-term, prospective studies can generate adequate samples and data for rigorous statistical analysis, though this is clearly more difficult to accomplish in female adolescents than in males. The present study attempts to demonstrate some basis for this optimism.

Clarifying the nature of suicide risk in adolescents is one step toward our ultimate goal of reducing preventable suicide in young people to a minimum. The even more formidable task of improving treatment and management still confronts us. It is of interest that skills in communicating and relating to others emerge as important elements in this empirical investigation as well as in clinical studies. These are the primary means by which we attempt to exert a therapeutic influence on young people, whether it be in terms of overcoming "existential bad faith"[33] or of generating a "deeply felt encounter"[34] to try to help them discover what brings lasting meaning to life.

ACKNOWLEDGMENTS

This investigation was supported by Grant No. MH 25080, from the Mental Health Services Development Branch, National Institute of Mental Health.

David C. Heilbron, PhD and Richard P. Juster, PhD from the University of California, San Francisco, Computer Center, assisted with the statistical aspects of the study.

REFERENCES

1. Friedman P (ed): *On Suicide.* New York, International Universities Press, 1967.
2. Balser B, Masterson J: Suicide in adolescents. *Am J Psychiatry* 1959;116:400–404.
3. Mason P: Suicide in adolescents. *Psychoanal Rev* 1954;41:48–54.
4. Barter J, Swaback D, Todd D: Adolescent suicide attempts: A follow-up study of hospitalized patients. *Arch Gen Psychiatry* 1968;19:523–527.
5. Mattsson A, Seese L, Hawkins J: Suicidal behavior as a child psychiatric emergency: Clinical characteristics and follow-up results. *Arch Gen Psychiatry* 1969;20:100–109.
6. Welner A, Welner Z, Fishman R: Psychiatric adolescent inpatients: Eight- to ten-year follow-up. *Arch Gen Psychiatry* 1979;36:698–700.
7. Tishler C, McKenry P, Morgan K: Adolescent suicide attempts: Some significant factors. *Suicide Life Threat Behav* 1981;11:86–92.
8. Topol P, Reznikoff M: Perceived peer and family relationships, hopelessness and locus of control as factors in adolescent suicide attempts. *Suicide Life Threat Behav* 1982;12:141–150.
9. Shaffer D: Diagnostic considerations in suicidal behavior in children and adolescents. *J Am Acad Child Psychiatry* 1982;21:414–416.
10. Garfinkel B, Froese A, Hood J: Suicide attempts in children and adolescents. *Am J Psychiatry* 1982;139:1257–1261.
11. Berman A, Cohen-Sandler R: Childhood and adolescent suicide research: A critique. *Crisis* 1982;3:3–5.
12. Sanborn D, Sanborn C, Cimbolic P: Two years of suicide: A study of adolescent suicide in New Hampshire. *Child Psychiatry Hum Dev* 1973;3:234–242.
13. Shaffer D: Suicide in childhood and early adolescence. *J Child Psychol Psychiatry* 1974;15:275–291.
14. Petzel S, Cline D: Adolescent suicide: Epidemiological and biographical aspects, in Feinstein S, Giovacchini P (eds): *Annals of the American Society for Adolescent Psychiatry.* Chicago, University of Chicago Press, 1978, vol 6, pp 239–266.
15. Cohen-Sandler R, Berman A: A follow-up study of hospitalized suicidal children. *J Am Acad Child Psychiatry* 1982;21:414–416.
16. Motto J: Suicide attempts: A longitudinal view. *Arch Gen Psychiatry* 1965;13:516–520.
17. Pokorny A: A follow-up study of 618 suicidal patients. *Am J Psychiatry* 1966;122:1109–1116.

18. Heilbron D, Bostrom A: Selection of variables in estimating suicide risk: Some statistical considerations. Paper read at 9th Annual Meeting of the American Association of Suicidology, Los Angeles, California, April 30, 1976.
19. Neuringer C: Problems in predicting adolescent suicidal behavior. *Psychiatric Opinion* 1975;12:27–31.
20. Beck A, Kovacs J, Weissman J: Hopelessness and suicidal behavior. *JAMA* 1975;234:1146–1149.
21. Peck M, Schrut A: Suicidal behavior among college students. *Health Services and Mental Health Administration Health Reports* 1971;86:149–156.
22. Jan-Tauch J: Studies of children, 1960–1963, in *New Jersey Public School Studies.* Trenton, NJ, State of New Jersey, Department of Education, 1963.
23. Schrut A: Suicidal adolescents and children. *JAMA* 1964;188:1103–1107.
24. Meeks J: *The Fragile Alliance.* Baltimore, Williams & Wilkins, 1971.
25. Miller D: *Adolescence: Psychology, Psychopathology and Psychotherapy.* New York, Jason Aronson, 1974, pp 365–376.
26. Motto J: Development of a suicide risk assessment instrument. Paper read at 15th Annual Meeting of the American Association of Suicidology, New York, NY, April 16, 1982.
27. Greer S: The relationship between parental loss and attempted suicide. *Br J Psychiatry* 1964;110:698–705.
28. Dorpat T, Jackson J, Ripley H: Broken homes and attempted and completed suicide. *Arch Gen Psychiatry* 1965;12:213–216.
29. Levi L, Fales C, Stein M, et al: Separation and attempted suicide. *Arch Gen Psychiatry* 1966;15:158–164.
30. Stanley E, Barter J: Adolescent suicidal behavior. *Am J Orthopsychiatry* 1970;40:87–96.
31. Jacobs J: *Adolescent Suicide.* New York, Wiley-Interscience, 1971.
32. Carlson G, Cantwell D: Suicidal behavior and depression in children and adolescents. *J Am Acad Child Psychiatry* 1982;21:361–368.
33. Shamblin W: Existential bad faith and psychotherapy with acting-out teenagers. *Highland Highlights* 1982;7:11–14.
34. Ishii K: Adolescent self-destructive behavior and crisis intervention in Japan. *Suicide Life Threat Behav* 1981;11:51–61.

APPENDIX

Data Coded for Each Subject

Demographic Data

Age
Sex
Race
Present marital status
Duration of present marital status
Number of living children
Number of times married
Number of times divorced
Birth rank order
Number of children in sibship
Age separation and gender of next older sibling
Age separation and gender of next younger sibling

Type of residence
San Francisco residence lifelong?
Country of acculturation
Present religious affiliation
Formal education (years)
Occupation of subject
Present employment status

Suicide Attempt Data

Method
Communication of intent
Help sought before attempt
Help sought after attempt
Suicide note left?
Seriousness (injury)

Seriousness (intent)
Effect of attempt on consciousness
Attitude toward attempt

Suicidal Thoughts

Method contemplated
Availability of method contemplated
Preparation of contemplated attempt
Action taken toward contemplated
  attempt
Termination behavior

*Consideration of Future
Suicide Attempt*

Method contemplated
Availability of method contemplated
Preparation of contemplated attempt
Action taken toward contemplated
  attempt

Present Life Situation

Acuteness of precipitating circumstances
Loss of significant person(s)
Threatened loss of significant
  person(s)
Other significant loss
Other threatened loss
Alcohol abuse?
Drug addiction or abuse?
Homosexuality (overt)?
Special isolating factor
Present state of health
Other stress
Present occupation (lethality)

Past Life Situation

From broken home?
Emotional disorder in family:
  relationship
Emotional disorder in family:
  type of disorder
Suicide in family (number)
Suicide in family (relationship)
Prior psychiatric hospitalization(s)
  (number)
Prior suicidal ideas
Prior suicide attempts (number)

Physical health for past year
Care required for physical illness
Prior efforts to obtain help
Results of prior efforts to obtain help
Stability of job pattern
Stability of present marital relationship

Present Depressive State

Sleep
Appetite
Weight loss
Despondency
Euphoria
Crying
Loss of prior interests
Feelings of hopelessness
Guilt–shame–remorse
Apathy
Suicidal thoughts
Suicidal impulses
Acuteness of suicidal ideas
Feelings of confusion
Ideas of persecution
Fears of "losing mind," of cancer or
  rare disease
Feelings of being a burden to others
Verbal expression of anger
Motor expression of anger
Attitude toward hospitalization
Attitute toward interview
Degree of psychosis
Readiness to accept help

Resources

Other-person resource available
Financial resources
Ability to relate to others
Ability to relate to interviewer
Ability to communicate with others
Ability to communicate with interviewer
Overall stability of prior pattern
Capacity to control behavior
Motivation for help
Church as resource
Intelligence
Capacity for self-scrutiny
Capacity for self-understanding
Interviewer's reaction to subject

CHAPTER 15

SOME DIFFICULTIES IN ASSESSING DEPRESSION AND SUICIDE IN CHILDHOOD

ERNA FURMAN

The focus of this chapter is on three areas: 1) uncertainties in defining and diagnosing nonpsychotic depression prior to adulthood are explored, and tne theoretical problems and clinical pitfalls in using a descriptive definition are highlighted and exemplified; 2) some personality factors which allow or compel suicidal actions in children and adolescents are pin-pointed, especially the manner in which sadomasochistic fixations and early deficiencies in bodily self-love contribute to self-hurting tendencies; and 3) the relationship between depression and suicide is discussed, when these pathologies do and do not coexist, and how this affects the chances of helpful therapeutic intervention.

UNCERTAINTIES IN DEFINING AND DIAGNOSING DEPRESSION

My interest in assessing and understanding depressed children began in connection with studying parental bereavement in childhood.[1] At that time, a group of child psychoanalysts, affiliated with the Cleveland Center for Research in Child Development and the Hanna Perkins Therapeutic Nursery School and Kindergarten, pooled and researched the psychoanalytic data we had gained from the long-term treatments of 23 children who had lost a parent through death. My colleagues and I decided to focus one aspect of our research work on depression because some of our patients showed depressive symptomatology prior to and/or during periods of their treatments,[2] and because object loss had often been linked with depression in psychoanalytic writings. We found that there was a dearth of data gathered from the analyses of depressed children. The limited available clinical material stemmed from the observations of infants and from diagnostic or brief psychotherapeutic contacts with older children.

Although many authors had addressed the topic, they did not agree upon a metapsychological definition or any aspects of it — the genetic origins, the pertinent dynamic and structural conflicts within the personality, the specific economic investments and shifts of psychic energy, and the adaptational factors. The links between depressive phenomena at different phases in childhood and in adulthood were tentative, mostly theoretical and insufficiently documented. There was not even a generally accepted descriptive clinical definition of depression. In our dismay we took comfort from Sandler and Joffe[3] who found themselves in a similar quandary and introduced their paper on childhood depression by stating, "The research worker who aims to investigate the subject of depression in childhood must inevitably find his task extraordinarily difficult."

Although much has been said and written on childhood depression in more recent years, the basic obstacles to definition, diagnosis and metapyschological understanding of childhood depression are still with us. This chapter will attempt to clarify some of these difficulties with the help of some of my clinical experiences.

I shall adhere to the definition of depression we ultimately used in our study of bereaved children.[2] We decided to exclude depressive psychoses because neither we nor others[3,4] had encountered this illness in children; none of our adolescent patients were psychotic; and we considered psychotic illness not a mere variation or extension of neurotic disturbances but a disease entity with different and additional organic components. We limited ourselves to the terms "depressed," "depressive reaction or response," "neurotic depression," and agreed on a working definition based on descriptive clinical manifestations: A dejected, helpless mood; a restriction of motility; a restriction of interest in the world and in objects; a loss of self-esteem." This definition is close to Bibring's,[5] and is not far from the mainstream of current psychiatric usage.

Difficulties Encountered in Using the Descriptive Definition

Some difficulties with this definition are at once apparent. It does not apply to babies in its exact form. The term "loss of self-esteem" would have to be changed, perhaps to a phrase like "loss of well-being" or "narcissistic depletion." This points up the problem of comparing manifestly depressive phenomena in patients at different phases of personality development. They may all look depressed, but this does not allow us to infer that they suffer from the same affliction, that the same causes are operative, or that their minds cope with them in like manner. The depressed 10-month-old, 4-year-old, schoolchild, adolescent, and adult, may each be dealing with different internal and external factors. Even when the depressive symptoms continue from one developmental phase to another or recur at a later stage, we cannot assume that the patient is still, or again, suffering from the same illness.

We know, for example, that obsessional symptoms in young preschoolers indicate a psychic disorder that is very different from the obsessional neurosis of the latency child or adult, although their rituals and ceremonials may appear identical; we also know that in some instances in which the young schoolchild's and adult's obsessional neurosis is the same in its psychic factors, the child's manifest symptoms may be altogether different due to the defensive externalization and interaction with the parental figures.[6,7] Likewise, the fears of the toddler and the phobias of the older preschooler are psychologically quite differently structured, though manifestly alike,[8] and anxiety attacks, though psychologically identical, typically show themselves in the form of temper tantrums during the preschool years and even during early latency, in sharp contrast to the well-known anxiety symptoms we observe in later phases and adulthood.[6,9]

Further, we know that the 2.5-year-old bedwetter who is still enuretic at age 9 has developed a disturbance that bears little relation to his or her earlier incontinence.[10] In regard to depression, such terms as "underlying depression" or "depressive equivalents"[11] point in this direction, but they do not help us diagnostically. Whether or not a nondepressive symptom wards off or contains a depressive response cannot be ascertained by observation. It can only be revealed and understood in the course of psychoanalysis or, in some instances, psychoanalytically oriented psychotherapy.

Another difficulty with the descriptive definition of depression is that one or another of its parts may be lacking in the manifest clinical picture or may be supplanted by its opposite. For example, instead of restriction of motility we see, not infrequently, hyperactivity or alternation between the two states.[2] Such substitutions confuse clinicians and tempt them to focus on one or another criterion instead of all, or to infer multiple substitutions. When the definition is so loosely applied, it may lead us to include a considerable variety of disturbances under the heading of "depression" instead of helping us to refine our diagnostic accuracy.

In my work as consultant to several social agencies and treatment centers, for example, the following cases were presented with a diagnosis of "depression": A prepubertal girl refused to attend school, often remained in her room, and seemed to gain little pleasure from activities and social contacts. Closer scrutiny revealed that her "restricted motility and restricted interest in people and activities" was primarily due to a severe phobia. In a second case an older adolescent boy complained that he could not get up in the morning and was always quite late for school; did not complete his assignments in spite of repeated extensions; tended to absent himself from home and described himself as depressed. Detailed investigation and coordination of information showed that his apparently "slowed down activity," "lack of interest in work," "distance in relationships" and "depressed affect" were due to a psychopathic disturbance. He lived by his instinctual pleasures (eg, excitement with a pile of pornographic magazines interfered with his getting up on time) and he manipulated his environment to escape responsibility. Even his faked self-professed "depression" served that end and had misled two psychiatrists into prescribing antidepressant medication for him.

Many disturbed adolescents, with mixed long-standing pathologies, exacerbated by internal developmental conflicts and external stress, present real puzzles to the clinician and do not readily fit into diagnostic categories. It is easy to misread their primitive instinctual excesses and drug abuse as defense against depression, and their feelings of guilt and inadequacy as a confirmation of it; to attribute their lack of phase-appropriate investment in ego functions and activities to depressive restriction; and to regard their difficulty in pursuing and achieving success to dejection and helplessness.

The depressive affect, often viewed as the cornerstone of the descriptive syndrome, poses its own special diagnostic problem, even when the patient is not trying to "con" us. Always present is the potential discrepancy between the clinician's observation and the patient's experience. One of our parentally bereaved children, 8-year-old Jim,[2] had frequent "depressed" periods which were of concern to his family. He would sit motionless, stare for hours with a dejected facial expression, withdrawn into himself and unresponsive to the approaches of his surroundings. In his analysis it was a surprise to find that Jim did not *feel* depressed at all at these or other times. He was totally apathetic and felt nothing. In his case, the apathy turned out to be a defense against sadness and painful memories, but apathy, a poorly understood phenomenon in itself,[2] does not necessarily represent a defense against sadness or against depression. When we observe apparently "depressed" infants, however, we cannot, in contrast to Jim, correct our impression with the help of their verbalized analytic material and may be off the mark. Even older children do not always recognize, observe and share their own feelings during diagnostic interviews and therefore with them, too, our perception of their affective experiences may be erroneous.

Perhaps the most common difficulty in assessing the patient's affect is the easy confusion between feeling sad and feeling depressed. The depressed feeling is marked by dejection, helplessness and hopelessness, and it is accompanied by lowered self-esteem. None of these are characteristic of sadness. Sadness occurs in relation to an internal or external loss. Though the loss is acknowledged, the loving investment of the mental representations of self and object is maintained and what was lost is actively longed for. The depressed feeling may or may not be attributed to a specific inner or outer loss but tends to spread and encompass all the psychic experiences. What is lost is internally surrendered and the self is thereby diminished. The investment of the mental representations is depleted and even inner restoration is given up as hopeless. Hence, the depressed person feels impoverished, while the sad person feels unhappy but relatively rich.

Experiences in Understanding the Psychic Mechanisms of Depression in Childhood

Our work with depressed bereaved children showed only one characteristic shared by all, namely their depressive response, in each instance, represented an unconscious defense against the affect of sadness and/or its true content. Some of the children were weepy during their depressed periods but attached their feeling to a displaced content; some realized neither their sadness nor its cause, its ideational content. Their depression lifted when the analytic work revealed the hitherto unconscious sadness and related content, and enabled them to be aware of being sad and of what they were really sad about.[2] If these children had been treated in a supportive psychotherapy, perhaps to bolster their self-esteem, or if they had been given antidepressant medication, their pathological defenses against the unconscious affect and content would have been reenforced rather than diminished. This may have produced a temporary improvement in their depressive symptoms but would not have helped them in the long run, because the unconscious factors would have continued to be active and forced the personality once again to resolve the inner tensions with the help of pathological compromise formations.

As to the underlying causes of our patients' depression, I may add that the unconscious content was not their parental bereavement, their loss of the love object. Instead it was a variety of internal and external experiences.[2] Unfortunately, our data were not ample enough to formulate a coherent theory about the metapsychological aspects of depression or to construct its developmental line in childhood and to relate it to adult depression.

This brief mention of the underlying causes of depression brings us to a group of children who, as a rule, clearly exhibit all the aspects of the descriptive clinical depressive syndrome, but are rarely diagnosed as depressed. I am referring to dying children — either children whose death is actually imminent or who suffer from potentially fatal illnesses. I have worked with such children over many years, sometimes directly in psychotherapy, sometimes indirectly as consultant to child-life workers in several pediatric hospitals.[12]

The professional staff, including mental health professionals, and the parents usually deny both the child's depression and its content, ie, the child's approaching death. They tend to view the patient as un-cooperative, resistant, stubborn, lazy, self-willed, spoiled, manipulative, overly sensitive to pain and discomfort, and/or they attribute his or her behavior to neurotic factors. My findings suggest that the dying or fatally ill child, at a certain point in the course of the disease, senses his or her deterioration, consciously or unconsciously. I am not implying that these children were told about their condition or that they have a specific concept of death. Rather, they register from internal bodily signals the waning of life's energy, the decrease of pleasure in bodily and mental functions.

Dying children of all ages have been observed to show depressive symptoms and to experience relief from them, depending on whether their parents and other caring adults could accept and understand their depleted, realistically helpless state, and could respect and meet their special needs at that critical time. When the caring adults do not recognize and accept the child's status but intrude upon him or her with demands for responsiveness and activity and interfere with the child's at-tempts to preserve any remaining sense of well-being by imposing pain-ful stimuli which are intended to better or cure the disease, the child is left alone with an excessive internal burden. He or she withdraws, becomes inactive and dejected and reacts to external demands with irrita-tion or lack of response.

By contrast, when the caring adults accept the child's dying or potentially dying state, share and understand his or her sense of dying, protect the child from excessive stimulation and help maintain minimal comfort, the child's depression subsides. He or she becomes able, often to a surprising extent, to utilize remaining energies for the pleasurable in-vestment of people and activities. With the help of the adult's shared awareness and acceptance of his or her dying state, the child can then also bear his or her own sense of dying, at times keeping it in conscious awareness and at times finding relief from it by means of unconscious defense mechanisms. It seems impossible for the child to employ such helpful defenses unless the adults are fully aware of the child's condition.

The experiences with dying depressed children may give us a pointer toward comparable states at the beginning of life — in earliest infancy, where perhaps primitive forerunners of later, more comlex depressive reactions, originate.

UNCERTAINTIES IN LINKING SUICIDE
AND DEPRESSION

It is not uncommonly held that depression and suicide are directly proportional, ie, the more depressed a patient is, the more likely is he or she to commit suicide. In addressing the topic of suicide I shall, as with depression and for the same reasons, exclude psychoses.

Children in prepuberty, adolescence and, more rarely, in latency who are clinically depressed may indeed be suicidal, but there are also many depressed youngsters who neither endanger nor harm their bodies. Depressed patients may think about dying and wish they were dead but this does not necessarily lead them to bring it about or to do it. Even healthy youngsters, especially in adolescence, *think* about death and perhaps most, if not all, have at one or another time *wished* they were dead, in despair, in anger, or with fascination. It seems to me that the potential for suicide is not directly related to the depressive response but to other personality factors which may or may not be present along with the depression. Suicide attempts and/or suicidal behaviors occur also in children and adolescents who are not manifestly depressed or whose pathology includes only some depressive features.

What then are the personality factors that allow or compel suicidal actions? Here, I find myself in a quandary. To clarify and substantiate my findings and tentative conclusions requires detailed data gathered from the work with individual patients. I do not lack such data. They derive from a few patients seen in daily psychoanalytic sessions over a period of years, and from more extensive but more superficial experiences as consultant to outpatient agencies and residential treatment centers, and to child-life workers who see such youngsters in the hospital following admission for suicide attempts. Unfortunately, I am unable to use any of these data for reasons of confidentiality and of concern lest revealing their material exacerbate the patients' disturbance. I therefore have to limit myself to generalities and a few diluted vignettes. It is my hope, nevertheless, that the reader will bear with me and that those who work with such patients may recognize, or be alerted to, similar circumstances in their experiences and will be able to follow my thinking.

The Role of Primitive Excitement
and Aggression in Self-hurting

The manifest events that the patients, and others, often view as the precipitating cause of the suicide attempt tend to be stressful but not of overwhelming proportions. For example, they include difficulties or failure at school, rejection by a boyfriend or girlfriend, parents leaving town temporarily, or contacts with family members who live elsewhere and are usually absent, such as a divorced parent or the parent of a child in placement. Quite often, the events would contain pleasure for other people; for example, impending graduation from high school, prospects of going away to college, success in being accepted at the school or job of his choosing, parties and outings with peers.

Only closer scrutiny reveals that these events were experienced, not only in terms of hurt feelings, loss of love, humiliation, fear of losing the loved ones and/or proof of inadequacy or guilt, but that they, or something associated with them, also excited the patient and unleashed intolerable impulses. In some instances genital sexual feelings and homo- or heterosexual activities were actually experienced but, even when this is the case, it is not this excitement which directly contributes to the suicidal attempt. The developmentally more advanced genital feelings and experiences either stimulated concurrent, more primitive sadomasochistic impulses or proved so threatening to the personality that it regressed defensively to such a more primitive level. It is this primitive sadomasochistic excitement which contributes to the danger of self-damage, because in it violence and mutual hurting provide gratification and death may take the place of surrender or orgasm.

Suicidal youngsters often act out these exciting doing-and-being-done-to fantasies. They provoke attacks, insults, rejections and humiliations or they perceive and misconstrue the words and behavior of others in these terms even when the reality does not warrant it. Sometimes they exhibit their excitement by means of exaggerated or unrealistic tales of woe and usually succeed in involving their audience by evoking pity or guilt or anger at the presumed perpetrators of cruelty to the patient. For example:

A 16-year-old boy provoked his teachers by not completing his work, then experienced their grant of extensions as humiliating torture, their ultimate deadline as an attack, and finally forced his school into suspending him, their supreme cruelty. He was quite unaware how, at the same time, he had hurt and upset his teachers and rendered them helpless.

A 17-year-old girl aggressively seduced her boyfriend into intercourse and deceived him by telling him that she was using contraceptives. She then experienced pregnancy, abortion, and the boyfriend's hurt withdrawal as torture, and masochistic punishment to which she surrendered.

A 13-year-old boy withdrew into stoic silence after his mother's criticism of his inconsiderate behavior and provoked her to tears with his refusal to have anything to do with her. In his treatment he similarly rejected the therapist and tried to provoke her to intrude upon him with aggressive questioning or to berate him for his lack of cooperation. His fantasies revealed that he was preoccupied with a hurting interaction between them.

Relationships with therapists tend to be drawn into all aspects of the hurting excitement. They are tortured and humiliated as the patient makes them anxious and helpless. They are perceived as tormentors and forced to take active "punitive" steps, and they are put into the position of the participating audience as patients reveal their excited distressing experiences or subject them to silent imperviousness. The patients who are most seriously driven to self-hurting and suicide may not share their difficulties or involve their therapists manifestly at all. They appear cooperative and may even feign improvement while they actively prepare for suicide. Casual acquaintances who are in no position to help such patients may receive signals of the impending danger, but the therapists are kept in the dark and receive their own sadistic punishment when they suddenly learn of the patients' suicides.

I am not implying that the patients are aware of their pathological excitement, contained in their behavior and/or fantasies, or that they consciously manipulate their relationships to gratify it. On the contrary, these manifestations are largely defensive and serve to protect them against the internally perceived danger of sadomasochistic masturbatory activities and fantasies centered on the infantile parental figures. Unfortunately, the defense is not always successful because the interactions with others also stimulate excitement so that they may create a vicious cycle.

Many of these patients are very afraid of being alone because this increases the threat of masturbation. This is one reason for their distress at being left by love objects or at being uninvited to participate in peer activities. Many suffer from sleep disturbances or escape into sleeping. Their reported masturbation often includes self-hurting practices and fantasies of being beaten, tortured or humiliated and of inflicting such suffering on the loved ones. The suicidal act may represent several aspects of the internal struggle — defense and gratification.

The primitive, raw, unattenuated aggression, attached to their sadomasochistic sexual life, often invades other aspects of these patients' personalities. It may manifest itself in breakthroughs of temper outbursts, physical violence and sarcasm, in their periodic lack of care for themselves and their possessions, and in their inability to protect their interests and to allow themselves to achieve and enjoy success. It may also rage at them from within, berating and belittling them in the form of lowered self-esteem and in the form of a harsh conscience which does not serve as an integrated inner monitor and guide but viciously "beats up" on them, meting out cruel punishments. In this way the doing-and-being-done-to excitement is reenacted within the psychic scenario. This aspect of the inner conflict may also lead to suicide.

Origins of Sadomasochistic Pathology

Where does such an intense sadomasochistic sexuality come from and why is the aggression that accompanies and coexists with it so unattenuated? We know, of course, that these manifestations are a normal part of toddler development and do resurface in prepuberty and early adolescence, along with other infantile impulses.[6,13] In our patients, however, they are not only unusually intense but so pervasive that they take precedence instead of subsiding. The personality is unable to progress to more mature genital functioning with considerate object relationships and modulated expression of aggression. When we have opportunity to observe the development of such difficulties long term in early childhood, and/or to explore it psychoanalytically in retrospect, we find that the crucial fixation points occurred in the preschool years, that their manifestations, for example, in the form of sadomasochistic masturbatory fantasies and activities, were relatively contained during latency, and then intensified in adolescence when the increased strength of the developing impulses could no longer be matched by the ego's resources of control and defense.

The early intensification of these impulses and the child's inability to resolve and overcome them during the preschool years may be due to a variety of factors. Among the patients I have worked with, pathology in the early parent-child relationships proved most important. In some cases there was marked ambivalence toward the child, manifested in a great deal of physical punishment, sadistic verbal humiliation, exposure to the parents' sadomasochistic relationship with each other and to their sexual activities. The young child perceived such sexual activities as violent fights which, in his mind, coalesced with the sadomasochistic interactions he experienced in daytime. With other patients, the most significant factor was the mothering person's inability to be sufficiently and consistently available and to protect the child from harm during the crucial early years. This resulted in overwhelming experiences at the hands of substitute caretakers or others outside the family. In some cases important contributory factors were repeated early medical and surgical treatments. These were experienced as sadistic attacks to which the patients had to submit without protest.

In all these situations the toddler's and young preschooler's affectionate bonds proved too weak or too inconsistent to outweigh, fuse and modify his or her aggression in the relationship to the loved ones. The child could not achieve the necessary measure of drive fusion that allows the personality to progress to and master subsequent developmental phases without undue interference from earlier levels; to surpass the sadomasochistic impulses; and to develop consideration for others and kindness to oneself in spite of mixed feelings.

The worst intensification of sadomasochistic pathology in later phases occurred in those patients whose vulnerable areas were again stimulated by interactions with the parental difficulties at such a later time because these interplays stirred or repeated the early pathology. For example, a father who had sadistically humiliated and beaten his boy in early childhood was once again drawn into teasing and belittling him in puberty as well as regaling him with florid tales of his (the father's) sexual exploits. The father's behavior unconsciously excited and infuriated the son, intensified his already present homosexual sadomasochistic fantasies, and interfered with his progressive sexual development and his age-appropriate task of transferring his emotional investment from the parent to new love objects outside the family.

I am not suggesting that these were not caring and concerned parents. Nor did they and their children lack love and affection which can indeed exist side by side with the disturbed features merely because the fusion between love and aggression is inadequate. The parents were completely or largely anaware of their pathology and of its impact on the growing child. A number were well-functioning families, in good social and economic standing, with admirable achievements in their professional or business pursuits. They were eager to do well by their offspring and often supportive of their intellectual and athletic activities.

The Role of Bodily Self-love as a Barrier to Self-injury

The persistence of intense, unfused early aggression in its sexualized sadomasochistic form and in its invasion of self-esteem and conscience is not, however, the only important factor contributing to suicidal actions. More important still is the difficulty which already precedes and later interacts with the toddler pathology — namely, an insufficient, loving self-investment of the infant's own body image during the first and second years of life.[14]

Usually, by the middle of the first year, babies have experienced enough pleasurable well-being that they can begin to build an idea of a primitive limited bodily self whose sense of comfort they want to preserve. They do not chew and bite themselves, they protest vigorously when they are hurt, they seek and accept comfort and welcome feeling good again. In short, they like their bodies and like to keep them feeling good. During the subsequent early years, the images of self and mother become increasingly differentiated and the inner image of the bodily self comes to include all parts of the body. The child's own pleasurable bodily experiences, together with the mother's loving ministrations, protection from harm and comfort of pain, help to build the liking of one's body, help it to take a firm hold and to create a lasting barrier against self-injury.

During toddlerhood, we commonly see indications that children are still struggling to take this developmental step; for example, when they turn down mother's food, mess their pants, or provocatively dash into the street to hurt and enrage mother, they show that they have not yet sufficiently differentiated themselves from her to appreciate that they are causing more harm to themselves than to her, and that their fun in engaging her in an excited tug-of-war outweighs their pleasure in being kind to themselves. The mother may facilitate progressive development by pointing out the reality and by not becoming a party to her toddler's provocation, or she may perpetuate and confirm his or her infantile gratifications by responding to the toddler at his or her level.

In some instances infants cannot complete these crucial developmental steps. It may be due to physical distress from illness or treatments which the mother is unable sufficiently to alleviate, or it may be due to deficits in handling, such as meeting the infants' needs in a way that prevents pleasurable gratification, failing to comfort them enough at times of bodily stress, or not protecting them from harm. When the parent actually inflicts hurt on children's bodies through rough care, in anger, excitement, or by way of punishment, such children cannot develop a proper liking for their bodies. They identify with the parental mistreatment of their bodies and may even come to enjoy and seek pain and discomfort in pathological gratification instead of avoiding and protesting such experiences. Early signs of such a development can be seen in not complaining when hurt, not seeking help and comfort, delay in learning to avoid common dangers, repeated injuries, accident proneness, self-hurting "comfort" habits, such as headbanging, violent scratching, hair pulling, injurious masturbatory activities, and in provocations to physical attack and punishment.

Children's failure to develop their protective bodily self-love is paralleled by a failure in the concomitant step of differentiation between self and object. When their raw and/or sexualized aggression is directed against themselves, it may therefore also represent aggression to the parental figures, vengeance upon them, or excited violent interaction with them. The more shaky and inadequate the earliest loving bodily investment, the more prone are patients to self-damaging and suicidal actions, with or without pathological admixture from later phases. This includes not only active self-hurting but passive inability to care for themselves, which can be just as life threatening.

The patients I worked with showed, in each instance, a considerable interference in the early development of liking their own bodies and consistently striving to protect them. Their psychological, though not their physiological pain barrier was inadequate to maintain self-preservation and, under stress, failed to protect them from self-injury when later impulses and conflicts drove them to it. The vulnerable substructure of their personality constituted an acute suicidal danger when it combined at the early level with strong sadomasochistic tendencies, poor self and object differentiation and inadequate fusion of aggression, and was later augmented by the adolescent increase in impulses, by conflicts inherent in achieving emotional independence, and by environmental stresses which strained already limited means of mastery and/or further stimulated existing pathology. These factors may be present in a variety of nonpsychotic personality disturbances. They may or may not accompany a depressive reaction. The extent to which they are inherent in the personality structure determines the suicidal risk in depressed youngsters.

Whenever a patient's depression or other disturbance occurs in the context of such early pathology, the therapeutic task is extraordinarily difficult and, at best, limited. By contrast, depressed patients who show no or minimal signs of weakness at the described early levels are often able to utilize psychological treatment that can help them to uncover and master the unconscious psychic contents.

For purposes of clarity, these statements are very concise and definite. This may be misleading because the reported findings are actually quite complex, with intricate individual ramifications. Thus, these conclusions are tentative and may need to be modified in the light of further clinical data.

REFERENCES

1. Furman E: *A Child's Parent Dies*. New Haven, Yale University Press, 1974.
2. Furman E: Observations on depression and apathy, in Furman E (ed): *A Child's Parent Dies*. New Haven, Yale University Press, 1974, pp 184–197.
3. Sandler J, Joffe WG: Notes on childhood depression. *Int J Psychoanal* 1965;46:88–96.
4. Anthony J, Scott P: Manic-depressive psychosis in childhood. *J Child Psychol Psychiatry* 1960;1:53–72.
5. Bibring E: The mechanism of depression, in Greenacre P (ed): *Affective Disorders*. New York, International Universities Press, 1953, pp 13–48.
6. Freud A: *Normality and Pathology in Childhood*. New York, International Universities Press, 1965.
7. Furman E: Some aspects of a young boy's masturbation conflict, in Marcus IM, Francis JJ (eds): *Masturbation From Infancy to Senescence*. New York, International Universities Press, 1975, pp 185–204.
8. Freud A: Fears, anxieties, and phobic phenomena. *Psychoanal Study Child* 1977;32:85–90.
9. Freud A: The symptomatology of childhood: A preliminary attempt at classification. *Psychoanal Study Child* 1970;25:19–44.

258

10. Katan A: Experience with enuretics. *Psychoanal Study Child* 1946;2:241–256.
11. Toolan JM: Depression in children and adolescents. *Am J Orthopsychiatry* 1962;32:404–415.
12. Furman E: Helping children cope with dying. *Archives Foundation Thanatology* 1981;9:3.
13. Freud S: Three Essays on the Theory of Sexuality, 1905 *The Complete Psychological Works of Sigmund Freud*, standard ed. London, Hogarth Press, 1953, vol 7, pp 125–243.
14. Hoffer W: Development of the body ego. *Psychoanal Study Child* 1950;5:18–23.

CHAPTER 16

EARLY INDICATORS OF SELF-DESTRUCTIVE BEHAVIORS IN CHILDREN AND ADOLESCENTS: Primary Detection by the Pediatrician

MATILDA S. McINTIRE
PAUL FINE
PAMELA R. FAIN

Pediatricians are invaluable to society for detecting and preventing suicide and other self-destructive behaviors. As diagnosticians they may be among the first to witness early indicators of self-destructive behaviors, and as primary care clinicians they have unique opportunities to influence children and families at risk within the community.[1]

This chapter is based on a brief survey of Nebraska pediatricians' opinions and involvement with self-destructive children and adolescents. Results of the survey are reviewed, and implications for the detection and management of self-destructive cases are discussed.

BACKGROUND

The problem of self-destruction among children and adolescents is complex, extensive, and diagnostically nonspecific. Clinical studies suggest that general factors such as chronic inner tension, rage, frustration, repeated losses, and escalating stress correlate most closely with self-destructive patterns, and that a diagnosis of depression, although present in many cases,[2,3] is absent in most.[4]

Mortality studies reinforce the impression that childhood self-destruction is a general problem. For example, despite a gradual decrease in all forms of violent death during the past 75 years, parallel rates of increase for suicide, homicide, and fatal accidents in the group between the ages of 15 to 24 years have been noted during the last 20 years. The pattern of increase is thought to reflect a continuum from overt to covert self-destruction, with social and family conditions determining each particular form of expression.[5]

Most pediatricians encounter the entire continuum of self-destructive cases, at least to the extent that they practice total health care. Moreover, self-destructive cases in pediatric practice probably represent the general population more closely than cases in psychiatric practice. For example, psychotic children and adolescents demonstrate higher rates for suicide than patients in nonpsychotic categories.[6] However, character-disordered cases also demonstrate increased risk for self-destruction,[4] and these less overt cases-at-risk probably are more frequent in the general population and in pediatric practice.

Disrupted personal, family, and social patterns have been described as "the new morbidity" for pediatrics.[7] Self-destructive cases almost certainly fall into this category, yet there are indications that pediatricians have not adequately engaged the problem in practice. For example, a survey of upstate New York pediatricians found that pediatricians in the study were likely to obtain mental health consultations for overtly suicidal situations, but did not screen routinely for signs and symptoms of self-destruction. Moreover, when the medical examiners' records for completed suicides were compared with the pediatricians' records from the same time period, it was found that few cases that actually completed suicide had been identified premorbidly by the pediatricians.[8]

There is little doubt that pediatricians could play a more significant role in identifying and managing self-destructive cases, but the task is subtle and extensive. Younger children who become self-destructive usually are not overtly or lethally suicidal. In fact, the mortality rate for suicides between ages 10 and 14 is less than one per 100,000, and completed suicides below the age of 10 are a rare occurrence.[9] Moreover, family-destructive patterns are difficult to separate from self-destructive patterns in the younger age group; personal decisions for self-destruction are less autonomous; and younger children lack a clear conception of death as final.[10] However, subtle self-destructive episodes during childhood can escalate to suicidal proportions as patients become adolescent.[11] These childhood cases, despite their low lethality and complicated perturbations, present an opportunity for prevention which, hopefully, could lower general mortality and morbidity.

Mortality and morbidity from adolescent self-destruction is more overt and appears easier to define. For example, the suicide mortality rate for the group between the ages of 15 and 19 years is 7.6 per 100,000, accounting for about 8% of all deaths in the age group and about 6% of all suicides.[9] However, other studies suggest that for every fatal suicide at least 50 additional adolescents intentionally injure themselves.[12] Completed suicides are more frequent among male adolescents, but nonlethal suicide attempts, usually involving self-poisoning, probably are more frequent among females.[19] In view of the seriousness of these situations, steps to reduce morbidity as well as to predict mortality are indicated for each case in which self-destruction is considered a possibility.

Pediatricians, along with other professionals, have found that self-destructive youngsters frequently come from problem families. For example, suicide attempters presenting at a pediatric emergency room in one study described a negative view of their parents, and the parents scored lower on a scale of marital adjustment than did a control group of parents.[13] Moreover, pediatricians can expect to encounter families of self-destructive patients from high as well as low socioeconomic status. High socioeconomic, overdemanding families have been found most likely to produce drug ingesters with a high lethality of intent.[14] In contrast, suicide attempters from low socioeconomic, inner-city areas are likely to be socially isolated and are from more disrupted families than would be a comparable group of nonsuicidal patients.[15]

In broad perspective, pediatricians could become a cornerstone for suicide prevention with high-risk families. Organizational characteristics of suicide attempters' family systems are known to include a lack of generational boundaries, severely conflicted spouse relationships, intrusive parent-child relationships, and inflexibility.[16] We believe that high-risk families can assimilate structure, value support, and accept referrals from a family pediatrician, particularly if the physician-patient relationship is secure and long-standing. This is not to suggest that pediatricians should undertake extensive counseling with self-destructive families, only that they could screen and coordinate access to appropriate resources and reinforce corrective efforts.

As a first step toward more effective suicide prevention, it appeared necessary to survey pediatricians concerning their interest and opinions about early diagnostic indicators for self-destruction and programs for intervention.

METHOD

In October of 1982, a questionnaire was sent by the authors to 110 physicians included on the current list of members of the Nebraska Chapter of the American Academy of Pediatrics. The questionnaire was kept brief to insure a reasonable rate of response, and items were chosen to include queries about general problems of self-destruction, including: 1) attitudes about management and referral practices concerning suicide attempters, accident-prone children, and abusive or neglectful parents, 2) the perceived degree of risk associated with certain broadly chosen indicators of self-destructive behaviors, 3) opinions concerning the relative effectiveness of a small sample of programs for suicide prevention, and 4) characteristics of the physicians, including age, sex, years of practice, proportion of time spend in practice, and population size of the community served.

Because the questionnaire was brief and relatively subjective, no attempt was made to determine the actual number of self-destructive cases seen by the pediatricians. Rather, we sought opinions and indications of interest in managing a variety of situations. Accident proneness was included in the survey because accident-prone children are vulnerable to suicide as they get older.[17] Abusive and neglectful parenting was included because destructive family patterns correlate with self-destructive personal patterns among children from these families.[18]

Indicators for screening self-destructive behaviors were chosen broadly from the literature[3,17] for economy of presentation and to sample the group's emphasis. Indicators were then organized for purposes of analysis into personal-clinical, family, and precipitant factors.

We realize that other important indicators, such as chronic physical illnesses and psychiatric diagnoses, were not included on the list and that, in any case, a weighted scale combining various factors would be necessary to predict degrees of risk in practice. However, since developing a scale for prediction was not the purpose of this study, items were considered sufficient to sample the pediatricians' range of opinions and level of involvement. Items for a short list of programs for suicide prevention also were chosen to sample pediatric options.

RESULTS

Questionnaires were returned by 65 pediatricians for a response rate of 59.1%. Actuarial data were compiled for members of the Academy using the questionnaire format and based upon personal knowledge and statistics provided by Academy listings. As indicated in Table 16-1, respondents provided a reasonable representation of Nebraska Academy members with respect to age, sex, time in practice, size of community, and years of experience.

MANAGEMENT AND REFERRAL PRACTICES

A summary of attitudes concerning management and referral is given in Table 16-2.

Results suggest that two thirds of the pediatricians who responded to the survey do not manage suicide attempters. However, all but one of these physicians indicated that they refer disturbed suicide attempters for help elsewhere.

This group of pediatricians is most likely to refer severely disturbed attempters to psychiatrists for help. Moreover, they rarely or infrequently refer to psychologists, social workers, social service or mental health

Table 16-1
Characteristics of Respondents Compared to All Academy Members*

	Respondents		All Members	
	Number	Percent	Number	Percent
Age				
20–30	0	–	5	4.5
30–40	27	42.2	42	38.2
40–60	28	43.8	49	44.5
over 60	9	14.0	14	12.7
Sex				
Male	54	84.4	91	82.7
Female	10	15.6	19	17.3
Type of Practice				
Full-time	56	87.5	97	88.2
Part-time	8	12.5	13	11.8
Size of Community				
1000– 25,000	3	4.7	8	7.3
25,000–100,000	7	10.9	9	8.2
100,000–250,000	12	18.8	22	20.0
Over 250,000	42	65.6	71	64.5
	Mean	*SD*	*Mean*	*SD*
Years of Experience	16.4	11.8	14.9	11.3

*One respondent did not complete this section of the questionnaire.

agencies. Among pediatricians who said they manage suicide attempters, all but one indicated that they also refer disturbed self-destructive patients to psychiatrists, and these pediatricians usually manage suicide attempters in a hospital rather than as outpatients.

As a group, the pediatricians who responded to the survey suggested that they are more likely to manage accident-prone children and abusive or neglectful parents than to manage suicide attempters. However, they are not likely to refer accident-prone children, and approximately one fourth of the pediatricians sampled neither manage nor refer accident-prone children.

There were no apparent differences in patterns of management and referral of suicide attempters when compared by the pediatricians' age group, size of community, and other identifying variables. However, pediatricians from smaller communities, with a population of less than 250,000, were significantly more likely to manage accident-prone children (82% vs. 56%, P < .05), and a similar trend was observed for the management of abusive and neglectful parents (76% in smaller communities vs. 61% in larger).

264

Table 16-2
Management and Referral Patterns for Self-Destructive Children Among 65 Nebraska Pediatricians (Percentages)

	Yes	No
Do you manage manipulative or attention-seeking suicide attempters?	34	66
If yes, do you usually manage these cases as outpatients or in the hospital?		
Outpatients	35	65
Hospital	75	25
Do you refer patients who attempt suicide and are psychotic or severely disturbed?	97	3
If yes, where do you usually refer these patients?		
Social Service Agency	7	93
Psychiatrist	91	9
Mental Health Agency	12	88
Psychologist or Social Worker	4	96
Do you manage children who are seriously accident-prone?	67	33
Do you usually refer them?	33	67
Do you manage abusive or neglectful parents?	67	33
Do you usually refer them?	73	27

RATINGS OF SELF-DESTRUCTIVE INDICATORS

The pediatricians' perceptions of risk associated with selected indicators of self-destructive behavior are summarized in Table 16-3.

Personal factors that were considered by a majority of the group as significant for extreme risk were a history of suicide attempts, severe psychiatric disorders, and alcohol or drug abuse. Impulsive or dangerous behaviors, school dropout, and a lack of close friends also were considered extreme risk factors by a large minority. However, mood swings and vegetative symptoms of depression were not considered indicators of extreme risk by most of this group of pediatricians.

Certain family factors also were considered significant indicators for at least some risk by most of the physicians. These factors included a family history of suicide, suicide attempts, severe mental disorders, poor communications within the family, and economic poverty.

Precipitating factors, such as the recent death of a family member, loss of a romantic attachment, pregnancy and parental divorce, were considered indicators of some risk by most of the pediatricians. However, few considered an acute precipitant, per se, as indicating an extreme risk.

Risk factors were analyzed in terms of age, sex, type of practice, community size, and years of experience for differences among the pediatricians. In this instance, the only notable trend related to differences in the age of respondents. Age differences in the degree of risk assigned to various risk factors are summarized in Table 16-4.

Table 16-4 indicates that although the degree of risk assigned to various family-related factors was similar for the two age groups of pediatricians, younger pediatricians consistently ranked personal-clinical factors as more extreme in terms of risk for self-destructive behavior. These differences reached statistical significance for impulsive behavior, school achievement, and extreme mood swings.

Table 16-3
Risk Associated with Indicators of Self-Destructive Behaviors as Perceived by 65 Pediatricians (Percentages)

	Not Much Risk	Some Risk	Extreme Risk
Personal Clinical Factors			
Personal history of suicide attempt	0	5	95
Severe psychiatric disorder	2	23	75
Alcohol or drug abuse	5	42	53
Impulsive or dangerous behavior	0	56	44
School dropout or serious underachievement	4	57	39
Lack of close friends	7	56	37
Extreme mood swings	2	70	28
Poor appetite, sleep disorders, or hypochondriasis	14	78	8
Family Factors			
Family history of suicide or suicide attempts	5	56	39
Family history of severe mental disorder	16	62	22
Poor family communications	8	71	21
Economic poverty	36	64	0
Precipitating Events			
Recent death of a family member	8	67	25
Recent loss of romantic attachment	8	72	20
Recent divorce of parents	4	78	18
Pregnancy	27	60	13

Table 16-4
Percent of Sample Who Classified Risk Factors for Self-Destructive Behavior as Extreme, by Age

Risk Factors	Under 40 Years	Over 40 Years
Personal Clinical Factors		
Personal history of suicide attempt	100	91.7
Severe psychiatric disorder	74.1	75.0
Alcohol or drug abuse	59.3	47.2
Impulsive or dangerous behaviors	59.3	33.3*
School dropout or serious		
underachievement	55.6	25.0*
Lack of close friends	44.4	33.3
Extreme mood swings	48.1	13.9*
Poor appetitie, sleep disorders,		
or hypochondriasis	11.1	5.6
Family Factors		
Family history of suicide or suicide		
attempts	37.0	38.9
Family history of severe mental		
disorder	22.2	19.4
Poor family communications	22.2	19.4
Economic poverty	0.0	0.0
Precipitating Events		
Recent death of a family member	25.9	25.0
Recent loss of romantic attachment	25.9	16.7
Recent divorce of parents	14.8	20.6
Pregnancy	7.4	13.9

*$P < .05.$

PROGRAMS FOR SUICIDE PREVENTION

Table 16-5 summarizes the pediatricians' view of programs for suicide prevention.

None of the programs listed was considered extremely effective by a majority of the physicians. Many thought that family life classes at school, routine guidance by the pediatrician, and referring problems to social agencies were ineffective. However, screening high-risk cases for treatment or referral seemed at least somewhat effective to 95% of the group. In addition, a large majority of the respondents claimed they would welcome a short, continuing medical education course concerning suicide and other self-destructive behaviors.

CONCLUSIONS AND IMPLICATIONS

Logical roles for pediatricians in suicide prevention include early identification of high-risk cases, referrals to appropriate resources, and

Table 16-5
The Pediatricians' View of the Effectiveness of Programs for Suicide
Prevention and the Need for Additional Training (Percentages)

	Not Very Effective	Somewhat Effective	Extremely Effective
Family life classes in high school	34	61	5
Routine guidance by the pediatrician	30	59	11
Referring problem to social agencies	21	71	8
Screening high-risk cases for treatment of referral	5	58	37

	No	Yes
Would you welcome a continuing medical education course concerning suicide and self-destructive behiavors?	21	79

coordination of services. The survey of these Nebraska pediatricians suggests that they are knowledgeable about and interested in self-destructive cases, but do not consider themselves primarily responsible for prevention or management.

Pediatricians in the study demonstrated a clear awareness that self-destructive incidents are multicausal and may include personal, family, and precipitant risk factors. As a group, the pediatricians' hierarchy of ratings for high-risk factors placed an emphasis on previous suicide attempts, severe psychiatric disorders, and alcohol or drug abuse.

Only three items from among 16 on the list appeared discrepant concerning risk. These items were pregnancy as a precipitant factor, and extreme mood swings and vegetative symptoms as personal-clinical factors.

Pregnancy was rated by most of the physicians as carrying only some risk. However, the actual risk for suicide has been found higher by a factor of 10 for adolescents and young adults who have experienced pregnancies, and teenagers who have experienced abortion may be particularly at risk.[19] Very few pediatricians in this study rated mood swings and vegetative disorders as indicators of extreme risk. However, mood swings and vegetative disorders are classic symptoms of a dangerous depression, the most common psychiatric correlate with overt self-destruction. Our interpretation of this apparent discrepancy is that appetite and sleep disorders are frequent in pediatric practice and probably connote a serious psychiatric disorder only when accompanied by other indicators.

Pediatricians under the age of 40 in this study were more likely to emphasize mood swings and other social and psychiatric factors as indicators of risk than were their older colleagues. We believe that this finding may indicate that the younger generation has become more attuned to subtle indicators of risk.

It should be noted that a significant minority of pediatricians who responded to the survey discounted items that the majority of their colleagues, in common with the literature, considered significant as indicators of self-destructive behaviors. It is this group, perhaps, that is most in need of effective, time-efficient approaches to the problem. This finding suggests that an efficient, weighted, paper-and-pencil scale of early indicators for self-destructive behaviors would be helpful. Several rating scales are available to identify depressions,[20] but there is currently no scale adequate to measure general problems of self-destruction.[21] Specific research toward a screening instrument is necessary and justified to meet the need. For best results, a screening instrument would be accompanied by a flow chart of procedural options and a list of specific local resources.

Psychiatrists clearly are utilized by pediatricians to care for disturbed, suicidal patients in Nebraska. This relationship between the two medical specialties is not surprising, since the psychiatric disturbance most commonly associated with suicidal behavior is depression; psychotic patients also are at risk, and psychiatrists have relatively effective means to treat patients with these diagnoses, including pharmacotherapy and hospitalization. However, severe personality disorders, alcoholism, and drug abuse as frequent pediatric correlates of self-destruction are more likely to require a wider network of community resources, but other mental health professions were not emphasized by the pediatricians in this survey.

Closer linkages between pediatricians and all relevant mental health professionals appear indicated, not only for suicidal cases, but also on behalf of children who are accident prone, suffer parental abuse, or are being raised in destructive family circumstances. Moreover, improved linkages are required not only during crisis periods, but also during an extensive prodromal period for self-destruction during childhood. Referral patterns from the Nebraska survey of pediatricians suggest that psychiatrists may be the most available group to help bring pediatricians into meaningful contact with other relevant mental health and other social services.

Pediatricians in this study indicated that they would welcome a continuing medical education program, and further steps are indicated to organize what is known about self-destruction so that it can be taught and applied on a broad and meaningful scale.

In the final analysis, pediatricians may be more likely to become engaged in suicide prevention when other members of the helping community recognize the pediatrician's essential role as family physician. Pediatricians from smaller communities in the Nebraska study were more likely to manage certain types of destructive family situations and, presumably, in a smaller community, medical services are more integral. Pediatric-based hospital referral centers for high-risk families, including consulting psychiatrists, and built on the model of poison control centers, may provide an approach to the general problem in any community. Hopefully, then, supportive ongoing primary physician-patient relationships with families could become a cornerstone for suicide prevention.

With the economic constraints of health and human services of the 1980s, careful consideration must be given to the outcome of funds expended on a target population. Despite massive anti-drug, rehabilitation and drug enforcement programs in all sections of the United States, drug and toxic substance abuse by adolescents has increased along with more violent forms of self-destructive behavior during the past two decades, leaving unintended death and personal catastrophes in its wake.

Inpatient psychiatric therapy, the most expensive approach to self-destructive cases, while necessary and required for selected indications, will not be possible in the majority of cases, yet a high recurrence rate chastens neglect. Primary detection and prevention by the pediatrician, in the form of directing high-risk cases toward appropriate, balanced, comprehensive, and coordinated services in the community, is an important priority.

REFERENCES

1. McIntire MS, Angle CR: Suicide as seen in poison control centers. *Pediatrics* 1971;48:914.
2. Carlson GA, Cantwell DP: Suicidal behavior and depression in children and adolescents. *J Am Acad Child Psychiatry* 1982;4:361–368.
3. Shaffer D: Suicide in childhood and early adolescence. *J Child Psychol Psychiatry* 1974;15:275–291.
4. Cohen-Sandler MA, Berman AL, King RA: Life stress determinants of suicidal behavior. *J Am Acad Child Psychiatry* 1982;21:178–186.
5. Holding TA, Buglass D, Duffy JC, Kreitman N: Parasuicide in Edinburgh — A seven year review 1968–1974. *Br J Psychiatry* 1977;130:534.
6. Inamdar SC, Lewis DO, Siomopoulos G, et al: Violent and suicidal behavior in psychotic adolescents. *Am J Psychiatry* 1982;139:932–935.
7. Haggerty RJ, Roghmann KJ, Pless IB (eds): *Child Health and the Community.* New York, John Wiley & Sons, 1975.
8. Hodgman CH, Roberts FN: Adolescent suicide and the pediatrician. *Adolesc Med* 1982;101:118–123.

9. Shaffer D, Fisher P: The epidemiology of suicide in children and young adolescents. *J Am Acad Child Psychiatry* 1981;20:545–565.
10. McIntire MS, Angle CR, Struempler LJ: The concept of death in midwestern children and youth. *Am J Dis Child* 1972;123:527–532.
11. Renshaw DC: Suicide in children. *Am Fam Physician* 1981;24:123–127.
12. Jacobziner H: Attempted suicide in adolescence. *JAMA* 1965;191:101.
13. McKenry PC, Tishler CL, Kelley C: Adolescent suicide: A comparison of attempters and nonattempters in an emergency room population. *Clin Pediatr* 1982;21:266–270.
14. McIntire MS, Angle CR, Wikoff RL, et al: Recurrent adolescent suicidal behavior. *Pediatrics* 1977;60:605–608.
15. Rohn RD, Sarles RM, Kenney TJ, et al: Adolescents who attempt suicide. *Pediatrics* 1977;90:636–638.
16. Pfeffer CR: The family system in suicidal children. *Am J Psychother* 1981;35: 330–340.
17. McIntire MS, Angle CR: The taxonomy of suicide and self poisoning: A pediatric perspective, in Wells CF, Stuart IR (eds): *Self-Destructive Behavior in Children and Adolescents*. New York, Van Nostrand Reinhold, 1981, pp 224–249.
18. Mehr M, Zeltzer LK, Robinson R: Continued self-destructive behaviors in adolescent suicide attempters. *Adolesc Health Care* 1981;1:269–274.
19. Tishler CL: Adolescent suicides following elective abortion: A special anniversary reaction. *Pediatrics* 1981;68:670–671.
20. Kazdin AE, Petti TA: Self-report and interview measures of childhood and adolescent depression. *J Child Psychol Psychiatry* 1982;23:437–457.
21. Pierce DW: A predictive validation of a suicide intent scale: A five year follow-up. *Br J Psychiatry* 1981;139:391–396.

CHAPTER 17

PSYCHOLOGICAL RECONSTRUCTION OF COMPLETED SUICIDE IN CHILDHOOD AND ADOLESCENCE

MOHAMMAD SHAFII
J. RUSSELL WHITTINGHILL
DAVID C. DOLEN
VERNON D. PEARSON, Jr
ANN DERRICK
SHAHIN CARRIGAN

During the last few years in the Child Psychiatric Services, University of Louisville School of Medicine, we have observed a significant increase in the number of referrals of children and adolescents with self-destructive and suicidal behaviors such as actively thinking about, threatening or attempting suicide. For example, in 1973 only 23 children and adolescents were seen on an emergency basis for suicidal behaviors, but in 1980, 145 were seen—an alarming 530% increase. Comparatively, the total number of new evaluations increased by 143%. At the present time, 16% to 18% of all referrals to the Child Psychiatric Services are related to suicidal behaviors.

This significant increase prompted us to explore the incidence and patterns of completed suicide in children and adolescents locally. We then compared our data with the national incidence. The findings led to the development of a research project for the psychological reconstruction of the factors that contribute to completed suicide in children and youths 19 years of age or younger.

INCIDENCE AND PATTERNS OF COMPLETED SUICIDE IN CHILDREN AND ADOLESCENTS IN JEFFERSON COUNTY

Jefferson County, Kentucky, includes the city of Louisville and surrounding area with a population of 684,793 in the 1980 census. Eighty-three percent of the population is white and 17% nonwhite, mostly

271

black. Children and adolescents under 19 years of age represent 32.3% of the population.

In reviewing and analyzing the coroner's data in Jefferson County from 1975 through 1980, we found 657 cases of completed suicide established beyond a reasonable doubt.[1] Sixty, or 9.4% of these cases, were children and youths between the ages of 10 and 19 years. Using the year 1975 as a baseline, we noticed that the incidence of suicide in children aged 10 to 14 years in 1975 in Jefferson County was 1.5 per 100,000 per year as opposed to 0.8 per 100,000 in this age group nationally. In youths aged 15 to 19 years, the incidence was 7.1, slightly less than the 7.6 national incidence.

During the five years 1976 through 1980, with some fluctuations, the "mean incidence of suicide in children aged 10–14 years was 2.74 per 100,000 per year — an increase of 83% over 1975. In ages 15–19, the mean incidence was 14.3 per 100,000 as opposed to 7.1 in 1975 — a more than 100% increase."[1] In the population aged 20 and older, the incidence in 1975 was 25.8 per 100,000, but it declined by 17% to 21.3 per 100,000 mean incidence from 1976 to 1980.

Regarding the patterns of suicide in the 60 cases reviewed from 1975 through 1980, slightly more than 15% were committed by children between the ages of 10 and 14 years, 18% were female, 12% were black. Ages 17 and 18 were the most vulnerable; 49% of all suicides occurred within this age group. The most common methods of committing suicide were by gunshot wound 57%, hanging 23%, chemical overdose 9%, and carbon monoxide poisoning 5%. In females, suicide by the use of firearms, hanging, and overdose were approximately equally distributed.

PSYCHOLOGICAL STUDIES
OF COMPLETED SUICIDE

Although a number of papers have been published on suicidal behaviors and the incidence and patterns of completed suicide in children and youth, there is a paucity of clinical case studies and psychological reconstruction of completed suicide within this age group.[2-10]

Litman et al[11] were the first to use a "psychological autopsy" in cases of "equivocal deaths" to assist the coroner (Los Angeles County) in deciding whether a death was by accident or suicide. According to Diller, the psychological autopsy helps "the coroner in making an informed judgment by providing a detailed account of events immediately preceding the person's death. To fulfill this purpose, information includes medical and other family history, patterns of reaction to stress and tension, and the role of alcohol or drugs or both if present."[12] The investigating team felt that the psychological autopsy was not only helpful in assisting the coroner determine the cause of death, but also made it possible for the survivors to receive some psychological help in their bereavement.

Barraclough and Shepherd[13] of England surveyed the survivors' reaction to the coroner's inquest following suicide. They concluded that the public nature of the inquest and the resulting publication of it in the media significantly distressed and aggravated the bereaved families.

Herzog and Resnick,[14] in a "Clinical Study of Parental Response to Adolescent Death By Suicide With Recommendations for Approaching the Survivors," reported significant difficulties in getting parents to agree to be interviewed. In cases in which the parents agreed to be interviewed, the research team was barraged with an avalanche of hostility and distrust. On the whole, the authors felt that contact with these families was futile and unproductive. The longer the time lapse between the suicide and the postvention interview, the more difficult it was to establish rapport and communicate with the family.

Cantor reported an attempt to study the families of 500 cases of "youthful suicide" which occurred over a five-year period in the state of Maryland and New York City. Cantor randomly selected 100 of these families and sent them a questionnaire. Less than "10% of the question-naires were returned and many of the questionnaires which were returned had numerous questions left unanswered."[15] Most frequently, the families who responded to the questionnaire were the ones in which the suicide had occurred recently and was drug related.

Whitis[16] discussed a case of a 10-year-old boy who was referred for outpatient psychiatric treatment for severe temper tantrums, depression, frequent crying, withdrawal, and suicide threats. These symptoms began three months after his 13-year-old brother committed suicide by hang-ing. The author attributed the patient's symptoms to the inability of the family to express their feelings about the loss of their son and their lack of being supportive with each other.

Resnick[17] described the insurmountable difficulties of working with families who have lost a child to suicide and suggested that immediate (within 24 hours) psychological intervention with the family may be of benefit for rehabilitation and renewal.

RESEARCH OBJECTIVES

The investigators decided to interview all the families who had lost a child or adolescent under 19 years of age to suicide in Jefferson County, Kentucky, beginning January 1, 1980. Our plan was to also interview friends and other meaningful people in the victim's life. The purpose of this study was: to develop methodology for initiating contact and effec-tive followup with bereaved family and friends; to explore and identify

274

contributing factors to suicide (psychological reconstruction); and to attempt to prevent future suicides in bereaved families and friends by being available as a point of contact for support, education, and referral.

This chapter includes a discussion of the development of methodology in interviewing bereaved families and the psychological reconstruction of completed suicide in childhood and adolescence using three cases as examples.

RESEARCH DESIGN AND METHODOLOGY

Research on and clinical work with families who have lost a child to suicide have been ignored for many years. Several reasons may account for this: the depressing nature of the work, the enormous time and effort required, the lack of clinical training in this area, the possible reluctance of the bereaved family, and above all, the physical and psychological toll on the researchers.

The two original investigators (MS and JRW) have had considerable clinical experience in working with suicidal children, adolescents, and their families. However, they felt apprehensive about and lacked experience in interviewing a family who had a child or adolescent commit suicide. This was especially true because the family was not asking for help and was being approached by the investigators for research purposes. The investigators found that the following approach was helpful in interviewing a bereaved family:

1. Remembering that the family members are not patients, and, therefore, the model of the clinician-patient relationship will most probably not be effective, especially in the initial phase;
2. Keeping in mind that our purpose is to *learn* from the family;
3. Following the family's lead;
4. Avoiding confrontation, interpretation, or asking questions either directly or indirectly that would imply blame or guilt for them or anyone else;
5. Experiencing the family's feelings and being cognitively and emotionally in communion with them;
6. Avoiding judging either verbally or nonverbally;
7. Avoiding false reassurance, false promises, and platitudes;
8. Being flexible in the length of the interview and the nature of questioning;
9. Appreciating the opportunity to intrude upon the family's grief and sorrow.

The investigators decided that the sooner they contacted the family the better the chances of establishing rapport. Based on this premise, the coroner asked his deputies to call us as soon as they received a request for a death investigation for possible suicide in an adolescent aged 19 years or younger. The plan was for one of the research team to go to the scene of the possible suicide.

We found it useful to establish a Suicide Research Team (SRT) comprised, in our situation, of a child psychiatrist as senior investigator, experienced master's degree social worker, a master's degree clinical psychiatric nurse specialist, and a research assistant. (These professionals had many other teaching and clinical responsibilities and spent approximately 10% to 20% of their time on this project, with the exception of the research assistant who devoted 30% to 40% of his/her time.)

It was also helpful to have two researchers participate in the initial interview with the family, if it was possible, in order to more effectively support the family and particularly for immediate debriefing of each other afterwards.

Weekly research meetings were held for all members of the team lasting about two hours for expressing feelings, observations, and reactions to childhood and adolescent suicide, and specifically to the cases being investigated. These weekly meetings facilitated the group supervisory process and lent support without becoming group therapy. They resulted in sharpening the researchers' ability for observation, data collection, documentation, and enhanced empathy toward bereaved families and friends.

Contacting the Bereaved Family

Initially, the Suicide Research Team (SRT) was supposed to be notified immediately of a suspected child or adolescent suicide by the attending deputy coroner so that a member of the team could come to the scene. However, for various reasons, the team was not usually immediately notified. Generally, the SRT learned about an incident of suicide through the daily review of the obituary section of the local newspaper or, on occasion, through a telephone call from the deputy coroner either hours or one to two days after the death.

As soon as the SRT learned about a suicide, the deputy coroner was contacted and the names of the parents, their address, and telephone number were obtained. The SRT member assigned to the case contacted the parents by telephone and explained the research project. The SRT member emphasized concern for the family's well-being and sought permission to visit at their earliest convenience. In most cases, initial contact was made at the funeral home during visitation hours. At this time, the SRT member assessed the family's reaction to the untimely death and recommended an interview later in their home, not only with them, but also with siblings and possibly the victim's friends. The home visit and interview usually occurred a couple of days or a week following the funeral. In some cases, it occurred two to four weeks later depending on the availability of the family.

Initial Interview

The initial interview was unstructured in order to encourage the development of rapport and to allow the family to express their feelings, thoughts, and ideas concerning the victim openly. Two or three interviews were often necessary during the first month in order to cover the following issues:

1. Description of the method of suicide;
2. Developmental history of the victim;
3. Past medical, psychiatric, and school history of the victim;
4. Social and family history;
5. Significant life events (losses, deaths, previous suicide attempts, or completed suicide);
6. Description of victim's behavior and attitude during the preceding year, week, and last 24 hours before suicide.

Special attention was given to the following factors: possible changes made within the last days, weeks, or months before suicide; previous suicidal behavior in self, family, friends, or idols; symptoms of depression, hopelessness, hostility, aggression, isolation, loneliness; changes in human relationships; changes in work and school habits; drug and alcohol abuse; legal history; recent medical illness; and the nature of parental controls and expectations.

The initial interview usually lasted three to four hours. It was frequently a cathartic experience for the family and a draining experience for the SRT members. Sometimes two to three additional interviews were arranged, for instance, with the parents together or separately, individual siblings, girl or boyfriend, close friends, clergy, teachers, classmates, or others. These interviews helped to develop a careful description and psychological reconstruction of the victim's life.

Followup

To explore how the family and friends coped with this major loss and to provide assistance for prevention of possible suicidal behaviors, the research team arranged face-to-face interviews or, if that was not possible, telephone interviews. Generally, the family and significant members of the above group were contacted one, two, three, six, and nine months following suicide and also at one year, the "anniversary interviews." After that, they were contacted every six months for up to three years.

We have found that friends frequently gave much more detailed information about the victim's life-style, behavior, pattern of drug and alcohol abuse, and previous suicidal preoccupation.

Standardized Data Collection

Psychological Profile of Suicide In addition to writing a careful description of the interviews, we have developed a 109-item questionnaire for the interviewers to use in documenting and assessing in a standardized manner a psychological profile of the suicide victim. This questionnaire is called the Psychological Profile of Suicide (PPS).

Behavioral checklists The parents filled out the Louisville Behavior Checklist (LBC) which is a 164-item true–false questionnaire assessing emotional disorders in childhood and adolescence. If indicated, the teacher was also asked to fill out a similar questionnaire called the School Behavior Checklist (SBC).[18-20]

Millon Clinical Multiaxial Inventory In order to systematically assess parental psychopathology, the parents were asked to complete the Millon Clinical Multiaxial Inventory (MCMI) which is a 175-item true–false questionnaire.

Control Group

Usually, a friend of the victim was chosen as a control subject because of similarity in age, sex, race, education, and socioeconomic status.[21] Permission was sought by the parents of the victim to call the friend and his or her family to see whether they were willing to act as controls. If the friend and the parents were willing to participate, initial and followup interviews were arranged similar to that of the victim's family. Information was sought from the controls to identify significant differences or similarities between these two groups.

PSYCHOLOGICAL RECONSTRUCTION – JEFFERSON COUNTY STUDY

From January 1, 1980 until the end of December 1982, there were 21 cases of completed suicide in children and adolescents aged 19 years and younger. During 1980, there were nine cases, in 1981 seven cases, and in 1982, five cases. Of all of these families, only one refused to participate in this study. The participation rate was 95%.

The following cases were chosen as representative of initial interviews with the family and friends of completed suicide in childhood and adolescence for the purpose of psychological reconstruction.

Prototype of the Initial Interview: Suicide of a 17-Year-Old Male

Although the following initial interview with a bereaved family occurred a few months before the formalization of the Suicide Research Project, it has served as a prototype for the subsequent interviews and, because of this, will be described in some detail.

At about 10:15 PM one fall evening, the deputy coroner called our research assistant and said, "I am going to a suicide investigation of a 17-year-old white boy, Robert Gordon. (All names have been changed for the sake of confidentiality.) Can you meet me at the victim's house?" When the research assistant arrived at the house, approximately 45 minutes following the suicide, the police investigators and the deputy coroner had completed their preliminary investigation of the scene and were removing the gun from Robert's body. Robert was found in his bedroom lying on his back with a gunshot wound to his head. A 12-gauge Mossberg pump shotgun was lying on him with his toe on the trigger.

Interview with the family pediatrician We wondered how we could get in touch with the family to ask them if they would participate in our research study. Considering the family's acute state of grief, and their possible lack of receptivity, we felt that the best approach was through the family minister or pediatrician. The senior investigator called Dr. B., the family pediatrician, who had been in close contact with the family regarding Robert. He was most receptive and agreed to an interview within 36 hours after the suicide.

Dr. B. is a well-known and highly respected pediatrician, who has been practicing in this community for many years. He was upset and grieved by this incident, and said:

Robert came to our practice at age 15 months when the parents moved here from another city. The last office visit I had with Robert was just one month before he killed himself. Mrs. Gordon brought him to the office. Young Robert complained of hearing difficulties. He had wax impacted in his ears. He had a history of allergy problems in the form of upper respiratory symptoms. When the weather was cold, his sinuses bothered him. He also complained of abdominal pain and discomfort.

A week before Robert's death, his mother called the office and said, "I need help. Robert is depressed and moody. He has a hard time going to sleep. His personality has changed. We are concerned about it. Robert's father and I need help. Is there anyone that you can recommend?" I recommend the name of a young, practicing child psychiatrist and also prescribed a barbiturate for sleeping.

A week later around 10:00 PM, Robert's father called me and said, "I am afraid of Robert. He is incoherent and belligerent. We are worried that he is taking drugs. When I went to his room, he didn't want to be bothered." Also, the father mentioned that Robert had been drinking recently. We talked a little about the use and abuse of alcohol and drugs. I mentioned that there may be a need for hospitalization. I asked whether Mrs. Gordon had pursued counseling for Robert. The father didn't know anything about this. Four or five minutes later, the father called me back and said, "I heard a gun. Robert has shot himself." I called Emergency Medical Services (EMS). Ten to 15 minutes later, one of the neighbors called me and said, "Robert is dead. EMS is here along with the police and the coroner." I drove to their house. Everyone was in a state of shock. I didn't view the body. I went up to his bedroom after the coroners had left. His body had been covered by the people from the funeral home. The shot was through the left eye. They found three shells on the bedside table. The neighbors were thinking it might have been an accident. They thought he might have been looking through the gun barrel and by accident shot himself. But the detective found that he had lain down in bed and triggered the gun with his toes. An empty bottle of tequila was found under the bed.

When I asked Dr. B. whether Robert had any symptoms of emotional problems, he replied: "To be frank, I didn't know Robert that well. I can't say. Robert might have been depressed. . . . ". Dr. B. was very helpful in arranging for us to interview the family.

Interview with the family Eight days later, on a sunny Saturday afternoon, we visited the Gordons in their home. The Gordons live in an established middle-class area. The neighborhood is quiet and attractive. When we drove up, Mr. Gordon, their older daughter, Mary, and a couple of teenaged boys were talking out in front of the house by a red sports car. These boys were friends of Robert and were coming to rake the lawn for the Gordons. Mr. Gordon and Mary greeted us and invited us into the house. Mrs. Gordon, Robert's aunt, and his younger sister, Jane, joined us. The mother and the two daughters sat on the couch, the father in a comfortable chair. Robert's aunt sat in a rocking chair on the other side of the room. The living room was tidy and nicely arranged. A heavy fog of oppressive sorrow hung in the air.

Mrs. Gordon is a black-haired, fair-skinned woman who was dressed in a black blouse and dark brown skirt. She wore very little or no makeup. She appeared to be in her late 30s. There was a quiet but deep sadness in her face. Mr. Gordon is in his early 40s. He was casually dressed and seemed somewhat cautious and wary. Mary, aged 14, was sad but willing to relate. Jane, aged 9–10 years, appeared pleasant, puzzled, and wide-eyed. The aunt, who was in her mid-60s, was pale and sadly quiet.

We were planning on spending one to two hours with the family, but we were there four hours. Robert's mother did most of the talking.

Robert's father and sisters, after initial inhibition, joined the conversation. We asked them whether they had any idea why we were there. Mrs. Gordon said:

Dr. B. asked us whether it would be all right if you contacted us. We thought about it a great deal. We finally decided that it would be okay. He mentioned suicide is a problem in this community and that you were doing research on it. We thought that if we could help someone else, we wouldn't mind at all.

Then Mrs. Gordon described in detail what had happened:

That afternoon, Robert came home and went to his room. At approximately 9:15 PM, I went upstairs. I saw Robert going into the bathroom down the hall. He stumbled and tripped over a chair, knocking it over. I thought that he had taken something. After going back to his room, I smelled the glass that he had gotten a drink of water from to see if it smelled like liquor. . . . You see, in July, we found out that Robert was drinking his father's beer, gin, and whiskey. We were angry about it, and when we asked him why he was doing it, he said that he couldn't go to sleep, and that drinking helped him to go to sleep. You know, because of that, I called Dr. B.'s office about one week before Robert's death and told him that Robert had a hard time going to sleep and that he looked depressed. I felt Dr. B.'s office thought I was overreacting. Dr. B. prescribed sleeping medication for him and said that he might need some counseling. But we didn't think it was that serious. I wish we would have taken him to see Dr. B. a week ago, or to see a psychiatrist. We never thought he would do such a thing to himself.

A quiet silence took over the room. Both mother's and father's eyes began to tear, but at no time during the four-hour interview did any of the family cry openly. The only thing that broke the silence was the parents' continuous cigarette and cigar smoking.

After a while, Mrs. Gordon continued:

I did not notice the smell of alcohol in the glass in the bathroom, but I was concerned about his stumbling, and I mentioned to my husband that I thought Robert was taking something—drugs or pills. A few minutes later, my husband went upstairs.

I turned to Mr. Gordon, who was sitting tensely on the edge of his chair biting on his cigar, and asked him, "Can you share with us what happened?"

He said:

I was sitting here and watching you, and I felt that at any moment, if you or your friend were trying to hurt any of us by your questioning, I would have kicked you out of the house and said, "Get the hell out of here!" But fortunately, I don't need to do that.

His explosive anger caught me by surprise. After a moment, I said, "I don't blame you. I'm sure that you were quite concerned and wondered what the hell we wanted from you and your family." A tense laughter filled the air. Afterward, everyone seemed more at ease, and the father began:

> I went upstairs to see what was happening. I went to Robert's room and said to him, "Have you taken any drugs?" He sounded angry and belligerent, and he couldn't speak right. But he said something like, "Get out of my room. Leave me alone." I became more angry and belligerent, and said, "We'll get to the bottom of this. I'm going to find out what kind of drugs you're taking. I'll leave you now." And while I was leaving the room, Robert screamed, "Yeah! I took hundreds. I'm spaced out!" I came downstairs. I was just furious and felt helpless and didn't know what to do. I decided to call Dr. B. and ask for help. Dr. B. suggested, "Let him sleep it off." After I hung up, we heard a sound from Robert's room like a book hitting the floor. We thought that Robert was getting mad and throwing a fit. I asked my wife to go up and see what it was. His door was closed when she got upstairs, and she was afraid to go in. I came upstairs and went to the room. The room was dark. I turned the light on and found him lying in blood on the bed. I closed the door and didn't let my wife and children go to the room. I immediately called Dr. B. again, and you know the rest.

Smoke was filling the living room. Jane, the youngest daughter, was becoming impatient and jittery. Looking at the children, I said, "It is too much for anyone to take." Both of the kids suddenly exploded, "It is unreal. We just can't believe it!" Jane said that she was getting tired. I suggested, "Let's all pause for a while." Everyone sighed in relief.

At this time, the family asked us if we would like iced tea or lemonade. We asked for iced tea. A few moments later, the mother and Mary, the oldest daughter, brought the grownups iced tea and the children lemonade.

Mary was a bright, articulate person, who for the most part shielded her sadness. She seemed intensely perplexed and baffled by her brother's suicide. She went over the details again of what happened that afternoon and evening adding:

> The kids in school rumored that my brother was taking too many drugs. I don't believe that. I noticed that he was drinking, and sometimes he would come home after school and drink Dad's gin or whiskey; but I don't think he took dope.
>
> I'm scared to sleep upstairs. I'd rather sleep downstairs with my aunt. That night, I was sleeping. I went to bed about 8:30 PM. Suddenly, I woke

up to the sounds of so many noises. Then I found out that Robert shot himself. The neighbors are saying that it was an accident; but I really don't think so because he knew how to use the gun. He and Dad have gone hunting so many times and skeet shooting and target practicing.

At this time, the mother interjected, "Mary, the neighbors want to be nice to us — you can't blame them. I would also like to believe it was an accident." The father added, "Oh, so badly I want to believe it was an accident." I said, "I'm sure it would be much easier to feel that it was an accident. . . . Sometimes the truth hurts a lot."

The father added:

Yes, it hurts a lot. But how could we say it was an accident? He knew how to handle the gun very well. The neighbors say that he might have been cleaning the gun, and it accidentally went off. But when I went to the room, the lights were off, so how could he have been cleaning his gun in the dark? We gave him that gun for his birthday just a few months ago. I know he called a few of his friends between 7 and 9 PM that evening. He wanted to go camping next week. The funny thing is, he had done his homework, but then we found a few of his birthday cards in his trash can. It breaks my heart. I don't know what state of mind he was in. You know, he didn't leave a note. I blame myself a million times. I feel I pushed him over the brink.

A number of times, I asked Jane how she felt about all of these things. All through the interview, Jane had a book in her hand. At times, she was listening intently, and, at times, she appeared to be reading the book. She was the only one who did not show any outward sign of sorrow. She was exuberant and effervescent and said, "Oh! I don't think about it." When I asked her what memories she had of Robert, she said, "Oh! Lots of good memories. He was so good to me. He was fun to play ball with. He taught me how to play baseball, how to catch and hit the ball. He tickled me. . . ." Then she burst into laughter.

Finally, we asked the aunt about her feelings and reactions. The aunt, with much sadness, spoke of Robert in glowing terms. She said he was very thoughtful and considerate. He would come and help her.

Later, the parents added that Robert was a very sensitive boy. He was an average student and had to work very hard to get B's and C's. Last winter, he was depressed for two to three weeks because of his schoolwork. He was small for his age and was quite concerned about not dating. Mother said, "He was immature for his age. I wanted him to stay home the first year of college and go to school here." Father added:

We had a close relationship when Robert was younger. We were active in Boy Scouts, and we did a lot of sports together. Recently, I sensed he did not seem as close to us as before. About a week before his death, I saw Robert becoming belligerent and out of control. I suspected he was using drugs or alcohol. He said that he had only one beer. I was surprised that one beer could have so much effect on him. He told me one of the girls that he wanted to date was using him and manipulated him and that he was furious about it. Finally, we had an argument about his beer drinking. He said to me, "Don't push me; you will be sorry."

At this time, Mother added, "Robert usually was even tempered, but he would sometimes stomp out. If he didn't like someone, he would tell us frankly that he didn't like them. I would say that he should be more polite. Generally, he was shy, polite, and considerate."

The parents denied any history of suicidal behavior in Robert or in the family, except, Mother said:

I have a tendency towards depression. The first time I felt depressed was after having Jane nine years ago. For a few months, I was down in the dumps and blue. Then I get some Triavil from our family doctor. About a year ago, I felt quite depressed again. I felt that I had spent a great deal of my life on my kids and my husband and hadn't achieved anything for myself. I think I told that to Robert. He said, "Mom, you are disappointed in me. I didn't turn out as well as you wanted me to." Of course, that was not true, but I think about it a lot now. I feel that I am responsible for his death. He inherited the depression from me.

Mrs. Gordon denied ever having any active suicidal thoughts or ideas. Later on, we learned from Mary that one of Robert's friends had been hospitalized in a psychiatric facility for attempted suicide a couple months earlier.

At the end of the interview, we wondered whether we could see Robert's room. At this time, tears swelled in the father's eyes, and he said that the children and mother had not gone to Robert's room. We said, "Of course, it's up to you, but it might be helpful if the children decided for themselves whether or not they want to visit Robert's room." Both children said they wanted to.

Robert's room was small and simply decorated. It had a twin bed and a couple of small pieces of antique furniture. Father proudly mentioned that he had refinished the antique furniture himself and had given a couple of pieces to Robert. On the desk there were a couple of books which Robert had been reading recently. One was *Blind Ambition* and another, *All the President's Men*. Mother said, "Robert loved to read. He and I were the readers in the house. When he was small, they called him 'Little Professor'." On the other side of the room was a cabinet with stereo equipment and a number of rock music tapes. Robert's wire-rimmed glasses were on top of the dresser by the door. Jane picked up his glasses and tried them on. The air was filled with strange feelings of loneliness and communion. We all were alone there and feeling empty. At the same time, there was a feeling of relief and comfort that everyone was in the room. Jane spontaneously said, "I tried to not even look at Robert's door when I came upstairs. I was afraid his ghost would come out." Mary laughed nervously and, in obvious relief, said, "Gee, I was scared to death of the same thing. I knew it couldn't be true, but I was still afraid that he might come out of the door any moment."

At the end, the parents said they were concerned about Jane, who had not shown her emotions and did not appear to be in mourning. We said that each individual dealt with loss and mourning differently. We added that it was important that the family be open and honest with each other and share their thoughts and feelings about Robert, but, at the same time, if any of them did not want to, or were not ready to express their feelings, that was all right. It seemed at this time, Jane was not ready to show her feelings. Also, we asked the family to give us a call if they were concerned about anything and assured them we would be happy to talk with them. Otherwise, we would get in touch with them in one month. We advised the family to remove all guns from the home, and also to put drugs in a locked place out of reach because each family member and friends were at a high risk for suicide. Also, we asked for the names of Robert's friends, and if we could get in touch with them.

Initial impression   After leaving the Gordons' home, the two of us were simultaneously exhausted, keyed up, and overwhelmed. We both felt that the family interview had gone well and seemed to provide a means of relief. We talked for about one and one-half hours sharing our feelings and reactions. We hypothesized that Robert had been somewhat depressed for some time. It appeared that, under the influence of alcohol, he experienced a state of pathological intoxication in the form of episodic dyscontrol which led to his suicide.

Suicide of an 11-Year-Old Male

On a mid-January evening, Jerry Hedrick, an 11-year-old white male, was found dead in his bedroom closet. Jerry had a rope around his neck, tied to the clothes bar. He was kneeling on a sack of clothes. The coroner ruled that his death was a "suicide." However, some friends and relatives viewed it as "accidental" or "foul play."

Initial interview with the family   The following evening, two members of the Suicide Research Team (SRT) interviewed the family in their home. The Hedricks live in a public housing project. Mrs. Hedrick has six children. The oldest, an 18-year-old half-sister to Jerry, lives with her husband in another neighborhood. The other four children, twin brothers, aged 15 years, and two younger brothers, aged 10 and 7, live with their mother and stepfather. The family members were in a state of shock and seemed very distressed. Mrs. Hedrick was friendly and pleasant and, although quite tearful, warmly welcomed us.

Developmental history Mrs. Hedrick reported that her pregnancy with Jerry was essentially normal with occasional bleeding after the sixth month. Labor was uneventful. According to the mother, "Jerry was a very healthy and normal child." He walked at age 14 months and was toilet trained by age 2. He was enuretic until age 10. He had a slight build, and a recent picture showed a good-looking boy with blonde hair, bright blue eyes and an engaging smile.

Medical history Jerry never had any major medical illness except for some scratches and stitches due to falling or playing.

School history At the time of his death, Jerry was a fifth grader in a public school. He had performed poorly in the third grade. In the fourth grade, he had a "sensitive and thoughtful teacher" with whom he established a close relationship. Jerry was this teacher's protege. He did so well in the fourth grade that according to this teacher "he accomplished the work of two academic years in one." He only missed two days of class during the entire school year.

However, Jerry and his fifth grade female teacher "did not get along very well." Jerry described her as "fair" but "hard." He skipped school often, and his grades dropped substantially. His school behavior deteriorated. At the same time, however, at the request of his former fourth grade teacher, Jerry participated in some extracurricular activities. He was awarded a "recognition certificate" for a paper he wrote on an environmental protection issue just two months prior to his suicide.

Family history When Jerry was 4 years old, his mother took all six children and left his father. The father apparently had raped his 11-year-old stepdaughter. Mrs. Hedrick commented that he had been a very good father and husband up to that time, and the kids loved him very much. After this incident, the children all resented him and did not want him back. The separation, she stated, "had a very profound effect on Jerry." He loved his father "dearly" and "took it very hard," but eventually "he got over it." According to his mother, "he was never told about the incident." However, the mother felt that "he must have heard rumors in the family and among friends about what caused the separation."

Mrs. Hedrick impressed the interviewers as a verbal, intelligent woman. However, she did not have an opportunity to go beyond high school. She reported having had a traumatic childhood. Her father was an alcoholic who abused her mother and the children. He was shot to death by her mother in "self-defense" when Mrs. Hedrick was only 11 years old. Her mother later married a "nicer" person. However, the tragic event "left a scar on all of us."

Mrs. Hedrick described herself as a strong-willed, self-confident and determined individual with a very definite opinion about right and wrong. She is critical of those who are unsure of themselves or who disagree with her. She sees herself as being sociable. She loves intense competition and likes to be in a leadership position. She mentioned that she has "an IQ of 137."

One of Jerry's 15-year-old twin brothers has a special ability in sketching. However, because of truancy from school, he is voluntarily going to a special school for children with discipline problems. Recently, the other twin was also referred to this same school because the mother is afraid that "he is going to get into trouble." Jerry's 10-year-old brother is an average student. His youngest brother, the 7-year-old, ranked in the 90th percentile in mathematics among his age group in the nation, and is doing well in school.

Profile of Jerry Jerry was described by his family, friends, teachers, and neighbors as a nature-oriented and athletic child who loved horses and animals. He was "bothered that he could not live in the country and have animals and horses." He was a likeable child, but at times he would become argumentative, and, when upset, would become violent. He could not handle anger, and as one of his brothers stated, "he would throw things around, kick the walls and tear the room apart." Mrs. Hedrick added that Jerry cried easily, whined and complained often, and was aloof, withdrawn and, at times, unresponsive. She revealed that he was involved in occasional shoplifting.

Jerry, according to the Louisville Behavior Checklist completed by his mother, was a very quiet, shy and introverted child who would keep things to himself and did not share his problems with others. These characteristics were also substantiated by his teachers, friends, and the school principal.

According to his favorite teacher, "Jerry had a mind of his own. He had a lot of potential, but was not a high achiever and would do only things he like to do." The teacher felt that although Jerry looked forward to seeing him and doing things with him, "he never got close to me."

A year prior to the suicide During the year before his suicide, Jerry experienced a number of tragic losses. One of his close friends drowned while they were swimming together. Another friend was killed by an automobile while he and Jerry were attempting to walk across the expressway. Later, a third friend was severely injured by an automobile when he and Jerry tried to run across the same expressway. A few months before his suicide, Jerry was suspended from school because of a disciplinary problem. He had smeared feces on a school window.

The day before the suicide The day before his suicide, Jerry brought home a rope and hid it in his closet. That night, he and his 7-year-old brother came home late, around 11 PM. Their parents were worried and upset and reprimanded both boys by sending them to their rooms and grounding them. Apparently, later that night, Jerry tied the rope on the bar. "No one thought anything of it because it was ordinary for the kids in that neighborhood to play hangmen and walk with a rope around their necks," according to one of the brothers.

The day of the suicide After school, around 4:00 PM, Jerry told a classmate, an 11-year-old girl, that he intended to go home and "kill myself." The friend did not take this threat seriously because she said, "he used to tease me and tell me that he would steal my dog or would break into a neighbor's house."

Evidently, that same day, one of Jerry's brothers told their mother that Jerry had crossed the freeway that day, something he was not supposed to do. When Jerry came home, he was sent to his room and was again grounded. Forty-five minutes later, when his 10-year-old brother opened the door to Jerry's closet, he found him kneeling on the sack of clothes with a rope around his neck. He was dead. All family members were home at that time.

Postvention Jerry's suicide has had a very profound effect on family members, friends, neighbors, and the children and the teachers at school. Mrs. Hedrick vacillates between thinking that Jerry's death was accidental or intentional. She stated that if she accepts the suicide ruling, it would mean that she had provided such a terrible life for her child that he wanted to terminate it. On the other hand, she does realize that the evidence tends to support this ruling. At the present time, she has come to the conclusion that Jerry's death may have been an "impulsive, unmeditated act of self-destruction as a way to retaliate for being punished. He wanted to teach those who picked on him a lesson. However, he went too far in his plan and was not able to reverse the consequences."

Jerry's brothers are afraid to be alone, afraid they may see "Jerry's ghost." The younger ones demand to sleep with the older ones. All of the brothers cry frequently, are very distressed, and have resumed shoplifting in recent days. The family is being treated in outpatient psychotherapy at Child Psychiatric Services. A day after Jerry's funeral, a close friend, an 11-year-old boy, attempted suicide. He tried to hang himself with a tie, but it broke. Jerry's family contacted the SRT. We arranged an emergency psychiatric evaluation and immediate hospitalization. While in the hospital during the second week, he made a second suicide attempt by hanging by a belt from the bathroom ceiling.

A second friend, an 11-year-old girl, was taken to the inpatient Child Psychiatric Service two months after Jerry's death. She had attempted to kill herself by ingesting some "nerve pills."

Five days after Jerry's suicide, the school principal asked the SRT members if they could come to school to talk with some teachers and students. The teachers had observed that several fifth graders were quiet and withdrawn, crying in class and asking to go home. The teachers were concerned that some of the children might imitate Jerry's suicidal act. Two members of the SRT went to the school. They talked to a group of 110 students and the teachers. They tried to answer their questions and helped them verbalize their concerns and worries. They let the students and teachers know that they would be available for further consultation.

Suicide of an 18-Year-Old Male

In late March shortly after midnight, Jason French, aged 18, committed suicide. He sealed off the garage, turned on the family car and killed himself by carbon monoxide poisoning. He had not ingested any alcohol or drugs prior to his death. Shortly before Jason died, he had a lengthy and emotional phone conversation with his girlfriend that ended with a statement that he "would not be around much longer to trouble anyone." Jason was crying when he hung up.

Initial interview with the family   The family and several friends were contacted at the funeral home and seen within 30 hours following the time of death. Everyone was receptive to the SRT's approach. A few days later, a home visit was made to the family.

Jason's family lived in a new middle-class suburban neighborhood. Their two-story stone home was immaculately kept. Jason lived with his natural mother, adoptive father, and an elementary school-age sister.

Developmental history   During the mother's pregnancy with Jason, the natural father physically and mentally abused her. As a result of this, she was hospitalized twice. In the second month of pregnancy, the natural father "accidentally" shot the mother when he intended to use the pistol as a club to beat her. The pregnancy lasted 9½ months. Labor was uneventful.

In late infancy, Jason had "constipation." He did not crawl, but stood at 5 months, walked at 9 months. According to the mother, he spoke words at 6 months and sentences at 16 months. He fed himself by 18 months, was toilet trained by age 2, and "was able to dress himself by age 3." Jason was the largest child in the first grade. He had facial hair at age 15. He was active in sports, especially football. At the time of his death, he was 6'5" tall and weighed 210 pounds.

Medical history   Jason received second-degree abdominal burns at age 18 months when he knocked over a hot iron. According to the mother, he had anemia twice at ages 5 and 16 in the form of borderline iron deficiency. He also had a rapid growth spurt between the ages of 13 and 14 years when he grew from 5'7" to 6'3", more than six inches in one year. The anemia in adolescence was thought to be the result of this rapid growth spurt. At age 16, he had a tonsilectomy. Also at age 16, he developed a blood clot in his right leg which reruptured after a minor car accident. This prevented him from playing any more football in his last year of high school. Jason was athletic and this upset him very much. He had seen the family doctor one month prior to his death for a "throat infection."

School history   Jason was an above average student, making "B" grades. According to his mother and closest friend, his grades began to decline at age 15 after "he was bussed." Bussing broke up several of his relationships. His grades fell to C's and D's. In the first semester of his senior year, he received one F. In spite of this, he still had accumulated enough credits to graduate from high school after this first semester. Early graduation resulted in "a premature separation from his graduation class."

Family history   Mrs. French divorced Jason's natural father when Jason was an infant because of the father's history of explosiveness and irrational behavior. For instance, Mrs. French said Jason's father would call her on the phone, threaten suicide, fire a gun and drop the phone on the floor. Mrs. French said that "Jason's paternal grandmother had shot herself to death in front of Jason's father when the father was about 10 years old." Jason was 2 years old when his mother remarried. He was adopted by her new husband, Mr. French. Jason had no contact with his natural father since infancy.

When Jason was 13 years old, Mrs. French told him that he was adopted. He became very upset and rebelliously confronted his adoptive father. Then Jason became very curious about his biological father. Mrs. French said that she told Jason that his father "was not a person she could live with in peace."

One year prior to the suicide   The first known serious deterioration of Jason's behavior occurred 12 months before his death when he told his girlfriend that he would kill himself if she left him. In the coming months Jason made a number of similar threats to his girlfriend. At one time he even brandished a knife, threatening to use it on himself.

A family friend observed that Jason's personal adjustment problems dated back to two years before his death. "He wouldn't talk much, and seemed wrapped up in his own problems."

Jason's best friend said that during the nine to 10 months before Jason died, he had "mentioned carbon monoxide poisoning . . . several times . . . in everyday conversation." Jason also commented to this best friend that he believed his long absent biological father was "crazy" and "I am crazy like my father." He hoped to locate his father and "beat him up" for the father's past abuse of his mother. Jason's girlfriend said every time they broke up, "he threatened suicide" telling her, "I'm like my real dad. I'm just crazy."

Another turning point in Jason's life came when he developed a severe thigh muscle injury and could not play any more football in his senior year. Football was very important to him. His mother said, "Jason was always pressured to be the best athlete" because of his size. He had been previously considered for an athletic scholarship. Following this setback, Jason's attitude changed dramatically. He would not keep part-time jobs. He started experimenting with marijuana and occasionally used alcohol. He was involved in a minor car accident. As the months passed into winter, he became more and more petulant, withdrawn, and explosive. His grades had dropped to C's and D's and one F. Jason became prone to crying when he was not allowed to drive the car. Repeated tardiness at school caused a disciplinary action (three days' detention hall) a few months before his death. Jason started sleeping a lot. His friends were applying for college, and he did not know what he wanted to do with his life.

Two months before Jason's death, a young male relative, only slightly older than he, committed suicide following a "setback in a girl-friend relationship."

One week before the suicide During the last week of his life, Jason talked to his girlfriend about the suicide of his relative. He commented to her that if a person were going to commit suicide, carbon monoxide was the easiest way. Jason's relationship with his girlfriend became less certain, and he had another fight with her. He started staying away from home overnight after arguments with his parents.

A few days before Jason's death, his mother told him that she had just made an appointment for him to see someone at a mental health clinic because of his withdrawal from the family, sitting around staring, and having problems with his friends. His mother said that he resented this and told her that he did not need help.

Final 24 hours Jason's mother reported in the final 24 hours before his suicide, Jason "seemed more relaxed." He had a pleasant and peaceful day and evening with his family and a visiting neighbor and friend, an adolescent male. Even though he had seen a movie that evening on mass suicide, he told his mother "it was awful" and that he would "never do anything like that." Jason gave "no indication" to his family that he was "troubled or upset in any way." He had joked with his mother. "For the first time, Jason seemed to have his future in focus."

At midnight, Jason talked with his girlfriend and made another "veiled threat," but since he had made so many threats over the past 12 months, she was not alarmed by what she heard. Jason changed clothes, straightened up his room, sealed off the garage, turned on the family car engine and died some time after midnight. No suicide note was found.

Postvention The victim's girlfriend was extremely despondent, blaming herself for Jason's death. Soon afterwards, one more contact was made with the girlfriend, but she decided that she did not want any additional contacts. In the following months, the girlfriend went through a lengthy period of marked social withdrawal. Several months after

Jason's death, the girlfriend saw a relative of Jason's and experienced an anxiety attack that was so severe that she was unable to walk and had trouble breathing. She developed headaches and had difficulty sleeping. She would not respond to phone calls or letters sent by the SRT. We learned that she married two years later.

Several home visits were made in the following months and contacts were made with close friends. This tragedy had marked effects on the family as they struggled with their guilt feelings. The victim's mother observed that her friends were uncomfortable and were avoiding her. The parents found it most difficult for them to discuss together their feelings about Jason's suicide.

Two years following Jason's death, his younger sister began to withdraw and isolate herself. She developed a preoccupation with death, sleep disturbance, and deterioration of academic performance. She adopted Jason's nickname and his musical interests. She started writing letters to movie stars talking about her brother's death. Then she wrote a "will." This significant change in behavior was discovered during a scheduled followup interview. The parents were encouraged to seek immediate psychiatric care for her.

SUMMARY

Significant increases in the referrals of young people with suicidal behavior encouraged the investigators to review and analyze the coroner's records for completed suicide of children and adolescents 19 years of age and younger in Jefferson County, Kentucky, from 1975 through 1980.

We found 657 cases of completed suicide established beyond a reasonable doubt. Sixty, or 9.4% of these cases, were children and youth 19 years of age and younger — the youngest being 10 years old. Slightly more than 15% were aged 10 to 14 years, 18% were female, and 12% were black. Ages 17 and 18 were the most vulnerable — 49% of the suicides occurred within this age group.

These findings led to the development of a research project, beginning in 1980, for the psychological reconstruction of completed suicide in childhood and adolescence in order to explore and identify contributing factors. In this chapter, we have discussed the methodology of interviewing bereaved families, friends, and other significant persons. The families and friends are then followed for at least three years. The purpose of the followup is to assess how the bereaved families and friends coped with the loss of a young person to suicide and to attempt to prevent possible suicide in these survivors by being available as a point of contact for support, education, and referral.

Three case examples of psychological reconstruction of young people who have committed suicide were discussed. We have found that the following are frequently common factors in completed childhood and adolescent suicide:

1. Ages 17 and 18 appear the most vulnerable;
2. Variety of physical complaints, such as sleep disturbance, pain, and allergies along with anger outbursts, irritability, and depressive symptoms during the previous four to six weeks;
3. Contact with a physician for above symptoms, but emotional state, including the possibility of depression, suicide, and drug and alcohol abuse, not assessed or taken seriously;
4. Breakdown of meaningful communication with parents or friends;
5. Direct or indirect mention of suicidal intentions;
6. Previous suicide attempt(s) in some cases;
7. Large amount of alcohol consumed during final few hours in many cases;
8. Major confrontation with a meaningful person during last 24 hours;
9. Desperate attempt to contact a friend(s) by telephone.

CONCLUSION

Based on our extensive work with bereaved families and friends of children and adolescents who have committed suicide, we have reached the following conclusions:

1. All suicidal messages and behaviors should be taken seriously;
2. The suicidal idea of yesterday frequently becomes the suicidal threat or attempt of today and the completed suicide of tomorrow;
3. The common denominator in all cases of completed suicide is the prevailing sense of loneliness and isolation during the months prior to suicide;
4. The final precipitating factor is actual or perceived loss of human contact;
5. An overwhelming feeling of "disappointing" parents or other loved ones prevails;
6. As opposed to previous reports, a vast majority of survivors are receptive to and appreciative of mental health support;
7. There is a significant increase in the incidence of depression, pathological grief, and particularly chronic preoccupation with suicidal thought, threats, and attempts in survivors;

8. Initial contact and regular followup with the survivors through the method of psychological reconstruction may decrease the possibility of suicide in this group.
9. We strongly urge the development of special training programs for mental health professionals, physicians, nurses, clergy, school counselors, teachers, and others who work with children and adolescents to increase their sensitivity and receptivity to suicidal messages. It is extremely important to move decisively in providing effective therapeutic intervention.
10. We recommend the development of a Mental Health Awareness Program in the school system, including universities, as part of the required curriculum which would increase sensitivities and awareness of the signs and symptoms of the emotional problems of living, with specific emphasis on suicide. The role of friends and peers in early recognition of suicidal behavior and prevention of suicide cannot be overemphasized.

ACKNOWLEDGMENTS

The authors acknowledge the contributions of Sharon Lee Shafii, RN, BSN; Pam Gilliam, RN, MS; and the continuous support of Richard Greathouse, MD, Coroner of Jefferson County, Kentucky. We are grateful for the grant from the George W. Norton Foundation, Louisville, Kentucky, which has made it possible to continue this project.

REFERENCES

1. Shafii M, Shafii SL: Self-destructive, suicidal behavior, and completed suicide, in: *Pathways of Human Development: Normal Growth and Emotional Disorders in Infancy, Childhood and Adolescence.* New York, Thieme-Stratton Inc, 1982, pp 164–180.
2. Bakwin RM: Suicide in children and adolescents. *J Am Med Wom Assoc* 1973;28:643,647,650.
3. Barter JT, Swaback DO, Todd D: Adolescent suicide attempts, a follow-up study of hospitalized patients. *Arch Gen Psychiatry* 1968;19:523–527.
4. Frederick CJ: Current trends in suicidal behavior in the United States. *Am J Psychotherapy* 1978;32:172–200.
5. Holinger PC: Adolescent suicide: An epidemiological study of recent trends. *Am J Psychiatry* 1978;135:754–756.
6. Otto U: Suicidal acts by children and adolescents. *Acta Psychiatr Scand (Suppl)* 1972;233:7–123.
7. Seiden RH: Suicide among youth: A review of the literature, 1900–1967. *A Supplement to the Bulletin of Suicidology*, National Clearinghouse for Mental Health Information. Washington, DC, US Government Printing Office, 1969.
8. Shaffer D: Suicide in childhood and early adolescence. *J Child Psychol Psychiatry* 1974;15:275–291.

9. Shafii M, Whittinghill JR, Healy MH: The pediatric-psychiatric model for emergencies in child psychiatry: A study of 994 cases. *Am J Psychiatry* 1979;136:1600–1601.
10. Teicher JD: Suicide and suicide attempts, in Noshpitz J (ed): *Basic Handbook of Child Psychiatry*. New York, Basic Books, 1979, vol 2, pp 685–697.
11. Litman RE, Curphey T, Shneidman ES, Farberow NL, Tabachnick N: Investigations of equivocal suicide. *JAMA* 1963;184:924–929.
12. Diller J: The psychological autopsy in equivocal deaths. *Perspect Psychiatr Care* 1979;17(4):156–161.
13. Barraclough BM, Shepherd DM: The immediate and enduring effects of the inquest on relatives of suicides. *Br J Psychiatry* 1977;131:400–404.
14. Herzog A, Resnick HLP: A clinical study of parental response to adolescent death by suicide with recommendations for approaching the survivors, in Farberow NL (ed): *Proceedings of 4th International Conference for Suicide Prevention*. Los Angeles, International Association for Suicide Prevention, 1968, pp 381–390.
15. Cantor P: The effects of youthful suicide on the family. *Psychiatric Opinion* 1975;12:6–11.
16. Whitis PR: The legacy of a child's suicide, in Cain AC (ed): *Survivors of Suicide*. Springfield, IL, Charles C Thomas, 1972, pp 155–166.
17. Resnick HLP: Psychological resynthesis: A clinical approach to the survivors of a death by suicide, in Cain AC (ed): *Survivors of Suicide*. Springfield, IL, Charles C Thomas, 1972, pp 167–177.
18. Miller LC: Louisville behavior checklist for males, 6–12 years of age. *Psychol Rep* 1967;21:885–896.
19. Miller LC: *Louisville Behavior Checklist Manual*. Los Angeles, Western Psychological Services, 1977.
20. Miller LC: Parental assessment of emotional disorders in childhood and adolescence, in Shafii M, Shafii SL: *Pathways of Human Development: Normal Growth and Emotional Disorders in Infancy, Childhood and Adolescence*. New York, Thieme-Stratton Inc, 1982, pp 234–242.
21. Detre K, Wyshak A: A matching procedure for epidemiological studies. *J Chronic Dis* 1971;24:83–92.

CHAPTER 18

DIAGNOSIS:
Review and Comment

HOWARD S. SUDAK
AMASA B. FORD
NORMAN B. RUSHFORTH

The preceding six chapters fall into three categories: diagnosis and aspects of psychological development in children (Pfeffer, Furman); in adolescents (Gammon, Friedman); and aspects of prediction, detection, and failure of detection (McIntire, Motto, Shafii). Each will be reviewed separately following some general remarks. The chapter will conclude with a brief consideration of subintentional suicide behavior.

It is not yet possible to predict suicide positively with any statistically meaningful accuracy. As Murphy showed in his paper on predicting infrequent events[1] and as more recently expressed by Pokorny,[2] the odds are always against a positive prediction. Thus, the prediction of "no suicide" for a given individual is almost always correct. What demographics can do, in addition to providing general etiological clues and suggesting methods of primary prevention, is to alert us to subgroups with higher risks of suicide. Greater precision in this area could lead to isolating subgroups with such high-risk rates that accurate predictions of suicide could be made. We are approaching such accuracy for groups such as physicians (or other professionals) who have lost their licenses to practice (or been disbarred) or who have been arrested and publicly humiliated. For these groups, the completed suicide rates for the year following the event approach 20% (20,000 per 100,000).[3] Similarly, depressed patients with markedly elevated 17-hydroxycorticosteroid levels or low norepinephrine-to-epinephrine ratios have been shown to have extremely high completion rates.[4-6]

When we leave such known high-risk groups, however, and turn to children and adolescents, we have fewer clues regarding which groups, if any, have comparably high rates. This is particularly so when evaluating the risk for a given youngster. We need to avoid the ecological fallacy described by Robinson[7] in which incorrect assumptions are made concerning associations among variables related to individuals employing relationships observed for these variables on the basis of ecological correlations.

Demographic data should only be used to alert the evaluator to especially high-risk groups when one is trying to appraise a given child or adolescent. For instance, knowing that the rates are relatively low for young black females does not mean one can automatically discount the risk for the specific depressed young black female being evaluated at the moment. She must be assessed on the status of her individual diagnosis, controls, helplessness, supports, etc, before one may conclude she does not require hospitalization. This is one of the major dangers with suicide scales — not only are they simplistic but they may falsely reassure the examiner that the risk is low because the score is low. The SAD PERSONS scale,[8] for instance, is useful as a mnemonic device to help the inexperienced therapist insure that he or she has inquired about most of the correct areas, but should not be facilely employed by itself to rule out suicidal risk.

The issue of which diagnosis or combination of diagnoses are most germane to suicide attempts and completions is the subject of these six chapters. Some chapters focus on symptoms, symptom clusters, other developmental or personal characteristics, or types of social and intrafamilial conflicts rather than on diagnosis per se. None follows this format so strictly that it does not digress into other aspects of suicidology as well, but in this review we will try to hold to the narrower focus.

Strictly speaking, since suicidal ideas, thoughts and acts are symptoms, not diseases, we should not speak of "diagnosing" suicide any more than we would speak of diagnosing a fever. Fever is a symptom of an underlying disease or disorder just as suicidal acts are the product of underlying diagnosable disorders. Epidemiological or sociological approaches focus on group effects, incriminating society, economics, etc, whereas a psychological focus seeks intrapsychic causes. A biopsychosocial view attempts to be more comprehensive, but often ends up paying lip-service to the balance since, in order to study anything, one generally focuses on one variable at a time. The proper application of multivariate techniques of analysis should prove to be a most useful tool with which to solve such problems, however. When we speak of "diagnosing" suicide we really mean either "predicting" suicide or diagnosing the relevant underlying problem.

Must there always be such an underlying problem? Is suicide ever normal? These questions are generally reducible to semantic or philosophical issues, since "rational" adults attempt suicide so rarely in our culture — particularly if one excludes the very elderly or those terminally or chronically ill or in severe physical pain. What is "normal" (ie, typical or average) is to employ the defense mechanism of denial to maintain a hopeful attitude. This is what keeps us from being suicidal in the face of adversity. What is remarkable is that the rate of suicide was not higher in concentration camps or for terribly impoverished people. Hope and denial maintain us. How ironic to note that Elisabeth Kubler-Ross,[9] one of the most eloquent spokespersons regarding medicine's failure to deal realistically with the dying patient, is allegedly apparently facilitated in her work with the dying by her own total denial of death! If one can talk with souls who have been there and come back or sense the spirits of people leaving their bodies, then there is no death — merely a transition to a "different" level of existence.[10] Religious faith can go a long way toward sustaining hope and denial for its adherents.

DIAGNOSIS IN CHILDREN

Cynthia Pfeffer reviews some of the literature on incidence and diagnosis, citing both her own and others' work. Readers should note that, in the child literature, suicidal ideas or thoughts are often cited as "suicidal," whereas for adults "threats" may be considered suicidal but ideation alone is so common as to be generally discounted.

Both the concept of suicidal ideas and threats being a normal part of the developmental turmoil of childhood and the belief that children do not get depressions like adults are strongly refuted by Pfeffer. Citing her own work as well as Carlson and Cantwell's[11] she indicates that acute and chronic depressions significantly correlate with the severity of suicidal preoccupations and actions. It is of interest, however, that suicidal ideas and depression correlated better with one another than suicidal acts and depressions. Is this because personality or character structure (Axis II) plays a more critical role in determining who will act on his or her suicidal ideas than Axis I diagnoses? Along these lines, how can we distinguish between depressed children who become suicidal and those who do not? Pfeffer reviews Cohen-Sandler's work,[12] showing that suicidal children appear to have undergone more stressful early childhoods as they matured than either nonsuicidal depressed children or children with other psychopathology. Her own studies suggest that the triad of depression, preoccupation with death, and suicidal tendencies in the child's family portend a particularly high risk.

Some clinically useful points relate to the therapist's countertransference and anxieties in the management of suicidal children. Pfeffer illustrates the treatment dilemmas that may arise from such feelings. Therapists may be comforted by realizing the ubiquitousness of discomfort with such children.

Although child psychiatrists have been too reluctant in the past to diagnose depression in children, Erna Furman's chapter warns us against too quickly appending such labels. If one diagnoses depression descriptively, one may be seriously misled. In her study of bereaved children, many of those who appeared depressed were found not to be so when studied more closely. Furman points out that similar symptoms at various developmental phases can have very different psychodynamics, just as similar psychodynamics across various developmental phases can lead to vastly different symptoms. Many of the children in her sample appeared to use depression as a defense against sadness (ie, against a real sense of loss or longing). Psychoanalytic work enabled them to give up the defense, become sad, and then work through their sadness. Premature "treatment" of these "depressions" by antidepressant medication, supportive therapy, etc, might, paradoxically, only facilitate the use of such pathological defenses against unconscious affect and content. Although the child might appear to be improved, particularly initially, long-range ill effects would likely ensue.

From the psychoanalyses of suicidal children, Furman has been able to extract a number of relevant phase-specific antecendents. All of these lead more to abnormal personality development (with a propensity toward self-hurting) than to intrapsychic (neurotic) depressions. The first of these relates to the role of primitive excitement and aggression in self-hurting so that, in later life, when events occur that excite adolescents and children and unleash intolerable homo- or heterosexual feelings, the patients may regress to (safer) earlier sadomasochistic levels. They are also apt to reenact such sadomasochism in their relationships with their therapists, she warns.

The second paradigm focuses on the origins of sadomasochistic pathology in the preschool years. Due to pathology in the parent-child relationships, such as excessive ambivalence, sadomasochism in the parent, or the parent being "unavailable" to protect the child from harm, or due to undergoing many medical or surgical procedures, the child's affectionate bonds are insufficient to bind the aggression. Furman's third model stems from insufficient bodily self-love to serve as a barrier against self-injury. Such early failures (in the first or second year) lead to poor differentiation between self and object so that later self-injury may also represent aggression toward others.

DIAGNOSIS IN ADOLESCENTS

Chapters 12 (Gammon) and 13 (Friedman) both address the problem of diagnosis in adolescents. The former group, at Yale, supports the use of structured diagnostic interviews in their chapter. Employing the Kiddie SADS-E, with data sets separately derived from a) mothers and b) patients, they compared diagnoses generated by these two sources with c) diagnoses in each case that they derived from any and all of the total information contained on the patient's charts, as well as d) all the clinical diagnoses made in each case plus e) an overall "best estimate" diagnosis. In addition, in the absence of a suitable scale for children or adolescents, in order to test the hypothesis that the more viable an individual's social support network was, the less likely depression and suicidal behavior would be, they originated their own. The small sample size hampered assessing adequately the validity of the premise using this "social adjustment scale," but preliminary results suggested that the hypothesis was correct.

Mother-informant versus child-informant K-SADS showed excellent concordance, and these both correlated extremely well with the ultimate best estimate diagnosis. There was much poorer agreement between diagnoses generated by their chart review and the diagnoses recorded by the patients' physicians. The former favored Axis I and the latter Axis II. The authors point out that the K-SADS and chart reviews are more apt to favor Axis I and downplay Axis II as compared with clinical interviews. They based this interpretation on the "data" being different based on the source. The Editors feel this may also relate to the fact that, despite DSM-III's explicit criteria for both axes, Axis II diagnoses tend to be more intuitive, ie, the interviewer's feelings are used to alert him or her to possible Axis II pathology and then he or she may substantiate the hunch by filling in the criteria. What was more striking was that six of the 17 adolescents were diagnosed as bipolar disorder on the basis of the K-SADS, but none of them had chart diagnoses for bipolar disorder. Also, in support of the value of the structured interview they found, via K-SADS, that four of the adolescents had prior suicidal attempts, whereas only two of these were noted in the patients' charts. This is a serious omission in view of the importance of a previous suicide attempt as a prediction of subsequent suicide behavior.

Friedman's group at Columbia also focused on the relationship between diagnosis and suicide attempts in adolescent inpatients and explored some of the Axis I versus Axis II interplay. They found an alarming association between frequency and severity of suicide attempts in patients with coexistent Borderline Personality Disorder (BPD) and Affective Disorder diagnoses. Over half of their 76 patients were diagnosed as having an Affective Disorder. Approximately one third of the affective group had coexistent Axis II diagnoses (virtually always BPD). Of the affective patients without BPD, males equaled females; of the ones with BPD, there was a great preponderance of females. Over half of the affective patients had made one or more lifetime suicide attempts, whereas only one of the nonaffective (3%) had done so. All of the patients with Affective Disorder with BPD had one or more attempts, but only half of the Affective Disorder alone group. Half of the Affective and BPD had made moderate to severe attempts, but only one tenth of the Affective Disorder alone.

Each of the patients with BPD met the criteria retrospectively for affective disorder. In all cases of Major Depression and BPD the Major Depression occurred first, leading the authors to wonder if BPD would have developed if the Affective Disorder had been diagnosed and treated at its onset (in other words, were these adolescents misdiagnosed as BPD?).

Since this apparently malignant combination of depression and BPD is most frequent in females, many of whom (undoubtedly influenced by their characterological problems) have made prior rather histrionic-appearing attempts, they are precisely the wrong group to dismiss as not being seriously suicidal. The authors also warn us against a glib dismissal of Dysthymic Disorders as being less serious than other Axis I depressive disorders. Four of Friedman and co-workers' patients with Major Depressive Disorder had carried earlier diagnosis of Dysthymic Disorder. Also, all of their study patients with Dysthymia and BPD had prior suicide attempts (and 55% of their study patients with Dysthymia but no BPD).

Their caveat regarding Dysthymia was repeated at the May 1983 American Psychiatric Association Meetings in New York City by Maria Kovacs.[13] She reported on 65 children aged 8 to 13 who were followed for five years with the diagnoses of Major Depressive Disorder, Dysthymia, or Adjustment Disorder with Depressed Mood. Dysthymia had earlier onset than Major Depressive Disorder (Adjustment Disorders in the middle); the recovery rates were slowest, about three years (faster for Major Depressive Disorder — 8½ months approximately; fastest for Adjustment Disorders — 6 months approximately). After recovery, the probability of a recurrence of a Major Depressive Disorder was greater and more rapid if there was a preexisting diagnosis of Dysthymia. Of children with the diagnosis of Dysthymia alone, 34% developed a Major Depressive Disorder within two years, and 73% within five years.

The implication of Friedman's study is that Axis I diagnosis should be vigorously treated despite the presence of Axis II pathology. His group refutes the bias that regards the latter as psychogenic and, consequently, in need of psychotherapy before one can treat the more organic Axis I disorder. The reverse is more likely true; if one treats the depression one improves the patient's ego functioning to the point where he or she can be a more effective ally in treating the personality disorder. Many patients will, therefore, require both psychotherapy and pharmacotherapy.

Readers of the two chapters in question are likely to note a discrepancy in diagnoses across Long Island Sound. In New York the diagnosis of Borderline Personality Disorder is far more common than in New Haven (or, for that matter, than in most of the rest of the country). Such local variation complicates comparisons and diagnostic studies across regions.

PREDICTION, DETECTION,
FAILURE OF DETECTION

Prospective studies of attempted suicide are uncommon in the literature. Thus, Motto's chapter holds extra merit, since it shows that such studies are not only feasible but can also provide us with data different from retrospective studies of attempters. Over a five-year period, he amassed a study sample of 122 adolescents and young males admitted to hospitals for depression and/or suicide attempts and then followed them for a mean seven-year period. Eleven suicided (9% of the total or 1.3% per year). Significantly correlating with completed suicide were fears of losing one's mind or fears of disease, and a moderate ability to communicate (good ability subjects and poor ability subjects were at less risk). Trends were noted for high suicide risk to be associated with "little or no drug use" and "absence of preparation for a suicide attempt." This might suggest that impulsivity is indicative of a particularly high risk for completed suicide and that therapists should not feel reassured merely because the patient does not make any "preparations." Motto's studies also suggest that a normal sleep pattern may be associated with high risk, rather than the converse. Carefully avoiding premature speculations, Motto illustrates the difficulties in prediction and urges more prospective studies to help identify predictive variables. Since fears of losing one's mind and fears of dying correlated with completed suicide, the Editors wondered if some of these individuals might have been preschizophrenic — a group whose considerable suicide risk is often underestimated.

Matilda McIntire's group focuses on the role of pediatricians in primary and secondary prevention. He or she is on the front line, and detection by the pediatrician could lead to very early referral and treatment. According to the authors, the "new morbidity" for pediatricians is that which arises secondary to the disrupted personal–familial–social patterns. Unfortunately, many pediatricians are insufficiently attentive to these aspects of their patient's lives. McIntire and her colleagues surveyed the Nebraska pool of pediatricians to assess their attitudes toward suicidal children and to study their management of self-destructive cases. Sixty-five of 110 potential subjects responded (59%). Pediatricians downplayed mood swings, vegetative symptoms, and acute precipitants as indicative of high risk. Younger pediatricians, however, tended to rank such factors as more serious than older ones. The authors noted that most referrals are to psychiatrists rather than to other mental health professionals and suggest that more education be provided regarding high-risk factors and the role of nonpsychiatrists in the mental health network.

The failure of detection by professionals and families is poignantly, painfully, described in the chapter by Shafii and his group. He and his collaborators interviewed all families in Louisville who had a child or adolescent of less than 19 years who committed suicide between January 1, 1980 and December 1, 1982. The extreme emotions experienced by such families immediately following a suicide have made it extremely difficult to conduct psychological postmortems until long after the event — thereby making the data less reliable. Defenses have had time to reconsolidate or new coping mechanisms appear, both of which may obscure the field. Shafii's group has been remarkably successful in interviewing families within hours of the event and then following the families for up to three years.

Three cases are presented in depth. These detail not only the apparent denial on the parents' part of the obvious (at least, in retrospect, obvious) pathology, depression, and even prior suicide attempts of their children, but also the chain of upsets in the surviving siblings and friends of the decedents. All of the families appeared to have been saying, "X was a perfectly normal, happy child . . . we never expected this." The ripple effect will be discussed further in the last section of this book under Intervention in Schools. Shafii's group feels that, in addition to their research leading to clues as to why these youngsters killed themselves, their work with the surviving family members may help to prevent additional suicides in them.

SUBINTENTIONAL SUICIDAL BEHAVIOR

The classification of conscious, deliberate suicidal behavior is so complex and our understanding so partial that we are not presenting a chapter on the still-murkier, twilight phenomena often called subintentional suicide. We cannot totally ignore this area, however, since it encompasses some very common behaviors as well as unusual ones. For instance, how does one classify wrist-cutting or other self-mutilation, alcohol and drug abuse, delinquency, anorexia or hyperobesity, accident-proneness, runaway behavior, promiscuity, truancy, polysurgery, religious cults, compulsive gambling, daredevil behavior, failure to comply with medical regimens, etc? Do we "diagnose" them? Do they help us better "predict" the degree of suicidal risk?

There are many classificatory schemes from which we may draw. The most complex, at least linguistically, is probably Shneidman's[14] who categorizes the basic orientations toward cessation into the following divisions: intentional (death-seekers, death-initiators, death ignorers, death-darers); subintentional (death-chancer, death-hastener, death-capitulator, death-experimenter); unintentioned (death-welcomer, death-accepter, death-postponer, death-disdainer, death-fearer); and contraintentioned (death-feigner, death-threatener).

Farberow[15] refers to Indirect Self-Destructive Behavior (ISDB) for behaviors in which there is not a conscious attempt to harm oneself. He divides these behaviors into present or absent underlying physical conditions and into actual versus only potential damage resulting from the activity (eg, smoking in the former and criminal activity in the latter categories).

Pattison and Kahan[16] proposed that the deliberate self-harm syndromes (eg, wrist-cutting, burning oneself) warrant a separate designation in a classification of self-destructive behavior and proposed a differential classification of all self-destructive behaviors. Their classification divides self-destructive behavior according to the following scheme:

	DIRECT	INDIRECT
HIGH LETHALITY	Suicide attempt	Termination of treatment such as dialysis
	SINGLE EPISODE	SINGLE EPISODE
MEDIUM LETHALITY	Suicide attempts	High-risk performance (stunts)
	MULTIPLE EPISODE	MULTIPLE EPISODE
	Atypical deliberate self-harm syndrome	Acute drunkenness
	SINGLE EPISODE	SINGLE EPISODE
LOW LETHALITY	Deliberate self-harm syndrome	Chronic alcoholism, severe obesity, heavy cigarette smoking
	MULTIPLE EPISODE	MULTIPLE EPISODE

The book edited by Farberow[15] provides one of the most comprehensive surveys of indirect self-destructive behavior (ISDB). Three of his authors (Litman, Achte, and Filstead) concluded that ISDB is one kind of defense used to ward off devastating feelings of depression or despair. Hendin's chapter on Delinquency focuses on delinquent behavior as the expression of the interplay between the adolescent and his or her family—conditioned, of course, by society.

All of these classificatory schemes are helpful ways to organize a complex, heterogeneous collection of behaviors but do not, per se, lead to increased understanding. None of their originators is simplistic enough to assume that similar behavior always has similar underpinnings. For instance, high-risk sports may, for some practitioners, represent an unconscious suicidal risk while, for others, it may represent mastery over fears of death, inadequacy, etc. Since we have no dipsticks into the unconscious, it is difficult in an individual instance to assess underlying motives. Subtle gradations of "intent" also complicate our taxonomy. Is smoking indirectly suicidal? Possibly, but if so, should one

304

also consider its effects on those around the smoker as "indirect homicide"? What about the use of artificial sweeteners? Any activity increases risks, but, on the other hand, passivity does not adequately protect one. It is only relatively safer inside the womb than out of it, so, from conception onward, we are all, to one degree or another, risk-takers. Where do we draw the line as to "pathology?" We usually do this pragmatically by defining anything out of the ordinary as abnormal. Obviously this leaves room for much subjective ("If I do it, it's not abnormal") and cultural biases. Nonetheless, indirect suicidal behavior does exist and must be carefully evaluated. Whether truly suicidal or not, much behavior of this sort is indicative of deficits in coping and warrants intervention.

CONCLUDING REMARKS

In children and adolescents, just as for adults, it appears that the most important aspect of prediction is a high index of suspicion on the therapist's part. Children who make threats of suicide or who are depressed, borderline, or dysthymic appear to be at particular risk. Biological tests such as the dexamethasone suppression test (DST) and structured diagnostic interviews may also help to indicate or confirm the risk for clinicians. What we need are better diagnostic indices, more prospective studies, more specific and more sensitive biological markers, better education and training for pediatricians and family physicians, and a clearer understanding of the meaning and implication of indirect suicidal behavior.

REFERENCES

1. Murphy GE: Clinical identification of suicidal risk. *Arch Gen Psychiatry* 1972;27:356–359.
2. Pokorny AD: Prediction of suicide in psychiatric patients. *Arch Gen Psychiatry* 1983;40:249–257.
3. Crawshaw R, Bruce JA, Eraker PL, et al: An epidemic of suicide among physicians on probation. *JAMA* 1980;243:1915–1917.
4. Bunney WE, Fawcett JA, Davis JM, et al: Further evaluation of urinary 17-hydroxycorticosteroids in suicidal patients. *Arch Gen Psychiatry* 1969;21:138–150.
5. Asberg M, Traskman L, Thoren P: 5-HIAA in the cerebrospinal fluid: A biochemical suicide predictor? *Arch Gen Psychiatry* 1976;33:1193–1197.
6. Ostroff R, Giller E, Bonese K, et al: Neuroendocrine risk factors of suicidal behavior. *Am J Psychiatry* 1982;139:1323–1325.
7. Robinson WS: Ecological correlations and the behavior of individuals. *Am Soc Rev* 1980;15:351–357.
8. Pattison WM, Dohn HH, Bird J, et al: Evaluation of suicidal patients: The SAD PERSONS scale. *Psychosomatics* 1983;24:343–349.
9. Kubler-Ross E: *On Death and Dying*. New York, Macmillan, 1969.

10. Lindsey R: "An Early Leader in Comfort for the Dying Moves Into Spiritualism," Special Report, *New York Times*, September 17, 1979.
11. Carlson GA, Cantwell DP: Suicidal behavior and depression in children and adolescents. *J Am Acad Child Psychiatry* 1982;21:361–368.
12. Cohen-Sandler R, Berman AL, King RA: Life stress and symptomatology: Determinants of suicidal behavior in children. *J Am Acad Child Psychiatry* 1982;21:178–186.
13. Kovacs M: Longitudinal Course of Childhood Depression, Symposium #34B, American Psychiatric Association, New York City, May, 1983. Paper accepted for publication in *Arch Gen Psychiatry*.
14. Shneidman ES: Suicide thoughts and reflections, 1960–1980. *Suicide Life Threat Behav* (special issue) Winter 1981;11(4):232–253. ("Orientations Toward Death: Subintentional Death and Indirect Suicide.")
15. Farberow NL (ed): Indirect self-destructive behavior: Classification and characteristics, in *The Many Faces of Suicide: Indirect Self-Destructive Behavior*. New York, McGraw-Hill, pp 15–27.
16. Pattison EM, Kahan J: The deliberate self-harm syndrome. *Am J Psychiatry* 1983;140:867–872.

CHAPTER **19**

TREATMENT OF CHILD AND ADOLESCENT SUICIDE ATTEMPTERS

PAUL D. TRAUTMAN
DAVID SHAFFER

This chapter reviews major areas of psychopathology associated with suicide attempts and some specific treatments that are available for their management. Four therapies which have been suggested for use with adolescent suicide attempters are discussed: insight-oriented psychotherapy, cognitive-behavioral, family, and group therapy. Noting the paucity of empirical treatment studies and the criteria for good comparative treatment research design, we review evidence, largely from studies of adults, for the effects of treatment on improving psychiatric condition and social adjustment and reducing the probability of further suicidal behavior.

Our present knowledge about suicidal behavior in children and adolescents does not allow us to say that a suicide attempt is a specific diagnosis nor that any constellation of symptoms and life experiences inevitably produces a suicide attempt. The wide variety of individual, familial and interpersonal factors associated with attempted suicide, and the sometimes contradictory nature of these factors, suggest that there may be multiple syndromes associated with suicide attempts. In two studies using cluster analytic methods[1-3] two broad subtypes emerge, even though they consider different populations (one adult, one adolescent) and use different variables for analysis. One subtype (Henderson type II, Facy type I and II) includes patients with formal psychiatric illness and multiple adverse psychosocial factors who use highly dangerous suicide methods; the second (Henderson type III, Facy type III and IV) includes patients who make an attempt judged to be of lower risk of death, lack formal psychiatric illness, and are responding to acute familial or interpersonal crisis. The adolescent study found a predominance of younger children and girls in the second subtype. These findings are supported by other evidence that one subtype acts out of hopelessness and the other for operant or manipulative reasons.[4,5]

SPECIFIC FOCI FOR TREATMENT

In the absence of clear-cut diagnostic criteria, syndrome(s) of prognostic value and comprehensive treatments of empirically demonstrated efficacy, the clinician must consider the total range of problems in each patient making a suicide attempt and direct intervention toward each problem. At a general level, it is well to remember that the complexity of human adaptation to stress cannot be understood simplistically as a dose-response relationship. Rather, individual characteristics such as cognitive ability and coping skills, and external factors such as social support networks, mediate between stress and emotional-behavioral outcome.[6] Treatment geared toward modification of these individual and external mediators should favorably affect outcome. Empirical evidence for this hypothesis is found in two recent reports[7,8] on the prevention of relapse in schizophrenia. These studies demonstrate the merits of a systematic program of family and patient education, instruction in behavior modification methods, modeling, feedback, social reinforcement and dynamic interpretation to enhance coping skills, reflective listening, reciprocity of conversations, social contacts, marital relations, interpersonal experiences, and intrapersonal attributes such as personality development, defense mechanisms and cognitive skills. These techniques seem well suited and adaptable to the complex personal and interpersonal problems of the young suicide attempter who generally is living at home.

Suicidal behavior The method of the suicide attempt dictates the first medical intervention and it is the attempt itself, rather than associated factors, that is now mobilizing the patient and family to seek treatment. This mobilization may rapidly disintegrate once the patient is medically cleared. The family's response is often inadequate and even counter-productive, as illustrated by parents' common attempt to keep the adolescent under constant surveillance once he or she has returned home. Thus, engagement of the family and patient is the vital first step of treatment. Careful diagnostic assessment and history-taking will quickly identify problems requiring intervention, and these problems and appropriate interventions can be listed to the family. This is likely to meet with a better response than simply saying "Come back on Tuesday and we'll talk," particularly for the patient for whom conversation is unsatisfying or foreign. People understand and accept treatment plans and prescriptions far more readily than a suggestion to explore feelings.

It is not within the scope of this chapter to discuss medical treatment of drug overdose or of other methods of suicide attempt, nor to discuss criteria for medical or psychiatric hospitalization. Relatively few of the people who make a suicide attempt ever see a physician and only a minority of these require medical hospitalization.[9] In making a decision to discharge, one must consider age, sex, race, lethality of method, isolation, efforts to avoid discovery, and the patient's statements about premeditation, intent to die, and present suicidal intent. The presence of psychiatric illness, particularly affective disorder, is the most important other consideration at initial assessment (see below). A detailed exploration of the precipitating events of the attempt and of the adolescent's contradictory thoughts, wishes and expectations at that time will serve as a guide to intrapsychic and interpersonal difficulties. Healthy family members or friends who can be relied upon to keep an eye on the patient, to dispose of means of further attempts, and help insure continuity of treatment are a therapist's powerful allies.

Major Depressive Disorder Depressive Disorder powerfully increases the risk of suicide attempts in adults.[10] Variables cited as predictive of suicidal behavior are often those associated with depression.[11-13] Mattsson et al[14] noted that 25% of 55 suicidal girls (48% of whom had made an actual suicide attempt) were depressed for at least one month prior to interview. Carlson[15] has drawn attention to the distinction between primary and secondary affective disorders in adolescents.

The existence of Major Depressive Disorder in adolescents is now widely accepted, although the criteria for diagnosis are in dispute.[16] Symptoms include persistent sad mood, irritability, guilt, self-denigration, pessimism, loss of concentration, loss of interest in usual activities, and vegetative signs. These symptoms must be elicited by direct interview of the child with corroboration by the parent. There is modest evidence for the effectiveness of imipramine (IMI) and desmethylimipramine (DMI) in prepubertal depressive disorder,[17] but an open study using IMI in adolescents showed poor response and poor correlation between serum drug levels and clinical improvement (J. Puig-Antich, personal communication, 1983). (See Chapter 6 by Ambrosini, Rabinovich, and Puig-Antich, in this volume.)

Empirical evidence for the effectiveness or ineffectiveness of psychotherapy for adolescent depression is lacking, but cognitive therapy of depression has demonstrated effectiveness in adults (see below). Other research in adults has demonstrated the effectiveness of psychotherapy for impaired interpersonal relations and social performance that are associated with depression, and that are unaffected by tricyclic antidepressant response.[18] In general, psychotherapy is held to be effective only after depressive symptoms have been cleared.[19] These findings are relevant for children and adolescents as psychological relationships, particularly verbal and affective communication, are often impaired in families of depressed children, and these problems persist after recovery of mood (Puig-Antich, Lukens et al, unpublished data, 1983).

Associated physical illness Adolescent suicide attempters have higher rates of current medical illness — 30% to 50% by recent reports — than age-matched peers.[20,21] Physical illness is found more often in older adolescents, males, and in patients who have multiple adverse family factors, poor work and school achievement, and who have previously attempted suicide.[2] Pregnancy or feared pregnancy is often associated with suicide attempts in girls.[22,23] Therapy must be directed not only to the medical condition but also to education of the adolescent about the nature, treatment, and prognosis of his condition and to the limitations imposed on normal adolescent life-style, particularly peer contact and sexual relations.

Drug and alcohol abuse High rates of drug and alcohol use — 37% by two recent reports — have been found in young suicide attempters.[20,24] Conversely, suicide attempts are common in drug abusers.[2,25] An impulsive or even accidental overdose in an intoxicated individual should be distinguished from a suicide attempt in a depressed patient who is, or is becoming, an alcoholic. High rates of alcoholism (30% to 40%) in parents and family members of child and adolescent suicide attempters[11,20] suggest that familial depressive spectrum disease[26] may underlie both the suicide attempt and drug abuse, and should be a primary focus of treatment. Cognitive-behavioral techniques and group therapy techniques have been described for alcoholic adolescents, and the effectiveness of Alcoholics Anonymous is widely accepted.[27,28] Treatment of drug abuse is not notably successful.[28]

Parental psychiatric illness Rates of psychiatric disturbance, including alcoholism, of up to 50% have been reported in the parents of adolescent suicide attempters.[20,29-33] There are a number of ties between parental psychopathology and suicidal behavior in their children. First, all members of the family may share a genetic predisposition to depressive illness. Second, parental psychopathology may directly impinge on the child's mental state, pushing him toward chronic unhappiness and hopelessness. For example, depressed women show diminished emotional involvement, disaffection and increased hostility toward their children.[34] The clinician has ample opportunity to observe the pall of hopelessness and frustration which can envelop the family of a depressed patient, and how harsh or coldly distant a depressed mother can be. Third, parents may overtly or covertly push the child toward suicide as a solution to their problems.[35,36] Finally, parental suicidal behavior or ideation may serve as a model for childhood suicidal behavior.[22,37]

In general, the child is particularly vulnerable to any of these ties when parental symptoms are overt and when no healthy adult is available to protect him. Parental mental illness not only impinges directly on the child's well-being but also contributes to the high rates of foster and group home placement among young suicide attempters. Placement often results in increased psychiatric disorder in children.[38] Treatment of the parent should include both antidepressant or other medication and psychotherapy focusing on social adaptation and interpersonal relations after symptomatic recovery of mood.[39]

Marital conflict   Adolescent suicide attempters come from homes with high rates of marital conflict[40] and are more likely to have heard recent talk of divorce or separation than are psychiatric controls.[30] Persisting marital discord, especially when it has a marked social impact or is associated with gross irritability toward the child, is associated with child psychopathology.[41] Marital discord has a greater impact on boys than on girls.[42,43] Marital therapy focussed on reduction of conflict, or at least parent counseling to avoid conflict in front of the children, is indicated.

Parent-child conflict   Recent parent-child conflict is frequently associated with suicide and suicide attempts.[2,32] The relationship between parental psychopathology and parent-child contact has been discussed, above. However, parent-child conflict need not occur in the context of parental mental illness. Parent-child conflict is probably the most important external factor in the emotional disturbances of adolescent suicide attempters[44] who perceive their parents as hostile, indifferent and exhibiting extremes of expectations and control.[45] One frequently encounters rigid, overcontrolling, critical parents whose children despair of living until they are old enough to move out of the house. Disturbance results not just from conflict but also from illogical, inconsistent expectations on the parents' part. For example, one mother allowed her 14-year-old daughter no allowance, insisted that she not "hang out" after school, and never allowed her to visit the homes of friends whose parents she (the mother) had not met, yet never questioned the records and posters the girl regularly brought home nor noticed that $900 was missing from a purse she kept in the girl's bedroom. Others have noted parental indifference, withdrawal, and lack of responsivity to adolescent crises.[46] Parents are easy to blame, but it is equally possible that personality and temperamental factors within the child or adolescent contribute to parent-child conflict.[47] Treatment should focus on conflict reduction, increased communication, parental acknowledgment of the child's level of distress, and effective discipline. Techniques have been described for tension reduction[48] and improving parent-child communication[49,50] and parent effectiveness.[51]

WHAT TREATMENTS HAVE BEEN SUGGESTED?

Individual psychotherapy   Advocates of individual psychotherapy generally follow Freud's[52] formulation that depression and suicide may be understood as the expression of anger towards an introjected, ambivalently regarded, lost object.[53,54] Adolescent suicide attempts are regarded as a specific manifestation of the second phase (ie, the adolescent phase) of the separation-individuation process. The goal of therapy is to bring these ambivalent feelings into consciousness, to accommodate to feelings of rejection and deprivation, and to allow the patient to separate from the lost object. Leaving aside the question of whether this formulation is "correct" (see discussion by Beck[55]), it may be said that while psychotherapies in general are superior to no treatment for a variety of problems,[56] we still lack convincing evidence that psychoanalytically oriented psychotherapy is superior to other techniques. This may be so because it is so difficult to distinguish the relative efficacy of interpretation, technique, therapist characteristics and the therapist-patient relationship itself in effecting change. It is safe to say that an atmosphere of positive regard is essential to keep the adolescent patient in treatment, to bolster self-esteem, and to give hope.[54,57] The therapeutic relationship may serve temporarily as the adolescent's only positive relationship, particularly when parents are hostile, uncaring, or resistant to efforts to alter family dynamics. The therapist must be aware of countertransference feelings of malice and aversion that suicidal patients can arouse.[58]

Cognitive-behavioral therapy Cognitive therapy for the treatment of suicide attempts and suicidal preoccupation has been chiefly described in work with adults.[59-61] This therapy operates from the assumption that the patient acts dysfunctionally on the basis of irrational ideas about himself and the world. The goal of treatment is to teach the patient to identify, rationally examine and test the validity of these thoughts and to develop more realistic and rational ideas and behaviors. Learning the technique of rational self-examination allows improvements to generalize. Specific tasks for use with suicide attempters have been described.[59] These include: a) a discussion of the patient's suicidal ideas, both for purposes of ventilation and acquisition of a more objective view of these ideas; b) listing the patient's reasons for dying and living; c) assessment of feelings of hopelessness about the patient's current life situation, self and future; d) teaching problem-solving, including generation of alternate solutions; and e) stress-inoculation, ie, role-playing and mental rehearsal of solutions to stressful situations. Nidiffer[62] and Kiev[63] have also described cognitive-behavioral techniques which the patient can be taught to employ in stress situations. These include both behavioral coping responses, (eg, playing the guitar to take one's mind off the situation, or walking away from an argument until a self-protective, nonprovocative response is rehearsed) and repetition of positive self-statements (eg, "I'm a good guitar player," "I'm a pretty girl"). The only behavioral technique — in fact, the only specific therapy — which has been empirically tested with suicide attempters is social skills training[64] (see discussion of this paper, below). Assertiveness training, problem-solving training, and operant shaping also seem applicable to the adolescent who attempts suicide,[6,65,66] but have not been systematically evaluated.

Family therapy Family treatments are based on the idea that a symptom in any family member is related to and is maintained by transactional difficulties in the family organization. Hence, the symptom exists in the family and the family is regarded as the patient. Richman[67] has paraphrased Durkheim[68] by saying that "suicide varies inversely with the degree of integration between the individual and the social group of which he is a part." Disturbances of family structure,[69] including role conflicts and blurring of role boundaries (eg, the child who is given a parental role, or the mother who undermines her parental authority by saying "Johnny, stop yelling! Okay?"), dysfunctional alliances across boundaries (eg, a child who joins one parent in discrediting the other), failures of communication and secretiveness, and rigidity with inability to accept change or tolerate crisis, have been posited to promote suicidal acting out.[67,70,71] An acceptance of these theoretical systems approaches leads to the definition of tasks of treatment (eg, getting the parents to unite on a plan of rules for their child's behavior, or removing parental responsibilities from the adolescent), but sidesteps more longitudinal issues such as temperamental incompatibilities, individual psychopathology, familial depressive disorder, and conflicts of separation and individuation in both parent and child. Also, it is not always clear whether dysfunctional family structure produces suicidal acting out or whether individual factors lead both to suicidal acting out and current family structure. Others have discussed the effects of parental psychopathology, particularly suicidal preoccupation in the mother and conscious and unconscious wishes to be rid of the child, on the development and precipitation of suicidal behavior.[35,36,72]

Group therapy   Group therapy with hospitalized adolescent suicide attempters has been described by Glaser[73] who suggests that it fosters verbal skills at the same time it suppresses purely physical expression of feelings. The therapeutic effects of group therapy include learning that others in the world share one's problems, support by peers, acquisition of social skills such as conversational skills and the use of eye contact, ventilation and role-modeling.[74] A skillful leader is required to ensure that role-modeling does not work negatively, with hopelessness, suicidal ideation and suicidal behavior spreading contagiously to all group members. Furthermore, there is evidence for the relationship between suicidal and aggressive behavior.[32] With its greater opportunities for frustration and provocation, a group experience may be more likely than individual treatment to bring out aggression in a suicidal person[75] and this may be meted out on other group members.[76] It has been suggested that group therapy may be a useful alternative to family therapy for the adolescent in florid rebellion against his parents.[73]

WHAT CONSTITUTES AN IDEAL TREATMENT STUDY?

At the present time, there are virtually no reported treatment studies of child and adolescent suicide attempters, and there are only two comparative treatment studies in adults (see below). Because the intra- and interpersonal problems of the young suicide attempter are so diverse, and because so many different treatment approaches have been suggested, well-designed comparative treatment studies are needed to demonstrate the efficacy and superiority of specific treatments for suicide attempters and the problems they present. Ideally, a comparative treatment study has the following characteristics: 1) the patient population is well-defined in terms of demographic variables, current problems, and diagnoses; 2) a description of the procedures for selection and allocation of patients is provided; assignment is random; patients refusing treatment are described; 3) there is a sufficiently large sample size to detect moderate to large effect size;[77,78] 4) each treatment is operationally defined and treatment techniques and their sequence are specified; blind raters must be able to distinguish the treatments (at a minimum) and attention is given to process research;[56] and 5) outcome measures are defined, have construct validity, and are sensitive to change. Design should also consider therapist characteristics and their effect on the success or failure of a given treatment.[19,79]

REPORTED TREATMENT STUDIES

Studies have generally failed to show the effectiveness of suicide prevention centers ("primary prevention") in decreasing the suicide rate and suicide attempt rate.[6] This may be so because of the unreliability of the data in this type of study, because only a small proportion of people making an attempt uses a "hot line," or because anonymous phone contact may not be sufficient to deter a serious suicide. Comparative studies of inpatient vs. outpatient treatment have not been conducted, but because of the problems associated with hospitalization (cost, separation from family, school and peers, and discontinuity of care), it is reasonable to focus on outpatient treatment.

Studies of secondary prevention are few, there are none of children and adolescents, and most use recurrent suicidal behavior rather than improvement of psychosocial adaptation as an outcome measure. These are summarized in Table 19-1. These studies vary markedly in followup time and percent of sample followed up. Brief followup has less validity than longer followup. The short interval between attempt and reexamination may not allow improvements resulting from contact or treatment to measurably affect the patient's mental state or behavior; conversely, contact and treatment may only temporarily delay suicide or a repeated attempt without providing lasting protection, so that an apparent beneficial effect will disappear over time. Low completion rates are difficult to interpret because so much is unknown about lost subjects. It seems likely that a low followup rate may underestimate the beneficial effects of contact and treatment since patients not appearing in the emergency room, psychiatric clinic, or morgue may be doing reasonably well.

Two adult studies contrast treated and untreated groups and lend support to the effectiveness of contact (but not psychiatric treatment, per se) in reducing repetition. Greer and Bagley[80] identified suicide attempters who had been discharged (due to oversight by staff) from an emergency room without psychiatric evaluation or referral and compared them with subjects who had had only one or two outpatient psychiatric visits (T1) and more than two visits (T2). A further suicide attempt occurred in 39% of the untreated, 26% of the T1, and 20% of the T2 subjects. The difference between the untreated and T2 groups is significant (P = .02). T1 subjects who received additional treatment at other centers were significantly less likely to repeat than those who did not receive treatment. The seriousness of the initial attempt was unrelated to outcome. It is not possible to say whether psychiatric contact was crucial since these patients were self-selected.

In the second study, Motto[81] followed up 853 persons admitted to nine psychiatric inpatient facilities because of a "depressive or suicidal state" who had discontinued their outpatient therapy program within one month of discharge. Half of these were randomly assigned to a contact group; the other half was not contacted. During followup, 43% were lost or refused further contact and 48% were still being followed at the time of publication. At the fourth year of followup, 20/242 (8.3%) no-contact subjects and 12/230 (5.2%) contact subjects had committed suicide. While not significant, the author noted that if the curves of the two groups continued to diverge at the same rate as in the first four years, significance would be reached in the fifth year.

Several other studies have assessed the effects of outreach and aftercare on the suicide reattempt rate. Welu[82] randomly assigned 63 patients seen in an emergency room to a special outreach program and contrasted these with 57 patients who were only given a followup appointment at a community mental health center. All subjects were residing at home and had the same range of services available to them. At the end of four months, 90% of the experimental group and 54% of the control group had had at least one outpatient therapy visit. The experimental subjects made significantly fewer suicide reattempts and significantly fewer were abusing alcohol.

A study by Ettlinger[83] found no beneficial effects of outreach, but the low completion rates make conclusions difficult. She followed up 681 subjects admitted to an intensive care unit with contact visits at one, six, and 12 months (or more, if necessary) after discharge. These were contrasted with 670 subjects treated before the institution of the contact-outreach program. The same range of services was available to both

Table 19-1
Treatment Studies of Suicide Attempters

Ref. No.	Age	N	Treatment		Followup	Percent Followup	Outcome Measures	Significant Effects
80	Unstated–adults	211	OP followup after ER visit		18 mo (12–24)	97%	Attempted suicide	2+ visits
				N				
			No followup	47				
			1–2 visits (T1)	76				
			2+ visits (T2)	88				
81	Unstated–adults	853	OP followup of hospitalized patients who discontinue OP visits		x̄ = 38 mo	48%	Completed suicide	(See text)
				N				
			No contact	242				
			Telephone and mail contact	230				
82	x̄ = 29 yrs minimum 16 yrs	120	OP followup after ER visit		4 mo	99%	Attempted suicide	+
							Alcohol abuse	+
				N			Accidents	−
			Appointment only	57			Drug abuse	−
			Appointment and phone, home, clinic contact	63				

Ref	Age	Treatment / N	Follow-up	%	Outcome measures	Results
83	Unstated– 8% less than 20 yrs	1351 — OP followup after ICU admission; No contact; Telephone and home contact, emergency phone — *N* 670, 681	5 yrs	51% of no contact, 80% of contact	Suicide; Attempted suicide; Registered sickness; Criminality; Offense for drunkenness; Pension/social assistance	—; —; —; —; —; —
84	Unstated– 38% less than 30 yrs, 16% older than 50 yrs	155 — OP followup after 2nd ICU admission; OP appointment only 84; Walk-in services, emergency telephone, home visit if appt. not kept — *N* 71	6 mo	100%	Attempted suicide; Mental state and behavior; Social state	—; —; +
85, 86	17–81	539 — OP treatment after ER visit; Task-centered case-work 200; Routine service 200; excluded 139 — *N*	4 mo; 18 mo; 12 mo	80%; Unstated; Unstated	Social problems; Attempted suicide; Use of psychiatric services	+ (4 mo); − (18 mo); − (12 mo); +(12 mo)
64	18–47 yrs	8M, 16F — Hospital treatment, OP followup; Insight-oriented therapy 8; Behavioral therapy 8 — *N*	2 yrs	100%	Depression; Fear; Assertiveness; MMPI; Suicidal ideation; Attempted suicide	+; +; +; −; +; −

groups. This study is flawed because of the low completion rate in the control group (49% were lost). None of the outcome measures significantly differed in the two groups.

Chowdhury et al[84] followed subjects admitted to an intensive care unit who had at least one prior ICU admission for a suicide attempt. Subjects were interviewed in the hospital and given outpatient psychiatric appointments. Subjects in the experimental group were also offered outpatient walk-in services and an emergency telephone service, and were visited at home if they did not keep their first outpatient visit. At six-month followup, the groups did not differ in reattempt rate (23%) nor in mental state or behavior, but the social state (defined as financial, housing, and employment problems) was significantly improved in the experimental group. It may be that the effect of the relatively small outreach effort was overwhelmed by other factors, for example, psychiatric clinic attendance by both groups.

Two studies of adults have compared two different treatments. The first[85,86] examined 539 adult deliberate self-poisoners seen in an emergency room during a one-year period. Two hundred subjects were randomly assigned to time-limited (three months) task-centered casework, 200 to "routine service" (54% saw a general practitioner, 33% a psychiatrist, and 13% "other"), and 139 subjects were excluded because of immediate suicidal risk or formal psychiatric illness requiring immediate treatment, or because they were already receiving psychiatric or social work intervention. The excluded group differed from the casework and routine service groups in that excluded subjects were of lower social class, included a higher proportion of men, and had higher scores on intent-to-die and prediction-of-further-attempt scales. Four months after the attempt, a random half of the casework and routine service groups was reinterviewed; only 80% could be located. The casework group had significantly fewer social problems (self-rated). Eighteen months after the attempt, the other half of each group was reinterviewed (percent not located unstated). The groups no longer differed in percent showing improvement in social problems. One year after the attempt, hospital and GP records were searched for documented repetition of self-poisoning and use of psychiatric and social work services. The casework and routine service groups did not differ in repetition (13.5% and 14.5%, respectively) whereas the excluded group had a significantly higher rate (36%). The casework group had significantly less psychiatric service than the routine service group in the year following the index attempt, although this apparently excludes the three-month, time-limited social work intervention for the casework group but includes all intervention for the routine service group. The results of this study are also difficult to interpret because the number of subjects for whom no information was available at the one-year followup is unstated and apparently grouped with the number who actually did not repeat or who actually did not have ongoing psychiatric service.

The second comparative treatment study is that by Liberman and Eckman.[64] This study is of eight men and 16 women who had made at least two suicide attempts within the last two years and had at least one prior psychiatric hospitalization. All carried a diagnosis of Major Depressive Disorder, Dysthymic Disorder or Adjustment Disorder with Depression. Subjects were randomized to behavior therapy (social skills training, anxiety management, and contingency contracting with family members) or insight-oriented therapy (individual, group, and family treatment). Each subject received 32 hours of inpatient therapy over eight days and no medication was used. At discharge, the behavior therapy group had significantly improved scores on rating scales of depression, fear and assertiveness. Regular followup revealed greater improvement in the behavior therapy group on psychological tests in 22 of 30 assessments. This group also had significantly fewer suicide threats, thoughts, urgency of thoughts, and plans at several followup points. The number of suicide reattempts did not differ in the two groups (21%). Aftercare for this population was not uniform but did not differ from the two groups.

In summary, there is evidence that contact, and perhaps psychosocial treatment, can lower the rates of completed and attempted suicide and suicidal ideation and improve mental state and social adjustment. The patient samples in these studies differ markedly; a history of suicide attempt and increased severity of attempt probably decrease the likelihood that treatment will be effective. However, in this regard, the Liberman and Eckman study is encouraging because it shows beneficial effects of treatment in a rather severely disturbed group of patients.

CONCLUSIONS

In this chapter we have attempted to show that a suicide attempt is not a diagnosis and that no one currently described treatment is adequate for the child or adolescent with this symptom. Rather, it is possible to identify a variety of problems in any given patient and to prescribe more or less specific interventions for each problem. Usually, management will require the application of several different treatment modalities.

It is true that there is more than one way to effect change, and that only comparative studies, using operationally defined treatments and sensitive measures of change in well-defined patient populations, will elucidate which treatment is the most effective for a given problem or problem cluster. For example, systems theory allows that a change in family organization can be effected by a change in an individual's behavior, yet we lack evidence that assertiveness training of the adolescent is any more or less effective in changing parent-child relationships than is structural family therapy.

Well-designed treatment studies are almost nonexistent in the literature, yet there is evidence that treatment can favorably affect social adjustment, mental state, and suicide reattempt rate. There is great need for additional research in the treatment of the young suicide attempter.

ACKNOWLEDGMENTS

Preparation of this material was assisted by grants from the W.T. Grant Foundation, NIMH Research Training Grant #5T32MH16434-03, and NIMH Psychiatry Education Branch Grant #MH07715-19.

REFERENCES

1. Henderson AS, Hartigan J, Davidson J, et al: A typology of parasuicide. Br J Psychiatry 1977;131:631-641.
2. Facy F, Choquet M, Lechevallier Y: Researche d'une typologie des adolescents suicidants. Social Psychiatry 1979;14:75-84.
3. Choquet M, Facy F, Davidson F: Suicide and attempted suicide among adolescents in France, in Farmer R, Hirsch S (eds): The Suicide Syndrome. London, Croom Helm, 1980.
4. Bedrosian RC, Beck AT: Cognitive aspects of suicidal behavior. Suicide Life Threat Behav 1979;9:87-96.
5. Kovacs M, Beck AT, Weissman A: The use of suicidal motives in the psychotherapy of attempted suicides. Am J Psychother 1975;29:363-368.
6. Clum GA, Patsiokas T, Luscomb RL: Empirically based comprehensive treatment program for parasuicide. J Consult Clin Psychol 1979;45:937-945.
7. Falloon IRH, Boyd JL, McGill CW, et al: Family management in the prevention of exacerbations of schizophrenia—A controlled study. N Engl J Med 1982;306:1437-1440.
8. Leff J, Kuipers L, Berkowitz R, et al: A controlled trial of social intervention in the families of schizophrenic patients. Br J Psychiatry 1982;141:121-134.
9. McIntire M, Angle CR: Suicide Attempts in Children and Youth. Hagerstown, Harper & Row, 1980.
10. Hagnell O, Lanke J, Rorsman B: Suicide rates in the Lundby study: Mental illness as a risk factor for suicide. Neuropsychobiology 1981;7:248-253.
11. Cohen-Sandler R, Berman R, King RA: Life stress and symptomatology: Determinants of suicidal behavior in children. J Am Acad Child Psychiatry 1982;20:178-186.
12. Shaffer D: Diagnostic considerations in suicidal behavior in children and adolescents. J Am Acad Child Psychiatry 1982;21:414-416.
13. Pfeffer CR: The family system of suicidal children. Am J Psychother 1981; 35:330-341.
14. Mattsson A, Seese LR, Hawkings JW: Suicidal behavior as a child psychiatric emergency. Arch Gen Psychiatry 1969;20:100-109.
15. Carlson G: The phenomenology of adolescent depression, in Feinstein S et al (eds): Adolescent Psychiatry—Developmental and Clinical Studies. Chicago, University of Chicago Press, 1981, vol 9.

16. Klein DF, Gittelman R, Quitkin F, et al: *Diagnosis and Drug Treatment of Psychiatric Disorders: Adults and Children*. Baltimore, Williams & Wilkins, 1980.

17. Puig-Antich J, Perel JM, Lupatkin W, et al: Plasma levels of imipramine (IMI) and desmethyl imipramine (DMI) and clinical response in prepubertal major depressive disorder: A preliminary report. *J Am Acad Child Psychiatry* 1979;18:616–627.

18. Klerman GL: Combining drugs and psychotherapy in the treatment of depression, in Greenblatt M (ed): *Drugs in Combination with Other Therapies*. New York, Grune & Stratton, 1975.

19. Weissman MM: The psychological treatment of depression. *Arch Gen Psychiatry* 1979;36:1261–1269.

20. Garfinkel BD, Froese A, Hood J: Suicide attempts in children and adolescents. *Am J Psychiatry* 1982;139:1257–1261.

21. Hawton K, O'Grady J, Osborn M, et al: Adolescents who take overdoses: Their characteristics, problems and contacts with helping agencies. *Br J Psychiatry* 1982;140:118–123.

22. Teicher JD, Jacobs J: Adolescents who attempt suicide: Preliminary fiindings. *Am J Psychiatry* 1966;122(part 2):1248–1257.

23. Jacobs J: *Adolescent Suicide*. New York, Wiley Interscience, 1971.

24. Herjanic B: Adolescent suicide. *Advances in Behavioral Pediatrics* 1980; 1:195–223.

25. Frederick CJ, Resnick HLP, Wittlin BJ: Self-destructive aspects of hard core addiction. *Arch Gen Psychiatry* 1973;28:579–585.

26. Van Valkenburg C, Lowry M, Winokur G, et al: Depression spectrum disease versus pure depressive disease. *J Nerv Ment Dis* 1977;165:341–347.

27. Marlatt GA: Alcohol use and problem drinking: A cognitive-behavioral analysis, in Kendall PC, Hollon SD (eds): *Cognitive-Behavioral Interventions — Theory, Research and Procedures*. New York, Academic Press, 1979.

28. Nystrom KF, Bal AL, Labrecque V: Substance abuse, in Nospitz JD (ed): *Basic Handbook of Child Psychiatry*. New York, Basic Books Inc, 1979, vol 2.

29. Schrut A: Suicidal adolescents and children. *JAMA* 1964;188:1103.

30. Stanley EJ, Barter JT: Adolescent suicidal behavior. *Am J Orthopsychiatry* 1970;40:87–96.

31. Hudgens RW: *Psychiatric Disorders in Adolescents*. Baltimore, Williams & Wilkins, 1974.

32. Shaffer D: Suicide in childhood and early adolescence. *J Child Psychol Psychiatry* 1974;15:275–291.

33. Marks P, Haller D: Now I lay me down to sleep for keeps: A study of adolescent suicide attempts. *J Clin Psychol* 1977;33:390–400.

34. Weissman MM, Paykel ES, Klerman GL: The depressed woman as a mother. *Social Psychiatry* 1972;7:89–108.

35. Sabbath JC: The suicidal adolescent — The expendable child. *J Am Acad Child Psychiatry* 1969;8:272–289.

36. Sabbath JC: The role of the parents in adolescent suicidal behavior. *Acta Paedopsychiatr (Basel)* 1971;38:211–220.

37. Tishler CL, McKenry PC: Parental negative self and adolescent suicide attempts. *J Am Acad Child Psychiatry* 1982;21:404–408.

38. Wolkind S, Rutter M: Children who have been "in care": An epidemiological study. *J Child Psychol Psychiatry* 1973;4:95–105.

39. Weissman MM, Klerman GL, Paykel, ES, et al: Treatment effects on the social adjustment of depressed patients. *Arch Gen Psychiatry* 1974;31:771–774.

40. Brook EM (ed): *Suicide and Attempted Suicide*. Public Health Papers, No. 58, Geneva, World Health Organization, 1974.
41. Rutter M, Quinton D, Yule W: *Family Pathology and Disorder in Children*. London, Wiley, 1977.
42. Rutter M: Parent-child separation—Psychological effect on the child. *J Child Psychol Psychiatry* 1971;12:233–260.
43. Hetherington M, Cox M, Cox R: Play and social interaction in children following divorce. *J Social Issues* 1979;35:26–49.
44. Lukianowicz N: Attempted suicide in children. *Acta Psychiatr Scand* 1968; 44:415–435.
45. McIntire M, Angle CR: Psychological "biopsy" in self-poisoning of children and adolescents. *Am J Dis Child* 1973;126:42–46.
46. Yusin A, Sivay R, Nihira K: Adolescents in crisis: Evaluation of a questionnaire. *Am J Psychiatry* 1972;129:574–577.
47. Rutter M, Hersov L (eds): *Child Psychiatry, Modern Approaches*. London, Blackwell Scientific Publishers, 1977.
48. Falloon IRH, Boyd JL, McGill CW, et al: Family management training in the community care of schizophrenia, in Goldstein MJ (ed): *New Developments in Interventions with Families of Schizophrenics*. San Francisco, Jossey-Bass, 1981, pp 61–77.
49. Robin AL: A controlled evaluation of problem-solving communication training with parent-adolescent conflict. *Behavior Therapy* 1981;12:593–609.
50. Guerney B, Coufal J, Vogelsong E: Relationship enhancement versus a traditional approach to therapeutic/preventative/enrichment parent-adolescent programs. *J Consult Clin Psychol* 1981;49:927–939.
51. Patterson, GR: *Families—Applications of Social Learning to Family Life*. Champaign, IL, Research Press, 1975.
52. Freud S: *Mourning and Melancholia*. London, Hogarth Press, 1917, vol 14.
53. Friedman M, Glasser M, Laufer E, et al: Attempted suicide and self-mutilation in adolescence: Some observations from a psychoanalytic research project. *Int J Psychoanal* 1972;53:179–183.
54. Gould RE: Suicide problems in children and adolescents. *Am J Psychother* 1965;21:228–245.
55. Beck AT: *Depression: Clinical, Experimental and Theoretical Aspects*. New York, Hoeber Medical Division, Harper & Row, 1967.
56. Parloff MB: Psychotherapy research evidence and reimbursement decisions: Bambi meets Godzilla. *Am J Psychiatry* 1982;139:718–727.
57. Schrut A, Michels T: Adolescent girls who attempt suicide—Comments on treatment. *Am J Psychother* 1969;23:243–251.
58. Maltsberger JT, Buie DH: Countertransference hate in the treatment of suicidal patients. *Arch Gen Psychiatry* 1974;30:625–633.
59. Beck AT, Rush AJ, Shaw BF, et al: *Cognitive Therapy of Depression*. New York, The Guilford Press, 1979.
60. Kovacs M, Ruch AJ, Beck AT, et al: Depressed outpatients treated with cognitive therapy or pharmacotherapy—A one-year follow-up. *Arch Gen Psychiatry* 1981;38:33–39.
61. Rush AJ, Beck AT, Kovacs M, et al: Comparative efficacy of cognitive therapy and imipramine in the treatment of depressed outpatients. *Cognitive Ther Res* 1977;1:17–37.
62. Nidiffer FD: Combining cognitive and behavioral approaches to suicidal depression: A 42 month follow-up. *Psychological Reports* 1980;47:539–542.
63. Kiev A: Psychotherapeutic strategies in the management of depressed and suicidal patients. *Am J Psychother* 1975;29:345–354.

64. Liberman R, Eckman T: Behavior therapy vs. insight-oriented therapy for repeated suicide attempters. *Arch Gen Psychiatry* 1981;38:1126–1130.
65. Bostock T, Williams C: Attempted suicide as an operant behavior. *Arch Gen Psychiatry* 1974;31:482–486.
66. Frederick DJ, Resnik HL: How suicidal behaviors are learned. *Am J Psychother* 1971;25:37–55.
67. Richman J: Family treatment of suicidal children and adolescents, in Stuart IR, Wells CF (eds): *Self-Destructive Behavior in Children and Adolescents.* New York, Van Nostrand Reinhold Co, 1981.
68. Durkheim E: *Suicide: A Study in Sociology.* Glencoe, IL, The Free Press, 1951.
69. Minuchin S: *Families and Family Therapy.* Cambridge, Harvard University Press, 1974.
70. Fishman HC, Rosman BL: A therapeutic approach to self-destructive behavior in adolescence: The family as the patient, in Stuart IR, Wells CF, (eds): *Self-Destructive Behavior in Children and Adolescents.* New York, Van Nostrand Reinhold Co, 1981.
71. Richman J: The family therapy of attempted suicide. *Family Process* 1979; 18:131–142.
72. Margolin NL, Teicher JD: Thirteen adolescent male suicide attempts — Dynamic considerations. *J Am Acad Child Psychiatry* 1968;7:296–315.
73. Glaser K: The treatment of depressed and suicidal adolescents. *Am J Psychother* 1978;32:252–269.
74. Yalom ID: *The Theory and Practice of Group Psychotherapy.* New York, Basic Books, 1970.
75. Mullan H, Rosenbaum M: The suitability for the group experience, in Rosenbaum M, Berger MM: *Group Psychotherapy and Group Function.* New York, Basic Books, 1975.
76. DeRosis L: Karen Horney's theory applied to psychoanalysis in groups, in Rosenbaum M, Berger MM: *Group Psychotherapy and Group Function.* New York, Basic Books, 1975.
77. Cohen J: *Statistical Power Analysis for the Behavioral Sciences.* New York, Academic Press, 1977.
78. Landman JT, Dawes RM: Psychotherapy outcome: Smith and Glass' conclusions stand up under scrutiny. *Am Psychologist* 1982;37:504–516.
79. Bierman R: Dimensions of interpersonal facilitation in psychotherapy and child development. *Psychol Bull* 1969;72:338–352.
80. Greer S, Bagley C: Effects of psychiatric intervention in attempted suicide. *Br Med J* 1971;1:310–312.
81. Motto JA: Suicide prevention for high-risk persons who refuse treatment. *Suicide Life Threat Behav* 1976;6:223–230.
82. Welu TC: A follow-up program for suicide attempters: Evaluation of Effectiveness. *Suicide Life Threat Behav* 1977;7:17–30.
83. Ettlinger R: Evaluation of suicide prevention after attempted suicide. *Acta Psychiatric Scand* 1975(suppl 260);135:1–135.
84. Chowdhury N, Hicks RC, Kreitman N: Evaluation of an aftercare service for parasuicide (attempted suicide) patients. *Soc Psychiatry* 1973;8:67–81.
85. Gibbons JS, Butler J, Urwin P, et al: Evaluation of a social work service for self-poisoning patients. *Br J Psychiatry* 1978;133:111–118.
86. Gibbons JS: Management of self-poisoning: Social work intervention, in Farmer R, Hirsch S (eds): *The Suicide Syndrome.* London, Croom Helm, 1980.

CHAPTER 20

PSYCHOTHERAPEUTIC TREATMENT OF SUICIDAL CHILDREN AND ADOLESCENTS

JAMES M. TOOLAN

In this chapter the author initially addresses the issues involved in evaluating suicidal children and adolescents. Efforts to measure the seriousness of their attempts will especially emphasize the effect of their behavior upon their environment, whether it be their immediate family, a boarding school, or a college. In the case of youngsters still living at home, the importance of understanding the parents' involvement in the behavior of a suicidal youngster and of having the parents participate in any ongoing therapeutic plan are stressed. Although the evaluation of these youngsters may take place in an infirmary or hospital, the treatment discussed will be primarily in an outpatient setting. The premise upon which the therapy is based is that suicidal children and adolescents require long-term rather than crisis-oriented therapy, primarily on an individual basis. Thus, the author discusses, in depth, transference and countertransference issues in working with suicidal youngsters. The role of depression and impulsivity in these patients is also looked at in some detail. The use of antidepressant medication is explored. Semisuicidal behavior, such as accidents, drug abuse, and anorexia nervosa are also considered.

Suicide and suicidal attempts are not rare phenomena in children and adolescents. This fact was overlooked or denied for some time by almost all professionals in the mental health field; it is only within the last few years when statistics have shown an increase in suicides among young people that the full significance of this observation has been appreciated. In large measure the oversight may have been due to the mistaken belief that children and adolescents do not experience depression and therefore are unlikely to commit suicide. Freud early exploded the myth of sexual innocence in children; the myth of childhood happiness has lasted much longer and has been even more difficult to shatter. Not only parents but even mental health professionals find it extremely disconcerting to accept the fact that children and adolescents may be depressed and, even worse, suicidal.[1] The reality is that the suicide rate among adolescents in this country has increased notably over the past 20 years.[2] Until very recently, the suicide rate was highest among the elderly and lowest among the young. At the present time this ratio is being significantly altered, both in the United States and in other countries. Suicide is now the second most common cause of death in the 18- to 24-year-old age group, and the third most common cause of death in the 15- to 19-year-old age group.[2] Only accidents, homicides, and malignant neoplasms surpass self-destruction. There is no simple explanation for this rise. Better statistical reporting may play a role, but increased stresses of various types, eg, educational pressures, higher divorce rates, the breakdown of family structure, and increased alcohol and drug abuse are probably significant factors.

All rates of suicide tend to be underestimated, especially those for children and adolescents. Many well-meaning individuals, including physicians, medical examiners, and parents, are loath to accept the fact that a youngster has killed himself. They will go to great lengths to deny the fact unless they actually find a note written by the youngster or other undeniable proof that death was due to suicide, preferring to call the death an accident. Although there are no precise figures available, the evidence is that most youngsters are less likely to leave suicide notes than are adults.[3]

If statistics for completed suicides are unreliable, the figures for suicidal attempts are less valid. Few communities require the accurate recording of suicidal attempts, and most hospital records will show a suicidal attempt as simply slashed wrists or an overdose of medication. Many more people attempt suicide than complete the act. Statistics in all countries show that males of all age groups *commit* suicide more frequently than females. On the other hand, records show that females generally *attempt* suicide in significantly greater numbers than males; only among children do males attempt suicide as frequently as females. This gender discrepancy may indicate that males tend to use more lethal methods such as guns or hanging, whereas females are more likely to use methods such as wrist-slashing or an overdose of medication in which a large margin for error exists and a higher rate of rescue occurs. The statistics leave unanswered the question of *why* females attempt suicide more frequently than males. Suter[4] has recently suggested that females place more value on interpersonal relationships than males and when these fail the females becomes suicidal. Rosenthal[5] in another recent study has suggested that the young male may have a macho-like need to prove that he is not afraid of death and this may influence his drive to complete the suicidal act.

All statistics show that accidents tend to be the leading cause of death among young people. Pertinent to this finding is the estimate of the Suicide Prevention Center of Los Angeles that as many as 50% of all suicides are disguised as accidents. It is certainly clear that many accidents are at best thinly veiled attempts at self-destruction. At times the intention of the victim may be ambivalent, but a suicide impulse is present in a significant number of accidents. In the few instances where psychological autopsies have been performed following accidents the above conclusion has been consistently supported. It should not be overlooked that an individual attempting suicide with an overdose of medication may not be aware of all the lethal properties of the medication ingested, or the individual may expect someone to save him by arriving at an expected time and the delay may prove fatal. Many youngsters attempting suicide may indeed have ambivalent intentions, but their behavior must always be seriously and carefully evaluated before jumping to the conclusion that it was only a gesture. Anyone of any age who attempts suicide requires therapy. Suicidal attempts may in reality be a cry for help. A good number of suicidal youngsters earlier in their lives have run away from home with the thought, "You'll be sorry." This is similar to the fantasies of many suicidal individuals who may visualize themselves in the coffin with family and friends passing by, saying, "We're sorry we treated him so badly." Suicidal attempts may be used to punish or to manipulate another person or even an institution, but I believe we must always ask whether an individual who resorts to such drastic behavior to influence another is not overly dependent, insecure, or threatened by overwhelming feelings of loneliness, helplessness, and hopelessness. There are more constructive ways of influencing other people than suicidal behavior and it is essential that we probe for the reasons why a youngster must resort to such behavior. It is also important to realize that if a suicidal attempt is a cry for help and is ignored or belittled, the youngster may be indirectly encouraged to try again and possibly succeed.

One of the great difficulties in discussing suicide is that self-destructive behavior of all kinds is often linked with suicidal behavior. It is likely that much adolescent behavior, such as alcohol and drug abuse, sexual promiscuity, illegitimate pregnancy, automobile and motorcycle racing, is self-destructive. The same is true, if not more so, of adult behavior such as cigarette smoking, overeating, drug and alcohol abuse. The difficulty arises when we must decide whether to lump all such behavior in one category or to put it in separate categories. It is my opinion that most self-destructive behavior is at least subconsciously suicidal and, consequently, may be even more difficult to evaluate and to treat than a straightforward suicidal attempt. Certainly eating disorders, such as anorexia and bulimia, appear self-destructive and potentially suicidal. It also seems that these disorders are now seen more frequently than they were in the past. It should be borne in mind that there is a relatively small subgroup of individuals, almost entirely female, who are frequently considered suicidal because they habitually slash their wrists, arms, and genitalia.[6] These individuals are not as a rule overtly suicidal but appear to have serious problems with body-image boundaries and marked disturbances in early object relations, or they may use such behavior to narcotize unpleasant feelings or to experience feelings in the absence of emotion. There are occasions when youngsters may slash themselves superficially and also be suicidal, as with Case 1:

> An 18-year-old college freshman was referred for consultation after she had inflicted numerous superficial cuts to both arms with a razor. She had cut herself to diminish feelings of anger and rage she was experiencing after the break-up of a close relationship. She indicated that she wished to remain at school (in order to please her parents) and to enter therapy. While waiting to hear from her former therapist before making a final decision as to the best therapeutic plan, only 48 hours after her first attempt to vent her feelings she took an overdose of medication. Although she requested help almost immediately and recovered medically with little difficulty, she had clearly made a definite suicidal attempt, probably in order to have a reason to leave school and enter a psychiatric hospital.

There is no doubt that certain individuals, notably those in penal institutions, will use suicidal behavior in a purely manipulative fashion. They correctly sense that our society is more frightened by a suicidal act than by more destructive behavior such as severe aggression or even homicide. It appears that a purely manipulative act should be handled differently than a genuine suicidal act, but I believe it behooves those making the evaluation to prove that such is the case rather than jumping to a facile conclusion. Many persons confined in correctional and penal institutions may be truly overwhelmed by their situation and be unable to conceive of any more effective way of communicating this feeling than a suicidal attempt.

Another important issue in the evaluation of suicidal behavior concerns the youngster's concept of death. It is debatable at what point a child or adolescent views death in the same manner as an adult, namely as an irreversible fact. If we follow Piaget's[7] developmental theory, such a concept should occur in a child by mid-adolescence. We often underestimate the child's ability, and, in addition, overestimate the adult's ability to conceptualize death. Almost all cultures subscribe to a concept of an afterlife, whether it be heaven, hell, nirvana, or the transmogrification of souls. Such beliefs clearly reflect the inability of most individuals to accept the finality of death, so perhaps adults are not that different from children in this regard. But even if there were a significant difference in the child's view of death it would not explain why children attempt suicide less frequently than adolescents and adults. If anything, the opposite should be true—if a child views death as reversible why would he hesitate to attempt suicide? It should appear easier for the young child than the older adolescent to view death as a temporary and a pleasant state of existence. The differences in suicidal rates do raise an intriguing question which has only recently been asked: Is there some innate protection that shields children from suicidal acts?[8]

HISTORICAL BACKGROUND

As Haim[1] has pointed out, until very recently there have been surprisingly few studies of suicidal ideation and suicidal attempts in children and adolescents. In 1937 Bender and Schilder,[9] working in Bellevue Hospital in New York City, described 18 youngsters under 18 years of age who had either threatened or attempted suicide. The authors felt that these children were attempting to cope with intolerable living situations which caused them to become very angry and to turn their anger into guilt. It was not until 1959 that Balser and Masterson,[10] working in a private hospital setting, reported that of a group of 500 adolescents 37 had attempted suicide. Shortly thereafter in 1962, the present author[11] noted that of 900 admissions to the Adolescent Service of Bellevue Hospital, 102 had seriously threatened or actually attempted suicide, a much higher rate than that reported by Bender and Schilder in the same institution 23 years earlier.

In 1964 Schrut[12] reported on 19 adolescent suicidal patients, and in the last few years there has been a veritable explosion of literature concerning suicidal children and adolescents. Pfeffer,[13,14] studying both inpatients and outpatients in a city hospital in New York, noted a much higher incidence of suicidal behavior than did the present author in the previously mentioned study. Pfeffer reported that 33% of an outpatient psychiatric group of youngsters displayed suicidal ideas, threats, or attempts, and 72% of an inpatient psychiatric population was considered a suicidal risk. Recently, numerous authors have addressed the issue of childhood and adolescent suicidal behavior. Haim[1] reported on his study of adolescent suicide in France in a monograph published in 1974. Holinger and Offer,[2] in a study called "Perspectives on Suicide in Adolescents," have offered the most thorough review of the literature on completed adolescent suicides to date. Recent issues of the *Journal of the American Academy of Child Psychiatry* and the annual publication of the *Society for Adolescent Psychiatry* have devoted significant space to this topic. It appears that a once-overlooked and ignored issue has finally come to the fore.

It is noteworthy that depression in children and adolescents has had a similar treatment. For many years, textbooks and publications in the field of childhood and adolescent psychiatry did not even mention the topic of depression. When this author first wrote on the subject of depression in children and adolescents in 1962, his work met with considerable resistance, much of which derived from circular reasoning, ie, children are incapable of being depressed, therefore depression cannot exist in children. It is of note that as studies of suicidal attempts in children and adolescents have increased, so have studies of depression in children and adolescents. The fact that children and adolescents can be truly depressed was officially recognized when depression in children was included in the Diagnostic and Statistical Manual III (DSM-III)[15] as a diagnostic entity. I do not believe that these two events, namely the increase in studies of suicidal behavior in children and adolescents and the increase in studies of depression in children and adolescents are purely coincidental. As I will attempt to demonstrate later in this chapter, depression is a significant component of suicidal behavior.

Another important topic that has recently gained attention, is the study of the families of suicidal children and adolescents. Studies such as those by Pfeffer,[13,14] Tishler and McKenry,[16] and Garfinkel et al[17] have shown that parents of suicidal children are frequently very depressed with suicidal ideation, and tend to abuse alcohol to a significant degree. Pfeffer's studies have let to her recommendation that every young psychiatric patient should be seriously evaluated for suicidal potential, and that parents should always be involved in the treatment of suicidal youngsters.

THEORETICAL CONCEPTS

It is clear that the first step in working with suicidal patients of any age is to evaluate as thoroughly as possible the suicidal risk. This is difficult even with adult patients, but is more so with children and adolescents because parents often complicate the issue by insisting that the child's suicidal attempt was only a mistake; or parents may even become angry with the child, asking, "How could you do this to me?" For these reasons, it is desirable to see the child apart from the parents so that they do not unduly influence the child's willingness to discuss his or her behavior. It has been my personal experience that children are less reluctant to acknowledge suicidal ideation than are adults, but most children will not volunteer such information unless they are questioned.

As a consultant, I have frequently been impressed by the fact that a youngster may have been in therapy for a considerable period of time without the therapist's asking the child if he or she has thought of suicide. Like the parents, it would seem that the therapist is in collusion with those who believe children and adolescents cannot have such painful thoughts. When these same youngsters are asked in consultation about suicidal ideation, they tend to be quite open about acknowledging such thoughts and often seem to feel relieved that they no longer need to hide their dreadful feelings. It is a well-known fact that many suicidal patients of all ages have been seen previously by physicians and mental health workers who have failed to properly evaluate the suicidal potential. Professionals often overlook the fact that youngsters with a history of running away from home, as well as those who abuse alcohol and drugs, frequently have a higher suicidal potential than the average youngster. This fact is illustrated by Case 2:

A 14-year-old adopted boy was first seen after running away from home. He was very depressed with some suicidal ideation. I recommended a period of evaluation in a hospital, but the youngster was not interested in any therapeutic intervention and his family was reluctant to force treatment against his will. He was seen initially just before the end of the school year, and over the next few months the father spent a considerable amount of time with his son, who had a good summer and voluntarily requested therapy. On entering therapy, the boy was found to be still depressed but less so than when last seen, and he was not suicidal. He was placed on desimipramine and continued in regular therapy. The youngster was very apprehensive about returning to school, but for the first month was able to handle the special program arranged by the school. Suddenly, one morning as he got off the school bus, he panicked and instead of entering the school he ran home. He said that none of the other students had harassed him. Over the next few days he became increasingly withdrawn and depressed and refused to return to school. As arrangements were being made for hospitalization he became more and more agitated; he wrecked his room and openly threatened suicide. Immediate hospitalization became necessary.

Until recently, many professionals believed it was dangerous to question children or adults about suicide lest it suggest such behavior to them. This absurd thinking appears to be less prevalent today; any therapist would be delighted if patients were so suggestible, as therapy would be greatly simplified if such were the case. Other cliches seem to have endured longer, such as the theory that people with strong religious beliefs such as Catholics will not attempt suicide because their religion considers it a serious moral offense. Any experienced therapist is aware that this is not true; one recent study even indicated that Catholics may attempt suicide more frequently than non-Catholics.[18]

The initial step in working with suicidal patients of any age is to evaluate the suicidal risk, but in addition one should thoroughly evaluate the individual's physical and psychiatric condition. Such an evaluation can be conducted in an office or outpatient setting, in the inpatient unit of a community hospital, or in the infirmary of a school or college. It is seldom necessary initially to refer a child to a psychiatric hospital, which may frequently be at a considerable distance from the youngster's home. A period of separation between the child and parents, however, is often of value because it interrupts the interaction between child and parents and allows objective personnel, such as nurses, to observe the youngster's behavior.

With suicidal patients of any age, it is of the utmost importance to understand the circumstances surrounding the act, such as whether the individual attempted to injure himself or herself when alone or whether the act occurred when he or she was in the vicinity of others, and how quickly the suicidal action was communicated to others. As already mentioned, we cannot take comfort from the fact that a nonlethal dose of medication was ingested; what is important is not the physician's knowledge of pharmacology but that of the youngster. We cannot dismiss minor gestures such as superficial wrist slashing as insignificant because the youngster may be attempting to convey a message of importance, and if we fail to recognize it he or she will see no choice but to make a more serious attempt in the future.

Denial frequently occurs after a suicidal act, which is why it is so important to speak to the individuals who first encounter the suicidal person. For example, it is not unusual for a patient upon awakening from an overdose of a drug(s) to convey to a nurse or attendant his or her unhappiness at not succeeding in committing suicide; yet a few hours later the same individual may say it was all a mistake and suicide was never intended. It must also be borne in mind that a suicidal attempt often has a temporary purgative effect and the individual may feel relieved for a brief period of time afterward. For that reason, as well as the difficulty in evaluating suicidal youngsters, I believe that we should not complete the evaluation in one brief hour, or even in one or two days in a hospital setting. It is preferable to observe a suicidal child or adolescent for several days before arriving at a final evaluation and treatment plan. It is equally important to evaluate the functioning of the parents and the family structure, especially if the youngster is to return home.

In addition to the usual psychiatric evaluation, scales have recently been developed[13] which are helpful in judging the risk of suicide in youngsters as well as adults. These scales, while still new and also time-consuming, may nevertheless be of great assistance in the overall evaluative process. Psychological testing may be of additional assistance, although we must bear in mind that such tests may fail to show the usual clinical signs of depression as seen in adults and may be heavily weighted towards angry, impulsive behavior.

It has been my experience that it can be very helpful to interview friends, teachers, or clergy who may have been involved with the suicidal youngster. Parents are often the last to know how a youngster feels, and it is most important to know the details leading up to the suicidal act. I have also found that many adolescents, especially females, tend to keep detailed journals. If possible, I always attempt to gain the youngsters permission to read these journals and have found over the years that they are extremely helpful in understanding the emotional processes that may have led to the suicide attempt.

At the end of the observation period, a therapeutic plan should be outlined to the youngster and to the parents and other involved individuals such as school personnel. The majority of suicidal young people are able to return home or to remain in their current school placement provided that adequate therapy is available. Some youngsters are either so disturbed or the home is so chaotic that placement in a hospital or residential treatment setting is necessary. I *firmly* believe that anyone of any age, but especially a child or adolescent who attempts suicide requires therapy, which usually proves to be both intensive and extensive and should involve significant members of the family. Even though a suicidal attempt may be used to manipulate or punish another, an individual who resorts to such drastic behavior to influence someone is either severely depressed, insecure, or frightened by overwhelming feelings of loneliness, helplessness, and hopelessness. Certainly, therapeutic assistance is required if the youngster is to cope with all of these feelings.

It has been my experience that the difficulty in treating the suicidal youngster lies not so much with the child, who is usually only too willing to accept help, but with the parents who wish to pretend that everything is fine, or with the school authorities who are frightened of allowing such a youngster to remain with them lest the child make another suicidal attempt. I am constantly impressed with the fact that many school and correctional institution personnel will tolerate youngsters who abuse alcohol and drugs or who indulge in angry outbursts against other youngsters, yet are frightened of any suicidal behavior. I believe that if the young person is capable of functioning academically and if an adequate therapeutic program can be arranged, he or she should remain in school. If school itself is the main problem, or if the youngster cannot concentrate on his academic work, a medical leave of absence is indicated.

It should be clear that no one treatment plan is suitable for all youngsters who attempt or threaten suicide. We must first have a diagnostic and psychodynamic formulation, as well as an evaluation of the strengths and weaknesses of the members of the family or the institution where the youngster resides. Diagnostic accuracy, especially in the case of children and adolescents, has been very poor until recently. With the advent of DSM-III and the Research Diagnostic Criteria, as well as the demise of the wastebasket diagnosis of Adjustment Reaction, psychiatry is becoming more precise. It is still difficult if not impossible, however, to compare the diagnostic categories of various authors, especially those published more than two or three years ago.

Some suicidal children or adolescents are clearly schizophrenic and may even be responding to auditory hallucinations that urge them towards suicide. These individuals require psychotropic medication in order to help control their psychotic thinking disorder, as well as psychotherapeutic assistance. Many suicidal youngsters who exhibit angry and impulsive behavior and act out their emotions with few if any restraints are best diagnosed as having behavioral and character disorders. This group is particularly hard to plan for as their behavior is so unpredictable. Such youngsters may appear to be functioning adequately at one moment and be actively suicidal the next.

I believe, however, that the majority of suicidal individuals of all ages are basically depressed.[11,19-21] Carlson and Cantwell[22] recently studied 102 psychiatrically referred children and adolescents and found that severe suicidal ideation increased around puberty and correlated with increasingly severe depression. They concluded that 63% of their subjects who were depressed were suicidal, versus 34% who were suicidal but were not depressed. They used the CDI (Children's Depressive Inventory) as part of this study. These scales, as well as the Kiddie-SADS-E (a structured diagnostic interview of children and adolescents) and the CAS (Child Assessment Schedule),[23] are helping us towards a more precise definition of depressed children. It is of interest that Carlson and Cantwell[22] did not find hopelessness to be a distinguishing feature of suicidal attempts in children and adolescents as did Beck[24] in adults. Goldney and Pilowsky[25] report that 50% to 75% of youngsters making suicidal attempts are depressed.

We may ask why all depressed youngsters are not suicidal. I believe they are, potentially. The question is then why some attempt suicide and others do not. Is the reason related to the degree of impulsivity in the youngster, or the ability to tolerate pain and discomfort, or the ability to conceive of a more hopeful future, or the support of family and friends? I suggest that any or all of these reasons may be involved in each case.

When I first began to write about depression in children and adolescents in 1960 I emphasized, as did other authors such as Lesse,[26] Glaser,[27] and Gould,[28] that most youngsters do not exhibit overt signs of depression but tend to manifest their depression by behavioral symptomatology. Controlled studies by Carlson[29] and Cytryn and McKnew[30] and numerous others indicate that many more children and adolescents exhibit overt signs of depression than was previously appreciated. DSM-III[15] has acknowledged that conclusion, although it does indicate that youngsters will show symptoms of depression in various ways at different developmental levels. Ostroff et al,[31] in a recent study of adult males, describe neuroendocrine tests that may reflect not only depressive features but may even be valuable as a predictive tool of suicidal risk. If these tests should prove valid for children and adolescents, it would significantly assist our efforts to evaluate and treat suicidal youngsters. Cohen-Sandler et al[32] recently reported that life stresses were more important in understanding the suicidal risk in children than any other factor. This study has not been confirmed to date, and it should be borne in mind that the authors used very rigid criteria for suicidal behavior. Pfeffer[33] and Tishler and McKenry[16] have emphasized that parental negative self-images, which are introjected by the child, are significant factors leading to suicidal attempts in both children and adolescents. Sabbath[34] has described children who are considered expendable by the parents. Peck[35] has described a group of youngsters whom he calls loners, who represent a subtype of suicidal adolescents.

It is of interest that little has been written concerning the therapy of suicidal youngsters. Almost all studies have emphasized epidemiology, psychodynamics, the youngster's attitude toward death, the attitude of the adult and society toward suicide, diagnostic factors, and the relation of depression to suicide, but very few writers have addressed the specific issue of therapy with suicidal children and adolescents. Exceptions are Haim,[1] Mintz,[36] and Tabachnick.[37]

Personally, I prefer individual, psychoanalytically oriented therapy for the suicidal child or adolescent as well as a similar program for the parents, even if the youngster is living away from home. Beck[38] has emphasized the value of cognitive therapy for adults, relatively few studies to date have described the effect of this approach on children and adolescents. I also prefer that the same therapist work with both the suicidal child and his parents, as this allows for a deeper understanding of the dynamics between child and parents and diminishes the opportunity for child and parents to play one therapist against another.

Most therapists who work with adolescents stress the complete separation of parents and youngster in the therapeutic process in order to demonstrate confidentiality, particularly from the adolescent's point of view. Confidentiality is certainly a valid issue, but it obscures even more important issues such as the necessity of improving communication and strengthening ties between the youngster and his or her parents. I believe the crucial issues are trust and respect, and if parents and youngster trust the therapist and the therapist respects the confidences of both parties, the model of a single therapist is viable. Such a plan allows the youngster to be seen alone, the parents to be seen alone, or all together with or without other family members. When two therapists are involved it does not resolve the issue of confidentiality; in fact, it may obscure the issue as neither parents nor child may be fully aware of how completely or how inadequately the two therapists confer. It is my practice to let each party know that they are entitled to confidentiality; for example, if one of the parents is having an extramarital affair, it is not the therapist's responsibility to disclose this fact to the child, nor would the parents be entitled to know about personal sexual events in the life of the child. However, a single therapist can significantly improve communication among family members on the important issues that relate to the youngster's suicidal ideation and behavior.

With this model, one becomes aware of the frequent instances of family secrets, usually, on the part of the parents, such as their own suicidal behavior or that of significant relatives, which is often of vital therapeutic importance. On the other hand, with the usual model of two therapists, such information may not be disclosed for a much longer time. A single therapist, while respecting the youngster's individuality, is able to comprehend the family structure, recognizing that it is still a vital necessity to the youngster. It should be noted that there is more resistance to this therapeutic approach on the part of therapists than on the part of children and adolescents or their parents. There are occasions when therapy cannot be provided by a single individual as when the child is away at school or college and the distance is too great, or when the paranoia of either party is extreme. When such is the case, it is important that the therapists working with members of the same family communicate frequently and with the knowledge of both youngster and parents.

The literature constantly refers to the difficulty of working with adolescent patients with all types of disorders. This is certainly true, but we often overlook the fact that working with the parents can be even more difficult because they fear therapy on account of guilt and are often only too willing to have the child treated provided that they are left alone. The initial stages of therapy must of necessity emphasize ego-supportive efforts for both the child and parents. It is especially important to help the youngster recognize his or her strengths and assets, as depressed suicidal youngsters as well as depressed adults tend to emphasize their perceived deficiencies. It is necessary to help the parents face their fear, anger, and guilt as quickly as possible lest the youngster feel compelled to "become well" in order to placate his or her parents.

Most therapists are aware that suicidal and depressed patients often respond favorably during the early stages of therapy. Soon thereafter, there is a natural inclination for both the youngster and his parents to say that everything is fine and to wish to terminate therapy. I would like to stress again that I believe most suicidal patients require prolonged therapy, and the therapist is wise not to terminate therapy prematurely. It is often emphasized and hoped that therapy of suicidal individuals will prevent loss of life; in my opinion, this is only one reason to stress intensive, long-term therapy with suicidal children and adolescents. The number of such youngsters who may actually commit suicide is admittedly rather modest, but I believe that those suicidal children and adolescents who do not receive appropriate therapy will continue to exhibit serious psychopathology throughout their adult lives and will frequently pass it on to their offspring. This is why I believe that short-term, crisis-oriented therapy may be like a Band-Aid applied to a malignancy.

Whether our approach be psychoanalytic or cognitive, a critical factor in all therapy of suicidal children and adolescents is the relationship between therapist and patient. Suicidal and depressed individuals of all ages, but especially children and adolescents, find it difficult to believe that anyone could truly care for them or be concerned about their welfare. They will often taunt the therapist with the words, "You don't really care about me — only your fee. It's your job to care." They will often test the therapist by coming late, missing sessions, angry outbursts, and threatening to discontinue therapy. These youngsters not only test the patience of the therapist but that of their friends as well, as in Case 3:

An 18-year-old college freshman had made a serious suicidal attempt towards the end of her senior year in high school and had been hospitalized over the summer. When seen in therapy in the fall she was very depressed and distant. Even more outstanding was her mistrust of her therapist and her friends. For example, her roommate had a car and volunteered to drive her to most of her therapy sessions. Connie (as we shall call her) took this for granted and never thanked her roommate or offered to reimburse her for her gasoline. One day Connie arrived for a session in a furious mood saying, "I knew it all along — my roommate hates me!" When asked why she thought so, Connie responded that her roommate had told her she was too busy to drive her that one day and suggested that she take a taxi. In brief, one disappointment (rejection) overcame numerous generous acts.

Difficult as it is to relate to such youngsters, I do believe that it is possible with the majority of them. I personally attempt to make them share the responsibility for their therapy, to help them realize that I have no magic, that I cannot prevent them from killing themselves if they so choose, but with their help will do my best to assist them to avoid such behavior. Many therapists stress an actual written contract, with the patient agreeing to certain conditions such as no suicidal attempts without calling the therapist. While I have no objection to such a contract I prefer to enlist the patient's verbal and voluntary agreement to assume responsibility for all aspects of his or her therapy, eg, coming to sessions regularly, calling for help if necessary, taking medication if it is prescribed. If a suicidal youngster is not willing and/or able to enter into such an agreement, I would hesitate to accept him or her in therapy, outside of a hospital setting. In working with actively suicidal patients I believe that we must, within reasonable limits, make ourselves available when patients need us by allowing them telephone access and by scheduling extra sessions. A good example of the demands made by depressed and/or suicidal patients and the flexibility required to respond adequately is David, Case 4:

David withdrew abruptly from college early in his freshman year. When seen shortly thereafter he was significantly depressed and withdrawn. He entered therapy mainly at the urging of his parents. The initial stages of therapy were slow and laborious. He gave numerous reasons for his depression, none of which seemed adequate. He became progressively more depressed until finally he reluctantly agreed to accept antidepressant medication, although it was evident he was not taking it faithfully. As his depression worsened I suggested a period of hospitalization which he angrily rejected. After leaving a session one day, he attempted to purchase a handgun but fortunately the dealer refused his request. He called me shortly after this act, finally admitting his extreme depression and suicidal thoughts. He and his parents were seen that evening and immediate hospitalization was arranged, but he found hospitalization a most painful experience and eloped to his home after several weeks. At that time he had shown little or no improvement.

David and his parents were seen in therapy over the next two weeks, during which time the question of certification to a hospital was discussed. Suddenly David entered a manic phase for the first time at which point he said he felt wonderful and did not need further therapy or medication; however, he did agree to continue in therapy at the urging of his parents. Although clearly manic, he refused to consider lithium. Finally, after being dismissed from a job because of inappropriate behavior and because he wished to return to college in a few months he agreed to take lithium. The response was dramatic—his moods stabilized. When warned that he had a bipolar illness and that a recurrence of his depression was a distinct possibility, he stated that everything was fine.

He reentered college in the fall and for the first months all went well until once again he suddenly became depressed, but failed to contact me. In a few days he took an overdose of lithium in a serious suicidal attempt. He did ask for help almost immediately and physically he recovered quickly. Only after his suicidal attempt was he able to face the fact that he had a serious problem that required both medication and psychotherapy—a problem that might last indefinitely. At that point it can be said that psychotherapy began; he acknowledged his despair, loneliness, emptiness, and fear of mental illness. Without the strong support of his parents and the availability and flexibility of the therapist, the outcome might have been much different.

The use of antidepressant medication for suicidal children and adolescents has recently come to the fore. Puig-Antich,[39] working with depressed children, has found that tricyclic medication is frequently efficacious and may facilitate the patient's ability to engage in the therapeutic process and reduce the suicidal risk. We must keep in mind that antidepressant medication, even when effective, takes two to three weeks to produce its full therapeutic effect. Suicidal youngsters who clinically appear to be angry do not respond to antidepressant medication as well as more overtly depressed youngsters. The dexamethasone suppression test, which has been widely used in diagnosing depression in adults, has recently been reported by Poznanski[40] as being useful in prepubertal depressed children. If this report proves valid, it will be an additional tool for therapists working with suicidal children and adolescents. It would help determine the importance of the role of depression as well as whether antidepressant medication is indicated.

Puig-Antich[39] has clearly described the cardiotoxic effects of tricyclic antidepressants in children. It therefore behooves therapists when prescribing such medication for children to work closely with a pediatrician or internist and to monitor such youngsters with EKGs. It is my belief that, even when antidepressant medication is effective, psychotherapy is also indicated. As Puig-Antich's studies have shown, even when his patients responded favorably to medication and were no longer clinically depressed, their general level of social interaction with other youngsters was not significantly improved.

In any discussion of medication for suicidal patients, mention must be made of the use of sedation. The majority of depressed persons have sleep disturbances, although the evidence to date indicates that this may be less true of children than of adolescents. I believe that barbiturates should be strictly avoided, not only because they present a suicidal potential but because there are better ways to improve the disturbed sleep pattern. If a sedative is temporarily needed, flurazepam hydrochloride or diazepam appear to be quite safe. If an antidepressant is warranted, the sleep disturbance can be ameliorated by selecting a more sedative type (such as amitriptyline); in any event the insomnia should abate as the depression lifts.

COUNTERTRANSFERENCE ISSUES

Countertransference (the therapist's unconscious reactions to the patient) is a problem in working with all patients, but is especially significant in our work with suicidal youngsters. The therapist may become frightened of the burden of working with suicidal individuals and find him or herself ruminating about such patients. The therapist may feel that his or her reputation will suffer if a patient were to commit suicide, especially if the patient comes from a well-known family. It is not unusual for a suicidal patient to test the therapist with a comment such as, "What would happen to your reputation if my death hit the newspapers?" Some therapists clearly would be well-advised not to work with suicidal patients, just as some do not do well with schizophrenic patients. As a general rule it is wise for most therapists not to have more than one or two acutely suicidal patients in therapy at the same time, especially in an outpatient setting, lest the therapist become emotionally depleted. This is especially important if the therapist works alone and has no one with whom to share his fears, worries, and concerns. A close colleague or a supervisor can be of great value at such times.

The therapist who is overly frightened of working with suicidal patients may prematurely or unnecessarily refer such individuals to a hospital simply because he or she is too uncomfortable with the level of self-anxiety experienced. On the other hand some therapists who, in their grandiosity, may believe that they can handle any problem may not be sufficiently alert to the suicidal risk and fail to refer such patients to the protective environment of a psychiatric hospital when this is necessary. If a therapist is to work successfully with suicidal patients of any age, but especially with children and adolescents, he or she needs to be able to share the pain and anguish experienced by these patients. Just as some physicians cannot help their dying patients face that painful knowledge, some therapists cannot help their patients face their painful emotions of depression, anger, despair, and loneliness. It has been my experience, as well as that of many others[37] working with suicidal youngsters, that these emotions tend to be the central dynamics which must be dealt with if therapy is to prove successful. The reluctance of some therapists to help their patients face and explore these feelings explains why many therapists may be only too willing to agree when the patient and parents suggest a premature termination of therapy. By such termination the therapist, as well as the patient, avoids many painful and uncomfortable sessions which are necessary if we are to resolve the basic problems of suicidal individuals.

OUTCOME STUDIES

Followup studies of therapy are few and often poorly controlled; adequate followup studies of suicidal children and adolescents are especially lacking. There have been a few followup studies of suicidal adults who have had psychiatric hospitalization, but the majority of suicidal patients never enter a psychiatric hospital. We do not even have a baseline from which to compare suicidal youngsters who have had various types of therapy with those who have had none. A recent study by Cohen-Sandler et al[41] compared suicidal and nonsuicidal children and adolescents who had been referred as psychiatric emergencies. They indicated that approximately half of the suicidal children repeated their suicidal behavior during a followup peroid, whereas not one of the nonsuicidal children attempted suicide during the same period. This study raises several intriguing possibilities, one of which may be that some children or adolescents who attempt suicide utilize such behavior for secondary gain, probably because they have learned that suicidal behavior may be rewarding.

Under the present circumstances we can only offer tentative conclusions. In my opinion the majority of youngsters who attempt suicide never receive adequate treatment. Nevertheless, most of them survive. We do not know how many of these untreated or inadequately treated youngsters continue to lead depressed lives, to abuse alcohol and drugs, to exhibit acting out and delinquent behavior, nor how many will pass their problems along to the next generation. I believe that a sizeable percentage will continue throughout life as emotionally handicapped individuals. It has been my experience that the majority of suicidal youngsters with whom I have had the opportunity to work in intensive and extensive therapy have done well. These patients have tended to become involved in therapy, to appreciate its value, and to be pleased that another person has taken their problems seriously. Their prognosis, not only for survival but for successful resolution of their underlying problems as a whole, has been good.

REFERENCES

1. Haim A: *Adolescent Suicide*. New York, International Universities Press, 1970.
2. Holinger PC, Offer D: Perspectives on suicide in adolescence, in Simmons R (ed): *Research in Community and Mental Health*. Greenwich, CT, Jai Press Inc, 1981.
3. Miller D: Adolescent suicide: Etiology and treatment, in Feinstein SC, Looney JG, Schwartzberg AZ, et al (eds): *Adolescent Psychiatry*. Chicago, University of Chicago Press, 1981, vol 9, pp 327–342.
4. Suter B: Suicide and women, in Wolman BB, Krauss HH (eds): *Between Survival and Suicide*. New York, Gardner Press, 1976.
5. Rosenthal MJ: Sexual differences in the suicidal behavior of young people, in Feinstein SC, Looney JG, Schwartzberg AZ, et al (eds): *Adolescent Psychiatry*. Chicago, University of Chicago Press, 1981, vol 9, pp 422–442.
6. Doctors S: The symptom of delicate self-cutting in adolescent females: A developmental view, in Feinstein SC, Looney JG, Schwartzberg AZ, et al (eds): *Adolescent Psychiatry*. Chicago, University of Chicago Press, 1981, vol 9, pp 443–461.
7. Piaget J: *The Construction of Reality in the Child*. New York, Basic Books, 1954.
8. Shaffer D: Suicide in childhood and early adolescence. *J Child Psychol Psychiatry* 1974;15:275–291.
9. Bender L, Schilder P: Suicidal occupations and attempts in children. *Am J Orthopsychiatry* 1937;7:225–234.
10. Balser B, Masterson JF: Suicide in adolescents. *Am J Psychiatry* 1959;115:400–405.

342

11. Toolan JM: Suicide and suicidal attempts in children and adolescents. *Am J Psychiatry* 1962;118:719–724.
12. Schrut A: Suicidal adolescents and children. *JAMA* 1964;188:1103–1107.
13. Pfeffer CR, Conte HR, Plutchik R, et al: Suicidal behavior in latency-age children: An empirical study. *J Am Acad Child Psychiatry* 1979;18:675–692.
14. Pfeffer CR, Conte HR, Plutchik R, et al: Suicidal behavior in latency-age children: An outpatient population. *J Am Acad Child Psychiatry* 1980;19: 703–711.
15. American Psychiatric Association Task Force on Nomenclature and Statistics: *Diagnostic and Statistical Manual of Mental Disorders*, ed 3. Washington, American Psychiatric Association, 1980.
16. Tishler CL, McKenry PC: Parental negative-self and adolescent suicide attempts. *J Am Acad Child Psychiatry* 1982;21:404–408.
17. Garfinkel H, Froise A, Hood J: Suicide attempts in children and adolescents. *Am J Psychiatry* 1982;139:1257–1261.
18. Gabrielson IW, Klerman LV, Currie JB, et al: Suicide attempts in a population of pregnant teenagers. *Am J Public Health* 1970;60:2289–2301.
19. Toolan JM: Depression in children and adolescents. *Am J Orthopsychiatry* 1962;32:404–415.
20. Toolan JM: Suicide in children and adolescents. *Am J Psychother* 1975;29: 339–344.
21. Toolan JM: Depression and suicide in children: An overview. *Am J Psychother* 1981;35:311–322.
22. Carlson GA, Cantwell DP: Suicidal behavior and depression in children and adolescents. *J Am Acad Child Psychiatry* 1982;21:361–368.
23. Hodges, K, McKnew D, Cytryn L, et al: The child assessment schedule (CAS) diagnostic interview: A report on reliability and validity. *J Am Acad Child Psychiatry* 1982;21:468–473.
24. Beck AT, Kovacs M, Weissman A: Hopelessness and suicidal behavior: An overview. *JAMA* 1975;234:1146–1149.
25. Goldney RD, Pilowsky I: Depression in young women who have attempted suicide. *Aust NZ J Psychiatry* 1980;14:203–211.
26. Lesse S: Hypochondriacal and psychosomatic disorders masking depression in adolescents. *Am J Psychother* 1981;35:356–365.
27. Glaser K: Psychopathologic patterns in depressed adolescents. *Am J Psychother* 1981;35:368–382.
28. Gould RE: Suicide problems in children and adolescents. *Am J Psychother* 1965;19:288–295.
29. Carlson GA: The phenomenology of adolescent depression, in Feinstein SC, Looney JG, Schwartzberg AZ, et al (eds): *Adolescent Psychiatry*. Chicago, University of Chicago Press, 1981, vol 9, pp 411–421.
30. Cytryn L, McKnew DH, Bunney WE Jr: Diagnosis of depression in children: A reassessment. *Am J Psychiatry* 1980;137:22–25.
31. Ostroff R, Giller E, Bonese K, et al: Neuroendocrine risk factors of suicidal behavior. *Am J Psychiatry* 1982;139:1323–1325.
32. Cohen-Sandler R, Berman AL, King RA: Life stress and symptomatology — Determinants of suicidal behavior in children. *J Am Acad Child Psychiatry* 1982;21:178–186.
33. Pfeffer CR: The family system of suicidal children. *Am J Psychother* 1981; 35:330–341.
34. Sabbath JC: The suicidal adolescent — The expendable child. *J Am Acad Child Psychiatry* 1969;8:272–285.

35. Peck ML: The loner: An exploration of a suicidal subtype in adolescence, in Feinstein SC, Looney JG, Schwartzberg AZ, et al (eds): *Adolescent Psychiatry*. Chicago, University of Chicago Press, 1981, vol 9, pp 461–466.
36. Mintz T: Clinical experience with suicidal adolescents, in Feinstein SC, Looney JG, Schwartzberg AZ, et al (eds): *Adolescent Psychiatry*. Chicago, University of Chicago Press, 1981, vol 9, pp 493–496.
37. Tabachnick N: The interlocking psychologies of suicide and adolescence, in Feinstein SC, Looney JG, Schwartzberg AZ, et al (eds): *Adolescent Psychiatry*. Chicago, University of Chicago Press, 1981, vol 9, pp 399–410.
38. Beck AT: *Depression: Clinical, Experimental, and Theoretical Aspects*. New York, Hoeber, 1967.
39. Puig-Antich J, Perel JM, Lupatkin W, et al: Plasma levels of imipramine (IMI) and desmethylimipramine (DMI) and clinical response in prepubertal major depression disorder. *J Am Acad Child Psychiatry* 1979;18:616–627.
40. Poznanski E, Carroll BJ, Banegas MC, et al: The dexamethasone suppression test in prepubertal depressed children. *Am J Psychiatry* 1982;139:321–324.
41. Cohen-Sandler R, Berman AL, King RA: A follow-up study of hospitalized suicidal children. *J Am Acad Child Psychiatry* 1982;21:398–403.

CHAPTER 21

COGNITIVE THERAPY OF DEPRESSED AND SUICIDAL ADOLESCENTS

RICHARD C. BEDROSIAN
NORMAN EPSTEIN

Cognitive therapy, as developed by Aaron T. Beck and his associates at the University of Pennsylvania, has shown considerable promise as an effective treatment for depression[1-4] and as a systematic approach to the sense of hopelessness that is associated with suicidal ideation and behavior among depressed individuals.[5] The cognitive approach has also spawned new assessment instruments for suicidal ideation and behavior.[6] The present chapter describes how the cognitive model and cognitive treatment techniques can be applied to depressed and suicidal adolescents.

COGNITIVE MODEL OF DEPRESSION AND SUICIDAL WISHES

The cognitive model of depression assumes that the patient's idiosyncratic interpretations, expectations, and basic assumptions generate unpleasant affective states, undesirable behaviors, and other symptoms of psychological distress.[7] Knowledge of the private meaning a person attaches to a particular situation allows one to predict his or her subsequent emotional reaction.

Beck[7] used the term "cognitive triad" to describe the hallmark of the depressed patient's thinking: negative views of the self, the world, and the future. The depressed person views him/herself as defective, blameworthy, or worthless; the world as cold, frustrating, devoid of opportunity or gratification; and the future as offering nothing but continued suffering. The depressed person processes new information in such a way as to continually validate depressogenic (ie, depression-producing) assumptions. Information that is discrepant with a negative view of the self and the world is often overlooked or disqualified in some manner (eg, "You say you love me, but you'd hate me if you knew me better"). Consequently, the depressed person becomes trapped in a vicious cycle in which distorted ideas are constantly reconfirmed, thereby maintaining and reinforcing the depressed mood. A considerable number of studies have identified distorted self-perceptions and other dysfunctional attitudes associated with depression.[8,9]

Given that an individual perceives the self as worthless, the world as barren, and the future as hopeless, he or she may begin to consider suicide as a viable option. The role of hopelessness in suicidal intent and ideation has been documented at a number of research sites, with various patient populations.[6,10,11] The cognitive model assumes that for each individual the conclusion that his or her life situation is hopeless will be based upon a unique interpretation or chain of reasoning that must be identified and modified if the individual's hopelessness and suicidal intent are to be decreased.

Degree of belief Every idea has a certain degree of belief attached to it. Cognitions with very high degrees of belief include those which stem from sensory data, delusions, and rigid, perfectionistic standards. It is possible to hold two contradictory beliefs at once, particularly if neither idea has a very high degree of belief attached to it. Such a contention is well illustrated by data which indicate that a high percentage of suicide attempters both wish to live and wish to die at the time of the attempt.[12]

Strongly held beliefs are more resistant to change, produce more intense affective reactions, and may stimulate more pressure to act. Regardless of the actual ideational content, if the suicidal wish is based upon beliefs that are so strongly held as to be impervious to change, the risk of harm to the individual will persist.

For example, a young woman believed that since she had undergone an elective abortion, it was God's will that she would ultimately kill herself. No therapeutic interventions seemed to affect the belief, even after an interview with a sympathetic priest. Despite improvements in mood and substantial alterations in life circumstances, the woman remained at risk for suicidal behavior as long as the basic suicidal cognition remained unchanged.

Consistency The nature and extent of an individual's distorted thinking may vary over time, in association with depressed mood, events in the environment, and other factors. Degree of belief in a particular cognition such as "Death is the only way out for me," may therefore fluctuate widely over time and/or across situations. In fact, patients may report having few or no suicidal thoughts in certain settings, but may feel overwhelmed by self-destructive thoughts in other situations. Risk assessment itself can be complicated by the fact that the relative safety and security of the clinical setting may diminish the intensity of suicidal ideation for some patients.

Sustained bouts of suicidal rumination produce a vicious cycle. Prolonged suicidal ideation leads to sustained (and even increased) depressive affect and symptomatology. As the depression deepens, the patient's ability to perceive nonsuicidal options diminishes, which in turn leads to continued self-destructive thoughts and more depressive affect.

COGNITIVE ASSESSMENT

It is assumed that a strong collaborative relationship between therapist and patient is a necessary component of effective cognitive assessment and therapy. Contrary to misconceptions of cognitive therapy,[13] the cognitive therapist does not simply get the patient to "change his or her mind" through argument, browbeating, or other didactic techniques. The therapist and patient(s) work together to identify the connections between specific thoughts, unpleasant emotions, and maladaptive behaviors. Likewise, once the salient cognitions have been identified, the therapist and patient collaborate to evaluate the validity and/or utility of each belief or interpretation. The term *collaborative empiricism* has been used to describe the assessment and treatment process in cognitive therapy.[14]

When adolescents enter treatment, most are well aware of the external difficulties they may be experiencing (eg, parents and school), but few patients recognize the cognition that mediate the relationships between external events and subsequent affect and behavior. Moreover, few teenagers are aware of the powerful influence exerted by their interpretations and attitudes upon their relationships with other people.

The cognitive therapy literature[14,15] contains descriptions of various methods for assessing dysfunctional cognitions. Reporting on one's thought processes is a skill which a patient can learn during the therapy hour. The therapist may ask the patient to reexperience a troublesome situation through imagery and to reveal the "automatic thoughts" (stream of consciousness cognitions) associated with the incident. Similarly, problem situations that involve interpersonal interactions can be recreated through the use of role playing. The goal is for the cognitive therapy patient to begin recording his or her dysfunctional cognitions in vivo between sessions.

Many teenagers find it difficult to tolerate face-to-face encounters with a therapist. As discussed elsewhere,[16] the therapist may include activities and games as part of the interview, in order to help the adolescent warm up to a discussion of sensitive issues. Even when the therapist has established good rapport and a relaxed therapeutic atmosphere, the adolescent may still offer very little workable material. In such instances, the therapist may provide the patient with alternative ways to express his or her thoughts. Instead of speaking directly to a therapist, adolescents can keep diaries, write letters, speak into tape recorders, pick out popular songs which reflect their experiences, and so on. Some teenagers who initially seem to be poor candidates for therapy will flourish in treatment if they can find a comfortable method by which to communicate with the therapist.

Below are excerpts from diaries and letters written by depressed adolescents who initially had offered the therapist very little information in direct discussion. The typical depressive themes such as negative self-image, expectation of rejection, hopelessness, and victimization at the hands of others are notable.

> "For awhile I was trying to think positive. Maybe school is nice, but it's not. I tried to think of good things, but I can't keep lying to myself. I wish I was the type of person that runs away, but I'm not. P.S. This is not my idea of how life should be!"

> "You know how I've been depressed? Well yesterday when I was at work, my boss yelled at me for leaving early Sunday. He said everyone was mad at me. I felt awful for doing that. I felt wicked, sick, like I could kill myself. I can't stand it when someone doesn't like me."

> "I feel my biggest problem has been the way I look. I'm so goddam ugly, it's pathetic. I've been ugly all my life. I wish I was dead! I have no boyfriends. They all think I'm shitty looking. I wish I was better looking, smarter, different. I'll never go to college or make people proud of me. I just can't take it anymore!!!"

As the therapist begins to gather information on the salient issues in the patient's life (a process which may be protracted in the case of an adolescent), he or she needs to probe, by means of patient, empathic questioning, beneath the surface of the individual's statements. For example, if a 17-year-old says she wants to kill herself because "I just can't go on since my fiance dumped me," under no circumstances should one assume that one knows exactly what she means. The patient's contention that things are hopeless for her could be based on any of a wide variety of cognitions. Some possibilities might include:

> "I have failed at the one important relationship in my life, so now there's no point in living."
> "This rejection proves I'm worthless, stupid, unattractive, etc."
> "No one else would ever want me."
> "I can never be happy without him."
> "I could never be close to anyone again."
> "I can't tolerate the shame and embarrassment of people knowing about this."

The clinician needs to identify the chains of reasoning and associated evidence that have led to the patient's statements. What does she believe will happen to her now in her boyfriend's absence? What had led her to conclude that she failed? How does she know she will be unable to enjoy another relationship? Has she ever been close to anyone other than her fiance? Has her relationship with him been her only source of gratification in life?

Cognitive assessment begins with the monitoring of the automatic thoughts or suicidal states. It then proceeds to the identification of more stable underlying assumptions or schemata that may make an individual susceptible to depression and suicidal ideation when activated by stressful life events.[17] Thus, in the above example, the patient's automatic thoughts regarding failure in relationships may be based on a long-standing belief (dormant unless activated by a disruption in her relationships with significant others) that one must be loved by others in order to be a worthwhile person. Providing evidence to challenge an automatic thought such as "No one else would even want me" is likely to decrease the intensity of belief in that cognition as well as the associated depressive symptoms; however, similar upsetting automatic thoughts may be elicited by relationship problems in the future unless the individual's underlying assumption about the necessity of relationships for her happiness is modified as well.

ASSESSMENT OF SUICIDAL IDEATION

The Scale for Suicide Ideation, developed by Beck, Kovacs, and Weissman,[18] serves as an excellent outline for the initial assessment of suicidal cognitions (it can be obtained from Dr. Aaron T. Beck at the Center for Cognitive Therapy, University of Pennsylvania). The SSI is a 19-item scale designed to be administered by a clinician in a semi-structured interview format. With practice, a clinician can easily incorporate the content of this instrument for use in a more informal manner. The items assess the frequency and duration of suicidal thoughts, as well as the patient's attitudes toward them; the extent of the wish to live and the wish to die; the current desire to make an active suicide attempt, and details of any plans; subjective feelings of control regarding the suicidal ideation; and so on. The following paragraphs are intended to provide the clinician with additional questions to consider in order to build upon the data base provided by the SSI.

Situational analysis The clinician needs to conduct a situational analysis of the suicidal cognitions. How frequent is the ideation? Does it occur in short bursts or for extended periods? Are there consistent situations or stressors associated with the ideation? Do the situations favor self-control or impulsivity? Can the patient avoid these situations? Are the stressors predictable or unpredictable, controllable or uncontrollable? Does the hopelessness relate more to the immediate stressors (eg, "I'm better off dead because I'll never find a job in this economy"), or to more pervasive basic beliefs ("I've never been anything but a loser all my life")? The more chronic and persistent the cognitive underpinnings are for the suicidal wishes, the greater the continuing risk of suicidal behavior.

Just as it is important to understand the nature of the suicidal ideation at its worst, it is useful to determine whether there are times when the patient's degree of belief in the suicidal cognitions wanes, or when he or she experiences a greater sense of control over the ideation. Does hopelessness ever lift enough for the patient to consider other options? How does the patient view his or her situation when he/she is comparatively lucid?

Wish to live, wish to die Because many suicide attempters report opposing wishes,[12] it is necessary to inquire about the strength of each wish separately. The clinician needs to ask whether the patient's reasons for living outweigh those for dying, or vice versa. Passive suicidal ideation, in which a person fails to take life-protecting action, is also a concern with patients such as diabetics, who are in a position to act upon such ideas quite readily.

In addition to focusing on the cognitions related to the wish to die, the clinician should review the reasoning behind the patient's wish to live. Does the desire to live rest primarily on deterrents to suicide (eg, pain it would cause to relatives), or does the patient cite any positive reasons for staying alive? Does the patient have a specific date targeted for suicide?

Conception of suicide The adolescent may view the idea of suicide with horror, relief, equanimity, or a perverse sense of romanticism. Does the young person believe that he or she is somehow destined to commit suicide? Does the patient identify with real or fictional characters who have died by suicide? What exactly does death offer the patient? Needless to say, these issues will assume even greater importance if the patient has experienced the loss of a significant other through suicide.

One 17-year-old described persistent suicidal ideation starting at age 12. As a suicide attempter, she viewed herself as part of a select group, whom others in society could not possibly understand. She read works of authors such as Sylvia Plath, and frequented plays and movies that dealt with the topic of suicide. Not only did she suffer from very low self-esteem and a pervasive sense of hopelessness, she now viewed herself as a *suicidal person*.

Attitudes toward the ideation The patient's response to treatment may well depend on his or her attitude toward the suicidal ideation. Patients will be less likely to become engaged in treatment regarding the issue of self-destructiveness as long as they experience thoughts of suicide as sources of comfort or relief. Of course, any possibility that the adolescent will conceal the presence or content of suicidal wishes increases risk. Conversely, a patient who is frightened or appalled by suicidal wishes may be willing to work with a therapist to learn how to resist the ideation, despite a fairly high degree of belief in the reasons for suicide.

Sense of control How strong is the patient's sense of control over the suicidal ideation or actions? In what situations are the controls effective or ineffective? What types of self-control strategies does the patient utilize? Typical controls include distraction, disputing the suicidal ideas, utilizing social supports, and engaging in alternative behaviors. Does the patient already use self-control techniques in other situations that can generalize to the suicidal ideation?

It is vital for the clinician to examine carefully any factors that might undermine controls or stimulate impulsive behavior at some point in the future. Prime concerns include alcohol abuse, as well as the abuse of other drugs such as marijuana, minor tranquilizers, amphetamines, barbiturates, and even caffeine. The presence of psychotic symptomatology or any past history of impulsive behavior similarly increases risk.

Depression and anxiety can sometimes mask or precede psychotic symptoms in adolescent patients. Consequently, the clinician needs to routinely inquire as to the presence of "command hallucinations" (ie, those which order the patient to do something), which can occur in the absence of more overt psychotic symptoms. It is also noteworthy that in a delinquent population suicide attempts seem to occur quite impulsively, without being preceded by substantial periods of depression and suicidal rumination.[19]

All of the above factors increase the risk of suicidal behavior markedly because they potentially nullify other favorable prognostic signs (eg, deterrents, sense of control, wish to live), cultivate impulsivity, and give rise to tragic miscalculations (eg, harming oneself when the overall suicidal intent is actually low). Because of the unpredictable cognitive content and controls, a suicidal individual with ongoing substance abuse or psychotic symptoms is best treated in an inpatient setting.

Deterrents Patients most frequently cite religion, family members, and the possibility of an unsuccessful attempt resulting in further suffering as deterrents to suicidal behavior. If an adolescent asserts "I wouldn't kill myself because of my parents," for example, it is necessary to ask questions such as, "What do you think would happen to them if you did kill yourself?" The evaluator needs to assess the chain of cognitions related to a particular deterrent and the associated degrees of belief. Are there competing cognitions which might undermine the power of a deterrent to prevent suicidal behavior (eg, "Sometimes I think my parents would be better off without me")?

Plans A completed suicide is often the result of well-articulated plans. How much actual preparation for the attempt has the patient engaged in? Is the contemplated method readily available? Does the patient have backup plans? Has he or she planned methods for providing isolation during the attempt and thwarting subsequent discovery? Has the patient engaged in any other activities in anticipation of death (eg, giving away possessions, writing notes)?

A note of caution needs to be sounded against equating suicidal intent with the medical lethality of the attempt, and thus labeling low lethality attempts (or contemplated attempts) as "gestures." Medical lethality is only one aspect of suicidal intent.[20] In order to estimate suicidal potential realistically, it is vital to assess a variety of factors, such as the patient's conception of the method's lethality and his or her expectation of death as a result of the proposed method.

TREATMENT GUIDELINES

As mentioned earlier, cognitive therapy proceeds best when an atmosphere of collaborative empiricism exists between the therapist and patient. Unlike adults, adolescents seldom enter treatment with clearly articulated complaints. Moreover, even the teenager with a fair degree of insight needs time to warm up to the therapist and the whole notion of therapy. It is vital for the therapist to give the adolescent patient a strong sense of control over the agenda of each session. The therapist may need to emphasize that he or she is neither willing nor able to read the teenager's thoughts. Questioning should proceed in an empathic manner, one which expresses benign concern rather than skepticism or implied ciriticism. Power struggles with the adolescent are to be avoided at all costs, and the therapist must ultimately respect the patient's refusal to discuss certain topics. Later in treatment, the teenager may well raise the issue spontaneously, particularly if the therapist has maintained a noncoercive stance.

At times, discussion of rather crucial topics such as suicide can lead to conflict with the youthful patient. The therapist may be able to focus on the relevant issues while avoiding an unproductive power struggle, as the following vignette illustrates.

A 15-year-old male was hospitalized after he had attempted suicide by ingesting minor tranquilizers. Despite his depressed, apathetic demeanor, he participated willingly in ward activities. Nonetheless, the youth replied to any attempt to discuss his suicidal ideation with the assertion "I'm going to kill myself sooner or later and there's nothing you can do to stop me." The more the staff tried to discuss suicide with the young man, the more determined he appeared to kill himself.

The inpatient unit requested a consultation with a cognitive therapist, who agreed to interview the adolescent. The young man proved to be cooperative and reasonably communicative, as long as suicide was not the focus. He discussed his interest in foreign films, an interest the therapist shared. Although he was suicidal, the patient did have vague hopes of a future career as a film director. The therapist was able to touch on some of the cognitions (eg, "The only place you can learn to be a director is Paris, and I don't speak French"), which prevented the young man from learning how to pursue such a career. Since the discussion of films and film-making dealt directly with the patient's hopelessness, it was hardly irrelevant to the issue of suicide. While the yong man seemed to become more alert and animated as the interview progressed, he withdrew into a hostile silence. The therapist recommended that the inpatient unit approach the topic of suicide gently, while encouraging the adolescent to attend films, select movies for his peers to watch, and inquire further into a career as a director.

By discussing an adolescent's interests or engaging in games, sports, and other activities, the therapist works to decrease threat and increase rapport. A common interview format involves alternating symptom-oriented discussion with periods of more informal conversation and activities. The adolescent who is able to express his or her interests or play games in the treatment setting may well experience a positive affect shift, upon which the therapist can build other interventions. Some adolescents will discuss sensitive issues only over a board game or while playing cards. Moreover, the adolescent's tastes in music, attitudes toward competition, and so on, all may provide the therapist with more relevant cognitions to explore.

Therapists of all orientations who work with adolescents learn that they must tolerate a high degree of frustration. Although cognitive therapy works best as a problem-focused treatment, the pace of therapy is slower and the scope of the therapist's data base is narrower with the adolescent patient. Adult norms for self-disclosure and prolonged self-exploration are not appropriate for most teenagers. Developing one or two treatment themes in a session is a major accomplishment for the therapist who works with adolescents.

It would be useful to reiterate a few recommendations made earlier[16,21,22] regarding the application of cognitive therapy techniques to adolescents:

1. Utilize briefer sessions than the traditional 50-minute hour.
2. Tolerate a modicum of noncompliance with treatment norms (eg, lateness, missed appointments).

3. Maintain ongoing family contact, so that systems interventions can occur on a continuing basis.

4. Respect the adolescent's sense of privacy and remember that not all sensitive topics require attention during one course of therapy. Distorted cognitions can be corrected by the adolescent in the years ahead, in the course of maturation, without professional help.

5. Avoid assigning complex homework assignments to adolescents who may already be experiencing school and/or learning difficulties: use more concrete, behavioral tasks between sessions.

FAMILY ISSUES

The contention that suicidal adolescents come from troubled family systems finds ample confirmation both in clinical practice and in the research literature.[23] Certainly for some suicidal teenagers the family system is so pathogenic that removal of the identified patient to a group home or foster family is desirable and perhaps necessary in order to prevent self-injury. In other instances, the adolescent will remain in the home, but the therapist will need to work toward modifications in the system of family interaction before individual change on the part of the teenager becomes a realistic possibility. It seems quite unlikely that there would be an instance in which treatment of a suicidal adolescent would not involve ongoing therapeutic contact with significant others. As described elsewhere,[16,22,24-27] cognitive interventions and family systems interventions can be readily interwoven by therapists with training in both modalities. The current chapter will not do justice to the complexities involved in blending the family and cognitive approaches because the primary purpose here is to introduce readers to the latter modality.

It is advisable to conduct the initial family interview with the entire family present. Haley[28] offers a particularly useful format for the first family interview.

The present authors' clinical impressions indicate that except for teenagers who attempt or threaten suicide, few adolescents are referred for treatment specifically for complaints associated with depression. Most adolescents enter treatment as a result of poor school performance, substance abuse, precocious sexual behavior, or defiance toward authority figures. Adolescents, their families, and even referral sources in the community often fail to recognize the underlying depression. The parents may describe the teenager as rebellious, lazy, hostile, manipulative, or immoral, and then attribute the presenting problems to their child's inherent character defects. Conversely, the adolescent may externalize blame for his or her difficulties onto parents, school, or siblings.

Parents and teenagers then may become locked into mutually destructive power struggles, while the real issues remain unaffected. Consequently, the first task of the therapist is to clarify the nature of the presenting problems.

The therapist often needs to work at the outset to change the family's attributions regarding the presenting complaints. Through constant criticism and conflict, the family may be continuously reinforcing the adolescent's negative self-image. Relabeling the problem as a depressive episode or a self-esteem deficit enables the therapist to reduce the tangible pressures on the teenager by blocking scapegoating in the family and restructuring parental expectations.

A 16-year-old female with no previous psychiatric contacts suffered an acute psychotic depression which required two months' stay in an inpatient unit. The girl was an excellent student, attractive, popular, and a skilled athlete. Her father was nearly 70, while her mother was over 20 years younger. The six children were all involved in the long-term antagonism between the parents. The house was in poor repair, and money was in constant short supply despite open talk of a small fortune saved by the father. While the father showered criticism and unreasonable demands upon the children, his wife calmly sabotaged his every move. Meanwhile, she would drink until she passed out each evening on the living room couch, in full view of the entire family.

Shortly after her discharge from the hospital, the teenager resumed her active life-style. The chronic parental friction was now available for comment by everyone in the family, and by the therapist. The mother had stopped her drinking entirely, and the father had modulated his harsh treatment of his daughter. Although neither spouse showed even the faintest desire to improve their relationship, the therapist was able to use their daughter's condition repeatedly as leverage to obtain changes in their behavior.

The marital tension persisted, but the identified patient knew that instead of quietly withdrawing into another depressive episode, she could raise any troubling family issues in the conjoint treatment sessions. By now, two of her siblings were raising similar concerns in the family meetings. The ongoing family treatment enabled the girl to avoid being overwhelmed by the chronic parental conflicts. As she neared her high school graduation, the therapist worked to help her separate more from the family. Family therapy cannot be a panacea, however. Even as she was able to separate from her parents, many of her own dysfunctional attitudes remained in need of change.

It is not surprising that depressed teenagers often are labeled as stubborn or defiant by their parents, because they are prone to fail in school, engage in acting-out behavior, or break family rules. As a consequence, parents may submit the identified patient to excessively harsh restrictions, such as being confined to home for unreasonably long periods of time. Rather than provide motivation for improved performance, these restrictions drive the teenager deeper into a sense of hopelessness and helplessness. The risks of runaway episodes and suicidal behaviors increase in such situations. It is the therapist's task to prevent the parents from cutting off the teenager from sources of reinforcement outside the home and to help them provide the adolescent with a mechanism for earning back privileges on an incremental basis. In accomplishing this task, the therapist will need to restructure parental attitudes and expectations.

Parental cognitions are frequently the targets of therapeutic work, in a variety of contexts. For example, a divorced mother sought treatment for her 12-year-old son who exhibited behavior problems both at home and at school. He had joined with neighborhood youths in episodes of vandalism, truancy, and drinking, and had threatened suicide numerous times. His mother's response to the unacceptable behavior was one of uncontrolled rage, and, predictably, prolonged escalating arguments resulted between them. When she became angry with her son she would think, "He is just like his father, and I couldn't control him either." The thought that her son was following in the footsteps of his sociopathic, alcoholic father both frightened and enraged her.

The therapist repeatedly pointed out the connections between her son's low self-esteem and his destructive behaviors. The mother slowly came to acknowledge that the boy's acting out reflected his poor self-image and his hunger for recognition, rather than his inherently anti-social character. The therapist asked the mother a number of times to describe the differences between her son and her ex-husband, so that she could learn to resist the tendency to scapegoat the boy. She was unable to think of such differences the first time the therapist presented this task, but over time she was able to recognize meaningful differences between the boy and his father. The therapist also focused on some of her general ideas about men, involving her son, ex-spouse, and the man she dated. She gradually began to react to her son's provocative behavior in a more calm, less hysterical fashion. From a more detached position, she was able to recognize more clearly the effects of his strong sense of inadequacy (and her negative attitudes) upon his behavior. She was surprised to see that as she changed, his behavior changed as well.

Consistent with a systems view of family interaction, the therapist also needs to examine how the depressed adolescent's own cognitions and behaviors can elicit parental responses that in turn reinforce the adolescent's own low self-esteem and hopelessness. In other words, a teenager may unwittingly create a self-fulfilling prophecy by expecting (and fearing or resenting) negative reactions from his or her parents and then engaging in acting-out behaviors that elicit these negative parental responses. Modification of such cyclic patterns in which one family member influences another's dysfunctional responses can be facilitated when the therapist assesses and intervenes with each person's cognitions and associated negative behaviors that maintain or exacerbate conflict in the family relationships.

CHANGING COGNITIONS

To reiterate a point elaborated earlier, cognitive therapy proceeds best in a spirit of collaborative empiricism, whereby therapist and patient work together to evaluate the validity and/or utility of the latter's cognitions. The therapist avoids a didactic or judgmental position, but consistently encourages the adolescent to examine his or her cognitions more closely. Cognitive changes seem to come about in a variety of ways. Some ideas will change because new information or gaps in reasoning come to light as a result of questioning by the therapist. Other ideas change because the patient has conducted "behavioral experiments" which fail to confirm them. The latter involve specific plans to take particular actions and to observe the consequences. For example, an adolescent who expects rejection by peers can first practice basic social skills during therapy sessions, and then experiment with brief interactions with school classmates. The therapist would structure the experiment in a manner that would maximize the probability of the adolescent's success and disconfirm the expectation of rejection.

Most typically, patients require repeated disconfirmatory experiences both in and outside the therapy hour, until gradually the bulk of the evidence supports a more functional way of viewing the self, the world, and the future.

The therapist chips away at the dysfunctional cognitions, looking for flaws in reasoning and opportunities to construct tests of certain ideas, but stops short of reassuring or arguing with the patient. A severely depressed teenager is likely to find a way to disqualify a compliment or other reassuring remark from a therapist (eg, "You wouldn't like me if you really knew me," "You're just trying to make me feel better"). Trying to argue a patient out of a strongly held belief has even more negative consequences, however. Brehm's theory of psychological reactance[29] would predict that an individual who perceives that his or her freedom to hold a particular belief was being threatened would respond by adhering even more strongly to that belief. If they feel attacked by the therapist, some patients, particularly adolescents, will expend considerable time and effort defending their right to feel hopeless, suicidal, self-critical, and so on. The cognitive therapist tries to move from less to more strongly held beliefs, while backing off quickly when a debate with the patient seems to be occurring.

The typical cognitive therapy techniques are intended to modify dysfunctional cognitions by exposing their underlying irrationality. However, there are occasions when, despite a very high level of belief in the dysfunctional cognitions, an individual may be able to acknowledge that it is simply not useful (and is probably harmful) to reiterate such ideas. Consequently, a patient with a seemingly ironclad rationale for committing suicide may allow little or no questioning of the rationale to occur, but may be willing to engage in techniques aimed at reducing the frequency of the suicidal cognitions (eg, thought-stopping or distraction procedures). As long as the cognitions underlying the suicidal wishes remain undisturbed, some measure of risk will persist. However, procedures that reduce the frequency and intensity of suicidal ideation can themselves reduce dysphoric affect and thereby serve as a bridge to changing the underlying cognitions.

Teenagers can learn to employ suicidal cognitions or any other upsetting ideation as cues to engage in distraction or other self-control strategies. Some strategies used by patients include exercising, walking around malls or shopping centers, calling a trusted friend or family member, writing down the negative thoughts and disputing them, and calling the local hotline or suicide prevention service.

The following sample dialogues from typical cognitive therapy sessions are offered in order to illustrate some of the concepts and procedures described in this chapter. The first dialogue occurred with Sherry, a severely depressed 17-year-old with a history of chronic suicide ideation and two prior attempts:

> Pt: I've got big problems. Bruce's parents say he can't see me any more. I'm gonna lose him.
> Th: How do you know that?
> Pt: He's the kind of guy who does what his parents want.
> Th: Have you spoken to him?
> Pt: No, but I will tonight or tomorrow.
> Th: So you don't know for sure yet if you're even going to lose him. Let's say you do, what's going to happen to you?
> Pt: I'm gonna have a rough time. He means a lot to me.
> Th: Do you think you'll make it?
> Pt: I don't know.
> Th: Will you try to kill yourself?
> Pt: I don't think so. But I know I'll be real depressed.
> Th: Do you remember what you told me when you broke up with Carl?
> Pt: That no one else would ever want me again.
> Th: Then what happened?
> Pt: I met Bruce. I didn't think I'd meet anyone again.
> Th: You're not even sure you're going to lose Bruce, yet. If you do, I'm sure it will be a big disappointment. But, I want you to remember that when you lost Carl you told yourself that things were hopeless and it turned out they weren't.

In this instance, the therapist was able to remind Sherry of some of her previous distortions regarding loss of an earlier boyfriend. The therapist also encouraged her to think beyond the perceived catastrophe of losing Bruce, while emphasizing that as yet the loss was by no means a certainty.

The following conversation took place with Mike, a 16-year-old who found it extremely difficult to approach girls even when he knew they might be interested in him. A year earlier, a girlfriend of his had rejected him in favor of an older boy.

Pt: I know this girl in biology class likes me. I've talked to her a few times and she's real nice, but I just can't make myself ask her out.

Th: What thoughts are holding you back?

Pt: I guess I figure there are guys who are better looking and who have more money than I do. Sooner or later, she'll find one of them.

Th: Like your old girlfriend did?

Pt: Yeah. Most of the girls I see around her go for looks and money.

Th: You mean all the girls you know are going to treat you like she did?

Pt: That's how it looks to me.

Th: Did you ever ask any girls what they look for in a guy?

Pt: No.

Th: I don't know what was in your girlfriend's mind when she dropped you, but I do know that sometimes guys don't always know what women want from them. Are there any girls around your age you could ask about this?

Pt: Yeah. I could ask my cousin and my brother's girlfriend.

Th: You won't feel embarrassed?

Pt: No. I want to hear what they have to say.

In this example, the therapist set up an experiment through which Mike could test his overgeneralization about girls. The therapist and Mike went on to rehearse the kinds of questions Mike would ask the girls he planned to approach and to anticipate possible meanings of some of the answers he might receive. Any such behavioral experiments shoud be set up by the therapist as a "no-lose" situation, with all outcomes considered beforehand. Otherwise the results may only reinforce the dysfunctional cognitions. An alternative route the therapist might have taken would have been to explore more fully with Mike what qualities he thought he lacked, since his remarks suggested that his self-image might have been a problem.

Generating Rational Responses

With practice, patients can learn to dispute their own dysfunctional cognitions. Under no circumstances does the therapist "spoon feed" rational responses to the patient. Rational responses develop as a direct result of the learning experiences encountered in the course of therapy. To be effective, a rational response requires at least a modest degree of belief on the part of the patient, and it may require a full session of therapeutic work to produce one or two effective rational responses.

The ability to generate rational responses during an actual stressful situation and thereby decrease emotional arousal represents the end point of a learning process that begins when the patient first starts observing his or her automatic thoughts. The therapist avoids giving the patient unrealistic or magical expectations, by emphasizing that the acquisition of rational responses is a slow process. Initially, the therapist and the patient jointly formulate and rehearse the rational responses in the treatment. If the teenager will record and respond to his or her thoughts between sessions, so much the better. Rational responses can address the utility of pursuing a particular line of thought, as well as the validity of the specific cognitions (eg, "Dwelling on mistakes I've made just depresses me and gets in the way of thinking of new solutions that will help solve problems. I can make more progress by figuring out ways to approach situations.").

Dealing with Boredom and Apathy

Depressed adolescents may complain of boredom with school, friends, family, and activities in a whining manner that communicates a sense of being "entitled" to things and antagonizes adults. Consequently, the depressed state of a withdrawn, possibly sullen teenager may go unrecognized by adults in the environment.

Stimulating the patient's participation in activities selected to increase his or her experiences of mastery and pleasure is a major component in the cognitive therapy of depression developed by Beck and his colleagues.[14] The therapist should take care to tailor any behavioral assignments as closely as possible to the adolescent's interests and areas of competency. Otherwise, the therapist may simply join the chorus of adults who make unreasonable demands upon the teenager.

As mentioned earlier, any behavioral assignment should be presented as a learning experience, so that the patient views it as a no-loss situation. Naturally, discussion of any prospective activities will elicit cognitions (eg, "I can't do it," "I won't like it," "I'll look stupid"), so that the behavioral assignment will allow the teenager to test some of his or her hypotheses. Of course, the depressed patient may well *not* enjoy new activities at first, so the therapist should prepare him or her for such a possibility.

Identity and Self-Esteem

Even for the well-adjusted teenager, preserving a positive self-image in the face of rapid physical development and changing role expectations represents a formidable task. Few adolescents possess the personal or environmental resources to cope with severe reductions in self-esteem. Since depressed adolescents are already acutely sensitive to their perceived deficiencies, they tend to overreact to any teasing or criticism they receive from peers, authority figures, or family members.

Teenagers often express rigid, all-or-nothing beliefs, eg, "People only respect the jocks," or "Guys will never be attracted to overweight girls." Adolescent peer groups reinforce such rigid beliefs by overemphasizing conformity and punishing deviation from narrow group norms.

A depressed 16-year-old girl stated, "At our school there are the 'stats' (high status), the 'jocks' and the 'druggies.' If you're not in one of those groups, you can just forget about a social life." Although many of the girl's peers did participate in the strict social regimentation she described, the therapist questioned her further about the young people who did not associate with one of the three groups. Were they all bored and lonely? What interests did she share with them? What reasons would people have for not liking her? What other activities were available to her that did not involve the same kids and same old rules? It may be necessary, as it was with this young woman, to focus on changing friendship patterns.

Success experiences in the natural environment seem to do more to bolster self-esteem than any interventions in the consulting room. It is advisable to become familiar with the appropriate resources (eg, YMCA, Police Athletic League, Catholic Youth Organization, Dungeons and Dragons Club) in the community. With some imagination and investigation, most teenagers can find something at which they can feel competent. Moreover, even the most disadvantaged communities offer training and support for a surprising variety of skills. In the course of treatment, the therapist will want to use any success experiences encountered by the patient to challenge hopelessness and self-denigration.

Depressed adolescents may isolate themselves from peers in part because they believe that other individuals do not struggle with similar troublesome thoughts and feelings. Consequently they persist in viewing themselves as different from and therefore inferior to others. Group therapy, bibliotherapy, and self-disclosure by parents or other significant adults in the environment all allow teenagers to discover that other people cope with similar difficulties. Teenagers are often shocked to learn that parents and other adults, whom they viewed as super-adequate, also struggled with thoughts of despair and inferiority at one time or another.

Rejection and Loss

A number of studies have found a strong relationship between loss of a parent and suicidal behavior in adolescents.[30-32] The deaths of significant others, parental separation or divorce, and loss of dating partners all may leave the teenager vulnerable to depressogenic thinking. Clinical experience indicates that a high percentage of suicidal adolescents reveals a history of multiple losses and/or rejections. Teenagers lack the psychological resources to cope with losses, while they also find it hard to ask for and receive the support from others that nurtures so many of their adult counterparts through similar stressful periods. Lastly, a depressed adolescent tends to see rejection or disapproval from others as reflections of their personal worth (or worthlessness).

Lilly, a 13-year-old, attempted suicide by taking 30 to 40 aspirin tablets a few weeks after her best friend moved to another state. A family interview revealed that when Lilly was 8 years old, a teenage brother died as a result of a "Russian roulette" incident. Two years later, her father left the family and moved several hundred miles away. She rarely spoke with him or saw him. Both Lilly and her mother became tearful when the father or the deceased brother were mentioned.

Lilly's mother appeared depressed, passive, and unable to manage the home. Lilly's 19-year-old brother lived in the home with his 15-year-old girlfriend. The couple, who seemed to run the house at times, flaunted their drinking and drug abuse in front of the mother.

Despite her friendly demeanor and her pretty, expressive face, Lilly was ridiculed by her peers at school for being too tall. She seemed to live for the approval of others and had few other interests, although her abilities in several areas seemed to be above average. She experienced the loss of her friend, who had served as her confidante and primary source of support, as a catastrophe.

The therapist consistently implied that Lilly's improvement would be tied to the mother's resolution of her own grief issues. He spent time discussing their various losses with Lilly and her mother. An older sister who lived in a nearby town also attended the sessions. She offered Lilly warmth and encouragement, while she served as a competent, confident role model. She also consistently allied with the therapist in pushing the mother to be more assertive in her own affairs.

The therapist stressed repeatedly the apparent irreversibility of the parents' separation, while questioning why the mother had not yet filed for divorce, dated other men, or made a number of important financial decisions. Slowly she assumed a less passive posture. The mother eventually developed a relationship with a man, ejected her son and his girlfriend from the house, and filed for divorce. With coaxing from everyone involved, Lilly began to be more involved in social and extracurricular activities, and boys suddenly took an interest in her. The family terminated treatment after five months of intermittent contact.

A year after treatment ended, Lilly's guidance counselor learned that she was again thinking of suicide and called the therapist to arrange for an immediate appointment for the girl. When she came for her session later that day, Lilly was tearful and agitated. The precipitant was another loss, this time rejection by her boyfriend. She explained, "He was the only guy who liked me. I'll never find anyone else. Nobody else could ever love me," and so on.

The therapist asked Lilly to pretend that he was a friend of hers who needed help because he had just lost his girlfriend. The following dialogue ensued:

Th: I know it's my fault she doesn't like me. There must be something wrong with me.
Pt: Maybe it's her problem. Maybe there's something wrong with her.
Th: No. It must be me. She left me so it's my problem.
Pt: Just because she left you doesn't mean there's something wrong with you.
Th: She was the only girl who ever wanted me. I'll never find anyone else.
Pt: You'll find someone else. You found her, didn't you?
Th: I'm too short to get another girl.
Pt: There are a lot of short girls. Besides, plenty of short guys get girls.
Th: But I probably won't find a girl I like as well as I liked her.
Pt: You might find one you like better.

One by one, Lilly provided splendid rational responses to the therapist's dysfunctional cognitions which of course were nearly identical to her own. The therapist was not easily convinced, however, so he maintained his lament for several minutes. Midway through the exercise, Lilly burst into a smile.

Lilly experienced a powerful affective shift by the end of the session, as she adopted a more realistic perspective on the loss of the boyfriend. The therapist met with Lilly and her mother for a few sessions subsequently, primarily to focus on the effects of the mother's boyfriend having moved into the house. The family terminated treatment within three

364

months, but the therapist was confident that Lilly would request his services again if she became depressed in the future.

CONCLUSION

The treatment of suicidal adolescents with any modality is a challenging enterprise, fraught with potential frustrations. Cognitive therapy has a directness that seems to appeal to teenagers. The assessment of cognitive factors such as hopelessness and low self-esteem provides the therapist with specific targets for intervention, which is especially helpful when dealing with suicidal individuals. The cognitive therapy procedures outlined in this chapter, including both cognitive and behavioral techniques, constitute a fairly structured approach that can help the depressed adolescent develop problem-solving skills, as well as enhance self-esteem and a realistic optimism. The therapist must be prepared to exercise considerable flexibility in the application of cognitive therapy with adolescent patients, and at least some intervention with parents and other significant people in the adolescent's life often will be essential. Consequently, experience with both cognitive and family systems approaches will be beneficial to clinicians working with depressed and suicidal adolescents.

REFERENCES

1. Blackburn IM, Bishop S, Glen AIM, et al: The efficacy of cognitive therapy in depression: A treatment trial using cognitive therapy and pharmacotherapy, each alone and in combination. *Br J Psychiatry* 1981;139:181–189.
2. Hollon SD, Beck AT, Bedrosian RC, et al: Combined cognitive pharmacotherapy versus cognitive therapy in the treatment of depression. Paper presented at the Annual Meeting of the Society for Psychotherapy Research, Oxford, England, 1979.
3. Rush AJ, Beck AT, Kovacs M, et al: Comparative efficacy of cognitive therapy and pharmacotherapy in the treatment of depressed outpatients. *Cog Ther Res* 1977;1:17–37.
4. Shaw BF: Comparison of cognitive therapy and behavior therapy in the treatment of depression. *J Consult Clin Psychol* 1977;45:543–551.
5. Epstein N: Hopelessness: The role of negative expectancy in suicidal behavior. Paper presented at the Annual Meeting of the American Association of Suicidology, New York, April, 1982.
6. Bedrosian RC, Beck AT: Cognitive aspects of suicidal behavior. *Suicide Life Threat Behav* 1979;9:87–96.
7. Beck AT: *Cognitive Therapy and the Emotional Disorders*. New York, International Universities Press, 1976.
8. Beck AT, Rush AJ: Cognitive approaches to depression and suicide, in Serban G (ed): *Cognitive Defects in the Development of Mental Illness*. New York, Brunner/Mazel, 1978.

9. Fleming B, Simon KM, Pretzer JL, et al: Beck's cognitive theory of depression: Current status of the empirical literature. Unpublished manuscript, University of Pennsylvania, 1982.
10. Beck AT, Kovacs M, Weissman A: Hopelessness and suicidal behavior: An overview. *JAMA* 1975;234:1146–1149.
11. Wetzel RD: Hopelessness, depression, and suicide intent. *Arch Gen Psychiatry* 1976;33:1069–1073.
12. Kovacs M, Beck AT: The wish to live and the wish to die in attempted suicides. *J Clin Psychol* 1977;33:361–365.
13. Ledwige B: Cognitive behavior modification: A step in the wrong direction? *Psychol Bull* 1978;85:353–375.
14. Beck AT, Rush AJ, Shaw BF, et al: *Cognitive Therapy of Depression*. New York, Guilford, 1979.
15. Bedrosian RC, Beck AT: Principles of cognitive therapy, in Mahoney MJ (ed): *Psychotherapy Process: Current Issues and Future Directions*. New York, Plenum, 1980.
16. Bedrosian RC: The application of cognitive therapy techniques with adolescents, in Emery G, Hollon SD, Bedrosian RC (eds): *New Directions in Cognitive Therapy*. New York, Guilford, 1981.
17. Beck AT, Epstein N: Cognitions, attitudes, and personality dimensions in depression. Paper presented at the annual meeting of the Society for Psychotherapy Research, Smugglers Notch, Vermont, June, 1982.
18. Beck AT, Kovacs M, Weissman A: Assessment of suicidal intention: The scale for suicide ideation. *J Consult Clin Psychol* 1979;47:343–352.
19. Miller M, Chiles J, Barnes V: Suicide attempters within a delinquent population. *J Consult Clin Psychol* 1982;50:491–498.
20. Beck AT, Schuyler D, Herman I: Development of suicidal intent scales, in Beck AT, Resnick HLP, Lettieri DJ (eds): *The Prediction of Suicide*. Bowie, MD, Charles Press, 1974.
21. Bedrosian RC: The adolescent in cognitive therapy. Paper presented at the Annual Convention of the American Psychological Association, Montreal, 1980.
22. Emery G, Bedrosian RC, Garber J: Cognitive therapy with children and adolescents, in Cantwell DT, Carlson G (eds): *Children's Affective Disorders*. New York, Spectrum, in press.
23. Haider I: Suicidal attempts in children and adolescents. *Br J Psychiatry* 1968; 114:1133.
24. Bedrosian RC: Ecological factors in cognitive therapy: The use of significant others, in Emery G, Hollon SD, Bedrosian RC (eds): *New Directions in Cognitive Therapy*. New York, Guilford, 1981.
25. Bedrosian RC: Using cognitive and systems interventions in the treatment of marital violence, in Barnhill L (ed): *Clinical Approaches to Family Violence*. Rockville, MD, Aspen, 1982.
26. Epstein N: Cognitive therapy with couples. *Am J Fam Ther* 1982;10:5–16.
27. Epstein N, Pretzer JL, Fleming B: Cognitive therapy and communication training: Comparison of effects with distressed couples. Paper presented at the Annual Meeting of the Association of Advancement of Behavior Therapy, Los Angeles, November, 1982.
28. Haley J: *Problem Solving Therapy*. San Francisco, Jossey-Bass, 1976.
29. Brehm JW: *A Theory of Psychological Reactance*. New York, Academic Press, 1966.

30. Crook T, Raskin A: Association of childhood parental loss with attempted suicide and depression. *J Consult Clin Psychol* 1975;43:277–282.
31. Dorpat T, Jackson J, Ripley H: Broken homes and attempted suicide. *Arch Gen Psychiatry* 1965;12:213–216.
32. Stanley E, Barton J: Adolescent suicidal behavior. *Am J Orthopsychiatry* 1970;40:87–96.

CHAPTER 22

GROUP COUNSELING FOR SUICIDAL ADOLESCENTS

CHARLOTTE P. ROSS
JEROME A. MOTTO

The identification of adolescents at high risk for suicide presents us with the formidable challenge of providing effective intervention and treatment. Based on the apparent relationship of suicide in this age group to family instability, interpersonal stress and alienation, the Suicide Prevention and Crisis Center of San Mateo County, California, developed a group counseling program for suicidal adolescents designed to address these conflicts. Seventeen youngsters participated in the program, which included 35 group meetings over a period of 40 weeks and an ongoing individual relationship with a special staff member. Twelve girls and five boys took part, of whom 10 had attempted suicide (26 attempts among them) and seven had threatened suicide. The focus was on 1) providing a supplemental support system, 2) learning constructive ways of dealing with stress, 3) enhancing self-esteem, 4) learning supportive techniques ("befriending") and 5) developing effective means of coping with dysphoria.

The development and implementation of the program are detailed, including unanticipated problems, special measures used, and prominent themes in the group process. No suicides or subsequent suicide attempts were found among the 14 group members available for a two-year followup. Further exploration of this approach appears warranted.

Social and professional concerns about rising suicide rates in adolescents have led to a number of studies, focusing primarily on psychosocial antecedents and characteristics of young people who are likely to engage in suicidal acts. These investigative efforts tend to reaffirm the close relationship of family instability, interpersonal conflict and alienation to self-destructive behavior in this age group.[1-4]

Identification of those adolescents at high risk for suicide leads us to the challenging task of planning and carrying out an intervention program for them. The acceptance of professional help by a troubled teenager is a big step in suicide prevention efforts, but is often only the

367

beginning of a long and arduous task. The treatment of adolescents and their families is frequently difficult, and at times the situation may even be considered "unworkable" with available treatment methods. Even in the most resourceful settings, the outcomes can leave much to be desired.[5-6]

The Suicide Prevention and Crisis Center of San Mateo County began a special prevention and intervention program for suicidal adolescents in 1975, focusing on early detection using a health education approach in the public high schools.[7] This program resulted in a significant increase of requests to the Center for both consultation and direct services for suicidal teenagers. The number of adolescents contacting the Center rose from 8% to over 20% of the Center's client population. In seeking to meet the special clinical needs of these young people, we began exploring the feasibility of group counseling for suicidal adolescents.

The concept of group work with depressed and suicidal adults is not new,[8-11] and various types of therapy groups for adolescents have also been reported.[12-15] We were able to find only two reports, however, of adapting the special potentials of the group approach to the unique clinical demands of adolescents at high risk for self-destructive behavior.[16,17] No specific guidelines were provided for such an effort outside a hospital, however, and the feasibility of such a group in an outpatient setting remained to be established.

The thought of taking on six to eight high-risk adolescents at once was somewhat intimidating, but our positive experience with adults in the same setting[18] encouraged us to pursue the possibility. The present discussion details our preparation and clinical experience in this effort.

ORGANIZATION AND STRUCTURE

The Suicide Prevention and Crisis Center is a contract agency of the San Mateo County Department of Health. The County Adolescent Services Unit, an integral part of the community mental health system, offered to collaborate with the Center in developing and implementing a group counseling program for adolescents at high risk for suicide.

It was agreed that the directors of the two agencies would serve as consultants to the program, and that each agency would provide one group leader. Primary responsibility for the group was assigned to the leader provided by the Center, a marriage, family, and child therapist with 12 years experience as a high school teacher and counselor. The County Adolescent Unit provided, as the co-leader, a psychology intern with special interest and training in working with young people.

To supplement the planning, two outside consultants were used for a critical review of plans, methods and goals. One brought a background of theoretical and clinical interest in suicide prevention, and experience with group therapy for high-risk adults (Jerome A. Motto, MD), and the other was a recognized leader in the theoretical and clinical aspects of group therapy (Irving Yalom, MD).

The goals of the group were to 1) provide a supplemental support network for its members, 2) help the participants learn strategies and skills for dealing with stress, 3) improve self-esteem, 4) learn supportive ("befriending") techniques, and 5) develop effective ways of handling dysphoria that would serve as alternatives to suicide.

The support network was planned to consist of the group leaders, the group members, and the Center's 24-hour crisis service, which offered both around-the-clock telephone and face-to-face "drop-in" services.

The original plan called for a "closed" group, with an unchanging set of members meeting for an hour and a half, 4:00 to 5:30 PM, weekly for 12 weeks. The meeting was subsequently advanced to 3:30 to 5:00 PM because the members preferred to come to the group directly from school. The duration of the group was also changed when some group members began expressing anxiety about the group ending at the 12th meeting. The group leaders shared some of this anxiety, and the decision was made to continue the group at least through the remainder of the school term. It was also decided that new members could be added as attrition allowed. The sessions were scheduled in a conference room in the same building that housed the Center, but not in the space occupied by it.

It should be emphasized that the group was designed to augment — not replace — other forms of therapy. Participants who were not in treatment when they entered the group were asked to see a therapist from the community health system, at least for an assessment interview, for the purpose of assigning a "therapist of record." The majority of members did this, but the resistance to it became so great that the idea was later abandoned.

In considering referrals to the group, an effort was made to accept any high-risk adolescent except those individuals whose symptoms indicated psychosis or violence, and those whose primary clinical problem was alcohol or drug abuse.

The name chosen for the group, "Peer Befriender Group," was derived from an earlier program developed by the Center, The Befrienders, which in turn was patterned after the long-established Samaritan organization based in Great Britain. In The Befrienders program, volunteers were assigned to "befriend" clients who might benefit from a supportive, goal-oriented relationship. Since a goal for the group was to help the members learn to befriend each other and themselves, the selection of this name seemed appropriate.

Formation of the Group

Candidates for the group were identified from three sources: the adolescent clients of the Center, referrals from high schools in the San

Mateo area, and Youth Service Bureaus. School referrals were generated by sending an information sheet about the project to the school nurses. This one-page description of the "Peer Befriender Group" invited referral of appropriate candidates of high school age to one of the group leaders.

The Center's background of prior collaboration with the school system facilitated referrals from school personnel. A high school "Suicide Prevention Education Program" had been carried out by the Center in the form of classroom discussions, followed by an offer of consultation for students about whom questions regarding suicide arose.[19] Thus, communication channels were already open between the Center and school personnel regarding any concerns the latter had about their students.

In addition, the group leader arranged to speak at a meeting of the San Mateo County school counselors and nurses to explain the program. She wanted them to meet her, ask questions, and discuss possible referrals and ways to facilitate offering the group to appropriate students.

Ongoing adolescent clients of the Center who were considered to be in need of additional support services were screened by the leaders and the Center director for admission to the group. Priority was given to those who seemed to be at greatest risk or in greatest need.

The invitation to join the group was presented by some variation of the following: "We are starting a support group for high school students who are depressed. It will be the sort of group in which members can learn that others may have similar problems, find ways to deal with their situation, and know where help is available. There is no fee charged for this group."

Additional information was provided in response to the youngsters' questions. The most frequently asked questions were:

Are you a teacher/nurse/counselor at my school? The concerns that lay behind this query were gently explored and found to deal with whether the group leader could influence the student's passing or failing, being transferred or having a notation of "unstable" entered in the school records.

The group leader did acknowledge that she was a teacher and a counselor, but made it very clear that her role with the group was a separate and different one. She explained that the group was a service offered by the Suicide Prevention and Crisis Center, and was not a part of the school system. From the adolescent's point of view, the group's separateness from the school was seen to be an asset, as it had no power or authority over its members, did not give homework, did not grade or discipline, and did not report to any other authority.

Who will know that I'm a member of the group — if I join it? Who will know what goes on in the group? This concern with confidentiality was a major and constant theme. The group leader assured them that their desire for privacy was understood and would be respected. She pointed out that, having been a teacher for several years, she knew many students and people in the school system. However, she promised that if she were even to pass a group member on the street, she would not say hello or acknowledge knowing them in any way unless they indicated first that it was permissible. They expressed appreciation for this sensitivity to their social structure.

Is my family supposed to come to the meetings? Will my family know? Will they have to give permission? We learned that most of their experience with "helping" resources had been limited to services which were, by law or custom, responsible to their parents, eg, school counselors, nurses, county health agencies, or the juvenile justice system. In addition, the majority of these students described their families as resistant to mental health treatment. In some instances, they indicated that their families might approve of their participation, but would do so principally as verification that the child, rather than the parent, was the source of the problem. In other instances, the parent's resistance seemed to stem only from lack of information and it was felt there was good potential for improving communication and gaining family cooperation. Two youngsters indicated unwillingness to consider the group if it required any family involvement, and subsequently described home situations in which their families warned them not to discuss "family problems" (ie, parental alcohol/drug abuse, battering, or incest) with "outsiders."

The group leader explained that, while she would like very much to have their family involved, she would respect their judgment regarding the risks they felt existed. They were told that they were free to tell their families as much or as little as they wished about the group, and that we would encourage but not require communication with their families.

California law enables a minor who has attained the age of 12, as well as designated maturity and intellectual levels, to receive mental health treatment or counseling on an outpatient basis without the consent of a parent or guardian. The professional person providing such service has the psychotherapist-patient privilege as regards confidentiality.[20]

Are you a psychiatrist? Will I have to see a psychiatrist? The adolescent's fear of being different is well known, but these youngsters' fear of being very different or even "crazy" was compounded by a fear that others would discover their shameful secret, which added to their distrust. They were assured that being in pain was very different from being "crazy" and that we (and/or their teacher/counselor/nurse) were concerned about the pain they were feeling. The leaders explained that there were many ways to deal with pain and despair, that one of these ways was to talk with others who were suffering similar feelings, that it was possible to learn new ways to handle problems, and that the group was intended to be a learning experience, not a psychiatric treatment program.

Each explanation and each piece of information was seen as an opportunity to develop the student's trust and confidence in the group leaders. In addition, a key factor in gaining their acceptance was our willingness to go into their territory, rather than requiring them to come to ours. In arranging an evaluation interview, the leader asked each youngster where he or she would find it easiest to talk. Most often, they preferred meeting at their school, although sometimes they requested that the interview be held at a neighborhood coffee shop. Again, we found that sensitivity to their problems concerning transportation, schedules and privacy was important and appreciated.

Sixteen adolescents were invited in this way, of whom 10 expressed an interest in coming to the Center to discuss it further, and made an appointment to do so. All 10 kept their appointments, which consisted of informal one-hour interviews with the two group leaders to resolve any remaining questions as to the desirability of participating. Of the 10 candidates interviewed, eight accepted the invitation to join the group, and two were seen by the interviewers as better served by other resources since they were seriously involved with alcohol and drugs. Those who elected to take part were given the date, time and place of the first meeting.

Composition of the Group

The selection procedures described above resulted in eight adolescents, five girls and three boys, being chosen to start the group. Six had a history of prior suicide attempts, and two were severely depressed and threatening suicide. Four were from the pool of Center clients, three were referred from the schools, and one was from a Youth Service Bureau. One of the boys made a suicide attempt before the first meeting, and following hospitalization, was sent outside the state, reducing the initial group to seven. They can be briefly described as follows:

Aileen, age 17, had severe family problems and had been referred to as a "pathological liar." She stated "I can make myself and everyone else believe *anything*." She had taken overdoses of aspirin or alcohol and drugs six times, saying she was not really trying to kill herself, but was angry with herself and wanted to punish her body. Aileen was referred by her school.

Jane, age 15, was physically abused as a baby and still had the resulting scars on her body. She was adopted at age 3 by older parents who were very strict and "old-fashioned." During a period of depression, she took an overdose while at school and was hospitalized for two weeks. She was referred by the Center, where she had been a frequent caller.

Arthur, age 18, had problems with his family and his girlfriend. He had made a recent suicide attempt with carbon monoxide that led to a two-week psychiatric hospitalization, but continuing psychiatric help was cut short by lack of funds. He was referred by his school.

Elaine, age 15, had a history of sexual abuse from the age of 9 and she had an abortion at 13. Her mother was bisexual. Chronic truancy and three suicide attempts (all overdoses) led to her calling the Center frequently, in spite of being very withdrawn. She was referred by the Center.

Carol, age 17, was referred by her school because of severe depression. The youngest of seven children in a violent family with an alcoholic father, she could barely contain her anger and had, on several occasions, pounded her fist through a wall. She had taken an overdose twice and had been hospitalized once for psychiatric care.

Erik, age 14, had problems with his family and school and had been in Juvenile Hall and other detention facilities. His father drank heavily and Erik used both drugs and alcohol. After two group sessions, Erik was sent to another state to avoid further detention. He had been referred by the Center.

Betty, age 14, had problems at school and with her family. She had been in detention homes three times for running away, and had abused drugs. Her mother suffered from alcoholism. She was severely depressed, and had been a frequent caller to the Center, from which she was referred.

Subsequent selection procedures led to the addition of 10 more participants. Six of these joined the group at the 13th meeting, by which time attrition had reduced the original group to three members. One more member was added at the 16th, 17th, 22nd and 24th meetings. Of these new participants, five had a history of prior suicide attempts, one had threatened suicide, and four were seriously depressed. Two were from the pool of Center clients, six were referred from the schools, one by her mother, and one by a friend. They can be briefly described as follows:

Georgia, age 15, was a homosexual student with severe health problems. She was referred from her school. She had a history of early physical and sexual abuse, and had used alcohol and drugs. She had made six suicide attempts with pills and alcohol, and had one psychiatric hospitalization.

Diane, age 16, was referred by her school due to two suicide attempts by overdose. She came from a seriously disturbed family in which she had been the victim of sexual abuse, and was still torn between allegiance to her divorced parents. She lived with the family of a friend, and intermittently returned to her father who was using drugs heavily.

Charles, age 18, was referred by his school after he attempted suicide by crashing his car following a quarrel with his homosexual partner. He made excellent grades, but when his homosexuality surfaced, he began to use drugs heavily. Conflicts in the family, especially with his father, had been reflected earlier by persistent truancy.

Adam, age 18, was referred to the group by his mother. She was concerned because Adam had not worked since graduating from high school, and he was severely depressed. Sexual identity issues were present, and he was full of rage at his overprotective parents. Adam only came to the group one time and withdrew because the girls were "not interesting" and the boys had "other issues."

Wynette, age 15, came from a broken home in which the paternity of the two children was not clear. Her mother lived with many men and was a heavy user of drugs and alcohol. Her mother was 14 when Wynette was born, and reiterated that she was sorry she ever gave birth to her. Wynette had taken overdoses of drugs on two occasions, "hoping I would sleep and not wake up." She also had a history of truancy.

Wanda, age 13, lived with her divorced mother who was very career oriented. Wanda got attention by taking drugs and staying out overnight with a boyfriend. Her mother was unable to set firm limits. Wanda was referred by the Center, which Wanda had called in a depressed state, threatening suicide.

Matthew, age 16, came from a very strict Catholic family that felt it was being punished by having a son like Matthew. His father was an attorney and his mother was very active socially. Matthew got attention by using drugs, driving fast, burning himself, and being active sexually. He had been expelled from school and from a summer program, and was working at a gas station. He was referred by a friend.

Christine, age 15, was referred by her school after two overdoses and one hospitalization. Her mother, father and stepfather were alcoholic. She and her older sister had been sexually abused, and she was struggling to get along with her stepfather and to maintain peace in the home when her parents were drunk. She felt very unattractive, and was beginning to experiment with drugs so she could be more accepted.

Louise, age 16, Christine's sister, was sexually active and in conflict with her stepfather about restrictions on her behavior. She had previously been an excellent student, but her school work had deteriorated. She had not attempted suicide, but was depressed and acting out sexually. She was referred to the group by her school.

Clarice, age 14, lived with her mother and two younger sisters. She was often left to babysit for her siblings and felt resentful at all the time her mother spent away from home. She used drugs to relieve her feelings of alienation and depression, but had made no suicide attempts. She was referred by the Center.

Three youngsters, two boys and one girl, withdrew from the program after only one or two meetings, thus they were not able to make use of the ongoing group process. The number of participants who were finally included in the counseling program was, therefore, 14 — 11 females and 3 males.

A total of 35 group sessions were held over a period of 40 weeks. The average attendance was 5.5 (range 2–11), and the average number of sessions each adolescent attended was 13.4 (range 7–29) over a mean period of 19.5 weeks (range 8–40). These data are detailed in Table 22-1.

OBSERVATIONS ON THE GROUP PROCESS

The Early Group Meetings

The first meeting began by the leaders introducing and giving background information about themselves. Each offered brief statements regarding his/her personal life. Both focused their comments on their involvement with adolescents, and their choice to work with youth because they liked and valued such relationships and experiences.

Table 22-1
Summary of Group Participation

Name	Age	No. of First Session Attended	No. of Sessions	Duration of Participation (Weeks)
Arthur	18	1	10	12
Aileen	17	1	10	9
Betty	14	1	19	18
Carol	17	1	29	40
Elaine	15	2	10	11
Jane	15	3	25	31
Erik	14	3	2*	1*
Louise	16	13	7	13
Georgia	15	13	15	28
Christine	15	13	17	28
Adam	18	13	1*	1*
Charles	18	13	15	28
Diane	16	13	7	8
Wanda	13	16	8	17
Wynette	15	17	8	13
Clarice	14	22	1*	1*
Matthew	16	24	8	17
Total			188	273
Mean			13.4	19.5

*Not included in totals or means.

The leaders next spoke of "rules," specifically, 1) being on time, 2) letting the leaders know if they would be unable to attend, 3) not smoking in the meeting room, 4) not using drugs or alcohol when attending group, and 5) protecting confidentiality. These were presented as issues of consideration and caring about each other and themselves, ie, not keeping others waiting or wondering, not polluting others' air, giving their full attention (nondrugged) in the meetings, and respecting each others' confidences by establishing trust and reliability. Thus, the rules were presented simply as "fair" ways of treating each other and themselves. All agreed to their appropriateness and to abide by them.

As a means of getting started, all the participants were asked to play the Name Game, which involved telling their name, where it came from, and how they felt about it. This provided the opportunity for members to begin talking about themselves and their families, to express some feelings, and to indicate their preference about their names or nicknames.

There was a lot of shyness in the beginning. Carol spoke of feeling shy in groups, avoiding dating, and sometimes putting people down as a way of distancing. Betty said very little and looked at the floor much of the time. Arthur spoke of moving back to live with his father and stepmother, but did not mention his recent suicide attempt or hospitalization. Aileen mentioned relatives she felt close to who lived in the midwest. Generally, during the process of getting to know each other, the participants stayed on safe ground.

The last point before breaking up was to emphasize the importance of communication, and the suggestion was made that members call the leaders or the Center if any need arose. To facilitate this, the leaders provided cards with their home telephone numbers.

In the second meeting, the group got off to a more dramatic start. Arthur had attempted suicide the day before the meeting by slashing his abdomen, and was hospitalized. Upon learning of this, the group leader had visited him at the hospital. She asked what he wanted her to tell the group. His immediate response was, "Anything you want," but after he talked about what had occurred (a fight with and rejection by his girl friend, and learning of an uncle's suicide), he asked that she explain it to the group just as it had happened.

The group members expressed shock, concern, curiosity, and caring. After the meeting, Aileen, Betty and Carol each asked if it would be permissible to visit Arthur in the hospital, and each did so. Aileen took flowers. Carol went to a great deal of trouble to get there, traveling an hour by bus.

Jane, who had missed the first meeting, did not appear at the second meeting either, and the group was told the reason: she was also in a hospital, after taking an overdose of drugs. The leader reported she had spoken to Jane and her physician, and Jane had asked permission to attend the group the following week.

These attempts brought the suicide issue clearly before the group. The reality of each member's thoughts and the consequences of their actions could not be avoided. It was sobering and frightening. Their reaction appeared to be to pull together, as each seemed to try to say to the other — wait, don't do that; it's not worth it.

Carol's "running away from home" to a girlfriend's house, which was discussed at length by the group, seemed almost mundane in the setting of the two suicidal actions. No effort was made by the group leaders to relate these acting-out episodes to starting the group counseling program, though much could be said about perceived expectations, low self-image and testing behavior. The subject was explored at some length by the staff outside the group, but no interpretations were suggested to the group itself.

At the third meeting, Arthur obtained permission from his doctor to come from the hospital to join the group (the Center is located in an annex to the hospital). Arthur spoke of how much the visits and phone calls from the group members had meant to him. In one call from Aileen, she had told him that she had taken an overdose of aspirin and was feeling sick. He immediately had the hospital crisis team and the Suicide Prevention Center contact her and make sure she was all right. Discussion of this in the group was dominated by Arthur's anger at Aileen, and at any group member who was so "stupid" and "selfish" as to attempt suicide instead of calling the group leader or other members to talk to them about their feelings.

The group leader drew out the feelings of being criticized and hurt that these comments evoked, and the group members were quick to assure Aileen that it was caring and not criticism they were trying to express. One said tearfully how sad and angry she would be if anyone in the group "really did it." This led to a discussion of how painful it is to lose someone important to you, like a best friend or a favorite uncle. It also led to a discussion of other sources of anger, such as parental discord, drinking, and excessive demands.

As members mentioned their families, they began to speak of sources of tension, especially parental behaviors, disciplinary methods, expectations from parents and teachers, and sibling conflicts. They also began expressing needs — the need for more unstructured time for themselves, male/female needs for recognition, and acceptance of their sexuality.

At the end of this session, telephone numbers were exchanged by all members of the group. Phone calls were eagerly solicited and promised in order to help a beleaguered member get through the weekend, if that became necessary.

The Adolescents' Befrienders

The enormous needs of these youngsters became painfully apparent within the first few weeks. They immediately began to turn to each other for support and, in addition, made frequent use of the Center's 24-hour telephone service. Their primary resources, however, were the group leaders, whom the youngsters called apparently at every critical point in their crisis-filled lives. Our concern that the members' needs for companionship, guidance, comfort and "rescuing" would exhaust the group leaders led us to seek an additional level of support for them. Thus was born the Adolescents' Befrienders.

We reasoned that to create what these youngsters most seemed to need and to be asking for, we would need to provide each member with a "therapeutic friend" on whom he or she could lean during a period of stress. It would be someone who understood the issues with which they were trying to deal, could support their positive efforts toward growth, and could serve as a role model. This description was not dissimilar to that of the Center's "Befrienders," the group of volunteers who gave large amounts of time to "befriend" and to work with individuals toward achieving specific goals and areas of growth.

From among the Center's volunteers, six people were selected on the basis of personality, attitudes, age, sex, and appropriateness as a "match" for the needs of each youngster. These volunteer Befrienders were required to make themselves available for personal contact several hours a week and whenever possible by telephone. In addition, they were to attend a supplemental three-hour training class to prepare them for their task, and then regular weekly staff meetings for ongoing supervision.

The first two Befrienders selected, a 20-year-old male and a 19-year-old female—both college students—were introduced to Arthur and Aileen just prior to the fourth group meeting. At that meeting, other members were asked if they would like to meet Befrienders. All said they would, and the "matching" proceeded over the next few weeks.

Four of the six Befrienders were young (19 to 24), and assumed the role of surrogate big brother or sister. The other two were a graduate student in her early 30s, and a professional woman in her 40s.

The Befrienders quickly became a significant part of the group experience. It appeared that the group had become a "family," and the Befrienders had extended the family to include that special person from whom each could seek advice, and whose behavior could be closely observed for alternative ways of relating to others. This extension of resources for the group members was particularly important because of the critical role that losses of significant persons had played in each member's life. It was inevitable that further losses would occur during the group experience; indeed, the group itself would eventually end.

Although time limitations were very real, the potential for providing a model for identification through the Befriender part of the program seemed essential. Even if it went no further than preparing for loss, coping with loss, and reordering one's life after a loss, it could provide the youngsters in the program with a source of strength, however modest, for many losses still to come.

Group Themes

The first three sessions introduced the primary themes that were to engage the group over the ensuing nine months: family relationships, peer relationships, loss–grief–pain, anger, suicidal impulses, and what to do when these are experienced as overwhelming.

Family relationships, and the absence of family relationships, provided the bulk of the material for discussion, as every group member shared a need to resolve conflicts in this area. Every possible conflict seemed to surface: parental expectations and demands, parental alcoholism and depression, parental child abuse and incest. There was too strict limit-setting ("No matter what I want to do, my father says, 'No'") and not enough limit setting ("I can do anything I want and she doesn't say anything"). There were struggles to get away from the parents ("I just want out!") and strivings to find "real" biological parents, after a series of foster parents ("My foster parents are going to help me find my real parents!" Rejoinder: "I've never seen my real father, but I met my mother once, and I hope I never see her again"). Perceived role reversal was also a recurrent source of family stress ("I want to leave, but then Mom would have nobody to take care of her").

The theme of peer relationships centered around issues of dating, what thoughts one person had about another, the pain of perceiving others' thoughts about the self as negative, and the disbelief of perceiving them as positive. The group members were quick to support or to reassure each other as the situation required, without much weighing of all the elements involved. There was intensified discussion of boy-girl relationships when Christine and Matthew began to come early to see each other before the group met, held hands during the group meeting, and arranged to get together at a vacation area where both families were going in the summer. This precipitated some antagonistic comments from Carol about "not trusting men," and extended discussions about boyfriends and their vagaries, especially if they used alcohol. It also provided an opportunity to discuss the good feeling of a "natural high" when the euphoric mood of Christine and Matthew led them to laugh and giggle inappropriately when group members were speaking of serious issues. The resentment of feeling "laughed at" by the offending couple was settled with appropriate apologies. Christine apparently wanted to keep the good will of the group, but seemed to find it difficult to empathize when she felt so fortunate to have Matthew as her "first real boyfriend."

The theme of boyfriends was tied to anxiety about losing peer relationships, and how painful it was when that happened. The problem of coping with that pain absorbed the attention of the group repeatedly, extending to the loss of family members, and even of pets. In one situation (at the 32nd session), the insistence of her foster parents that Jane give up a pet dog precipitated a serious suicidal episode. She tried to use alcohol to ease the pain, but it did not help. Feelings were stirred of not being "any good at anything," of being "unrecognized," and "unwanted," and a five-page suicide note said that she felt "her heart had been cut out" when the dog was taken to the Humane Society. She "saw no reason to go on living." The group leader arranged for her to be in a protected setting for a time, and the group came up with a plan to find a good home for the pet. The crisis gradually subsided without suicidal behavior, but a good deal of group time and energy was absorbed by it.

The theme of suicide was accepted as the kind of impulse that arises when you hurt badly. So many experiences proved to be a source of hurt that the specter of self-destructiveness was never very far away, though a number of meetings went by without explicit mention of it. The content was more on recounting the means of fending it off—using alcohol or drugs, running away, arguing with key persons, getting help from the group leaders, other group members, or from a Befriender.

Though despondency was made evident in many ways, anger was the predominant affect expressed verbally, playing some part in essentially every situation that touched these youngsters' lives. Thus, the persistent themes of loss, pain and self-destructive impulses were consistently intertwined with manifestations of anger as well, usually in the form of defiance of parent figures, school personnel, or employers.

The major theme of the counseling effort was the acknowledgment and acceptance of these feelings, and what to do when they threatened to overwhelm the person experiencing them. The essence of the communication was, first, there are people who care, second, this is who they are, third, this is how to get in touch with them, fourth and most important, if you give them a chance to express their caring, they can help you. The help may be simply in listening, understanding and providing emotional support, or it may be in any number of more active ways that will ultimately lead to a lessening of the pain of the experience. The most encouraging aspect of the group counseling project was that both the Center staff and the young people in the group became increasingly aware that these simple principles seemed to work in practice.

Group Characteristics

It must be asked how this group differs from those composed of suicidal adults and from other adolescent counseling groups. Though adolescents are unique in their individual characteristics, a few generalizations were suggested by this experience.

A striking issue was the degree of need these youngsters brought to the group. This need was not only for emotional support to help cope with self-destructive impulses, but evident in practically all aspects of their lives. As the themes noted above suggest, the family turmoil, peer pressures, and demands of parents or parent figures, jobs, school and internal needs, in combination posed a formidable challenge. Even the numerous crisis and decisions of everyday living (eg, transportation, temporary shelter) were brought to the group and group leaders in such abundance that exhaustion appeared inevitable unless the support system was increased beyond that ordinarily provided in group work with either adolescents or adults.

A second characteristic, closely related to the sustained high level of need, was the intensity of feeling that was generated by stress situations. This is a well-recognized characteristic of the adolescent period that has made helping efforts for this age group a difficult task whatever modality is offered. With youngsters who turn to suicidal behavior when in despair, the extreme emotionality demonstrated in the group setting poses a very special concern. For example when Jane had to relinquish her pet dog, it was an anguish that she seemed unable to bear without help from all the elements in the support system. Similarly, when Arthur was vehemently critical of Aileen for taking an overdose of aspirin, he seemed unaware of the ludicrousness of doing so from the hospital where he had been admitted for a serious suicide attempt of his own.

A third characteristic of the group was its high level of communication among group members, between individual members and the elements of the support system, and among the supporting elements. Thus, a telephone call from one member to another might result in a serious problem being made known to the second person's Befriender, who would call the Befriender of the member in trouble, who in turn would call that member and also let the group leader know of the situation. The group leader might invite the individual to share the matter with the group at the next meeting, though she usually let the group member decide the time and extent of engaging the group in the problem. There tended to be so intense a feeling of cohesion in the group atmosphere, especially when a member was in a crisis, that the usual adolescent concern for confidentiality did not seem to be an issue. It was as though a message to anyone in the system was a message to the entire system.

382

Even after one member (Betty) moved to another state, letters were exchanged with others in the group, who then shared the interchange at the next meeting.

This communicative openness apparently had only one condition: the person should mean what he or she said. As long as that requirement was fulfilled, no matter how distorted or exaggerated the content, immediate support and emotional strokes were forthcoming from the other group members. It seemed as though a need to be needed and to be a source of help vitiated any need for critical listening and careful weighing of the different sides of the issue. Empathic responses were unreserved and undiscriminating. The practical problems involved were left largely to the group leaders; the peer group was thus quite predictable and dependable as an ally of any member in a crisis situation. This differs markedly from what so often occurs in traditional group settings, in which a serious suicidal state in one member tends to result in the other members becoming acutely anxious, and drawing away from the one in crisis.

When the condition of honesty was not fulfilled, the group could feel so offended and betrayed that hostility and rejection would be triggered just as uncritically as support was offered under the usual circumstances. Thus, when it was learned, in the course of trying to find help for one member (Elaine), that the member had given a false age and had concealed information about her earlier contacts with the health system, the group was unequivocal in expressing its rejection. Even the group leaders were unable to find reason to protect Elaine from the group's feeling that it had been "conned," and they arranged for her referral back to her prior therapist. It is pertinent here that the group had responded with a great deal of feeling to Elaine's life experiences, which were particularly painful and touching. Having evoked this very intense emotional response, Elaine was felt by the group to have used them and their feelings dishonestly, and there was little evidence of understanding or compassion on the part of the group for her having done so.

Issues of sexuality were not prominent in the group setting, though this was recognized by the group leaders as an important developmental issue. Two group members spoke openly about sexual matters, but not in the context of conflict. One (Georgia) was lesbian, and spoke freely of her difficulties and disappointments with her sexual partners. The other (Wynette), in the context of seeking a definition for "genuine feelings of love," spoke of the sounds she overheard when her mother was with various boyfriends. Though some discussion of sexuality ensued, the group seemed uncomfortable with the topic, with some clear embarrassment when sexual activity was discussed openly, and the subject was not explored in depth.

In view of the frequency of incest and of conflict with parents regarding sexual activity, this seemed surprising at first. Resentment about limits being placed on their own sexual behavior shared the broader theme of "problem parents" and conflicts around discipline. The issue of incest, however, was clearly taboo. The five group members with such experience were reluctant to discuss it in the group, or allow the group leader to explore it. In individual discussions, it became clear that they saw themselves as different from everyone else because of their experience, that their self-esteem was greatly diminished by it, and that the powerful emotional block to exposure was intensified even more by the presence of males in the group. In most instances, the history of incest was not realized until the youngsters gradually let it be known to the group leader after several weeks or months of group participation. The need for a special group to deal with this subject led to the subsequent development of a Family Stress Service at the Center, which collaborated with the County Children's Protective Services in appropriate cases.

School activity was also an important issue that received relatively little time in the group. Its significance as a source of stress was clear in some instances, but the most prominent role of the school seemed to be as an instrument for the expression of anger and independent striving. Truancy or inadequate effort in the schoolroom were means of punishing a parent, asserting autonomy, or simply a means of withdrawing from a painful situation, akin to running away from home. Support was given for the idea of doing well in school, but the issue did not demand a significant amount of group time or energy.

Direct encouragement to take constructive action in various situations was provided, usually as a way to stimulate learning new coping methods. For example, when Matthew expressed reluctance to participate in family therapy, Georgia spoke convincingly about how helpful it had been for her, and Matthew was persuaded to try it. On another occasion, when Carol stated that an attractive boy's interest in her could not be due to any attractiveness on her part, the group reassured her that she was indeed a pretty girl, and encouraged her to accept that as a basis for handling the relationship. When Matthew was doubtful of the value of using a punching bag as a way of getting hostile feelings out, Christine was able to get him to accept one simply by her persistent encouragement that he do so.

The strong nurturing personality and highly involved, maternal style of the primary group leader had an enormous impact on the group. From the first session, she demonstrated that her involvement was not limited to the one and a half hours of the group meeting, and her support was not limited to merely discussing their problems. Members began "testing" her commitment from the outset, and continued to do so repeatedly throughout the program by calling for help at all hours of the day and night. Some of the active interventions undertaken by the group leader in response to such calls were:

- Immediately going to visit members of the group who were hospitalized.
- Going out at midnight to pick up and take home a group member who left home after being beaten by her brother; notifying police of her action, and providing shelter for three days for a cooling off period for the family.
- Providing cautious support for Jane in her search to find her biological parents; helping with placement in a temporary foster home, and subsequently with placement in a group home.
- Meeting with the California Youth Authority to explore options and negotiate actions for Betty that would be in her best interest.
- Accompanying Georgia to the police department to report rape, and to the hospital for a physical examination.

TERMINATION

The 12-week prearranged time limit for the group had been set in order to avoid asking the youngsters for a commitment of time which would appear to be either vague or excessive. Although this limited commitment may have been appealing to the youngsters when considering entering the group, it became a source of anxiety when considering leaving it. As members began to express their concerns ("I don't know what I'll do when I can't come to group anymore"), Center staff explored ways to deal with their anxiety. Although the befrienders were seen as an aid in bridging the stress of the termination process, it appeared that the group needed more time. All staff members were aware of the association of attempted suicide with the termination of a supportive and meaningful relationship, and the need for a gradual transition to a modified support system.

Both the group leader and co-leader were scheduled to leave the area within two months following the originally planned termination date. It was decided that new leaders would be brought into the group and that the departing leaders' remaining time would be used for a period of transition. The group could then continue at least through the end of the school term. The transition period also involved a number of external changes for the group — the ending of the school year, the demands of summer jobs, and "enforced" vacations (two members were sent to spend the summer with a divorced parent living in another area).

Another factor affecting the termination of the group was the different style and personality of the new group leader. The original leader took a very active role, as described above, becoming deeply involved with each member. She dispensed encouragement, support and firmness with a confidence and vitality that commanded trust and tended to rivet the group into a close unit. The style of the new leader was more introspective, and her caring was expressed in a less active way. Her ability to elicit feelings, and to encourage expression of them, was geared more toward developing individual growth and problem solving than in furthering strong group ties.

Consequently, as the time for ending the group again approached, and the issue of termination was again raised, the members appeared ready to deal with it. Their feelings of apprehension about "making it" were intermingled with increased confidence in their ability to use what they had learned "on the outside."

It has been stated that, "if the therapist has done his job properly, the patient no longer needs him and breaks all contact."[21] This appears to be an admirable goal, indeed, but it was not seen as appropriate to our group. Members were encouraged to continue contact with the Center, and were assured that future requests for help — or just someone to talk to — would not indicate failure on their part, but would demonstrate taking good care of oneself.

FOLLOWUP

Followup calls two years after termination of the group provided information about all but three of the group members (Table 22-2), two of whom (Betty and Clarice) had moved away, and one (Elaine) could not be located. No suicides or subsequent suicide attempts were reported to the followup interviewer.

Two members had brief psychiatric hospitalizations. Louise reported that she had been a patient on a psychiatric inpatient unit, and then had lived in a half-way house for six months. At followup she had been seeing a psychiatrist on an outpatient basis for the prior six months, but "can't open up to her because she (the therapist) is not emotionally involved." Louise asked if she could come back into the group.

Jane was placed in a group home shortly after the group ended. She did well there, "graduated," and moved to a group home for older girls. This move precipitated a severe depression and she was again hospitalized. At followup she was living with a foster family, would soon graduate from high school, and was looking forward to college. She had kept in touch with the Center and referred to Center staff as her "real" family.

Table 22-2
Followup Status of Group Members after Two Years

Name	In School Yes	In School No	Has Job Yes	Has Job No	Lives with Parents Yes	Lives with Parents No	In Treatment Yes	In Treatment No	Overall Status Improved	Overall Status Same	Overall Status Variable	Overall Status Worse
Arthur		X	X		X			X	X			
Aileen	X		X		X			X	X			
Betty			living in another state									
Carol		X		X	X			X				X
Elaine			unable to locate									
Jane	X			X		X		X			X	
Erik	X			X	X			X		X		
Louise	X			X	X		X					X
Georgia	X			X	X		X		X			
Christine			X		X			X	X			
Adam		X		X		X		X		X		
Charles			X			X	X		X			
Diane	X		X		X			X	X			
Wanda	X		X		X			X	X			
Wynette		X	X			X		X		X		
Clarice			living in another state									
Matthew		X	X			X		X	X			

Adam, who attended only one meeting, and Erik, who was sent away after his second meeting, were found to have problems similar to those that originally brought them to the group. Adam's mother reported that he had again lost his job and spent most of his time on the streets. Erik was again having difficulty getting along with his parents.

Carol spoke sadly of the many difficulties she had faced since the group. She had been abandoned by her boyfriend, had an abortion, and a friend of 11 years had recently died. She did not have a job and was living at home. She quoted the group leader as having once told her that she was "too strong to commit suicide," and said she often repeated this to herself in order to keep going. She added that the group had enabled her to survive a very difficult time in her life, and expressed a wish to talk to the group leader again.

Arthur reported he was working as a house painter and "doing great." He said he had not suffered any further bouts of depression and had sought no other therapy.

Aileen stated that she was attending a community college and holding three part-time jobs. She added that she would like to be in a group again, if she "could be of further help to the members."

Christine, now a high school senior, was working as a salesgirl. She reported that things were "O.K." with her and she did not need or want any further counseling. She added that she had made friends at school, her life was busy, and she felt she was handling things satisfactorily.

Georgia stated that she was still seeing her therapist, and "everything is going well."

Charles was trying to start a gardening business, and reported that "starting a business is rough," but he did not get depressed as he had before. Following the group, he had continued in individual therapy with the co-leader through a county program.

Diane reported that she was "doing fantastic." She graduated from high school, was attending a community college, and working in sales. She was still living with her father, who had developed an appropriate relationship with her. She commented that the group was a "wonderful experience" and had enabled her to survive a "horrible time" of her life. She added that she missed the group leader.

Wanda was a high school junior, working as assistant manager of a telephone answering service. She was very proud of earning an impressive salary. She reported that she still saw her Befriender, talked to her at least two times a week, and referred to her as her "best friend in the whole world." She stated "I'm really doing great now."

Wynette dropped out of school after completing the 11th grade. She obtained a job, moved in with a girlfriend, and decided that she would not return to live with either her mother or father, who battled continually over her custody.

Matthew joined the army shortly after the group ended. His mother reported that he seemed to be doing well, and added that nothing else had reached or influenced him in the positive way the group had.

DISCUSSION

The essence of group counseling may be seen as the creation of a supplemental or substitute family designed to facilitate growth. For suicidal adolescents, that process involves primarily two tasks: The gratification of extreme dependent needs while supporting realistic independent strivings, and the nurturing of a healthy and realistic sense of self, or identity. Group work with nonsuicidal adolescents differs primarily in the amount of energy, disruption and social concern that are associated with self-destructive behavior.

A suicidal state is considered by some to be a contraindication to group therapy,[22] but this cannot apply when reduction of the impulse toward self-destruction is a primary goal in the formation of the group, and coping with that impulse is a powerful element in group unity and cohesiveness. The structure of a family-like resource for this task has enormous demands put on it. The first task is to understand earlier life experience, how family and peer patterns are perceived by the adolescent, and how the resulting stresses are defended against by self-destructive actions. The second, and most demanding task is to persevere in standing by the youngster supportively while encouraging a more constructive way of handling painful feelings.

The process of carrying out such an effort with troubled adolescents is an exacting task, even without the presence of suicidal states. Bates[23] points out the need to be prepared for unexpected confrontation at any time, and observes further how inexperienced group counselors may at first be naively confident, on the basis of their individual counseling skills, but that "it requires only a few grueling sessions to raise their panic level to the red button stage."

It seems clear that adolescents are more responsive to an "active relatedness" on the part of group leaders than to an introspective style. Ott et al[17] found themselves using a number of structured activities, such as pictures or stories, to stimulate active interchange in the group. They attributed the inertia problem to the overwhelming depressive state of the participants, as well as to their age.

When undertaken in a hospital setting, structuring a support system is made easier by the staff members' proximity and accessibility. For example, Ott et al[17] were able to provide a combination of individual evaluation, family therapy, psychodrama using puppets, milieu therapy, social education, and group therapy with nine suicidal adolescents on a neuropsychiatric ward. The group sessions were considered the nucleus of the treatment program. After a four-month period of this multidimensional approach, they observed improved social adaptation, and 18 months after discharge reported the participants doing satisfactorily in school or at work, and with no further suicide attempts.

In an outpatient setting, caring adults whom the adolescent trusts and can reach at any hour are more difficult to provide. Our initial assumption — that the group members, group leaders, around-the-clock telephone crisis service, and individual counselors would suffice — proved incorrect, and necessitated the addition of the Befrienders. That these were trained volunteers suggests that, given current resources, perhaps only through collaboration with volunteer agencies can an adequate support system for suicidal adolescents be achieved for outpatient groups.

Though difficult to assess, the peer support system provided by the group deserves attention. During group meetings, it appeared to have a clearly positive effect. Outside the group, much undoubtedly transpired which was not reported in the group. In spite of this, we feel that the very presence of the peer network exerted a supportive influence, and probably reduced the demands placed on the group leaders and the Center. Though group workers have tended to take a negative view of outside contacts between group members,[21] in this setting we see it as a necessary and valuable resource. A program established for suicidal adolescents in Krakow and Lublin, Poland, focuses largely on the stabilizing influence of social interaction between the participating young people, their friends and families. In this multifaceted program, the "Social Club" is a synonym for the "Suicide Prevention Center."[24]

The only previous report of an outpatient group specifically for suicidal adolescents, to our knowledge, is that of Hadlik.[16] It was carried out in Brno, Czechoslovakia, in response to an increasing suicide rate in this age group. Hadlik cites "adolescent emotionality" as a characteristic requiring a special approach, noting that young people form groups more easily than adults, and participate more actively and spontaneously. He observed five prominent patterns in the group process: 1) by recognizing that their problems were the same as others, the youngsters' self-confidence increased, and by discussing those problems, they achieved a better understanding of their parents' and their own behavior, 2) a tendency of some adolescents to model their behavior after that of other group members, 3) maximum group communication stabilized self-confidence, 4) sympathetic support was elicited from other group members, and 5) through the process of being helped, motivation to help others was generated.

An initial plan that could not be carried through was to obtain serial ratings on a scale measuring suicidal potential, and on the self-administered Rosenberg Self-Image Questionnaire. Though theoretically and methodologically indicated, the consensus was that the clear advantages of such a testing program were outweighed by the risk of alienating the participants before the group counseling program was even underway.

CONCLUSIONS

Group counseling for suicidal adolescents is seen to be a feasible program in an outpatient setting. In the project discussed here, the experience, knowledge, skill and dedication of the group leader were recognized as key elements in the group's development.

The critical factors in the group process appeared to be the understanding and involvement of staff members, and the subsequent facilitation of communication in the group. The group members gradually came to speak of their own painful feelings as well as express supportive responses to the anger, guilt and despair of the others. A sense of connectedness akin to a feeling of "family" gradually developed, which provided a safe setting to share feelings, to seek refuge in the group's caring and support, and to reach out to help others.

There is a great need for trials of group counseling for suicidal young people in various clinical settings, mindful of the unique strengths inherent in the group structure as well as its requirements for back-up support. It can be of special value in those instances when the young person has no family available or the nature of the family interaction precludes it having a supportive role. Though current practice puts much emphasis on family therapy as an essential part of an adolescent's treatment program, in those situations in which that is not feasible, we should not be dissuaded from offering the best substitute we have.

Lastly, in the face of our increasing problem of suicide in youth, group therapy for suicidal adolescents can be considered a promising supplement to the traditional treatment modalities of individual therapy and family therapy. Ever-present peer support can provide a stabilizing mechanism that goes beyond the usual counseling relationship, and can help make it possible for the traditional modalities to proceed more effectively.

REFERENCES

1. Berman A, Cohen-Sandler R: Suicidal behavior in childhood and early adolescence. Paper presented at 13th Annual Meeting of the American Association of Suicidology, Nashville, TN, 1980.
2. Tishler C, McKenry P, Morgan K: Adolescent suicide attempts: Some significant factors. *Suicide Life Threat Behav* 1981;11:86–92.
3. Shaffer D: Diagnostic consideration in suicidal behavior in children and adolescents. *J Am Acad Child Psychiatry* 1982;21:414–416.
4. Topol P, Reznikoff M: Perceived peer and family relationships, hopelessness and locus of control as factors in adolescent suicide attempts. *Suicide Life Threat Behav* 1982;12:141–150.
5. Meeks J: *The Fragile Alliance.* Baltimore, MD, Williams & Wilkins, 1971.
6. Stone M: The parental factor in adolescent suicide. *Int J Child Psychother* 1973;2:163–201.
7. Ross C: Mobilizing schools for suicide prevention. *Suicide Life Threat Behav* 1980;10:239–243.
8. Farberow N: Vital process in suicide prevention: Group psychotherapy as a community of concern. *Life Threat Behav* 1972;2:239–251
9. Motto J, Stein E: A group approach to guilt in depressed and suicidal patients. *J Religion Health* 1973;12:278–285.
10. Billings J, Rosen D, Asimos C, Motto J: Observations on long-term group psychotherapy with suicidal and depressed persons. *Life Threat Behav* 1974; 4:160–170.
11. Asimos C: Dynamic problem-solving in a group for suicidal persons. *Int J Group Psychother* 1979;29:109–114.
12. Westman J: Group psychotherapy with hospitalized delinquent adolescents. *Int J Group Psychother* 1961;11:410–418.
13. Kaufman P, Deutsch A: Group therapy for pregnant unwed adolescents in the prenatal clinic of a general hospital. *Int J Group Psychother* 1967;17: 309–320.
14. Bratter T: Group therapy with affluent, alienated, adolescent drug users. *Psychother Theory Res Pract* 1972;9:308–313.
15. Berkovitz I (ed): *Adolescents Grow in Groups.* New York, Brunner/Mazel, 1975.
16. Hadlik J: Group psychotherapy for adolescents following a suicide attempt, in Fox R (ed): *Proceedings of the International Congress for Suicide Prevention*, London, 1969. Vienna, International Association for Suicide Prevention 1970, pp 57–59.
17. Ott J, Guyer M, Schneemann K: Multidimensional clinical psychotherapy of a group of children and adolescents after attempted suicide. *Psychiatr Neurol Med Psychol (Leipz)* 1972;24:104 – 110 (in German).
18. Frey D, Motto J, Ritholz M: Group therapy for persons at risk for suicide: An evaluation using the intensive design. *Psychother Theory Res Pract* (in press).
19. Ross C: Teaching children the facts of life and death, in Peck M, Litman R, Farberow N (eds): *Youth Suicide.* New York, Springer (in press).
20. California Civil Code, Section 25.9; California Evidence Code, Section 1014.5.
21. Yalom I: *The Theory and Practice of Group Psychotherapy.* New York, Basic Books, 1975.

22. Horwitz L: Indications and contraindications for group psychotherapy. *Bull Menninger Clin* 1976;40:505–507.
23. Bates M: Themes in group counseling with adolescents, in Berkovitz I (ed): *When Schools Care*. New York, Brunner/Mazel, 1975, pp 56–68.
24. Pluzek Z: Efficacy of a treatment program for attempted suicides among youth, in Aalberg V (ed): *Proceedings of the 9th International Congress for Suicide Prevention*, Helsinki, Finland, 1977. Helsinki, Finnish Association for Mental Health, 1978, pp 114–118.

CHAPTER 23

THE FAMILY THERAPY
OF SUICIDAL ADOLESCENTS:
Promises and Pitfalls

JOSEPH RICHMAN

This chapter deals with a method of treating suicidal adolescents and their families, describes some of the barriers in the way of effective therapy, and discusses how to surmount these. The goal of these interventions is to release the forces of growth and caring, so that the adolescent can become more autonomous and the family move from being a destructive or helpless force to a self-help group. The basic working premises are that all healing is self-healing, that the family as a system possesses similar properties in the form of a family growth process, and that the main task of the therapist is to remove the barriers to maturity, individuation, caring, and cohesion.

Family therapy for suicidal adolescents requires special skills and training in the therapist, including such personal qualities as sensitivity, empathy, self-awareness, and a working through of his or her own destructive and self-destructive proclivities. Required, too, is a background in family therapy, with experience in the treatment of suicidal persons. While the need for such qualifications appears obvious, it may be necessary to insist upon the point since too many therapists lack the background for treating the suicidal person and are not aware of such deficits. One therapist commented after the suicide of one of his patients, "We tried family therapy, but it did not work." The therapist, however, possessed no background in family therapy and none in the family therapy of suicidal persons.

There is no need to go deeply into the scope of the problem and the reasons for the almost epidemic increase in suicidal behavior among the young since that is discussed in other chapters of this work. The author notes, however, that the dynamic basis of suicide in young people whom he saw 20 years ago is no different from what he sees today. The increase in suicide must be related to social mores and conditions, especially changes in the family and the increasing alienation of adolescents from parents. The changes that may be most relevant are those most conducive to anomie and alienation. These include the dramatic increase in the divorce rate and the increase in so-called sexual freedom and permissiveness. Many young people are forced prematurely into situations of failure in their sex-role functioning.

Another change is the increasing pressure some adolescents feel to leave home as soon as possible. While such separation can be salutary and contribute to individuation, it can be "deadly" in those who are not ready. Unfortunately, we tend to confuse physical separation and isolation from the family with personal autonomy, ie, mistaking pseudo-independence for true independence. In addition, many teenagers who run away from home are not "leaving home" in the sense of a movement towards personal freedom, but are responding to a crisis in the family which requires a change in the family's structure and functioning. The running away prevents any genuine change and thus preserves the family's status quo. That is often true, paradoxically, of divorce: a necessary change in the marital and family relationship is stopped or prevented by stopping the marriage.

Other considerations for the increased rate of adolescent suicide may include speculations regarding the romanticization of suicide among the young (both as an expression of social protest and a permissible form of "doing your own thing") and, finally, the fact of "The Bomb" and our apparently suicidal search for still more lethal forms of killing, with the specter of the destruction of the entire human race.

The implications are for a greater alertness and attention to the special problems of suicide in adolescents, both in our day-to-day clinical work and in the training of mental health professionals. In particular, the concept of suicide as the expression of a family with a problem it cannot resolve is of prime value for the understanding, assessment, and treatment of teenaged, self-destructive persons. What is needed today are greater training opportunities in the family approach to suicide prevention. A properly conducted family approach is the most effective form of treatment for those undergoing a suicidal despair, in this writer's opinion.

THE NATURE OF THE SUICIDOGENIC FAMILY

While the author's work rests upon clinical experience and observations, these in turn are based upon the great literary contributions to psychiatry and the mental health field. Among these, this writer suggests that the following belong in the library of every family therapist who works with the suicidal.

The work of John Bowlby[1,2] is helpful because of the importance of separation and loss in self-destruction. Freud's *Mourning and Melan-*

cholia[3] is a monumental contribution to understanding not only the vicissitudes of the aggressive impulse, but also the roles of incorporation and introjection and the positive function of mourning. Melanie Klein[4] and the object-relations school contributed to the further understanding of splitting, introjects, and projective identification in suicide. Last, yet first in many ways, is *Suicide* by Emile Durkheim.[5] Durkheim's brilliant presentation of anomie and alienation in suicide, and the place of social integration in the prevention of suicide represents the basis for the theory and practice of family therapy for suicidal situations.

In the family therapy literature, Nagy and Spark's[6] work is valuable because of their profound discussion of family loyalties and the related topics of justice and reciprocity, which are so vital a part of the dynamics of suicide. Bowen,[7] Haley,[8] Minuchin and Fishman,[9] and Whitaker[10] have provided valuable guides in the practice of family therapy, even though they have addressed themselves but peripherally to the topic of suicide. This writer's own studies[11,12] are of value for the direct application of family therapy to the treatment of suicide. Langsley and Kaplan et al[13] are invaluable for their pioneering work in family crisis intervention. Finally, *In A Darkness*, by James Wechsler and the Wechsler family,[14] and *Vivienne* by Mack and Hickler[15] provide moving accounts of a teenage suicide and the failures of therapy, which is both thought provoking and challenging.

In addition, based upon direct experience with over 500 families with a suicidal member whom the author has studied, assessed, and treated, a number of family characteristics consistently stood out at the time of the suicidal act. These salient features are summarized in Table 23-1.

As one may infer from Table 23-1, many of these characteristics overlap with families faced with other disturbances, including the psychoses, addictions, and psychosomatic illnesses. That is not entirely surprising, since most, perhaps all, of these family characteristics can be seen as due to stress or responses to stress and anxiety; and many of the emotional and psychiatric illnesses are stress related. There is, of course, an overlap between suicide and emotional disturbances since these are not two different groups. The presence of mental illness, physical illness, and alcoholism, for example, are associated with an increased risk of suicide.[16]

However, there are features within the family that are suicide-specific, especially at the time of the suicidal crisis. One is a particularly close association between separations and death, based upon early traumatic experiences in both the suicidal individual and the relatives. This is sometimes repeated over many generations and currently may be perceived by the family as a struggle for its survival.[17] Second is the isolation of the suicidal person within the family while intimacies with

Table 23-1
The Family under Suicidal Conditions*

   I. An inability to accept necessary change
      A. An intolerance for separation
      B. A symbiosis without empathy
      C. A fixation on infantile patterns and the primary relationship
      D. A refusal to mourn past persons or situations
  II. Role conflicts, failures, and fixations
 III. A disturbed family structure
      A. A closed family system
      B. A prohibition against intimacy outside the family
      C. An isolation of the potentially suicidal person within the family
      D. A quality of family fragility
  IV. Affective difficulties
      A. A one-sided pattern of aggression
      B. A family depression
   V. Unbalanced or one-sided intrafamilial relationships
      A. A specific kind of scapegoating
      B. Double-binding, sadomasochistic relationship
      C. The potentially suicidal individual becomes the bad object for the
         entire family
  VI. Transactional difficulties
      A. Communication disturbances
      B. An excessive secretiveness
 VII. An intolerance for crises

---

*Adapted from Richman 1971.[19]

persons outside are forbidden. The well-known social isolation and loneliness of the suicidal individual is invariably related to such covert and unconscious family rules. Third is the dynamics of the expression of aggression and other drives,[18] especially the family rules regarding instinctual discharge. Fourth, is the nature of the communication pattern, most strikingly the presence of overt and covert messages involving suicide, and how they are received.

Sometimes these suicidogenic features in the family are very subtle. Nevertheless, the experienced and astute family clinician can usually identify a person and family at risk of suicide through the nature of the interaction during the family interview.

IMPLICATIONS FOR ASSESSMENT

How we intervene depends upon our view of the nature and causes of suicide. In the author's view, suicide is based upon four major factors, all of which are intimately related to the family factors listed in Table 23-1.

First, an exhaustion of the ego resources and coping mechanisms of the individual at risk takes place so that he or she can no longer deal with the demands and vicissitudes of life.

Second, there follows an exhaustion of the emotional resources and coping mechanisms of the family system and social network, so that they are no longer able to help and support the suicidal member of the family.

Third, a crisis occurs which is perceived as insoluble by everyone. It is the proverbial last straw that precipitates the suicidal act, although it possesses certain salient characteristics that makes it suicidogenic. The crisis always involves the individual and the family; and the crisis always involves separation and loss. These experiences are so much related to the typical developmental tasks of youth that adolescents are particularly vulnerable to suicidal and other self-destructive reactions. The family becomes progressively less able to deal with the problem within its midst. There are good reasons for the intensity of the turmoil that arises, since the family believes it is struggling for its survival.

The major variables outlined in Table 23-1 escalate sharply at the time of the suicidal crisis. The presence of strong symbiotic ties within the family are central, especially between the potentially suicidal adolescent and a key family member or members, most often the mother. The parents of the suicidal adolescent exhibit a great attachment to the primary figures, especially their own parents and grandparents. Through a process of projective identification, the potentially suicidal person represents such primary figures, sometimes extending back through three generations and more. The threatened loss or separation of this adolescent, therefore, may be experienced almost literally as a loss of the part of the self of the family members and of a threat to the very foundations of the family. To counter this threat, the family reacts to the outside world as a danger and attempts to keep the adolescent at risk from forming close relationships with external institutions and persons.

At this point, however, a double bind may develop. As Erikson[20] and others have noted, the key tasks of the adolescent include the achievement of personal autonomy, self identity, and the pursuit of goals and activities in school, work, and among peers; all of which move him or her outside the purview of the family, no matter how strong the symbiosis. As a result of these conflicts, progress and growth become seen as threat and loss. The family usually wants the adolescent to succeed, yet paradoxically takes steps to restore the old, unfortunately untenable homeostasis. The adolescent may then remain home or run away (for running away is part of a family transaction, a form of banishment), or the adolescent may be completely isolated. Isolation or banishment is the other side of the coin of symbiotic merging; in symbiosis there is no in-between. Extreme rage, meanwhile, escalates to dangerous proportions. Thus does the crisis develop, culminating in the attempted or completed suicide of the adolescent.

There is a fourth factor, for even the above vicissitudes are not enough for the situation to culminate in a suicidal act. The last requirement is the concept of suicide as an acceptable and possible solution. Once again, the acceptability of suicide is a systems phenomenon, and not only an individual decision.

In order to evaluate the acceptability of suicide, I ask each member of the family to read out loud and agree to a no-suicide pledge during the first family interview. The statement reads: "No matter what happens I shall not kill myself, accidentally or on purpose, at any time."[21] This request becomes a basis for current and future negotiations and agreements.

In families in which attempted suicide is a presenting complaint, the family members will often refuse to agree to a no-suicide pact, even those relatives who are ostensibly not suicidal. In families in which the identified patient is not suicidal, the patient as well as family members agree readily to the no-suicide contract. It appears that the idea of suicide as an acceptable solution for the vicissitudes of life is based on the experiences of early separation from symbiotic primary attachments, at a time when a temporary separation and a permanent death were not differentiated.

No assessment of suicide potential is complete unless it takes into account all four variables: the ego resources or their decompensation in the suicidal person; the coping abilities and ability to help (or else the exhaustion of the resources of the family and members of the social network); the nature of the current crises; and the perception of suicide as an acceptable solution. All four variables are assigned a numerical score or rank. Many errors of assessment occur because one or more of these were neglected.

FAMILY ASSESSMENT PROCEDURES

The methods of family assessment interviewing utilized are relatively brief and appear effective. When a person is suicidal, the author sees each member of the family individually to obtain his or her perception of the events leading up to the suicidal act or impulse and to obtain at least one Figure Drawing. This is a very effective screening device for suicidal potential.[22,23] The therapist also expresses appreciation for their coming, and invites them to collaborate with him in the therapeutic endeavor. Then the whole family is seen together.

These individual meetings perform several valuable functions. They afford an opportunity to make contact and establish rapport with each member of the family quickly and effectively. They are especially helpful to the relative newcomer in the practice of family therapy, since it enables the therapist to practice his or her skills in individual interviewing. The procedure helps undercut or reduce the unfortunate tendency of many beginning family interviewers to take sides, which in a family in which suicide is an issue may lead to quickly losing the case.

FROM ASSESSMENT TO THERAPY

The most important part of the assessment interview is the family meeting itself, in which the ability of the family to help or harm and to become a force for growth and healing become most apparent. Since the first session is an assessment interview, this writer is relatively inactive, especially during the early part of the session. The family members are instructed to form a semicircle, face each other, and share their perceptions and understandings, and what they can all do to prevent such events in the future. The author then sits back and insists they communicate among themselves. Almost invariably they do; most often complaints, tensions, and dissensions are expressed and escalate, often with much scapegoating and expression of marked anger and even overt death wishes.

Such outbursts are welcomed because they indicate that the family is accessible and are likely to get better. This attitude runs counter to the prevailing wisdom that the therapist should not countenance such behavior in his or her office. With suicidal persons, however, since such behavior will occur in the home, it is preferable for it to take place in a therapeutic context, where its destructive effects can be examined and, hopefully, transformed. In addition, the context changes the meaning of the behavior. The participants know at some level that they are present in order to better the situation. Most important, such outbursts clear the air and have a cathartic effect. The family sees that it has survived the encounter, that no one has died, the family is still intact, and, in fact, the separation and death anxiety, which is behind the rage and destructive outbursts, has been reduced.

It is evident by now that the family assessment of suicidal potential cannot be separated from family therapy; both occur simultaneously. It is also true that the outbursts described above can be considered an expression of the first crisis in therapy; and how it is handled represents the first crisis intervention. Many therapists, however, who are inexperienced or unskilled in the family therapy of suicidal persons mistakenly read these outbursts as evidence of failure, and erroneously think that the family is not suitable for family therapy. They may even interrupt treatment and send the patient to a group home or some long-term treatment facility. In contrast, when such a blow-up or crisis does *not* occur in the family with a suicidal member, the author becomes suspicious, and inquires into why not. If they do not appear spontaneously, one may inquire into the presence of depression and suicidal impulses in the suicidal member, and of death wishes and exhaustion of resources in all the family members. The procedures vary, depending upon the circumstances and the family.

One might, for example, ask the identified suicidal member if he or she feels the family is fed up with him or her, if he or she thinks that he or she is a burden, and that they would be better off if he or she were dead. The other family members are asked if they do, in fact, feel they have been burdened, and did they ever think they might be better off if he or she were dead. The responses are used, whatever they are, to encourage further dialogue as well as to clarify the nature of the stresses within the family and between the different members. Death wishes are openly expressed with impressive frequency. They are labeled for what the author believes they are: the expression of feelings of complete frustration, exasperation, helplessness, and hopelessness, indicating that the family members no longer know how to deal with the situation. The family, including the suicidal representative, is thus provided with an alternative to what may otherwise be seen as a literal and concrete instruction to the individual to commit a self-destructive act.

The results of such loaded inquiries have uniformly been positive, when appropriately conducted, and in the author's personal clinical experience have never resulted in an escalation of suicidal and self-destructive behavior. Essential, of course, is the comfort of the therapist with what he or she is doing and his or her ability to be sensitive, empathic, and in touch with all the family members. On the basis of the assessment of the family, the individual suicidal person, the crises, and acceptance or rejection of a dangerous suicidal resolution, the decision is made where and how to treat.

THE SUICIDAL CRISIS

Whatever the setting, in hospital, crisis center, clinic, or private office, a suicidal situation is a crisis, and crisis intervention methods are utilized at the outset. The procedures follow the established crisis intervention principles of establishing rapport, pinpointing the crisis, determining the amount of suicidal potential, intervention, and followup.[13]

Suicide is based upon a problem in the present which has its basis in unresolved crises in the past which, in turn, precipitates a major crisis, the fate of which may determine the future. In a sense, all of the patient and family's past and present history and future fate is condensed in the suicidal moment. Such a crisis also presents a great therapeutic opportunity.

Many suicidal persons are resistant to bringing in the family, and many families of suicidal persons are extremely threatened when a suicidal young person enters into psychotherapy. The family is afraid of what the patient will say about them and what secrets he or she will reveal. The members fear he or she will be disloyal. Above all, they fear losing the young person through therapy. However, when an attempted suicide does take place and the person is admitted into the emergency room or directly into the medical wards or intensive care unit, the family is often more emotionally accessible than ever before. If a therapist or team trained in crisis intervention, especially family crisis intervention, is available at that moment, it may be possible to involve the family in treatment and begin a process of healing and growth. The implication is that every hospital should have a crisis intervention team immediately available on a 24-hour basis.

At first, the intervention is intensive, with daily contacts, if possible. The therapist or team keeps in touch and uses medication, if called for, until the current crisis is resolved. The family, including the suicidal member, may then decline to continue; or a decision may be reached by the family and therapist to remain in longer term family psychotherapy, or to refer one or more family members for individual or group therapy.

SOME GENERAL PRINCIPLES

A few considerations apply to all successful therapies of suicide, variable as the procedures might otherwise be.

One is a sensitivity by the therapist to issues of separation. That includes such situations as leaving home, admission to a hospital (which means leaving home); and discharge from a hospital. Leaving a hospital may be a separation that recapitulates all the other unbearable separations in the past. Separation and death anxiety are also aroused when the therapist goes on vacation or is away for any reason. The rest of the family cannot always be a support at such times, because they have not learned how to help each other through separations. I used to think that, since the presence of the family does reduce the intensity of the transference, such separations were not as traumatic in family therapy, but I was mistaken. The entire family may respond in an extreme manner to such separations, as though they were forever and identical to death.

A second consideration is a tolerance in the therapist for great hostility during the family meetings, ranging from loud and aggressive exchanges to deviousness and the manipulative sabotage of treatment. An appreciation of the ambivalence in suicidal situations can help the therapist benignly survive much rage, including that which is so often directed upon himself. Ambivalence is a characteristic of the family, not only the individual. That means that behind the hate and death wishes is also love and a wish for the adolescent to succeed in his or her efforts at autonomy.

Third, is the central importance of hope as a major attitude in the therapist. That is especially important in those very suicidal persons and families in which hope has been surrendered. Hope is the one major affect that helps the family move from a suicidal despair to renewed living. The effective therapy of suicide relies upon the hope and faith of the therapist in the family and a refusal to give up.

Another important approach by the therapist is an emphasis upon the positive. For example, when an intense and seemingly destructive quarrel arises, the family members are commended for being open and doing their job as good patients.

Attributing positive intent and meanings to the participants is also an example of relabeling or reframing. An example was given earlier, in which the expressions of death wishes were labeled or interpreted as the result of feelings of frustration, exasperation, and an admission of helplessness; *not* as direct or covert instructions to kill oneself. Reframing can also be considered as examples of "universe changing," a term applied by the philosopher D. H. Monro[24] to the analysis of humor. Universe changing refers essentially to the ability to see and present a situation in a new, alternative, or different light.

Underlying all of these approaches and procedures is the view of the therapist as "merely" a catalyst who helps release the healing and growth forces of the family. That may be one reason why the paradoxical and brief therapies work.

The concept of second order changes, for example, refers essentially to the activation of growth forces. Watzlawick, Weakland, and Fisch[25] describe first order changes in therapy (and in life), which make no fundamental difference; and second order changes, which constitute a fundamental improvement. These can occur spontaneously and not necessarily in the more restricted situation of formal therapy. An example they give concerned a severe agoraphobic patient whose condition had become so unbearable that he decided to commit suicide. He drove his car towards a mountain top, believing that the anxiety generated would precipitate a heart attack and kill him. Instead, he was cured of his phobia.

PITFALLS AND ROADBLOCKS

Some prevailing attitudes exist among the general public and even the professional community which can greatly hamper the help-giving and help-receiving process. A major stumbling block is the belief that if someone is suicidal there is nothing anyone can do about it. Such myths emphasize the importance of public education. However, it is surprising how frequently a similar attitude is found among mental health professionals. Sometimes this assumes the form of a fatalistic attitude concerning the inevitability that a troubled and seriously suicidal person will commit suicide.

A second roadblock is the belief that if you are suicidal it must be kept a secret. This is another area in which public education is vital, and one in which the mental health field should take the lead. Once again, however, the professionals are often as secretive as the general public.

Third is the belief that if someone confides in you that he or she is planning suicide, but it is a secret, you must respect that confidence. This is nonsense which ignores the ambivalence of the suicidal person, the complexities of the human communication, and the wish at some level to be saved. However, suicidal persons and their families do tend to be extraordinarily secretive. In *Vivienne*,[15] for example, the 14-year-old heroine takes her sister and girlfriend into her confidence regarding her decision to kill herself, and both felt obligated to honor the confidence. But, in addition, the family went into family counseling, in which her suicidal behavior was not mentioned during the sessions. It must be emphasized that the family counselor must be open just because the family is not.

Fourth, many people believe you should not ask someone if he or she is suicidal, because that might precipitate the deed. The opposite is the case. No one, to my knowledge, has been harmed by being asked about suicidal problems. However, many died because they were not asked and therefore did not obtain help. On the other hand, it is true that sometimes people do not ask for fear the person would acknowledge he or she is suicidal, and the questioner would not know what to do with the response. The professional, certainly, and concerned others in addition, should know not only how to inquire but also how to help or obtain help for the suicidal person, the relatives, and friends.

Fifth is the belief that people should not mourn, because it is more important to go on with the business of living than to keep thinking of the dead. Such an attitude goes far towards inhibiting living and preventing growth, because mourning is a necessary process. The failure to mourn leads to stagnation at best, or regression and illness, while successful mourning enlarges the self. One rule in pinpointing the suicidal crisis is to ask who or what remains to be mourned.

Sixth is the view that one should not see a psychiatrist because it would mean that you are crazy. Besides, they twist minds and turn people away from their families. Such attitudes are part of that closed family system of those who cannot seek help for their feelings or hopelessness and despair. Such views are best countered by working with the family as well as the individual.

These are among the major barriers to the successful therapy of the suicidal person. It is evident that many therapists are not free of such misconceptions. What is required is a greater degree of self-examination and of openness and sharing within the mental health profession.

CONCLUSION

Suicidal behavior in adolescents presents us with a challenge as well as an opportunity, not only to improve the lot of the unhappy teenager, but to help construct a foundation for a more successful and satisfactory later life. As a developmental psychologist, whose more recent work has been with geriatric patients, the author can affirm that many unhappy and suicidal old people had been suicidal as adolescents. Proper treatment then might have prevented much heartache later. Taking the process one generation further back, the most effective suicide prevention for the adolescent is the successful treatment of depression and suicidal problems in the parents.

We, as professionals, have helped a great deal through our recognition and treatment of troubled and suicidal individuals and their families. However, we are usually called in when the house is already on fire, and are rarely involved in preventive efforts. From a still broader social outlook, suicide is everyone's business. Suicidal people are affected by others and they affect other people. They often choose a rescuer, as Jensen and Petty[26] pointed out a quarter of a century ago. The rescuer may be a crisis center volunteer, a policeman, a fireman, a teacher, a doctor, a school counselor, another teenage friend, a parent, or you, or me. What are we all to do?

The answer is a program of public enlightenment. The new frontier in suicide prevention will be in education; the modification or elimination of false and destructive ideas and attitudes; and the striving for a society that permits the optimal conditions for growth and life in its youthful members. We shall then have gone a long way toward eliminating these tragic and unnecessary deaths.

REFERENCES

1. Bowlby J: *Attachment and Loss.* New York, Basic Books, 1969, vol 1.
2. Bowlby J: *Attachment and Loss.* New York, Basic Books, 1973, vol 2.
3. Freud S: *Mourning and Melancholia,* standard ed. London, Hogarth Press, 1957, vol 14, pp 243–258.
4. Klein M: A contribution to the psychogenesis of manic-depressive states, in *Love, Guilt, and Reparation and Other Works.* New York, Delacorte Seymour Lawrence, 1975.
5. Durkheim E: *Suicide.* Spaulding JA, Simpson G (trans). New York, The Free Press, 1951.
6. Nagy IB, Spark GM: *Invisible Loyalties.* New York, Harper & Row, 1973.
7. Bowen M: *Family Therapy in Clinical Practice.* New York, Jason Aronson, 1978.
8. Haley J: *Leaving Home: Therapy With Disturbed Young People.* New York, McGraw-Hill, 1980.
9. Minuchin S, Fishman HC: *Family Therapy Techniques.* Cambridge, Harvard University Press, 1981.
10. Neill JR, Kniskern DP (eds): *From Psyche to System. The Evolving Therapy of Carl Whitaker.* New York, Guilford, 1982.
11. Richman J: Family therapy of attempted suicide. *Family Process* 1979;18:131–142.
12. Richman J: Mass suicide as a family affair: The People's Temple in Guyana, in Selkin J (ed): *Proceedings, 12th Annual Conference of the American Association of Suicidology.* Denver Colorado, American Association of Suicidology, 1979.
13. Langsley DG, Kaplan DM, Pittman SS, et al: *The Treatment of Families in Crisis.* New York, Grune & Stratton, 1968.
14. Wechsler JA: *In A Darkness.* New York, WW Norton, 1972.
15. Mack JE, Hickler H: *Vivienne. The Life and Suicide of an Adolescent Girl.* Boston, Little Brown & Co, 1981.
16. Dublin LI: *Suicide: A Sociological and Statistical Study.* New York, Ronald, 1963.
17. Gehrke S, Kirschenbaum M: Survival patterns in family conjoint therapy. *Family Process* 1967;6:67–80.
18. Rosenbaum M, Richman J: Suicide: The role of hostility and death wishes from the family and significant others. *Am J Psychiatry* 1970;126:128–131.
19. Richman J: Family determinants of suicide potential, in Anderson D, McClain LJ (eds): *Identifying Suicide Potential.* New York, Behavioral Publications, 1971, pp 33–54.
20. Erikson EH: *Childhood and Society.* New York, WW Norton, 1953.
21. Drye RC, Goulding RL, Goulding MM: Monitoring of suicidal risk, in Goulding RL, Goulding MM (eds): *The Power is in the Patient.* San Francisco, TA Press, 1978, pp 125–133.
22. Richman J: The clinical use of human figure drawing in the evaluation of suicidal potential, in Litman RE (ed): *Proceedings, 6th International Conference on Suicide Prevention.* Ann Arbor MI, Edwards Brothers, 1972.
23. Richman J, Pfeffer C: Figure drawings for the assessment of suicide potential in children, in Achte K (ed): *Proceedings, 9th International Congress for Suicide Prevention.* Helsinki, Finland, International Association for Suicide Prevention, 1977.

24. Monro DN: *Argument of Laughter*. New York, Cambridge University Press, 1951.
25. Watzlawick P, Weakland J, Fisch R: *Change. Principles of Problem Formation and Problem Resolution*. New York, WW Norton, 1974.
26. Jensen VW, Petty TA: The fantasy of being rescued in suicide. *Psychoanalytic Quarterly* 1958;27:327–339.

CHAPTER 24

INTERVENTION AND
POSTVENTION IN SCHOOLS

WILLIAM H. HILL

The compulsory school system in our country may provide a viable location for intervention and postvention work. This chapter presents anecdotal evidence of how suicide prevention centers have provided service to adolescents in the school setting, both by a planned intervention/consultation program, and by responding to schools requesting assistance after an adolescent has committed suicide. In the latter case, the author describes how postvention efforts with peer groups of the deceased revealed a four-phase bereavement sequence: the initial reaction of crying, withdrawing and flight; the second phase of asking why the death occurred; the third of blaming self or others; and the final phase of overfocusing or overgeneralizing. A group meeting with the peer group appears to address this sequence and assist the group members into further bereavement. Finally, there is discussion about how intervention and postvention in the schools are interrelated, and how these activities ought to be carried out by suicide prevention and mental health centers.

The increase in adolescent suicide has been a catalyst for new research and prevention programs.[1] The aftermath of suicide has also generated a need for caregivers to respond to the needs of the family, peers and teachers.[2,3] In some communities, support groups have been formed for relatives of people having committed suicide.[4] Suicide prevention centers[5] are being called upon to conduct postvention programs, and it is to this context — postvention in the school setting — that this chapter is set.

Postvention refers to a series of procedures conducted after a suicide with family and friends of the deceased. Shneidman has urged the professional community to focus on postvention as a means of prevention in subsequent decades and generations.[2] The literature about postvention has, indeed, increased.[2-10] However, little is available of a descriptive nature about postvention in the schools.

The school system has been recommended as a viable setting for prevention and, to some extent, intervention.[5] The important fact that school attendance is compulsory in this country serves as a monitor for the withdrawn adolescent who might otherwise remain physically isolated. The captive audience of students, and therefore teachers, creates a setting in which education and intervention are possible. Whether or not teachers feel a responsibility to add yet another task to an ever-expanding role is addressed by Susan E. Gordon in her dissertation on adolescent suicide—teacher knowledge and attitudes.[11] Gordon's data provide a basis for identifying, by demographics and by attitude, teachers who might be positive candidates for training and intervention purposes. Her findings also support the need for teacher preservice and inservice education about adolescent suicide and intervention.

On behalf of a suicide prevention center, the author responded to three large suburban and two private high schools requesting assistance with the peers of teenagers who had committed suicide. The Suicide Prevention Center in Cleveland provided emergency evaluation and referral services to a large metropolitan county in Ohio. In addition to conducting psychiatric evaluations, referrals, and research, the center offered community education and training programs. It was the exposure to the school systems via the education and training program that resulted in the schools calling back for postvention services. The immediate impetus for these requests was apparently for the school to demonstrate that, as an institution, it was doing something in response to the tragic death of one of the students.

The suicide prevention center was the logical agency to call upon for several reasons. First, the suicide center had been providing educational and training programs for both teachers and students in the community and so was a familiar agency. Second, the very presence of the center in the community provided an avenue for the schools to look outside themselves for reasons for the death—perhaps in order to externalize the initial feelings of responsibility that some administrators and faculty felt for these untimely deaths. Underlying the reasons seemed to be the feeling that somebody ought to do something. A student had committed suicide. The very fact that it was a student brought focus on the school. What might the school have done (or failed to do) to have averted this death? Now that there had been a death, the school was under implicit, and sometimes explicit, pressure to do something. Such pressure came from within as well as outside the school system. Calling the suicide prevention center for help was a response to this need to respond— perhaps in self defense—but a response, nonetheless, to the suicide.

It was a time of crisis for the students and the school. It was a time of disequilibrium, and somehow the balancing factors had to be restored.[12] After a sudden loss, feelings ran high; judgment was impaired, and guidelines for establishing protocol did not exist. How many students should be excused to attend the wake and funeral? Should a letter be sent to all the students' parents? Perceptions remained unclear of just what problems really had to be addressed. The group of students closest to the teenager actually provided some grounding for the schools. At least the school administrators could say they were going to start somewhere and the peer group seemed to be an identifiable place to start. The purpose of a meeting was to provide some mode of intervention for a group whose emotions were awash with guilt, anger and anxiety. These normal feelings could build toward a depression. There always lurked the fear that if this potential for depression was not addressed, would these friends somehow be caught up in a contagion-like force and become suicidal themselves?[13]

Lindeman and Greer[13] suggest the group itself can feel a real wound from the suicide of one of its members. The death threatens cohesiveness and is responded to as though it were a subversive act. Although the peer group has to work through its own grief, the members can be a valuable source of comfort to the deceased's family. Due to our cultural emphasis on competence and strength, there is a lack of social validation for expressing emotions after death by any cause — perhaps especially death by suicide. The peer group can be very helpful to the parents by just being present. After all, how can the parents solicit support from a society that will be very quick to suspect them guilty of causing or, at least facilitating, this death in the first place?[3] At a time when protocol for mourning does not exist, it is all the more important for someone to address the issues with the survivors. The major issue was to help initiate the grief work so the surivors could begin the task of breaking the emotional ties with the one who had been lost.[14]

In each case there was only one meeting held with the students. Another meeting was held for faculty on two of the five occasions. The meetings of intervention were arranged by school and Center personnel. Most often the choice was to meet with the immediate peer group in the school during school hours. The meetings were held within 24 to 48 hours after the suicide. This particular time frame was not always planned as such, but seemed appropriate for addressing the emotions that were beginning to surface following the initial outbursts. The 24-hour lapse also reduced the chance for encountering the psychic numbing effect sudden trauma can provoke. Although some students reported feeling "nothing" at first, within a day they were able to report the emergence of feelings that were not present the first few hours following hearing the news.

Meetings took place at the schools in a lounge or classroom where privacy was maintained from the rest of the student body. The group composition was identified by the school counselor or administrator who had the most contact with the group initially. On two occasions, the guidance counselor sought out the peer group and, on the other three occasions, the group or a representative of the group approached the counselor for some help about the suicide. The size ranged from five to 15.

One public high school called the center several weeks after a suicide and reported they had an assembly the day after a suicide "for anybody wishing to talk about the tragedy." A large group responded — in excess of 50 students — and the meeting quickly disintegrated into a chaos of bragging and comparing about how bad their own lives were. The guidance counselors who called the large meeting never anticipated so many students would respond to this general announcement and were unprepared to divide the group into smaller sessions. In that instance, the immediate peer group of the student who committed suicide left the large assembly and went to one member's house to talk.

In another instance, students in a small group conducted by the author disclosed how angry they felt at other students who overtly displayed their upset feelings but who allegedly were, at the most, casual acquaintances of the deceased. One peer group member said, "These were kids just trying to get out of schoolwork by pretending to be upset about the death of somebody they didn't even know." These accusations of false grieving occasionally led to verbal confrontations in the school between the peer group members and those perceived as outside the "known" circle of friends.

Most often there was no school official present in the meetings. As the teenagers struggled with their feelings, school teachers and administrators became displaced targets of blame for the death. These reactions were not so freely expressed with school personnel present. Naturally, a lot depended on the preexisting relationships between teachers and students, but these small groups tended to function better without school personnel attending. It was, however, vital that the worker not lose sight of school faculty's needs. In two schools, meetings were held with the faculty later the same day. For students, the optimal size group seemed to be about 10. For faculty, a bit larger was manageable.

Meetings lasted around one and a half hours. They were time-limited so as to provide structure at a time when some students were fearing their own loss of control. The meetings began with the school counselor or assistant principal introducing the worker, "This is Mr. Hill from the Suicide Prevention Center. He's here to try to help us understand a little better what might have happened. All of you are excused from your next two classes and are to stay until I come back in about an hour and a half." The worker then reintroduced himself and explained what he knew about the circumstances of the death. This explanation was an attempt to create some consensus regarding the "facts" surrounding the death which were not always accurate. Additional information was added by group members, but even this early in the meeting, frustrations were verbalized about not being able ever to have all the facts. At the outset, the worker focused on the deceased by asking about what kind of person he was and calling him by name and using the past tense. "I have some knowledge about suicide and how come people kill themselves, but I never met Bob. Can you tell me a little about him so I can try to understand what kind of person he was?" By going around the group eliciting information, the worker was able both to learn about the person who suicided as well as some of the characteristics of each member and his perception of the relationship to the deceased.

This initial exercise of eliciting a response from each member was both a fact-finding and diagnostic step and helped the worker plan some of the content for later in the meeting. This exercise also helped initiate some grieving and enabled the worker to identify the uniqueness of each member's relationship to the deceased. Latitude was permitted in the responses. Some members had to be restrained gently from monopolizing the time while others who were quiet were invited to participate but allowed to remain silent.

The adolescents' responses to the suicide followed a sequence which was partially observed in most of the meetings. If not observed, the content of the meeting discussion revealed that phases had, indeed, developed. First, there had been the initial reaction upon hearing the news. Crying, silence, withdrawal and flight were common responses. The flight would either be to cars or home or occasionally to a school counselor's office. Such early responses appeared to be a retreating to a safe place.

By their own account, the students reported that once they were somewhat isolated (generally in small peer groups) they began to ask each other questions. This was the second phase. The shock of receiving the news had been experienced, and now, somewhat attenuated by being in the safe place with safe friends, they could ask questions. The search for *Why?* began in this phase. "Why did he do it?" "How could she do such a thing?" "How could anybody do it?" "What caused her to do it now?" "Whey did he choose that way to kill himself?" "If she killed herself, what about so-and-so; he might do it too?" As these questions were asked again and again, both silently and to friends, and as the answers failed to satisfy or even materialize, the third phase emerged. The teenagers began to formulate their own answers. A major question was who to blame for this death?

This blame question led to one of two answers. One answer resulted in self-blame and more questions. "What did I do to cause this death?" "What didn't I do?" The other answer was to externalize the blame. The cause of this death was an act of commission or omission on the part of the deceased's parents, or teachers, or other friends or enemies, maybe alcohol or drugs, or maybe even the world. Internalized blame, motivated by guilt, actually seemed to enhance the adolescent's sense of omnipotence, thereby inducing an increased perception of responsibility for the death. Externalized blame often appeared to be displaced or projected guilt and was frequently contaminated by other issues the student had with the external person or situation.

In the latter case, one student was furious at a teacher's somewhat glib remark upon hearing of the suicide. The student said, "People kill themselves because of dumb teachers like that." The student later disclosed he had received a low grade from that teacher on the same day as the suicide. Self-blame is overfocusing the responsibility for the death. One of the variables for whether the blame was overfocused or overgeneralized appeared to be the intensity of the friendship. The closer, the more self-blame. The less close, the more overgeneralized. Some students, struggling with increasing ambivalence, would vacillate from self-blame to other-blame.

The fourth and final phase occurred as intervention began to address the overfocusing and overgeneralizing. The worker explained that suicide is a complex phenomenon and that people rarely kill themselves for a single reason. Considerable effort was placed on separating the apparent precipitant to the suicide from the possible causes. The "if only" remarks were acknowledged as genuine showing of concern, but these remarks were also challenged by the worker. "I'm sure you were a very good friend of Tom's, but when you went on a camping trip with your parents in the past without him, suicide was not the outcome. How could you have expected it to be the outcome this time?" As some of the group members began to feel some relief, or if some felt less responsible for the death, they supported the worker's tack of supporting–confronting–supporting.

The worker's response was different with the members of the groups who overgeneralized the causes of death. Anger was more pervasive, and projections of this anger had to be acknowledged, but not reinforced. If the school system was seen as the reason the adolescent committed suicide, the worker acknowledged how hard it must be to be so closely affiliated with the same place within which a suicide occurred, or a place that carried so much influence and power over students. Then, proceeding in as nondefensive a manner as possible, the worker would add that the whole school system, as such, could not possibly be aware of all the details of the student's life and probably could not ever have had a lot of control due to that lack of knowledge. Thus, similar to the above, the worker's tack was acknowledging–confronting–supporting.

The bereavement process could never be completed with each member, nor for the group as a whole, in one meeting. The meetings were never planned with that expectation. Given that overfocusing and overgeneralizing were, in part, normal defenses, the worker had to guard against stripping them all away. Rather, the worker, cast as an authority about the causes of suicide, attempted to unhook the omnipotent-feeling, overfocusing members from their own single sense of responsibility. Likewise, the worker tried to pull in, or blunt the pervasive feeling that the whole world was to blame as felt by those overgeneralizing members. The major goal was always to free or focus the group members so their mourning process could begin.

Along with the peer group intervention, was intervention with school faculty in two of the five occasions; once by a sort of spontaneous request, the other by specific plan. The group process in both cases was different from the students' groups. Rather than question why the suicide occurred, the more frequent question was what might the teachers have done to be more attuned to this particular suicide victim's behavior and possibly prevented the event? The faculty wanted to know how to respond to the students now. How much demonstration of upset and bereavement should be permitted in the classroom? Somewhat predictably, the answers to these questions were directly proportionate to the closeness of the teacher to the student, and to the teacher's own defenses against his or her perceived responsibility for the death.

Similar to the students' group, the worker made a brief statement about how complex an issue suicide causation was and that each person who knew the deceased may feel a sense of responsibility, but that indeed the adolescent who committed suicide had a world outside the school setting that had to be acknowledged too. By and large, in the experience of this author, the faculties as a whole were less verbal and open than those in the peer group. Some explanations for this may be that adults have more sophisticated defenses in place; that not all the faculty knew the deceased well; and that there was reluctance to show one's own vulnerability among fellow teachers and administrators. The worker tried to act as a permission-giver for the wide range of emotions and thoughts that were expressed or implied. Concrete suggestions were welcomed such as allowing the students time to talk in each class, yet structuring the class since school work had to be conducted too. It was not a time for long lectures or major exams but, indeed, work had to progress despite how badly many students felt. Finding this balance between recognizing the tragedy and conducting school work became the major focus of the teachers in one group. Their responses were in direct correlation to their closeness to the deceased and their own ambivalence about what this death had elicited in themselves.

Repeatedly, both the students and faculty wanted answers. The worker, cast as the authority, emphasized that answers could not be definitive, but at least a perspective on the death might emerge. This perspective in and of itself was comforting to group members. Because the

worker spent time with the student and faculty group only on single occasions, this "authority" or "expert" power was vital. The group members'
vulnerability after a suicide created an opportunity for the expert to provide not only perspective, but some relief. The goal of the group meeting
was not so much to settle everybody down, as it was to provide some
framework within which the group members' could safely react and then
begin their mourning process.

There was some follow through with postvention efforts. The
worker was accessible by phone to group members. This was arranged
via the community agency's 24-hour telephone availability. The school
representative to the peer group was encouraged to monitor the group
members' behavior in the days following the meeting. Consultation was
made available to the counselors because individual case finding was a
logical and crucial next step. Students who did not appear to be moving
on with their grief work needed to be identified and referred to additional
resources for individual counseling or some other form of therapy.
Again, the suicide center was used as the primary source of help to assist
in followup efforts.

Prevention

Charlotte Ross reported that the Suicide Prevention and Crisis
Center of San Mateo County (California) conducted a pilot project in
one high school district (six schools) and one community college, and included workshops, training courses, and inclass presentations at the high
school and college level.[5] Brochures, training kits, media presentations,
and an educational film were produced. Questions concerning duty-to-
warn as opposed to confidentiality and how teachers should handle
suicide attempts were addressed. The Center staff continued to be
available in the followup consultation role. Ross reported an increased
number of requests for backup support and services made from the
schools to the Center. In fact, following the presentations, the Center
received an increase in requests for consultation with school personnel in
their own management of suicidal patients. Prior to the presentations,
the more frequent requests were for direct counseling services following a
suicide attempt. As a result of a rather thorough training program, the
schools took a greater responsibility for intervention, but used the
Center as a significant authority for consultation.

A major issue is how a suicide center can, in fact, become an integral
part of the secondary educational system in the community it serves.
Personal outreach to guidance counselors and school administrators
about what a suicide center can offer is one way. Mass mailings of pam-

phlets is another, but schools are inundated with mailings so that pamphlets are not consistently distributed to appropriate faculty or administrative personnel. In the Cleveland area, positive regard for the presentations seemed to spread from teacher to teacher, and subsequently, system to system.

Establishing a reputation for being expert in suicidology and bereavement is the responsibility of the local suicide prevention center's or mental health center's community education program. Once a Center is known, requests will abound from secondary schools for speakers, films, pamphlets and bibliographies. The topics of suicide, teenage suicide, suicide prevention, and postvention appear throughout high school curricula of health, psychology, sociology, contemporary problems, death and dying, literature, and human resources. Opportunities to conduct training sessions are present in groups such as student government, peer counseling, faculty meetings, administrative retreats, and all-school professional days.

The presenter to these classes and groups must develop clear educational objectives and tailor the presentations to the uniqueness of each group. Nonsensational, but lively presentations create an atmosphere of openness. In every case, from a 40-minute class to a whole-day workshop, clear objectives and time for questions are mandatory components of a presentation. The presenter must demonstrate both expertness by providing accurate information and sensitivity to each participant by allowing and encouraging questions.

As a community agency's reputation increases for providing information and training about suicide, credibility is enhanced, thus adding legitimacy to the expertness needed when postvention is required. Such a reputation can be created rather quickly depending on the size of the community to be served and the latitude of the community agency's availability. When the education and training programs are perceived as helpful, word among the school systems spreads; requests for speakers increase, and the reputation builds.

In summary, this author's experiences reflect the conviction that some postvention is better than none; that educational programs about suicide are preferable to their absence; and that the two are interdependent. Staff providing these services must cultivate a knowledge of crisis intervention; of group work with adolescents; and of how to conduct viable community education and training programs about suicide prevention, intervention, and postvention. There are rewards for staff conducting these programs. When students and school personnel recognize that the worker is comfortable talking about suicide, their questions and responses reinforce the very processes of learning and grieving that the worker hopes to facilitate.

REFERENCES

1. Tischler CL, McKenry PC, Morgan KC: Adolescent suicide attempts: Some significant factors. *Suicide Life Threat Behav* 1981;11:86–92.
2. Cain AC (ed): *Survivors of Suicide*, Springfield, Ill, Charles C Thomas, 1972.
3. Cantor P: Effects of youthful suicide on the family. *Psychiatric Opinion* 1975;12:6–11.
4. Hatton CL, Valente SM: Bereavement group for parents who suffered a suicidal loss of a child. *Suicide Life Threat Behav* 1981;11:141–150.
5. Ross CP: Mobilizing schools for suicide prevention. *Suicide Life Threat Behav* 1980;10:239–243.
6. Danto B: *Suicide and Bereavement*. New York, MMS Info Corp, 1977.
7. Grollman EA: *Suicide: Prevention, Intervention, Postvention*. Boston, Beacon Press, 1971.
8. Klagsbrun F: *Youth and Suicide: Too Young To Die*. New York, Pocket Book, 1977.
9. Wallace S: *After Suicide*. New York, John Wiley and Sons, 1973.
10. Wekstein L: *Handbook Of Suicidology*. New York, Brunner/Mazel, 1979.
11. Gordon SE: An analysis of the knowledge and attitudes of secondary school teachers concerning suicide among adolescents and intervention in adolescent suicide. Dissertation, North Texas State University, 1979.
12. Aguilera DC, Messick M: *Crisis Intervention*. St. Louis, CV Mosby Co, 1974.
13. Lindeman E, Greer IM: A study of grief: Emotional responses to suicide, in Cain AC (ed): *Survivors Of Suicide*. Springfield, Ill, Charles C Thomas, 1972, pp 63–69.
14. Simos BG: Grief therapy to facilitate health restitution. *Soc Casework* 1977;58:337–342.

CHAPTER **25**

THERAPIES AND INTERVENTION:
A Review

HOWARD S. SUDAK
AMASA B. FORD
NORMAN B. RUSHFORTH

What is the "best" therapy for suicidal patients? As Trautman and Shaffer have indicated in Chapter 19, there is, of course, no single answer to such a question. In their chapter they review four types of treatment for suicide attempters using evidence from adult studies primarily. We will approach the issue by looking at five related questions: Inpatient versus outpatient therapy? Pharmacotherapy versus psychotherapy (or both)? Individual or group or family psychotherapy? Psychoanalysis or psychoanalytically oriented or behavioral/cognitive psychotherapy? Finally, what is the role of intervention and postvention in schools?

Inpatient versus outpatient therapy Of the above questions, this is certainly the one about which consensus can most easily be reached. If a therapist has any serious concerns about any acute self-destructive tendencies of a child or adolescent, immediate arrangements for inpatient care should be made. When in doubt, it is preferable to err on the conservative side. Obviously, less harm is done by a relatively unnecessary admission than by a needless death. Unfortunately, it has become fashionable to adopt a laissez-faire attitude toward the involuntary hospitalization of some suicidal adults. Freedom becomes equated with "free-doom," and therapists are told not to play God or degrade patients or rob them of their dignity by infantalizing them through involuntary hospitalization. Mental illness becomes viewed as a myth.[1] Therapists can evade their professional responsibilities and rationalize behind such a "stance" because responsibility can be left to the patient.

Such a view totally ignores the fact that a majority of suicidal individuals suffer from depressions of one sort or another and these are among the most treatable illnesses — often, even without the patients' cooperation. Since it is clear that for children and adolescents, whether

417

or not one believes in mental illness per se, therapists and "the state" have the responsibility to prevent them from self-harm, the issue of "don't hospitalize them against their will" is not nearly so evident. Dealing with minors who can be signed into hospitals by their parents also, of course, helps to obviate this issue.

Pharmacotherapy versus psychotherapy (or both) If the therapist believes the child or adolescent has a depression that is primarily biological/genetic in origin, it is not unreasonable to attempt a course of antidepressant medication. Unfortunately, it is not so easy to estimate the role of biology in a given case. A strong family history may help as may a biological test such as the DST. Ambrosini, Rabinovich and Puig-Antich, in Chapter 7, are sanguine about the DST and other chemical-marker tests in children and adolescents, although Targum and Capodanno[2] found a predictive value of only 23% for major depressive disorder in their study using the DST in 120 adolescents. Even in the adult literature there is a growing disenchantment with the DST for its lack of sensitivity and specificity. Perhaps we embraced the test with too much zeal since it appeared to be the first biological marker applicable to our field.

Certainly, pharmacotherapy is faster and cheaper than psychotherapy so that a trial of medication for equivocal cases of major depressive disorder would appear expedient. Such a trial is not to be undertaken capriciously, however, for it may not be free from undesirable consequences. First of all, what might it do to the child or adolescent's self-image were he or she to view himself or herself as having an intrinsic, genetic, probably life-long, predisposition to mental illness? If it is valid, fine — the individual will need to come to grips with this sooner or later and, hopefully, adapt and destigmatize him or herself. If it is not valid, there is the danger that the therapist may have inadvertently added a burden to an individual whose psychological functioning is already compromised by an exogeneous (reactive, neurotic) type of depression. Furthermore, as Furman pointed out in Chapter 15, such biological treatment may sometimes get in the way of doing the work that can only be done through intensive psychotherapy. The issue of combined pharmacotherapy and psychotherapy was dealt with in Chapter 13 by Friedman et al.

Individual, group, family psychotherapy It would make things much easier for patients (consumers) if the behavioral sciences had sharper indices for which illnesses need which treatments. Most internists would agree that an uncomplicated right lower lobe bacterial pneumonia in an otherwise healthy and nonallergic adult should be treated with penicillin. Although diagnostic consensus in psychiatry may approximate that seen in other branches of medicine, agreement regarding the best therapy for psychiatric diagnoses is much poorer, particularly if we exclude treatment of psychoses (for which consensus is best). Both quantitative and qualitative differences of opinion are of great magnitude. For example, a patient with a few neurotic symptoms may only feel he needs these attended to — a tune-up so to speak; the evaluator may feel he is an excellent prospect for an analysis — and suggest an overhaul. Conversely, patients with similar symptoms may want very different amounts of remediation: some people are very intolerant of anxiety, set high standards for their own mental functioning, and seek intensive therapy, while others, with far more anxiety, would never dream of consulting a psychiatrist. Thus, both the buyer and the seller can have very dissonant and varying perspectives on just what is indicated for what.

Furthermore, the biases of the therapist will generally be crucial regarding treatment approaches for neurotic or characterological problems. If one is trained in a "family-oriented" program and believes in it, then family therapy is the approach of choice. The same for Freudians, Horneyians, Rankians, Jungians, Adlerians, Rogerians, Sullivanians, Gestalt therapists, transactional analysts, group therapists, behaviorists, cognitive therapists, etc. And these are just a few of the more traditional approaches from which to select. There are also the newer, affect-for-affect's sake, instant therapies such as EST, primal scream, re-birthing, etc. While these have in common the contention (usually correct) that people need to get in better touch with their affects (feelings), they share what appears to be the specious assumption that long-lasting changes in coping and defensive styles can occur virtually instantly, and that (artificial) discharge of affect (sanctioned by the other group members and the therapist) will be therapeutic by itself.

For suicidal patients, of course, the situation is no different, ie, children and adolescents will be referred for the treatment of any underlying neurotic or characterological problems, in accord with the referrer's biases, for individual, group, or family therapy (or combination). So far, fortunately, children and adolescents seem to have been better protected from referrals to the affect-for-affect's sake type of therapies.

Richman's chapter reflects his view that, in children and adolescents, suicidal behavior is the expression of a family with a problem it cannot resolve. Consequently, family therapy is the best and most logical approach. He describes some characteristics of the family under suicidal conditions and explains that they are not unique but are characteristic of any family under stress. Part of the problem, of course, is that it is difficult to separate cause from effect. Is the family under stress because it contains a suicidal family member rather than vice versa? It is similar to some of the research dilemmas growing out of family approaches to schizophrenia. The schizophrenic child or adolescent was often viewed by theorists as playing a role in order to meet some covert need of the family's, eg, was sick in order to keep the parents together. Family dynamics could be seen which appeared to foster such a role, maintain disordered communication, etc. Again, which is effect and which cause? Are the family dynamics disordered and does the family appear to have unusual communication patterns because of the need to adapt to such a disturbed child or adolescent? It is hard to envision schizophrenia merely as a purposive (conscious or unconscious) stance a child takes to maintain some family homeostasis.

Richman does feel there are some unique features to the suicidal child or adolescent's family, however. Namely, a close association between separations and death and the isolation of the suicidal individual within the family. Despite this, outside intimacies are prohibited for him or her, special family rules and dynamics exist concerning the expression of aggression or other drives, and overt or covert messages regarding suicide are present. Four specific factors lead to suicide: diminished ego resources with which to cope in the individual; similar diminished resources in the family collectively; the occurrence of a crisis (always involving separation and loss); and suicide becomes seen as an acceptable solution.

He employs crisis techniques in his work with these families and stresses the opportunity the crisis situation may present for meaningful change. He encourages more open communications within the family including the expression of hostility. Only after such feelings are made manifest can they be dealt with and defused. Suicide is seen as "based on a problem in the present based on an unresolved crisis in the past which, in turn, precipitates a major crisis, the fate of which may determine the future." He views all healing as really self-healing and feels that the family, as a system, can grow and heal. The therapist's task is to help remove the barriers to the family's growth. Therapists (individual and family) must constantly be alert to separation issues to forestall suicides; must teach families how to anticipate their (pathological) ways of dealing with them and, hopefully, to learn more adaptive ways.

Ross and Motto do not argue that group therapy is preferable to individual therapy for suicidal adolescents but, instead, describe in Chapter 22 their experiment with group treatment in combination with other therapies for 17 adolescents. The amount of responsibility that would be felt by group leaders, were the group sessions the only therapy received by suicidal adolescents, makes it unlikely that many therapists would undertake such treatment. Some Eastern European reports are cited by the authors along these lines, however. The Suicide Prevention and Crisis Center of San Mateo County in collaboration with the County Adolescent Services Unit enrolled in the group program 10 adolescents who had made suicidal attempts and seven who had threatened. Charlotte Ross was able to recruit Jerry Motto and Irving Yalom as consultants; 35 group meetings over 40 weeks were held (the mean number of sessions attended per participant was 13; over a mean duration of 20 weeks). They were able to do a two-year followup on 14 subjects.

The goals were to provide supplementary support; to help learn strategies for dealing with stress; increase self-esteem; to learn befriending techniques; and to develop alternative ways to handle dysphoria rather than through suicidal threats or acts. They utilized a large support network consisting of the group leaders, the group members, and the crisis services of the Suicide Prevention Center (SPC). Their combined efforts augmented any individual therapy the subjects were receiving. In addition, they elected to supply befrienders: six volunteers from the SPC who each gave several hours per week on the phone or in person to individuals in the group. The group became like a family with the befrienders extending this as "special friends" to individuals within the family.

It is clear that the high anxiety levels generated by the work and the intense needs of these adolescents prompted the leaders to provide a much more extensive support network than they otherwise might have. It also prompted them to delay the predetermined termination date; to encourage peer contacts in between group sessions (despite the usual arguments against this); and to encourage contacts with the befrienders after the group terminated.

The leaders were tactful, nurturing, and, most of all, quite active with their cases. As readers familiar with Ross and Motto might expect, they make no extravagant claims for their work. There were no suicides or suicide attempts in the two-year followup period, and the authors suggest that the group therapy and support systems may have helped these young people find healthier ways to cope.

Psychoanalysis or psychoanalytically oriented versus cognitive/behavioral treatment The determining factor, in addition to the usual diagnostic, economic, and temporal constraints, regarding the suitability of a suicidal child or adolescent for analysis, is often the degree of "suicidalness" of the patient. Analysts are not generally eager to treat children or adolescents whose analyses are apt to be interrupted by one or more hospitalizations necessitated by suicidal threats or acts. A fair amount of ego strength, control, and a reasonably cooperative family is called for. Some of the reasons to press for psychoanalytic treatment of such children and adolescents have been presented in Chapter 8 by Novick and in Chapter 15 by Furman.

A much wider net is cast by proponents of psychoanalytically oriented psychotherapy, however. Toolan, in Chapter 20, stresses the need for long-term, intensive, individual treatment, and deplores the trend toward "patching things up" via brief crisis therapy. He warns against premature termination despite pressure from the patients and their families. Even when the risk of completed suicide following such termination does not appear to be great, he feels these children and adolescents will have a high risk of developing serious problems in the future and are at risk for passing on their problems to their future children if inadequately treated. He also is in favor of the same therapist periodically seeing the parents of the child being seen individually. Although this can generate some rather sticky confidentiality problems, he feels the benefits outweigh the risks.

In common with Pfeffer (Chapter 11), Toolan stresses the counter-transference problems inherent in dealing with suicidal youngsters. Children and adolescents are apt to test the therapist and provoke or alarm him or her. It is helpful if the therapist can enlist the parents to share some of the responsibility for treatment. Since these cases are such a burden, he suggests that therapists carry only one or two such cases at a time. It is helpful to have a colleague or supervisor with whom to share one's feelings. The fear of the child or adolescent's death and fears of any ensuing notoriety contribute to the unpopularity of such cases and, often, to the desire to terminate the cases as soon as possible.

Bedrosian and Epstein present a strong case for cognitive therapy of depressed and suicidal adolescents in Chapter 21. The precision, logic, and apparent directness of such an approach is made clear in their over-view. They cite Beck's cognitive triad of depression: a negative view of oneself, the world, and the future. Such selective attention validates the individual's negative views. Part of therapy requires a cognitive assess-ment in which patient and therapist work together in a "collaborative empiricism" and learn to monitor some of these negative thoughts. They warn that work with adolescents requires that the therapist expect less directness and may have to be more flexible than he or she would be with adults (eg, agreeing to shorter sessions or irregularly scheduled ones). Families may not be able to be counted on to recognize the adolescent's depression and to warn the therapist. Their work with adolescents entails changing cognitions. To do this may require some behavioral experi-ments to challenge dysfunctional cognitions.

Much of what these authors write will be familiar to therapists of other persuasions, of course. Psychodynamically, we know that patients selectively scan for what they need to see in their environments. De-pressed patients wear dark glasses through which the past, the present, and the future all appear gloomy, and they lose hope. We all try to help our patients shift their perspectives toward more optimistic ones. Where disputes are more apt to occur is, again, in the area of cause and effect. Cognitive therapists believe that because the patient thinks depressed he comes to feel depressed. Noncognitive therapists are more apt to believe that because the patient feels depressed (due to biological or psychologi-cal causes or both) he comes to think depressed. The former school puts more emphasis on correcting the faulty cognitions and the latter on the affect, per se. (Why is the patient depressed? What were the losses? What anger is being directed inward? Who is being identified with? What is in it for the patient to feel depressed? What are the biological predisposi-tions to depression?)

In *Suicide in America*[3] and elsewhere[4] Hendin presents a very positive view of individual psychotherapy with suicidal patients but warns that the therapist in the role of controller, manager, or rescuer of the suicidal patient may only worsen the problem. Suicidal patients should not be manipulated, told to live "for the sake of others," or be allowed to use suicidal acts or threats to coerce those around them. The therapist's task is to help the patient understand what is making him or her feel suicidal, the way he or she uses the threat of death, and to help the patient wish to live for his or her own sake. There are, of course, inevitable situations in which therapists are forced into being rescuers but, as Hendin would undoubtedly agree, the crucial aspect will be does such behavior get analyzed so that the patient can understand the wishes and the patterns and find more adaptive ways of dealing with his or her needs.

Individual therapy also affords the opportunity for therapist and patient to explore in depth the meaning of the suicidal method attempted or contemplated.[3] Both cultural and personal (conscious and unconscious) factors figure prominently in the methods conceived or executed and much can be learned regarding the details and circumstances involved (eg, who was expected to find the individual).

Prevention, intervention, postvention The final topic considered in our Treatment Section was involvement with schools regarding suicide prevention, intervening when an attempt is threatened or made, and "postvening" following a completion to deal with some of the aroused affects.

Hill's chapter on these topics (Chapter 24) presents some of the efforts of the Cleveland SPC, with particular emphasis on postvention. He feels that, following a completed suicide in a high school student, there are four phases that ensue. The first of these is a retreat to a safe place via flight. This is generally to the home of one of the decedent's friends. Crying, silence, and/or withdrawal may be part of the picture. The second phase is a preoccupation with why did the death occur? Third, a need to blame oneself or others. The closer the student is to the decedent the more likely that the blame will be on the self. If less close, blame tends to be externalized. Fourth is a tendency to either overfocus or overgeneralize. Students are attempting to separate the precipitating events from more substantive causes but frequently overfocus on single, simple causes, or overgeneralize—for instance, blaming everything on the school.

The school is in some ways an ideal location in which to carry out postvention since compulsory education means that both students and teachers are captive—even the withdrawn adolescent. Work with students and faculty requires repeated acknowledging, confronting, supporting. Just as with their students, the faculties wanted to know how they could have detected the suicide. They also want help in dealing with other students' upsets. Naturally, the closer the teacher was to the student, the more upset he or she became personally. Ironically, Hill noted that the faculty tended to be less open than the students.

In his chapter Hill cites some of Charlotte Ross's pioneering work on postvention and intervention in schools.[5] Ross feels that the ones in the best position to know of an incipient suicide attempt are the close friends of the student in question. Thus, peer-counseling techniques and education regarding signs of depression and behavior which should be suspected as presuicidal (eg, giving away one's record collection) are provided. Considerable emphasis is placed upon the duty to warn (dispelling any notions of confidentiality, the need to keep things secret, betrayal by disclosure to parents or other outsiders). Ross is quite aware of needing to avoid the excitement and contagion/suggestion effects that might result from getting students all stirred up regarding suicide, while still being able to provide the beneficial suicide prevention effects. Such efforts call for considerable tact and discretion on the part of the interviewer.

Hill and Ross both stress the role of the SPCs as backups to their efforts. According to Hill, the SPC must earn a reputation as having helpful experts available. After his school sessions, counselors call him at the SPC for further advice. Ross employed educational materials such as training kits, brochures and bibliographies from her SPC in her work with schools. Although Lester,[6,7] Weiner,[8] and Barraclough[9] question the efficacy of SPCs in preventing suicide, a conclusive test of this remains to be performed. In any event, their role in community education should be better exploited. As Hill points out, "some prevention is better than none; education about suicide is preferable to its absence; and the two are interdependent."

CONCLUDING REMARKS

It is clear that there are no satisfactory objective data to tell us which therapies are best. Each school of psychotherapy claims approximately the same percent of cures (two-thirds to three-fourths), leading some observers to believe that the theoretical underpinnings of each school are irrelevant and that the only relevant factor is one held in common by all the schools: an unusual dyad is established between patient and therapist in which there is much trust of the therapist, implicit or explicit support from the therapist, and a relatively neutral, nonjudgmental attitude on the therapist's part—thus, "the relationship" is seen as the critical variable. Most practitioners eschew such lumping and maintain the superiority of their own split. Unfortunately, there are little objective data to confirm our biases. Subjective, anecdotal data are abundant but lack scientific precision. An enormous number of "objective" outcome studies of psychotherapy have been carried out over the years, most of them flawed by either the lack of suitable control groups or discrete indices of change.

Recently, attempts have been made to compensate for the methodological deficits of such studies by combining data (eg, cancelling out sampling error by building up a huge sample size). Can one produce validity by averaging out invalid studies? It seems unlikely that the mental health field can create silk purses this way or that we should have and immunity to the GIGO principle of computers. Such studies were reviewed by Parloff[10] who noted that they may fail to reflect proportionately the most frequently used therapies. Parloff also reported that approximately 500 rigorously controlled studies have shown that all forms of psychological treatments (psychodynamic, behavioral, cognitive; short or long term) appear comparably effective and clearly superior to the no-treatment control groups.

Thus, families are left to pick and choose along the line of their own biases for what sort of therapy is best for a given child or adolescent. Either that or they will have the decision made for them through the biases of others (eg, whomever they rely on in the mental health referral/delivery system). Fortunately, the prognosis for most such children, adolescents, and their families is favorable regardless of what channel is selected so long as some meaningful help is sought.

It appears clear that what is most needed are studies that avoid parochial approaches to the question of childhood and adolescent suicide. It is unlikely that we can explicate such complicated, multifaceted phenomena as if a unitary approach could provide an answer. Demographic and sociologic knowledge and lines of inquiry need to be interdigitated with the more individual studies from biological and psychological perspectives. Intriguing issues remain to be confronted from multidisciplinary vantage points. For instance, there is as yet no satisfactory answer to the male-female disparity question (high male completions but high female parasuicides); nor black/white disparities, nor what "protects" black females, nor why do rates for black males peak in young adults and then decrease?

There are some studies which have begun to cross-apply methodology from separate disciplines. For example, Phillips's studies (see Chapter 5); Pokorny's recent article on the difficulties of suicide prediction[11]; cohort and population model approaches (see Chapters 1 and 2); and Waldron's work.[12] In her paper with Eyer, Waldron relates the increased rate of adolescent suicide in the 1960s to an increase in potentially overwhelming life problems, including an increased parental divorce rate, alcohol abuse, illegitimate pregnancies, a relative decline in income for young persons as compared to their parents, and increased social isolation brought about by a decreased marriage rate among young adults.

The question of why the alarming increase in suicide rates in adolescents and young adults over the past 20 years is most apt to be answered by studies enriched by interdisciplinary methods and cooperation. Issues such as those cited above by Waldron and others need to be further tested and understood as well as related ones such as concern about nuclear catastrophies, handgun availability, and more subtle disruptions in our large sociopolitical–economic–religious institutions as well as the smaller, nuclear institution, the family. Hopefully, with such answers will come some practical clues which will help us reverse this pattern.

REFERENCES

1. Szasz TS: *The Myth of Mental Illness*. New York, Harper & Row, 1961.
2. Targum SD, Capodanno AE: The dexamethasone suppression test in adolescent psychiatric inpatients. *Am J Psychiatry* 1983;140:589–591.
3. Hendin H: *Suicide in America*. New York, WW Norton, 1982.
4. Hendin H: Psychotherapy and suicide. *Am J Psychotherapy* 1981;35:469–480.
5. Ross CP: Mobilizing schools for suicide prevention. *Suicide Life Threat Behav* 1980;10:239–243.
6. Lester D: The myth of suicide prevention. *Compr Psychiatry* 1972;13:555–560.
7. Lester D: Effect of suicide prevention centers on suicide rates in the United States. *Health Serv Rep* 1974;89:37–39.
8. Weiner IW: The effectiveness of a suicide prevention program. *Ment Hygiene* 1969;53:357–363.
9. Jennings C, Barraclough BB: The effectiveness of the samaritans in the prevention of suicide, in Farmer R, Hirsch S (eds): *The Suicide Syndrome*. London, Crom Helm, 1980, pp 195–200.
10. Parloff MB: Psychotherapy research evidence and reimbursement decisions: Bambi meets Godzilla. *Am J Psychiatry* 1982;139:718–727.
11. Pokorny AD: Prediction of suicide in psychiatric patients. *Arch Gen Psychiatry* 1983;40:249–257.
12. Waldron I, Eyer J: Socioeconomic causes of the recent rise in death rates for 15–24 year olds. *Soc Sci Med* 1975;9:383–395.

INDEX

Abraham, K., 140
Accident-proneness, 98, 302
  referrals for, 263
Accidents
  alcoholism and drug abuse and,
    40
  data classification problems with,
    17, 147, 163, 327
  population changes and, 16,
    18–26, 47, 160
  self-destructive behavior and, 16,
    98, 162
  see also Automobile accidents;
    Nonvehicular accidents
Achenbach, T.M., 188
Acting out, 252
Addiction, see Alcohol abuse and
  alcoholism; Drug abuse
Adjustment Disorder, 319
Adjustment Reaction, 222
Adult suicides
  adolescent suicide attempts
    compared with, 235–236, 237,
    238
  automobile accidents and, 76–79
  time series regression analysis of,
    72–74
  urban community study of,
    50–54
Affective disorders, 153, 184, 185
  attempted suicide and, 211
  Borderline Personality Disorder
    (BPD) and, 217, 299–300
  diagnosis of, 204, 211
  DSM-III definition of, 212
  inpatient diagnostic profile of,
    213, 217
  parental, 217
  psychological autopsy method
    with, 150
  social adjustment and, 187
  suicide in children and, 173–174

  treatment considerations and,
    223–224
Age
  cohort analysis of suicide rates
    by, 10–12
  concepts about death and, 177
  official statistics on, 142–143
  profile analysis and, 2–10
  risk group in, 183–184
  self-destructive behavior and, 265
  white male suicide rates and, 34
Aggression and aggressive behavior,
  155
  black suicide rates and, 144
  bodily self-love and, 257
  death instinct and, 136
  female suicide and, 143
  sadomasochistic pathology and,
    253, 254, 255
  self-hurting and, 251–254
  suicide attempts and, 236
  suicide sequence example with,
    125, 128–129, 130, 133, 134
Akiskal, H.S., 215, 217
Alcohol abuse and alcoholism
  accidents and, 40
  blacks and, 38–40, 161
  depressive disorder with, 82–83
  legal drinking age and, 40
  mother's awareness of, 198
  native American Indian suicide
    rates and, 38–40
  parental, 153, 173, 175, 240,
    310, 355, 395
  psychiatric disease model of sui-
    cide and, 141
  psychological autopsy method
    with, 150
  psychological reconstruction
    method with, 272
  self-destructive behavior and,
    264, 302

428

438

442